Intelligent Techniques in Recommendation Systems:

Contextual Advancements and New Methods

Satchidananda Dehuri
Fakir Mohan University, India

Manas Ranjan Patra
Berhampur University, India

Bijan Bihari Misra
Silicon Institute of Technology, India

Alok Kumar Jagadev
SOA University, India

T0338617

Managing Director:	Lindsay Johnston
Editorial Director:	Joel Gamon
Book Production Manager:	Jennifer Romanchak
Publishing Systems Analyst:	Adrienne Freeland
Development Editor:	Hannah Abelbeck
Assistant Acquisitions Editor:	Kayla Wolfe
Typesetter:	Erin O'Dea
Cover Design:	Nick Newcomer

Published in the United States of America by
Information Science Reference (an imprint of IGI Global)
701 E. Chocolate Avenue
Hershey PA 17033
Tel: 717-533-8845
Fax: 717-533-8661
E-mail: cust@igi-global.com
Web site: http://www.igi-global.com

Library of Congress Cataloging-in-Publication Data

Intelligent techniques in recommendation systems: contextual advancements and new methods / Satchidananda Dehuri, Manas Ranjan Patra, Bijan Bihari Misra, Alok Kumar Jagadev, editors.
     pages cm
  Includes bibliographical references and index.
  Summary: "This book is a comprehensive collection of research on the latest advancements of intelligence techniques and their application to recommendation systems and how they could improve this field of study"-- Provided by publisher.
  ISBN 978-1-4666-2542-6 (hardcover) -- ISBN 978-1-4666-2544-0 (print & perpetual access) -- ISBN 978-1-4666-2543-3 (ebook) (print) 1. Decision support systems. I. Dehuri, Satchidananda.
  T58.62.I5695 2013
  658.4'038011--dc23
                        2012023122

British Cataloguing in Publication Data
A Cataloguing in Publication record for this book is available from the British Library.

Table of Contents

Chapter 14

Detailed Table of Contents

This chapter pays attention to the automatic generation and recommendation of teaching materials for teachers who do not have enough time to learn how to use authoring tools for the creation of materials to support their courses. To overcome the difficulties, the research is intended to solve the problem of time needed to create adapted case studies for teaching decision-making in network design. Another goal is to reduce the time required to learn the use of an authoring tool to create teaching materials. Thus, the authors present an assistant that provides adapted help for teachers, generates examples automatically, verifies that any generated example fits in the class of examples used by the teacher, and recommends personalized examples according to each teacher's preferences. They study the use of data related to teachers to support the recommendation of teaching materials and the adaptation of Web-based support. The automatic generation and test of examples of network topologies are based on a probabilistic model, and the recommendation is based on Bayesian classification. This investigation also looks at problems related to the application of Artificial Intelligence (AI) to support teachers in authoring learning sessions for Adaptive Educational Hypermedia (AEH).

The aim of this chapter is to provide a model for requirement specification, useful in developing efficient e-assessment applications with personalized feedback, which is enhanced by calling a recommender engine. The research was done in the context of using educational technology to facilitate learning processes. The data used to build the requirement model was collected from a set of interviews with the users and creators of an e-assessment application in project management. Requirement analysis assumes human effort and thus introduces uncertainties. To minimize the subjective factor, the data extracted from interviews with the users and the developers of the existing e-assessment application are clustered using a fuzzy logic solution into classes of requirements. These classes are the units of the model. The connections between classes are also mentioned: relations such as "if-then," "switch," or" contains" are explained. The requirements analysis conducts a smart set of specifications, obtained in a collaborative manner, useful for the design of e-assessment applications in project management or other similar domains.

Chapter 3

This chapter presents an overview of the field of recommender systems and describes the current generation of recommendation methods with their limitations and possible extensions that can improve the capabilities of the recommendations made suitable for a wide range of applications. In recent years, machine learning algorithms have been considered to be an important part of the recommendation process to take intelligent decisions. The chapter will explore the application of such techniques in the field of network intrusion detection in order to examine the vulnerabilities of different recommendation techniques. Finally, the authors outline some of the major issues in building secure recommendation systems in identifying possible network intrusions.

In this chapter, the authors describe Reperio, a flexible and generic industrial recommender system able to deal with several kinds of data sources (content-based, collaborative, social network) in the same framework and to work on multi-platforms (Web service in a multi-user mode and mobile device in a mono-user mode). The item-item matrix is the keystone of the architecture for its efficiency and flexibility properties. In the first part, the authors present core functionalities and requirements of recommendation in an industrial context. In the second part, they present the architecture of the system and the main issues involved in its development. In the last part, the authors report experimental results obtained using Reperio on benchmarks extracted from the Netflix Prize with different filtering strategies. To illustrate the interest and flexibility of the architecture, they also explain how it is possible to take into account, for recommendations, external sources of information. In particular, the authors show how to exploit user generated contents posted on social networks to fill the item-item matrix. The process proposed includes a step of opinion classification.

A business case describes a problem present in all insurance companies: portfolio risk evaluation. Such analysis deals with determining the risk level as well as main risk factors. In the specific case, an insurance company is faced with market share growth and profit decline. Discovered knowledge about the level of risk and main risk factors was not used to increase premium for the riskiest portfolio segments due to a specific market situation, which could lead to loss of clients in the long run. Instead, additional analysis was conducted using data mining methods resulting in a solution, which stopped further profit decline and lowered the risk level for the riskiest portfolio segments. The central role for the unexpected revealed knowledge in the chapter acts as the REFII model. The REFII model is an authorial mathematical model for time series data mining. The main purpose of that model is to automate time series analysis, through a unique transformation model of time series.

Chapter 6

Giuliano Armano, University of Cagliari, Italy
Alessandro Giuliani, University of Cagliari, Italy
Eloisa Vargiu, University of Cagliari, Italy & Barcelona Digital Technology Center, Spain

Information Filtering deals with the problem of selecting relevant information for a given user, according to her/his preferences and interests. In this chapter, the authors consider two ways of performing information filtering: recommendation and contextual advertising. In particular, they study and analyze them according to a unified view. In fact, the task of suggesting an advertisement to a Web page can be viewed as the task of recommending an item (the advertisement) to a user (the Web page), and vice versa. Starting from this insight, the authors propose a content-based recommender system based on a generic solution for contextual advertising and a hybrid contextual advertising system based on a generic hybrid recommender system. Relevant case studies have been considered (i.e., a photo recommender and a Web advertiser) with the goal of highlighting how the proposed approach works in practice. In both cases, results confirm the effectiveness of the proposed solutions.

Chapter 7

Sagarika Bakshi, ITER, SOA University, India
Sweta Sarkar, ITER, SOA University, India
Alok Kumar Jagadev, ITER, SOA University, India
Satchidananda Dehuri, Fakir Mohan University, India

Recommender systems are applied in a multitude of spheres and have a significant role in reduction of information overload on those websites that have the features of voting. Therefore, it is an urgent need for them to adapt and respond to immediate changes in user preference. To overcome the shortcomings of each individual approach to design the recommender systems, a myriad of ways to coalesce different recommender systems are proposed by researchers. In this chapter, the authors have presented an insight into the design of recommender systems developed, namely content-based and collaborative recommendations, their evaluation, their lacunae, and some hybrid models to enhance the quality of prediction.

Chapter 8

M. Hemalatha, M.A.M. College of Engineering, India

The foremost theme of this chapter is to utilize the subtractive clustering concept for defining the market boundaries in the fuzzy-based segmentation. In this sense, the present work starts by analyzing the importance of segmenting the shoppers on the basis of store image. After reviewing the segmentation literature, the authors performed a segmentation analysis of retail shoppers in India. Researchers often use clustering analysis as a tool in market segmentation studies, the results of which often end with a crisp partitioning form, where one member cannot belong to two or more groups. This indicates that different segments overlap with one another. This chapter integrates the concept of application of subtractive clustering in fuzzy c means clustering for profiling the customers who perceive the retail store based on its image. Fuzzy clustering is also compared with hard clustering solutions. Then the authors predict the model using discriminate analysis. Further, the chapter concentrates on the answer tree model of segmentation to identify the best predictor. Main conclusions with implications for retailing management are shown.

Recommender systems represent a prominent class of personalized Web applications, which particularly focus on the user-dependent filtering and selection of relevant information. Recommender Systems have been a subject of extensive research in Artificial Intelligence over the last decade, but with today's increasing number of e-commerce environments on the Web, the demand for new approaches to intelligent product recommendation is higher than ever. There are more online users, more online channels, more vendors, more products, and, most importantly, increasingly complex products and services. These recent developments in the area of recommender systems generated new demands, in particular with respect to interactivity, adaptivity, and user preference elicitation. These challenges, however, are also in the focus of general Web page recommendation research. The goal of this chapter is to develop robust techniques to model noisy data sets containing an unknown number of overlapping categories and apply them for Web personalization and mining. In this chapter, rough set-based clustering approaches are used to discover Web user access patterns, and these techniques compute a number of clusters automatically from the Web log data using statistical techniques. The suitability of rough clustering approaches for Web page recommendation are measured using predictive accuracy metrics.

The objective is intelligent recommender system classification unit design using hybrid neural techniques. In particular, a neuroscience-based hybrid neural by Buabin (2011a) is introduced, explained, and examined for its potential in real world text document classification on the modapte version of the Reuters news text corpus. The so described neuroscience model (termed Hy-RNC) is fully integrated with a novel boosting algorithm to augment text document classification purposes. Hy-RNC outperforms existing works and opens up an entirely new research field in the area of machine learning. The main contribution of this book chapter is the provision of a step-by-step approach to modeling the hybrid system using underlying concepts such as boosting algorithms, recurrent neural networks, and hybrid neural systems. Results attained in the experiments show impressive performance by the hybrid neural classifier even with a minimal number of neurons in constituting structures.

Because of their mathematical backgrounds and coherent structures, Artificial Intelligent-based methods and techniques are often used to find solutions for different types of problems encountered. In the related context, nature-inspired algorithms are also important for providing more accurate solutions. Because of their nature-based, flexible process structures, the related algorithms can be applied to different types of problems. At this point, recommendation systems are one of the related problem areas where nature-inspired algorithms can be used to get better results. In the literature there are many research studies that are based on using nature-inspired algorithms within recommendation systems. This chapter aims to discuss usage of some newly developed nature-inspired algorithms in typical recommendation systems. In this aim, features and functions of some new nature-inspired algorithms will be explained first. Later, using the related algorithms in recommendation systems will be discussed. Following that, there will be a discussion on future of nature-inspired algorithms and also their roles in the recommendation approach or system-based applications.

Chapter 12

The neural network is a very useful tool for approximation of a function, time series prediction, classification, and pattern recognition. If there is found to be a non-linear relationship between input data and output data, it is difficult to analyse the system. A neural network is very effective to solve this problem. This chapter studies the applied neural network model in relation to clearance sales outshopping behaviour. Since neural network theory can be applied effectively to this case, the authors have used neural network theory to recognise the retail area satisfaction and loyalty. To measure the impact among the retail area attributes, retail area satisfaction, and retail area loyalty, the authors have used the neural network model. In this chapter, they have treated twenty seven factors as the input signals into the input layer. Therefore, they find the weights between nodes in the relationship between the value of all twenty seven factors and the retail area satisfaction and loyalty. The development of the model by retail area attributes, and their interpretation, was facilitated by a collection of data across three trading areas. This neural network modeling approach to understand clearance sales outshopping behaviour provides retail managers with information to support retail strategy development.

The objective is a neural-based feature selection in intelligent recommender systems. In particular, a hybrid neural genetic architecture is modeled based on human nature, interactions, and behaviour. The main contribution of this chapter is the development of a novel genetic algorithm based on human nature, interactions, and behaviour. The novel genetic algorithm termed "Buabin Algorithm" is fully integrated with a hybrid neural classifier to form a Hybrid Neural Genetic Architecture. The research presents GA in a more attractive manner and opens up the various departments of a GA for active research. Although no scientific experiment is conducted to compare network performance with standard approaches, engaged techniques reveal drastic reductions in genetic operator operations. For illustration purposes, the UCI Molecular Biology (Splice Junction) dataset is used. Overall, "Buabin Algorithm" seeks to integrate human related interactions into genetic algorithms as imitate human genetics in recommender systems design and understand underlying datasets explicitly.

Chapter 14

The technology behind personalization or Web page recommendation has undergone tremendous changes, and several Web-based personalization systems have been proposed in recent years. The main goal of Web personalization is to dynamically recommend Web pages based on online behavior of users. Although personalization can be accomplished in numerous ways, most Web personalization techniques fall into four major categories: decision rule-based filtering, content-based filtering, and collaborative filtering and Web usage mining. Decision rule-based filtering reviews users to obtain user demographics or static profiles, and then lets Web sites manually specify rules based on them. It delivers the appropriate content to a particular user based on the rules. However, it is not particularly useful because it depends on users knowing in advance the content that interests them. Content-based filtering relies on items being similar to what a user has liked previously. Collaborative filtering, also called social or group filtering, is the most successful personalization technology to date. Most successful recommender systems on the Web typically use explicit user ratings of products or preferences to sort user profile information into peer groups. It then tells users what products they might want to buy by combining their personal preferences with those of like-minded individuals. However, collaborative filtering has limited use for a new product that no one has seen or rated, and content-based filtering to obtain user profiles might miss novel or surprising information. Additionally, traditional Web personalization techniques, including collaborative or content-based filtering, have other problems, such as reliance on subject user ratings and static profiles or the inability to capture richer semantic relationships among Web objects. To overcome these shortcomings, the new Web personalization tool, nonintrusive personalization, attempts to increasingly incorporate Web usage mining techniques. Web usage mining can help improve the scalability, accuracy, and flexibility of recommender systems. Thus, Web usage mining can reduce the need for obtaining subjective user ratings or registration-based personal preferences. This chapter provides a survey of Web usage mining approaches.

Preface

Recommendation systems have become an important research area in the fields of cognitive science, approximation theory, information retrieval, and management sciences. Since the first papers on collaborative filtering were published in the mid 1990s, researchers in industry and academia have expanded the field and, over the last decade, developed new computational methods for recommender systems. This area remains a problem-rich research area due to the profusion of practical applications that help users to deal with information overloads and provide them with personalized recommendations, content, and services. For example, most on-line shopping sites have adopted approaches like Amazon. com's to recommend books, CDs, and other products, and now even publishers' sites like Elsevier, IEEE, ACM, IGI, etc. recommend journal articles.

However, despite all these advances, the current generation of recommendation systems still requires further improvements to make recommendation methods more robust, intelligent, effective, and applicable to an even broader range of real life applications, including ones for vacation planning, financial services and investing decision-making, and smart shopping cart technologies. Researchers and designers need better methods for employing intelligent techniques like evolutionary algorithms, neural networks, swarm intelligence, fuzzy theory, and rough theory to represent user behavior and gather, determine, and present information about recommended items. More advanced recommendation modeling methods—ones that incorporate various contextual information into the recommendation process, utilize multi-criteria ratings, feature less intrusive and more flexible recommendation methods—also rely on the measures that more effectively determine performance of recommender systems.

Recommendation systems are software tools and techniques providing suggestions for items (e.g., CDs, news, songs, books, etc.) to be of use to a user by considering his/her preferences.

Recommendation systems are primarily directed towards individuals who lack sufficient personal experience or competence to evaluate the potentiality overwhelming number of alternative items that a web site, for example, may offer.

This book consists of 14 chapters of the latest advances of intelligent techniques and their possible applications in recommendation systems, with an attention to how intelligent methods for recommended systems could advance the field. Further, the standard recommender systems work in pull mode: the user is supposed to ask (pull) for a suggestions and therefore is required to enter information about his preferences, needs, and constraints. However, a new kind of recommender systems instead prompts the user with a recommendation, when the user is in a contextual state that the system considers as suitable for that suggestions. Hence, to build such a system, an intelligent technique with an active learning methodology will have to be considered. In this context, this book can be a source of inspiration for developing an intelligent recommender system by considering the contextual state of a user rather than his/her preferences.

ORGANIZATION OF THE BOOK

Chapter 1 pays attention to the automatic generation and recommendation of teaching materials for teachers who do not have enough time to learn how to use authoring tools for the creation of materials to support their courses. To overcome the difficulties, this work is intended to solve the problem of time needed to create adapted case studies for teaching decision-making in network design. Another goal is to reduce the time required to learn the use of an authoring tool to create teaching materials. Thus, the author presents an assistant that provides adapted help for teachers, generates examples automatically, verifies that any generated example fits in the class of examples used by the teacher, and recommends personalized examples according to each teacher's preferences. A. Rodriguez studies the use of data related to teachers to support the recommendation of teaching materials and the adaptation of Web-based support. The automatic generation and test of examples of network topologies are based on a probabilistic model, and the recommendation is based on Bayesian classification. This investigation also looks at problems related to the application of Artificial Intelligence (AI) to support teachers in authoring learning sessions for Adaptive Educational Hypermedia (AEH).

The aim of chapter 2 is to provide a model for requirement specification, useful in developing efficient e-assessment applications with personalized feedback, which is enhanced by calling a recommender engine. The research was done in the context of using educational technology to facilitate learning processes. The data used to build the requirements model was collected from a set of interviews with the users and creators of an e-assessment application in project management. Requirements analysis assumes human effort and thus introduces uncertainties. To minimize the subjective factor, the data extracted from interviews with the users and the developers of the existing e-assessment application are clustered using a fuzzy logic solution into classes of requirements. These classes are the units of the model. The connections between classes are also mentioned: relations such as "if-then," "switch," or "contains" are explained. The requirements analysis conducts to a smart set of specifications, obtained in a collaborative manner, useful for the design of e-assessment applications in project management or other similar domains.

Chapter 3 presents an overview of the field of recommender systems and describes the current generation of recommendation methods with their limitations and possible extensions that can improve the capabilities of the recommendations made suitable for wide range of applications. In recent years, machine learning algorithms have been considered to be an important part of the recommendation process to make intelligent decisions. The chapter will explore the application of such techniques in the field of network intrusion detection in order to examine the vulnerabilities of different recommendation techniques. Finally, Panda et al., outline some of the major issues in building secure recommendation systems in identifying possible network intrusions.

Meyer et al., in chapter 4, describe REPERIO, a flexible and generic industrial recommender system able to deal with several kinds of data sources (content-based, collaborative, social network) into the same framework and to work on multi-platforms (Web service in a multi-user mode and mobile device in a mono-user mode). The item-item matrix is the keystone of the architecture for its efficiency and flexibility properties. In the first part, the authors present core functionalities and requirements of recommendation in an industrial context. In the second part, the architecture of the system and the main issues involved in its development are presented. The last part reports experimental results obtained using REPERIO on benchmarks extracted from the Netflix Prize with different filtering strategies. To illustrate the interest and flexibility of the architecture, the authors explain how it is possible to take into account, for recommendations, external sources of information. In particular, the authors show how to exploit user generated contents posted on social networks to fill the item-item matrix. The process proposed includes a step of opinion classification.

A business case describes a problem present in all insurance companies: portfolio risk evaluation. Such analysis deals with determining the risk level as well as main risk factors. In the specific case, an insurance company is faced with market share growth and profit decline. Discovered knowledge about the level of risk and main risk factors was not used to increase premium for the riskiest portfolio segments due to a specific market situation, which could lead to loss of clients in the long run. Instead, additional analysis was conducted using data mining methods resulting in a solution, which stopped further profit decline and lowered the risk level for the riskiest portfolio segments. The central role of unexpectedly revealed knowledge in chapter 5 acts as the REFII model. The REFII model is an authorial mathematical model for time series data mining. The main purpose of that model is to automate time series analysis, through a unique transformation model of time series.

Information filtering deals with the problem of selecting relevant information for a given user, according to her/his preferences and interests. Chapter 6 considers two ways of performing information filtering: recommendation and contextual advertising. In particular, this chapter studies and analyzes them according to a unified view. In fact, the task of suggesting an advertisement to a Web page can be viewed as the task of recommending an item (the advertisement) to a user (the Web page) and vice versa. Starting from this insight, this chapter proposes a content-based recommender system based on a generic solution for contextual advertising and a hybrid contextual advertising system based on a generic hybrid recommender system. Relevant case studies have been considered (i.e., a photo recommender and a Web advertiser) with the goal of highlighting how the proposed approach works in practice. In both cases, results confirm the effectiveness of the proposed solutions.

Recommender Systems are applied in a multitude of spheres and have a significant role in reduction of information overload on those websites that have the features of voting. Therefore, it is an urgent need for them to adapt and respond to immediate changes in user preference. To overcome the shortcomings of each individual approach to design the recommender systems, a myriad of ways to coalesce different recommender systems are proposed by researchers. In this chapter, Bakshi et al., in chapter 7, have presented an insight into the design of recommender systems developed, namely content-based and collaborative recommendation, their evaluation, their lacunae, and some hybrid models to enhance the quality of prediction.

The foremost theme of chapter 8 is to utilize the subtractive clustering concept for defining the market boundaries in the fuzzy-based segmentation. In this sense, the present work starts by analyzing the importance of segmenting the shoppers on the basis of store image. After reviewing the segmentation literature, this work performed a segmentation analysis of retail shoppers in India. Researchers often use clustering analysis as a tool in market segmentation studies, the results of which often end with crisp partitioning forms, where one member cannot belong to two or more groups. This indicates that different segments overlap with one another. This study integrates the concept of application of subtractive clustering in fuzzy c-means clustering for profiling the customers who perceive the retail store based on its image. Fuzzy clustering is also compared with hard clustering solutions. Then this work predicts the model using discriminate analysis. Further, it concentrates on the answer tree model of segmentation to identify the best predictor. Main conclusions with implications for retailing management are pointed out.

Recommender systems represent a prominent class of personalized Web applications, which particularly focus on the user-dependent filtering and selection of relevant information. Recommender Systems have been a subject of extensive research in AI over the last decade, but with today's increasing number of e-commerce environments on the Web, the demand for new approaches to intelligent product recommendation is higher than ever. There are more online users, more online channels, more vendors, more products, and most importantly, increasingly complex products and services. These recent developments in the area of recommender systems generated new demands, in particular with respect to interactivity, adaptivity, and user preference elicitation. These challenges, however, are also in the focus of general Web page recommendation research. The goal of chapter 9 is to develop robust techniques to model noisy data sets containing an unknown number of overlapping categories, and apply them for Web personalization and mining. In this chapter, rough set-based clustering approaches are used to discover Web user access patterns, and these techniques compute the number of clusters automatically from the Web log data using statistical techniques. The suitability of rough clustering approaches for Web page recommendations are measured using predictive accuracy metrics.

The objective of chapter 10 is to design an intelligent recommender system classification unit using hybrid neural techniques. In particular, a neuroscience-based hybrid by Buabin is introduced, explained, and examined for its potential in real world text document classification on the modapte version of the Reuters news text corpus. The described neuroscience model (termed Hy-RNC) is fully integrated with a novel boosting algorithm to augment text document classification purposes. Hy-RNC outperforms existing works and opens up an entirely new research field in the area of machine learning. The main contribution of this chapter is the provision of a step-by-step approach to modeling the hybrid system using underlying concepts such as boosting algorithms, recurrent neural networks, and hybrid neural systems. Results attained in the experiments show impressive performance by the hybrid neural classifier even with a minimal number of neurons in constituting structures.

Because of their mathematical backgrounds and coherent structures, AI methods and techniques are often used to find solutions for different types of problems encountered. In the related context, nature-inspired algorithms are also important for providing more accurate solutions. Because of their nature-based, flexible process structures, the related algorithms can be applied to different types of problems. At this point, recommendation systems are one of the related problem areas that nature-inspired algorithms can be used to get better results. In the literature, there are many research studies that are based on using nature-inspired algorithms within recommendation systems. This chapter aims to discuss the usage of some newly developed nature-inspired algorithms in typical recommendation systems. In this aim, features and functions of some new nature-inspired algorithms will be explained first. Later, using the related algorithms in recommendation systems will be discussed. Following that, there will be a discussion on the future of nature-inspired algorithms and also their roles in the recommendation approach or system based applications (chapter 11).

The neural network is a very useful tool for approximation of a function, time series prediction, classification, and pattern recognition. If there is found to be a non-linear relationship between input data and output data, it is difficult to analyse the system. A neural network is very effective to solve this problem. This work applied the neural network model to study the clearance sales outshopping behaviour. Since neural network theory can be applied effectively to this case, the author has used neural network theory to recognise the retail area satisfaction and loyalty. To measure the impact among the retail area attributes, retail area satisfaction and retail area loyalty, the author has used neural network model. In this study, twenty-seven factors have been treated as the input signals into the input layer. Therefore, M. Hemalatha will find the weights between nodes in the relationship between the value of all twenty-seven factors and the retail area satisfaction and loyalty. The development of model by retail area attributes, and their interpretation, was facilitated by collection of data across three trading areas. This neural network modeling approach to understanding clearance sales outshopping behaviour provides retail managers with information to support retail strategy development (chapter 12).

The objective is neural-based feature selection in intelligent recommender systems. In particular, a hybrid neural genetic architecture is modeled based on human nature, interactions, and behaviour. The main contribution of this chapter is the development of a novel genetic algorithm based on human nature, interactions, and behaviour. The novel genetic algorithm termed "Buabin Algorithm" is fully integrated with a hybrid neural classifier to form a Hybrid Neural Genetic Architecture. The research presents GA in a more attractive manner and opens up the various departments of a GA for active research. Although no scientific experiment is conducted to compare network performance with standard approaches, engaged techniques reveal drastic reductions in genetic operator operations. For illustration purposes, the UCI Molecular Biology (Splice Junction) dataset is used. Overall, "Buabin Algorithm" seeks to integrate human-related interactions into genetic algorithms, so as imitate human genetics in recommender systems design and understand underlying datasets explicitly (chapter 13).

The technology behind personalization or Web page recommendation has undergone tremendous changes, and several Web-based personalization systems have been proposed in recent years. The main goal of Web personalization is to dynamically recommend Web pages based on the online behavior of users. Although personalization can be accomplished in numerous ways, most Web personalization techniques fall into four major categories: decision rule-based filtering, content-based filtering, and collaborative filtering and Web usage mining. Decision rule-based filtering reviews users to obtain user demographics or static profiles, and then lets Web sites manually specify rules based on them. It delivers the appropriate content to a particular user based on the rules. However, it is not particularly useful because it depends on users knowing in advance the content that interests them. Content-based filtering relies on items being similar to what a user has liked previously. Collaborative filtering, also called social or group filtering, is the most successful personalization technology to date. Most successful recommender systems on the Web typically use explicit user ratings of products or preferences to sort user profile information into peer groups. It then tells users what products they might want to buy by combining their personal preferences with those of like-minded individuals. However, collaborative filtering has limited use for a new product that no one has seen or rated, and content-based filtering to obtain user profiles might miss novel or surprising information. Additionally, traditional Web personalization techniques, including collaborative or content-based filtering, have other problems, such as reliance on subject user ratings and static profiles or the inability to capture richer semantic relationships among Web objects. To overcome these shortcomings, the new Web personalization tool, nonintrusive personalization, attempts to increasingly incorporate Web usage mining techniques. Web usage mining can help improve the scalability, accuracy, and flexibility of recommender systems. Thus, Web usage mining can reduce the need for obtaining subjective user ratings or registration-based personal preferences. Chapter 14 provides a survey of Web usage mining approaches.

Satchidananda Dehuri
Fakir Mohan University, India

Manas Ranjan Patra
Berhampur University, India

Bijan Bihari Misra
Silicon Institute of Technology, India

Alok Kumar Jagadev
SOA University, India

Chapter 1

A Recommender System Supporting Teachers to Author Learning Sessions in Decision-Making

Arnoldo Rodríguez
Universidad de Costa Rica, Costa Rica

ABSTRACT

This chapter pays attention to the automatic generation and recommendation of teaching materials for teachers who do not have enough time to learn how to use authoring tools for the creation of materials to support their courses. To overcome the difficulties, the research is intended to solve the problem of time needed to create adapted case studies for teaching decision-making in network design. Another goal is to reduce the time required to learn the use of an authoring tool to create teaching materials. Thus, the author presents an assistant that provides adapted help for teachers, generates examples automatically, verifies that any generated example fits in the class of examples used by the teacher, and recommends personalized examples according to each teacher's preferences. He studies the use of data related to teachers to support the recommendation of teaching materials and the adaptation of Web-based support. The automatic generation and test of examples of network topologies are based on a probabilistic model, and the recommendation is based on Bayesian classification. This investigation also looks at problems related to the application of Artificial Intelligence (AI) to support teachers in authoring learning sessions for Adaptive Educational Hypermedia (AEH).

INTRODUCTION

The main question to answer here is how to provide Web-based context-sensitive help to teachers engaged in authoring Adaptive Educational Hypermedia (AEH). This chapter is intended to address and solve their problems of time needed

to learn the use of an authoring tool and to create examples and additional teaching materials.

Our solution seeks to provide teachers with an easy to use access to an adaptive help and an authoring tool that will enable any qualified teacher to create his own course-work with minimal programming effort.

DOI: 10.4018/978-1-4666-2542-6.ch001

Although some AEH facilitate the development of supporting material for teaching, dealing with an AEH entails multiple challenges to combine and organize topics and resources. AEH systems are based on the hypertext structure, and they use information of each student to adapt learning to his needs (Brusilovsky, 2001). Most authoring tools used to create AEH remain difficult to learn and use. Authoring tools are programs used for the production of intelligent tutoring systems (Johansson, 2001).

To overcome the difficulties, in this chapter we will view the teacher as a trainee who needs to be instructed not only in the different pedagogical strategies involved in teaching a subject, but in the usage of an authoring tool for the creation of AEH (Vázquez-Abad, Rodríguez, & Aïmeur, 2003).

Consequently, this chapter also presents an assistant, ARIALE (Authoring Resources for Implementing Adaptive Learning Environments), that involves the recommendation of examples and the application of adapted help techniques. Our assistant generates examples automatically and verifies that any generated examples fits in the class of examples used by the teacher (the teacher's teaching style). The generation and test of examples of network topologies are based on a probabilistic model, and the recommendation is based on techniques of artificial intelligence, such as Bayesian classification (Keller, 2002) and Case-Based Reasoning (CBR) (Cortés, et al., 1994).

The recommendation in this research is also based on the automatic generation of examples according to the teacher's preferences, on the addition and reuse of existing examples in a case base, and on the learning of the teacher's decisions related to which examples to use (Rodríguez, 2008).

ARIALE includes an authoring tool for the creation of teaching materials and a Teacher Model with information related to each teacher's preferences. The Teacher Model belongs to a knowledge base that supports personalized help for teachers and the different decisions that ARIALE makes.

Decisions about how to provide recommendations and adapt help are based on teacher's data stored in a Teacher Model, and ARIALE learns from these decisions to improve future support to teachers. Data related to used examples models each teacher's teaching style. Each style evolves according examples changes (Rodríguez, 2011). This view of the Teacher Model is new and helpful, because our Teacher Model is part of a knowledge base that allows our system to be more flexible than a classical AEH with a static Pedagogical Model.

Regarding the aspects described previously, this investigation answers the following questions:

1. What can be the general structure and functionality of an assistant to support teachers authoring learning session in decision-making?
2. Which specific functionalities and characteristics of an authoring tool can allow implementer teachers to adapt teaching material according to their pedagogical goals?
3. How can the assistant generate and recommend examples to support teaching decision-making?
4. How does the assistant make decisions about which kind of help content to show, and which media to use for displaying the content?
5. How does the assistant learn to help teachers in a personalized or customized way?

In the following sections we discuss other projects related to our research, the problem focused on this research, the solutions, the knowledge base that ARIALE uses to make decisions, the adaptive help applied, a process to generated and recommend examples, a mixed method for developing our system, the results of an evaluation of the system and our conclusions.

LITERATURE REVIEW

As a result of the review of literature related to our research subjects, we defined a series of concepts that supports our approach and that we applied in our system.

In our Pedagogical Model, we apply the Cognitive Load Theory (CLT) (Sweller, 1988) and Payr's model for teaching and learning (Payr, 2003). A fundamental idea is using "worked-out examples" to reduce the cognitive load that teachers may experience while they are learning new concepts. Using worked-out examples requires that the Teacher Model keeps data related to which examples a teacher can reuse. In addition, worked-out examples are stored as cases that ARIALE manipulates applying artificial intelligence techniques.

We also focus on concepts related to the application of artificial intelligence in human-computer interaction, particularly adaptation, machine learning, artificial intelligence techniques such Case Base Reasoning (CBR) and Bayesian Learning, intelligent help systems, automatic generation of case studies and recommender systems. While the application of intelligence or adaptation in help, namely desktop on-line help, Web-based help, on-line documentation, or any help system, is not commonly used, the use of artificial intelligence techniques for adaptation in help systems is not frequent (Delisle & Moulin, 2002).

Although research is not focusing on on-line intelligent and adaptive/hypermedia that helps instructors to teach using authoring tools, some authors have mentioned the lack of research on the instructor modelling and the advantages of using information of teachers to improve Intelligent Tutoring Systems (ITS) (Kinshuk, Hong, & Patel, 2001). An ITS is a system that uses artificial intelligence to provide customized learning and supports students in their learning (Shiri-Ahmadabadi, 1999). There are also projects related to the application of Bayesian Networks and user modelling (Henze & Nejdl, 1999).

In the area of assistance for users, some research aims at guiding workers while they are working, such as ADAPTS, an adaptative hypermedia ITS to guide in maintaining complex equipment (Brusilovsky & Cooper, 1999). Other examples of Web-based adaptive help are found in Interbook (Brusilovsky & Schwartz, 1997), a system intended to support students learning computer science. CACTUS has an authoring tool to create ITSs and an agent that monitors users to guide them on using the tool (García, 2000). Using a teacher model, WEAR helps authors on how to teach (strategy), and allows teachers to share exercises among themselves (Virvou & Mondriduo, 2007).

An important concern is the automatic generation of user support. An interesting antecedent is the automatic generation of quiz questions proposed in MULTIBOOK (Fischer & Steinmetz, 2000). In this system, a static number of components is combined to generate a limited set of questions. Another earlier study in this area is HYPER-ITS, a system that includes a random problem generator which "selects concepts that will be treated independently given and creates instances of these concepts by randomly generating values within specified boundaries" (Kinshuk, Patel, & Russell, 1999, p. 276).

Some authors have proposed methods that use machine learning techniques for the generation of network topologies with low cost and a minimal acceptable delay (Pierre, 1998; Pierre & Elgibaoui, 1997; Pierre & Legault, 1998).

AIMS includes recommendations in its functions of intelligent help for authors, but these recommendations are limited to leaning support and they do not include problem-solving support, as in our case (Aroyo, Cristea, & Dicheva, 2002). In addition, automatic generation of teaching materials is not usually adapted to each teacher's characteristics and style (Kinshuk, et al., 1999; Virvou & Mondriduo, 2007).

The contribution of our system is not only the generation of examples in a probabilistic manner, but also the use of these generated examples to increase the knowledge base of the system. By classifying examples, our system also learns the class of examples that the teacher prefers.

In conclusion, we found that the purpose and goals of our research are justified because they are pertinent, important, and attack relevant problems that other researchers have not studied with an approach similar to ours.

A RECOMMENDER SYSTEM

The Problem

The complexity of creating a Web site is out of the hands of a typical professor. For professors, it is difficult and time-consuming to create a Web site. Many guides, books, tools, and companies are available to develop Web sites, but they do not make it easier for teachers to use information technology really.

Some universities have specialized units to teach teachers how to use Web-based technologies and how to apply information and communication technologies in education. The problem has two faces: the technical issues about to create a Web site and the more complex aspects referred to how to design effective architectures to structure information according to pedagogical goals.

Although some AEH facilitate the development of supporting material for teaching, they are complex systems, and most authoring tools used to create AEH remain difficult to learn and use. Usually, teachers do not have enough time to learn how to use authoring tools for the creation of their courses. Indeed, most people are eager to use any application with no previous test and training and they prefer the "on-the-job training" style focused on real tasks to be performed.

Sometimes help can be available, but it is not really accessible because users do not know how to access it or access is difficult, or the help is available and accessible, but not adapted to the users' needs (Brusilovsky & Schwartz, 1997; Leung, 2001).

We assume that when an author is creating teaching material with an authoring tool, he faces two main barriers: he requires specific information related to his current task (personalized and specific help according to each teacher's characteristics), and he finds it difficult to locate this information to perform the task (Capobianco, 2002). Finding the right help and adapting it can be complicated and time-consuming jobs for a teacher.

In many cases, the teacher's goal is not the same as the explicit task that the authoring tool was designed for. A descriptive example of this type of problem is analyzed by Guzdial (1999). It is clear that the teacher's main goal is to create materials for teaching; rather than learn how to use the authoring tool. A teacher is an expert whose goal is not learning to use a tool, but rather to achieve an objective with the help of the tool.

As Draper (1999) points out, a teacher has some goals, and learning is just a by product. Many teachers are attempting training while they are impatient and under pressure because they have goals different to learning to use software.

The scenario of a teacher authoring a learning session could be very complex because the teacher must pay attention to teaching, which is the main task, but, at the same time, she must know how to manipulate the authoring tool, and if she needs help, she would also have to interact with the help. Her mind would be involved in three cognitive processes: teaching, manipulating the authoring tool, and dealing with the help features.

Thus, teachers authoring learning sessions may well experience a cognitive overload when learning how to use an authoring tool. In the context of learning, cognitive overload is a situation in which the processing demands required by learning a task may need more effort than the capacity of a teacher's cognitive system (Mayer & Moreno, 2003). For example, university teachers face two barriers when they are authoring teaching materials for their courses:

1. Teachers do not have enough time to create teaching materials.
2. Teachers do not have enough time to learn how to use the tools that could reduce the time required for the creation of materials.

Studies about university teachers report that the amount of time required in learning to use new technologies is the second problem they face after general equipment failures (Butler & Sellbom, 2002). Some authoring tools include different types of help such as wizards, tutorials, and context-sensitive online help, but teachers ask for more personalized support on technical and pedagogical aspects (Weiss-Lambrou & Raymond, 2002). A survey showed that 57% of teachers, who do not use this type of new technology, claim technical support is not adapted to the reality of university teaching (Karsenti, 2004).

Additionally, a learning session is an instance of specific sequences of activities, tasks, steps and actions that uses certain resources to teach one or more groups of students. While a teacher is authoring a learning session, he has to include examples that students will analyze. The creation of examples is also a time-consuming task for teachers.

Solutions and Recommendations

To solve the problems described above, we will view the teacher as a trainee who needs adaptive support to be instructed not only in the different pedagogical strategies involved in teaching a sub-

ject, but also in the usage of an AEH for teaching complex decision-making that takes into account multi-criteria combinatorial (Vásquez-Abad, Rodríguez, Ng, Zukerman, & Warfield, 2001).

To provide teachers with an easy to use authoring environment, we developed ARIALE (Authoring Resources for Implementing Adaptive Learning Environments), an assistant that simplifies the situation for the teacher. ARIALE has a client-server architecture with a three-tier structure that includes most processes working on the server-side, the database on the server-side, and a client-side.

We also take into account a general principle that says more functionality and flexibility or generality in systems implies less usability, but more usability would allow non-programmers to build an AEH. To improve the usability in our research, we forget the breadth to favour depth and usability of our system ARIALE (Murray, 1999). In accordance with this approach, we provide an authoring tool with a limited functionality in a specific domain: decision-making in Network Design. This authoring tool is part of an AEH system with an adaptive interface to train authors. Then, our system supports teachers in two ways by:

1. Recommending examples to be edited or reused. This function implies generating, testing and recommending examples to teachers.
2. Providing tools, resources, and help to create examples. This option includes an authoring tool for the creation of learning sessions to teach decision-making in Network Design and an adaptive help system. The help system offers adaptive context-sensitive and Web-based support about how to use the authoring tool.

ARIALE applies knowledge base adaptation to profit information stored in the Pedagogical Model, the Teacher Model, the Curriculum, and a

Example-base of our system. The most important components of the knowledge base are detailed in the next section.

The Pedagogical Model

The Pedagogical Model provides a model of the teaching process, which is adapted to the different needs of each student. Based on the student model, the Pedagogical Model can make pedagogical decisions about what aspects of the domain knowledge should be presented to the learner, when to review, when to present a new topic, and which topic to present. The Pedagogical Model contains the knowledge about how to teach. The Pedagogical Model is the set of knowledge, teaching strategies and techniques that an ITS or an AEH can apply to teach students.

Consequently, a question to answer is what should the Pedagogical Model, methods and the teaching strategies to teach decision-making expertise and support teachers involve?

Our Pedagogical Model focuses on decision-making in Network Design. More specifically, ARIALE is intended to support teaching Multi-Criteria Decision-Making (MCDM). MCDM deals with multiple conflicting criteria in decision-making for planning process.

The Pedagogical Model behind this research breaks down the study of complex decision-making into three specific tasks or teaching strategies for the integration of knowledge related to the main concepts used in the decision-making process. We are implementing three strategies to teach students: comparison of examples of network topologies, modification of an example of a network topology, and competition to find the best solution to a problem. The final activity integrates the concepts studied in previous activities (Vásquez-Abad, et al., 2001).

ARIALE includes the teaching content and its organization or sequence in its Pedagogical Model. The designer of a curriculum has to create the structure (units or activities) and contents to be taught. To perform this task, it is possible to use a high-level authoring tool similar to Aha! (De Bra, et al., 2003). However, the system can also be programmed directly, as we do. Our system has a curriculum or plan with the main concepts used in the decision-making process that the students will learn in terms of actions and performances.

In order to learn the concepts, students and ARIALE interact in an environment of discovery learning, a pedagogical strategy where the learner can construct his own knowledge by interacting with a domain in order to infer rules from the results of the experiments (Van Joolingen, 1999).

Direct strategies are a group of discovery strategies that includes among others: learning by examples, learning by storytelling, learning by doing, learning by games, learning by analogy, learning by induction, by abduction. Learning by doing is a pedagogical strategy that allows the learners to be involved in hands-on experiences manipulating simulated devices or following procedures.

For students, ARIALE uses "Learning by doing." In this Pedagogical Model, "learning by doing" with worked-out examples the learner can develop the skills to recognize patterns in the provided examples. In this way, the student develops the expertise to retrieve patterns from his long-term memory to compare them with the examples and identify differences and similarities. This view is close to Case-Based Reasoning (CBR) (Cortés, et al., 1994), an artificial intelligence technique, and to the case studies method widely used in teaching business administration (DeLacey & Leonard, 2002). In CBR, learning is a by-product of problem solving.

In addition, our system has two curricula:

1.   The curriculum to be taught to the students; and

2.   The curriculum used to help teachers, which in turn actually entails two aspects: the

learning help about the author tool, and the problem-solving support to create examples of network topologies.

The curriculum used to help teachers works parallel to the curriculum for teaching students. Traditional AEH uses a Pedagogical Model that only take into account the strategies to teach students, but in our case, we also use strategies and techniques to support the tasks that teachers must perform while authoring learning sessions with ARIALE.

For example, each learning session adapted to a specific teacher is composed of two parallel hypermedia: the authoring environment and the corresponding help. For each activity in a curriculum there are one or more parallel help nodes; for each task in an activity there is a parallel help node for the corresponding task. The help nodes that adapt to the progress of the teacher are Adaptive Context-Sensitive Help (AC-SH). The help that does not adapt continuously as the teacher progresses (help for menus, for example) is Non Adaptive Context-Sensitive Help (C-SH). Figure 1 shows the structure of a curriculum hypermedia and the help hypermedia, based on the layered authoring model proposed by (Cristea & Mooij, 2003).

Accessing help is a type of navigation through the help hypermedia. When a teacher clicks links to view help or when the system provides active help, this interaction allows the teacher to traverse the nodes of the help hypermedia.

Our Pedagogical Model applies an on-the-job-training approach to support teachers while they are using the authoring tool for the creation of learning sessions. The on-the-job-training approach is intended to supply support while the teacher is authoring instead of offering training before authoring. We consider that "on-the-job training" is more appropriate for Web-based help than classical methods which include previous training, pre-test, post-test, and other techniques to evaluate the learning of a tool.

The Teacher Model

A teacher should be able to define his pedagogical goals for the activities that he proposes to the students. For example, specifying some criteria to be applied in a particular type of analysis that his students must develop. This view is also supported by the concepts human teacher model (Kinshuk, et al., 2001) and local implementer teacher (Kinshuk, 2003). These concepts refer to the teacher as a person with particular characteristics and preferences, who wants to adjust or adapt an existing ITS or AEH according to his interests and expertise.

The focus of this research is the implementer teacher (Kinshuk, et al., 2001). By implementer teachers, we mean university professors who are using a Web-based authoring tool to create courseware for a subject or course prepared by a designer. These teachers may be experts in the subject, but not necessarily skilled at using Web-tools.

A human teacher model includes personal characteristics of each teacher, information about how he teaches and, in our system, information about how he acquires more knowledge and experience using an authoring tool. For example, a human Teacher Model keeps the teacher's name, his age, the course he teaches, and the type of examples that he prefers to use.

Sometimes a teacher is not sure about what information he needs, and then the system has to infer and predict what information the teacher might need. If the system knows what information is required, the system can adapt to different user's actions to supply appropriate information (Brusilovsky, 2001). Consequently, the system needs information about the teacher's context (user data, usage data and environment data) to support its decisions about what information to find for the teacher (Kobsa, Koenemann, & Pohl, 2001).

A Teacher Model is a set of data referring to a particular teacher. A Teacher Model profiles the characteristics of the teacher. It is also possible to classify the characteristics according to cognitive

Figure 1. Curriculum and help are parallel hypermedia layers that interact

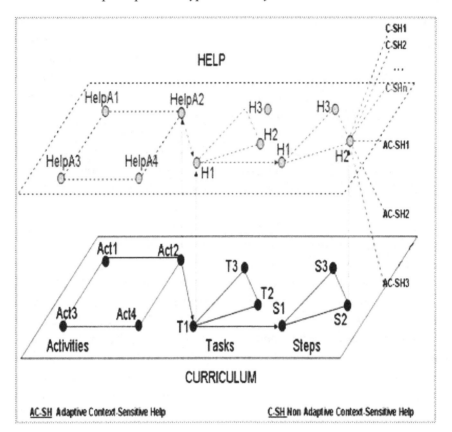

factors related to the knowledge, interests and skills of the users, as well as affective aspects.

Modelling a teacher also implies to store information about the teacher's preferences, his activities and interests (frequent sessions, exercises), his level of expertise (Virvou & Mondriduo, 2002), his goals and plans, his experience and skills (Encarnaçao, 1997), his teaching style, his prior knowledge about the platform, his discipline subject to teach, his learning ability, and the capabilities of the computer hardware and software he is using (Patel, Russell, Oppermann, & Rashev, 1998).

We have adapted the view of the teacher as learner of new technologies (Brusilovsky & Schwartz, 1997) to that of a trainee who requires only adaptive contextual help and support to solve problems, rather than learning to use the author-

ing tool in order to be evaluated (Guzdial, 1996). In this scenario, the teacher's learning becomes a by-product of the support that he receives. We see the teacher as a worker who can learn while he is on the job. We see a teacher as a trainee or a teacher as learner (Vásquez-Abad, et al., 2003).

Based on the Teacher Model, ARIALE helps teachers in the workplace with adapted learning support and problem-solving support (Aberg, 2002) by:

1. Recommending examples to be edited or reused. This function implies generating, testing and recommending examples to teachers.
2. Providing tools, resources, and help to create examples. This option includes an authoring tool for the creation of learning sessions to

teach decision-making in Network Design and an adaptive help system. The help system offers adaptive context-sensitive and Web-based support about the authoring tool.

Teachers have different tendencies in teaching, for example formal authoritarian, demonstrative, suggestive, facilitative, collaborative, delegative (Grasha, 1996). According to Cristea and Garzotto (2004), a teaching style can be problem solving, case-based, progressive, and sequential and others. A teaching style can be described by the way in which he deals with a subject, audiovisual or text based pedagogical strategies, examples, simulations, and demonstrations used to teach. We modelled the teaching style as the class of examples that a teacher uses most frequently. For example, if a teacher uses topologies of high reliability and low cost, these networks can be classified in a particular class, and so the teaching style of this teacher will be associated with this class. In addition, we establish that a teacher classified in a category has a similar teaching style to that of other teachers in the same category. ARIALE takes into account the teaching style information in the Teacher Model to recommend examples that can be useful for a particular teacher. Then, the data (examples) stored in the Teacher Model can be used as a basis to chose and recommend examples which characteristics are similar to the characteristics of the examples that a teacher uses. The main function of our Teacher Model is to allow the system to adapt to different teaching styles in order to recommend appropriate examples.

Automatic Generation, Classification, and Recommendation

Other questions to be answered by this chapter are how can the assistant generate and recommend examples to support teaching decision-making, and which specific functionalities and characteristics of an authoring tool can allow implementer

teachers to adapt teaching material according to their pedagogical goals?

Learning support and problem solving support are two approaches in supporting users with teaching material and help adapted to their pedagogical goals (Aberg, 2002). While some systems only provide learning support, ARIALE offers both.

Problem-solving support helps the user in solving a problem. Instead of helping the user to achieve a goal step-by-step, problem-solving support provides the solution to the problem. This situation occurs when a user is not interested in spending time learning how to use a system or how to solve a problem, and prefers to use the application directly to finish his tasks.

Problem-solving support can be implemented by means of a recommender system. A recommender system learns about a person's needs in order to identify and recommend information that meets his needs (Callan, et al., 2003). Our methods for problem-solving support include the automatic generation, test and the recommendation of examples of network topologies.

An example is a topology to be studied. Examples are topologies that have equivalent measures of performance; the number of link can or not be the same. Equivalent examples are classified in the same class. The topologies in Figure 2 are networks that have equivalent measures of performance, but different number of links. Table 1 shows the measures of performance of network topologies A and B.

Recommending examples is a help technique to support teachers while they are authoring learning sessions. To recommend topologies, our system accesses a case base that stores topologies and selects a series of examples matching the teacher's teaching style (teaching style is the class of topologies that a teacher prefers). If the teacher does not accept to reuse any example that our system recommends, ARIALE generates, tests, and recommends additional examples by using a probabilistic method, which assigns at random

Figure 2. Two topologies A and B are equivalent and belong to a same class

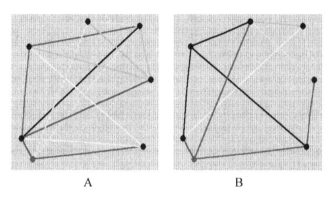

A　　　　　　　　B

the links between the nodes of a topology. An important remark is that ARIALE creates and not only reuses topologies that match teachers' characteristics. Automatically generated teaching materials are not usually adapted to each teacher's characteristics in other AEH. Once a teacher accepts a new generated topology, this example is included in the ARIALE's knowledge database and the system has learned new knowledge to support its future performance in an improved manner. The method for testing examples by Bayesian classification is described later.

Our system uses a hybrid method to recommend examples: one is based on the teacher's characteristics and the other takes into account the examples that the teacher uses to teach.

First, to solve the cold-start problem (Schein, Popescul, Ungar, & Pennock, 2002) when the

Table 1. Measures of performance of network topologies A and B

Measures	Topologies	
	A	B
Reliability	3	3
Capacity	Medium	Medium
Cost	Medium	Medium
Number of links	14	11

teacher has not authored any example, the system uses a collaborative filtering method that takes into account the similarities between teachers according to their teaching styles (Eirinaki & Vazirgianis, 2003). This method allows the system to recommend examples created by teachers with similar backgrounds and preferences.

The reasoning behind the recommendation mechanism of our system is based on CBR, and the hypothesis is that the examples the teacher will use in the future depend on the ones used previously by teachers classified in the same category. If the system knows which examples the teacher has used in the past or which have been used by other teachers of the same category, it can reasonably choose examples that the teacher will probably be able to use.

ARIALE uses Bayesian classification to find similarities between a teacher that has not authored any example and teachers with examples created and teaching styles defined. Bayesian classification or Bayesian learning is an artificial intelligence technique for classification that uses probabilities (Keller, 2002). The system believes that teachers sharing similar characteristics in the same category can also share a teaching style or pattern. In order to recommend examples, the system classifies the teacher in a class or category of teachers with similar characteristics. Doing this, ARIALE detects the type of examples that the teachers in the particular category use. After that, the system recommends examples of this type to the new teacher (Rodríguez, 2008).

Bayesian classification is a method to classify new evidence according to given prior evidence. This type of classifier can classify sets of inputs and learn novel inputs in order to anticipate behaviour or a result (Rothrock, Koubek, Fuchs, Hass, & Salvendy, 2002). This method is based on Bayesian theory, which uses previously known results to calculate more probabilities. A conditional probability or posterior probability is the probability of an event given some evidence.

Second, when the teacher has created at least one example, the system uses a content-based filtering method that looks for examples that are similar to the example used by the current teacher (Eirinaki & Vazirgianis, 2003). Filtering examples by taking into account the preferred examples of a teacher allows the system to recommend examples that are close to his current teaching style.

Our system has a particular module, the Generator, which creates examples automatically. This module generates examples according to the criteria defined by the designer, and verifies that any generated topology fits in the class of examples used by the teacher (the teacher's teaching style). If the generator creates an example that is out of the scope that the teacher prefers, the example is aborted and a new one is generated. The following procedure details how the Generator creates and tests examples for a teacher.

- Procedure Generate examples () {
  - ○ Given 7 nodes and a set of types of link
  - ○ M=<twisted, coaxial, fiber, infrared, microwave, satellite>
  - ○ WHILE the example does not belong to the teacher's class of examples nor matches his preferred measures of performance DO
    - ▪ FOR each link L_{ij} connecting node i to node j DO {

- ▪ At random, select a type of link from M
- ▪ Or do not assign any link
- ▪ Assign the selected type of link to L_{ij}
- ▪ }
  - ○ Locate a concentrator at random
  - ○ Calculate the measures of performance of the generated example
  - ○ Verify the example belonging to the teacher's class of examples
  - ○ END of WHILE
  - ○ Display the topology in the editor
  - ○ }

The generation and test of topologies are based on a probabilistic model, and the recommendation is also based on Bayesian learning. We use Bayesian learning to test if a generated example matches the teacher's teaching style; if the example matches his style, ARIALE recommends the topology.

A network topology can be represented as a vector of four measures: the network reliability, the number of links, the total network capacity and the network cost. We are using some of the measures of performance for the characterization of computer networks proposed by Pierre and Gharbi (2001). The measures of performance (global values) are functions of the values of the attributes of the links in a topology. To check if the topology matches the teacher's preferences, the system must calculate the probabilities for each measure of performance to compare them to the measures of the type of topologies the teacher prefers. By classifying a generated example in the teacher's preferred class of examples, the Generator verifies if the example fits his preferences or must be discarded.

After calculating the measures of performance of the generated example, it is possible to multiply the probabilities of each measure of performance to appear in a class in order to obtain the global probability of the vector to belong to a particular class. The maximal probability obtained determines to which class the topology can belong, according to Equation (1)

$$v(E) = \underset{v_j \in |A,B|}{\arg\max} P(v_j) \prod_i P(a_i \mid v_j) \qquad (1)$$

where:

- {A,B } is the set of the different classes to classify examples.
- E is the example to be classified.
- v_j is each class of examples.
- a_i is the value of each attribute (reliability, capacity, cost and number of links) tested for each class.

Unfortunately, the Bayesian classifier performs poorly when the number of instances with a particular attribute a_i is very small, or in the worst case when it is zero and produces zero as the final probability. To solve this problem, the naïve Bayesian classifier uses m-estimate of probabilities and applies Equation (2) to calculate the probability of each attribute of belonging to each class of examples (Keller, 2002).

$$P(a_i v_J) = \frac{n_c + mp}{n + m} \qquad (2)$$

where:

- a_i is the value of each attribute a_i tested for each class v_j.
- n is the total number of instances in each class v_j.
- n_c is the number of instances with attribute a_i and class v_j.
- p is a priori estimate for $P(a_i|v_j)$. According to Keller (2002) p means the probability of a_i having one of its possible values.
- m is a constant used to avoid the possible consequences if $n_c = 0$ (in this case the cal-

culation would be zero). We use m = 4 as a constant because we have four attributes (reliability, capacity, cost and number of links).

Learning

If the teacher does not like an example generated by the system, the system can prompt the teacher to edit the offered example until he is satisfied with it. If the teacher does not want to edit it, the generator continues to produce examples until it gets one that the teacher accepts. This validation method is intended to recommend examples that fit the specific teacher's teaching style. ARIALE applies a type of knowledge acquisition that models each teacher's expertise in teaching a subject.

ARIALE has a knowledge base with data that supports its decisions about providing learning support and problem-solving support. The knowledge in this base must improve to offer better support. ARIALE uses classification learning and an overlay model in the Teacher Model to improve its knowledge. Once an example is accepted, it is classified and included in the knowledge base of the system. This is a kind of learning, but how does the assistant learn to help teachers in a personalized or customized way?

Bayesian learning is a method that allows the system to learn new input in order to anticipate a teacher's request for support. Each time a new example is included in the database, the system learns from it. A Bayesian classifier can keep a summarized image of the frequency with which different characteristics of an example appear in a base of examples. After the classification of each new example, ARIALE updates the data (summarized image) which is necessary for making decisions about learning support and problem-solving support. Then, learning in naïve Bayesian classifier derives from updating the probabilities based on the frequencies of each attribute a_i to appear in a particular class.

The system also learns by monitoring the teacher's accesses to learning support, the changes in his preferences, and the tasks he has performed. The information about accessing help is in the Teacher Model and the system makes decisions based on it (Rodríguez, Aïmeur, & Vásquez-Abad, 2004a). These decisions are not always the same, and they change as the teacher progresses, receives more help, and improves his experience working with the authoring tool. In addition, if a teacher frequently uses a particular type of example in his teaching, the system should remember this tendency (teaching style) to offer examples of the same type. Learning also allows our system to deal with unforeseen situations, such as when a teacher changes his teaching style.

Using a Bayesian classifier makes the generalization, scalability, and reusability in ARIALE easier. An evaluation compared the accuracy of our Bayesian classifier to a k-NN (k=1 Nearest Neighbour) method in recommending network topologies and showed that a Bayesian classifier not only is efficient in this case, but also reduces the latency between requests and answers via Internet (Rodríguez, 2008).

Adaptive Help

In this section, we answer the following question: how does the assistant make decisions about which kind of help content to show, and which media to use for displaying the content?

The learning support helps the teacher to perform some tasks. According to Encarnação (1997), there are four types of user support:

1. On-line support tools (help, guidance, on-line manuals);
2. Off-line documentation;
3. Training; and
4. Advice.

This research focused on the on-line support tools such as help and guidance. Intelligent help should be able to support the teacher whenever he needs help on any related topic.

An intelligent system can perform some tasks by means of artificial intelligence techniques. In general terms, an intelligent system chooses actions based on knowledge to achieve a main objective. Some characteristics of an intelligent system are the representation of information, the reasoning using the information representation, the ability to learn from its experience and the generation of new information.

A more specific means to support users is intelligent help. Intelligent help is a sort of adaptive support that the user might need at a particular time, or in a specific situation or context. We use the concept Intelligent Help Systems (IHS) as equivalent to Adaptive Help Systems (AHS) and according to the definition of Brusilovsky and Schwartz (1997).

Adaptive systems can change their parameters and behaviour in order to meet a goal. Two general categories of adaptation are:

1. **Adaptability:** Users have the possibility to select different types of presentation and interaction.
2. **Adaptivity:** The system possesses the capability to monitor user interaction to generate automatic adaptation that suits different users or contexts of use (Stephanidis, 2001).

IHS provide personalized, dynamic, and contextual support by using artificial intelligence techniques for adaptation (Lorés, et al., 2002). "Contextualized" means supporting the user, taking into account the current plan, and the user's context, and the situation in which the user-computer interaction occurs (Aberg, 2002; Wang, 2001). Context-sensitive help provides information that relates to the specific field of the

Web page in which the user is working currently (Self, 1998).

To help users, it is possible to apply the minimalist approach and layering technique used by Selbach, Sieckenius, and Barbosa (2003), and the techniques of incremental learning and adaptive help proposed by Brusilovsky and Schwartz (1997). The minimalist approach means that the users receive small chunks of information to support them while performing a task or learning how to do it.

Incremental learning and layering technique mean that the system adapts to the user as he learns and progresses from beginner to advanced. According to Brusilovsky and Schwartz (1997), it is necessary:

1. To track the user's actions to know the user knowledge.
2. To use task models to deduce the goal of the user.

Tracking the user's actions, the system can obtain information in three ways:

1. A dialog can be developed between the user and the system.
2. The user can provide an example of what he wants to the system.
3. The system can infer new information based on information previously received.

Personalized Web-Based Help

Information in the Pedagogical Model, the Teacher Model, the Curriculum, and an Example-base, make up a knowledge base of our system (Fischer, 2001). This knowledge base supports the different decisions that ARIALE makes. ARIALE uses knowledge representation and reasoning based on models of users, domains, tasks and media to personalize and improve the interaction between the system and the teacher. As a particular teacher interacts with the system authoring, accessing

help, and getting experience, ARIALE stores data related to this interaction. This data allow the system to adapt help according to the teacher's evolution.

ARIALE takes into account data about the teacher's skills, checks the plan to follow, and decides the type of learning. This decision depends on the events triggered in each Web page. For example, when the teacher is a beginner with no sessions in progress and a Web page is loaded, our system offers problem-solving support by providing a worked-out example to reuse. In all cases, learning support is displayed when the teacher moves the mouse over a link (Rodríguez, Aïmeur, & Vásquez-Abad, 2003).

Our system is efficient to provide learning support because help contents are indexed to each field of each Web page, following the same idea as in ADAPTS (Brusilovsky & Cooper, 1999). However, different to ADAPTS, our system adapts help contents not only to the plan but also to the teacher's skills and personal attributes. Then resources to be displayed are not always the same for a certain field. Then, ARIALE will take into account:

- The ability of the teacher to perform a certain task;
- The complexity of the tasks to be done; and
- The type of content (curriculum) and media (multimedia resources) required to help the instructors with what task to do and how to perform that task (Rodríguez, Aïmeur, & Vásquez-Abad, 2004b).

We can classify teachers in three basic categories according to their ability and experience in teaching and using the system: beginner, intermediate and advanced users.

The support for users at the three levels could include: demonstrations, guidance, and assistance in free explorations. A user may only require guidance about the usage of the authoring tool. Another user can need demonstrations about the usage of the tool, guidance on pedagogical strategies to teach decision-making and assistance about some concepts related to a domain namely "Network Design," for instance. These strategies use text based explanations, graphics, and multimedia resources (Rodríguez, et al., 2004a). Our system selects the help strategy and techniques to deliver support, the kind of help content to show, and the media to display the content adapted to the teacher's preferences, such as language or media.

BUILDING THE SYSTEM

Previous sections explained data and procedures behind ARIALE and now we detail the general structure and functionality of an assistant to support teachers authoring teaching materials.

ARIALE is a prototype of a Web-based adaptive hypermedia assistant made up of an authoring tool and an Intelligent Help System (IHS). The authoring tool and the intelligent help system depend on three components:

- Information that supports the decisions of the system (knowledge).
- Resources used to build Web pages.
- Processes that use information and resources to build Web pages.

The data that the system needs for decision-making is related to the definition of the system and includes the curriculum, order of concepts to be presented, teacher's data, environment data, pedagogical strategies, structure of sessions and examples, and rules that the system uses to make decisions. This set of components is a part of the knowledge of the system. The resources are the texts, images, and multimedia files used to generate menus, forms for the authoring tool, and help messages in the Web pages. The system is a "decision-maker" that uses knowledge to guide the construction of Web pages by selecting low-level

resources such as a string of text or an image file. Figure 3 shows a scheme of our system.

ARIALE has a client-server architecture with a three-tier structure that includes most processes working on the server-side, the database on the server-side, and a client-side.

On the server side, the system includes components such as Curriculum, Teacher Model, Pedagogical Model, Sessions Base, Resources, a Session Manager, a Planner, and a Helper. On the client side, an interface agent interacts with the user, thereby monitoring his environment and sending information to the server (Vázquez-Abad, et al., 2003).

Guidelines

One of the most important questions related to ITS is which method or guidelines should be followed by designers when they use an ITS authoring environment (Kimiavi, 1998). Extending the question to authoring AEH, the development of ARIALE was based on two main aspects or answers from different authors:

1. Data and implementation are independent; thus, content adaptation must be easier (Costagliola, Ferrucci, & Francese, 2002). This means that no template has a static component such as text, or image and each template is filled dynamically.
2. The system has a typical three-layer model (Costagliola, et al., 2002; Cristea & Mooij, 2003; De Bra, et al., 2003; Koch, 1999):
   a. A presentation level, to display information;
   b. A storage level, with the physical representation of data (files and database entries);
   c. A logical level, with the correspondences between data stored in databases and the structure of the templates; these correspondences are according to the teacher's skills, plans and preferences.

Figure 3. The system depends on information about the teacher, the environment, and the resources

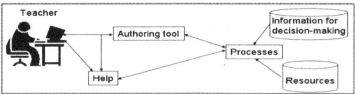

Taking into account those two main aspects, we had to create the following method to build our hypermedia system because we did not find a complete method to develop intelligent help systems for authoring tools. This method integrates fragments from other methods and guides for building ITSs (Kimiavi, 1998), AEH (Wu, Houben, & De Bra, 1998), help systems (Selbach, et al., 2003), and adaptive interfaces (Rothrock, et al., 2002). This mixed method has two parts: the first is a typical software engineering method intended to create the general functionality of a Web site and authoring tool; the second part includes the intelligent help. Each part encloses several steps to be followed.

Implementing the Authoring Tool

The steps of the first part are requirement analysis, task analysis, definition of contents and a prototype.

Requirement Analysis

In this phase, the needs of the course designer were partially defined in order to be mapped to initial Web pages. The expert content required was also defined, the general tasks that the implementer teacher (author) had to perform were identified (Vásquez-Abad, et al., 2001), and the most important areas of problem-solving support and learning support were also detected.

Task Analysis

The general tasks for authoring a learning session were broken down in sequences of more detailed tasks and these were refined until they identified specific actions (click a button, write an instruction) that an author had to perform in order to create a learning session. Once these actions were identified, the different types of support were also defined.

Definition of Authoring Tool Contents

In this phase, the contents to be displayed as part of the authoring tool were defined and included in the database.

Prototype of the Authoring Tool

A first prototype of the authoring tool is produced with no help nor adaptation added. This phase involves many activities:

- Implementing the Web site.
- Creating the Teacher Model, the Curriculum, the resources for the authoring tool and all the components required in order to have a functional Web site.
- Building the interface.
- Creating Web pages.
- Coding the different fields in each template in order to make the integration of help easier.
- Implementing the navigation between Web pages.

A page-builder engine was developed to generate Web pages dynamically (Rodríguez, et al., 2004b).

Integrating the Help System

To design and integrate the Help System, we applied the following steps.

Adaptive Interface Design

We used the guide to adaptive interface design proposed by Rothrock et al. (2002) that has three rules for designing an adaptive interface:

1. Identify variables that call for adaptation;
2. Determine modifications to the interface;
3. Select the inference mechanism.

Identify Variables that Call for Adaptation

In this step, it was necessary to define the information that the system had to take into account for the adaptation. In ARIALE, the main sources of adaptation are (Rothrock, et al., 2002):

- User Performance (mouse events, for example).
- User Goals (plan to be performed).
- User Knowledge (previous experience teaching a subject, for example).
- User Groups (recommending to the user something that is common to the user's group).
- User Personality and Cognitive Style (preferences and examples used for teaching).

Related to these sources of adaptation, we use three more specific types of variables that call for adaptation: variables activated by a system event, such as when a Web page is loaded or unloaded; variables that are activated when the teacher performs events explicitly, such as clicking a link; and, variables that are activated without any explicit intention of the user, but result from his interaction with the system.

Determine the Type of Adaptation to be Performed

In this case, the help content, the medium to display help messages, and the help techniques are the most important aspects that are adapted in ARIALE (Rodríguez, et al., 200b). In the case of help techniques, the recommendation of examples was also one of the types of adaptation determined.

Define the Inference Mechanism

This is the mechanism that reacts to changes in the teacher's information or triggers functions when an event occurs and decides what modifications have to be made in the interface (Rothrock, et al., 2002). For example, generation, testing and recommending a topology that matches the teacher's teaching style is a process that the system performs when the teacher clicks a button to generate a new topology in the network editor (Rodríguez, 2008).

Definition of Help Contents

The actual texts, images, animations and video for the help were defined in this step (Selbach, et al., 2003). The generator of examples was also created.

Definition of the Content Structure

The organization of the help content included not only defining attributes to classify help resources but also defining the classes of examples to be classified and developing an example classifier.

Definition of the Relations between Fields in Templates and Contents

In this step, we linked the help to the interface components (indexation).

User Interface Layout

The tool used to generate and edit network topologies is the topology editor (Figure 4). This editor allows teachers to edit examples of the type of network they want their students to analyse. It also allows teachers to try changing links and nodes until they get the network they want the students to receive. The editor was designed to provide an easy tool to create examples of network topologies and, it allows the teacher to create a static model of a network.

While the teacher is authoring a session, he can use this editor to define the configuration of a network topology. Using the graphical editor, the teacher can manipulate nodes and links as drag-and-drop objects with different properties.

In many applications, a teacher must switch from one window to another window or frame to check the help information. In order to offer less disruptive help, our system has a standard layout where the left area of the screen is used to display the menu for navigation, the authoring area uses the middle area of the screen, and the right area of the screen is used to display help information. Figure 4 shows the Web page layout including the editor (generator) of network topologies.

These decisions to display help are based on the following four criteria:

- **Parallelism:** Means that information required by the user can be displayed simultaneously in a parallel manner, for example, a column of information on the left side accompanied by a column with complementary information on the right (Yu, 2002; Yu, Min, & Spenkelink, 2003).

- **Embedded help:** Displayed in the same screen and window that the user is working on (Weber, 2000).

- **Shortened line of text:** The line length of text used in this layout is between 35 and

Figure 4. The interface of the system: menu (left), the author tool and the generator (center), and graphic help (right)

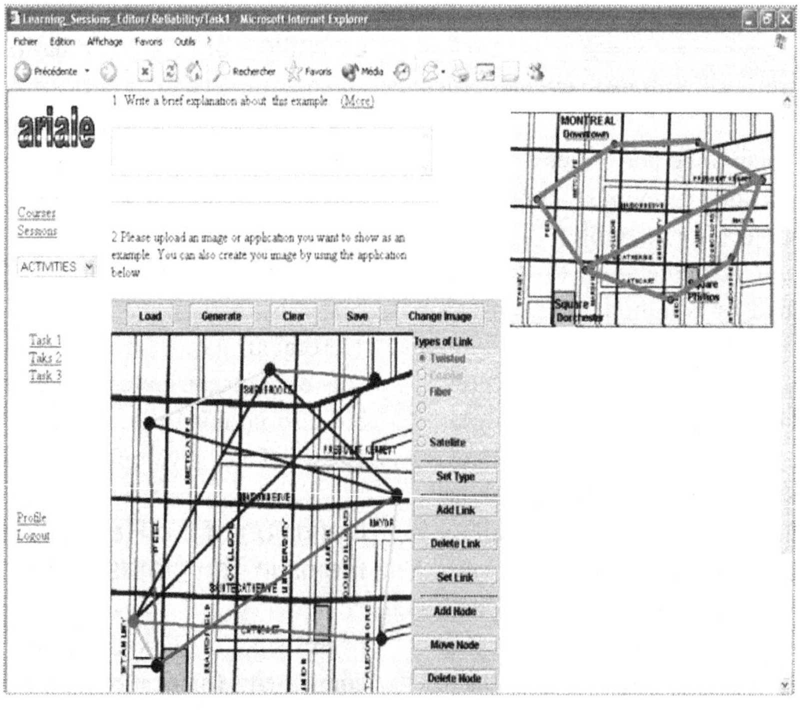

70 characters to avoid excessive movements of the eye and neck from the end of one line to the beginning of the next line (Lynch & Horton, 2001).

- **Short paragraphs:** Enable the teacher to scan instead of read. Shorter paragraphs and shorter lines of text allow the user to quickly scan and find the information he is looking for (Spool, 1999).

Teachers′ data collected by means of a survey support the affirmation that personalized and embedded help makes the learning support for teachers more comfortable than traditional help (Rodríguez, 2007).

EVALUATION

Two aspects of the support that ARIALE provides were evaluated:

1. The accuracy of ARIALE in recommending examples of network topologies (problem-solving support), and
2. The acceptance of the ARIALE help approach by teachers.

We applied the accuracy criterion to check if the system recommends good examples. An example is a network topology with different number and types of links and three basic measures of performance (reliability, capacity, and cost). In our validation, we not only tested the accuracy of our Bayesian classifier but also compared it to a k-NN (k=1 Nearest Neighbour) method (Rodríguez, 2008, 2007). The accuracy of our recommendation method was validated by the following two ways:

- 10-fold cross-validation of each of the three classifiers.
- Comparison of the performance of the Bayesian classifier based on measures of performance with the other classifier.

Cross-Validation

Cross-validation consists of dividing the training dataset data into a number k of partitions. Testing is performed by extracting one partition from the dataset; each example of the extracted partition is classified to measure the error rate of the classifier. After finishing with a partition, it is reinserted into the dataset and another block of examples is tested. These operations are repeated for each partition, and finally, an average of the number of errors is calculated (Stone, 1977). The inverse of this average shows the degree of accuracy of the classifier.

We ran 10-fold cross-validation to validate the accuracy of our classifiers, and the results are:

- The accuracy of the Bayesian classifier based on the measures of performance is 94% (6% error), according to the test developed with a training dataset of 200 topologies (20 topologies for testing and 180 for training for each test). This classifier works with six classes of topologies.
- The accuracy of a k-NN (k=1 Nearest Neighbour) classifier based on the measures of performance is 96% (4% error), according to the test developed with the same training dataset of 200 examples. This classifier also works with our six classes of topologies. This k-NN classifier measures the dissimilarity between the measures of performance of a given topology and the measures of performance of each network in a set of topologies. We measure the dissimilarity between each pair of topologies by using Euclidean distance (Euclidean similarity). As the dissimilarity measure increases, the two topologies become more different.

Although the result of testing the accuracy of k-NN classifier (96%) is better than the result obtained by the Naïve Bayes classifier (94%), a Bayesian classifier is more flexible and easy to adapt to different domains and number of attributes. The Naïve Bayes algorithm is easy to implement and a k-NN classifier requires a lot of work and tests (Rodríguez, 2008). Another argument in favour of naïve Bayesian classifiers is that they reduce the latency between requests and answers via Internet (Webb, Pazzani, & Billsus, 2001; Miyahara & Pazzani, 2002). A recommender system that uses a Bayesian classifier as ours is scalable because the number of examples can increase without affecting the time to respond highly.

Evaluation of the Help Approach

The evaluation of the acceptance of the help approach used in ARIALE was implemented by means of a survey applied to 27 teachers that work in the Universidad de Costa Rica (a public university in San José, Costa Rica) and had used a Web site to teach a course at least (Rodríguez, 2007). We selected those 27 teachers because they have used an authoring tool to create their Web sites and they were receptive to answer the survey. In this group, we find 13 women and 14 men, and all people ages are between 30 and 55 years old, except two teachers who are younger than 30 years old. Each of the 27 teachers was interviewed personally and they answered 25 questions related to:

- Automatic generation and recommendation of examples (problem-solving support) to save time in creating teaching materials, and
- Learning support to reduce the time that teachers need to learn how to use authoring tools.

Although most teachers are not using teaching materials that can be generated automatically, an important percentage of the interviewed teachers accept the automatic generation of examples, exercises or cases, and the recommendation of them in a personalized mode, which is better than just sharing materials between teachers with no adaptation to each teacher's characteristics. According to the survey, more that the half of teachers does not use teaching material that can be generated automatically, but 45% (12) of teachers think that the automatic generation and recommendation of examples reduces the time required to produce teaching materials (Rodríguez, 2007).

Regarding the acceptance of recommendations by teachers, we found that 92% (25) of the teachers accept that a computer or software recommends teaching materials for teaching, and this percentage of teachers also accept that software uses teachers' data related to their preferences to recommend examples, exercises and cases similar to the ones that they apply in their courses. Additionally, 44% (12) of teachers accept software that generates and recommend examples, cases or exercises according to their preferences.

According to the survey, 70% of opinions (19 teachers) consider that a personalized context-sensitive help that appears in the same window where a teacher is working, as used in ARIALE, reduces the time they need to learn how to use software or applications to create teaching materials.

The interviewed teachers not only think that our approach saves time in learning to use an application or authoring tool, but they also prefer our method to display learning support or help contents embedded in the same window where the teacher is working (Rodríguez, 2007). More specifically, 48% (13) of teachers prefer to receive help embedded in the same window they are working, as implemented in ARIALE.

Teachers' data collected by means of our survey support the affirmation that personalized help makes the support for teachers more comfortable than traditional help (Rodríguez, 2007). However, although this survey is an important study, we think that its results are restricted to this research and can not be generalized to other universities.

FUTURE RESEARCH

At the beginning of this research, we thought of using a planner (partial order-planner) for generating examples of network topologies (Russell & Norvig, 2002). Ultimately, we switched to a probabilistic generator. However, an alternative that could improve the generation of examples would be a probabilistic planner that selects the operators at random. A planner is a method to transform an initial state into a final state by performing operations that generate a series of temporal states. A complementary option is that a probabilistic planner can transform cases from a case-base.

Although some studies (Koychev, 2000; Leung, 2001) have analyzed forgetfulness in help and recommender systems, more investigation in this field is required. For example, teachers can forget how to use a function or how to author a task. This problem is linked to the need to develop the functionality of adapting the classes and the classification of examples according to the evolution of teachers' activity. For example, substitution of classes no longer in use for new ones can result in splitting frequently used classes. In this case, the systems would forget an unused class of examples.

We must recognize that a limitation of our research is the current implementation of the teachers' teaching style. Our definition of teaching style is helpful for the recommendation of examples and it is a step forward in the study of modelling the teaching style of implementer-teachers. However, more comprehensive study of a definition of teaching style in decision-making is necessary. A major aspect in decision-making in Network Design is the criteria that each teacher applies in the analysis of case studies. For example, in the case of network design, one teacher may prefer to analyze network configurations on the basis of their reliability and cost, while another teacher might prefer to use capacity and delay as

his criteria. Including these criteria in the Teacher Model can be a valuable complement to improve the teaching style and the recommendations.

CONCLUSION

ARIALE is using a recommender that reduces the complexity of finding an appropriate example for a particular teacher. Simple sharing of examples is an old type of collaboration between teachers, but providing more personalized examples (problem-solving support) makes collaboration between teachers more intelligent than simple sharing of teaching materials.

We focus on concepts related to the application of artificial intelligence in human-computer interaction, particularly adaptation, intelligent help systems, knowledge based help, Web-based help, automatic generation of examples and recommender systems.

The generation of examples uses a probabilistic method that provides a great variety of examples. The system can generate new examples according to the teacher's preferences and add each new example to the base of cases. To test and recommend or not each example generated automatically, ARIALE applies principles and techniques of artificial intelligence (machine learning), such as a classification learning (Bayesian classifier) and the Case-Based Reasoning (CBR) approach. Using classification learning, ARIALE learns when it identifies the class of examples of topology that a teacher prefers. The system also learns when the teacher switches to use topologies from another class because information is updated in the Teacher Model.

The application of the Teacher Model is an important improvement over previous AEH that did not take into account teachers' differences and the evolution of their teaching styles. In addition, the recommendation of learning sessions and examples, the automatic generation of examples, and the learning of the teacher's decisions related to teaching style and help, are important contributions of this research.

This chapter is also a portrait of the complexity of building an adaptive educational hypermedia. The importance of this portrait is that it shows the integration of many methods and procedures that are usually studied unconnectedly. This integration results in a methodology to build our assistant in two steps and it is needed because the authoring tool and the help must be coordinated.

Our experience studying teachers' reactions to computer-based technology in education (Rodríguez, 1997) has taught us that regardless of the number of hours of training they receive, teachers can be excluded from using new information technology because they do not have time to practice the theoretical contents learned in the training phase; the edition of resources is time consuming; and there is not a logical connection between training and real tasks to be performed. We consider that our support approach that involves on-the-job training is a good alternative to training when there is no enough time available. Consequently, a recommender system can play an important role to provide adapted problem-solving support for teachers.

ACKNOWLEDGMENT

This research was supported by the Universidad de Costa Rica, the Consejo Nacional para Investigaciones Científicas y Tecnológicas (National Commission to Scientific and Technological Investigations), and the Ministerio de Ciencia y Tecnología de Costa Rica (The Ministry of Science and Technology of Costa Rica). This work is also supported partially by the National Sciences and Engineering Research Council of Canada (NSERC), the Fonds Québécois de la Recherche sur la Nature et les Technologies (FCAR), and Valorisation Recherche Québec (VRQ) of the governments of Canada and Quebec.

REFERENCES

Aberg, J. (2002). *Live help systems: An approach to intelligent help for web information systems.* (Ph.D. Thesis). Linköpings Universitet. Linköping, Sweden.

Aerts, A., Bierhoff, P., & De Bra, P. (1999). Web-CS: Infrastructure for web-based competitions. In *Proceedings of the WebNet 1999 Conference,* (pp. 69-74). WebNet.

Aroyo, L., Cristea, A., & Dicheva, D. (2002). A layered approach towards domain authoring support. [ICAI.]. *Proceedings of the ICAI, 2002,* 615–621.

Brusilovsky, P. (2001). Adaptive educational hypermedia. In *Proceedings of the 10th International Peg Conference (Peg 2001),* (pp. 8-12). Peg.

Brusilovsky, P., & Cooper, D. (1999). ADAPTS: Adaptive hypermedia for a web-based performance support system. In *Proceedings of 2nd Workshop on Adaptive Systems and User Modeling on WWW at 8th International Word Wide Web Conference and 7th International Conference on User Modeling.* Retrieved October 15, 2002 from http://wwwis.win.tue.nl/asum99/brusilovsky/brusilovsky.html

Brusilovsky, P., & Schwartz, E. (1997). User as student: Towards an adaptive interface for advanced web-based applications. In *Proceedings of the 6th International Conference on User Modeling,* (pp. 177-188). IEEE.

Butler, D., & Sellbom, M. (2002). Barrier to adopting technology for teaching and learning. *EDUCAUSE Quarterly, 2.* Retrieved March 16, 2003 from http://www.educause.edu/ir/library/pdf/EQM0223.pdf

Callan, J., Smeaton, A., Beaulieu, M., Borlund, P., Brusilovsky, P., & Chalmers, M. … Toms, E. (2003). *Personalisation and recommender systems in digital libraries*. Joint NSF-EU DELOS Working Group Report. Retrieved April 24, 2004 from http://www.dli2.nsf.gov/internationalprojects/working_group_reports/perso-nalisation.htm

Capobianco, A. (2002). *Stratégies d'aide en ligne contextuelles: Acquisition d'expertises, modélisation et évaluation expérimentale*. (Thèse de Doctorat). Université Henri Poincaré. Nancy, France.

Cortés, U., Moreno, A., Armengol, E., Béjar, J., Belanche, L., & Gavaldá, R. … Sánchez, M. (1994). *Aprendizaje automático*. Catalina, Spain.

Costagliola, G., Ferrucci, F., & Francese, R. (2002). Web engineering: Model and methodologies for the design of hypermedia applications. In Chang, S. K. (Ed.), *Handbook of Software Engineering & Knowledge Engineering* (*Vol. 2*, pp. 181–199). Singapore, Singapore: World Scientific. doi:10.1142/9789812389701_0009

Cristea, A., & Garzotto, F. (2004). Designing patterns for adaptive of adaptable educational hypermedia: A taxonomy. [AACE.]. *Proceedings of ED-MEDIA*, *2004*, 808–813.

Cristea, A., & Mooij, A. (2003). LAOS: Layered WWW AHS authoring model and their corresponding algebraic operators. In *Proceedings of the 12th International World Wide Web Conference (WWW 2003)*. Retrieved March 23, 2004 from http://wwwis.win.tue.nl/~acristea/HTML/Minerva/papers/WWW03-cristea-mooij.doc

De Bra, P., Aerts, A., Berden, B., De Lange, B., Rousseau, B., & Santic, T. … Stash, N. (2003). AHA! The adaptive hypermedia architecture. In *Proceedings of the ACM Hypertext Conference,* (pp. 81-84). ACM Press.

DeLacey, B., & Leonard, D. (2002). Case study on technology and distance in education at the Harvard Business School. *Journal of Educational Technology & Society*, *5*(2), 13–28.

Delisle, S., & Moulin, B. (2002). User interfaces and help systems: From helplessness to intelligent assistance. *Artificial Intelligence Review*, *18*(2), 117–157. doi:10.1023/A:1015179704819

Draper, S. (1999). Supporting use, learning, and education: Commentary on Guzdial's supporting learners as users. *Journal of Computer Documentation*, *23*(2), 19–24.

Ehlert, P. (2003). *Intelligent user interfaces: Introduction and survey*. Research Report DKS03-01/ICE 01. Delft, The Netherlands: Delft University of Technology. Retrieved November 7, 2002 from ftp://ftp.kbs.twi.tudelft.nl/pub/ice/Ehlert.P.A.M-report_IUI.pdf

Eirinaki, M., & Vazirgianis, M. (2003). Web mining for web personalization. *ACM Transactions on Internet Technology*, *3*(1), 1–27. doi:10.1145/643477.643478

Encarnação, M. (1997). Multi-level user support through adaptive hypermedia: A highly application-independent help component. In *Proceedings of the International Conference on Intelligent User Interfaces (IUI 1997)*, (pp. 187-194). IUI.

Erkol, E. (1998). *A multi-agent extension of Negoplan and its application to a business strategy game*. (Master Degree Thesis). University of Ottawa. Ottawa, Canada.

Fischer, G. (2001). User modeling in human computer interaction. *User Modeling and User-Adapted Interaction*, *11*(1-2), 65–86. doi:10.1023/A:1011145532042

Fischer, S., & Steinmetz, R. (2000). Automatic creation of exercises in adaptive hypermedia learning systems. In *Proceedings of the Eleventh ACM Conference on Hypertext and Hypermedia,* (pp. 49 – 55). ACM Press.

García, F. (2000). CACTUS: Automated tutorial course generation for software applications. In *Proceedings of the 5th International Conference on Intelligent User Interfaces,* (pp. 113–120). IEEE.

Grasha, A. (1996). *Teaching with style*. New York, NY: Alliance Publishers.

Guzdial, M. (1999). Supporting learners as users. *Journal of Computer Documentation, 23*(2), 3–13.

Hartley, R. (2003). An interactive computer-based simulation environment for supporting and developing complex decision-making skills. *International Journal of Continuing Engineering Education and Lifelong Learning, 13*(3-4), 212–231. doi:10.1504/IJCEELL.2003.003279

Henze, N., & Nejdl, W. (1999). Student modeling in an active learning environment using Bayesian networks. In *Proceedings of 7ᵗʰ Conference User Modelling*. Retrieved March 23, 2003 from http://www.cs.usask.ca/UM99/Proc/posters/Henze.htm

Johansson, A. (2001). *Authoring tools for developing intelligent tutoring systems*. Uppsala, Norway: Uppsala University. Retrieved October 11, 2002 from http://www.csd.uu.se/~alj/ATDITS.html

Karsenti, T. (2004). Prof branches: Un sondage révèle que 71% des formateurs emploient les TIC. *Forum, 38*(31), 1–2.

Keller, F. (2002). *Naive Bayes classifiers.* Saarlandes, Germany: Universit¨at des Saarlandes. Retrieved January 16, 2004 from http://homepages.inf.ed.ac.uk/keller/teaching/connectionism/lecture10_4up.pdf

Kimiavi, S. (1998). *ITS author: A framework for building hypermedia-based intelligent tutoring systems for the world wide web*. (Ph.D. Dissertation). George Washington University. Washington, DC.

Kinshuk, H. (2003). State-of-the-art in adaptive learning: Keynote address pedagogies & communication. In *Proceedings of the International Conference on Open & Online Learning (ICOOL 2003)*. Retrieved March 18, 2004 from http://icool.uom.ac.mu/2003/papers/file/keynote/kinshuk.zip

Kinshuk, H., & Patel, A. (2001). Extended ITS framework with human teacher model. In C. H. Lee, S. Lajoie, R. Mizoguchi, Y. Yoo, & B. du Boulay (Eds.), *Enhancement of Quality Learning Through Information & Communication Technology (ICT), Proceedings of ICCE/SchoolNet 2001 Conference*, (pp. 1259-1262). ICCE/SchoolNet.

Kinshuk, H., Patel, A., & Russell, D. (1999). HyperITS: A web-based architecture for evolving a configurable learning environment. *Staff and Educational Development International Journal, 3*(3), 265–280.

Kobsa, A., Koenemann, J., & Pohl, W. (2001). Personalized hypermedia presentation techniques for improving online customer relationships. *The Knowledge Engineering Review, 16*(2), 111–155. doi:10.1017/S0269888901000108

Koch, N. (1999). *A comparative study of methods for hypermedia development*. Technical Report 9905. Munich, Germany: LudwigMaximilians–Universitt. Retrieved November 20, 2002 from http://www.dsic.upv.es/~west2001/iwwost01/files/contributions/NoraKoch/hypdev.pdf

Koychev, I. (2002). Tracking changing user interests through prior-learning of context. *Lecture Notes in Computer Science, 2347*, 223–232. doi:10.1007/3-540-47952-X_24

Leung, M. (2001). *Towards a generic approach to providing proactive task support*. (Ph.D. Dissertation). University of Waterloo. Waterloo, Canada.

Lorés, J., Abascal, J., Cañas, J., Gea, M., Gil, A., & Martínez, A. … Vélez, M. (2002). *Introducción a la interacción persona-ordenador*. Retrieved August 6, 2003 from http://griho.udl.es/ipo/descarga.html

Lynch, P., & Horton, S. (2001). *Web style guide: Basic design principles for creating website*. Retrieved June 22, 2004 from http://www.webstyleguide.com/type/lines.html

Mayer, R., & Moreno, R. (2003). Nine ways to reduce cognitive load in multimedia learning. *Educational Psychologist, 38*, 43–52. doi:10.1207/S15326985EP3801_6

Miyahara, K., & Pazzani, M. (2002). Improvement of collaborative filtering with the simple Bayesian classifier. *IPSJ Journal, 43*(11). Retrieved May 6, 2004 from http://www.ics.uci.edu/~pazzani/Publications/IPSJ.pdf

Murray, T. (1999). Authoring intelligent tutoring systems: An analysis of the state of the art. *International Journal of Artificial Intelligence in Education, 10*, 98–129.

Patel, A., Russell, D., Oppermann, K., & Rashev, R. (1998). An initial framework of contexts for designing usable intelligent tutoring systems. *Information Services & Use, 18*(1-2), 65–76.

Payr, S. (2003). The virtual university's faculty: An overview of educational agents. *Applied Artificial Intelligence, 17*, 1–19. doi:10.1080/713827053

Pierre, S. (1998). Inferring new design rules by machine learning: A case study of topological optimization. *IEEE Transactions on Man, Systems, and Cybernetics, 28A*(5), 575–585. doi:10.1109/3468.709602

Pierre, S., & Elgibaoui, A. (1997). A tabu search approach for designing computer network topologies with unreliable components. *IEEE Transactions on Reliability, 46*(3), 350–359. doi:10.1109/24.664006

Pierre, S., & Gharbi, I. (2001). A generic object-oriented model for representing computer network topologies. *Advances in Engineering Software, 32*(2), 95–110. doi:10.1016/S0965-9978(00)00081-8

Pierre, S., & Legault, G. (1998). A genetic algorithm for designing distributed computer network topologies. *IEEE Transactions on Man, Systems, and Cybernetics, 28*(2), 249–258. doi:10.1109/3477.662766

Rodríguez, A. (2007). Evaluación de un tipo de ayuda en línea destinada a profesores que deseen crear sitios educativos en Internet. *Intersedes, 7*(11), 99–117.

Rodríguez, A. (2008). Generation, testing and recommendation of teaching materials using classification learning. *International Journal of Advanced Media and Communication, 2*(3), 308–324. doi:10.1504/IJAMC.2008.020182

Rodríguez, A. (2011). Teacher model for an educational adaptive hypermedia that supports the teaching of decision-making. In *Proceedings of INTED 2011 Conference*, (pp. 91-100). INTED.

Rodríguez, A., Aïmeur, E., & Vázquez-Abad, F. (2003). Training teachers in teaching decision-making skills. In *Proceedings of the 2nd International Conference on Multimedia and Information & Communication Technologies in Education*, (pp. 1964-1968). IEEE.

Rodríguez, A., Aïmeur, E., & Vázquez-Abad, F. (2004a). Adaptive help techniques to reduce the teachers' cognitive overload. In *Proceedings of the International Conference on Computers in Education (ICCE 2004)*, (pp. 1741-1750). ICCE.

Rodríguez, A., Aïmeur, E., & Vázquez-Abad, F. (2004b). E-learning for complex decision-making with the support of a web-based adaptive ITS. In *Proceedings of the International Conference on Knowledge Engineering and Decision Support (ICKEDS 2004)*, (pp. 47-54). ICKEDS.

Rothrock, L., Koubek, R., Fuchs, F., Haas, M., & Salvendy, G. (2002). Review and re-appraisal of adaptive interfaces: Toward biologically-inspired paradigms. *Theoretical Issues in Ergonomics Science, 3*(1), 47–84. doi:10.1080/14639220110110342

Schein, A., Popescul, A., Ungar, L., & Pennock, D. (2002). Methods and metrics for cold-start recommendations. In *Proceedings of the 25th Annual International ACM SIGIR Conference on Research and Development in Information Retrieval*, (pp. 253-260). ACM Press.

Selbach, M., Sieckenius, C., & Barbosa, S. (2003). A method of semiotic engineering for the online help systems construction. In *Proceedings of the Latin American Conference on Human-Computer Interaction*, (pp. 167-177). IEEE.

Self, T. (1998). Implementing a web-based help system. In *Proceedings of the Help for the Web Symposium*. Retrieved May 6, 2004 from http//:www.help4web.org/publication/self1.htm

Shiri-Ahmadabadi, M. (1999). *Étude et modélisation des connaissances et raisonnement de l'apprenant dans un STI*. (PhD Dissertation). Université de Montréal. Montreal, Canada.

Spool, J. (1999). *Web site usability: A designer's guide*. San Francisco, CA: Morgan Kauffman Publishers Inc.

Stephanidis, C. (2001). Adaptive techniques for universal access. *User Modeling and User-Adapted Interaction, 11*, 159–179. doi:10.1023/A:1011144232235

Stone, M. (1977). Asymptotics for and against cross-validation. *Biometrika, 64*, 29–35. doi:10.1093/biomet/64.1.29

Sweller, J. (1988). Cognitive load during problem solving: Effects on learning. *Cognitive Science, 12*, 257–285. doi:10.1207/s15516709cog1202_4

Towle, B. (2001). *Authoring tools for building how-to simulations*. (Ph.D. Dissertation). Northwestern University. Evanston, IL.

Van Joolingen, W. (1999). Cognitive tools for discovering learning. *International Journal of Artificial Intelligence in Education, 10*, 385–397.

Vázquez-Abad, F., Rodríguez, A., & Aïmeur, E. (2003). Training the teacher: A new approach for authoring ITSs for teaching decision-making. In *Proceedings of the International Conference on Open & Online Learning (ICOOL 2003)*. Retrieved May 18, 2004 from http://icool.uom.ac.mu/2003/papers/file/Rodriguez.pdf

Vázquez-Abad, F., Rodríguez, A., Ng, A., Zukerman, M., & Warfield, R. (2001). Bridging theory and practice in network design using web-based simulation. In *Proceedings of the 12th Annual Conference of the Australasian Association for Engineering Education (AaeE 2001)*, (pp. 40-45). AaeE.

Virvou, M., & Moundridou, M. (2002). Adding an instructor modelling component to the architecture of ITS authoring tools. *International Journal of Artificial Intelligence in Education, 12*, 185–211.

Wang, J. (2001). *Toward the usability of hypermedia adaptive intelligent interfaces*. (PhD. Dissertation). The George Washington University. Washington, DC.

Webb, G., Pazzani, M., & Billsus, D. (2001). Machine learning for user modeling. *User Modeling and User-Adapted Interaction, 11*, 19–20. doi:10.1023/A:1011117102175

Weber, J. (2000). Editing online help. *Weber-Woman's Wrevenge*. Retrieved from http://www.wrevenge.com

Weiss-Lambrou, R., & Raymond, D. (2002). *Rapport du sondage sur: L'utilisation de WebCT à l'Université de Montréal et l'appréciation du soutien offert par le programme SUITE*. Montreal, Canada: Université de Montréal. Retrieved October 12, 2003 from http://www.cefes.umontreal.ca/Documents/CEFES_SondageA01_Resultats.pdf

Wu, H., Houben, G., & De Bra, P. (1998). AHAM: A reference model to support adaptive hypermedia authoring. In *Proceedings of the Zesde Interdisciplinaire Conferentie Informatiewetenschap*, (pp. 77-88). Academic Press.

Yu, T. (2002). *Empirical study to cognitive load and the PI theory with well-designed products for procedure skills and parallel instructions*. Retrieved July 25, 2004 from http://projects.edte.utwente.nl/pi/Papers/indexYu.html

Yu, T., Min, R., & Spenkelink, G. (2003). E-learning environments on the world wide web, based on the concept of parallelism. In *Proceedings of the EARLI Conference*. Retrieved March 23, 2004 from http://wwwis.win.tue.nl/~acristea/HTML/Minerva/papers/report4jOfCompAssLearning-YuMinSpenkelink.doc

ADDITIONAL READING

André, E., & Rist, T. (2002). From adaptive hypertext to personalized web companions. *Communications of the ACM, 45*(5), 43–46. doi:10.1145/506218.506243

Bengio, Y., & Granvalet, Y. (2003). *No unbiased estimator of the variance of k-fold cross-validation*. Technical Report 1234. Montreal, Canada: Université de Montréal. Retrieved December 5, 2004 from http://www.iro.umontreal.ca/~lisa/pointeurs/TR1234.pdf

Brusilovsky, P., & Cooper, D. W. (2002). Domain, task, and user models for an adaptive hypermedia performance support system. In Y. Gil & D. B. Leake (Eds.), *Proceedings of 2002 International Conference on Intelligent User Interfaces*, (pp. 23-30). ACM Press.

Carreira, R., Crato, J., Gonçalves, D., & Jorge, J. (2004). Evaluating adaptive user profiles for news classification. In *Proceedings of the 9th International Conference on Intelligent User Interface*, (pp. 206 – 212). IUI.

Conati, C., Gertner, A., & Vanlehn, K. (2002). Using Bayesian networks to manage uncertainty in student modeling. *User Modeling and User-Adapted Interaction, 12*(4), 371–417. doi:10.1023/A:1021258506583

Davis, J., Leelawong, K., Belynne, K., Bodenheimer, B., Biswas, G., Vye, N., & Bransford, J. (2003). Intelligent user interface design for teachable agent systems. In *Proceedings of the 8th International Conference on Intelligent User Interfaces*, (pp. 26-33). IUI.

Fritze, P. (2003). *Innovation in university computer-facilitated learning systems: Product, workplace experience and the organisation*. (PhD Dissertation). RMIT. Melbourne, Australia.

Funk, P., & Conlan, O. (2003). Using case-based reasoning to support authors of adaptive hypermedia systems. In *Proceedings* of *Workshop on Adaptive Hypermedia and Adaptive Web-Based Systems*, (pp. 113-120). IEEE.

Gallagher, L., & Daigle, J. (2002). *Creating online help*. Retrieved June 16, 2004 from http://www.techcomplus.com/CreatingOnlineHelpHandout-WithTables.pdf

Gerjets, P., & Scheiter, K. (2003). Goal configurations and processing strategies as moderators between instructional design and cognitive load: Evidence from hypertext-based instruction. *Educational Psychologist, 38*, 33–41. doi:10.1207/S15326985EP3801_5

Heffernan, N. (2001). *Intelligent tutoring systems have forgotten the tutor: Adding a cognitive model of human tutors*. (PhD Dissertation). Carnegie Mellon University. Pittsburgh, PA.

Herlocker, J., Konstan, J., Terveen, L., & Riedl, J. (2004). Evaluating collaborative filtering recommender systems. *ACM Transactions on Information Systems, 22*(1), 5–53. doi:10.1145/963770.963772

Johnson, A., & Taatgen, N. (2003). User modelling. *The Handbook of Human Factors in Web Design*. Retrieved May 8, 2004 from http://www.ai.rug.nl/~niels/publications/usermodels.pdf

Johnson, W., Shaw, E., Marshall, A., & LaBore, C. (2003). Evolution of user interaction: the case of agent adele. In *Proceedings of the 8th International Conference on Intelligent User Interfaces,* (pp. 93-100). IUI.

Koelle, D. (2002). *Intelligent user interfaces: An independent study project*. Retrieved June 15, 2004 from http://www.davekoelle.com/intint.jsp

Kumar, V. (2002). Embedding human reasoning in soft computing. *International Conference on Hybrid Intelligent Systems*. Retrieved June 16, 2004 from http://www.sfu.ca/~vivek/personal/papers/HIS2002.pdf

Lavesso, N. (2003). *Evaluation of classifier performance and the impact of learning algorithm parameters*. (Master Thesis). Blekinge Institute of Technology. Blekinge, Sweden.

Light, M., & Maybury, M. (2002). Personalized multimedia information access. *Communications of the ACM, 45*(5), 54–59. doi:10.1145/506218.506246

Maybury, M. (2003). Intelligent user interfaces: An introduction. *The MITRE Corporation*. Retrieved November 2003 from http://www.iuiconf.org/tutorial1.html

Meisner, E. (2003). *Naive Bayes classifier example*. Retrieved October 12, 2003 from http://www.cs.rpi.edu/courses/fall03/ai/misc/naive-example.pdf

Moreno, R. (2004). Decreasing cognitive load for novice students: Effects of explanatory versus corrective feedback in discovery-based multimedia. *Instructional Science, 32*, 99–113. doi:10.1023/B:TRUC.0000021811.66966.1d

Murray, T. (2002). Content design issues in adaptive hyperbooks. *International Journal of Computer Applications Technology on Designing Technology Supported Learning*. Retrieved March, 2003 from http://helios.hampshire.edu/~tjmCCS/papers/IJCAT2002ML/IJCAT2002.htm

Papanikolaou, K., Grigoriadou, M., Kornilakis, H., & Magoulas, G. (2003). Personalizing the interaction in a web-based educational hypermedia system: The case of INSPIRE. *User Modeling and User-Adapted Interaction, 13*(3), 213–267. doi:10.1023/A:1024746731130

Purchase, H., & Worril, J. (2002). An empirical study of on-line help design: Features and principles. *International Journal of Human-Computer Studies, 56*(5), 539–567. doi:10.1006/ijhc.2002.1009

Rezazad, H. (2003). *An approach to the development of intelligent agents to assist with network configuration design problem*. (PhD Dissertation). George Mason University. Washington, DC.

Syme, A., Dickinson, A., Eisma, R., & Gregor, P. (2003). Looking for help? Supporting older adults' use of computer systems. In Rauterberg, M., Menozzi, M., & Wesson, J. (Eds.), *Human-Computer Interaction* (pp. 924–931). Dordrecht, The Netherlands: IOS Press.

Virvou, M., & Kabassi, K. (2002). Intelligent help in a graphical user interface. In *Proceedings of the 2002 IEEE International Conference on Systems, Man and Cybernetics,* (pp. 170-175). IEEE Press.

Virvou, M., & Moundridou, M. (2001). Student and instructor models: Two kinds of user model and their interaction in an ITS authoring tool. In *Proceedings of the 8th International Conference,* (pp. 158-167). Academic Press.

Wooldridge, M. (2002). *An introduction to multi-agent systems*. London, UK: John Wiley & Sons Ltd.

Wu, H. (2002). *A reference architecture for adaptive hypermedia applications*. (PhD. Dissertation). Universiteit Eindhoven. Eindhoven, The Netherlands.

KEY TERMS AND DEFINITIONS

Adaptation: Adaptive systems can change their parameters and behaviour in order to meet a goal. Two general categories of adaptation are: 1) adaptability: users have the possibility to select different types of presentation and interaction from among the ones included in the system prior to the initiation of interaction; 2) adaptivity: the system possesses the capability to monitor user interaction to generate automatic adaptation that suits different users or contexts of use (Stephanidis, 2001).

Automatic Generation of Examples: Case studies, examples to be analyzed or, more specifically, network topologies can be generated automatically by a system instead of provided by a teacher or expert. The system requires functions or programs that follow rules and procedures to generate examples according to a expert criterion.

Bayesian Classification (Bayesian Learning, Classification Learning): Bayesian classification is a method to classify new evidence according to given prior evidence. This type of classifier can classify sets of inputs and learn novel inputs in order to anticipate behaviour or a result (Rothrock, et al., 2002). This method is based on Bayesian theory, which uses previously known results to calculate more probabilities. According to this theory, an event has unconditioned probability or prior probability assigned in the absence of knowledge that supports its occurrence or absence. A conditional probability or posterior probability is the probability of an event given some evidence.

Case Base Reasoning: CBR is an artificial intelligence method that a system can use to learn. The idea is to allow a system to learn from its own experience. For example, an expert detects a new problem and compares it with the previous problems in the same domain that he solved before. If he finds a similar problem in his memory, in order to solve the new case he tries to reuse or adapt the same methods he used for solving the old problem (Cortés, et al., 1994).

Intelligent Help Systems: Intelligent help systems provide personalized, dynamic and contextual support by using artificial intelligence techniques for adaptation (Lorés, et al., 2002).

Recommender System: A recommender system is intended to "learn about a person's needs and then proactively identify and recommend information that meets those needs" (Callan, et al., 2003).

Similarity Measuring: This method calculates or measures the distance between two cases. This is a method to classify an example, taking into account examples classified previously. Each time a new instance has to be classified, the classifier method compares it to the stored examples to assign a distance value to the new example.

Chapter 2
Building Efficient Assessment Applications with Personalized Feedback:
A Model for Requirement Specifications

Constanta-Nicoleta Bodea
Academy of Economic Studies, Romania

Maria-Iuliana Dascalu
Academy of Economic Studies, Romania

ABSTRACT

The aim of this chapter is to provide a model for requirement specification, useful in developing efficient e-assessment applications with personalized feedback, which is enhanced by calling a recommender engine. The research was done in the context of using educational technology to facilitate learning processes. The data used to build the requirement model was collected from a set of interviews with the users and creators of an e-assessment application in project management. Requirement analysis assumes human effort and thus introduces uncertainties. To minimize the subjective factor, the data extracted from interviews with the users and the developers of the existing e-assessment application are clustered using a fuzzy logic solution into classes of requirements. These classes are the units of the model. The connections between classes are also mentioned: relations such as "if-then," "switch," or" contains" are explained. The requirements analysis conducts a smart set of specifications, obtained in a collaborative manner, useful for the design of e-assessment applications in project management or other similar domains.

INTRODUCTION

The role of educational technologies in improving the learning outcomes was always controversial: there are both positive and negative findings related to the use of technology in educational processes. Among positive aspects, there are: students learn more in less time when using computers, students are more attracted to the classes where computer are necessary, teachers improve their practices, by replacing stand-up lecturing with an interactive approach of teaching. Among

DOI: 10.4018/978-1-4666-2542-6.ch002

negative aspects, there are: computer didn't have positive impact on every area; the level of educational technologies' effectiveness depends on students' population, educator's role, level of student's access to technology, software design. The current chapter embraces the idea of increasing the efficiency and effectiveness of educational technology through a thorough software design, based on a collaborative approach of building software requirements.

Educational technology is seen not only as a solution for improving traditional learning methods, but also a way of "reducing the inequities in educational opportunities around the world". This aspect brings into discussion the reliability of educational software. The reliability issue is strongly connected to quality issues. Quality in educational software is critical, as a study developed by the European Quality Observatory has revealed (Ehlers, Goertz, Hildebrandt, & Pawlowski, 2005). The main quality characteristic is given by the degree of transformation made possible by an educational platform, meaning the increase in the degree of competence, as a result of the learning process: quality means obtaining "the best learning achievement" (Ehlers, Goertz, Hildebrandt, & Pawlowski, 2005).

Upon a study made by Learning Societies Lab (Gilbert, Gale, Warburton, & Wills, 2008), quality of educational technologies means: reliability, security, validity, accessibility, pedagogical appropriateness. Another study proposes a model for an interactive Web-based learning system (Barker, 1999), based on: pedagogical philosophy (knowledge comes from the instructor or knowledge builds itself in the mind of the learner), learning theory (emphasizes observable behavior or internal mental states), goal orientation (sharply focused or offers more than one solution to a problem), task orientation (academic, which focuses on traditional academic exercises or authentic, which focuses on exercises in authentic settings), source of motivation (extrinsic, outside of learning environment or intrinsic, inside of learning envi-

ronment), teacher role (didactic, meaning that the teacher is repository of knowledge or facilitative, meaning that the teacher guides the students), meta-cognitive support (no support for monitoring progress and adjusting to students' need or with such a support), collaborative learning strategies (students work individually or in pairs/ groups), cultural sensitivity (insensitive or respectful), and structural flexibility (fixed or open). The report supports the integration of a Web-based learning product to the above-mentioned criteria, thus obtaining the desired quality.

The importance of technologies to learning is highly mentioned by researchers (Buzzetto-More & Alade, 2006). As assessment is an important part of every learning process, technology also supports authentic assessment (Buzzetto-More & Alade, 2006). To underline the integration of assessment into a learning process, we mention the continuous assessment loop of Martell and Calderon: identification of learning goals and objectives, the gathering of evidence, analysis of evidence, report and discuss results, identify improvement opportunities, reflect and make changes (Martell & Calderon, 2005). The final purpose of an assessment is to improve students' outcome. A qualitative computer based tool for assessment doesn't mean to type good questions in the software application, but to translate the whole assessment process into the new medium (Gilbert, Gale, Warburton, & Wills, 2008). This translation can be successfully achieved only by active participation of all those involved in computer based assessment: learners, trainees, tutors, teachers, decision makers, technical experts.

The researchers involved in developing robust assessment applications are interested in bringing technical flavor to evaluations, without robbing anything from the intrinsic quality of the evaluative process: "The Cambridge Approach seeks to ensure that technology is used to enhance the process; reliability, validity, accessibility, efficiency, feedback, speed etc but does not dilute the quality" (Craven, 2009).

An innovative method to transform the e-assessment application into a useful tool in educational area is to endow it with a personalized feedback mechanism. The feedback mechanism is generally considered to be highly important for the formative dimension of an e-test (Biggam, 2010). Wang (2008) suggests timely feedback to be offered after each given answer. Black and Wiliam (2009) state that feedback is necessary to move the trainee forward. Sitthiworachart and Sutinen (2008) identify feedback as a success factor for e-assessment in computer science education. Still, there are different opinions regarding the impact of feedback to students' performance: Wieling and Hofman (2010) claim that feedback does not necessary increase students' performance, but a study which was held at Oxford Brookes University (JISC, 2010) proves that feedback has a tremendous role in diminishing the failure rate of students and, thus, increasing their performance. The role of feedback in formative e-assessment cycle is stressed out by Tuttle (2007): each question receives an answer, then a result is given to the student and, in order to understand the result, a feedback is also provided to the student. The feedback mechanism is the base of the active learning process.

The feedback activities are provided by both trainers/ teachers and colleagues or other external agents (JISC, 2010). Such an external agent can be a Recommender System (RS), which guides the trainee/student to further educational resources. The use of RSs in educational technology started to be a common practice. There are numerous deposits of educational digital resources, such as MERLOT (http://www.merlot.org/) or European Schoolnet's Learning Resource Exchange (http://lreforschools.eun.org/). In the plethora of educational resources, the users of online e-learning tools should benefit from services that help them fulfil their learning needs. In this context, the concept of recommendation sytems in education technology appeared (Manouselis, Drachsler, Vuorikari, Hummel, & Koper, 2010). The extraction of information from the Internet which is really useful to the end-user is a critical activity, but RSs are able to take intelligent decisions in complex situations (Göksedef & Gündüz-Ögüdücü, 2010). In education, they have more and more applications: some assist the students in establishing their schedule or choosing the proper subjects (Hsu, 2009), others are used in collaborative contexts, in sharing the right information to the right users, taking into account their roles, tasks, knowledge levels, others offer bibliographical recommendations (Mooney & Roy, 2000) or help students to learn English, as a foreign language (Hsu, 2008). As a follow-up of successful use of RSs in various educational systems (Manouselis, Drachsler, Vuorikari, Hummel, & Koper, 2010), theis use is proposed for e-assessment application, too. The main benefit would be the improvement of the feedback mechanism.

Such an application is described in the current chapter: the e-assessment application can easily offer a personalized feedback to the users in the form of a specific list of Web bibliography, obtained after accessing a recommendation engine. At the end, the students who took the tests can fill their knowledge gaps, by consulting the recommended Web documents. This kind of e-assessment has an important role in learning and teaching. It is well used in organizational learning (Bodea & Dascalu, 2010; Frey & Fisher, 2009), being known as "assessment for learning" (Birenbaum, Kimron, Shilton, & Shahaf-Barzilay, 2009). To increase the educational effect of the e-assessment, the recommendations are given to the trainees into a clustered form, using an educational ontology. Although the RS is meant to increase the quality of the e-assessment, the question whether the e-assessment application is good or not still remains. We consider that the e-assessment success fully depends on design contrains, which are an important part of Software Requirements Specification (SRS), together with other non-functional requirements, such as performance or quality constrains and with functional requirements.

The concern of developing a good e-assessment application has to be directed not only to the final product itself, but also to the customers' satisfaction. This principle is widely acknowledged in software products development, disregarding the software nature: more often, the software success depends more on customers' needs than on technical optimization (Kuschel, 2006). Because of the multidisciplinary nature of requirements, developers have to carefully select requirement techniques and practices for their software processes. The suitability of a requirement specification should be project oriented: it should be highly adapted to the context of the project (Jiang, Eberlein, Far, & Mousavi, 2008). There should be a strong connection between the attributes of a project and the ones of the requirement engineering techniques. In this way, a highly qualitative set of requirement specifications could be obtained, which will conduct to a high quality of the final products: there is a strong believe that "effective RE will continue to play a key role in determining the success or failure of projects, and in determining the quality of systems that are delivered" (Nuseibeh & Easterbrook, 2002). Current chapter offers a set of requirements specifications for assessment applications with an embedded recommender engine for personalized feedback. The method for providing this set of specification was highly elaborated, this ensuring its efficiency.

THE RESEARCH CONTEXT

Projects are the most spread organizational structure in today's society: for obtaining the success, project management professionals request for continuous competence development (Suikki, Tromstedt, & Haapasal, 2006). Among core concepts related to professional competency, there are competency assessment ("evaluating performance for the effective application of knowledge and skill in a work setting") and certification ("the formal recognition" of professional competency") (Lysagh & Altschuld, 2000). As the information

systems are more and more used in work environments (Raymond, Croteau, & Bergeron, 2009), e-assessment applications became a common tool for knowledge (the ground of competence) checking (Delcea & Dascalu, 2009).

As the preparation for a professional certification might be quite time consuming for an individual engaged in economic activities, the Romanian Association of Project Management offers an e-assessment tool for simulation purposes. This practice complies with the effort of digital economy to raise the accessibility level of information systems: individuals do not have to go the association's office and take a simulation test there; they can do that from anywhere, even from their office. The e-assessment, "CertExam," is available at http://www.pm.org.ro/certexam/. The workflow of the application which is available to trainees and students can be seen in Figure 1.

The online tests check knowledge related to three categories of competences (International Project Management Association, 2006):

- Technical competencies of delivering projects in a structured way, including the project management process.
- Contextual competencies in managing relations with projects within organizations, programmes and portfolios, based on the knowledge of project characteristics, projects in the organizational context, and project environment.
- Behavioural competencies for a positive, collective, and dynamic thrust in nurturing project management professionalism such as leadership, communication, results-orientation, ethics, negotiation, and so forth.

The users of "CertExam" can access tests, according to their desired level of knowledge in project management:

- **IPMA Level A:** At this level, the individual has to have demonstrated successful use of the competence elements in the coordi-

Figure 1. Workflow in project management assessment tool

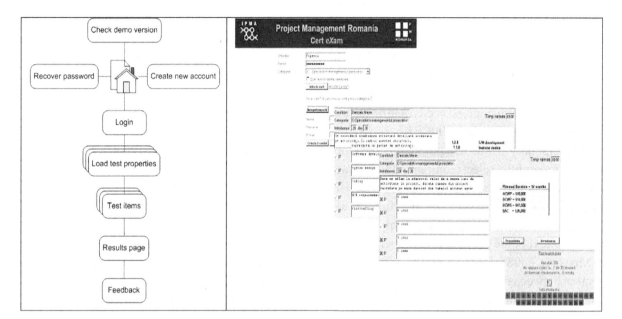

nation of programmes and/or portfolios; guided programme and/or project managers in their development and in the use of the competence elements; been involved in implementing the competence elements or relevant methodology, techniques or tools in projects or programmes; and contributed to the development of the project manager's profession by publishing articles or presenting papers on his experiences or by outlining new concepts.

- **IPMA Level B:** At this level, the individual has to have demonstrated successful use of the competence elements in complex project situations. She/he has also guide (sub) project managers in their application and implementation of the competence.
- **IPMA Level C:** At this level, the individual has to have demonstrated successful use of the competence element in project situations with limited complexity. He/she might need to be guided in the further development of the competence element.
- **IPMA Level D:** At this level, only knowledge related to the competence element is assessed by written examination.

The prototype of the e-assessment system is pretty complex and does not consists only in the Web interface presented in Figure 1. The system has several components: the admin module, the trainer module and the student module (see Figure 2). The admin module offers the possibility to accomplish operations on levels, competences, trainers, users or questions. The trainer module allows the creation of rules-based tests, visualization of previously created tests, and visualization of students. The student module contains the Web application used by the students to resolve online tests. These tests are created with various adaptation models. The models are implemented by the Adaptive test-building engine. Another important component of the system is the feedback module: after completing a testing session, each student has the possibility of revising the incorrectly answered questions and receiving future recommendations for filling the knowledge gaps.

The admin and the trainer module communicate with the database via a set of business services. The trainee module communicates with the database via a Web service (see Figure 3). The Web service can call the adaptive tests engine and the feedback engine. This service-oriented and components-based architecture ensures the system's flexibility.

The e-assessment tool can be used also as a self-directed tool for learning (Bodea & Dascalu, 2009). The knowledge creation through self-directed learning can be followed after the test is finished: once the user gets to the results report, he/she can go straight to the wrong answered questions by clicking the red buttons (see Figure 1). The correct answers for those questions are checked with green. The knowledge creation path is session dependent, meaning the second time a user takes a test, the knowledge path will be different.

Each question of an e-assessment session checks a certain number of concepts from the knowledge domain in project management. This knowledge domain is represented by an educational ontology. The recommender engine should search for Web documents related to the concept of the incorrectly answered question, but also for Web documents related to the parent node of the concept in the domain ontology and other child nodes of that parent. The lexical instances of these concepts are the entry points for the clustering algorithm. The concepts are converted to their lexical instances, using the educational ontology. The recommender engine is a C# Web-service.

Figure 2. The system architecture of web application for project management knowledge assessment

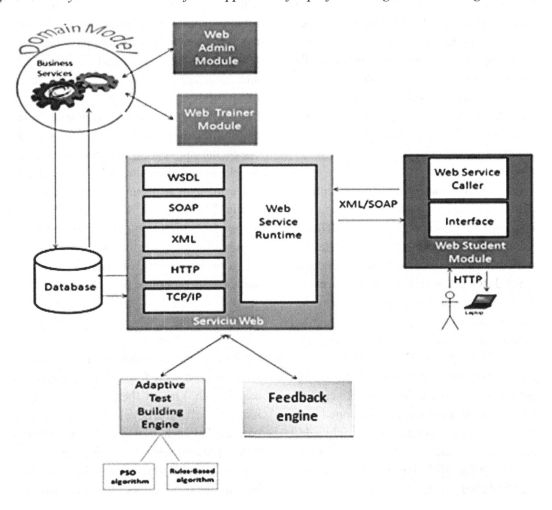

The mechanism of the recommender engine is presented in Figure 4.

According to Figure 4, the following steps are available in the recommender engine mechanism:

1. The user takes the test.
2. The user finishes the test and the 'user profile' is built: a set of concepts related to the incorrectly answered questions.
3. The user profile is mapped in the domain ontology, taking account a λ parameter used as an entry data: according to that parameter, child nodes from the initial set of concepts might be chosen. For all chosen concepts, lexical instances are extracted and further used for Web search.
4. The Web search is processed for the lexical instances from Step 3 and for the following admin parameters: the set of search engines to be used (the administrator of the e-assessment application can choose the available engines from a combo-box), the number of links per page, the number of clusters.
5. A clustering algorithm is applied. Clustering is realized after a predefined number of iterations.

This number will be determined experimentally in order to find a compromise between computing time and quality of clusters obtained. By default, we make 6 clusters, the 7th cluster representing unclassified documents and we use a threshold value of 0.3 for classification of instances in clusters. After each clustering, we recalculate the centroids and we reset the clusters' components. The new centroids are calculated using the average weigh of words reached in that cluster.

Figure 5 presents the results of the query "Mediul social extern al proiectulu" delivered as clusters. On the left side, there are mentioned four clusters induced for this search. On the right side, we can see the links and the related snippets for the cluster with the label "Partile interesate" (in English, "Stakeholders").

PURPOSE OF THE RESEARCH

The current chapter aims at enhancing the advantages and reducing the limitations of professional knowledge e-assessment. The authors argue that respecting a good requirements specification would definitely diminish the risk of failure in knowledge e-assessment. The main research question is related to what are the smart sets of requirements for efficient project management e-assessment: "What are the functional and non-functional requirements which lead to a good e-assessment experience?"

THE RESEARCH METHODOLOGY

This chapter embraces the collaborative practice research approach (Mathiassen, 2002), because the requirement specifications were obtained after a close interaction with the actual trainees and operatives, who used the e-assessment application offered by the Romanian Association of Project Management: "CertExam." The main research methods were: interviews with the users of the application and interviews with the developers. Recent studies of requirements engineering indicated some other useful techniques (Jiang, Eberlein, Far, & Mousavi, 2008), which helped us in improving our set of requirements: document mining (we thoroughly consulted other e-assessment use cases and documents) and field study (observations of people taking the e-tests).

Participants

Besides a practice research methodology, there were some driven forces who dictated our research path. One of them was the well-known issue in software development: achieving the balance between customers' requirements and product knowledge. The challenge in developing an e-assessment is that the customers are both trainers and trainees, teachers and students,

Figure 3. Web service architecture

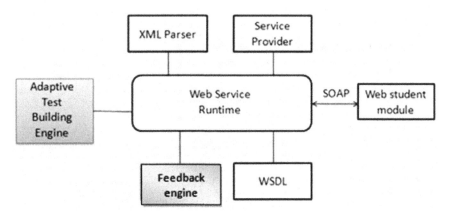

employers and employees. The dual nature of an e-assessment customer should be reflected in the requirements specification. Usually, the trainer/ teacher/employer is the one who is more listened in this case. The modern e-assessment should satisfy also the trainee/student/ employee. This was the reason for which we interviewed the ones who

actually took the "CertExam" tests. Therefore, the participants of our interviews were:

- Individuals who took the tests offered by "CertExam";
- Evaluators, members of the Romanian Association of Project Management;
- Software developers of "CertExam";

Figure 4. Feedback engine mechanism

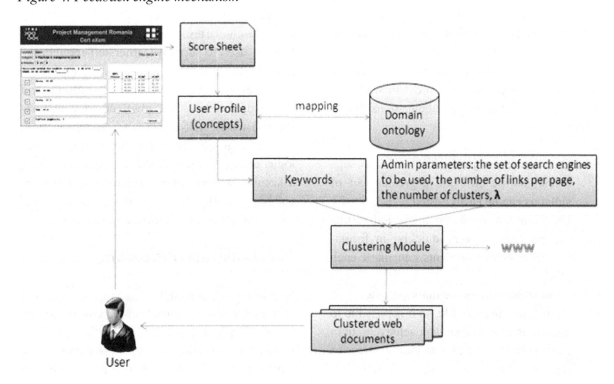

Figure 5. Search results delivered as clusters for the query "mediul social extern al proiectului" (external social environments of the project)

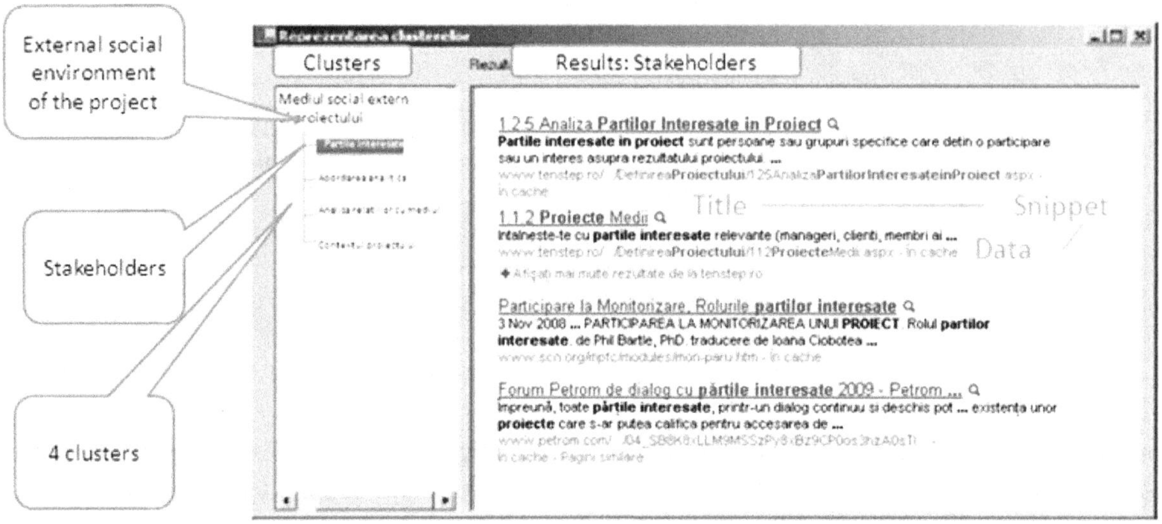

Context

As the number of individuals willing to take or prepare for project management certifications increased, the time and place constrains became a crucial requirement of these individuals, the Romanian Association of Project Management offered them an e-solution for knowledge assessment, based on multiple-choice questions. Some features of multiple-choice questions are presented, for shaping the context in which an e-assessment with such type of questions should be developed:

- Questions are objective;
- Questions are efficient, a greater part of syllabus can be easily tested;
- Questions are easily to mark and results can be returned very quickly; in formative assessments students can mark each other's;
- Scoring uses the entire marking range;
- Results are quantifiable, so it is possible to analyse the level of student achievement in each question; it is easy to identify areas of student difficulty or problematic questions;

- Provision of feedback can be targeted more effectively because of the limited ways in which students can have gone wrong;
- Setting right questions is time consuming and challenging;

According to other researches (Nicol, 2006), multiple-choice tests aren't just simple checks, but "can be used to support learner self-regulation" (Nicol, 2006), if some feed-back principles are to be respected: clarifying goals, criteria, and standards (students are involved in constructing the tests), self-assessment, and reflection, delivers high-quality feedback, encourages dialogue around learning, offers motivation, filling a knowledge gap, offers guidance to tutors or teachers. Starting from the above observations, the "CertExam" application was analyzed.

Data Collection Procedure

Interviews with a predefined set of goals (and not of questions) were made with 83 out of 153 users of "CertExam': see Table 1 for their profiles. In order to have time for all these respondents, most interviews took place by e-mails or on the

Table 1. Profiles of the "CertExam" users

E-Tests Level		
IPMA Level	**No. Users**	**No. Respondents**
A	0	0
B	11	2
C	35	12
D	106	69
Affiliation to Business Sector		
Business sector	**No. Firms**	**No. Participants**
IT	7	32
Consulting	9	29
Education	3	12
Other sectors	2	10

phone. The average rate for these interviews was about 15 minutes.

Longer interviews were taken to the members of the Romanian Association of Project Management: 9 such tutors were questioned. In order to complete the holistic image of the opinions about "CertExam," the 3 software developers involved in building the application were also interviewed.

All interviews aimed at finding out the balance between the expectations of the respondents and the real feeling left by the use/ development of "CertExam." Starting with simple questions, like: "Are you satisfied with the e-assessment application?" and continuing with more difficult ones, like: "Are you satisfied with the level of interactivity given by the application?" "Do you consider the application useful for developing your project management competences?" "Are the recommendations offered suitable or useful?" the interviews revealed the attributes considered necessary for an efficient e-assessment product.

Data Analysis with Fuzzy Clustering

The respondents' opinions were used to establish a set of requirements for improving "CertExam," especially and giving some guidelines for all project management e-assessment, in general. In order to obtain a more accurate set of requirements for

a good assessment application design, we decided to classify the requirements in three groups (see Figure 6): product' requirements, trainers' requirements and trainees' requirements. The voices of the product were the developers involved in the e-assessment implementation. The trainees were the individuals who took the tests. The trainers were the professors who used the e-assessment in class. The surprising element was when we realized that there were some overlapping requirements in the three groups. A fuzzy clustering seemed the proper solution for our problem.

According to the c-means algorithm (Taraskina & Cheremushkin, 2006), the input information for a fuzzy clustering is the matrix of observation. The matrix has the following dimensions:

$$l \times n$$

where:

- l represents the number of objects, in our case requirements;
- n represents the number of characteristic of each object, in our case the requirement's features;

The task of clustering is to partition the objects to a predefined number of clusters, with respect to some given criteria. As we established the three groups of requirements (trainer, trainee, product), we wanted to partition the requirements thought to be necessary for an e-assessment to three. Each object belongs to several or all clusters simultaneously, but with different degree of confidence. The cluster structure is specified by the membership matrix, which has the following dimensions:

$$c \times l$$

where:

- c represents the number of clusters, in our case 3;

- I represents the number of objects, in our case requirements;

The matrix M has elements between 0 and 1: 0 means that the object j doesn't belong to the cluster i; 1 means that the object j totally belong to the cluster i; 0.5 means that the object j belongs in a certain measure to the cluster I, where "j" is a column index and "i" is a row index. Each row sum should be greater than 0 and each column sum should be at least equal to 1. Two objects belong to the same cluster when the distance between them is minimal. A small distance can be translated, from the linguistic point of view, in a high degree of similarity. In our case, it means a great number of common attributes. The statistical parametric approach reduces the problem of clustering to the estimation of a mixture of densities parameters, obtained by the search for the Maximum Likelihood. The c-means algorithm minimizes the index of quality defined as sum of squared distance for all points included in the cluster space to the center of the cluster. The steps in c-means algorithm are the following:

Figure 6. Requirements groups for an e-assessment application

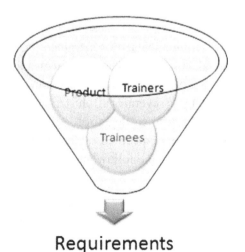

Requirements

- Assign randomly all training input vectors to a cluster, thus creating a partition;
- Calculate a cluster center as the mean of each vector component of all vectors assigned to that cluster;
- Repeat for all clusters;
- Compute all Euclidean distances between each cluster center and each input vector;
- Update partition by assigning each input vector to its nearest cluster center (minimum Euclidean distance);
- Stop if centers do not move any more, otherwise loop to the step in which a cluster center is calculated;

The results offered by the c-means algorithm depended on: amount of chosen cluster centers; sequence of pattern survey; geometric properties of the data. Our data was satisfactory. C-means algorithm has easy prototypes and is not very stable. Other clustering prototypes are: Self-Organizing Maps (SOM), splitting, merging, cluster swapping. Although SOM is more stable than c-means, it is much slower. Splitting algorithm is not always accurate. Merging is very slow. Cluster swapping is accurate, but slow. Taking into account all these considerations, we chose c-means for requirements clustering.

THE REQUIREMENTS MODEL

The main classes of the model are reflected in the membership matrix from Figure 7. The columns contain the clusters and the rows contain the requirements' classes. The clustering was realized using the attributes of the requirements indicated by users and developers in the interviews. Each of the class will be further explained.

Standardization is important, to both users (trainers and trainees) and developers. Standardization means interoperability, reusability, manageability, accessibility and durability of an e-assessment application (AL-Smadi, Guetl, &

Figure 7. Membership matrix of the requirements cluster for an e-assessment application

Requirement class/Cluster	Standardization	Design flexibility	Management & support for the entire assessment cycle	Adaptability	Modularity	Custom ability	Security & privacy
Trainee	0.1	1	1	1	0	0.3	0.8
Trainer	0.4	1	1	1	0.5	1	0.7
Product	0.5	0	0	0	0.8	0	0.2

Helic, 2009). Interoperability is expressed by the ability of an information system to share resources or services. This feature is very useful for developers, as they can reuse certain components, but also for the actors in an e-assessment environment, as they can bring their experience from other environments into the current one.

Reusability is strongly connected to the interoperability. An "if-then" relationship contains the two subclasses: if interoperability exists, then reusability exists. Manageability aims the tracking of all processes and activities in an e-assessment. This feature aims mainly the technical parts of the management process. Accessibility refers to the possibility given by the assessment application to be used from all over the places: the fact that it is a Web application is, for sure, a great plus in this direction, but the developers have to be sure that the application looks and acts the same, disregarding the browser type or version.

Durability means that "the learning content does not need any redesign or redevelopment" when the operating system is upgraded (Al Smadi, Guetl, & Helic, 2009). In order to increase the standardization and the configurability or custom ability of the e-assessment application, metadata can be a successful solution (Bodea & Dascalu,

2009). A standard-conformant e-assessment tool is a step forward to a global assessment process. The relationship between "standardization" and all the five subclasses discussed so far (interoperability, reusability, manageability, accessibility and durability) can be formalized through a "contains" relationship. The fact that the recommender engine was, somehow, external to the e-assessment application itself (it is called by the feedback mechanism, included in the Web service), supports the durability of the analyzed application.

Design flexibility refers to the user-friendly interfaces, respecting interactivity patterns, such as in-line help, tooltips or input feed-back. In addition, the cross-language support could be of tremendous help. All these components of design flexibility have a direct impact on raising the accessibility level.

Implementing the entire assessment cycle can be a challenging task for developers. Trainers are interested in: "exercises creation, storage and compilation for assessments, assessment performance, grading, and feedback provision" (Al-Smadi, Guetl, & Helic, 2009). According to our interviews, trainees are more interested in the feedback features, either immediately or timely.

The explanation for this is that they would like to use the e-assessment as a learning tool, so they would like to learn from their mistakes (Bodea & Dascalu, 2009).

Adaptability is a very challenging task for the developers: implementing a computer adaptive principle is not a straightforward thing. Still, it is a highly appreciated feature among the users. The trainers would like to have the possibility to create their own set of exercises, based on self-developed learning objectives and a set of criteria. More exactly, in project management, they would like to check, sometimes, a predefined set of ICB competences. Users would like the e-assessment to support guided and self-directed learning: each question should bring a challenge and should add value to their knowledge. A solution for the adaptive demanding is given by the use of ontological approaches and semantic networks in modeling the digital content (Bodea & Dascalu, 2009; Hardas, 2006). If computer adaptive principle is used, the security is also enhanced and supervision concerns are greatly diminished (Linacre, 2000).

The adaptation also is made for recommendation issues: the recommendations are meant to fill some knowledge gaps, which are different from user to user.

The modular design is a request from developers—it is easier to realize the maintainability tasks and from the trainers—they said it gives them the possibility to buy a new module and to integrate it or to sell a component. The service-oriented approach serves the modularity.

The custom ability can be translated, from the trainees' point of view, to the capacity of creating their own layout of the tests: for "CertExam," some said that they would have preferred to have the image in the right side or they would have liked to have all the answers unchecked. At "CertExam," when a new test item is opened, all the answers are checked, by default. For trainers, the custom ability is synonym with adaptability to their needs, for some and others would have liked to buy an e-testing solution and to adapt it for project management. For this, standardization would have been a "must."

Figure 8. Requirements model for a project management e-assessment application based on an empirical study

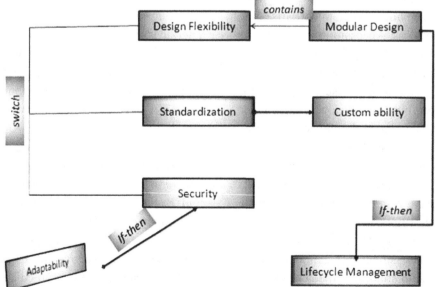

Security had different meanings for our interviewers. The developers mentioned assuring security of the data transferred over the network is a top priority for them. The trainees were more interested in privacy and results' security. The trainers were concerned about the security of their digital content. Other two features came into discussion when talking about security: fairness and reliability. Trainees mentioned their need of clear questions: if they are supposed to have the competence of starting a project, they should be asked about this. On other words, the test items should address the intended learning outcomes.

The trainers feel that they have to trust the e-assessment for providing them accurate results of the trainees' knowledge: proper grading mechanism was one extremely mentioned demanding among our interviewers. As this was a finding from our studies, we conclude that the reliability is a key issue in developing an efficient e-assessment application: "If a person passes on e-assessment he/she should have the essential knowledge for performing the relevant tasks for he/she holds a competency" (Gilbert, Gale, Warburton, & Wills, 2008). Increased security is obtained with a compromise: the user interfaces are slower and, sometimes, the accessibility has to be reduced. Therefore, a "switch" relation between security, standardization, and design flexibility is drawn in Figure 8. The relationships between our classes of requirements are also reflected in Figure 8.

FUTURE RESEARCH DIRECTIONS

As a follow-up of the current study, two future directions were established:

- At local level, "CertExam" will be improved, by: inserting services clustering, using semantic networks and concept space graphs for knowledge exploitation, using Computer Adaptive Testing principle to increase the self-directive learning features of the e-assessment application, increase the use of metadata, increase security;
- At global level, the requirements model will be improved, after another round of interviews, which are to be made on future versions of "CertExam"; an interesting issue would be to compare the proposed set of specifications (obtained after analyzing an e-assessment application which uses a recommender engine to enhance its feedback mechanism) to an e-assessment application which does not have this kind of feature; thus, one could establish whether the e-assessment applications with recommender engines are a special class of e-assessment tools or not.

Another improvement can be made at the clustering algorithm. The C-means clustering algorithm is very much dependent on the choice of the initial distribution of cluster centers. Therefore, the algorithm ends up in a local optimum, which can be far from real life global optimum, especially when a large number of data points and clusters are involved. A genetic C-means algorithm, insensitive to initial conditions, would be a nice step forward towards a more accurate clustering and thus a more effective requirements model.

CONCLUSION

The chapter provides a smart set of requirements for developing an e-assessment application, based on empirical study regarding the features and usability of an e-assessment application for project management. The authors tried to translate the fuzzy opinions of the trainers, trainees, and developers of the e-assessment tool into a clear model. For better understanding, the requirements were clustered into classes, with the aid of fuzzy logic. The fact that the findings are easily generalized for any domain complies with the need of a global e-assessment solution.

Based on user experience and on stakeholders' interests, the proposed model will be used to improve the performance of the e-assessment tool of the Romanian Association of Project Management.

As a conclusion to this study, for building and efficient e-assessment, one should take into consideration also: the type of tests (summative or formative), what you are trying to assess, how the tests will be marked, how your questions will be pilot.

REFERENCES

Al-Smadi, M., Guetl, C., & Helic, D. (2009). Towards a standardized e-assessment system: Motivations, challenges and first findings. In *Proceedings of the 4th International Conference on Mobile and Computer Aided Learning, ICML.* Amman, Jordan: ICML.

Amiel, T., & Reeves, T. C. (2008). Design-based research and educational technology: Rethinking technology and the research agenda. *Journal of Educational Technology & Society, 11*(4), 29–40.

Barker, K. (1999). *Quality guidelines for technology assisted distance education.* New York, NY: FuturEd Consulting Education Futurists.

Biggam, J. (2010). Using automated assessment feedback to enhance the quality of student learning in universities: A case study. In *Technology Enhanced Learning: Quality of Teaching and Educational Reform* (pp. 188–194). Athens, Greece: Springer. doi:10.1007/978-3-642-13166-0_27

Birenbaum, M., Kimron, H., Shilton, H., & Shahaf-Bar, R. (2009). Cycles of inquiry: Formative assessment in service of learning in classrooms and in school-based professional communities. *Studies in Educational Evaluation, 35*, 130–149. doi:10.1016/j.stueduc.2010.01.001

Black, P., & Wiliam, D. (2009). Developing the theory of formative assessment. *Assessment. Evaluation and Accountability, 21*(1), 5–31. doi:10.1007/s11092-008-9068-5

Bodea, C., & Dascalu, M. (2009). A parametrized web-based testing model for project management. In *Proceedings of the Advances in Web-Based Learning, ICWL,* (pp. 68–72). Aachen, Germany: Springer.

Bodea, C., & Dascalu, M. (2010). Competency-based e-assessment in project management and firm performance: A case study. In *Proceedings of the 4th Conference on European Computing Conference,* (pg. 76-81). Bucharest, Romania: WSEAS.

Buzzetto-More, N., & Alade, A. J. (2006). Best practices in e-assessment. *Journal of Information Technology Education, 5,* 251–269.

Commission of the European Communities. (2005). *Proposal for a recommendation of the European parliament and of the council on key competences for lifelong learning.* Brussels, Belgium: European Commission.

Craven, P. (2009). *History and challenges of e-assessment: The Cambridge approach perspective – e-Assessment research and development 1989 to 2009.* Cambridge, UK: Cambridge University Press.

Delcea, C., & Dascalu, M. (2009). Knowledge strategies tools for managing enterprise crisis. In Proceedings of *the 4th International Conference on Knowledge Management: Projects, Systems and Technologies,* (pp. 115-117). Bucharest, Romania: Carol I National Defense University.

Ehlers, U.-D., Goertz, L., Hildebrandt, B., & Pawlowski, J. (2005). *Quality in e-learning - Use and dissemination of quality approaches in European e-learning - A study by the European quality observatory.* Luxembourg, Luxembourg: Office for Official Publications of the European Communities.

Frey, N., & Fisher, D. (2009). Using common formative assessments as a source of professional development in an urban American elementary school. *Teaching and Teacher Education, 25,* 674–680. doi:10.1016/j.tate.2008.11.006

Gilbert, L., Gale, V., Warburton, B., & Willis, G. (2008). *Report on summative e-assessment quality (REAQ).* Southampton, UK: Joint Information Systems Committee.

Göksedef, M., & Gündüz-Ögüdücü, S. (2010). Combination of web page recommender systems. *Expert Systems with Applications, 37,* 2911–2922. doi:10.1016/j.eswa.2009.09.046

Hardas, M. (2006). *A novel approach for test problem assessment using course ontology.* Kent, OH: Kent State University.

Hsu, I.-C. (2009). SXRS: An xlink-based recommender system using semantic web technologies. *Expert Systems with Applications, 36,* 3795–3804. doi:10.1016/j.eswa.2008.02.062

Hsu, M.-H. (2009). A personalized English learning recommender system for ESL students. *Expert Systems with Applications, 34,* 683–688. doi:10.1016/j.eswa.2006.10.004

International Project Management Association. (2006). *IPMA competence baseline.* Nijkerk, The Netherlands: IPMA.

Jiang, L., Eberlein, A., Far, B., & Mousavi, M. (2008). *A methodology for the selection of requirements engineering techniques.* Berlin, Germany: Springer. doi:10.1007/s10270-007-0055-y

JISC. (2010). *Methods of assessment.* Retrieved February 25, 2011, from http://www.jiscinfonet. ac.uk/InfoKits/effective-use-of-VLEs/e-assessment/assess-methods

Kardan, A., Abbaspour, S., & Hendijanifard, F. (2009). A hybrid recommender system for e-learning environments based on concept maps and collaborative tagging. In *Proceedings of the 4th International Conference on Virtual Learning,* (pp. 200-207). ICVL.

Kuschel, J. A. (2006). *Conceptual framework for remote vehicle diagnostics services - Customer experienced needs as core business.* Paper presented at the 5th International Conference on Mobile Business. Copenhagen, Denmark.

Linacre, J. (2000). *Computer - Adaptive testing: A methodology whose time has come.* Chicago, IL: MESA Psychometric Laboratory.

Lysagh, R. M., & Altschuld, J. W. (2000). Beyond initial certification: The assessment and maintenance of competency in professions. *Evaluation and Program Planning, 23,* 95–104. doi:10.1016/S0149-7189(99)00043-9

Martell, K., & Calderon, T. (2005). Assessment of student learning in business schools: What it is, where we are, and where we need to go next. *Assessment of Student Learning in Business Schools: Best Practices Each Step of the Way, 1*(1), 1–22.

Mathiassen, L. (2002). Collaborative practice research. *Information Technology & People, 15*(4), 321–345. doi:10.1108/09593840210453115

Mooney, R., & Roy, L. (2010). Content-based book recommending using learning for text categorization. In *Proceedings of the ACM International Conference on Digital Libraries,* (pp. 195-204). San Antonio, TX: ACM.

Nicol, D. (2007). E-assessment by design: Using multiple-choice tests to good effect. *Journal of Further and Higher Education, 31*(1), 53–64. doi:10.1080/03098770601167922

Nuseibeh, B., & Easterbrook, S. (2002). Requirements engineering: A roadmap. In *Proceedings of the Conference on the Future of the Software Engineering,* (pp. 35-46). Limerick, Ireland: IEEE.

Raymond, L., Croteau, A.-M., & Bergeron, F. (2009). The integrative role of IT in product and process innovation: Growth and productivity outcomes for manufacturing. In *Proceedings of the Enterprise Information Systems, 11th International Conference,* (pp. 27-39). Berlin, Germany: Springer-Verlag.

Schacter, J. (1999). *The impact of education technology on student achievement: What the most current research has to say.* Santa Monica, CA: Milken Exchange on Education Technology.

Sitthiworachart, J., Joy, M., & Sutinen, E. (2008). Success factors for e-assessment in computer science education. In *Proceedings of World Conference on E-Learning in Corporate, Government, Healthcare, and Higher Education,* (pp. 2287-2293). Chesapeake, VA: AACE.

Suikki, R., Tromstedt, R., & Haapasal, H. (2006). Project management competence development framework in turbulent business environment. *Technovation, 26,* 723–738. doi:10.1016/j.technovation.2004.11.003

Taraskina, A., & Cheremushkin, E. (2006). The modified fuzzy c-means method for clustering of microarray data. In *Proceedings of the Fifth International Conference on Bioinformatics of Genome Regulation and Structure,* (pp. 180-183). Novosibirsk, Russia: IEEE.

Tuttle, H. G. (2007). *Formative assessment cycle in your classroom: Your technology use.* Retrieved March 13, 2011, from http://eduwithtechn.wordpress.com/2007/10/31/formative-assessment-cycle-in-your-classroom-your-technology-use/

Wang, T.-H. (2008). Web-based quiz-game-like formative assessment: Development and evaluation. *Computers & Education, 51,* 1247–1263. doi:10.1016/j.compedu.2007.11.011

Wieling, M., & Hofman, W. (2010). The impact of online video lecture recordings and automated feedback on student performance. *Computers and Education.* Retrieved from http://www.martijnwieling.nl/files/onlinevideo.pdf

Yang, S.-Y. (2010). Developing an ontology-supported information integration and recommendation system for scholars. *Expert Systems with Applications, 37,* 7065–7079. doi:10.1016/j.eswa.2010.03.011

Zhen, L., Huang, G., & Jiang, Z. (2010). An inner-enterprise knowledge recommender system. *Expert Systems with Applications, 37,* 1703–1712. doi:10.1016/j.eswa.2009.06.057

ADDITIONAL READING

Airasian, P. (1994). *Classroom assessment.* New York, NY: McGraw-Hill.

Arthur, N. (2006). Using student-generated assessment items to enhance teamwork, feedback and the learning process. *Synergy: Supporting the Scholarship of Teaching and Learning at the University of Sydney, 24,* 21–23.

Banks, D. (2006). *Audience response systems in higher education: Applications and cases.* Hershey, PA: IGI Global. doi:10.4018/978-1-59140-947-2

Boud, D. (2000). Sustainable assessment: Rethinking assessment for the learning society. *Studies in Continuing Education, 22*(2), 151–167. doi:10.1080/713695728

Boyle, J., & Nicol, D. (2003). Using classroom communication systems to support interaction and discussion in large class settings. *Association for Learning Technology Journal*, *11*(3), 43–57. doi:10.1080/0968776030110305

Crawford, L. (2005). Senior management perceptions of project management competence. *International Journal of Project Management*, *23*, 7–16. doi:10.1016/j.ijproman.2004.06.005

Ellul, J. (1980). *The technological system*. New York, NY: Continuum.

Feenberg, A. (2002). *Transforming technology*. Oxford, UK: Oxford University Press.

Granland, R., Bergland, E., & Eriksson, H. (2000). Designing web-based simulations for learning. *Future Generation Computer Systems*, *17*, 171–185. doi:10.1016/S0167-739X(99)00112-0

Hickman, L. A. (2001). *Philosophical tools for technological culture*. Bloomington, IN: Indiana University Press.

Higgins, R., Hartley, P., & Skelton, A. (2001). Getting the message across: the problem of communicating assessment feedback. *Teaching in Higher Education*, *6*(2), 269–274. doi:10.1080/13562510120045230

Hlynka, D. (2003). The cultural discourses of educational technology: A Canadian perspective. *Educational Technology*, *43*(4), 41–45.

Lunce, L. (2004). Computer simulations in distance education. *International Journal of Instructional Technology and Distance Education*, *1*(10).

Lundin, J. (2005). *Talking about work: Desiging information technology for learning in interaction*. Gothenburg, The Netherlands: Gothenburg University.

National Center for Postsecondary Education. (2001). *Student assessment in higher education: A comparative study of seven institutions*. Ann Arbor, MI: University of Michigan.

Nicol, D. (2006). *Increasing success in first year courses: Assessment re-design, self-regulation and learning technologies*. Paper presented at the ASCILITE Conference. Sidney, Australia.

Nicol, D., & Macfarlane-Dick, D. (2006). Formative assessment and self-regulated learning: A model and seven principles of good feedback practice. *Studies in Higher Education*, *31*(2), 198–218. doi:10.1080/03075070600572090

Novak, G. M., Patterson, E. T., Gavrin, A. D., & Christian, W. (1999). *Just-in-time-teaching: Blending active learning with web technology*. Upper Saddle River, NJ: Prentice Hall.

Pellegrino, J., Chudowsky, N., & Glaser, R. (2001). *Knowing what students know: The science and design of educational assessment*. Washington, DC: National Academy Press.

Ridgway, J., McCusker, S., & Pead, D. (2004). *Literature review of e-assessment*. Bristol, UK: Nesta Future Lab.

Scouller, K. (1998). The influence of assessment method on students' learning approaches: Multiple choice question examination versus assignment essay. *Higher Education*, *35*, 453–472. doi:10.1023/A:1003196224280

Turner, J. R. (1996). International project management association global qualification, certification and accreditation. *International Journal of Project Management*, *14*(1), 1–6. doi:10.1016/0263-7863(96)88794-1

Urciuoli, B. (2005). The language of higher education assessment: Legislative concerns in a global context. *Indiana Journal of Global Legal Studies*, *12*(1), 183–204. doi:10.2979/GLS.2005.12.1.183

Walvoord, B. E., & Anderson, V. J. (1998). *Effective grading: A tool for learning and assessment.* San Francisco, CA: Jossey-Bass.

Wiggins, G. (1990). The case for authentic assessment. *Practical Assessment, Research & Evaluation, 2*(2).

Wu, D., & Hiltz, R. (2004). Predicting learning from asynchronous online discussions. *Journal of Asynchronous Learning Networks, 8*(2), 139–152.

Yorke, M. (2003). Formative assessment in higher education: Moves towards theory and the enhancement of pedagogic practice. *Higher Education, 45*(4), 477–501. doi:10.1023/A:1023967026413

Zakrzewski, S., & Bull, J. (1999). The mass implementation and evaluation of computer-based assessments. *Assessment & Evaluation in Higher Education, 23*(2), 141–152. doi:10.1080/0260293980230203

KEY TERMS AND DEFINITIONS

E-Assessment: Is a Web-based software application, used to evaluate individuals' knowledge.

Educational Technology: Is the study and practice of facilitating learning and improving performance by creating, using and managing appropriate technological processes and resources.

E-Learning: Is a type of distance education, which is mediated by an environment set up by new information and communication technologies, in particular the Internet. Internet is both the material environment, as well as the communication channel between the actors involved.

Feedback: Is a mechanism which offers more explanations to the students regarding their knowledge gaps and gives them the possibility to revise their mistakes; when using feedback within an e-assessment system, the e-assessment gains formative value and becomes a learning tool.

Fuzzy Clustering: Is a method of grouping different elements, based on a set of attributes, where the same element can appertain to one or more groups.

Recommender System: Is an intelligent system, used for guiding the user to interesting objects (concepts) in a large space of possible options.

Requirements Specification: Is a set of rules, based usually on customers' wishes, which is used in developing software products.

Chapter 3
Building Recommender Systems for Network Intrusion Detection Using Intelligent Decision Technologies

Mrutyunjaya Panda
Gandhi Institute for Technological Advancement (GITA), India

Manas Ranjan Patra
Berhampur University, India

Sachidananda Dehuri
Fakir Mohan University, India

ABSTRACT

This chapter presents an overview of the field of recommender systems and describes the current generation of recommendation methods with their limitations and possible extensions that can improve the capabilities of the recommendations made suitable for a wide range of applications. In recent years, machine learning algorithms have been considered to be an important part of the recommendation process to take intelligent decisions. The chapter will explore the application of such techniques in the field of network intrusion detection in order to examine the vulnerabilities of different recommendation techniques. Finally, the authors outline some of the major issues in building secure recommendation systems in identifying possible network intrusions.

INTRODUCTION

Recommendation systems produce a ranked list of items on which a user might be interested, in the context of choosing a current item. Recommendation systems are built for movies, books, communities, news, articles, electronic commerce and other information access systems. Users have come to trust the recommendation software to reduce the burden of navigating large information spaces and product catalogues. The preservation of this trust is important both for the users and site owners, and is dependent upon the perception of

DOI: 10.4018/978-1-4666-2542-6.ch003

the recommender systems as objectives, unbiased and accurate. However, because recommendation systems are dependant on external sources of information, such as user profiles, they are vulnerable to attack. If a system generates recommendations collaboratively that is by user-to-user comparison, hostile users can generate bogus profiles for the purpose of biasing the systems' recommendations for or against certain products.

There are two main approaches to build a recommendation system- collaborative filtering and content based (Melville, Mooney & Nagarajan, 2002). Collaborative filtering computes similarity between two users based on their rating profile, and recommends items which are highly rated by similar users. However, quality of collaborative filtering suffers in case of sparse preference databases. Content based system on the other hand does not use any preference data and provides recommendation directly based on similarity of items. Similarity is computed based on item attributes using appropriate distance measures.

Some previous attempts at integrating collaborative filtering and content based approach include content boosted collaborative filtering (Melville, Mooney & Nagarajan, 2002), weighted, mixed, switching and feature combination of different types of recommender system (Bruke, 2002). But, none of them discuss about producing recommendation to a user without getting preferences. The authors conducted a pioneering study on the problem of the robustness of collaborative recommendations in (O'Mahoney, Silvestre & Hurley, 2004), where they use kNN-based collaborative filtering for vulnerability analysis. Lam and Riedl (2004) use some empirical studies of attacks against collaborative algorithms.

Intrusion detection is defined as the process of monitoring the events occurring in a computer system or network and analyzing them for signs of intrusions (Power, 2002). The need for effective intrusion detection mechanism for computer systems was recommended by Denning and Neumann (1985) in order to find reasons for intrusion

detection within a secure computing framework. The first major work in the area of intrusion detection was discussed by Anderson (1985) with an insight to the fact that certain types of intrusions to the computer system security could be identified through a detailed analysis of information contained in the system's audit trial. Three threats are identified by Anderson which could be: External Penetrations, as unauthorized users of the system; internal penetrations, as authorized system users who uses the system in an unauthorized manner; and finally Misfeasors, an authorized user who try to exploit their access privileges. But, it is Denning (1987), who proposed an intrusion detection model which is considered to be the fundamental core of most intrusion detection research in use today.

Approaches for intrusion detection can be broadly divided into two types: misuse detection and anomaly detection. In misuse detection system, all known types of attacks (intrusions) can be detected by looking into the predefined intrusion patterns in system audit traffic. In case of anomaly detection, the system first learns a normal activity profile and then flags all system events that do not match with the already established profile. The main advantage of the misuse detection is its capability for high detection rate with a difficulty in finding the new or unforeseen attacks. The advantage of anomaly detection lies in the ability to identify the novel (or unforeseen) attacks at the expense of high false positive rate.

In fact, intrusion detection is considered as a classification problem, namely, to identify the behaviour of the network traffic to fall either in normal or any one out of the four attack categories (i.e. Probing, Denial of Service, User to Root and Root to Local). Hence, the main motivation is to develop accurate classifiers that can effectively classify the intrusive behaviour than the normal one.

Despite number of approaches based on different soft computing paradigms have been proposed for intrusion detection, the possibilities of using the techniques are still considered to be under utilized. Hence, this chapter identifies key issues for the study of efficient recommendation, focusing particularly on the identification of attack models using different machine learning approaches.

BACKGROUND

The advent of the World Wide Web (WWW) and concomitant increase in information available online has caused information overload and ignited research in recommender systems. Recommender systems attempt to reduce information overload and retail customers by selecting a subset of items from a universal set based on user preferences (Perugini, Goncalves & Fox, 2004). Examples of such systems include movie (Alspector, Kolez & Karunanithi, 1998), and book (Mooney & Roy, 2000) recommenders, intelligent avatars (Andre & Rist, 2002) and advanced search engines (Chakrabarti et al., 2000). Recommender systems harness techniques which develop a model of user preferences to predict future ratings of artefacts, which ranges from keyword matching (Housmann & Kaskela, 1996) to sophisticated data mining of customer profiles (Adomavicius & Tuzhilin, 1999). Recommender systems are now widely believed to be critical to sustaining the Internet economy (Shapiro & Varian, 1999). In Computer Science research, several overlapping categories of recommender system approach are available. The first category consists of data analysis tools such as clustering (Berry & Linoff, 1997), classifier learning (Valient, 1984) and latent semantic indexing (LSI) (Papadimitriou et al., 1998), in which the goal is to infer a structure characterizing a given dataset. Clustering partitions the dataset into groups that are similar by some measure; classifier learning to build a hypothesis using the training data and validated with cross validation test; and LSI analyzes spectral properties of the term document matrix to cluster closely related documents for an efficient recommender system design.

Goals of the Recommender System

Recommender systems apply knowledge discovery techniques to the problem of making personalized recommendations for issues under considerations, which poses some key challenges due to the tremendous growth in the amount of information available to websites in recent years. One such challenge is the ability to be adaptive to environment where users have many completely different interests or items have completely different content. A recommender system can have the following reasons for its efficient implementation:

- An intrusion detection system can use such a powerful technology to increase its attack detection ratio by showing the normal and abnormal behaviour of the intruders to the system administrators to make efficient decisions.
- The system administrator further can take precautionary measures in order to protect the system from authorized users.
- Collaborative filtering (CF) can also be of immense useful for detecting the unseen or new attacks that fall under the rare attack categories.

Issues in Recommender System

The following are some of the issues that should be considered as a part of recommendation technologies to build an effective Recommender System.

- **Lack of Data:** This is considered as one of the biggest issues in designing recommender system, in the sense that they need huge amount of data to effectively make recommendations. Example of such data includes: Google, Amazon, UCI KDDD Cup Repository, etc. A good recommender system needs item data at first (either from a catalogue or any other form), then it must capture and analyze the data under evaluation to understand the behavioural trends and finally use the proposed algorithm to provide the useful insights. The more item and user data a recommender system has to work with, the stronger the chances of getting good recommendations. But it can be a chicken and egg problem i.e. to get good recommendations; you need a lot of users, thereby to get a lot of data for the efficient recommendations.

• **Changing Data:** Building a recommender system using past behaviour is always not a good assumption in situations especially where the trends are always changing. However, in case of fashion challenged people, item recommendations does not work because there re simply too many products attributes in fashion and each attribute to think fit, price, colour, style, fabric, brand etc. has a different level of importance at different times for the same consumer. However, social aspects of the recommender system may solve this problem.

• **User Preferences:** In this aspect, the recommender systems don't have correctly label users. For example: A person browsing Amazon.com today may be for new books for himself, but the very next day, the same user might be using Amazon to a birthday gift for some of his friend. So, changing user preferences should also be taken care of with utmost care while building an efficient recommender system.

• **Unpredictable items:** A data with unpredictable items for example the type of movie that people usually like or dislike. These types of items are quite difficult to make recommendations on, because the user reactions to them tend to be diverse and unpredictable.

MACHINE LEARNING AS INTELLIGENT DECISION TECHNOLOGY IN RECOMMENDER APPLICATIONS

The term machine learning in the context of recommendation system refers to describe the collection of analysis techniques used to infer recommendation rules or build recommendation models from large datasets. In this, the recommender system using machine learning algorithms make their recommendations using knowledge learnt from the actions and attributes of users. These systems are often based on the development of user profiles using algorithms like clustering, classification techniques, generation of association rules and the production of similarity graphs through techniques such as Horting.

Some clustering techniques present each user with partial participation in several clusters. The prediction is then average across the clusters, weighted by degree of participation. Clustering techniques usually produce less personal recommendations then other methods and in some cases, it produces worst accuracy than the traditional CF-based algorithms (Breese, Hackerman & Kadie, 1998). We will use some novel clustering algorithms by combining with classification techniques for useful recommendation in detecting network intrusions.

Classification techniques are used to build a recommender system (Schafer et al., 1999) using information about a product and a customer as the input, and to have the output category represent how strongly to recommend the product to the customer. Here, we propose to use some hybrid methodology for building an efficient recommendation system.

One of the best-known examples of machine learning algorithm in recommender systems is the discovery of association rules, or item-to-item correlations (Sarwar et al., 2001). In this, more powerful systems match an entire set of items, such as those in a customer's shopping cart, to identify appropriate items to recommend. Item-to-item correlation recommender applications usually use current interest rather than long-term customer history, which makes them particularly well suited for ephemeral needs such as recommending gifts or locating documents on a topic of short lived interest. A user merely needs to identify one or more "starter" items to elicit recommendations tailored to the present rather than the past. Here, we propose to discover some significant association rules to recommend the network administrator to take precautionary measures afterwards to prevent possible intrusions.

Intrusion Detection

Intrusion detection is defined as the process of monitoring the events occurring in a computer system or network and analyzing them for signs of intrusions (Power, 2002). The need for effective intrusion detection mechanism for computer systems was recommended by Denning and Neumann (1985) in order to find reasons for intrusion detection within a secure computing framework. The first major work in the area of intrusion detection was discussed by Anderson (1985) with an insight to the fact that certain types of intrusions to the computer system security could be identified through a detailed analysis of information contained in the system's audit trial. Three threats are identified by Anderson which could be: External Penetrations, as unauthorized users of the system; internal penetrations, as authorized system users who uses the system in an unauthorized manner; and finally Misfeasors, an authorized user who try to exploit their access privileges. But, it is Denning (1987), who proposed an intrusion detection model which is considered to be the fundamental core of most intrusion detection research in use today.

Approaches for intrusion detection can be broadly divided into two types: misuse detection and anomaly detection. In misuse detection

system, all known types of attacks (intrusions) can be detected by looking into the predefined intrusion patterns in system audit traffic. In case of anomaly detection, the system first learns a normal activity profile and then flags all system events that do not match with the already established profile. The main advantage of the misuse detection is its capability for high detection rate with a difficulty in finding the new or unforeseen attacks. The advantage of anomaly detection lies in the ability to identify the novel (or unforeseen) attacks at the expense of high false positive rate.

In fact, intrusion detection is considered as a classification problem, namely, to identify the behaviour of the network traffic to fall either in normal or any one out of the four attack categories (i.e. Probing, Denial of Service, User to Root and Root to Local). Hence, the main motivation is to develop accurate classifiers that can effectively classify the intrusive behaviour than the normal one.

Despite number of approaches based on different soft computing paradigms have been proposed for intrusion detection, the possibilities of using the techniques are still considered to be under utilized.

Intrusion Detection Datasets

KDDCup 1999 Dataset

In this section, we provided a brief overview of the KDDCup 1999 benchmark intrusion detection dataset. Under the sponsorship of Defence Advanced Research Projects Agency (DARPA) and Air Force Research Laboratory (ARFL), the Lincoln Laboratory at Massachusetts Institute of Technology (MIT) conducted the 1998 and 1999 evaluations of computer network intrusion detection systems (Mahoney & Chan, 2003; McHugh, 2000). DARPA dataset is the most popular dataset used to evaluate a large number of intrusion detection systems. The KDDCup 1999 dataset is a subset of DARPA dataset prepared by Stolfo and Lee (2000), which can be directly used for testing and evaluating the classifiers without further pre-processing.

Each connection record in the KDDCup 1999 dataset is labeled as either normal or anomalous (attack). There are 39 types of attacks which are grouped into four major categories: DoS (Denial of Service), U2R (unauthorized access to root privileges), Probing, and R2L (unauthorized access from a remote machine).

NSL-KDD Dataset

During last decade, KDDCup 1999 intrusion detection benchmark dataset is used by many researchers in order to build an efficient network intrusion detection system. However, recent study shows that there are some inherent problems present in KDDCup 1999 dataset (Tavallaee et al., 2009).The first important limitation in the KDDCup 1999 dataset is the huge number of redundant records in the sense that almost 78% training and 75% testing records are duplicated, which cause the learning algorithm to be biased towards the most frequent records, thus prevent it from recognizing rare attack records that fall under U2R and R2L categories. At the same time, it causes the evaluation results to be biased by the methods which have better detection rates on the frequent records. This new dataset, NSL-KDD dataset provided in (Tavallaee et al., 2009) is used for our experimentation and is now publicly available for research in intrusion detec-

tion. It is also stated that though the NSL-KDD dataset still suffers from some of the problems discussed in (McHugh, 2000) and may not be a perfect representative of existing real networks, it can be applied an effective benchmark dataset to detect network intrusions. More details about the inherent problems found in KDDCup dataset can be obtained from (Tavallaee et al., 2009). In this NSL-KDD dataset, the simulated attacks can fall in any one of the following four categories.

- **Probing Attack:** This is a type of attack which collect information of target system prior to initiating an attack. Some of the examples are Satan, ipsweep, nmap attacks.
- **DoS Attack:** Denial of Service (DoS) attack results by preventing legitimate requests to a network resource by consuming the bandwidth or by overloading computational resources. Examples of this are Smurf, Neptune, Teardrop attacks.
- **User to Root (U2R) Attack:** In this case, an attacker starts out with access to a normal user account on the system and is able to exploit the system vulnerabilities to gain root access to the system. Examples are eject, load module and Perl attacks.
- **Root to Local (R2L) Attack:** In this, an attacker who doesn't have an account on a remote machine sends packet to that machine over a network and exploits some vulnerabilities to gain local access as a user of that machine. Some examples are ftp_ write, guess password and imap attacks.

Table 1. Known and novel attack types (Adetunmbi et al., 2008)

Probe	DoS	U2R	R2L
Known Attacks			
ipsweep, satan, nmap, portsweep	Teardrop, pod, land, back, Neptune, smurf	Perl, loadmodule, rootkit, buffer_overflow	ftp_write, phf, guess_passwd, warezmaster, warezclient, imap, spy, multihop
Novel attacks			
saint, mscan	mailbomb, udpstorm, apache2, processtable	Xterm, ps, sqlattack, httptunnel	Named, snmpguess, worm, snmpgetattack, xsnoop, xlock, sendmail

The known and novel attack types available in NSL-KDD dataset are presented in Table 1.

PROPOSED RECOMMENDER SYSTEM

The components of our proposed recommender system are provided in Figure 1.

- **Naïve Bayes (NB):** Naïve Bayes is also called as Idiot's Bayes, Simple Bayes and independent Bayes, which is considered to be important for its simplicity, elegance and robustness. Naïve Bayes is an efficient and effective classification algorithm which assumes that all attributes are independent given the class (conditional independence assumption). But the attribute conditional assumption of Naïve Bayes rarely holds in real world applications. So, it needs to relax the assumption effectively to improve its classification performance.
- **Decision Trees (DT):** Decision trees construct easily interpretable models, which is useful for a system administrator to inspect and edit. It can also be used effectively in large data set which makes them useful in real time applications. The ability to detect the unseen or new attacks is made possible due to the generalization property of the decision trees.
- **Ensemble learning:** The learning procedure for ensemble algorithms can be divided into the following parts.
  - **Constructing base classifiers/base models:** The main tasks at this stage are
    - **Data processing:** Prepare the input training data for building base classifiers by perturbing the original training data, and
    - **Base classifier constructions:** Build base classifiers on the perturbed data with a learning algorithm as the base learner. In this work, we have used NB and DT (J48) as the base learners.
- **Voting:** The second stage of an ensemble method is to combine the base models built in the previous step into a final ensemble model. There are different types of voting systems, the frequently used ones are: weighted voting and un-weighted voting. In the weighted voting system, each base classifier holds different voting power. On the other hand, in the un-weighted system, individual base classifier has equal weight, and the winner is the one with most number of votes.

Figure 1. The proposed framework for NIDS

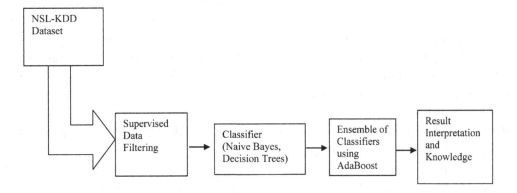

Table 2. Detection rate comparison

Methodology/ Detection Rate	Normal	Probe	DoS	U2R	R2L
NB+J48	0.972	0.71	0.819	0.045	0.057
AB+NB+J48	0.973	0.714	0.767	0.02	0.013
RotFor+NB+J48	0.969	0.702	0.756	0.015	0.02
BBN+TS	0.966	0.665	0.745	0.19	0.045
Dagging+SMO+Poly Kernel	0.931	0.532	0.752	0	2.17E-03
J48	0.972	0.709	0.819	0.045	0.057
AB+J48	0.974	0.682	0.828	0.04	6.89E-03
Nom2Bin+DMNB	0.973	0.441	0.803	0	0
NB+Random Forest	0.973	0.652	0.835	0.02	3.20E-02
Lazy LWL+LNN+J48	0.972	0.709	0.819	0.045	0.057

- **AdaBoost:** Boosting algorithms are a class of algorithms that have been mathematically proven to improve upon the performance of their base models in certain situations. AdaBoost (AB) has performed very well in practice and is one of the few theoretically motivated algorithms that have turned into a practical algorithm. However, AdaBoost can perform poorly when the training data is noisy, i.e. the inputs and outputs have been randomly contaminated (Dietterich, 2000). Noisy examples are normally difficult to learn. More details can be found in (Oza, 2004; Ratsch et al., 2001; Panda & Patra (2009). In order to enhance the accuracy of the classifiers, we propose to use the hybrid classifier by combining the Naïve Bayes and Decision Trees, as shown below in Figure 2.

This chapter combines Naïve Bayes (NB) with Decision Tree (DT) J48, which is called as hybrid NBDT, in order to build an efficient network intrusion detection model. This approach to the beat of our knowledge has not been used by any of the intrusion detection researchers using either KDDCup 1999 or NSL KDD dataset. In this model, Naïve Bayes and Decision tables can both be trained efficiently, and the same holds true for the combined model. The algorithm for learning the combined model (NBDT) proceeds in much the same way as the DTs alone. At each point in the search; it evaluates the merit associated with splitting the attributes into two disjoint subsets: one for the Naïve Bayes and the other for the Decision Trees. In this, forward selection is used, where at each step, selected attributes are modeled by NB and the reminder by the DT, and all attributes are modeled by the DT initially. We use leave-one-out cross validation to evaluate the quality of a split based on the probability estimates generated by the combined model. In this, we aim to use accuracy as our performance measures in a 2-class classification process in building a network intrusion detection system, as most of the anomaly detection schemes are concerned to obtain whether the particular instance belong either normal or attack without discussing much insight about the attack types. The class probability estimates of the Naïve Bayes and Decision Trees must be combined to generate overall class probability estimates.

PERFORMANCE EVALUATION

In this section, a detailed performance evaluation measures are highlighted.

- Detection Rate and Recall Rate are two widely used measures for evaluating the quality of results in statistical classification domain. Detection rate (Precision Rate) is defined as a measure of fidelity or exactness which provides an insight to understand how much efficiently all class labels are detected truly. In other words, detection rate (DR) is calculated as the ratio between the true positives to the sum of true positives and false positives. True positives are the number of items correctly classified as belonging to the class and which are incorrectly classified are termed as false positives. In contrast, recall (RR) is a measure of completeness. RR can be defined as the number of true positives divided by the total number of items that actually belong to the class.

- False positive rate (FPR) and false negative rate (FNR) are also important in finding the performance of any machine learning algorithms. False positive (FP) occurs when actually there is no attack occurred but alarm is raised, where as false negative (FN) gives an indication of a possible attack but there is no alarm raised.

- Cost sensitive classification is also considered as an important performance evaluation measures in order to find the cost of misclassification for intrusion detection. In this, with a given test set, the average cost of a classifier is calculated as follows:

$$\text{Cost} = = \frac{\sum_{i=1}^{5}\sum_{j=1}^{5} ConfM(i,j) * CostM(i,j)}{N}$$

where, ConfM (i, j) denotes the entry at row i, column j in the confusion matrix, CostM (i, j) is the entry at row i, column j in the cost matrix and N is the total number of connections in the intrusion detection test dataset. Numbering of network attacks categories along with the cost matrix are shown below in Table 1 and Table 2 respectively.

- Bias-Variance Dilemma is another measure that plays a vital role in the evaluation of a classifier. The principle can be stated as: datasets with too few parameters are inaccurate because of a large bias and thus have not enough flexibility, where as large variance occurs when there are too many parameters which mean too sensitivity to the sample.

Table 3. False positive rate comparison

Methodology/ False Positive Rate	Normal	Probe	DoS	U2R	R2L
NB+J48	0.056	0.034	0.078	8.4E-03	0.103
AB+NB+J48	0.083	0.033	0.096	8.6E-03	0.107
RotFor+NB+J48	0.084	0.035	0.098	8.66E-03	0.107
BBN+TS+SE	0.075	0.04	0.101	7.17E-03	0.108
Dagging+SMO+Poly Kernel	0.162	0.056	0.103	8.79E-03	0.108
J48	0.057	0.034	0.078	8.4E-03	0.1
AB+J48	0.066	0.036	0.074	8.45E-03	0.108
Nom2Bin+DMNB	0.089	0.06	0.087	8.79E-03	0.109
NB+Random Forest	0.059	0.039	0.074	8.62E-03	0.106
Lazy LWL+LNN+J48	0.057	0.034	0.078	8.4E-03	0.104

Table 4. Performance evaluation of various classifiers

Methodology	Kappa	RMSE	Build Time in Seconds	Number of Leaves and Trees	Average Cost of Misclassification
NB+J48	0.5921	0.1193	109.08	547, 662	0.643
AB+NB+J48	0.5868	0.119	777.92	697, 830	0.711
RotFor+NB+J48	0.583	0.1198	1350	867, 1027	0.7
BBN+TS+SE	0.572	0.1196	64.44	**********	0.698
Dagging+SMO+Poly Kernel	0.5379	0.155	859.56	**********	0.757
J48	0.5921	0.1193	98.44	547, 662	0.686
AB+J48	0.591	0.1186	980.22	1023,1142	0.679
Nom2Bin+DMNB	0.5443	0.1153	73.66	**********	0.742
NB+Random Forest	0.5904	0.1105	67.67	RF of 10 trees, with 6 random features and oob error=0.03	0.671
Lazy LWL+LNN+J48	0.5921	0.1193	104.02	547, 662	0.643

SOLUTIONS AND RECOMMENDATIONS

The experiments were conducted with NSL-KDD dataset, a variant of KDDCup 1999 benchmark intrusion detection dataset. We have performed 2-class classification (i.e. either normal or anomaly) to build our proposed hybrid intelligent system to detect network intrusions. All experiments were conducted on a Pentium-4 IBM PC with 2.8GHz CPU, 40GB HDD with 512 MB RAM using Java Environment (Witten & Frank, 2005).

To solve the issues mentioned earlier, we performed our experiments using general frame work and hybrid approach for detecting network intrusions on NSL-KDD dataset which contains 25192 training and 22544 testing instances with 42 attributes. All attributes are same to that of KD-DCup 1999 dataset. In order to test and compare the effectiveness of the proposed methodologies, we have used separate testing dataset and 10-fold cross validation method both for designing the intrusion detection model. The simulation results obtained using framework as per Figure 1 is provided for 5-class classification in Table 2 and Table 3 respectively for individual and multiple classifier systems. Finally, we provided the results obtained by many researchers in this area of research using KDDCup 1999 and NSL-KDD benchmark intrusion dataset in Table 4 and Table 5-6 respectively. From Table 2, it is observed that AB+J48 has highest accuracy of 97.4% for Normal category, AB+NB+J48 with 71.4% for probing attack, NB+Random Forest for DoS attack, Bayesian belief network (BBN) with Tabu search (TS) for U2R attacks with 19%, and

Table 5. Proposed hybrid methodology (part 1)

Algorithms Using 10-fold CV with NSL-KDD Dataset	Normal		Anomaly		Build Time in Seconds	RMSE
	DR (%)	FPR (%)	DR (%)	FPR (%)		
Naïve Bayes	91.25	10.5	87.69	10.33	3.5	0.3152
Decision Trees (J48)	99.55	0.51	99.57	0.38	26	0.0651
NBDT	99.55	0.51	99.57	0.38	29.95	0.0651

Table 6. Proposed hybrid methodology (part 2)

Algorithms using separate testing dataset with NSL-KDD Dataset	Normal		Anomaly		Build Time in Seconds	RMSE
	DR (%)	FPR (%)	DR (%)	FPR (%)		
Naïve Bayes	92.78	13.82	64.3	26.22	3.52	0.4816
Decision Trees (J48)	97.17	5.1	68.86	23.29	26.89	0.413
NBDT	97.17	5.1	68.86	2.83	29.11	0.413
AdaBoost+ NBDT	97.33	5.44	66.52	24.15	553.34	0.4399

Lazy locally weighted learning (LWL)+Linear neural network(LNN)+DT with 5.7% accuracy for R2L attacks.

Similarly, from Table 3, we can see NB+DT has lowest FPR with 5.6% for Normal, AB+NB+DT with 3.3% for Probe, NB+ Random Forest with 7.4% for DoS, BBN+TS with 7.17E-03 for U2R, and J48 with 10% for R2L attacks categories. The performance of the various classifiers with other important performance measures is shown in Table 4. The classifier with high kappa value, low Root mean square error (RMSE), less time, less number of leave and trees and finally low cost of misclassification is an obvious choice while designing a NIDS.

Further, based on the Hybrid Approach as shown in Figure 2, all the experiments are conducted using NSL-KDD dataset with 2-class classification. We have evaluated all our algorithms with various evaluation measures and the results are presented in Table 5 and Table 6. In Table 5, we use 10-fold cross validation test and separate testing dataset is used in Table 6, to understand the efficacy of the designed intrusion detection model.

From Table 5, it can be observed that the NBDT provides very high detection rate (99.57%) to detect network intrusions with low false positive rate (0.38%). We further test our model using separate NSL-KDD testing dataset with 22544 instances, which are different than the training dataset used, which is provided in Table 6. The results show that the accuracy to detect network intrusions is reduced in comparison to our earlier approaches. With this approach, the detection rate for NBDT restricted to only 68.86% and 68.47% respectively with somewhat more false positive rates in comparison to our 10-fold cross validation approaches. This is very difficult on our part to compare the proposed methodologies with others, due to unavailability of the research works using the NSL-KDD dataset to detect network intrusions.

Figure 2. A hybrid data mining approach to NIDS

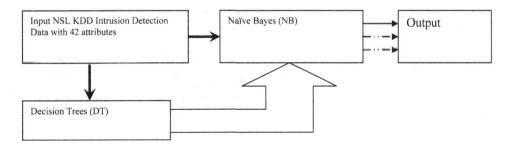

CONCLUSION AND FUTURE TRENDS

Recommender systems have emerged as powerful tools for helping users find and evaluate items of interest. These systems use a variety of machine learning techniques to help users identify the items that best fit their tastes or needs. While recommender systems may have stared as largely a passing novelty, they clearly appear to have moved into a real and powerful tool in a variety of applications, and that machine learning algorithms can be and will continue to be an important part of the recommendation process even in the area of Intrusion Detection.

The empirical analysis from this research suggests that our proposed approach using various machine learning methodologies using NSL-KDD dataset in place of KDDCup 1999 intrusion detection benchmark dataset because of its limitations as discussed earlier; performs reasonably well in all category of majority attacks while a poor detection rate in detecting U2R and R2L minority attacks because of their large bias available in dataset with low false positive rate. We perform a cost sensitive classification and found the models achieve low detection cost. However, it can be noted that no system is absolutely secure with a given set of best possible algorithms, while protecting our resources from network attacks. This makes the computer security is always an active and challenging area of research. To move further in this direction, we propose to evaluate more machine algorithms to detect minority attacks efficiently with acceptable false appositive rate and low cost of misclassification in future.

REFERENCES

Adetunmbi, A. O., Falaki, S. O., Adewale, O. S., & Alese, B. K. (2008). Network intrusion detection based on rough set and k-nearest neighbor. *International Journal of Computing and ICT Research*, *2*(1), 60–66.

Adomavicius, G., & Tuzhilin, A. (1999). User profiling in personalization applications through rule discovery and validation. In *Proceedings of the 5th ACM SIGKDD International Conference on KDD*, (pp. 377-381). San Diego, CA: ACM Press.

Alspector, J., Kolez, A., & Karunanithi, N. (1998). Comparing feature based and clique-based user models for movie selection. In *Proceedings of the 3rd ACM Conference on Digital Libraries*, (pp. 11-18). Pittsburgh, PA: ACM Press.

Anderson, J. P. (1985). *Computer security threat monitoring and surveillance.* Technical Report. Fort Washington, PA: J.P. Anderson Company.

Andre, E., & Rist, T. (2002). Form adaptive hypertext to personalized web companions. *Communications of the ACM*, *45*(5), 43–46. doi:10.1145/506218.506243

Berry, M. J., & Linoff, G. (1997). *Data mining techniques.* New York, NY: John Wiley.

Breese, J., Hackerman, D., & Kadie, C. (1998). Empirical analysis of predictive algorithms for collaborative filtering. In *Proceedings of the 14th Conference on Uncertainty in Artificial Intelligence*, (pp. 43-52). IEEE.

Bruke, R. (2002). Hybrid recommender systems: Survey and experiments. *Journal of User Modelling and User Adapted Interaction*, *12*(4), 331–370. doi:10.1023/A:1021240730564

Chakrabarti, S., Dom, B. E., Kumar, S. R., Raghaban, P., Rajgopalan, S., & Tomkins, A. (2000). Mining the web's link structure. *IEEE Computer*, *32*(8), 60–67. doi:10.1109/2.781636

Denning, D. E. (1987). An intrusion detection model. *IEEE Transactions on Software Engineering, 13*(2), 222–232. doi:10.1109/TSE.1987.232894

Denning, D. E., & Neumann, P. G. (1985). *Audit trail analysis and usage collection and processing.* Technical Report Project 5910. Menlo Park, CA: SRI International.

Dietterich, T. G. (2000). Ensemble methods in machine learning. *Lecture Notes in Computer Science, 1857,* 1–15. doi:10.1007/3-540-45014-9_1

Housmann, V., & Kaskela, E. (1996). State of the art in selective dissemination of information. In *Proceedings of IEEE Transactions on Engineering and Writing Speech,* (pp. 100-112). Stanford, CA: AAAI Press.

Lam, S. K., & Riedl, J. S. (2004). Recommender systems for fun and profit. In *Proceedings of the International World Wide Web Conference,* (pp. 393-402). New York, NY: ACM Press.

Lee, W., & Stolfo, S. J. (2000). A framework for constructing features and models for intrusion detection systems. *ACM Transactions on Information and System Security, 3*(4), 227–261. doi:10.1145/382912.382914

Mahoney, M., & Chan, P. (2003). An analysis of the 1999 DARPA/Lincoln lab: Evaluation data for network anomaly detection. In *Proceedings of Recent Advances in Intrusion Detection* (pp. 220–238). Berlin, Germany: Springer. doi:10.1007/978-3-540-45248-5_13

McHugh, J. (2000). Testing intrusion detection system: A critique of the 1998 and 1999 DARPA intrusion detection system evaluations as performed by Lincoln laboratory. *ACM Transactions on Information and System Security, 3*(4), 262–294. doi:10.1145/382912.382923

Melville, P., Mooney, R. J., & Nagarajan, R. (2002). Content–boosted collaborative filtering for improved recommendations. In *Proceedings of the 18th National Conference on Artificial Intelligence,* (pp. 187-192). Edmonton, Canada: AAAI Press.

Mooney, R., & Roy, L. (2000). Content based book recommending using learning for text categorization. In *Proceedings of the 5th ACM Conference on Digital Libraries,* (pp. 195-204). San Antonio, TX: ACM Press.

O'Mahoney, M., Silvestre, G., & Hurley, N. (2004). Collaborative recommendations: A robustness analysis. *ACM Transactions on Internet Technology, 4*(4), 344–377.

Oza, N. C. (2004). AdaBoost2: Boosting with noisy data. In F. Roli, J. Kittler, & T. Windeatt (Eds.), *Proceedings of the 5th International Workshop on Multiple Classifier Systems,* (pp. 31-40). Berlin, Germany: Springer-Verlag.

Panda, M., & Patra, M. R. (2009). Ensemble voting system for detecting anomaly based network intrusions. *International Journal of Recent Trends in Engineering, 2*(5), 8–13.

Papadimitriou, C. H., Raghavan, P., Tamaki, H., & Vempala, S. (1998). Latent semantic indexing: A probabilistic analysis. In *Proceedings of the 17th ACM Symposium on Principles of Database Systems,* (pp. 159-168). ACM Press.

Perugini, S., Goncalves, M. A., & Fox, E. A. (2004). Recommender system research: A connection centric survey. *Journal of Intelligent Information Systems, 23*(2), 107–143. doi:10.1023/B:JIIS.0000039532.05533.99

Power, R. (2002). CSI/FBI computer crime and security survey. *Computer Security Journal, 18*(2), 7–30.

Ratsch, G., Onoda, T., & Muller, K. R. (2001). Soft margins for AdaBoost. *Machine Learning, 42,* 287–320. doi:10.1023/A:1007618119488

Sarwar, B., Karypis, G., Konstan, K. A., & Riedl, J. (2001). Item based collaborative filtering recommendation algorithms. In *Proceedings of the 10th International Conference on World Wide Web,* (pp. 115-153). IEEE.

Schafer, J. B., Konston, J. A., Borchers, A., Sarwar, B., Herlocker, J., & Riedl, J. (1999). Combining collaborative filtering with personal agents for better recommendations. In *Proceedings of 16th National Conference on Artificial Intelligence*, (pp. 439-446). AAAI Press.

Shapiro, V., & Varian, H. R. (1999). *Information rules: A strategic guide to the network economy.* Boston, MA: Harvard Publisher School Press.

Tavallaee, M., Bagheri, E., Lu, W., & Ghorbani Ali, A. (2009). A detailed analysis of the KDD-Cup 1999 dataset. In *Proceedings of 2009 IEEE International Symposium on Computational Intelligence in Security and Defense Applications*, (pp. 1-6). IEEE Press.

Valient, L. G. (1984). A theory of learnable. *Communications of the ACM, 27*(11), 1134–1142. doi:10.1145/1968.1972

Witten, I. H., & Eibe, F. (2005). *Data mining -Practical machine learning tools and techniques* (2nd ed.). London, UK: Elsevier.

Chapter 4

REPERIO:
A Flexible Architecture for Recommendation in an Industrial Context

Frank Meyer
Orange Labs Lannion, France

Isabelle Tellier
LIFO Orléans, France

Damien Poirier
LIFO Orléans, France

Françoise Fessant
Orange Labs Lannion, France

ABSTRACT

In this chapter, the authors describe Reperio, a flexible and generic industrial recommender system able to deal with several kinds of data sources (content-based, collaborative, social network) in the same framework and to work on multi-platforms (Web service in a multi-user mode and mobile device in a mono-user mode). The item-item matrix is the keystone of the architecture for its efficiency and flexibility properties. In the first part, the authors present core functionalities and requirements of recommendation in an industrial context. In the second part, they present the architecture of the system and the main issues involved in its development. In the last part, the authors report experimental results obtained using Reperio on benchmarks extracted from the Netflix Prize with different filtering strategies. To illustrate the interest and flexibility of the architecture, they also explain how it is possible to take into account, for recommendations, external sources of information. In particular, the authors show how to exploit user generated contents posted on social networks to fill the item-item matrix. The process proposed includes a step of opinion classification.

INTRODUCTION

We are entering an era of huge catalogs and databases where one person cannot consider himself/herself to have an overview of what is available and what might interest him/her. Two types of systems were developed in parallel with the rapid

inflation of the available content: search engines, and automatic recommendation systems. Search engines are serving people who know what they want and who will, more or less easily, perform a search query. Automatic recommendation systems are often used as a support system for discovery, navigation aid or as a support system for decision-

DOI: 10.4018/978-1-4666-2542-6.ch004

making. Aid to discovery will be done by issuing personal recommendations. The navigation aid will be done by providing a contextual help such as similar products to the product being viewed. The support for decision making will be carried out by predicting, for a user, the potential value a product may have for him/her, for instance by predicting a rating for this product.

Automatic recommendation systems exist on subjects as diverse as Web pages, movies, TV programs, books, restaurants, humorous jokes, songs, people within a social network, etc. (Rao & Talwar, 2008) identified 96 recommendation systems on various subjects, academic or industrial. The general goal of automatic recommender systems is to help users to find products (items) that should interest them, from large catalogs. Items are defined as any object that can be consumed, bought, read or viewed.

Several recommender system typologies are known in the literature: the classical typology, with collaborative filtering, content-based filtering and hybrid filtering, for instance used in Adomavicius and Tuzhilin (2005), the typology of Rao and Talwar (2008) depending on the data sources used by the systems, the typology of Su and Khoshgoftaar (2009) restricted to collaborative filtering. In the first part of this chapter, we briefly review these typologies.

However, although the literature focuses on the score prediction, industry prioritization of functionalities is very different. In this context, we introduce another possible classification of the recommender systems, based on the types of functions available, rather than on data sources. This new typology distinguishes scoring-oriented systems and those similarity-based or recommendation-oriented. We show that systems based on item-item matrix are able to cover the all functionalities an industrial recommender system needs. A system that operates in industrial context should also satisfy some requirements like robustness, scalability and reactivity, adaptation to diverse

sources of data, cold-start management, etc. We describe an operational recommender system that integrates core functionalities of the recommendation and industrial requirements.

Next, we evaluate the efficiency of our industrial recommender system with an application in the field of movie recommendation. We built a benchmarks with data extracted from the Netflix challenge. We compare several filtering strategies with several kinds of sources (collaborative, content-based). As expected, the collaborative filtering approach is more efficient than the content-based one.

Finally, we also conducted experiments to exploit an original source of data: posts of users on a social network Web site concerning movies. The posts are short texts written in an SMS-like style. We show that they nevertheless express opinions that can be automatically recognized, and that these opinions can help to fill the item-item matrix on which the recommendations are based. Our experiments show that a collaborative filtering based on such a matrix is more efficient than a content-based filtering. This strategy opens interesting perspective to face the well-known cold-start problem.

MAIN TYPOLOGIES OF RECOMMENDER SYSTEMS

The typology currently found in the literature identifies three types of recommender systems: the collaborative filtering systems, the content-based (or thematic) filtering systems, the hybrid systems, using both collaborative and content-based techniques. This typology is based on the type of information used as input for the models (Adomavicius & Tuzhilin, 2005). Collaborative filtering uses logs of users, generally user ratings on items, sometimes with dates. Content-based filtering uses item metadata (i.e. intrinsic characteristics of the items, described by text, structural data—or information extracted from the items in some cases: acoustic features from songs for instance). In collaborative filtering logs of users are compared in some way in order to find usage correlations. In content-based filtering, metadata are compared to compute explicit or implicit user preferences. Unlike content-based filtering, collaborative filtering can be said "content agnostic": this means that a collaborative filtering system does not need data describing the items, which will be recommended: an "item ID" is enough. The hybrid filtering on the other hand is a combination of collaborative filtering and content-based filtering.

Su and Khoshgoftaar (2009) propose a sub-classification for purely collaborative systems that includes the hybrid techniques (which are necessarily collaborative) to classify them into hybrid collaborative methods. They distinguish three sub-categories of collaborative filtering:

- Memory-based approaches for type K-nearest-neighbors;
- Model-based approaches encompassing a variety of techniques such as: clustering, Bayesian networks, matrix factorization, Markov decision processes;
- Hybrid collaborative filtering, which combine another technical approach (mainly methods based on content recommendation) with collaborative filtering recommendation techniques.

Rao and Talwar (2008) propose a classification which depends on the sources of information used to recommend items:

- Content-based filtering (or thematic filtering) systems use item correlations to generate recommendations, and matching between item features and user profile to calculate a score for each item;

- Collaborative filtering systems are only based on logs of user usages on items;
- Demographic filtering systems use a priori knowledge on groups of users. This knowledge is used to build stereotypes (with information such as age, location) linked with particular lists of items to recommend;
- The last type is a hybrid filtering that makes use of collaborative filtering and content based filtering.

Rao and Talwar (2008) also mention two other systems, one based on a priori knowledge of relationships between items and users, said "knowledge-based recommender system," and another based on a notion of utility calculated for a user and an item, called "utility-based recommender systems."

RECOMMENDER SYSTEM IN AN INDUSTRIAL CONTEXT

Core Functionalities

Although the literature focuses on the score prediction, industry prioritization of functionalities is very different. Automatic recommender systems are often used on e-commerce Web sites. These systems work in conjunction with a search engine for assistance in catalogue browsing to help users find contents.

Many users of e-commerce Web sites are anonymous, and therefore the main feature is the contextual recommendation of items, for anonymous users. The purpose of these systems is also increasing uses (the audience of a site) or increasing sales, so the recommendation itself is more important than the score prediction. Moreover, prioritizing a list of items on a display page is a more important functionality than the prediction of a rating. Numerous exchanges between marketing and project teams in the Orange Company lead us to propose another typology of recommendation systems based on the four core functionalities that are estimated as crucial for a system in an industrial context. Seven important requirements follow from the core functions. We discuss these core functions and requirements in next sections.

The four functionalities that a recommender system in an industrial context must verify are the following:

- It must be able to make predictions of ratings or scores;
- It must be able to rank or order items by relevance criterion;
- It must be able to make contextual, unpersonalized recommendations of items for anonymous Web site user;
- It must be able to make personalized recommendations of items.

These features are essential because they cover the four essential needs of users facing huge catalogs of items: decide, compare, explore, discover.

The rating prediction functionality of the recommendation consists in computing a predictive rating a user u would give to an item i. The items for which the predicted ratings are highest are not necessarily the most useful items for the user. Indeed, we must distinguish the fact that a user likes an item and the fact that an item is already known by the user (Herlocker, et al., 2004). To recommend a movie the recommendation system must find an item that would probably be well rated by the user but also an item that the user probably does not know. The ranking can incorporate a notion of item utility and is not necessarily derived from the rating prediction score. It is a function of its own. For a profile S_u and a list L of items, a recommender system can provide a relevant score, which can sort the items in the list L. The ranking is an important feature allowing implementing filtering services coupled with a dedicated search engine.

The contextual item-to-item function consists in giving for an item i, a list of similar items $L(i)$. This is the classic item-to-item-recommendation, popularized by the e-commerce Web site Amazon (www.amazon.com) (Linden, et al., 2003). This mode is widely used in industry because it can make recommendations for anonymous users, based on the item he/she consults. This browsing aid in a catalog is simple and very effective.

The last function is usually called "Item-based Top-N recommendation" (Karypis, 2001; Deshpande & Karypis, 2004) in the literature. As the ranking must be well differentiated from rating prediction, the personalized recommendation of items must be seen as a specific function which is not necessarily deducted from the others. Here, one wants to provide a user with a shortlist $L(u)$ of p items from a catalog of items C.

The important requirements associated to the four core functions in an industrial recommender system can be listed as follows:

- The ability to be complaint with many data sources as industrial system have to be deployed on different services with different kinds of data and ideally the system must be designed to avoid switching manually from one data source to another;
- The robustness to noisy or possibly corrupted data, as some data sources may be more or less trusted;
- The management of the cold-start at the time of the recommender's launch. The cold-start is the problem for the system to start prediction on users or items without enough data: the predictions may be poor, if not impossible. To deal with the cold-start problem, a recurrent choice is the use of metadata with a content-based recommender. Another interesting choice is the use of external data, (for instance other known usages on the items to recommend). The use of external data will be necessary

until the service has enough user data (profiles, explicit and/or default profile);

- The scalability and reactivity of the system, as operation systems have to deal with volumetric and response time issues;

- The transparency and the explain ability: the transparency of a recommender system is its ability to explain how it works and to give a confidence index for its recommendations. There are important factors in acceptance of recommendations (Bilgic, 2004). It is important for the user but also for the service manager (marketing…) for the validation and the traceability of the service;

- The management of the "long tail," that is to say the management of all the items that are not often bought/seen but that we want to promote (Anderson, 2006; Celma, 2008). Indeed, it is essential for a commercial application to fully exploit its catalog.

The functions and requirements are summarized in Table 1 and Table 2.

Why Isn't a Scoring System Enough?

Many publications in the field of automatic recommendation focused exclusively on scoring-based systems, that is to say systems capable of predicting an appetence score of a user for a given item. This emphasis on scoring systems is the result of several factors we discuss below.

The first factor is the scarcity of public data sources. MovieLens and Netflix databases are the best known and both deal with logs of anonymous user rating on items.

The second factor is methodological. The evaluation of a scoring system is simple and well known in the community. Several measures exist (Root Mean Squared Error, Mean Average Error) and are well accepted. Instead it is impossible to establish the added value of an objective system issuing recommendations other than by an online service.

Of course, logs allow using a protocol with two sets, Learning and Test, to simulate recommendations based on profiles only known in the Learning set and to check if they correspond to existing items (case logs of usage) or appreciated items (if logs of ratings) in the Test set. Deshpande and Karypis (2004), for instance, describe this type of protocol. However, these principles of simulation present many problems of interpretation:

- They do not distinguish which of the recommendations are really useful, those that lead to a purchase that would not have happened without the recommendation;

- They prefer simple systems that recommend the most viewed or rated items, at the expense of systems performing risky but useful recommendations;

- Each recommendation which does not use content in the logs used for the test cannot be assessed.

Table 1. Summary of core features of an industrial recommender system

Industrial core features	Specification summary
Help users to Decide	given a user u and an item i, give a predictive interest score (rating)
Help users to Compare	given a user u and a list of items $i_1,...,i_n$, sort the items in decreasing predicted interest
Help users to Navigate	given an item i used as context, give n similar items to a user browsing the catalog, specifically appropriated for anonymous users
Help users to Discover	given a user u, give n interesting items for u

Table 2. Summary of requirements of an industrial recommender system

Industrial requirements	Specification summary
Multi data sources	deployment in different contexts, with heterogeneous data sources
Cold Start	ability to deal with few collaborative data
Robustness	ability to deal with noisy catalogs or logs
Scalability	the model must be computed quickly and manage huge data
Reactivity	fast reaction to user's feedback
Trusted relationship	transparency of the system and understand ability for users
Long tail	any item can be recommend, even those rarely viewed/bought/rated.

Only on-line experiments on real users, using measurements like conversion rate (percentage of recommendation triggering an act of consumption) or Lifetime Value (measure of the value generated by each client) via a A/B testing protocol can actually evaluate the quality of the pushed recommendation. Generally, academic studies do not report on such tests that are often confidential, except for rare exceptions like in Davidson et al. (2010).

A third factor is that the scoring function appears to be sufficient to produce the other functionalities of a recommender system. An implicit assumption is that a scoring system can make recommendations: simply browse the items in the catalog, scoring each item for a user and then return the result. This view, however, has very significant limitations:

- If there is no notion of similarity between two items, the item recommendation for anonymous users will not be possible: this recommendation is based only on the items data (characteristics or usages characteristics) and require a similarity function to link items;
- For personalized recommendation, the system will eventually not scale. It is impossible to regularly score all items in the catalog for each user to retain the most important scores. Consider an application for Web pages recommendation for users whose profiles are changing every day, if every profile change implies to browse the entire catalog (the Web site!) to keep the items with the highest score, the system will quickly collapse;
- The prediction of the highest rated item is not necessarily the most useful recommendation (Cremonesi, et al., 2010). For instance, the item with the highest predicted rating shall be already known by the user.

The Need for a Notion of Similarity between Items

As we discuss below, in an industrial context, a system based on a single rating prediction algorithm will be incomplete. In particular, the contextual item-to-item functionality can't be solved and yet this function is the main function used in real industrial systems like Amazon or YouTube (www.youtube.com) to make recommendations for anonymous users, based on the visited items. Neighborhood-based methods and especially those based on item-item matrix are legitimate candidate methods (Linden, et al., 2003; Koren, 2010). These matrices can directly make recommendations for anonymous users: for any item being viewed (and used as a context) a list of similar items can be displayed by direct access to the matrix.

SYSTEMS BASED ON ITEM-ITEM SIMILARITY MEASURE

We define as an item-item matrix based system any predictive system using a matrix (usually pre-calculated) linking pairs of items according to a similarity measure. These systems compare pairs of items. For each item, a list of similar items, with a similarity index, is associated. Several sources can be used: a log table for a collaborative mode or a catalog for a content-based mode.

The following notations will be adopted later: u, v denote users, i, j items, T_i all users who rated item i, S_u all items rated by u, $r_{u,i}$ the rating of user u for item i, $\bar{r}_i$ the mean rating of item i on all the logs of ratings, $\hat{r}_{u,i}$ the predicted rating by the scoring system of a user u for an item i.

Similarity Measure

The similarity measure between items is central to item-item approaches. A frequently measure used is the Pearson correlation proposed in Resnick et al. (1994). It corresponds to the Cosine of deviations from the mean which measures the tendency of users to rate items i and j similarly:

$$\text{Pearson}(i, j) = \frac{\sum_{u \in T_i \cap T_j} (r_{ui} - \bar{r}_i)(r_{uj} - \bar{r}_j)}{\sqrt{\sum_{u \in T_i \cap T_j} (r_{ui} - \bar{r}_i)^2 \sum_{u \in T_i \cap T_j} (r_{uj} - \bar{r}_j)^2}} \tag{1}$$

For these similarity measures, only the set of attributes in common between two vectors are considered. Thus, two vectors may be completely similar even if they only share one appreciation on one attribute. Such measures have drawbacks. For example, consider the case when one user is a fan of science fiction while another only watches comedies. Furthermore, these users have not rated any film in common so their similarity is null. Now, they both say that they like Men in Black, a science fiction comedy. These users thus become completely similar according to the previously presented measures, given that their only common reference point was equally rated (Deshpande & Karypis, 2004; Breese, et al., 1998).

The Jaccard similarity, however, does not suffer from this limitation since it measures the overlap that two vectors share with their attributes:

$$jaccard(i, j) = \frac{\left| \{T_i \cap T_j\} \right|}{\left| \{T_i \cup T_j\} \right|} \tag{2}$$

On the other hand, such a measure does not take into account the difference of ratings between the vectors. In this case, if two users watch the same films but have completely opposite opinions on them, then they are considered to be similar anyway according to Jaccard similarity. This similarity applies for services that only support binary events such as purchases (ratings are managed as constants and the Pearson similarity is ineffective: it returns always zero).

The values of Cosine-based similarity measures lie between -1 and 1 while the other similarity values lie between 0 and 1.

Scoring and Prediction Rule

The user's rating for an item is predicted using the ratings given by the user on the nearest neighbors of the target item:

$$\hat{r}_{ui} = \bar{r}_i + \frac{\sum_{\{j \in S_u\}} sim(i, j) \times (r_{uj} - \bar{r}_j)}{\sum_{\{j \in S_u\}} \left| sim(i, j) \right|} \tag{3}$$

This predictor assumes knowledge of average ratings on items of other users, which is not always the case. For example, in the case of a personal recommendation service embedded on mobile terminal, item means calculated on other users are not available. In the case of an autonomous embedded system, the following formula can be used (formula for a single user):

$$\hat{r}_{ui} = \frac{\sum_{\{j \in S_u\}} sim(i,j) \times (r_{uj})}{\sum_{\{j \in S_u\}} |sim(i,j)|} \qquad (4)$$

Evaluation

Several methods can be used to evaluate the performance of a recommender system (Herlocker, et al., 2004). Most of them address the rating prediction function or even the personalized recommendation one like error rate evaluation using cross-validation. Unpersonalized recommendation is more difficult to assess. Another kind of evaluation can be based on user satisfaction evaluation.

For the first approach, many measures can be used to compare the results of different recommender systems. The most widely used ones are:

1. Mean Absolute Error (MAE);
2. Root Mean Squared Error (RMSE);
3. Precision measures.

The first two measures evaluate the capability of a method to predict if a user will like or dislike an item, whereas the third measure evaluates its capacity to order a list of items based on user tastes. These measures thus carry different meanings (McNee, et al., 2006). In the first two cases, the method needs to be able to predict dislike, but there is no need to order items. In the last case, however, the method only focuses on items that users will like and the order in which these items are ranked is important.

Beyond the importance of the predictive performance of recommender systems, other elements may be taken into consideration in their evaluation. The scalability of the proposed system is for example an important characteristic that needs to be taken into account. The coverage of a method, that is the proportion of recommendations it can provide, can also be considered. Finally, the system's ability to provide a level of confidence in a

recommendation (Basu, et al., 1998) and to explain why a recommendation was made (Herlocker, et al., 2000; Bilgic, 2004) can be used to define its potential interest to the user.

Evaluating a recommender system based on real users' opinions is also important because, in many cases, recommending the set of items that maximise their predicted ratings does not necessarily lead to user satisfaction. For instance, users may estimate that such recommendations lack originality, or they may think that the proposed list of recommendations is not varied enough (Ziegler, et al., 2005). Users may also want to have some control over the system, rather than having little or no direct influence in the results.

INDUSTRIAL RECOMMENDER SYSTEM DESCRIPTION

Global Architecture

Reperio, our engine is a prototype of a hybrid recommender engine developed at Orange Labs between 2007 and 2010. It is composed of two branches: a centralized one (Reperio-C) that has a Web service and works exclusively on centralized servers. The other branch is embedded (Reperio-E), does not have Web service and works as a development library on any terminal with a Java Virtual Machine (JVM): this includes PCs and mobile java-based frameworks such as Google Android™'s smart phones. Reperio-E is adapted to limited resource systems and can be used for privacy preserving or unplugged services as the profile and the catalog are embedded (the catalog is cyclically synchronized on a server). The main characteristic of the architecture is its flexibility both in terms of application field and in terms of input data.

The Reperio engine has allowed us to test prototypes of services in several fields: DVD recommendation, Video on Demand recommendation, TV program recommendation (embedded engine on Android™ smart phone), and music recommendation. Reperio is currently tested as deployed system on the following recommendation services: books and radio stations. It has been designed to take into account all the basic needs of the recommendation and all the industry prerequisites presented in previous sections (Table 1 and Table 2). It manages globally the recommendation and not just one of its aspects, rating prediction or recommendation of items.

This recommender system is also a multi-data source engine operating in several modes: collaborative, thematic and hybrid scoring modes, item centered, user centered, or metadata centered recommendation modes, mono-user or multi-user scoring modes.

The last original feature of Reperio is that it operates on two types of platforms:

- In centralized mode, on a PC, with a possible very large data volumetry, as modeling is parallelizable;
- In embedded mode on Google's Android™ operating systems.

Reperio is composed of a database containing the data sources and the models of recommendation, and program modules composed of Java™ packages. It can handle four different data sources:

- Logs of users (shopping, browsing and ratings on items stored in the table User Logs);
- Catalog of items, with metadata describing the items (table Catalog);
- User preferences on product attributes (table User Preferences);
- Data of social networks (table User Friends).

The linker for the representation of items and user preferences is the descriptor, an association between an attribute (e.g. Genre, Title, Actor, Author, Date) and a value. For example, in a movie catalog, Gender and Actor are attributes and couples (Genre, Adventure), (Actor, Harrison Ford) are descriptors. Generally, we build similarity matrices between items, from logs of usages (collaborative filtering) or from a catalog (contend-based filtering). It is also possible to build matrices of similarities between users or between item's characteristics.

The core of our recommender system is made of several modules that handle:

- Similarity between objects (usually items, but it may also be users or descriptors);
- Computation of the similarity matrix;
- Scoring functions: prediction of ratings and ranking (sorting of the items by relevance);
- Recommendation functions.

Additional modules manage:

- Data importations (or catalog synchronization);
- Internal data access layer;
- Global view of user profiles, consisting in logs, preferences, and friends;
- Automatic benchmarking tools;
- Application Program Interface to use Reperio as a central engine or as an embedded engine.

Figure 1 is a schematic view of the global architecture and its components.

When installing Reperio, a setting defines which recommendation types will be available. In centralized mode, Reperio works with a cyclic batch process stating which data table sources are active and must be updated and which similarity tables are active and must be pre-computed, and when. In embedded mode, Reperio is intended to use the logs, preferences, and the catalog in mono user mode, and with relatively low data volumes. In embedded mode, similarity matrices are not pre-calculated: the similarities between items are

Figure 1. General architecture of Reperio

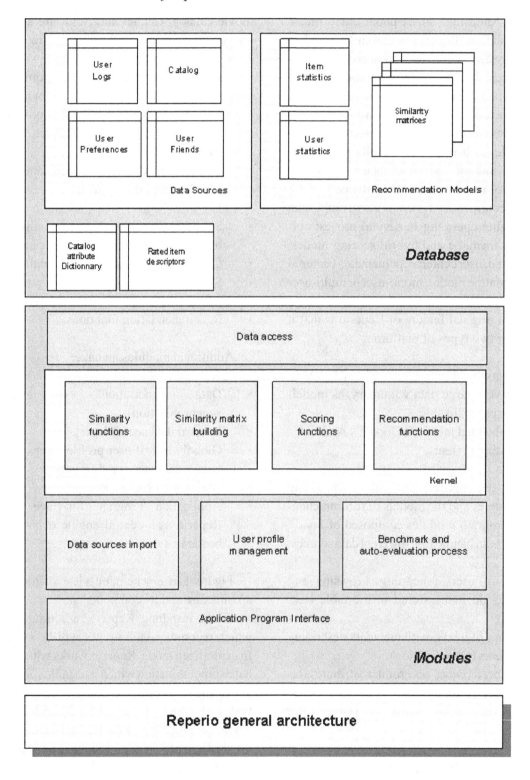

calculated online via appropriate optimized data structures (hash-tables and data caches). In the scope of the chapter, we restrict to the classical case of the recommended items, but it is also appropriate for the objects descriptors and users.

Reperio uses an adapted Pearson similarity in the case of logs of ratings, or Jaccard similarity in the case of binary log events, such as purchases or browsing, or catalog data (this makes inoperative the Pearson similarity: it returns always zero). To address both rating logs and purchase/browsing logs, a hybridization similarity of Jaccard and Pearson detailed in Candillier et al. (2008) is also used.

Implementation of the Core Functions

Rating prediction: The rating $\hat{r}_{u,i}$ predicted for a user u on an item i by the scoring system, in the multi-users case, is given by the formula:

$$\hat{r}_{ui} = \overline{r}_i + \frac{\sum_{\{j \in S_u\}} sim(i,j) \times (r_{uj} - \overline{r}_j)}{\left|\sum_{\{j \in S_u\}} sim(i,j)\right|} \tag{5}$$

where j denotes items, S_u all items rated by user u, $\overline{r}_i$ the mean rating of item i on all the logs of ratings, $r_{u,i}$ the rating of user u for item i. The predictor assumes knowledge of average ratings on users or items, which is not always the case, especially for the recommendation service embedded on mobile terminal. In this case, we use the mono user formula that is the same as above with all $\overline{r}_i$ set to zero.

$$\hat{r}_{ui} = \frac{\sum_{\{j \in S_u\}} sim(i,j) \times (r_{uj})}{\left|\sum_{\{j \in S_u\}} sim(i,j)\right|} \tag{6}$$

The multi-user scoring formula is used for the collaborative mode; the mono user formula applies on the thematic mode. Some default predictors are also implemented and activated when an item has no similarity with another one. In this case, the item is given a score that is the mean of the item or the mean of the user.

Ranking: The ranking functionality directly comes from the scoring functionality. The system produces a list of items ranked by predicted scores in decreasing order.

Item-to-item contextual recommendation: The recommendation to anonymous users is immediate with the item-item similarity matrix. An item is associated with the list of the most similar items from the similarity matrix.

Personalized recommendation: The functionality is based on the user profile's content. First, several items of reference are selected from the profile using randomized heuristics (some recent best rating items for example). Second, the engine searches for each reference, the similar candidate items thanks to the active similarity matrix, and try to select both long-tail and short head items. The items already known in the user profile are deleted from the set of candidates and then the candidates are ranked by relevance. Last, a subset of the candidates is returned to the user using a random-based diversity criterion. We propose some evaluation of this functionality, using several kinds of input data, at the end of this chapter.

Some filtering mechanisms are also included in the ranking, item-to-item and personalized recommendation functions to delete some items too similar to those of the user profile or not expected by the user

Implementation of the Industrial Requirements

We now discuss how the industrial requirements (Table 2) are taken into account in the architecture.

Ability to manage multiple sources: The format of the input tables of the similarity matrices is normalized (sparse matrix with 3 fields, row, column, value). All the sources of Reperio share this format. So, it is easy to generate item-item, user-user, and descriptor-descriptor similarity matrices and also to hybridize sources of different types.

Management of the cold start: For a new service without enough usage logs, the item-item similarity matrix can always be alimented by catalog metadata about items or log data from external users as explained below (Poirier, et al., 2010). Indeed, in the experiment part we describe a methodology allowing to extract logs from textual reviews coming from a social network.

Robustness to noisy or corrupted data: A feature weighting scheme has been implemented to manage descriptors suspected to be noisy in catalogs of items. Reperio can combine linearly several similarity matrices (collaborative item-item matrix with fake users with thematic item-item matrix from confident catalog) to reduce the impact of fake users.

Scalability: The computation of one similarity matrix can be parallelized and executed on several machines.

Reactivity: Personalized recommendation functions of the engine are based on the on-line user profile with linear complexity according to the size of this profile. The reactivity of the system is then good by construction. The profile is permanently updated. On the other hand, the similarity matrix evolving slowly, a cyclic refresh (every day or every week) is enough.

Transparency and ability to explain recommendations: Similarity matrices can be used to link a recommended item to other similar items already known by the user (i.e. in her/his profile) and the similarity indexes can be used as confidence indexes.

Management of the long tail: The long tail management is directly implemented in the personalized recommendation function, during candidate generation and randomization after ranking to insure diversification of the recommendations.

EXPERIMENTS

In this part, we evaluate Reperio and illustrate the interest of having an item-item similarity matrix as the kernel of a recommender system. To show this, we have conducted various experiments. First, we evaluate the system when used with a collaborative filtering approach, and when used with content-based filtering approach. Only results for personalized recommendation are described. Then, we evaluate the system when the matrix is computed from external textual data collected from a social network. We prove that a collaborative filtering recommender system based on such a matrix can be more efficient than a content-based filtering one. We also evaluated the system over speed performances.

The chosen domain is movies. This field was preferred because the data required for recommendation are varied (logs or different kinds of descriptors), rich and easy to obtain. However, these kinds of data are more difficult to find, if not impossible, for items of other fields. In this case, it is necessary to obtain data in another way, so our global methodology can be very useful for these other domains.

To start, the methodology of these experiments is described. Then we present the results obtained from two data sets publicly available in the movies domain:

- The first data set comes from the Netflix prize (www.netflixprize.com) and contains millions of real ratings. It was used to evaluate the collaborative filtering method;

- The second data set comes from the Internet Movie Database (www.imdb.com) and contains a lot of movie descriptors which are used to evaluate content-based filtering.

To finish, we describe a way to obtain useful data from unstructured texts provided by a social network. We describe how to extract descriptors or logs from this texts allowing building item-item matrices. We then compare these matrices with those previously obtained with the Netflix and the IMDb data.

Methodology

The purpose of the experiments is to build item-item matrices thanks to different kinds of data and to compare the information contained in each of them. To do that, we use the same test base containing logs from the Netflix Price (Bennett & Lanning, 2007). The test base is composed of approximately 100 millions of logs (triplets user-movie-rating) concerning almost 480,000 users and 17,770 movies. Each item has an average of about 5000 user ratings. 90% of the logs of each user are used to define the user profiles whereas the remaining 10% are used for the evaluation of the recommendations. The Table 3 presents the main characteristics of the test base.

This test based is then used to compare the information contained in each item-item matrix. The Figure 2 presents the complete methodology used to compare the item-item matrices. Several similarity measures are used to build the item-item matrices, depending on the nature of the data (logs, descriptors, or texts): the cosine measure, the Jaccard index and the Pearson similarity.

The evaluation criteria chosen in these experiments is the RMSE in order to compare our

Table 3. Statistics concerning Netflix data

Quantity of logs	≈ 100,000,000
Quantity of users	≈ 480,000
Quantity of movies	17,770
Logs used for profiles	≈ 90,000,000
Logs used for evaluation	≈ 10,000,000

results with those obtained by the Netflix Prize participants.

Evaluation on the Two Usual Data Sets

Generally, collaborative filtering methods consist in applying the learning step (the building of the item-item matrix in our case) on users' profiles contained in the test base. To be more specific, the knowledge required to make recommendations is learning data concerning the same users as those who receive recommendations. That is what we did in order to evaluate our collaborative filtering approach: to start, we built the item-item matrix by measuring distances between items thanks to the ratings contained in the users' profiles and we predicted the missing ratings. The evaluation of recommendations was done by comparing predicted ratings with users' ratings kept for the evaluation using the RMSE measure. The result obtained with this method is 0.862.

Figure 2. Methodology

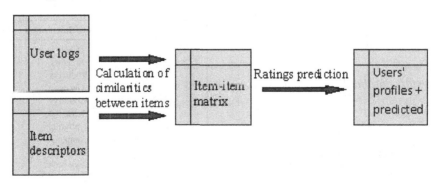

During the Netflix Prize, the best RMSE was 0.857. The Table 4 contains the best results obtained during the challenge for each year of its existence. We can see in this table that the improvement of performances was really wake during the last two years, compared to the first one. In fact, there is a step, situated around 0.86, were improvements required a lot of efforts. The winner score, 0.857 was obtained by using really expensive (in terms of computation capacity) techniques which are probably not possible to use in an industrial deployment. Concerning our result, 0.862 is very closed to the best one obtained in 2008. In fact, we did not use exactly the same data for the test (as the original data set is not publicly available) but our result seems to be a good one despite the constraints we have.

Concerning the evaluation of the content-based filtering, we used data coming from the Internet Movie Database. This public database is known as the Web site containing the most of information about movies, actors, directors, etc. We found 15,953 movies among the 17,770 of the Netflix corpus. Each item is described by a lot of information, which are listed in the Table 5. The RMSE obtained with this method is 0.921, which is much worse than the one obtained with the collaborative filtering method. It is already known than content-based filtering brings worse results than collaborative filtering, this is why the first one is used only in some situations, especially when logs are too few to allow good predictions with collaborative filtering. This case can happen when users have not produced enough logs (cold-start) for instance.

As we stated earlier, the cold-start is a recurrent problem in the field of recommendation. Different kinds of cold-start exist:

- The user cold-start happens for every new user which has not yet rated any item;
- The item cold-start happens when a new item is added to the catalog and has not yet received any rating;
- The system cold happens when launching a new service which does not have any user yet.

To remedy to the last two cold-starts, the item one and the system one, we propose a solution consisting of extracting the information required for recommendation from free texts written by Web users on blogs and community Web sites.

Focus on the Exploitation of Free Texts from Blogs

One of the main challenges to building an efficient recommender system to face is to collect enough data to "initialize" the recommendation process. The idea developed in this part is that it is possible to collect informative data from texts found on the Web. As a matter of fact, the Web is now a huge reservoir of information that is continuously growing, especially thanks to User Generated Content that appeared with the explosion of the Web 2.0 (O'Reilly, 2005). The

Table 4. Main results obtained during the Netflix prize

Year	2006	2007	2008	2009
RMSE	0.952	0.872	0.863	0.857

Table 5. List of descriptors extracted from IMDb

Kinds of descriptors
Cast
Directors
Producers
Genres
Country
Release date
Scriptwriters
Company
Language
Keywords

great majority of this content is composed of unstructured textual data (consumer reviews and opinions about products). A study of this rich information could build knowledge about users and items and overcome the lack of initial data, consequently bringing a significant contribution to the field of recommendation.

To make this study, we extracted a lot of movie reviews from the community Web site Flixster (www.flixster.com). This Web site is a platform where millions of users share everyday their opinions and appreciations concerning movies, actors, directors, etc. On this website, users can create a personal page where they can post, among other things, ratings and reviews about films. Reviews about films are connected to a user, a film, and a rating given by the author. The rating, which is between 0.5 and 5, summarizes the opinion expressed in the review. We extracted more than three millions of these reviews and their associated ratings. Texts were written by approximately 100,000 users and speak about 10,500 movies among the 17,770 contained in the Netflix corpus. Ratings are important for experiments because they can help to learn how to predict the opinion of reviews and they can also be used to evaluate and compare final results. Concerning the nature of the reviews, they are very short with an average of fifteen words and also contain very bad spelling, closed to SMS language. The Table 6 contains some examples of reviews.

As we saw earlier, two kinds of data can be used to make recommendations: descriptors and ratings (Figure 2).

The first possibility, which seems to be the more natural, consists in extracting descriptors from texts to feed a system based on content-based filtering. In this case, descriptors are words extracted from the reviews. We evaluated this approach by using a naive method consisting in deleting the more frequent and the less frequent words. The reason is because they are often considered as the less informative words. Distances between items are then computed by using the cosine measure. We

Table 6. Examples of reviews

| weeeeeeiiiiiiirrrrrddddddd movie |
| Very funny. Typical and quite predictable story but pretty hilarious. I had some good laughs.:) |
| I see it @ work everyday so this movie sucks! |
| OMG I LOVED THIS MOVIE!!!!!!!!!!!!!<3 |
| A little weird, but not bad... |
| It is a funny movie, but its not as funny as scary movie! |
| Soooo awsome i loved it..Tom Cruise did awsome in this movie.. |
| i liked this cuz this shit can really happen. |

obtained a RMSE of 0.922. This simple method allows matching results with those obtained with IMDb descriptors. This experiment shows that unstructured textual data can compete with a very rich structured collection of descriptors.

However, as we saw in the examples, reviews do not contain a lot of descriptive information about movies. They are very short and their authors go to the essential, i.e. the most part of these texts only express the opinion and sentiments felt during the viewing of the movie. In addition, we know that collaborative filtering is widely better than content-based filtering. For these reasons, we explored the conversion of texts into logs in order to make collaborative filtering. This approach requires an intermediate step called opinion classification, which is a task of opinion mining, consisting in classifying texts according to the opinion polarity they express. This polarity can then be interpreted as a rating given by the author on the subject of the review, which is

Table 7. Item-item similarity computations

	Time	Speed
Time slice (about 100 items)	~ 0.08s	~1 250 similarities /s
On 1 Day (about 1600 items)	~1.2s	~1 300 similarities /s

a movie. We can then extract logs from texts and make collaborative filtering thanks to this task of opinion mining.

Two main kinds of methods are used to classify a text according to its opinion: lexicon-based methods and machine learning-based methods. A mix of both approaches can also be used. In many cases, lexicon-based methods are used. This kind of methods consists in referencing as many opinion words as possible. Generally, an opinion word is a word expressing a feeling or an impression, with a positive or a negative polarity. It can also be a smiley, punctuation, or onomatopoeia. The building of opinion lexicons can be done by different ways, manually or automatically (Turney, 2002; Yu, et al., 2002; Kanayama, et al., 2006; Ding, et al., 2007; Hu, et al., 2004). Once this step has been done, lexicons are used to determine the polarity of texts. The basic method consists in counting positive and negative opinion words present in the text. A more advanced method takes into account adverbs in order to give more precision to opinion intensity (Benamara, et al., 2007). These methods do not necessarily require large learning corpora, but, if such corpora are available, machine learning-based methods become more efficient than lexicon-based ones (Pang, et al., 2002).

The most widely used machine learning-based methods for opinion classification come from the field of supervised machine learning. These techniques involve building a model from some classified examples. Then, the model is used to classify new unclassified texts. A lot of machine learning techniques have been tested for the opinion classification task, among which are Support Vector Machines (SVM) (Kobayakawa, et al., 2009; Abbasi, et al., 2008) or maximum entropy models (Kim, et al., 2006). Pang et al. (2002) compare SVM, maximum entropy and a naive Bayes classifier (NB) and show that SVMs and NBs are the two most adapted tools for this task. These approaches are rarely used alone. The majority of machine learning methods use Natural Language Processing (NLP) pretreatments, like spelling or stemming the words, in order to reduce the vocabulary size.

Concerning our experiments, we tried both different approaches and it was the machine learning approach, which brought better results. However, the machine learning approach requires examples (classified reviews) to be applied, which is the case for us. Indeed, the ratings associated to reviews allow using supervised learning techniques. Lexicon-based approach is not really adapted for our corpus because texts are really short and contain very few words. The probability to find a word from a lexicon is then lower. Furthermore, the big quantity of misspellings, abbreviations, or onomatopoeia makes the building of the lexicon very difficult. Concerning our experiments with the supervised learning approach, we tried different NLP pretreatments, different text representations, different tokenizations and different classification methods. The best results were obtained using a Support Vector Machine method, which is often the most efficient on this kind of sparse data (Joachims, 1999), and by doing a binary classification: positive reviews versus negative reviews. The best result obtained with this method is closed to 0.75 of F_{score} (which is calculated according to precision and recall). This is a pretty good result considering the characteristics of the corpus (short length and SMS language). By considering these polarities obtained, this first step then allows obtaining a log matrix containing triplets user-item-rating. This matrix allows making recommendations by using our collaborative filtering method. Indeed, users in the Learning set (coming from Flixster) and users in the Test set (coming from Netflix) are not the same and it is just because of the item-item matrix that we can make recommendations.

The RMSE obtained with this process is 0.889, which is much better than the results obtained with content-based filtering, with IMDb descriptors as well as words extracted from reviews. However, it is lower than the RMSE obtained with the Netflix corpus. Several reasons can explain this poorer performance:

- Flixster data is much more sparse than Netflix ones. Indeed, let us recall that Netflix users rated 180 movies in average when Flixster users rated only 30 of them;
- Concerning the experiment with the Netflix corpus, users during the learning step and during the test step are the same. It is not the case in this last experiment;
- The quantity of logs is most considerable in the Netflix corpus (90 millions) compared to the Flixster corpus (fewer than 3.5 millions). This difference seems to have its importance. Indeed, the Figure 3 shows that results could surely be improved by adding more reviews;
- We can also assume that ratings from both Web sites have not exactly the same meaning. Indeed, ratings from the Netflix corpus were attributed to a support (a DVD in most cases) and not to the movie alone as it is normally the case for Flixster's ratings. The difference is that for Netflix's ratings, users can also judge the thechnical quality of the DVD (image, sound), the interest of available bonus, etc. and also the service offer by Netflix as the delivery time for example.

Figure 4 shows main results obtained with our recommender system depending on input data. We can see that best result is obtained with the Netflix corpus which is the richest we have. The second best result is obtained with the ratings predicted on Flixster's reviews. We can see that this result is better than the one obtained with the true ratings given by authors' reviews. The only

explanation we have is that some authors write their reviews without modifying the default rating which is 0.5 on Flixster. This noise is then present in the experiment with the true ratings and is not by using the predicted ratings. Other important information showed by this Figure 3 is that result obtained with the opinion classification brings better result than content-based filtering applied on IMDb descriptors, which is a reference in the field. Indeed, IMDb can be regarded as the most complete database from the Web about cinema and the descriptors chosen are numerous. This result shows that for a beginner service, it could be more interesting to look for reviews written about catalog items to use descriptors, even if they are very rich. We can logically assume that even with a smaller quantity of subjective texts coming from blogs or forums, recommendations could be better than recommendations made by a recommender system based on content-based filtering. We can also assume that extracting written reviews about a new item coming in the catalog could allow remedying to the item cold-start problem.

Speed Performances

We give here some speed performances of Reperio, for similarity and rating generations (Tables 7-9), which are critical in deployments.

Reperio Embedded

The hardware configuration is: Android™ 1.5 specification with a 528 MHz ARM, 288 MB

Table 8. Rating prediction computations

	Time	Speed
Time slice (about 100 items)	~ 2.2s	~ 45 scores /s
On 1 Day (about 1600 items)	~ 35.3s	~ 46 scores /s

Table 9. Item-item similarity and rating prediction computations

	Time	Speed
Learning time of a item-item model for 90 million logs	~ 2 h 30	~17 500 similarities /s
Scoring time for 10 millions logs	~1 minute	~166 000 scores /s

Figure 3. Variation of RMSE according to quantity of reviews

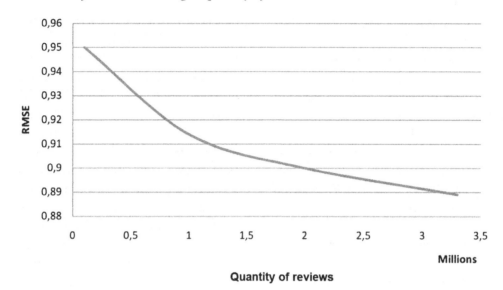

RAM: 288 MB Disk, Micro SD 2 GB. Reperio uses an electronic program guide of 60 TV channels (French channels) containing 15 attributes, with an average of 1600 items/day. Each TV program has an average of 15 descriptors. Scoring is done with a profile of 25 rated items, using a Jaccard similarity and mono-user scoring formula.

Reperio Centralized

The hardware configuration is: PC 64-bit 3.40GHz 2-cores CPU, 32GB RAM, 300 MB Disk. Reperio uses the Netflix's database: 100 million logs, 17 770 items, 480 000 users. Each item has an average of about 5000 user ratings. Scoring is

Figure 4. Main results

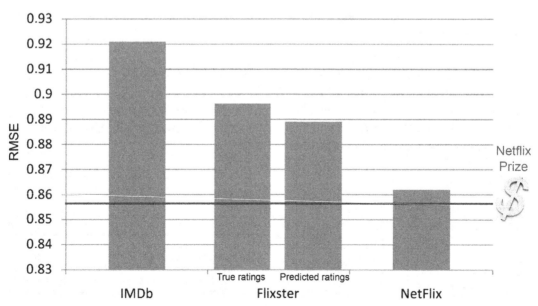

done with user profiles in the learning set (in the 90 millions logs), using Pearson similarity and multi-user scoring formulae.

CONCLUSION AND FUTURE RESEARCH

In this chapter, we presented an industrial prototype of recommender engine, generic and flexible. It has three main original particularities:

- It manages globally the recommendation and not just one of its aspect, taking into account all the basic needs of users;
- It runs both on a centralized platform with large databases, and on an embedded platform with reduced resources;
- It has several recommendation modes, mono-user and multi-user modes, collaborative, thematic, hybrid modes, possible generation of items, users or descriptors as recommended objects.

We experimentally proved that the architecture of this system was flexible enough to take into account external data. This property is particularly interesting for a beginner recommender system. As a matter of fact, for such a system, user generated textual data are often easier to collect than usage data. Therefore, this chapter is also a contribution about how to combine opinion classification and recommendation. Our experiments show that even if the texts are not very informative and if the classifier is not very good, the recommendation obtained is better than the one obtained with content-based filtering.

The prototype of Reperio is currently used in Orange™ Company in Web radio, video on demand and book recommendation services. The TV program embedded recommendation prototype on Android is not industrialized yet. In future work we would like to evaluate Reperio

on user-centered and descriptor- centered modes using social networks data and social tagging data. These are other external data that should also contribute to recommendations in the future.

REFERENCES

Abbasi, A., Chen, H., & Salem, A. (2008). Sentiment analysis in multiple languages: Feature selection for opinion classification in web forums. *ACM Transactions on Information Systems*. Retrieved from http://ai.arizona.edu/intranet/papers/AhmedAbbasi_SentimentTOIS.pdf

Adomavicius, G., & Tuzhilin, A. (2005). Toward the next generation of recommender systems: A survey of the state-of-the-art and possible extensions. *IEEE Transactions on Knowledge and Data Engineering, 17*(6), 734–749. doi:10.1109/TKDE.2005.99

Anderson, C. (2006). *The long tail: Why the future of business is selling less of more*. Berlin, Germany: Hyperion Verlag.

Basu, C., Hirsh, H., & Cohen, W. W. (1998). Recommendation as classification: Using social and content-based information in recommendation. In *Proceedings of the 15th National Conference on Artificial Intelligence,* (pp. 714–720). IEEE.

Benamara, F., Cesarano, C., Picariello, A., Reforgiato, D., & Subrahmanian, V. (2007). Sentiment analysis: Adjectives and adverbs are better than adjectives alone. In *Proceedings of the International Conference on Weblogs and Social Media (ICWSM),* (pp. 203–206). ICWSM.

Bennett, J., & Lanning, S. (2007). *The Netflix prize*. San Jose, CA: ACM Press.

Bilgic, M. (2004). *Explanation for recommender systems: Satisfaction vs. promotion.* (PhD Thesis). University of Texas at Austin. Austin, TX.

Breese, J., Heckerman, D., & Kadie, C. (1998). Empirical analysis of predictive algorithms for collaborative filtering. In *Proceedings of the 14th Conference on Uncertainty in Artificial Intelligence,* (pp. 43–52). San Francisco, CA: Morgan Kaufman.

Candillier, L., Meyer, F., & Fessant, F. (2008). *Designing specific weighted similarity measures to improve collaborative filtering systems.* Paper presented at the Industrial Conference on Data Mining. Leipzig, Germany.

Celma, O. (2008). *Music recommendation and discovery in the long tail.* Barcelona, Spain: Universitat Pompeu Fabra.

Cremonesi, P., Koren, Y., & Turrin, R. (2010). Performance of recommender algorithms on top-N recommender tasks. In *Proceedings of the Fourth ACM Conference on Recommender System (RecSys'10).* Barcelona, Spain: ACM Press.

Davidson, J., Liebald, B., & Liu, J. (2010). The YouTube video recommendation system. In *Proceedings of the Fourth ACM Conference on Recommender System (RecSys'10).* Barcelona, Spain: ACM Press.

Deshpande, M., & Karypis, G. (2004). Item-based top-N recommendation algorithms. *ACM Transactions on Information Systems, 22*(1), 143–177. doi:10.1145/963770.963776

Ding, X., & Liu, B. (2007). The utility of linguistic rules in opinion mining. In *Proceedings of the 30th Annual International ACM SIGIR Conference on Research and Development in Information Retrieval,* (pp. 811–812). ACM Press.

Herlocker, J., Konstan, J., & Riedl, J. (2000). Explaining collaborative filtering recommendations. In *Proceedings of the ACM Conference on Computer Supported Cooperative Work.* ACM Press.

Herlocker, J., Konstan, J., Terveen, L., & Riedl, J. (2004). Evaluating collaborative filtering recommender systems. *ACM Transactions on Information Systems, 22*(1), 5–53. doi:10.1145/963770.963772

Hu, M., & Liu, B. (2004). Mining and summarizing customer reviews. In *Proceedings of the Tenth ACM SIGKDD International Conference on Knowledge Discovery and Data Mining,* (pp. 168–177). ACM Press.

Joachims, T. (1999). Making large-scale support vector machine learning practical. In *Advances in kernel methods: support vector learning* (pp. 169–184). New York, NY: ACM Press.

Kanayama, H., & Nasukawa, T. (2006). Fully automatic lexicon expansion for domain-oriented sentiment analysis. In *Proceedings of the 2006 Conference on Empirical Methods in Natural Language Processing,* (pp. 355–363). IEEE.

Karypis, G. (2001). Evaluation of item-based top-N recommendation algorithms. In *Proceedings of the 10th International Conference on Information and Knowledge Management,* (pp. 247–254). IEEE.

Kim, S. M., & Hovy, E. (2006). Automatic identification of pro and con reasons in online reviews. In *Proceedings of the COLING/ACL on Main Conference Poster Sessions,* (pp. 483–490). COLING/ACL.

Kobayakawa, T. S., Kumano, T., Tanaka, H., Okazaki, N., Kim, J.-D., & Tsujii, J. (2009). Opinion classification with tree kernel SVM using linguistic modality analysis. In *Proceeding of the 18th ACM Conference on Information and Knowledge Management,* (pp. 1791–1794). ACM Press.

Koren, Y. (2010). Factors in the neighbors: Scalable and accurate collaborative filtering. *ACM Transactions on Knowledge Discovery from Data, 4*(1), 1–24. doi:10.1145/1644873.1644874

Linden, G., Smith, B., & York, J. (2003). Amazon. com recommendations: Item-to-item collaborative filtering. *IEEE Internet Computing, 7*(1), 76–80. doi:10.1109/MIC.2003.1167344

McNee, S., Riedl, J., & Konstan, J. (2006). Being accurate is not enough: How accuracy metrics have hurt recommender systems. In *Proceedings of the 2006 ACM Conference on Human Factors in Computing Systems*. ACM Press.

O'Reilly, T. (2005). *O'Reilly network: What is web 2.0*. Retrieved from http://www.oreillynet.com/lpt/a/6228

Pang, B., Lee, L., & Vaithyanathan, S. (2002). Thumbs up? Sentiment classification using machine learning techniques. In *Proceedings of the ACL-02 Conference on Empirical Methods in Natural Language Processing*, (pp. 79–86). ACL.

Poirier, D., Fessant, F., & Tellier, I. (2010). Reducing the cold-start problem in content recommendation through opinion classification. In *Proceedings of Web Intelligence* (pp. 204–207). Toronto, Canada: IEEE. doi:10.1109/WI-IAT.2010.87

Rao, K. N., & Talwar, V. G. (2008). Application domain and functional classification of recommender systems - A survey. *Journal of Library Information Technology, 28*(3), 17–35.

Resnick, P., Iacovou, N., Suchak, M., Bergstrom, P., & Riedl, J. (1994). Grouplens: An open architecture for collaborative filtering of netnews. In *Proceedings of the Conference on Computer Supported Cooperative Work*, (pp. 175–186). ACM Press.

Su, X., & Khoshgoftaar, T. M. (2009). A survey of collaborative filtering techniques. In *Proceedings of Advances in Artificial Intelligence*. IEEE.

Turney, P. D. (2002). Thumbs up or thumbs down? Semantic orientation applied to unsupervised classification of reviews. In *Proceedings of the 40th Annual Meeting of the Association for Computational Linguistics*, (pp. 417–424). ACL.

Yu, H., & Hatzivassiloglou, V. (2003). Towards answering opinion questions: Separating facts from opinions and identifying the polarity of opinion sentences. In *Proceedings of the 2003 Conference on Empirical Methods in Natural Language Processing*, (pp. 129–136). ACM.

Ziegler, C.-N., McNee, S., Konstan, J., & Lausen, G. (2005). Improving recommendation lists through topic diversification. In *Proceedings of the 14th International World Wide Web Conference*, (pp. 22–32). IEEE.

Chapter 5
Risk Evaluation in the Insurance Company Using REFII Model

Goran Klepac
Raiffeisen Bank Austria, Croatia

ABSTRACT

A business case describes a problem present in all insurance companies: portfolio risk evaluation. Such analysis deals with determining the risk level as well as main risk factors. In the specific case, an insurance company is faced with market share growth and profit decline. Discovered knowledge about the level of risk and main risk factors was not used to increase premium for the riskiest portfolio segments due to a specific market situation, which could lead to loss of clients in the long run. Instead, additional analysis was conducted using data mining methods resulting in a solution, which stopped further profit decline and lowered the risk level for the riskiest portfolio segments. The central role for the unexpected revealed knowledge in the chapter acts as the REFII model. The REFII model is an authorial mathematical model for time series data mining. The main purpose of that model is to automate time series analysis, through a unique transformation model of time series.

INTRODUCTION

The presented business case is concentrated on an insurance company, which decides to move its focus from a saturated life insurance market to a more profitable car insurance market. After two years, their profit and market share was up, but they also faced rising expenses due to increasing risk of their customers. A profile analysis was done to identify most risky clients. Their first intention, increasing price for the most risky segment, was rejected once they realized that the competitors might use it to differentiate. They did an additional

analysis on temporal data and found some new interesting patterns which marketing department used to develop a strategy resulting in increased loyalty level and lower losses.

Portfolio risk assessment is one of the fundamental analytic activities in the insurance industry. Risk based segmentation enables the development of the price strategy. As the riskiness of the portfolio may vary by time, insurance services prices must be corrected.

In lowering the prices, due to estimated decline of risk, there's no danger of market share loss and losing the customer to competitors (Berry, 1997).

DOI: 10.4018/978-1-4666-2542-6.ch005

Price increase on the other hand is accompanied by risk of losing clients. If the estimated cost of losing market share is less than the estimated cost of claims for a given risk segment, insurance companies decide to take that route.

In an ideal situation, one would be able to decrease the portfolio risk level while keeping the same or even lower prices. Data mining methods can sometimes be useful in pursuing this aim (Berry, 1997; Han, 2000; Kantardžić, 2003). There is no recipe for it and data mining methods must be applied in an interaction of multidisciplinary expert knowledge Thomas (2002). This interaction often includes trial and error methodology and participation of several organizational units.

Results of one analysis can lead to new hypothesis so that next step s in the analysis are focused on their approval/rejection. If the main factors, which affect the risk level, are found the unpopular price increase can be avoided.

BACKGROUND

As data mining techniques have become more popular, they have become increasingly involved in risk evaluation in insurance companies (Apte, 1999; Chidanand, 1999; Pyle, 1999; Smith, 2000). Who is the riskiest client, who could have a car accident with highest probability during the lifetime of the contract, which is the low risk segment in insurance portfolio? This, and similar questions preoccupy portfolio managers in insurance companies.

Applied data mining model for the risk evaluation in insurance companies could vary (Apte, 1999). It can be built using probabilistic models (Chidanand, 1999), Fuzzy logic (Derik, 1995), Neural networks (Alexander, 1995), logistic regression (Kolyshkina, 2002), or linear models (Samson, 1997).

For the risk evaluation in insurance companies there is no prescribed solutions for using data mining techniques. Each case demands a solution regarding its specific business environment and client profiles. This chapter represents one solution based on data mining techniques for a specific case in insurance business.

The central role for success is presented as a case study and time series analysis. In traditional time series data mining analysis, there is a lot of different methods which solve a particular kind of problem. As a result of this approach, we have a situation in which if we want to solve a problem of discovering patterns in time series, we could use methods which are described by Pratt (2001), Xsniaping (1998), and Han (2000).

Many different methods for different kind of problems exist in scientific works. There are many different methods for solving seasonal oscillations, recognition time segments, similarity search, etc.

The suggested solution for all mentioned problems presented in the chapter is REFII model (Klepac, 2005), as a fully automated preparation tool which gives solution for problems such as:

- Discover seasonal oscillation;
- Discover cyclic oscillation;
- Discover rules from time series;
- Discover episodes from time series;
- Discover similarity of time segments;
- Discover correlation between time segments;
- Discover rules from in domain of finances from time series;
- Connect time series and standard data mining methods;
- Analyze time series with the help of data mining methods (clustering of time segments, classification of time segments).

The chapter shows a few of mentioned functionalities, which lead us to the solution.

TOTAL MARKET SHARE GROWTH WITH PROFIT DECLINE

Safety First is an insurance company with 76% of its clients having car insurance and the rest having life, health, and property insurance. For the last five years, the company had a continuous growth in the number of clients. Despite this trend, the profit has been below the plan for the last two years.

An analysis done on the data warehouse revealed a trend of increasing number of accidents, mostly in the car insurance segment. In addition, the number and the amount of car insurance claims increased having a negative effect on profit. A decision was made to do a risk analysis of Safety First's clients, which would serve as a basis for strategic decisions aiming to increase profits.

Safety First has branches in almost all bigger Croatian cities and for the last three years had several successful promotional campaigns which resulted in a considerable increase in number of clients. Due to increasing competition in the insurance industry, Safety First decided three years ago that their strategically most important products are: obligatory car insurance, hull insurance, and innovative car insurance products. Management based this decision on market developments, which showed that competitors were focusing on life and property insurance while the total market for these segments was stagnating. Competitors were also decreasing their promotional activities and campaigns in the car insurance segment. Market analysis clearly shows an increasing trend of car sales on a global level accompanied by an increasing interest in basic car insurance as well as other insurance products related to car insurance. Having in mind that the competitors are mainly focusing their attention on stagnating products such as life and property insurance, Safety First decided to increase its market share and become a market leader in car insurance. Although other insurance products, such as life, health, and property

insurance, will continue to play a role, they will not be strategic products expected to increase its market share in the next few years. The reason for this was found in a cost-benefit analysis, which showed a very high cost per new client acquisition due to an intense competitiveness in these market segments.

With several promotional campaigns spread over a three year period, Safety First became a leader in the car insurance market. However, in the last 15 months the actual profit fell short of the planned one in respect to number of new insurance policies. Analysis based on data warehouse revealed a significant increase of claims, mostly by new customers. In order to reconcile the profit trend with the increasing number of new insurance policies, a decision was made to do a risk analysis, determine the risk profiles of car insurance clients, and accordingly correct the premiums.

Developing a Conceptual Solution Model

Due to a primary focus on car insurance clients, the analysis used only the data referring to this client segment. A large number of reports were generated using the existing information system in order to determine the risk profile of car insurance clients. These reports revealed some basic risk characteristics and served as a basis for further analysis using data mining methods.

Analysis strategy development was driven by the following basic questions:

- What are the shared characteristics of risky customers?
- What are the shared characteristics of non-risky customers?
- How to evaluate the risk level of new customers?
- Does the risk vary by specific time periods (day of the week, month, time of the day, etc.)?

Answers to these questions were supposed to bring the company closer to achieving the goal of the analysis: how to neutralize risk and by doing so lower its impact on profit decline in the future?

For a successful risk analysis, the first thing that needed to be done was data preprocessing, which was easier in this case due to availability of a data warehouse. After data preprocessing, attribute relevance analysis was done followed by modeling using decision tress, neural networks, and Bayesian networks. Depending on the outcome of the preliminary analysis, a dominant method will be used to create a model for risk assessment.

Bayesian networks were used for the basic model, while the model built with neural networks was used for prediction of the risk level of new insurance contracts. Due to the decision that detailed analysis should be done in order to find out whether riskiness vary by time periods, a risk analysis was done using time series analysis techniques based on REFII model. An analysis of seasonal oscillations using REFII model was done on the week level (due to observation period of 15 months) in addition to the analysis of customer characteristics impact on claims trends.

Results from these analyses are supposed to describe the risk profiles of risky as well as less risky clients, time periods when one might expect an increase in claims and customer characteristics which are most relevant in respect to increasing trends of claims in a time period. Making use of this information enables decision making which will affect the company's business policy in order to meet set goals. Prior to the analysis, an interview with risk managers and managers from accounting and controlling departments was conducted. In the initial phase, 74 candidate attributes were identified based on the database documentation. The interviews were aimed at supporting the attribute selection process by reducing irrelevant attributes in the initial phase. This was necessary in this case as well as in this kind of analysis generally, in order to:

- Identify the most relevant attributes affecting the goal/goal variable,
- Ease the development of the analytical model,
- Shorten the time for learning algorithm processing which is done on a large amount of data where the number of attributes used in the learning process significantly affects the time required.

The interview method is not and must not be the only method used for attribute relevance analysis. Besides the interviews, an algorithmic attribute relevance analysis was done which compared relevant attributes identified by experts and relevant attributes identified algorithmically. The aim was to find an optimal set of characteristics which best describes the goal variable of car accident risk assessment.

Attribute Relevance Analysis

In order to facilitate the analysis process, since the databases of the Safety First insurance company contained a whole series of attributes which could be utilised as input data for analysis, it was necessary to first carry out an attribute relevance analysis. The attribute relevance analysis was carried out with respect to the target variable risk level. The risk level variable was defined as a categorical variable and was assigned two basic values: yes and no. The choice of defining a categorical variable was made after carrying out detailed analysis using descriptive statistical methods and after the company management decided that it will not go into deeper categorisation of risk according to amount of damage incurred, but that the basic criteria for risk level assessment will be whether an accident resulting in damages above the specified amount occurred in the period observed. In order to carry out such an analysis a table with 74 potential attributes for analysis was derived from the data warehouse and the target value risk level was added based on the mentioned company management decision. Basic data analysis was then carried out using both descriptive statistics and data visualisation tools. Using attribute relevance assessment, the final analysis of attribute relevance was carried out.

Regarding attribute relevance analysis the most important variables was age, number of accidents, region, car class, engine volume, gender. Missing value rate was very low, because system recognised more fields as mandatory during the process of entry into the core system. Low missing values rate was recognised particularly on attributes recognised as most relevant.

On population of 7234 cases, the variable with worst performance regarding missing value was "car class" with 0.43% missing values in population.

Based on the Gini index, assessment of attribute relevance was performed with regard to the risk-level target value. The results obtained from attribute relevance analysis were compared to the projected relevant attributes which had been suggested by experts and after a work meeting was held, the obtained attribute set was somewhat expanded based on the experts' suggestions.

The basic data analysis which was carried out revealed a very low level of interdependency between the target variable and the variables suggested by the experts which did not show a very high level of relevance during the algorithmic attribute relevance analysis. The analysis performed significantly reduced the number of attributes to be included in further analysis which in turn, taking into account the amount of data to be processed, significantly reduced the machine learning time in the Bayesian and neural network models.

Bayesian Network Model for Risk Assessment

Creation of Model

As the aim of the analysis was recognition of the riskiest profile, Bayesian networks were chosen,

because in comparison with traditional models like logistic regression Bayesian networks has the power for fast profiling of risky segments using conditional probability.

In order to perform analysis using Bayesian networks, all input variables were first classified into categories. Classification of variables was carried out with the help of experts, based on a pre-processed table from the data warehouse, from which relevant attributes were then isolated. The table prepared in this way served as the basis for creating the Bayesian network model.

The Bayesian network structure can be created in three ways:

1. "Manually" designed networks by analysts.
2. Algorithmic network design by software tools based on the available data set.
3. Combined method in which the software tool suggests the structure based on detected interdependencies resulting from the data set, which can then be modified by analysts later on.

In the risk analysis carried out by the Safety First insurance company, the combined method for creating a Bayesian network model was used, using the Hugin Explorer software package.

To the categorised data set, the NPC (Necessary Path Condition) structural learning algorithm was applied, whereby a Bayesian network structure was suggested. The suggested model was in many ways identical to the hand-sketched model prepared during consultations with experts but the directions of links between categorical attributes had to be adjusted manually. During this structural learning process, the number of relevant attributes was further reduced. During structural design, the links between region, age and vehicle class were added according to the number of traffic accidents committed.

The structural model is the first step, which enables learning of conditional probabilities between categories of related variables, that is, the creation of a table of conditional probabilities between related categories. For this purpose, the EM-machine learning algorithm also included in the Hugin Explorer software package was used. The thus created structural model, supplemented by conditional probability tables using the EM-machine learning algorithm, became the basis for carrying out risk analysis.

The model basis consists of seven variables:

- Age
- Number of accidents
- Region
- Engine volume
- Vehicle class
- Gender
- Risk level

The risk level and number of accidents variables are especially interesting as predictors in the model.

Conducting Analysis

Bayesian network models for risk assessment are by nature very closely related to what-if analysis and sensitivity analysis. The risk assessment of car insurance clients in the Safety First insurance company must also be understood in this context. The defined model was used to calculate risk probability, with the aim to assess which category of policy holders is the one carrying the highest level of risk. Risk level assessment is done by defining the certain events (evidence) in the model and monitoring the level of probability in the target variable as shown in Figure 1.

By defining certain categories as certain events, risk probability is calculated. From the model shown in Figure 1, it is evident that under the conditions:

- Age between 36 and 45
- Number of accidents committed – none
- Region – North
- Vehicle class – middle

The risk level (probability) is 73.10, which is a very high probability of risk.

The model shows that the greatest increase in the level of risk is linked to the age group between 36 and 45 and that the risk level further increases if the policyholder is from the northern region, if he/she drives a middle class vehicle and has never provoked any car accidents.

The effect of each of the mentioned categories on risk level (with the exception of the age group between 36 and 45) is much smaller if we look at each category separately than if we look at their joint effect on the level of risk.

As regards effect on the probability of the number of accidents the model clearly shows that the probability of one or more accidents increases in the case of policy holders from the southern region who are under the age of 25.

Analysis Results

Using the Bayesian network model the first analytical goal—risk-level assessment, i.e. diagnosis of the high-risk market segment was achieved. A high-risk car insurance policy holder is between 36 to 45 years old, has not caused any traffic accidents to date, lives in the northern region and drives a middle class vehicle. The age group between 36 and 45 has the strongest effect on the risk level, which increases under the above-mentioned conditions that that the policyholder has not caused any traffic accidents to date, that he/she lives in the northern region and drives a middle class vehicle. These relations illustrate the principle according to which Bayesian networks, which are based on conditioned probabilities, function.

Based on the results of the analysis the next logical step would be to increase the premium for those clients who belong to the high-risk market segment. Before making this rather unpopular decision (market-wise), which in the long run may result in a fall in the number of clients belonging to this market segment, the company management wished to examine other options.

Figure 1. Bayesian network model

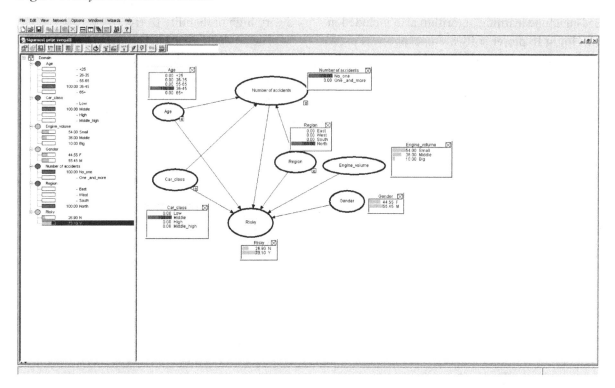

From the economic point of view, a reduction in the number of high-risk policyholders may in the long run result in higher profit. On the other hand, since the competition has uniform car insurance premiums, raising the price for this market segment would probably lead to dissatisfaction of these clients who would turn to the competition. Considering that in the previous period the competing companies also perceived a fall in demand for life insurance and property insurance policies and an upward trend in the demand for car insurance policies, in which field the Safety First insurance company established itself as the market leader in the previous period, there is the danger of losing a significant part of the market. Further confirmation that this hypothesis is correct was obtained through a market survey conducted by an independent agency via telephone poll on a random representative sample. For this reason, the adoption of this unpopular decision was postponed

in order to carry out other analysis on the basis of which the risk-level of the diagnosed market segment could be reduced in other ways.

RISK ASSESSMENT BASED ON TIME SERIES

Theoretical Basis of REFII Model

REFII Model can be defined as a unique time series transformation model which is used as the starting point for data mining from time series on various conceptual bases. The acronym REFII stands for Rise Equal Fall, second generation. The author of the model is Goran Klepac who provided an analysis of his model in his doctoral thesis (Klepac, 2005).

Former methods dealing with time series analysis focused mainly on a particular problem and functioned as a "black box" (Williams, 2001, 2002). Based on input parameters (time series) they provide information such as the existence of seasonal oscillations or recurrent patterns and the like. They all share a common feature—they have their own time series transformation models which are almost always adapted to the particular problem in question and in addition to being mutually incompatible, they cannot be extracted from the model as output values.

In the new approach introduced by the REFII model the transformation model is considered as the basis of analysis on which all further analytical methods are based.

Time series analysis based on a unique time series transformation model makes linking of different conceptual models of time series analysis possible, which represents a step forward from the traditional method of using a series of unconnected methods. It also enables time series analysis by application of traditional data mining methods. By connecting different time series analysis concepts within the REFII model, complex analytical tasks based on time series can be solved, such as market segmentation and detection of market patterns. In addition to linking different concepts, this model has an open structure, which allows new algorithms for machine learning from time series to be developed, depending on the problem we wish to solve. Before the REFII model was developed, the main problems were that it was impossible to connect methodological mining concepts in time series, to apply the traditional data mining methods on time series and to automatically pre-process time series for mining purposes.

Using the transformation model as the starting point for analysis also enables a more detailed time series analysis by chaining methods and the modelling of solutions for non-standard problems, ensuing from detection of market patterns and market segmentation.

Thoroughness in this case means that it is possible to carry out various types of analysis on a reduced set of data from the time series, obtained by processing before the application of the method or analytical approach, with the aim of solving complex tasks such as for example market segmentation on the basis of time series.

The REFII transformation model was designed to provide a uniform description of the time series curve by transforming the time series into a series of values, which represent the area beneath the time segment, the coefficient of the angle inside the time segment and trend movement.

The REFII model focuses on three basic segments, which uniquely define the curve, these being:

- Shape of curve (how the time series looks)
- Area beneath the curve (quantification of time series)
- Coefficient of the angle inside the time segment (trend "intensity")

The final algorithm must integrate all three parts and create the basis for the application of analytical procedures.

The time series transformation algorithm in the u REFII model works in several steps.

Time series can be expressed as a sequences of values $S(s1,..,sn)$, where S represents the time series and $(s1,..,sn)$ represent the elements in the S series.

Step 1: Time Interpolation

Creation of auxiliary time series $Vi(vi1,..,vin)$ on interval $<1..n>$ (days, weeks, months, quarters, years) with the value 0. Based on the created sequence, interpolation of the missing values in $S(s1,..,sn)$ with the value 0 based on the created sequence Vi is carried out. The result of processing is the series $S(s1,..,sn)$ with interpolated missing values from the series $Vi(vi1,..,vin)$.

Step 2: Time Granulation

In this step the degree of compression of time series $S(s1,..,sn)$ in the elementary time unit (day, week, month…) is defined. In the second step, the elements of the existing time series are compressed by using statistical functions such as sum, average, and mode on the level of the granulated segment. In that way, the time series can be converted to a higher degree of granulation (days into weeks, weeks into months…), resulting in the time series S(s1,..,sn) with a higher degree of granulation.

Depending on the objectives, we can return to this step during the process of analysis, which means that the processes described in the following steps must also be repeated.

Step 3: Standardisation

The standardisation procedure consists of transformation of the time series S(s1,..,sn) into the time series T(t1,..,tn), in which each element in the series is subjected to min-max standardisation on interval <0,1>, where:

1. Time series T consists of the elements (t1,.., tn), where ti is calculated as $ti=((si-min(S))/(max(S)-min(S))$, in which min(S) and max(S) represent the minimum and maximum value of time series S.

2. The time variation between elementary patterns (time complexity measure) of the segment on the X axis is defined as $d(ti,ti+1)=a$.

Step 4: Transformation to REF Notation

According to the formula Tr=ti+1- ti Tr > 0 =>R; Tr< 0 =>F; Tr=0 =>E, where Yi are elements of series Ns

Step 5: Calculation of Angle Coefficient

Angle coefficient=>

Tr > 0 (R) Coefficient = t i+1-t i

Tr < 0 (F) Coefficient = t i -t i+1

Tr = 0 (E) Coefficient = 0

Step 6: Calculation of Area beneath the Curve

Method of numeric integration based on the rectangle

$p= ((t i*a)+(t i+1*a))/2$

Step 7: Creation of Time Indexes

Building of a hierarchical index tree depending on the characteristics of the analysis, in which an element of the structured index can also be an attribute, such as the client code.

Step 8: Creating Categories

Creation of derived attribute values based on the area beneath the curve and the angle coefficient. It is possible to create categories by application of standard crisp logic or by application of fuzzy logic.

Step 9: Connecting the REFII Model Transformation Tables with Relational Tables containing Attributes that do not have a Temporal Dimension

These nine basic steps represent the basis of the algorithmic procedure on which the REFII model is based, the final result of which is the creation of a transformation matrix. The transformation matrix is the basis for conducting further analytical procedures with the aim of time series analysis.

REFII model is basically a concept made up of the three sub-models, with the primary goal being the transformation of time series into a series of indicators which uniquely define the time series. REF, the area beneath the curve and the angle coefficient are indicators, which uniquely describe the time series segment, while a series of such segments together make up the transformed time series. The series of indicators are arranged in the order in which they appear in the unit of time and are integrated into the joint conception structure of the transformed time series, which we call the transformation matrix.

Such a structure, viewed from the perspective of dynamic memory, can be a matrix 4x tn-1, or a file with 4 attributes of length tn-1, from the perspective of disc recording.

The structure is shown in Table 1.

Time segment indicators were calculated on the basis of co-ordinates of two neighbouring values in the time series. Thus, for example, the segment with index I1 was formed on the basis of the value of time series co-ordinates t0 and t1. The time segment index serves for unique identification of the time segment for the purpose of

Table 1. Transformation matrix

Time segment index	I1	I2	...	In
REF notation	REF1	REF2	...	REF n
Angle coefficient	Angle coefficient 1	Angle coefficient 2	...	Angle coefficient n
Area of time segment	P1	P2	...	Pn

its analysis i.e. for the creation of a base sample as already discussed in the presentation of the mathematical bases of the model.

The indexes can have complex structures and may contain hierarchical elements as well as association elements and elements linking them to other data sources.

The elements included in Table 1 are the basic elements of the REFII model, which can be used to uniquely describe the curve and to carry out all analysis for which the model was developed in the first place. Apart from the described indicators, it is possible to also include derived indicators, but that is an optional approach, which depends on the character of analysis. Indicators from Table 1 serve as the basis for all analysis for which this model was developed.

After transforming the time series using REFII model, a transformed time series was obtained in the form shown in Table 1.

These transformed data are processed by algorithmic methods in order to solve concrete problems in the domain of time series. The algorithmic methods and procedures which serve for solving concrete problems are part of the REFII model in the broader sense.

The character of analysis determines the approach to the transformed time series regarding the "division" of the structure thus formed into smaller logical units. If, for example, we are observing weeks, and the time series contains data for each day of the week throughout the whole year, then the series should be logically divided into weeks and the time segments analysed using a concrete algorithm. This procedure of "dividing" a time series into smaller, analytically comparable,

logical segments is related to the concept of time complexity. This measure determines the point of logical division of the time series, in view of the aim of analysis, and it is a part of the algorithmic analysis procedure. Thus, for example, the coefficient for a week can have the value 7 or 5 (working days in one week), taking into account the fact that in certain points of time no value exists, which this measure also has to deal with.

The model shown in the table is the universal starting point for all the above described analysis. The derived tables, closely linked with the individual sub-model are examined especially with regard to the aim of analysis.

It is important to mention that each of the three mentioned elements of the REFII model mutually complements each other. Yet in certain situations, some of the elements are irrelevant.

All this of course depends on the objective of the analysis and on the analytical approach embodied in the algorithmic procedure. The table may be procedurally processed through various algorithmic types, which ultimately provide the desired results. It is also possible to apply various types of algorithms to the same table and to compare the efficiency of their application in resolving the same problem. This transformation model is the universal starting point for all possible types of analysis which are conducted on time series and which this concept successfully solves.

Data Preparation

The object of risk level analysis based on time series was the time series, which represent the number of car accidents per day. From the data warehouse, two tables were created. The first contained two attributes, the date and the number of accidents on the daily level while the second table, relationally linked to the first table (one-to-many relation), contained details on all participants in accidents on the daily level (age, gender, vehicle class, region...). If for example 250 accidents occurred on one specific day, the second table contained 250 records for that day, having the same value as the date, to which were linked the values of the attributes describing each policyholder who participated in the car accident.

The first table is important for transformation to REFII model and for conducting analysis of seasonal oscillations, while the second table is important for analysing temporal effects and corresponds to the concept of temporal expansion in the REFII model.

The transformation of time series to REFII model was carried out using the Time Explorer software shown in Figure 2.

The time series from the first table created by using the data warehouse was transformed to

REFII model with the above mentioned software. The analysis was oriented towards the shape of the curve, with the aim of discovering potential oscillations on a weekly level. Secondary transformation of angle coefficients was carried out according to the definition included in the software program shown in Figure 3.

Through transformation, the transformation matrix was obtained in Table 2.

Where cycle corresponds to the ordinal number of the week in the year and the index value corresponds to the label of the day of the week. Based on the obtained transformation matrix it is possible to classify the area of the segments beneath the curve, as was done for the angle, but this was disregarded at this stage of analysis because the analysis focused on the shape of the curve which was used to conduct further analysis.

Analysis of Seasonal Oscillations

Using the REFII model, it is possible to carry out an analysis of seasonal oscillations in two ways.

Figure 2. Time explorer

The first method originates from the pattern discovery methodology and is based on conditional probabilities of corresponding segments in respect of time indexes, while the second, more simplified method is based on crosstabulation analysis of frequency of trend in respect of corresponding time segments. The second method was used for analysing seasonal oscillations of the car accidents under Safety First insurance policies.

The first crosstabulation table was created using the SPSS software package on the transformation matrix, on the level of the basic trends (labels R, E, F) in order to see whether any pattern exists in the trends:

Table 3 was obtained as the result of this analysis.

Trend indexes have the following meaning:

1. Trend of occurrence from Saturday to Sunday
2. Trend of occurrence from Sunday to Monday
3. Trend of occurrence from Monday to Tuesday
4. Trend of occurrence from Tuesday to Wednesday
5. Trend of occurrence from Wednesday to Thursday
6. Trend of occurrence from Thursday to Friday
7. Trend of occurrence from Friday to Saturday

The analysis showed that there are seasonal upward trends in the number of accidents occurring from Saturday to Sunday, with a 98.1% level of certainty, and in the number of accidents occurring from Thursday to Friday with a 75% level of certainty. From Friday to Saturday there is a downward trend in the number of accidents, with a level of certainty of 86.5%, the same as from Saturday to Sunday.

Taking into account the detected trend patterns, further analysis of the transformation matrix was carried out in respect of trend intensity (angle categories) from which the results in Table 4 were obtained.

Table 2. Part of the processing results

Cycle	Index	REF	Area	Angle category	Angle coefficient
1	3	R	65.5	Small rise	0.14893617
1	4	R	88.5	Small rise	0.046808511
1	5	R	94.5	Small rise	0.004255319
1	6	R	101.5	Small fall	0.055319149
1	7	F	80.5	Small fall	0.234042553
2	1	R	65.5	Small rise	0.106382979
2	2	R	88	Small rise	0.085106383
2	3	F	92	Small fall	0.05106383
2	4	F	82.5	Small fall	0.029787234
2	5	F	77.5	Small fall	0.012765957
2	6	R	93	Small rise	0.144680851
2	7	F	87	Small fall	0.195744681
3	1	F	55	Small fall	0.076595745
3	2	R	68	Small rise	0.187234043
3	3	R	98	Small rise	0.068085106
3	4	F	90	Small fall	0.136170213
3	5	R	86.5	Small rise	0.106382979
3	6	R	105.5	Small rise	0.055319149
3	7	F	90.5	Small fall	0.182978723
4	1	R	85.5	Small rise	0.140425532
4	2	R	107.5	Small rise	0.046808511
4	3	E	113	No change	0
4	4	F	95	Small fall	0.153191489
…	…	…	…	…	…

This table shows a more precise elaboration of seasonal oscillations, including the intensity of upward and downward trends in each specific time segment observed.

The analysis showed seasonal trends towards a small rise in the number of accidents occurring from Sunday to Monday as well as from Thursday to Friday.

From Saturday to Sunday, a trend towards a small fall in the number of accidents has been recorded, the same as from Friday to Saturday.

Taking into account the data on the structure of insurance policy users who had a car accident, on

Figure 3. Secondary transformation of angle coefficients

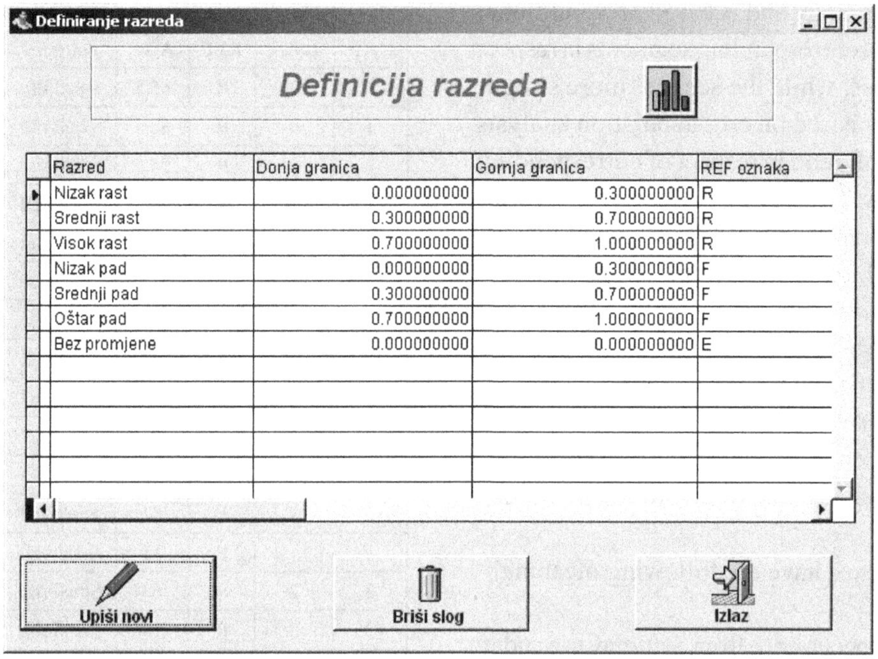

the basis of which this analysis was conducted, we see that these were generally middle-aged persons, with one or more children, with the average age of the car being 7.8 years. The results of the seasonal oscillations analysis clearly show that there is a downward trend in the number of car accidents during the weekend, while this number increases at the beginning and at the end of the workweek. From these indicators it may be concluded that these are family men who use their cars mostly for driving to and from work so that the probability of having an accident is higher at the beginning and at the end of the workweek. Also, the probability of an accident occurring is lower during the weekend, which may be attributed to the car being less used during the weekend or to increased caution on the part of the driver since, if they are going on a trip, they are probably driving their family with them, which additionally motivates them to drive cautiously.

These results were obtained on the level of the entire sample of committed car accidents.

In order to make the analysis more precise, the seasonal oscillation analysis was repeated on the segment of car insurance users, which were diagnosed as high-risk (age between 36 and 45, number of car accidents committed – none, region – north, vehicle class – middle). The obtained results were slightly different from the results obtained at the level of the entire sample of committed car accidents, where high-risk persons were

Table 3. Seasonal oscillations based on trends

Trend Index	REF		
	E	F	R
	Line %	Line %	Line %
1	1.9%	86.5%	11.5%
2	.0%	1.9%	98.1%
3	3.8%	51.9%	44.2%
4	1.9%	57.7%	40.4%
5	3.8%	42.3%	53.8%
6	.0%	25.0%	75.0%
7	.0%	86.5%	13.5%

Table 4. Seasonal oscillations based on angle category

Trend Index	Angle category				
	No change	Small fall	Small rise	Average fall	Average rise
	Line %	Line %	Line %	Line %	Line %
1	1.9%	84.6%	11.5%	1.9%	.0%
2	.0%	1.9%	86.5%	.0%	11.5%
3	3.8%	48.1%	38.5%	3.8%	5.8%
4	1.9%	48.1%	34.6%	9.6%	5.8%
5	3.8%	38.5%	51.9%	3.8%	1.9%
6	.0%	25.0%	67.3%	.0%	7.7%
7	.0%	76.9%	13.5%	9.6%	.0%

characterised as middle-aged, with one or more children, and with a somewhat lower average age of the car – 6.4 years.

Analysis of Temporal Effects

The aim of the analysis of temporal effects was to provide an answer to the question of whether the place of vehicle registration has a significant effect on accident trends i.e. whether there is a dominant factor (in the form of a specific attribute value) which has a significant effect on car accident trends. For the purpose of this type of analysis the principle of temporal expansion of the time segments of non-temporal attributes, contained in the second relational table, was used. After creating such a data structure, OLAP analysis was conducted as well as decision tree analysis. The result of the first, OLAP analysis is shown in Table 5, representing the effect that the place of vehicle registration has on the time segment trend.

The table shows that, for example, there is a higher probability that vehicles with Zagreb licence plates will be involved in car accidents in the periods in which there is a small rise in the time segment trend, while for example for vehicles with Križevci licence plates the probability of being involved in a car accident is higher in the periods in which there is a small fall in the time

segment trend. This type of analysis helps us to create conditional probabilities of involvement of cars with a certain licence plate in an accident, in respect of the expected occurrence trend. If we look at this analysis in the context of the analysis carried out to detect time patterns and seasonal oscillations, then we can see for example that from Sunday to Monday the probability of cars with Križevci licence plates being involved in a car accident is higher than in the case of cars with Zagreb licence plates, because in that period a seasonal oscillation of a small fall was recorded.

We can also observe the entire structure of the effect of vehicle licence plates on trend, where the frequency of occurrence of accidents in relation to the place of registration is more evident.

Table 6 was obtained.

The table shows the effect the place of registration has on trends, with emphasis on the frequency of accident occurrence. Here we can see that Zagreb dominates in the number of accidents in the periods of an average rise in time segment trends. These kind of results were somewhat expected, taking into account the number of insurance policy holders according to each region.

Further analysis was aimed at answering the question of whether there is a dominant factor (in the form of a certain attribute value) which significantly affects trends in car accident occurrence. For that purpose the transformation matrix

Table 5. Angles according to place of vehicle registration

License plate	Category				
	No change	Small fall	Small rise	Average fall	Average rise
	Line %	Line %	Line %	Line %	Line %
ZG	1.4%	38.3%	48.1%	3.5%	8.7%
ST	1.5%	40.9%	46.1%	3.9%	7.6%
PU	1.3%	42.9%	44.9%	3.6%	7.2%
RI	1.9%	39.9%	45.9%	4.1%	8.2%
OS	1.1%	36.7%	51.5%	2.4%	8.3%
ZD	.9%	40.7%	46.3%	5.3%	6.9%
ČK	1.9%	41.3%	46.5%	4.1%	6.1%
KA	1.4%	36.8%	49.7%	4.4%	7.7%
KR	2.3%	39.1%	45.4%	4.0%	9.3%
SK	1.3%	38.6%	47.3%	4.2%	8.6%
VŽ	1.6%	40.3%	45.9%	2.7%	9.4%
SB	1.5%	36.7%	46.1%	6.5%	9.2%
KC	1.3%	38.2%	47.9%	5.3%	7.4%
DU	1.7%	43.9%	43.2%	4.9%	6.3%
ŠI	2.3%	39.1%	48.8%	3.6%	6.1%
BJ	.8%	45.5%	46.8%	2.2%	4.7%
VK	1.2%	43.6%	46.5%	2.3%	6.4%
NA	1.5%	39.8%	47.5%	5.6%	5.6%
PŽ	.6%	41.7%	40.7%	7.1%	9.9%
VU	1.5%	43.5%	44.6%	1.9%	8.5%
DA	1.8%	40.3%	48.2%	2.7%	7.1%
BM	2.3%	34.5%	50.0%	5.5%	7.7%
DJ	1.0%	37.9%	47.1%	3.4%	10.7%
KT	2.5%	40.7%	42.6%	3.4%	10.8%
IM	.5%	43.1%	47.0%	1.5%	7.9%
VT	1.5%	46.4%	38.1%	6.2%	7.7%
KŽ	3.1%	44.3%	41.7%	2.6%	8.3%
NG	.5%	37.4%	50.5%	4.4%	7.1%
MA	1.7%	37.1%	50.3%	5.1%	5.7%
GS	1.7%	39.3%	48.0%	3.5%	7.5%
PS	2.5%	38.5%	48.4%	.8%	9.8%
ŽU	.0%	33.7%	57.1%	1.0%	8.2%
OG	.0%	43.3%	51.7%	.0%	5.0%
DE	.0%	34.6%	50.0%	.0%	15.4%

in REFII format was expanded with non-temporal attributes and analysed using a decision tree. The processing results are shown in Figure 4.

Figure 4 shows that the age group of insurance policy holders from 36 to 45 has the greatest effect on the average and small rise of the number of accidents.

Interpretation of Analysis Results from the Perspective of Business Planning

Time series analysis provided an alternative to making the unpopular decision to increase the amount of the insurance premium (although only for the market segment assessed as high-risk) and thereby risking to potentially loose part of the market while increasing profitability. The key role in achieving an increase in profit with respect to the market share was assigned to the public relations department and the marketing department, whose main goal was to take action aimed at the high-risk market segment, with the goal of reducing the level of risk.

Since the high-risk segment was found to be persons of the age between 36 and 45, with one or more children, number of accidents committed to date – none, region – north, vehicle class – middle, probability of accident – highest at beginning or end of the work week, it is clear that these persons have families, are employed and that they use their cars less or drive more cautiously during the weekend.

Based on these results, a poll was conducted on a randomly selected representative sample of high-risk policyholders, which additionally confirmed these hypotheses. The poll showed that most of the poll respondents are more stressed out at the beginning of the work week and this fact most likely has a significant effect on the occurrence of car accidents, just as they are in more of a rush at the end of the week because of staying

Table 6. Angles according to place of registration (structure)

License plate	Category				
	No change	Small fall	Small rise	Average fall	Average rise
	Column %	Column %	Column %	Column %	Column %
ZG	34.1%	33.8%	35.5%	32.4%	37.7%
ST	10.4%	10.5%	9.9%	10.6%	9.5%
PU	6.8%	8.2%	7.2%	7.4%	6.8%
RI	9.0%	6.9%	6.7%	7.5%	7.0%
OS	4.0%	5.1%	6.0%	3.6%	5.6%
ZD	1.8%	3.0%	2.9%	4.1%	2.5%
ČK	3.5%	2.9%	2.7%	3.0%	2.1%
KA	2.6%	2.5%	2.9%	3.2%	2.6%
KR	4.0%	2.6%	2.5%	2.8%	3.0%
SK	2.0%	2.3%	2.3%	2.6%	2.5%
VŽ	2.4%	2.3%	2.2%	1.6%	2.7%
SB	2.0%	1.8%	1.9%	3.4%	2.2%
KC	1.3%	1.5%	1.6%	2.2%	1.4%
DU	1.8%	1.7%	1.4%	2.0%	1.2%
ŠI	2.4%	1.5%	1.6%	1.5%	1.2%
BJ	.7%	1.4%	1.2%	.7%	.7%
VK	.9%	1.2%	1.1%	.7%	.9%
NA	1.1%	1.1%	1.1%	1.6%	.8%
PŽ	.4%	1.1%	.9%	2.0%	1.3%
VU	.9%	.9%	.8%	.4%	.9%
DA	.9%	.7%	.8%	.5%	.6%
BM	1.1%	.6%	.8%	1.0%	.7%
DJ	.4%	.6%	.7%	.6%	.9%
KT	1.1%	.7%	.6%	.6%	.9%
IM	.2%	.7%	.7%	.3%	.6%
VT	.7%	.7%	.5%	1.0%	.6%
KŽ	1.3%	.7%	.6%	.4%	.6%
NG	.2%	.6%	.6%	.7%	.5%
MA	.7%	.5%	.6%	.8%	.4%
GS	.7%	.6%	.6%	.5%	.5%
PS	.7%	.4%	.4%	.1%	.5%
ŽU	.0%	.3%	.4%	.1%	.3%
OG	.0%	.2%	.2%	.0%	.1%
DE	.0%	.1%	.1%	.0%	.2%

at work overtime to finish all the tasks they fell behind with during the week.

Instead of introducing the unpopular measure of increasing the premium amount for the high-risk market segment, the public relations department and the marketing department prepared information leaflets providing the policy holders with information on the effect that stress and rush at the beginning and end of the week has on increasing the risk of car accidents, suggesting that they use public transportation instead or use increased caution in traffic, especially at the beginning and at the end of the work week.

In the information leaflets, they also announced a prize contest in which all the persons who received the information leaflets who do not provoke a car accident in the following twelve months can participate and win the main prize—a car. The information leaflets accentuated the message that the insurance company cares for its clients and that this care and concern was the main reason for preparing and sending the leaflets.

This promotional material was sent to all those clients who belong to the high-risk segment.

ANALYSIS RESULTS

Due to the already mentioned intensive promotional activities aimed at a further increase in the market share, comparisons were made between the projected number of accidents (numerically and financially), in which the effect of the implemented campaign was not taken into account, and the actual number of accidents in the observed period.

In the first six-month period no significant effects which should have occurred because of the campaign being implemented were recorded, so that in the period of the first six months the campaign was borderline cost-effective. For this reason, the company management decided to make the necessary preparations for raising the premium for the high-risk segment of car insurance policy holders. Because of the highly competitive

environment in the field of car insurance, market research was carried out (survey on a randomly selected representative sample by the Agency for Market Research) in order to make an assessment of the effect of making these decisions on the loss/retention of market share. The survey results indicated a significant decrease in the market share especially in the segment diagnosed as high-risk. It was calculated that profitability would increase, but would lead to the loss of a significant part of the market, so that in the end, this would result in even lower profits in the long term. Given the assessed market situation, it was decided to continue with the previously initiated campaign even more intensely for the next six months, to delay the implementation of this decision for the next six months and to subsequently evaluate the effects of the campaign. Further encouragement to postpone raising the premium for the high-risk segment was based on analysis that showed that in the case of new clients, there was a significant reduction in the risk level of the market segment labelled as high-risk in the past six months. Regarding customer churning (non-renewal of policies upon expiry), these trends were satisfactory, and it could be concluded that the number of customer churnings and crossovers to other insurance companies was not significant. The sample of churning customers was in a very small percentage and did not show any pattern by any criteria, based on which it could be concluded that the reason for churning was not motivated by any targeted campaign of the competition.

Although the effects of the campaign were systematically monitored one year back, the main analysis was conducted in the semi-annual periods. The second semi-annual evaluation of the campaign gave much better results. The number of car accidents was cut almost in half, especially in the segment of clients aged between 36 and 45 who were identified as those with the highest risk level in the analysis. A significant decrease in the number of accidents was also recorded at the beginning and at the end of the workweek, on

Figure 4. Analysis of factors which affect car accident trends

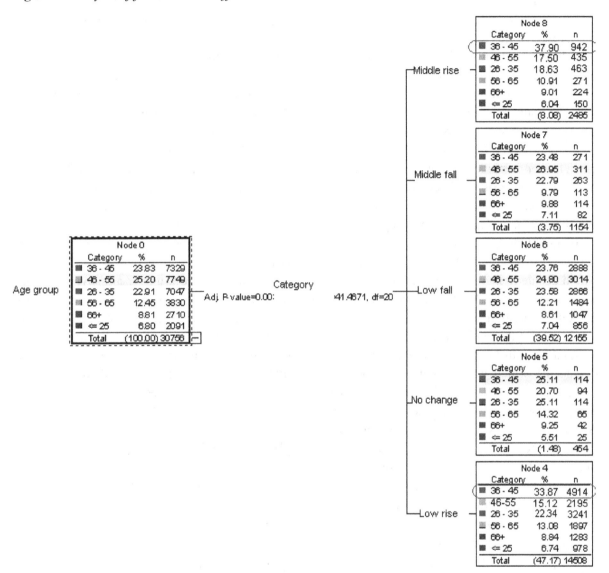

which policy holders aged between 36 and 45 had a significant impact. A reduction in the number of accidents was recorded with respect to the other characteristics of the high-risk segment as well, but the most significant results were visible precisely in relation to the age characteristic and to the period of accident occurrence related to the day of the week.

Given the estimated success of the campaign, it was decided that the unpopular measure of raising the premium for the high-risk segment of policyholders would not be introduced and that further implementation of the initiated campaign with reduced intensity would be continued in order to further decrease the level of risk and increase profits.

CONCLUSION

The presented business case shows that knowledge discovered from databases has a direct effect on certain types of decisions. Let us again look at the problem outlined at the beginning of this text: the company's profits for two years back were much smaller than expected, although based on the number of clients the company expected much higher earnings. The earnings were in fact reduced because of the increased number and higher amounts of insurance claims due to car accidents, which in turn lead to a drop in profit.

If no detailed analysis was conducted, it is very likely that the majority of company managers would decide to increase the price of taking-out an insurance policy. In conditions of intensified market competition, that measure could result in a reduction of the market share.

A more sophisticated approach would include diagnosing which market segment carries the highest risk, as was done in this business case, and based on this analysis, the company management could decide to raise the price of taking-out a car insurance policy for the high-risk market segment. This decision could also lead to a reduction of the market share in such highly competitive conditions, but the market share reduction would primarily pertain to the high-risk segment.

Understanding the models of behaviour of high-risk clients, and gaining insight into their profiles enabled a very different, defensive approach to be taken towards the high-risk market segment, aimed not only at reducing the level of risk and thus increasing the profit of the insurance company in the long-term, but also at strengthening customer loyalty. The decision to educate the high-risk policy holders, in a way in which they get the impression that the insurance company cares about them and their assets, can positively affect their opinion of the insurance company in which they contracted the insurance policy. The role of the public relations service which was responsible for preparing the appropriate informa-tion leaflets sent by mail to the high-risk segment of policyholders must also be stressed.

This example clearly shows the impact that knowledge discovered from databases can have on decision-making processes, where the actual situation on the market is taken into account and the risks that certain types of decisions entail is attempted to be reduced to a minimum. Discovered knowledge opens new possibilities in the process of decision-making. Other sources of information such as results of market research, statistical data, macroeconomic data and the like should also be taken into consideration. The only drawback, which is also the advantage of the process of discovering knowledge from databases, stems from the fact that there are no universal analytical recipes for certain types of problems. Although the process of discovering knowledge mostly depends on the skills and experience of the analysts, if they are designed well and implemented, they can provide high quality information that becomes the basis for making better business decisions.

REFERENCES

Aleksander, I., & Morton, H. (1995). *An introduction to neural computing*. New York, NY: International Thompson Computer Press.

Apte, C., Grossman, E., Pednault, E., Rosen, B., Tipu, F., & White, B. (1999). *Insurance risk modeling using data mining technology*. Report RC-21314. Yorktown Heights, NY: IBM Research Division.

Berry, J. A. M., & Linoff, G. (1997). *Data mining techniques for marketing sales and customer support*. New York, NY: John Wiley & Sons Inc.

Chidanand, A., Edna, G., Edwin, P. D., Pednault, B. K. R., Fateh, A. T., & Brian, W. (1999). Probabilistic estimation-based data mining for discovering insurance risks. *IEEE Intelligent Systems, 14*(6), 49–58. doi:10.1109/5254.809568

Derrig, R. A., & Ostaszewski, K. M. (1995). Fuzzy techniques of pattern recognition in risk and claim classification. *The Journal of Risk and Insurance, 62*(3), 447–482. doi:10.2307/253819

Hackerman, D. (1995). *A tutorial on learning with bayesian networks microsoft research. MSR-TR-95-06.* Seattle, WA: Microsoft.

Han, J., & Kamber, M. (2000). *Data mining: Concepts and techniques.* San Francisco, CA: Morgan Kaufmann.

Kantardžić, M. (2003). *Data mining: Concepts, models, methods and algorithms.* New York, NY: John Wiley & Sons. doi:10.1115/1.2123107

Klepac, G. (2005). *Time series rule discovering with unique model of transformation.* (Unpublished Doctoral Dissertation). University of Zagreb FOI. Varaždin, Croatia.

Klepac, G., & Mršić, L. (2006). *Poslovna inteligencija kroz poslovne slučajeve.* Zagreb, Croatia: Liderpress.

Kohonen, T. (2001). *Self-organizing maps.* Berlin, Germany: Springer. doi:10.1007/978-3-642-56927-2

Kolyshkina, I. (2002). *Modeling insurance risk: A comparison of data mining and logistic regression approaches.* London, UK: PricewaterhouseCoopers.

Pratt, K. (2001). *Locating patterns in discrete time series.* (M.Sc. Thesis). University of South Florida. Tampa, FL.

Pyle, D. (1999). *Data preparation for data mining.* San Francisco, CA: MKP.

Samson, D. (1986). Designing an automobile insurance classification system. *European Journal of Operational Research, 27,* 235–241. doi:10.1016/0377-2217(86)90065-2

Samson, D., & Thomas, H. (1987). Linear models as aids in insurance decision making: The estimation of automobile insurance claims. *Journal of Business Research, 15,* 247–256. doi:10.1016/0148-2963(87)90027-0

Smith, K. A., Willis, R. J., & Brooks, M. (2000). An analysis of customer retention and insurance claim patterns using data mining: A case study. *The Journal of the Operational Research Society, 51*(5), 532–541.

Thomas, L., Edelman, D., & Crook, J. (2002). *Credit scoring and its application.* New York, NY: SIAM. doi:10.1137/1.9780898718317

Tryfos, P. (1980). On classification in automobile insurance. *The Journal of Risk and Insurance, 47*(2), 331–337. doi:10.2307/252336

Vaughan, E. J., & Vaughan, T. M. (1996). *Fundamentals of risk and insurance* (7th ed.). New York, NY: Wiley.

Vose, D. (2000). *Quantitative risk analysis.* New York, NY: John Wiley & Sons.

Williams, J. G., Weiqian, L., & Mehmet, O. (2001). Temporal data mining using hidden Markov-local polynomial models. *Lecture Notes in Artificial Intelligence, 2035.*

Williams, J. G., Weiqiang, L., & Mehmet, A. O. (2002). An overview of temporal data mining. In *Proceedings of the 1st Australian Data Mining Workshop (ADM 2002),* (pp. 83-90). Canberra, Australia: University of Technology.

Xsniaping, G. (1998). *Pattern matching in financial time series data.* Retrieved from http://www.datalab.uci.edu/people/xge/chart

KEY TERMS AND DEFINITIONS

Bayesian Networks: Probabilistic models based on conditional probability.

Conditional Probability: Probability that some event will happen if some other event happened previously.

Conditional Probability Table: Integral part of Bayesian networks which shows conditional probabilities between interrelated nodes.

Data Mining: Discovering hidden useful knowledge in large amount of data (databases).

Neural Networks: Analytical models which structure and calculation methods are inspired with human brain.

NPC (Necessary Path Condition): Structural learning algorithm in Bayesian networks used for the purposes of learning from the data.

Risk Evaluation: Evaluation of possibility that some risky event will happened.

Chapter 6
Intelligent Techniques in Recommender Systems and Contextual Advertising:
Novel Approaches and Case Studies

Giuliano Armano
University of Cagliari, Italy

Alessandro Giuliani
University of Cagliari, Italy

Eloisa Vargiu
University of Cagliari, Italy & Barcelona Digital Technology Center, Spain

ABSTRACT

Information Filtering deals with the problem of selecting relevant information for a given user, according to her/his preferences and interests. In this chapter, the authors consider two ways of performing information filtering: recommendation and contextual advertising. In particular, they study and analyze them according to a unified view. In fact, the task of suggesting an advertisement to a Web page can be viewed as the task of recommending an item (the advertisement) to a user (the Web page), and vice versa. Starting from this insight, the authors propose a content-based recommender system based on a generic solution for contextual advertising and a hybrid contextual advertising system based on a generic hybrid recommender system. Relevant case studies have been considered (i.e., a photo recommender and a Web advertiser) with the goal of highlighting how the proposed approach works in practice. In both cases, results confirm the effectiveness of the proposed solutions.

DOI: 10.4018/978-1-4666-2542-6.ch006

INTRODUCTION

Information Filtering (IF) is aimed at presenting only relevant information to users. IF systems cover a broad range of domains, technologies, and methods involved in the task of providing users with the information they require (Hanani, et al., 2001). IF systems are, typically, able to handle large amounts of data with the following characteristics:

1. Primarily textual,
2. Unstructured or semi-structured, and
3. Based on user profiles. IF systems are also expected to remove irrelevant data from incoming streams of data items.

The current generation of IF systems requires improvements to make filtering methods more robust, intelligent, effective, and applicable to an even broader range of real life applications. In particular, focusing on a collaborative scenario like the Web 2.0, users need suggestions about online items (e.g., Web pages, news, photos, ads), according to their preferences and tastes. To this end, research activities in this field might be focused on defining and implementing intelligent techniques that rely, for instance, on machine learning, text categorization, evolutionary computation, and Semantic Web (Armano, et al., 2010).

IF is typically performed by Recommender Systems (RS). In particular, RS have been widely advocated as a way of coping with the problem of information overload in many application domains and, to date, many recommendation methods have been developed (Wei, et al., 2000).

Besides recommendation, an emergent field in IF is Contextual Advertising (CA). CA systems are devoted to suggest suitable advertisements (ads) to users while surfing the Web. Most ads on the Web are short textual messages usually marked as "sponsored links" (Deepayan, et al., 2008).

In the literature, RS and CA have been separately studied, despite the existence of common issues. In fact, the task of suggesting an ad to a Web

page can be viewed as the task of recommending an item (the ad) to a user (the Web page), and vice versa. In our opinion, a unifying view could be useful to study and experiment novel strategies to exploit benefits and experiences from both research fields (Armano & Vargiu, 2010). In this chapter, after a brief survey of relevant related work on both RS and CA, we test the reliability of the proposed unifying view by proposing a content-based RS devised a la mode of CA (Addis, et al., 2010a), and a novel hybrid CA system devised a la mode of RS. In the following, to show the effectiveness of both approaches, we present a relevant case study for each of them: a photo recommender and a Web advertiser, respectively. A discussion on further relevant unified solutions ends the chapter.

BACKGROUND

In this section, we first give a summary about IF –recalling the main contributions in this field. Subsequently, we concentrate on two specific subfields of IF: RS and CA (the former filters items according to users' interests and preferences, whereas the latter filters ads according to the content of the given Web page).

Information Filtering

Two major approaches characterize IF systems: knowledge based and user model based. IF systems that follow the former approach use artificial intelligence techniques to represent user profiles and to implement filtering and learning capabilities. In particular, these systems use production-rules (Malone, et al., 1987; Wolinski, et al., 2000), semantic-nets (Stefani & Strapparava, 1999; Asnicar & Tasso, 1999), and artificial neural networks (Jennings & Higuchi, 1992; Kantor, et al., 2000). The adopted user model in IF systems differs from each other mainly in the following aspects (Belkin & Croft, 1992): data acquisition, content model, and underlying architecture. As for data acquisition, there are two main approaches: the implicit approach, which is implemented by inference from some kind of observation (Thomas & Fisher, 1996; Avery, et al., 1999), and the explicit approach, which interacts with the users by acquiring feedback on information that is filtered (Oard, 1998; Fleming & Cohen, 1999; McCalla, et al., 1996). As for the content model: the shallow semantics model uses only keywords to represent user's interests (Jennings & Higuchi, 1993; Newell, 1997), whereas the enhanced user model attempts to infer high-level knowledge about the user by assigning values to parameters such as user background and past experience (Stefani & Strapparava, 1999; Shapira, et al., 1997). As for the underlying architecture, agent systems and neural networks are commonly used for automatically inferred model, while the vector space and latent semantic indexing are mostly used for explicit inference.

According to Hanani et al. (2001), a generic IF system includes four basic components: data analyzer, user modeler, filter, and learner. The data analyzer obtains or collects data items from information providers. Data items are analyzed and represented in a suitable format (e.g., as a vector of indexed terms). This information is provided as input to the filter. The user modeler, which explicitly and/or implicitly gathers information about users and their information needs, constructs user models (e.g., user profiles). In addition, the user-model is provided as input to the filter. The filter matches the user model with the represented data items and decides if a data item is relevant to the user. Sometimes the decision is binary (i.e., relevant or irrelevant) and sometimes is probabilistic (i.e., the data item gets a relevance rank). The filtering process can be applied to a single data item (e.g., a new blog post) or to a set of data items (e.g., a Web site). The user who gets the suggested data item is the only one that can state the real relevancy. Her/his evaluation enables further feedback, to be provided to the learner. The learner is aimed at improving the filtering ability, with the goal of dealing with the

difficulties that arise from modeling users and from changes in their information needs. In particular, the learning process is able to counteract shifts in users' interests by updating their model to avoid inaccuracies occur in profiles that might affect filtering results.

Recommender Systems

RS help users to navigate through large product assortments and to make decisions in e-commerce scenarios. Development of RS is a multi-disciplinary effort, which involves experts from various fields such as Artificial Intelligence, Human Computer Interaction, Information Technology, Data Mining, Statistics, Adaptive User Interfaces, Decision Support Systems, Marketing, and Consumer Behavior (Ricci, et al., 2010).

In this section, we first summarize the most relevant work in this research field and then we sketch a generic RS architecture that highlights the main tasks of a RS.

State of the Art

RS usually fall in the following categories, based on how recommendations are made (Adomavicius & Tuzhilin, 2005): content-based recommendations, collaborative filtering, and hybrid approaches.

Content-based RS suggest to users items that are similar to those they preferred in the past (Lops, et al., 2010). Many current content-based systems focus on recommending items containing textual information, such as documents and Web sites. The improvement over traditional information retrieval approaches comes from the adoption of user profiles that contain information about users' tastes, preferences, and needs. The profiling information can be elicited from users explicitly (e.g., through questionnaires) or implicitly learned from their transactional behavior over time.

Unlike content-based recommendation methods, collaborative RS (or collaborative filtering systems) try to predict the utility of items for a particular user based on the items previously rated by other users. There have been many collaborative systems developed in the academia and in the industry. The Grundy system (Rich, 1998), GroupLens (Resnick, et al., 1994), Video Recommender (Hill, et al., 1995), and Ringo (Shardanand & Maes, 1995) were the first systems that used collaborative filtering algorithms to automate prediction. Other examples of collaborative RS include the book RS from Amazon.com (Linden, et al., 2003), and the PHOAKS system that helps people to find relevant information on the Web (Terveen, et al., 1997).

The choice of the most suitable algorithm for a RS depends on many issues, including the specific type of service, the nature of items, together with the kind and amount of available information. For instance, if items are documents, an algorithm based on content matching is more appropriate because it is able to deal with problems related to the automatic analysis of text (Yan & Garcia-Molina, 1999; Stevens, 1993). If items are multimedia with scarce descriptions, but rated by a community of users, collaborative filtering could be more suitable (Sarwar, et al., 2001; Linden, et al., 2003).

Several RS use a hybrid approach, which combines collaborative and content-based methods (Burke, 2002). In so doing, certain limitations of content-based and collaborative systems can be overcome. The ways for combining collaborative and content-based methods fall in the following categories (Adomavicius & Tuzhilin, 2005):

1. Implementing collaborative and content-based methods separately and combining their predictions;

2. Incorporating some content-based characteristics into a collaborative approach;

3. Incorporating some collaborative characteristics into a content-based approach; and

4. Devising a unifying model that embodies both content-based and collaborative characteristics.

To support the recommendation process in social activities, group RS have also been proposed. These systems are aimed at providing recommendations to groups instead of individuals (Boratto & Carta, 2010). The way a group is formed affects the way it is modeled and how recommendations are predicted. Four notions of group have been defined (Jameson & Smyth, 2007):

1. Established group, i.e., a number of persons who explicitly choose to be a part of a group;

2. Occasional group, i.e., a number of persons who occasionally do something together;

3. Random group, i.e., a number of persons who share an environment in a given moment without explicit interests that link them; and

4. Automatically identified group, i.e., groups that are automatically detected considering user preferences and/or the available resources.

More recently, some work focused on combining information embedded in user profiles with contextual information (Adomavicius, et al., 2005; Adomavicius & Tuzhilin, 2008; Ramaswamy, et al., 2009). The underlying motivation is that taking into account both profiles and contexts in a recommendation process gives benefits to a RS for many reasons: users' preferences and ratings change according to their contexts (Stefanidis & Pitoura, 2008); traditional RS do not consider multiple ratings of the same content (Anand & Mobasher, 2007); and RS may fail in providing some valuable recommendations, as their similarity distance is uniformly applied to user's preferences without analyzing the discrepancies introduced by the context (Abbar, et al., 2009). In the literature, the term "context" is referred to "events which modify the user behavior" in the area of RS, and to "keywords used in search engines" in the area of CA. In this chapter, we adhere to the latter interpretation, disregarding context-aware RS.

A Generic Hybrid Architecture

The recommendation problem can be formulated as follows: let U be the set of all users[1] and let I be the set of all possible items that can be recommended (e.g., books, movies, and restaurants)[2]. Let f be a utility function that measures the usefulness of item i for user u, i.e., $f : U \times I \rightarrow R$, where R is a totally ordered set (e.g., non-negative integers or real numbers within a certain range). Then, for each user $u \in U$ we want to choose the item $i' \in I$ that maximizes the user's utility function. More formally:

$$\forall u \in U, \quad i'_u = \arg\max_{i \in I} f(u, i)$$

In RS, the utility function is typically represented by ratings and is initially defined only on items previously rated by the users. For example, in a book recommendation application (e.g., Amazon.com) users initially rate some subsets of books that they have read.

In this chapter, we are mainly interested in hybrid RS. As already recalled in the previous section, Adomavicius and Tuzhilin (2005) identified four ways to combine collaborative and content-based methods. According to this classification and considering how to incorporate collaborative characteristics into a content-based approach, in our view, a generic hybrid architecture could be designed as depicted in Figure 1. Let us note that it is just one of the feasible solutions for implementing a hybrid RS (a comprehensive study on variations deemed useful for implementing a hybrid RS is out of the scope of this chapter).

The architecture, composed by three modules, obtains information about items previously rated by the users from the User repository and information on available items from the Item repository.

Peer user extractor: This module is typical of collaborative RS. Its main purpose is to detect the "peers" of any given user u. Peer users are other users that have similar tastes. The underlying idea is that only items that are most liked by the "peers" of user u should be recommended.

In the literature, various approaches have been used to compute the similarity *sim(u, u')* between users in collaborative RS. The two most popular approaches are correlation-based (Resnick, et al., 1994; Shardanand & Maes, 1995) and cosine-based (Breese, et al., 1998; Sarwar, et al., 2001).

Formally, let I_{uv} be the set of all items co-rated by both users u and v, i.e., $I_{uv} = i \in I : r_{u,i} > \emptyset$ and $r_{v,i} > \emptyset$, where $r_{u,i}$ and $r_{v,i}$ are the rates given to item i by user u and v, respectively.

In the correlation-based approach, the Pearson's correlation coefficient is used to measure the similarity:

Figure 1. A generic hybrid architecture for RS systems

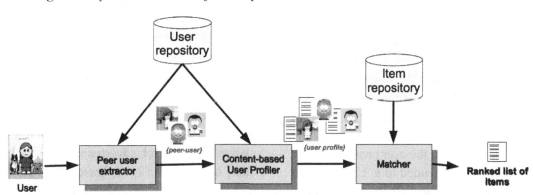

$$sim(u,v) = \frac{\sum_{i \in I_{uv}} (r_{u,i} - \overline{r}_u) \cdot (r_{v,i} - \overline{r}_v)}{\sqrt{\sum_{i \in I_{uv}} (r_{u,i} - \overline{r}_u)^2 \cdot \sum_{i \in I_{uv}} (r_{v,i} - \overline{r}_v)^2}}$$

In the cosine-based approach, users *u* and *v* are represented by two vectors in an *m*-dimensional space, where *m* is the cardinality of I_{uv}. Then, the similarity between two vectors can be measured by computing the cosine of the angle between them:

$$sim(u,v) = \frac{\sum_{i \in I_{uv}} r_{u,i} \cdot r_{v,i}}{\sqrt{\sum_{i \in I_{uv}} r^2_{u,i} \cdot \sum_{i \in I_{uv}} r^2_{v,i}}}$$

Content-based user profiler: This module, typical of content-based RS, is aimed at identifying the user profiles that belong to the users selected by the peer user extractor.

User profiling is typically either knowledge-based or behavior-based. Knowledge-based approaches engineer static models of users and dynamically match users to the closest model. Questionnaires and interviews are often employed to obtain this user knowledge. Behavior-based approaches build a model from user behavior, commonly adopting machine-learning techniques to discover useful behavioral patterns. In particular, behavioral logging is employed to obtain the data required to extract patterns. The user profiling approach used by most RS is behavior-based, commonly uses a binary class model to represent what users find interesting and uninteresting. Machine-learning techniques are then used to find potential items of interest with respect to the binary model. Kobsa (1993) provides a good survey of user modeling techniques.

Matcher: This module is common in every kind of RS. The main purpose of the matching is to find, starting from the user profiles, the set of items to be recommended to *u*. Each score is calculated by taking into account the extracted profiles, the characteristics of items, and the rates provided by users. Instead of using ratings, Sarwar et al. (2001) use the same correlation-based and cosine-based techniques used to compute the similarity between user pairs. This idea has been further extended in Deshpande and Karypis (2004) for the top-N item recommendations.

Contextual Advertising

Online Advertising is an emerging research field, at the intersection of Information Retrieval, Machine Learning, Optimization, and Microeconomics. Its main goal is to choose the right ads to present to a user engaged in a given task, such as sponsored search advertising or CA.

Sponsored search advertising (or paid search advertising) puts ads on the page returned from a Web search engine following a query. CA (or content match) puts ads within the content of a generic, third party, Web page. A commercial intermediary, namely ad-network, is usually in charge of optimizing the selection of ads with the twofold goal of increasing revenue (shared between publisher and ad-network) and improving user experience. In other words, CA is a form of targeted advertising for ads appearing on Web sites or other media, such as content displayed in mobile browsers. The ads themselves are selected and served by automated systems based on the content displayed to the user.

In this Section, we first summarize the most relevant work in this research field and then we sketch a generic CA architecture that highlights the main tasks of a CA system.

State of the Art

CA is the economic engine behind a large number of non-transactional sites on the Web. A main factor for the success in CA is the relevance to the surrounding scenario. Each solution for CA evolved from search advertising, where a search query matches with a bid phrase of the ad. A natural extension of search advertising is extracting phrases from the target page and matching them with the bid phrases of ads. Yih et al. (2006) propose a system for phrase extraction, which uses a variety of features to determine the importance of page phrases for advertising purposes. To this end, the authors proposed a supervised approach that relies on a training set built using a corpus of pages in which relevant phrases have been annotated by hand.

Ribeiro-Neto et al. (2005) examine a number of strategies to match pages and ads based on extracted keywords. They represent both pages and ads in a vector space and propose several strategies to improve the matching process. In particular, the authors explore the use of different sections of ads as a basis for the vector, mapping both page and ads in the same space. Since there is a discrepancy between the vocabulary used in the pages and in the ads (the so called "impedance mismatch"), the authors improved the matching precision by expanding the page vocabulary with terms from similar pages.

In a subsequent work, Lacerda et al. (2006) propose a method to learn the impact of individual features by using genetic programming. The results show that genetic programming helps to find improved matching functions.

Broder et al. (2007) introduces a semantic analysis by classifying both pages and ads according to a given taxonomy, and match ads to the page falling in the same node of the taxonomy. Each node of the taxonomy is built as a set of bid phrases or queries corresponding to a certain topic. Results show a better accuracy than that of classic systems (i.e., systems based on syntactic analysis only). Let us also note that, to improve performances, this system may be used in conjunction with more general approaches.

Another approach that combines syntax and semantics has been proposed in Armano et al. (2011b). The corresponding system, called ConCA (Concepts on Contextual Advertising), relies on ConceptNet, a semantic network able to supply commonsense knowledge (Liu & Singh, 2004).

Nowadays, ad-networks need to deal in real time with a large amount of data, involving billions of pages and ads. Therefore, several constraints must be taken into account for building CA systems. In particular, efficiency and computational costs are crucial factors in the choice of methods and algorithms. Anagnostopoulos et al. (2007) present a methodology for Web advertising in real time, focusing on the contributions of the different fragments of a Web page. This methodology allows to identify short but informative excerpts of the Web page by using several text summarization techniques, in conjunction with the model developed in Broder at al. (2007).

According to this view, Armano et al. (2011c) studied the impact of the syntactic phase on CA. In particular, they performed a comparative study on text summarization in CA showing that implementing effective text summarization techniques may help to improve the corresponding system.

Since bid phrases are basically search queries, another relevant approach is to view CA as a problem of query expansion and rewriting. Murdock et al. (2007) consider a statistical machine translation model to overcome the problem of the impedance mismatch between page and ads. To this end, they propose and develop a system able to re-rank the ad candidates based on a noisy-channel model. In a subsequent work, the authors used a machine learning approach, based on the model described in Broder et al. (2007), to define an innovative set of features able to extract the semantic correlations between the page and ad vocabularies (Ciaramita, et al., 2008a).

Many of the techniques used in CA to place ads in Web pages may be used to place ads in response to a user's query, as in Sponsored Search. Sponsored Search can be thought of as a document retrieval problem, where ads are documents to be retrieved in response to a query. Ads could be partly represented by their keywords. Carrasco et al. (2003) approach the problem of keyword suggestion by clustering bi-partite advertiser-keyword graphs. Joachims (2002) propose to use click-data for learning ranking functions resulting from a search engine as an indicator of relevance. Ciaramita et al. (2008b) studied an approach to learn and evaluate sponsored search systems based solely on click-data, focusing on the relevance of textual content.

A Generic Architecture

The CA problem can be formulated as follows: let P be the set of Web pages and let A be the set of ads that can be displayed. Let f be a utility function that measures the matching between an ad and a Web page, i.e. $f : P \times A \to R$, where R is a totally ordered set (e.g., non-negative integers or real numbers within a certain range). Then, for each page $p \in P$, we want to select an ad $a' \in A$ that maximizes the page utility function. More formally:

$$\forall p \in P, \quad a'_p = \arg\max_{a \in A} f(p, a)$$

Our view of CA is sketched in Figure 2, which illustrates a generic architecture that can give rise to specific systems, depending on the choices made on each involved module. Notably, most of the state-of-the-art solutions are compliant with this view. The architecture encompasses four modules, each corresponding to a specific task.

Pre-processor: Its main purpose is to transform an HTML document (a Web page or an ad) into an easy-to-process document in plain-text format, while maintaining important information. This is obtained by preserving the blocks of the original HTML document, while removing HTML tags and stop-words. First, any given HTML page is parsed to identify and remove noisy elements, such as tags, comments and other non-textual items. Then, stop-words are removed from each textual excerpt. Finally, the document is typically tokenized and each term stemmed. The stemmer algorithm mostly used in practice is the well-known Porter's algorithm (Porter, 1980).

Text summarizer: It performs a syntactic analysis. Its goal is to generate a short representation of the Web page with a negligible loss of information.

Extraction-based techniques are typically applied to the blocks that form a Web page (Kolcz, et al., 2001), e.g., appropriate paragraphs and titles of the page. The text summarizer outputs a vector representation of the original HTML document as Bag of Words (BoW), each word being weighted by TFIDF (Salton & McGill, 1984). Let us recall that, for each term t_k, the TFIDF determines the weight w_{jk} of t_k in the document d_j. Comparative experiments on text summarization techniques in CA are reported in Armano et al. (2011a).

Classifier: It is devoted to perform a semantic classification. Text summarization is a purely syntactic analysis and the corresponding Web page classification is usually inaccurate. To alleviate possible harmful effects of summarization, a semantic analysis is performed by classifying both page excerpts and ads according to a given set of categories (Anagnostopoulos et al., 2007). The corresponding Classification-based Features (CF) are then used in conjunction with the original BoW.

A typical solution consists of adopting a centroid-based classification technique (Han & Karypis, 2000), which represents each class with its centroid calculated starting from the training set. A page is classified measuring the distance between its vector and the centroid vector of each class by adopting the cosine similarity.

Matcher: It is devoted to suggest ads (a) to a Web page (p) according to a similarity score based on both BoW and CF (Anagnostopoulos et al., 2007). The matching is performed by taking into account the following formula (α is a global parameter that allows to control the emphasis of the syntactic component with respect to the semantic one):

$$score(p, a) = \alpha \cdot sim_{BoW}(p, a) + (1 - \alpha) \cdot sim_{CF}(p, a)$$

where, $sim_{BoW}(p, a)$ and $sim_{CF}(p, a)$ are cosine similarity scores between p and a using BoW and CF, respectively.

Figure 2. A generic architecture for CA

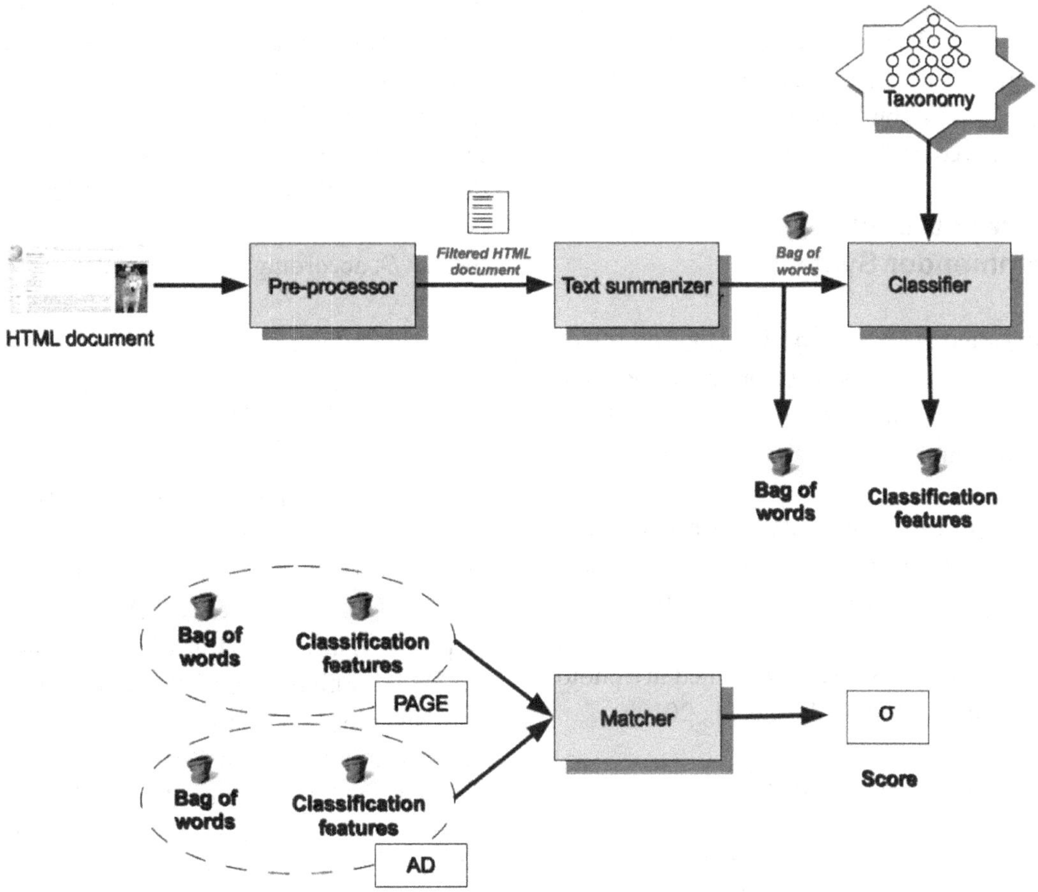

A UNIFYING VIEW

As discussed in Broder et al. (2007), CA is an interplay of four players:

- The advertiser, who provides the supply of ads;
- The publisher, who is the owner of the Web pages on which the ad is displayed;
- The ad-network, which, as a mediator between advertiser and publisher, is in charge of selecting the ads to put in the pages;
- Users, who visit the Web pages of the publisher and interact with the ads.

Nothing prevents from viewing a RS as an interplay of four players (Armano & Vargiu, 2010):

- The recommender, who provides the supply of items to be recommended;
- The publisher, who is the owner of the Web pages on which items are displayed for recommendation;
- The recommender system, which, as a mediator between recommender and publisher, is in charge of selecting the items to be recommended to a specific user;
- A user, who visits the Web pages of the publisher/recommender and interacts with the suggested items.

This new setting permits us to investigate the possibility of devising a RS a la mode of CA, and vice versa. The underlying motivation is that exchanging ideas from similar research fields may help in the task of building novel RS/CA systems with improved performances.

A Content-Based Recommender System

The first attempt aimed at proving the validity of the unifying view consists of building a RS a la mode of CA. In Addis et al. (2010a), the authors define and implement a content-based RS able to

1. Profile a user in terms of a set of given categories belonging to a taxonomy, and
2. Recommend new items to her/him.

The system has been experimented in a photo recommender system (Addis, et al., 2010b).

The Proposed Approach

Our approach for building a recommender system involves two steps: user profiling and recommendation.

For each user of the system, a profile is generated from a set of documents rated as relevant by the selected user (i.e., the user history). Then, new documents can be proposed to the user and added to her/his user history if they match the computed profile.

User Profiling

Figure 3 sketches the architecture of the proposed system, composed by four main modules: statistical document analyzer, semantic analyzer, semantic net handler, and profiler.

Statistical document analyzer: While analyzing documents rated as relevant by the user, this module is devoted to create the BoW, aimed at collecting all terms contained in the input texts,

suitably weighted. The statistical document analyzer removes from the BoW all non-informative words such as prepositions, conjunctions, pronouns, and very common verbs using a stop-word list. Subsequently, it calculates the weight of each term adopting the TFIDF measure. The statistical document analyzer calculates an overall TFDIF considering all documents contained in the user history D, according to the formula:

$$tfidf_D(t_k, D) = \frac{\sum_j tfidf_D(t_K, d_j)}{\#(D, t_k)}$$

where $\#(D, t_k)$ denotes the number of documents in D in which the term t_k occurs at least once (also known as the document frequency of t_k), whereas $tfidf_D(t_k, d_j)$ is the classical TFIDF value of t_k with respect to d_j (measured in D). Furthermore, the weights resulting from TFIDF undergo a cosine normalization. To reduce the dimensionality of the space, only the first N terms of the BoW are retained. The optimal value of N must be calculated experimentally. The set of terms stored in the BoW will be called features, hereinafter.

This module corresponds to the preprocessor and the text summarizer adopted in the previously described generic CA solution, devoted to perform a syntactic analysis.

Semantic word analyzer: This module creates the Bag of Synsets (BoS), which collects all synsets related to the selected features. To this end, the semantic document analyzer queries the online lexical database WordNet (Miller, 1995). In particular, for each feature, WordNet provides the corresponding synsets with a proper ID, the corresponding synonyms, and the meaning. After synset extraction, the semantic document analyzer assigns to each synset a weight according to the TFIDF of all related terms.

This module corresponds to a text summarizer based on semantic information. In fact, a semantic approach can be adopted in CA to improve the performances of the text summarization task.

Figure 3. The user profiler at a glance

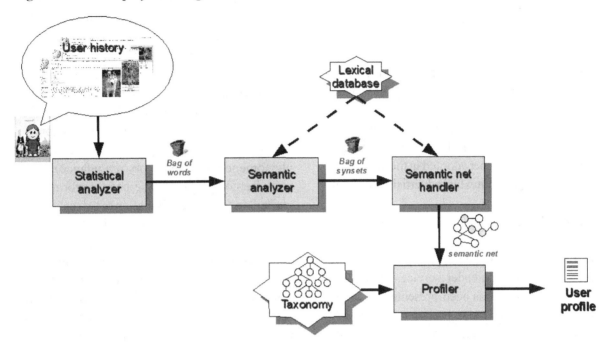

Semantic net handler: This module is aimed at performing the semantic analysis by building the semantic net from the BoS and at extracting its most relevant nodes. First, the semantic net is built in form of a graph, whose nodes are the synsets belonging to the BoS and whose edges are the semantic relations that hold between synsets. Four kinds of semantic relations are taken into account: hyponymy (sub-name) and its inverse, i.e., hypernymy (super-name); meronymy (has-part) and its inverse, i.e., holonymy (member-of). Then, the semantic net handler prunes the network by dropping non relevant nodes, identified according to their weight and to the number of connections with other nodes.

Profiler: This module is devoted to extract the user profile. To this end, it exploits the WordNet Domains Hierarchy, WNDH (Magnini & Cavagli, 2000), and associates the proper category to each selected node. Considering the selected nodes, together with their weights, the profiler is able to identify the real interests of a user in terms of WNDH categories. In particular, a user profile is represented as a set of pairs $c_k, w_k>$, where c_k is a WNDH category and w_k is the corresponding weight in the range *[0, 1]*.

The semantic net handler and the profiler modules correspond to the classifier module adopted in the previously described generic CA solution.

Recommendation

Once the profile of a user u has been generated, the system can rank a new item i to determine whether it could be of interest for the user (see Figure 4). This can be done by measuring the distance between the vector-based representation of the item, $\vec{V}(i)$, and the user profile vector $\vec{V}(u)$. In more detail, the textual information of an item i is processed in a way similar to that of profile extraction: a set of WDNH categories with the corresponding relevance ratio are computed for the item and the cosine distance between u and i is evaluated. In formula:

$$sim(i, u) = \frac{\vec{V}(i) \cdot \vec{V}(u)}{\left|\vec{V}(i)\right| \cdot \left|\vec{V}(u)\right|}$$

where the numerator represents the dot product of the vectors and the denominator is the product of their Euclidean lengths. Items that obtain a score greater than 0.5 are proposed to the user.

It is easy to note that the recommender corresponds to the matcher adopted in the previously described generic contextual advertising solution.

A Case Study

As a case study, we devised a Web application, i.e., a photo recommender service, in which a set of 700 photos[3] has been presented to 26 users, who were asked to express a rate from 1 to 5 for each photo according to their appreciation (1 means "not interesting at all," 5 means "very interesting"). Figure 5 shows a screen shot of user interface of the photo recommender (Agelli, et al., 2008).

First, to assess whether our approach can be adopted to profile users in terms of the categories they are interested in, we first adopted to the approach described in Addis et al. (2009) to build a dataset in which documents are classified according to WNDH categories. Selecting documents from such dataset allowed us to automatically create user histories. Several experiments have been performed, averaging on the number n of

categories (ranging from 1 to n) and keeping fixed (at a rate $1/n$) the amount of documents belonging to each category. Results, calculated for different numbers N of features (from 10 to 100), show that the best result is obtained for N=80.

Subsequently, we performed a preliminary study about the impact of changing the number of documents associated to a given category in a user history. As starting point for studying this phenomenon (say category imbalance), only pairwise comparisons have been performed. In particular, for each combination of two categories (say, A and B), experiments have been performed starting from 5% of documents belonging to A and 95% to B, incrementing such percentage up to 95% for A and vice versa for B (with a step of 5%). Experimental results point out that the filtering activity of the Statistical Document Analyzer is more effective when the user history is composed by a large amount of documents of a specific class. In our view, this is due to the fact that a strong bias on a given category facilitates the system in the task of identifying it. Moreover, the fact that in this case the remaining category has a lower range of variation has also a positive impact. Let us also note that this result is obtained by averaging all pairwise combinations of categories, without taking into account that some categories may be correlated (e.g., Medicine and Biology).

As for the photo recommender, the experimental setting is concerned with assessing the mean average precision of:

Figure 4. The recommender module at a glance

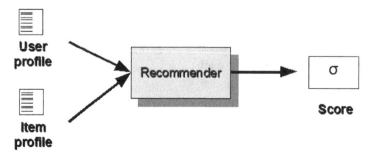

Figure 5. The photo recommender

step n. 2

Your Rating: Good

★ ★ ★ ★ ☆
CONTINUE

thailand beach

quick snap as i walked along the beach on west phuket, thailand

Author: adamskee

help

You can rate this image by clicking on the stars.

If you rate it with only 1 star, you think this image is awful. Otherwise, five stars mean that you think it's a beautiful image.

1. The proposed recommender system, say *CB*,
2. An item-based system, say *IB*, compliant with the state-of-the-art algorithm proposed in Sarwar et al. (2001), and 3) a hybrid system, say *H*, that embeds both.

The overall activity consists of 4 steps. The first step is devoted to collect preliminary information about users: to this end, each user is requested to rate 100 photos randomly selected from the 700 available. Once the first step is completed, the information is sent to *CB* and *IB*. Such information is used by the former to generate user profiles and by the latter to generate the initial user-item matrix. In the subsequent step, *CB* and *IB* select the 20 photos with the highest rating and the Web application displays them in random order. At this point, each user is required to rate the displayed photos. The step is considered completed only when all users have rated the whole set of 40 photos. Two additional steps, with the same characteristics of the one described above, have been performed with the goal of incrementally estimating the precision of each recommender in isolation from the other, as well as the precision of *H*. It is worth pointing out that the score of *H* is calculated by averaging the score of *CB* and *IB* according to a weighting schema that accounts for the corresponding precisions (each weight being in fact a normalized precision, updated at each step).

Results in terms of precision showed that the hybrid approach produces interesting results for some users, but not for all. The main reason is due to the constraining scenario, which is not particularly suitable for a content-based algorithm, since the textual descriptions of photos are scarce and often ambiguous. Moreover, most of the users probably rated more the beauty of photos rather than their subjects.

Figure 6. The proposed architecture for the hybrid CA system

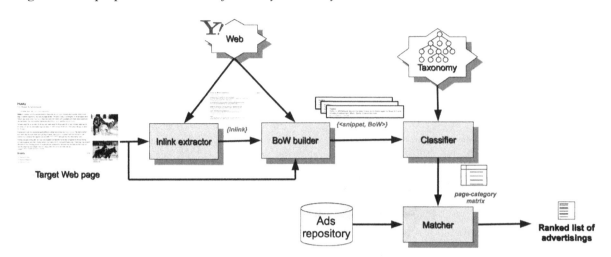

A Hybrid Contextual Advertising System

To show the validity of the unifying view we also built a CA a la mode of RS. In particular, we defined and implemented a hybrid CA that embeds collaborative characteristics into a content-based approach. The system has been experimented to put ads in a Web page.

The Proposed Approach

Our idea of a hybrid CA system relies in suggesting ads to a Web page p exploiting the "collaboration" of p with its peer pages and then analyzing the content of the peers. Figure 6 depicts the proposed high-level architecture. The architecture is composed of four modules: inlink extractor, BoW builder, classifier, and matcher.

Inlink extractor: This module is devoted to find, given a page p, the peer pages. Suitable peer pages appear to be all the inlinks of p, i.e., all pages that link to p. The underlying motivation is that a page q links a page p (i.e., it is an inlink of p) if, at least in principle, the topics of q are related to the topics of p (Koolen & Kamps, 2011). In principle, also outlinks could be taken into account, since in fact, an outlink o in p to q is an inlink to q from p. However, in the current version of the system we consider only the inlinks, as they

Figure 7. The adopted taxonomy

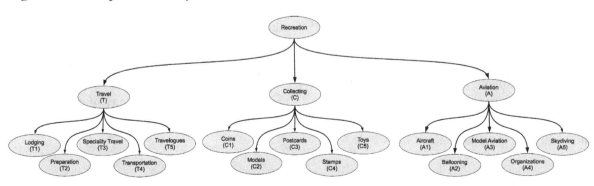

are, statistically speaking, more informative than outlinks.

The inlink extractor collects the first 10 inlinks of a given page querying the Yahoo! search engine[4]. Let us note that further solutions may be adopted, including the use of available tools (e.g., Page Inlink Analyzer5).

This module corresponds to the peer user extractor adopted in the previously described generic RS architecture.

BoW builder: Instead of considering the whole page, we first extract the snippet provided by Yahoo! From both the original page and each of its inlinks. The main purpose of this module is to process each snippet in order to remove stop-words and to stem each term by means of the Porter's algorithm. For each snippet, the module outputs a

vector representation of the original text as BoW, each word being weighted by TFIDF.

Classifier: To infer the topics of each inlink and of the original page, snippets are classified according to a given taxonomy. First, for each node of the taxonomy we merge all the queries into a single compound document. We then use it as a centroid for the Rocchio classifier (Rocchio, 1971), with only positive examples and no relevance feedback. Each centroid is defined as a sum of the TFIDF values of each term, normalized by the number of queries in the class:

$$\vec{c}_j = \frac{1}{|C_j|} \cdot \sum_{\vec{d} \in C_j} \frac{\vec{d}}{\|\vec{d}\|}$$

Figure 8. A fragment of the selected web page

Figure 9. The page-category matrix

	A	A1	A2	A3	A4	A5	C	C1	C2	C3	C4	C5	T	T1	T2	T3	T4	T5
The Rough Guides	0.033	0.024	0.009	0.040	0.015	0.012	0.029	0.018	0.012	0.006	0.023	0.026	0.045	0.033	0.032	0.024	0.014	0.039
The Savvy Traveler	0.008	0.004	0.004	0.006	0.008	0.003	0.014	0.014	0.006	0.005	0.007	0.007	0.158	0.076	0.129	0.074	0.072	0.163
University of Kansas Medical Center	0.066	0.034	0.011	0.061	0.063	0.034	0.066	0.063	0.041	0.018	0.036	0.023	0.059	0.029	0.058	0.062	0.014	0.026
Robert Wyatt interview	0.008	0.006	0.005	0.004	0.001	0.005	0.011	0.004	0.003	0.001	0.002	0.028	0.024	0.021	0.010	0.007	0.020	0.019
Travel Blog	0.002	0.000	0.002	0.002	0.001	0.001	0.010	0.005	0.002	0.002	0.006	0.015	0.042	0.018	0.040	0.021	0.021	0.038
Bur Dubai	0.025	0.021	0.010	0.025	0.017	0.007	0.033	0.024	0.018	0.007	0.016	0.032	0.056	0.051	0.035	0.020	0.029	0.039
Johnny Jet	0.015	0.013	0.001	0.015	0.014	0.005	0.005	0.001	0.007	0.002	0.000	0.005	0.231	0.240	0.073	0.098	0.222	0.097
Gardens of Paris with Dermot O'Neill	0.050	0.033	0.032	0.025	0.044	0.014	0.016	0.012	0.004	0.007	0.010	0.011	0.107	0.130	0.023	0.028	0.112	0.041
Travel Guides, backpacker info, budget travel	0.036	0.029	0.014	0.029	0.021	0.016	0.064	0.036	0.035	0.024	0.039	0.049	0.360	0.148	0.328	0.194	0.111	0.386
English Teaching Resources	0.016	0.005	0.001	0.026	0.013	0.006	0.016	0.003	0.018	0.006	0.004	0.021	0.016	0.009	0.002	0.013	0.013	0.017
Boeken over Rome	0.007	0.007	0.002	0.002	0.001	0.007	0.019	0.023	0.009	0.002	0.010	0.009	0.036	0.039	0.017	0.012	0.018	0.022
Sum:	0.266	0.177	0.090	0.235	0.198	0.110	0.283	0.203	0.156	0.079	0.154	0.226	**1.135**	**0.794**	0.747	0.553	0.646	**0.887**

where $\vec{c}_j$ is the centroid for class C_j and d ranges over the documents of a particular class. The classification is based on the cosine of the angle between the snippet and the centroid of the compound documents, in formula:

$$C_{\max} = \arg\max_{c_j \in C} \frac{\vec{c}_j}{\|\vec{c}_j\|} \cdot \frac{\vec{s}_j}{\|\vec{s}_j\|} = \arg\max_{c_j \in C} \frac{\sum_{i \in |F|} c^i \cdot s^i}{\sqrt{\sum_{i \in |F|} (c^i)^2} \sqrt{\sum_{i \in |F|} (s^i)^2}}$$

where F is the set of features. The score is normalized by the snippet and by the class length, to produce comparable score. The terms c^i and s^i represent the weights, based on the standard TFIDF formula, of the *i*th feature in the centroid of the class and of the snippet, respectively.

The classifier outputs the page-category matrix, whose generic element w_{ij} reports the score given by the classifier j (i.e., the classifier that represents the category) to the page i (which can be the given Web page or a page corresponding to one of its inlinks).

It is easy to note that the BoW builder and the classifier correspond to the content-based user profiler of the previously described generic hybrid RS system.

Matcher: This module is devoted to suggest ads to the Web page according to the corresponding categories, i.e., the content. First, the matcher calculates the three most relevant categories considering the sum of the scoring (i.e., summing the weights in column). Then, for each category, an ad is randomly extracted from the Ads repository: In the proposed system we assume that a repository in which ads are classified according to the given taxonomy is available.

This module corresponds to the matcher of the previously described generic hybrid RS.

A Case Study

As a case study, we considered the task of suggesting ads to a given Web page.

We first trained the classifier with a given dataset, i.e., a subset of DMOZ[6] Let us recall that DMOZ is the collection of HTML documents referenced in a Web directory developed in the Open

Directory Project (ODP). For our experiments we selected 18 categories, all belonging to the root Recreation, as depicted in Figure 7.

The selected Web page is the home page of the portal Rough Guides[7], an online guide that collects information useful for travelers, such as weather conditions, museums, points of interest, and photo galleries. A fragment of the home page is depicted in Figure 8.

First, the hybrid CA system queries Yahoo! asking for the first 10 inlinks. Subsequently, the corresponding snippets are pre-processed and classified, the output being a page-category matrix. Figure 9 shows the page-category matrix for the

Figure 10. The selected ads

given page, together with the sum of the scores for each category. The most significant categories are Travel (T), Travelogues (T5), and Specialty Travel (T3). Therefore, for each category, the system suggests an ad randomly extracted from the Ads repository (see Figure 10): an online travel agent, for the category Travel; an online shop of digital cameras and accessories, for the Travelogues category; and an online supplier for mountain bikes, road bikes, and accessories, for the Specialty Travel category.

The results obtained by the proposed system are compliant with the topics of the given page.

FUTURE RESEARCH DIRECTIONS

This is the first attempt to jointly study RS and CA. Since results are promising, we are encouraged to carry out further studies and experiments on this matter. In particular, we are currently studying how to improve the systems described in this chapter. As for the content-based RS, to better highlight the effectiveness of the approach, we are about to perform experiments in a scenario in which items are textual or contain textual information (e.g., implementing a system aimed at suggesting books or movies). Furthermore, we are also planning to add some collaborative features to the system (e.g., the ability of taking into account the profiles belonging to peer users). As for the hybrid CA system, we will extend the first module, to extract both inlinks and outlinks. Moreover, we are planning to modify the classifier adopting a hierarchical approach, such as the one proposed in Addis et al. (2010c). We expect that taking into account the taxonomic relationships among classes should improve the performance of classification.

Further research directions could be concerned with the study and development of RS and CA systems in social scenarios, i.e., applying them to social networks such as Facebook or Twitter.

CONCLUSION

RS and CA are IF techniques aimed at selecting and suggesting data (i.e., items and ads, respectively) to users. So far, these fields have been separately investigated and several solutions have been independently proposed in the literature. Nevertheless, in our view, some common features drive us to think that systems devised to solve one of the tasks could be easily adapted to solve the other.

In this chapter, we presented a first attempt to consider RS and CA according to a unified view. In particular, we deem that bringing ideas from CA may help to build novel RS with improved performance, and vice versa. Since CA is an emergent research field whereas RS techniques have been more and more applied in several real applications, we deem that studying CA as a RS problem may help in devising novel and effective CA systems that can be adopted in practice.

To support our insight, in this chapter we proposed and presented two novel systems, together with suitable case studies. We presented a RS inspired by a generic solution typically adopted to solve contextual advertising tasks. To show the effectiveness of the approach, we considered a photo recommender and we devised a hybrid system that embeds the proposed recommender system and a state-of-the-art item-based system. Results highlight that the proposed approach can improve the recommendations issued by the item-based system. Furthermore, we presented a novel CA system inspired by a generic (hybrid) solution typically adopted to build RS. The corresponding system has been put into practice to suggest ads to a Web page. Results showed that the suggested ads are relevant to the selected Web page.

ACKNOWLEDGMENT

This work has been partially supported by Hoplo srl. The authors would like to thank all CRS4 researchers that took part in the development of the photo recommender during the Distributed Agent-based Retrieval Tools (DART) project (http://www.dart-project.org). We would also like to thank Ugo Sirca for participating in the implementation of the hybrid CA system.

REFERENCES

Abbar, S., Bouzeghoub, M., & Lopez, S. (2009). Context-aware recommender systems: A service-oriented approach. In *Proceedings of the 35th Conference on Very Large Data-Bases*. IEEE.

Addis, A., Armano, G., Giuliani, A., & Vargiu, E. (2010a). A recommender system based on a generic contextual advertising approach. In *Proceedings of ISCC 2010: IEEE Symposium on Computers and Communications*, (pp. 859–861). IEEE Press.

Addis, A., Armano, G., Giuliani, A., & Vargiu, E. (2010b). A novel recommender system inspired by contextual advertising approach. In *Proceedings of IADIS International Conference Intelligent Systems and Agents 2010*, (pp. 67-74). IADIS.

Addis, A., Armano, G., & Vargiu, E. (2009). A novel semantic approach to document collections. *IADIS International Journal on Computer Science and Information Systems, 4*(2), 73–85.

Addis, A., Armano, G., & Vargiu, E. (2010c). Assessing progressive filtering to perform hierarchical text categorization in presence of input imbalance. In *Proceedings of International Conference on Knowledge Discovery and Information Retrieval*, (pp. 14-23). IEEE.

Adomavicius, G., Sankaranarayanan, R., Sen, S., & Tuzhilin, A. (2005). Incorporating contextual information in recommender systems using a multidimensional approach. *ACM Transactions on Information Systems, 23*(1), 103–145. doi:10.1145/1055709.1055714

Adomavicius, G., & Tuzhilin, A. (2005). Toward the next generation of recommender systems: A survey of the state-of-the-art and possible extensions. *IEEE Transactions on Knowledge and Data Engineering, 17*(6), 734–749. doi:10.1109/TKDE.2005.99

Adomavicius, G., & Tuzhilin, A. (2008). Context-aware recommender systems. In *Proceedings of the 2008 ACM Conference on Recommender Systems*, (pp. 335–336). New York, NY: ACM.

Agelli, M., Armano, G., Cherchi, G., Clemente, M. L., & Ghironi, D. (2008). Experimenting combinations of content-based and collaborative filtering with a photo recommender system. *Communications of SIWN, 5*, 33–38.

Anagnostopoulos, A., Broder, A. Z., Gabrilovich, E., Josifovski, V., & Riedel, L. (2007). Just-in-time contextual advertising. In *Proceedings of the 16th ACM Conference on Information and Knowledge Management*, (pp. 331–340). New York, NY: ACM Press.

Anand, S. S., & Mobasher, B. (2007). Contextual recommendation . In *Discovering and Deploying User and Content Profiles* (pp. 142–160). Berlin, Germany: Springer. doi:10.1007/978-3-540-74951-6_8

Armano, G., de Gemmis, M., Semeraro, G., & Vargiu, E. (Eds.). (2010). *Intelligent information access*. Berlin, Germany: Springer-Verlag. doi:10.1007/978-3-642-14000-6

Armano, G., Giuliani, A., & Vargiu, E. (2011a). Experimenting text summarization techniques for contextual advertising. In *Proceedings of the Italian Workshop on Information Retrieval, CEUR Workshop*, (Vol. 704). CEUR.

Armano, G., Giuliani, A., & Vargiu, E. (2011b). Semantic enrichment of contextual advertising by using concepts. In *Proceedings of International Conference on Knowledge Discovery and Information Retrieval*. IEEE.

Armano, G., Giuliani, A., & Vargiu, E. (2011c). Studying the impact of text summarization on contextual advertising. In *Proceedings of 8ᵗʰ International Workshop on Text-Based Information Retrieval*. IEEE.

Armano, G., & Vargiu, E. (2010). A unifying view of contextual advertising and recommender systems. In *Proceedings of International Conference on Knowledge Discovery and Information Retrieval,* (pp. 22–28). IEEE.

Asnicar, F. A., & Tasso, C. (1999) ifWeb: A prototype of user model-based intelligent agent for document filtering and navigation in the world wide web. In *Proceedings of the Workshop Adaptive Systems and User Modeling on the World Wide Web, Sixth International Conference on User Modeling*. IEEE.

Avery, C., Resnick, P., & Zeckhauser, R. (1999). The market for evaluations. *The American Economic Review, 89*(3), 564–584. doi:10.1257/aer.89.3.564

Belkin, N. J., & Croft, W. B. (1992). Information filtering and information retrieval: Two sides of the same coin? *Communications of the ACM, 35*(12), 29–38. doi:10.1145/138859.138861

Boratto, L., & Carta, S. (2010). State-of-the-art in group recommendation and new approaches for automatic identification of groups . In A. Soro, E. Vargiu, G. Armano, & G. Paddeu (Eds.), *Information Retrieval and Mining in Distributed Environments* (pp. 1–20). Berlin, Germany: Springer-Verlag. doi:10.1007/978-3-642-16089-9_1

Breese, J., Heckerman, D., & Kadie, C. (1998). Empirical analysis of predictive algorithms for collaborative filtering. In *Proceedings of the 14ᵗʰ Conference on Uncertainty in Artificial Intelligence,* (pp. 43–52). San Francisco, CA: Morgan Kaufmann.

Broder, A., Fontoura, M., Josifovski, V., & Riedel, L. (2007). A semantic approach to contextual advertising. In *Proceedings of the 30ᵗʰ Annual International ACM SIGIR Conference on Research and Development in Information Retrieval,* (pp. 559–566). New York, NY: ACM Press.

Burke, R. (2002). Hybrid recommender systems: Survey and experiments. *User Modeling and User-Adapted Interaction, 12*(4), 331–370. doi:10.1023/A:1021240730564

Carrasco, J., Fain, D., Lang, K., & Zhukov, L. (2003). Clustering of bipartite advertiser-keyword graph. In *Proceedings of the Workshop on Clustering Large Datasets, IEEE Conference on Data Mining*. IEEE Computer Society Press.

Ciaramaita, M., Murdock, V., & Plachouras, V. (2008a). Semantic associations for contextual advertising. *Journal of Electronic Commerce Research, 9*(1), 1–15.

Ciaramaita, M., Murdock, V., & Plachouras, V. (2008b). Online learning from click data for sponsored search. In *Proceeding of the 17ᵗʰ International Conference on World Wide Web*. ACM Press.

Deepayan, C., Deepak, A., & Vanja, J. (2008). Contextual advertising by combining relevance with click feedback. In *Proceeding of the 17th International Conference on World Wide Web,* (pp. 417–426). ACM Press.

Deshpande, M., & Karypis, G. (2004). Item-based top-n recommendation algorithms. *ACM Transactions on Information Systems, 22*(1), 143–177. doi:10.1145/963770.963776

Fleming, M., & Cohen, R. (1999). User modeling in the design of interactive interface agents. In *Proceedings of the 7ᵗʰ International Conference (UM 1999),* (pp. 67-76). IEEE.

Han, E. H., & Karypis, G. (2000). Centroid-based document classification: Analysis and experimental results. In *Proceedings of the 4th European Conference on Principles of Data Mining and Knowledge Discovery, PKDD 2000,* (pp. 424–431). London, UK: Springer-Verlag.

Hanani, U., Shapira, B., & Shoval, P. (2001). Information filtering: Overview of issues, research and systems. *User Modeling and User-Adapted Interaction, 11,* 203–259. doi:10.1023/A:1011196000674

Hill, W., Stead, L., Rosenstein, M., & Furnas, G. (1995). Recommending and evaluating choices in a virtual community of use. In *Proceedings of the SIGCHI Conference on Human Factors in Computing Systems,* (pp. 194–201). ACM Press.

Jameson, A., & Smyth, B. (2007). Recommendation to groups. *Lecture Notes in Computer Science, 4321,* 596–627. doi:10.1007/978-3-540-72079-9_20

Jennings, A., & Higuchi, H. (1992). A personal news service based on a user model neural network. *IEICE Transactions on Information and Systems, E, 75-D*(2), 198–210.

Jennings, A., & Higuchi, H. (1993). A user model neural network for a personal news service. *User Modeling and User-Adapted Interaction, 3*(1), 1–25. doi:10.1007/BF01099423

Joachims, T. (2002). Optimizing search engines using clickthrough data. In *Proceedings of the ACM Conference on Knowledge Discovery and Data Mining (KDD).* ACM Press.

Kantor, P. B., Boros, E., Melamed, B., Menkov, V., Shapira, B., & Neu, D. J. (2000). Capturing human intelligence in the net. *Communications of the ACM, 43*(8), 112–115. doi:10.1145/345124.345162

Kobsa, A. (1993). *User modeling: Recent work, prospects, and hazards.* Retrieved from http://www.isr.uci.edu/~kobsa/papers/1993-aui-kobsa.pdf

Kolcz, A., Prabakarmurthi, V., & Kalita, J. (2001). Summarization as feature selection for text categorization. In *Proceedings of the 10th International Conference on Information and Knowledge Management,* (pp. 365–370). ACM Press.

Koolen, M., & Kamps, J. (2011). Are semantically related links more effective for retrieval? In *Proceedings of the 33rd European Conference on Advances in Information Retrieval,* (pp. 92-103). Berlin, Germany: Springer-Verlag.

Lacerda, A., Cristo, M., Goncalves, M. A., Fan, W., Ziviani, N., & Ribeiro-Neto, B. (2006). Learning to advertise. In *Proceedings of the 29th Annual International ACM SIGIR Conference on Research and Development in Information Retrieval,* (pp. 549–556). ACM Press.

Linden, G., Smith, B., & York, J. (2003). Amazon.com recommendations. *IEEE Internet Computing, 7*(1), 76–80. doi:10.1109/MIC.2003.1167344

Liu, H., & Singh, P. (2004). ConceptNet: A practical commonsense reasoning tool-kit. *BT Technology Journal, 22,* 211–226. doi:10.1023/B:BTTJ.0000047600.45421.6d

Lops, P., de Gemmis, M., & Semeraro, G. (2010). Content-based recommender systems: State of the art and trends . In Ricci, F., Rokach, L., Shapira, B., & Kantor, P. B. (Eds.), *Recommender Systems Handbook* (pp. 73–105). New York, NY: Springer. doi:10.1007/978-0-387-85820-3_3

Magnini, B., & Cavagli, G. (2000). Integrating subject field codes into WordNet. In *Proceedings of LREC-2000, 2nd International Conference on Language Resources and Evaluation,* (pp. 1413-1418). LREC.

Malone, T., Grant, K., Turbak, F., Brobst, S., & Cohen, M. (1987). Intelligent information sharing systems. *Communications of the ACM, 30*(5), 390–402. doi:10.1145/22899.22903

McCalla, G., Searwar, F., Thomson, J., Collins, J., Sun, Y., & Zhou, B. (1996). Analogical user modeling: A case study in individualized information filtering. In *Proceedings of the 5ᵗʰ International Conference on User Modeling,* (pp. 13-20). IEEE.

Miller, G. A. (1995). WordNet: A lexical database for English. *Communications of the ACM, 38*(11), 39–41. doi:10.1145/219717.219748

Murdock, V., Ciaramita, M., & Plachouras, V. (2007). A noisy-channel approach to contextual advertising. In *Proceedings of the Workshop on Data Mining and Audience Intelligence for Advertising (ADKDD).* IEEE.

Newell, S. C. (1997). User models and filtering agents for improved internet information retrieval. *User Modeling and User-Adapted Interaction, 7*(4), 223–237. doi:10.1023/A:1008292003163

Oard, W. D. (1998). Implicit feedback for recommender systems. In *Proceedings of the American Association for Artificial Intelligent Workshop of Collaborative Systems (AAAI 1998),* (pp. 80-83). AAAI.

Porter, M. (1980). An algorithm for suffix stripping. *Program, 14*(3), 130–137. doi:10.1108/eb046814

Ramaswamy, L., Polavarapu, R., Gunasekera, K., Garg, D., Visweswariah, K., & Kalyanaraman, S. (2009). Caesar: A context-aware, social recommender system for low-end mobile devices. *IEEE International Conference on Mobile Data Management,* (pp. 338–347). IEEE Press.

Resnick, P., Iacovou, N., Suchak, M., Bergstrom, P., & Riedl, J. (1994). Grouplens: An open architecture for collaborative filtering of netnews. In *Proceedings of the 1994 ACM Conference on Computer Supported Cooperative Work,* (pp. 175–186). New York, NY: ACM Press.

Ribeiro-Neto, B., Cristo, M., Golgher, P. B., & Silva de Moura, E. (2005). Impedance coupling in content-targeted advertising. In *Proceedings of the 28ᵗʰ Annual International ACM SIGIR Conference on Research and Development in Information Retrieval,* (pp. 496–503). New York, NY: ACM Press.

Ricci, F., Rokach, L., Shapira, B., & Kantor, P. B. (Eds.). (2010). *Recommender systems handbook.* New York, NY: Springer.

Rich, E. (1998). User modeling via stereotypes. In Maybury, M. T., & Wahlster, W. (Eds.), *Readings in Intelligent User Interfaces* (pp. 329–342). San Francisco, CA: Morgan Kaufmann Publishers Inc.

Rocchio, J. (1971). Relevance feedback in information retrieval . In *The SMART Retrieval System: Experiments in Automatic Document Processing* (pp. 313–323). Upper Saddle River, NJ: Prentice Hall.

Salton, G., & McGill, M. (1984). *Introduction to modern information retrieval.* Columbus, OH: McGraw-Hill Book Company.

Sarwar, B., Karypis, G., Konstan, J., & Reidl, J. (2001). Item-based collaborative filtering recommendation algorithms. In *Proceedings of the 10ᵗʰ International Conference on World Wide Web,* (pp. 285– 295). New York, NY: ACM.

Shapira, B., Hanani, U., Raveh, A., & Shoval, P. (1997). Information filtering: A new two-phase model using stereotypic profiling. *Journal of Intelligent Information Systems*, *8*, 155–165. doi:10.1023/A:1008676625559

Shardanand, U., & Maes, P. (1995). Social information filtering: Algorithms for automating "word of mouth". In *Proceedings of the SIGCHI Conference on Human Factors in Computing Systems,* (pp. 210–217). ACM Press.

Stefani, A., & Strapparava, C. (1999). Exploiting NLP techniques to build user model for web sites: The use of WordNet in SiteIF project. In *Proceedings of the Second Workshop on Adaptive Systems and User Modeling on the World Wide Web, 8th International World Wide Web Conference*. ACM Press.

Stefanidis, K., & Pitoura, E. (2008). Fast contextual preference scoring of database tuples. In *Proceedings of EDBT,* (pp. 344-355). Nantes, France: EDBT.

Stevens, F. C. (1993). *Knowledge-based assistance for accessing large, poorly structured information spaces*. (PhD Thesis). University of California. Boulder, CO.

Terveen, L., Hill, W., Amento, B., McDonald, D., & Creter, J. (1997). Phoaks: A system for sharing recommendations. *Communications of the ACM*, *40*(3), 59–62. doi:10.1145/245108.245122

Thomas, C., & Fisher, G. (1996). Using agents to improve the usability an usefulness of the WWW. In *Proceedings of the 5ᵗʰ International Conference on User Modeling,* (pp. 5-12). IEEE.

Wei, Y. Z., Jennings, N. R., Moreau, L., & Hall, W. (2000). User evaluation of a market-based recommender system. *Autonomous Agents and Multi-Agent Systems*, *17*, 251–269. doi:10.1007/s10458-008-9029-x

Wolinski, F., Vichot, F., & Stricker, M. (2000). Using learning-based filters detect rule-based filtering obsolescence. In *Proceedings of the RIAO 2000 Conference,* (Vol 2, pp. 1208-1220). RIAO.

Yan, T. W., & Garcia-Molina, H. (1999). The SIFT information dissemination system. *ACM Transactions on Database Systems*, *24*(4), 529–565. doi:10.1145/331983.331992

Yih, W. T., Goodman, J., & Carvalho, V. R. (2006). Finding advertising keywords on web pages. In *Proceedings of the 15th International Conference on World Wide Web,* (pp. 213–222). ACM Press.

KEY TERMS AND DEFINITIONS

Classification: The task of determining and assigning class labels to data. In other words, given an input, classification consists of identifying the class(es) to which the input belongs.

Contextual Advertising (CA): A form of targeted advertising for advertisements appearing on websites or other media, such as content displayed in mobile browsers. Advertisements are selected and served by automated systems based on the content displayed to the user.

Information Filtering (IF): The task of exposing to users only the information that is relevant to them, according to their profiles and preferences.

Information Retrieval: The task of representing, storing, organizing, and accessing information items.

Lexical Database: A lexical resource, with has an associated software environment. Information typically stored in a lexical database includes lexical category and synonyms of words, as well as semantic relations between different words or sets of words.

Recommender System (RS): A specific type of information filtering system devoted to recommend information items that are likely to be of interest to the user.

Text Summarization: A technique aimed at producing summaries from textual documents. A summary is a text produced from one or more texts that conveys important information from the original text(s) with the mandatory constraint that the summary length must not be longer than half of the original text(s), but usually significantly less than that.

ENDNOTES

1. It can be very large, millions in some cases.
2. It can be very large, ranging in hundreds of thousands or even millions of items in some applications.
3. The photos were downloaded from flickr, among those fulfilling Creative Commons License and having a title and a description, which had to be related to some of the contexts included in WNDH.
4. http://www.yahoo.com
5. http://ericmiraglia.com/inlink/
6. http://www.dmoz.org
7. http://www.roughguides.co.uk/

Chapter 7
Revisiting Recommendation Systems:
Development, Lacunae, and Proposal for Hybridization

Sagarika Bakshi
ITER, SOA University, India

Alok Kumar Jagadev
ITER, SOA University, India

Sweta Sarkar
ITER, SOA University, India

Satchidananda Dehuri
Fakir Mohan University, India

ABSTRACT

Recommender systems are applied in a multitude of spheres and have a significant role in reduction of information overload on those websites that have the features of voting. Therefore, it is an urgent need for them to adapt and respond to immediate changes in user preference. To overcome the shortcomings of each individual approach to design the recommender systems, a myriad of ways to coalesce different recommender systems are proposed by researchers. In this chapter, the authors have presented an insight into the design of recommender systems developed, namely content-based and collaborative recommendations, their evaluation, their lacunae, and some hybrid models to enhance the quality of prediction.

INTRODUCTION

Over the past few decades, Web use has made its impact on various arenas like e-commerce, social networking sites, and digital libraries. However, the irony is that an enormous amount of available information is not accessible to the users since they are unaware that it exists. It is therefore necessary to broadcast in an efficient manner the relevant information to the Web users. This situation offers a very attractive framework for researching in the form of new accurate and efficient techniques designed to access this information (Campos, Luna, & Huete, 2008). Recommender Systems (RSs) are a type of information filtering system that gives advice on products, information, or services that a user may be interested in. They assist users with the decision making process when choosing items

DOI: 10.4018/978-1-4666-2542-6.ch007

with multiple alternatives. RSs are based on human social behavior where opinions and tastes of known acquaintances are taken into consideration while making decisions. RSs generate personalized recommendations incorporating various mathematical, probabilistic and soft computing techniques. Movie recommendation websites are probably the most well-known cases to users and are without a doubt the most well studied by researchers (Konstan, Miller, & Riedl, 2004; Antonopoulus & Salter, 2006; Yamada & Li, 2004) although there are many other fields in which RS have great and increasing importance, such as e-commerce (Jinghua, Kangning, & Shaohong, 2007), e-learning (Denis, 2007; Bobadilla, Serradilla, & Hernando, 2009), and digital libraries (Porcel & Herrera, 2010; Porcel, Moreno, & Herrera, 2009). Added to the meteoritic rise in dissemination of information, this decade has seen the development of many software products such as Web 2.0 that add to the generation of recommendations very abruptly. Therefore, it is a challenge for the researchers to design RS that can take into account many demographic, contextual and preference factors and predict useful items more efficiently. The core of a RS is its filtering algorithms namely knowledge, demographic, content, utility, collaborative-based or their combination, which when applied are called hybrid RS. Demographic based algorithm is established on the assumption that individuals with certain common personal attributes (sex, age, country, etc.) will also have common preferences, whilst content-based filtering recommends items similar to the ones the user preferred in the past. Utility-based and knowledge-based recommenders do not attempt to build long-term generalizations about their users, but rather base their advice on an evaluation of the match between a user's need and the set of options available. Utility-based recommenders make suggestions based on the computation of the utility of each object for the user. However, the issue is how to create a utility function for each user. Currently, Collaborative Filtering (CF) is the most commonly used and

studied technique based on the principle in which in order to make a recommendation to a given user, it first searches for the users of the system who have voted in the most similar way to this user, to later make the recommendations by taking the items most highly valued by the majority of their similar users (Fernando, Hernando, & Alca, 2011).Various approaches to recommend the items in a domain are:

- **Demographic Filtering (DMF):** The user is recommended those items similar to the ones other people with same demographic profile preferred. Lifestyle Finder uses demographic groups from marketing research to suggest a range of products and services.
- **Content-Based Filtering (CBF):** The user is recommended those items similar to the ones he preferred in the past. Example of such systems is News Weeder.
- **Collaborative Filtering (CF):** The user is recommended those items which people with similar tastes and preferences liked in the past. GroupLens, MovieLens, and Ringo are some examples of such systems.
- **Hybrid Filtering:** These techniques combine more than one filtering technique to enhance the performance like Fab, Amazon.com.

In this chapter an extensive study of content-based, collaborative, and hybrid filtering of recommender systems is done.

BACKGROUND STUDY

Specifically, recommender systems have:

- **Background data:** The information that the system has before the recommendation process begins.
- **Input data:** The information that user must communicate to the system in order to generate a recommendation.

• An algorithm that combines background and input data to arrive at its suggestions.

On this basis, five different recommendation techniques can be represented, as shown in Table 1 (Burke, 2002).

Basically, to build a RS using any filtering technique, a model for each user is required which must reflect the user preferences and taste. The key success of any filtering technique comes from the way it learns user models (Yahya, Shamri, & Bharadwaj, 2008). The CBF learns the model from the features describing the items the user has rated in the past, whereas CF learns the model from ratings of the items themselves. Basically, to build a RS using any filtering technique, a model for each user is required which must reflect the user preferences and taste. The key success of any filtering technique comes from the way it learns user models (Yahya, Shamri, & Bharadwaj, 2008). The CBF learns the model from the features describing the items the user has rated in the past, whereas CF learns the model from ratings of the items themselves. In real life, users put some priorities for each feature and these priorities need learning also. This makes the application of soft-computing techniques in the design of RS. Many hybrid R.S used the evolutionary search to learn these priorities tailoring the recommendation process to the preferences of each individual user. The main shortcomings of CBF are content limitations, which means only a very superficial analysis of certain kinds of content can be supplied, and over-specialization; the user is restricted to see items similar to those already rated by him only.

These systems are not suitable for dynamic and very large environments, where items are millions and inserted in the system frequently. The great power of CF relative to CBF is its cross-genre or 'outside the box' recommendation ability (Yahya, Shamri, & Bharadwaj, 2008). Moreover, CF is completely independent of any machine-readable representation of the items being recommended. However, CF suffers some weaknesses: new user problem (cold start problem), sparsity, scalability, and loss of neighbor transitivity. Usually each user rates only a very limited percentage of items, when compared to the total available. This leads to sparse user-item matrices; the set of users cross the set of items, therefore weak recommendations could be produced because the successful neighbors cannot be found. On the other hand, the computational cost of RS grows fast with both the number of users and items, thus giving rise to scalability problem. Moreover, both content-based and collaborative techniques suffer from the "portfolio effect," which means

Table 1. Recommendation techniques

Technique	Background	Input	Process
Collaborative	Ratings from U of items in I	Ratings from U of items in I	Identify users in U similar to u, and extrapolate from their ratings of i.
Content based	Features of items in I	u's ratings of items in I.	Generate a classifier that fits u's rating behaviour and use it on i.
Demographic	Demographic information about U and their ratings of items in I.	Demographic information about u.	Identify users that are demographically similar to u, and extrapolate from their ratings of i.
Utility based	Features of items in I.	A utility function over items in I that describes u's preferences.	Apply the function to the items and determines i's rank.
Knowledge based	Features of items in I. Knowledge of how these items meet a user's need.	A description of u's needs or interests.	Infer a match between i and u's need.

an ideal recommender would not suggest a stock that the user already owns or a movie she has already seen. The problem becomes quite tricky in domains such as news filtering, since stories that look quite similar to those already read may in fact present some new facts or new perspectives that would be valuable to the user.

To overcome the shortcomings of the above-mentioned systems, many hybrid algorithms have been proposed by researchers that could exploit the merits of each individual model. Added to it this decade has witnessed evolution of many soft-computing techniques that have been incorporated in the design of many recommender systems. Burke has analyzed the lacunae of various R.S and has provided a comparison of existing RS as following Table 2 (Burke, 2002).

In a hybrid model, two or more techniques could be integrated as in the following Table 3 (Burke, 2002).

A weighted hybrid recommender is one in which the score of a recommended item is computed from the results of all of the available recommendation techniques present in the system. For example, the simplest combined hybrid would be a linear combination of recommendation scores. The P-TangoA switching hybrid builds in item-level sensitivity to the hybridization strategy: the

system uses some criterion to switch between recommendation techniques. The DailyLearner system uses a content/collaborative hybrid in which a content-based recommendation method is employed first. If the content-based system cannot make a system recommendation with sufficient confidence, then a collaborative recommendation is attempted that uses such hybrid. Where it is practical to make large number of recommendations simultaneously, it may be possible to use a "mixed" hybrid, where recommendations from more than one technique are presented together. The PTV system uses this approach to assemble a recommended program of television viewing. It uses content-based techniques based on textual descriptions of TV shows and collaborative information about the preferences of other users. Recommendations from the two techniques are combined together in the final program. Another way to achieve the content/collaborative merger is to treat collaborative information as simply additional feature data associated with each example and use content-based techniques over this augmented data set.

For the inductive rule learner Ripper was applied to the task of recommending movies using both user ratings and content features, and achieved significant improvements in precision

Table 2. Trade-offs between various RS

Technique	Pluses	Minuses
Collaborative filtering (CF)	A. Can identify cross genre niches. B. Domain knowledge not needed. C. Adaptive: quality improves over time. D. Implicit feedback sufficient.	I. New user ramp-up problem. J. New item ramp-up problem. K. "Gray sheep" problem. L. Quality dependent on large historical data set. M. Stability vs. Plasticity problem.
Content based (CN)	B, C, D	I, L, M
Demographic (DF)	A, B, C	I, K, L, M N must gather demographic information
Utility-based (UT)	E. No ramp-up required F. Sensitive to changes of preferences. G. Can include non-product features	O. User must input utility function. P. Suggestion ability static.
Knowledge-Based (KB)	E, F, G H can map from user needs to products.	P Q. Knowledge engineering required

Table 3. Hybridization methods

HYBRIDIZATION METHOD	DESCRIPTION
Weighted	The scores (or votes) of several recommendation techniques are combined together to produce a single recommendation.
Switching	The system switches between recommendation techniques depending on current situation.
Mixed	Recommendations from several different recommenders are presented at the same time.
Feature Combination	Features from different recommendation data sources are thrown together into a single recommendation algorithm.
Cascade	One recommender refines the recommendations given by another.
Feature augmentation	Output from one technique is used as an input feature to another.
Meta-level	The model learned by one recommender is used as input to another.

over a purely collaborative approach. Unlike the previous hybridization methods, the cascade hybrid involves a staged process. In this technique, one recommendation technique is employed first to produce a coarse ranking of candidates and a second technique refines the recommendation from among the candidate set. The restaurant recommender EntreeC is a cascaded knowledge-based and collaborative recommender. In case of Feature Augmentation, a technique is employed to produce a rating or classification of an item and that information is then incorporated into the processing of the next recommendation technique. For example, the Libra system makes content-based recommendations of books based on data found in Amazon.com, using a naive Bayes text classifier. In the text data used by the system is included "related authors" and "related titles" information that Amazon generates using its internal collaborative systems. These features were found to make a significant contribution to the quality of recommendations. Many models and their lacunae have been studied and their enhancements have been evolved to cater to the needs of dynamic information overload. Some have applied traditional metrics, some have applied evolutionary techniques and some have incorporated many phases to build an intelligent system.

CONTENT-BASED RECOMMENDER SYSTEM

In the context based recommendation system an item is recommended to the user based upon a description of the item and a profile of the user's interest. Content-based recommendation systems may be used in a variety of domains ranging from recommending Web pages, news articles, restaurants, television programs, and items for sale. Although the details of various systems differ, content-based recommendation systems share in common a means for describing the items that may be recommended, a means for creating a profile of the user that describes the types of items the user likes, and a means of comparing items to the user profile to determine what to recommend. The profile is often created and updated automatically in response to feedback on the desirability of items that have been presented to the user.

User Profile

A profile of the user's interests is used by most recommendation systems. This profile may consist of a number of different types of information. However, most of the recommendation systems mainly focus on two types of information:

1. A model of the user's preferences, i.e., a description of the types of items that interest the user. There are many possible alternative representations of this description, but one common representation is a function that for any item predicts the likelihood that the user is interested in that item. For efficiency purposes, this function may be used to retrieve the n items most likely to be of interest to the user.

2. A history of the user's interaction with the recommendation system. This may include storing the items that the user has viewed together with the other information about the user's interaction such as whether the user has purchased the items or the ratings given by the user to an item.

Learning a User Model

Creating a user's preferences model from the user's history is a form of classification learning. The training data of the classification learner is divided into two binary categories, 'items the user likes' and the 'item the user doesn't like.' This is accomplished either through explicit feedback in which the user rates items via some interface for collecting feedback or implicitly by observing the user's interactions with items. Following is a Webpage of a R.S using explicit feedback (see Figure 1).

Given a new item and the user model, the function predicts whether the user would be interested in the item. Many of the classification learning algorithms create a function that will provide an estimate of the probability that a user will like an unseen item. This probability may be used to sort a list of recommendations. Alternatively, an algorithm may create a function that directly predicts a numeric value such as the degree of interest.

Nearest Neighbour Methods

In order to classify a new, unlabeled item, the algorithm compares it to all stored items using a similarity function and determines the "nearest neighbor" or the k nearest neighbors. The class label or numeric score for a previously unseen item can then be derived from the class labels of the nearest neighbors. The similarity function used by the nearest neighbor is depends on the type of data. In case of the structured data Euclidean distance metric is used. In case of the vector space model cosine similarity metric is often used. The vector space approach and the cosine similarity function have been applied to several text classification applications.

COLLABORATIVE RECOMMENDER SYSTEM

The most significant part of CF algorithms refers to the group of metrics used to determine the similitude between each pair of users (Ingoo, Kyong, & Tae, 2003; Adomabicius & Tuzhilin, 2005; Bobadilla, Seradilla, & Bernal, 2010), among which the Pearson correlation metric stands out as a reference for many models. Collaborative filtering algorithms can be classified as memory based or model-based algorithms. Memory-based algorithms are heuristics based algorithms, which utilize the entire rating history to arrive at predictions. These include the commonly implemented class of user-based and item based CF methods (Anand & Bharadwaj, 2011). Model-based recommender systems build a user-model in an off-line learning phase and then apply this model on-line for recommendation. The accuracy offered by memory-based RS, since they examine the entire rating database for prediction, and their simplicity, is the reason for their popularity.

Recommender systems that utilize memory-based algorithms and utilize a user-item matrix to generate a prediction fall under the memory

Figure 1. A recommendation system using explicit feedback (adapted from Pazzani, 2007)

based recommender systems category. There are three steps into processing a recommendation based on a CF system:

1. Representation
2. Neighbourhood Formation
3. Recommendation Generation

Generalized RecSys Framework

Step 1: Compute local user similarities $sim_L(i,j)$. Compute the similarities between all pairs of users.

Step 2: Compute the global user similarities $sim_G(i,j)$.

Step 3: Obtain predicted ratings using local and global neighbours which for an item k for active user u is based on Resnick's prediction formula:

$$pr_{i,k} = \bar{r_1} + \frac{\sum_{j \in N(i)} sim_{i,j} * (r_{j,k} - \bar{r_i})}{\sum_{j \in N(i)} |sim_{i,j}|}$$

Step 4: The predicted ratings from local and global neighbourhoods are combined using the following formula:

$$pr_{i,k} = (1 - \propto) * pr_{i,k}^L + \propto * pr_{i,k}^G$$

Similarity between two users can be computed from any of the following methods:

Let's say,

1. $v_{i,j}$ = vote of user i on item j
2. I_i = items for which user i has voted
   Mean vote for i is:

$$\overline{v_1} = \frac{1}{|I_i|} \sum_{j \in I_i} v_{i,j}$$

3. Predicted vote for "active user" a is weighted sum:

$$P_{a,j} = \overline{v_a} + k \sum_{i=1}^{n} w(a,i)(v_{i,j} - \overline{v_1})$$

Suppose user-item links were probabilities of following a link, then w (a,i) is the probability of *a* and i "meeting." This probability can be computed as follows:

1. k-nearest neighbor

$$w(a,i) = \begin{cases} 1 \_ if \_ i \in neighbors(a) \\ 0 \_ elsewhere \end{cases}$$

2. Pearson correlation coefficient (Resnick, 1994):

$$w(a,i) = \frac{\sum_j \dfrac{(v_{a,j} - \overline{v_a})}{(v_{i,j} - \overline{v_1})}}{\sqrt{\sum_j \dfrac{(v_{a,j} - \overline{v_a})\char`^2}{\sum_j (v_{i,j} - \overline{v_1})\char`^2}}}$$

3. Cosine distance (from IR)

$$w(a,i) = \sum_j \frac{v_{a,j}}{\sqrt{\sum_{k \in I_a} v_{a,k}^2}} \frac{v_{i,j}}{\sqrt{\sum_{k \in I_i} v_{i,k}^2}}$$

The cosine distance between two users a and i can be visualized as in Figure 2. The parameter α serves to adjust the weight that we give to global neighbours with regards to the weight that we give to the local neighbours. When the ratings matrix is dense then generally the local neighbourhood set is rich enough to enable prediction for the active user, in which case the predictions from local neighbourhood should be weighed more. However, when the ratings matrix is sparse, the meagre local neighbourhood set generated may lead to low quality recommendations, and therefore it needs to be enriched by the globally similar neighbours for better predictions.

Anand and Bharadwaj (2011) have proposed several sparsity measures which enable the global neighbors to be weighed according to the active user and the item whose vote needs to be predicted. The dependency of the α value on the user and item ensures that the local and global neighbors are weighed differently for every user and for every prediction. Prior to it fixed α schemes were proposed:

1. Fixed: A scheme 1 (Luo, et al., 2008).
2. Fixed: A scheme 2 (Luo, et al., 2008).

But improvising on the α scheme has provided better predictions.

1. Overall Sparsity Measure (OS):
    $$Overall sparsity measure = 1 - \frac{nR}{nUSERS * nITEMS}$$
    where, where nR is the total number of ratings which exist, nUsers is the total number of users in the system and nItems is the total number of items.

2. User Specific Sparsity measure (USS):
    $$user specific sparsity measure = 1 - \frac{n_a}{\max(n_u)}$$
    where n_u is the number of items rated by user u.

3. Local Global Ratio (LGR)
    $$LGR(u,i) = 1 - \frac{L_{u,i}}{G_{u,i}}$$
    where $L_{u,i}$ is the set of local neighbors of user u who have rated item i, $G_{u,i}$ is the set of global neighbors of user u who have rated item i.

4. User-Item Specific Sparsity measure 1 (UIS1):
    $$UIS1(u,i) = 1 - \frac{|L_u|}{|N_i|}$$
    where N_i is the set of users who have rated item i.

5. User-Item Specific Sparsity measure 2 (UIS2):
    $$U1S2(u,i) = 1 - \frac{|L_{u,i}|}{|L_u|}$$

where L_u is the set of local neighbours for user u.

6. Unified measure of sparsity (UMS)–GA approach

$$UMS = W_1 OS + W_2 USS + W_3 LGR + W_4 U1S1 + W_5 U1S2$$

where,

$$\sum_{i=1}^{s} W_i = 1$$

Evaluation

The evaluation of the recommender system was done by Anand and Bharadwaj (2011) as follows:

The MAE (u_i) for the active user u_i is:

$$MAE\left(u_i\right) = \frac{1}{|S_i|} \sum_{k=1}^{|S_i|} \left| pr_{i,k} - r_{i,k} \right|$$

where $|S_i|$ is the cardinality of the test ratings set of user u_i. The total MAE over all the active users, N_T can be computed as:

$$MAE = \frac{1}{N_r} \sum_{i=1}^{N_r} MAE\left(U_i\right)$$

A smaller value of MAE signifies better prediction quality. A related accuracy metric is the RMSE which squares the error before summing them.

The RMSE (u_i) for active user u_i can be defined as:

$$RMSE\left(U_i\right) = \sqrt{\frac{1}{|S_i|} \sum_{k=1}^{|S_i|} \left(pr_{i,k} - r_{i,k}\right)^{\wedge} 2}$$

The RMSE over all active users is the average of RMSE of individual active users.

$$RMSE = \frac{1}{N_r} \sum_{i=1}^{N_r} RMSE\left(u_i\right)$$

The error in prediction has been calculated (Anand & Bharadwaj, 2011) taking into consideration the above formulae and tabulated as Table 4.

Figure 2. Visualising cosine distance

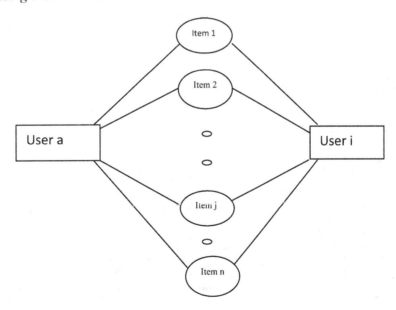

Inference

Of all the schemes UMS method outperforms under all configurations, both in terms of MAE as well as RMSE. UMS is able to offer better quality predictions. However, the computational complexity grows linearly with the number of customers and items. Therefore, hybrid models are to be adopted in order to provide be predictions with better accuracy.

HYBRID RECOMMENDER SYSTEM (CBBCHPRS)

The hybrid approach proposed named as CB-BCHPRS (Centering-Bunching Based Clustering Hybrid Personalized Recommender System [Shinde & Kulkarni, 2011]) extracts user's current browsing patterns using Web usage mining, and forms a cluster of items with similar psychology to obtain implicit users rating for the recommended item. The system architecture that they have designed has been partitioned into two main phases: offline and online. The phase I is offline. It does the pre-processing and clustering. In this phase, background data in the form of user-item rating matrix is collected and clustered. Once the clusters are obtained the cluster data along with their centroids are stored for future recommenda-

tions. The phase II is online in which the recommendation takes place for the active user. Here, similarity and density of clusters are calculated for choosing best clusters for making recommendations. The rating quality of each item unrated by active user is computed in the chosen clusters. To generate the recommendations, clusters are further selected based on rating quality of an item. The recommendations are then made by computing the weighted average of the rating of items in the selected clusters. The architecture of the system is shown in Figure 3 (Burke, 2002).

The working of the system can be demonstrated as follows:

Pre-Processing Phase

Normalization of Data

User-item rating taken from Jester dataset rated in the scale of -10 to +10 is normalized in the scale of 0 to 1, where 0 indicates that item is not rated by corresponding user.

Centering-Bunching Based Clustering

In the K-means, and new K-mediods clustering algorithm centroids were initially selected by the user. Therefore, performance of these algorithms depended on the manual selection of centroids.

Table 4. MAE and RMSE comparison of various weighing schemes on ML-300

Configurations	Error	Fixed-α Scheme 1	Fixed-α Scheme 2	LGR	US1	US2	OS	USS	UMS
10	MAE	0.852652	0.846077	0.832761	0.833769	0.834540	0.837084	0.838417	0.829230
	RMSE	1.047549	1.046703	1.041914	1.041470	1.040415	1.042390	1.043752	1.036936
15	MAE	0.834998	0.828519	0.799258	0.799396	0.799260	0.801574	0.802726	0.796225
	RMSE	1.024083	1.020234	0.996773	0.995680	0.993368	0.995504	0.996690	0.991263
20	MAE	0.832258	0.825387	0.795202	0.796822	0.795784	0.800076	0.800990	0.793316
	RMSE	1.016667	1.014926	0.994329	0.994564	0.991338	0.995320	0.996373	0.990454
25	MAE	0.823745	0.817562	0.791298	0.793779	0.791601	0.796753	0.797741	0.788414
	RMSE	1.011413	1.010889	0.990690	0.991102	0.987201	0.991261	0.992035	0.985489

Figure 3. System architecture of CBBCHPRS

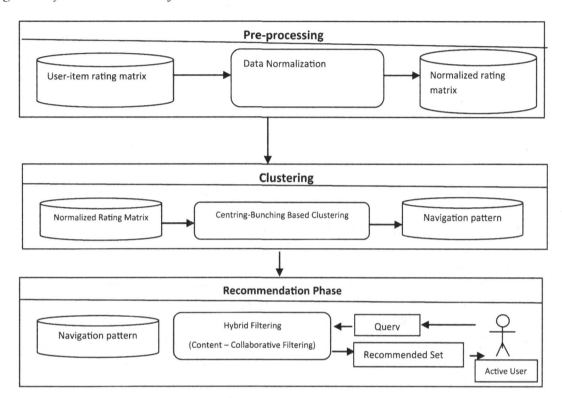

But in CBBCHPRS centroids are initially calculated appropriately, which resulted in the proper creation of the clusters. The clustering algorithm consists of three steps, determining the centroids, bunching and removing bunched patterns.

Recommendation Process for the Active User

Choosing the Appropriate Clusters

The cluster (s) to be chosen depends upon two factors viz., density of the cluster and similarity with active user profile. The probability Pi(t) that the cluster i is chosen for generating recommendations at time t is expressed as:

$$P_i\left(t\right) = \frac{\delta_i\left(t\right)sim_i}{\sum_{j=1}^{k}\delta_j\left(t\right).sim_j}$$

where sim_i is the value of similarity function to measure the similarity between the active user profile and the centroid of the ith cluster, $\delta i(t)$ is the density of ith cluster at time t and k is the total number of clusters.

The density of the cluster is determined by the following equation:

$$\delta_{i(t)} = \frac{Number of users in clustering}{Total number of users}$$

If the numbers of users in a cluster are more, the density is more and vice versa.

The similarity measure of the active user profile is calculated with each cluster in order to find clusters, which has user with similar preferences. There are number of possible measures for computing the similarity, for example the Euclidean distance metric, cosine similarity, and the Pearson correlations metric.

But in the CBBCHPRS the Euclidean distance formula is used, which is as follows:

$$sim_i\left(cent_i, U\right) = \left\{\sum_{j=1}^{d}\left|cent_{i,j} - U_j\right|^2\right\}^{1/2}$$

where d is dimension of data i.e. No. of attributes, $Cent_i$ is the centroid of the cluster i, U is active user profile, $cent_{i,j}$ is j^{th} attribute of the centroid profile in cluster i, and U_j is the jth attribute of the active user profile.

The clusters whose probability value lies in the range {(highest probability-0.1) <= probability <= (highest probability)} are chosen for generating recommendations for the active users instead of only the cluster with highest probability. This overcomes the limitation of Collaborative Filtering recommender system where recommendations are provided based only on the opinion of the user with most similar preferences.

Computing the Rating Quality of the Item in Each Chosen Cluster

The rating quality depends on the number of users in the cluster who has rated the items, the individual ratings for the item in the given rating matrix and how close the rating provided by the users is, to each other. The rating quality of the item, Q is computed as:

$$Q = \frac{\max\_rating + avg\_rating}{2*\max\_rating}$$

where, max_rating is equal to the highest rating of given item and avg_rating is equal to the average rating of the item in the chosen cluster. If the rating quality of item close to 1, indicates that user has provided good quality rating and vice versa.

Rating of Items

The rating of each item is then computed from the selected clusters by computing the weighted average of the ratings using the following equation:

$$Rating = \frac{\sum_{i-1}^{n}\left(Q_i \times avg\_rating\right)}{\sum_{i-1}^{n}Q_i}$$

where Q_i is a quality of the item in the selected cluster, n is number of clusters selected, and avg_rating is an average rating of the item in the selected clusters.

Provide Recommendations to Active User

Once the quality rating of each item is calculated, the recommendation to the active user is provided.

Inference

In traditional recommender system similarity is normally the only heuristic used in recommendation process where as in CBBCHPRS, similarity is combined with density of the clusters. This helps in the exploration of other clusters, which have similarity closer to the active user and provide him/her with good set of recommendations. Therefore, this incorporation of clustering methods aids in generation of better recommendations.

HYBRID RECOMMENDER SYSTEM (BAYESIAN NETWORK COLLABORATIVE RECOMMENDER SYSTEM)

Recommender systems enable users to access products or articles that they would otherwise not be aware of due to the wealth of information to be found on the Internet. The two traditional recommendation techniques are content-based and collaborative filtering. While both methods have their advantages, they also have certain disadvantages, some of which can be solved by combining both techniques to improve the quality of the recommendation. The resulting system is known as a hybrid recommender system. In the context of artificial intelligence, Bayesian networks, as demonstrated in Figure 4, have been widely and successfully applied to problems with a high level of uncertainty. The field of recommendation represents a very interesting testing ground to put these probabilistic tools into practice.

1. **Features nodes:** There will be an attribute node F_k for each feature used to describe a product. Each node has an associated binary random variable which takes its values from the set $\{f_{k,0}, f_{k,1}\}$ which means that the kth feature is not relevant (not apply), $\{f_{k,0}\}$ or is relevant (apply), $\{f_{k,1}\}$, for the description of the content of a product.

2. **Item nodes:** Similarly, there is a node I_j for each item. The random variable associated with I_j will take its values from the set $\{I_{j,0}, I_{j,1}\}$ meaning that the item is not relevant (not apply) or is relevant (apply), respectively, when it comes to predicting the user's rating.

3. **User nodes:** These U_i nodes used to predict the ratings of the target items, particularly they should represent how probable the user rates with s an item. The domain of this variable is therefore from the set $\{R \cup 0\}$. The additional value 0 is included to represent the lack of knowledge.

4. In this model, A is an active user. The system has used both the collaborative approach and the content based recommendation to give the prediction of the target item I_s.

Canonical Weighted Sum

Let X_i be a node in a BN, let $Pa(X_i)$ be the parent set of X_i and let Y_k be the kth parent of X_i in the BN. By using a canonical weighted sum, the set of conditional probability distributions stored at node X_i are then represented by means of following equation:

$$\Pr\left(X_{i,j} \middle/ Pa(X_i)\right) = \sum_{Y_k \in Pa(X_i)} w\left(Y_{k,1}, X_{i,j}\right)$$

The system design is illustrated in Figure 5.

Results and Evaluation

After a set of predicted votes is generated, it is compared with the actual votes made by the users. Based on this comparison precision and recall is calculated for each of this user.

$$recall = \frac{true\,positve}{true\,positive + false\,negative}$$

$$precision = \frac{true\,positive}{true\,positive + false\,positive}$$

The final measure F is calculated by:

$$F - measure = \frac{2 \times precision \times recall}{precision + recall}$$

PROBABILISTIC-BASED RECOMMENDER SYSTEM

By focusing on a probabilistic approach to recommender systems, many variants can be found. Generally, and in order to model the recommending problem with BN it is necessary to learn the structure from a set of observed data. There are two main approaches for finding the structure. The first approach poses a learning constraint satisfaction problem. By estimating properties of dependencies or independencies among the attributes in the data, a network that exhibits the underlying

Figure 4. Feature, user, and item layered Bayesian network

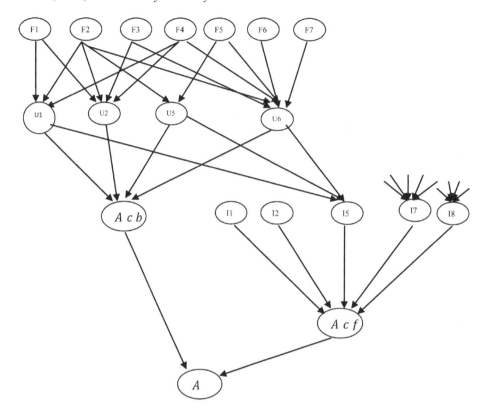

relationships is built. The second approach poses learning as an optimization problem. By means of a statistically motivated score, a search for an optimal structure that is optimum to the observed data is performed.

Thus, focusing on content-based RS, learning as constraint satisfaction problem is posed in Butz (2002) where the user profile is learnt considering contextual independences. Also, by assuming independence between variables, Bayesian classifiers have been used in Mooney and Roy (2000) and Pazzani and Billsu (1997) to estimate the probability that an item belongs to a certain class (relevant or irrelevant) given the item description.

Finally Campos, Fernandez, Gomez, and Huete (2005) and Campos, Fernandez, and Huete (2005) model the item descriptions with a BN and estimate the probability that a user rates an item with a value given the user preferences

(also represented by means of a subset of content features). In Junzhon, Liu, and Zhong (2004), learning is posed as an optimization problem and applies a Branch and Bound methodology to search for the structure optimizing the observed data with an scoring criterion and (Sehiaffino & Amandi, 2000) uses learning algorithms to built a user profile by combining BNs with case-based reasoning techniques

INCORPORATION OF SOFT COMPUTING TECHNIQUES IN DESIGN OF RS

Soft computing techniques can very well present various metrics to measure similarity between users, which is applicable in collaborative filtering processes carried out in recommender systems. Genetic Algorithms (GA) have mainly been used

Figure 5. System design of the hybrid recommender system (adapted from Kunaver, et al., 2007)

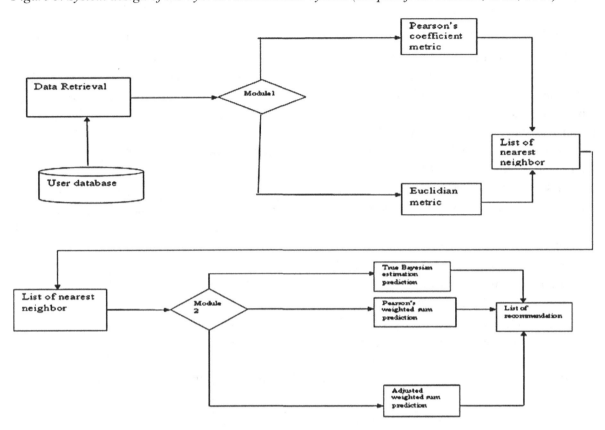

in two aspects of RS: clustering (Kim & Ahn, 2004, 2008; Zhang & Chang, 2006)and hybrid user models (Gao & Li, 2008; Ho, Fong, & Yan, 2007; Al-Shamri & Bharadwaj, 2008). The metric used by Jesus and Ortega (2011) was calculated via a simple linear combination of values and weights. Values were calculated for each pair of users between which the similarity is obtained, whilst weights are only calculated once, making use of a prior stage in which a genetic algorithm extracts weightings from the recommender system which depend on the specific nature of the data from each recommender system. The results obtained had presented significant improvements in prediction quality, recommendation quality, and performance. The RS hybrid user models commonly use a combination of CF with demographic filtering or CF with content based filtering, to exploit merits of each one of these techniques. In these cases, the chromosome structure can easily contain the demographic characteristics and/or those related to content-based filtering.

Design of New Similarity Method

The fundamental objective of including soft computing methods is to improve the results of CF by obtaining a metric that improves the accuracy (Herlocker, Konstan, Riedl, & Terveen, 2004; Giaglis & Lekakos, 2006; Bobadilla, Ortega, & Hernando, 2011) of CF based RS. For this purpose, a series of experiments were carried out by researchers on different metrics, different levels of sparsity (Papagelis, Plexousakis, & Kutasuras, 2005; Bobadilla & Serradilla, 2009), and different databases.

Values

We will consider a RS with a set of U users, {1, . . ., U}, and a set of I items {1, . . ., I}. Users rate those items they know with a discrete range of possible values {m, . . ., M} where m usually represents that the user keeps completely unsatisfied about an item, and a value M usually represents that the user is completely satisfied with an item. Recommender System normally uses m with value 1 and M with value 5 or 10. In this way, the range of possible ratings is usually {1, . . ., 5} or {1, . . ., 10}.

The ratings made by a particular user x can be represented by a vector, $r_x = (r_x^1, r_x^2, ..., r_x^1)$ with dimension l (the number of items in the RS) in such way that r_x^1 represents the rating that the user x has made over the item i. The expression $r_x^1 = $ to state that the user x has not rated an item.

Similarity

For each vector $w = (w^0, ... w^{(M-m)})$ the following similarity function is considered

$$\text{sim}_w(x, y) = \frac{1}{M - m + 1} \sum_{i=0}^{M-m} w^i v_{x,y}^i$$

- Since $w^{(0)} = 1$, this similarity function evaluates highly positively the number of items rated identically.
- Since $w^{(4)} = -1$, this similarity function evaluates highly negatively the number of items which have been rated in opposite way $\left(w_x^{(0)} = -1 \right)$.
- Since $w^{(2)} = 0$, this similarity function takes no consideration of those items over which the difference between the ratings made by both users is 2.
- Since $w^{(1)} = 0.5$, this similarity function evaluates with a positive intermediate value those items over which the difference

between the ratings made by both users is 1.
- Since $w^{(3)} = -0.5$, this similarity function evaluates with a negative intermediate value those items over which the difference between the ratings made by both users is 3.

Genetic Representation

Individuals of populations are represented in binary form as strings of 0s and 1s. Each component $w^{(i)}$ in the vector of w will be represented by 10 bits. Consequently, the vector $w = (w^0, ... w^{(M-m)})$ will be represented by the following string of 0s and 1s (with a length of $2^{10(M-m+1)}$ bits.

$$b_{M-m}{}^9 ...... b_{M-m}{}^1 b_{M-m}{}^0 b_{M-m-1}{}^9 ...... b_0{}^9 ...... b_0{}^1 b_1 b_1{}^0$$

where each component of the vector $w_i \in [-1, 1]$ can be obtained through the following expression:

$$w_i = \frac{2 \sum_{j=10}^9 2^j b_i{}^j}{2^{10} - 1} - 1$$

Initial Population

In order to choose the population size, we have considered the criterion of using a number of individuals in the population, which is the double of the number of bits used to represent each individual. Consequently, when using Movielens and Netflix the initial population will be of 100 individuals, in view that in both recommender systems M = 5 and m = 1, but when using FilmAffinity (where M = 10 and m = 1) the initial population would be of 200 individuals.

Fitness Function

The fitness function of a genetic algorithm is used to prescribe the optimality of a similarity function

sim_w (for the individual w). In our genetic algorithm, the fitness function will be the Mean Absolute Error (MAE) of the RS.

The MAE is obtained by comparing the real ratings with the predicted ratings made according to the similarity function. In order to calculate the MAE of the RS for a particular similarity function sim_w, we need to follow the next steps for each user x:

Deviation From Mean (DFM) as aggregation approach:

$$P_x^i = r_x + \frac{\sum_{n \in k_x} (sim_w(x,n) \times (r_n^i - \bar{r}_n))}{\sum_{n \in k_x} sim_w(x,n)}$$

where $\bar{r}_x$ is the average of ratings made by the user x.

Once every possible prediction according to the similarity function sim_w is calculated, we obtain the MAE of the RS as follows:

$$MAE(f) = \frac{1}{|R_{test}|} \sum_{r_{ui} \in R_{test}} |f_{u,i} - r_{u,i}|$$

Reproduction and Termination

When using the reproduction operator, 1000 individuals are generated in each generation using random crossover between the best-fit parent individuals. The number of individuals keeps constant through every generation. As it has stated above, the population is 100 when using Movielens and Netflix as recommender systems and 200 when using FilmAffinity as RS. We only keep the 5% of the best individuals from each generation to obtain the next one (elitist selection).

Figure 6. The process of a recommender system (adapted from Kim, et al., 2011)

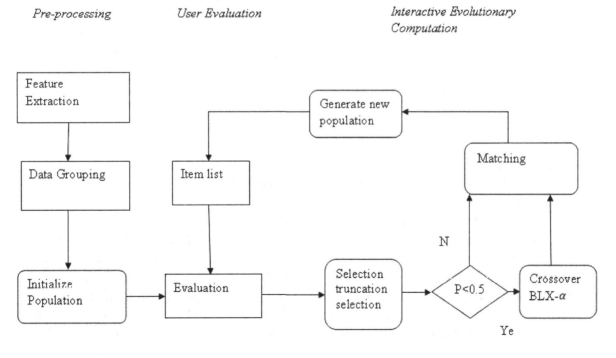

Combination of Evolutionary Computing with Data Mining Techniques

Hyun-Tae, Ahn, and Wook (2011) have proposed a novel recommender system that combines two methodologies, interactive evolutionary computation and content-based filtering method. Also, their system applies clustering to increase the time efficiency. It could effectively adapt and respond to immediate changes in user's preference. The system is shown in Figure 6.

Step 1: Feature Extraction

The feature extraction is a technique that derives properties from specific data, such as document, music, and photos. In the model they have employed a feature extraction tool i.e. CLAM (http://clam-project.org/) to analyze the properties of items. The CLAM is a software framework for research and application development on the audio and music field.

Step 2: Interactive Evolutionary Computation (IEC)

Evolutionary Computation (EC) is the general term for several computational techniques that are based on the evolution of biological life in the nature, among which Genetic Algorithms (GAs) are most widely used. GAs work on a population of candidate solutions; each solution has a fitness value indicating its closeness to the optimal solution of the problem. The solutions having higher fitness values than others are selected, and survive to the next generation. GAs produces better offspring (i.e., new solution) by the combination of selected solutions. The methods can discover, preserve, and propagate promising sub-solutions (Mitchell, 1998; Goldberg & Holland, 1988). Interactive Evolutionary Computation (IEC) is also

an optimization method as the genetic algorithm. However, a user takes charge of the evaluation of fitness value for candidate solutions (Takagi, 2001; Kim, Lee, & Ahn, 2010).

Step 3: Data Grouping – K-Mean Clustering Algorithm

A data grouping technique (i.e., clustering) is used to improve the computational efficiency in terms of accuracy and quality of recommendation. *K*-mean clustering algorithm (David, 2003), which is a technique commonly used to separate a data set into *k* groups had been incorporated in the model. This technique divides data set based on the features of data set. It starts by choosing *k* initial cluster centroid, and iteratively refines the given data set (Wagstaff, Cardie, Rogers, & Sehroedl, 2001).

The system is composed of three phases as follows: preprocessing, user evaluation and IEC phase.

Pre-Processing Phase

In this phase, it has first performed feature extraction to each music track using CLAM. It produces XML files as a result; the proposed system then parses the XML files to initialize individuals for IEC. We consider seven extracted features: Tempo, Pitch, Octave, Root, Mode, Desc, and Simil, which are real numbers.

User Evaluation

The proposed recommender system allows its users to evaluate the fitness value of each music track. A user can assign his or her own rating score, which is the most exact way for users to represent their subjective preferences. After having the given items rated by users, the proposed system evolves a population based on the evaluated data.

Interactive Evolutionary Computation (IEC) Phase

The IEC phase is a fundamental element for making recommendations since the system produces promising items to users based on their own evaluations. We consider two genetic operators, selection, and crossover; we exclude the mutation operator because it has the potential to make the population deviate from the common patterns of candidate solutions discovered by the evolutionary process. Figure 2 shows how to operate IEC phase in the proposed system. As shown in Figure 6, IEC works based on user evaluation and it divided by three steps: Selection, Crossover, and Matching.

SUMMARY AND DISCUSSION

Incorporation of evolutionary techniques in the design of the recommender systems definitely shows a reduction in the complexity of the same. In fact building a concise and representative user model off-line reduces the effect of user-item matrix sparsity. Added to that the incorporation of soft-computing techniques improve the accuracy of R.S. For example by employing Genetic Algorithms, each user priority of each feature is captured. This fine-tunes the off-line mode and helps the system learn better. Similarly, fuzzy distances are very well co-related to the human usage of terms.So integrating fuzzy-genetic approaches or Bayesian methods help in enhancing the prediction rating quality. So analysing the existing R.S, it could be found out that many of them have incorporated many traditional as well as evolutionary mechanisms. Every system has better statistical evaluations and some shortcomings. In order to overcome those limitations, the systems may be cascaded or integrated so as to yield better results. This dynamic information overload over the Internet adds many complex features to be resolved. So many approaches to work on the ratings in an offine mode can be resorted to. One more issue to be addressed is to generalize the proposed models to date on a broader domain to be applied in various networks.So all the possible combinations of data mining tools, evolutionary techniques and traditional methods can be wisely used as hybrid models to cater to the needs of users.

REFERENCES

Adomavicius, G., & Tuzhilin, A. (2005). Toward the next generation of recommender systems: A survey of the state-of-the-art and possible extensions. *IEEE Transactions on Knowledge and Data Engineering*, *17*(6), 734–749. doi:10.1109/TKDE.2005.99

Ahn, H., & Kim, K. (2004). Using a clustering genetic algorithm to support customer segmentation for personalized recommender systems. *Artificial Intelligence Simulations*, *3397*, 409–415.

Ahn, H., & Kim, K. (2008). A recommender system using GA K-means clustering in an online Shopping market. *Expert Systems with Applications*, *34*(2), 1200–1209. doi:10.1016/j.eswa.2006.12.025

Alcala, J., Bobadilla, J., Hernando, A., & Ortega, F. (2011). *Improving collaborative filtering recommender system results and performance using genetic algorithms*. Madrid, Spain: Universidad Politecnica de Madrid.

Al-Shamri. Bharadwaj, K. K., & Yahya, H. M. (2008). *Fuzzy-genetic approach to recommender systems based on a novel hybrid user model*. New Delhi, India: Jawaharlal Nehru University.

Al-Shamri, & Bharadwaj, K. K. (2008). Fuzzy-genetic approach to recommender systems based on a novel hybrid user model. *Expert Systems with Applications, 35*(3), 1386–1399. doi:10.1016/j.eswa.2007.08.016

Alcala, J., Bobadilla, J., Hernando, A., & Ortega, F. (2011). Improving collaborative filtering recommender system results and performance using genetic algorithms. *Knowledge-Based Systems, 24*, 1310–1316. doi:10.1016/j.knosys.2011.06.005

Alcala, J., Bobadilla, J., Hernando, A., & Ortega, F. (2012). A collaborative filtering similarity measure based on singularities. *Information Processing & Management, 48*(2).

Amandi, A., & Schiaffino, S. N. (2000). User profiling with case-based reasoning and Bayesian networks. In *Proceedings of the IBERAMIA-SBIA 2000 Open Discussion Track*, (pp. 12–21). IBERAMIA-SBIA.

Anand, D., & Bharadwaj, K. K. (2011). *Utilizing various sparsity measures for enhancing accuracy of collaborative recommender systems based on local and global similarities.* New Delhi, India: Jawaharlal Nehru University. doi:10.1016/j.eswa.2010.09.141

Antonopoulus, N., & Salter, J. (2006). Cinema screen recommender agent: Combining collaborative and content-based filtering. *IEEE Intelligent Systems, 21*(1), 35–41. doi:10.1109/MIS.2006.4

Bernal, J., Bobadilla, J., & Serradilla, F. (2010). A new collaborative filtering metric that improves the behaviour of recommender systems. *Knowledge-Based Systems, 23*(6), 520–528. doi:10.1016/j.knosys.2010.03.009

Billsu, D. S., & Pazzani, M. (1997). Learning and revising user profiles: The identification of interesting. *Machine Learning, 27*, 313–331. doi:10.1023/A:1007369909943

Bobadilla, J., Hernando, A., & Serradilla, F. (2009). Collaborative filtering adapted to recommender systems of e-learning. *Knowledge-Based Systems, 22*, 261–265. doi:10.1016/j.knosys.2009.01.008

Bobadilla, J., & Serradilla, F. (2009). The incidence of sparsity on collaborative filtering metrics. In *Proceedings of the Australian Database Conference ADC 92*. ADC.

Burke, R. (2002). *Hybrid recommender systems: Survey and experiments.* Fullerton, CA: California State University.

Burke, R. (2007). Hybrid web recommender systems. *Lecture Notes in Computer Science, 4321*, 377–408. doi:10.1007/978-3-540-72079-9_12

Butz, C. (2002). Exploiting contextual independencies in web search and user profiling. In *Proceedings of World Congress on Computational Intelligence*, (pp. 1051–1056). IEEE.

CALM. (2012). *Website*. Retrieved from http://clam-project.org/

Cardie, C., Rogers, S., Schroedl, S., & Wagstaff, K. (2001). Constrained k-means clustering with background knowledge. In *Proceedings of the 18th International Conference on Machine Learning*, (pp. 577-584). IEEE.

Chang, H. Y. A., & Zhang, F. (2006). Collaborative filtering algorithm employing genetic clustering to ameliorate the scalability issue. In *Proceedings of the IEEE International Conference on e-Business Engineering*, (pp. 331–338). IEEE Press.

Crow, J. F., & Kimura, M. (1979). Efficiency of truncation selection. *Proceedings of the National Academy of Sciences of the United States of America, 76*(1), 396–399. doi:10.1073/pnas.76.1.396

David, M. (2003). An example inference task: Clustering. In *Information Theory, Inference and Learning Algorithm* (pp. 284–292). Cambridge, UK: Cambridge University Press.

de Campos, L. M., Fernandez-Luna, J. M., & Huete, J. F. (2005). A decision-based approach for recommending in hierarchical domains. *Lecture Notes in Computer Science, 3571*, 123–135. doi:10.1007/11518655_12

de Campos, L. M., Fernandez-Luna, J. M., & Huete, J. F. (2005). Generalizing e-bay.net: An approach to recommendation based on probabilistic computing. In *Proceedings of the 1st Workshop on Web Personalization, Recommender Systems and Intelligent User Interface*, (pp. 24–33). IEEE.

de Campos, L. M., Fernandez-Luna, J. M., & Huete, J. F. (2008). *A collaborative recommender system based on probabilistic inference from fuzzy observations. Granada, Spain: Departamento de Ciencias de la Computacin e Inteligencia Artificial E.T.S.I.*

de Campos, L. M., Fernandez-Luna, J. M., & Huete, J. F., & RuedaMorales, M. A. (2010). Combining content-based and collaborative recommendations: A hybrid approach based on Bayesian networks. *International Journal of Approximate Reasoning, 51*, 785–799. doi:10.1016/j. ijar.2010.04.001

Denis, H. (2007). Managing collaborative learning processes, e-learning applications. In *Proceedings of the 29th International Conference on Information Technical Interfaces*, (pp. 345–350). IEEE.

Gao, L. Q., & Li, C. (2008). Hybrid personalized recommended model based on genetic algorithm. In *Proceedings of the International Conference on Wireless Communications Networks and Mobile Computing*, (pp. 9215–9218). IEEE.

Giaglis, G. M., & Lekakos. (2006). Improving the prediction accuracy of recommendation algorithms: Approaches anchored on human factors. *Interacting with Computers, 18*(3), 410–431. doi:10.1016/j.intcom.2005.11.004

Goldberg, D., & Thierens, D. (1994). Elitist recombination: An integrated selection recombination GA. In *Proceedings of the First IEEE Conference on Evolutionary Computation*, (pp. 508–512). IEEE Press.

Goldberg, D. E., & Holland, J. H. (1988). Genetic algorithms and machine learning. *Machine Learning, 3*(2-3), 95–99. doi:10.1023/A:1022602019183

Hae-Sang, & Jun, C. (2009). A simple and fast algorithm for K-medoids clustering. *Expert Systems with Applications, 36*(2), 3336–3341. doi:10.1016/j.eswa.2008.01.039

Herlocker, J. L., Konstan, J. A., Riedl, J. T., & Terveen, L. G. (2004). Evaluating collaborative filtering recommender systems. *ACM Transactions on Information Systems, 22*(1), 5–53. doi:10.1145/963770.963772

Herrera, F., Lozano, M., & Verdegay, J. L. (1998). Tackling real-coded genetic algorithms: Operators and tools for behavioural analysis. *Artificial Intelligence Review, 12*, 265–319. doi:10.1023/A:1006504901164

Herrera-Viedma, E., & Porcel, C. (2009). A multi-disciplinary recommender system to advice research resources in university digital libraries. *Expert Systems with Applications, 36*, 12520–12528. doi:10.1016/j.eswa.2009.04.038

Herrera-Viedma, E., & Porcel, C. (2010). Dealing with incomplete information in a fuzzy linguistic recommender system to disseminate information in university digital libraries. *Knowledge-Based Systems, 23*(1), 32–39. doi:10.1016/j. knosys.2009.07.007

Hill, & Terveen, L. (2001). Beyond recommender systems: Helping people help each other. In *HCI in the New Millennium*, (pp. 487–509). Reading, MA: Addison-Wesley.

Ho, K., & Lin, H. M. T. (2012). Design and implementation of an intelligent recommendation system for tourist attraction: The integration of EBM model, Bayesian network and Google maps. *Expert Systems with Applications, 39,* 3257–3264. doi:10.1016/j.eswa.2011.09.013

Ho, Y., Fong, S., & Yan, J. (2007). A hybrid ga-based collaborative filtering model for online recommenders. In *Proceedings of the International Conference on e-Business,* (pp. 200–203). IEEE.

Hyun-Tae, K., Jang-Hyun, L., & Wook, C. (2011). A recommender system based on interactive evolutionary computation with data grouping. *Procedia Computer Science, 3,* 611–616. doi:10.1016/j.procs.2010.12.102

Ingoo, H., Kyong, J. O., & Tae, H. R. (2003). The collaborative filtering recommendation based on SOM cluster-indexing CBR. *Expert Systems with Applications, 25,* 413–423. doi:10.1016/S0957-4174(03)00067-8

Jinghua, H., Kangning, W., & Shaohong, F. (2007). A survey of e-commerce recommender systems. In *Proceedings of the International Conference on Service Systems and Service Management,* (pp. 1–5). IEEE.

Karypis, G., Konstan, J., Riedl, J., & Sarwar, B. (2000). Analysis of recommendation algorithms for ecommerce. In *Proceedings of the 2nd ACM Conference on Electronic Commerce,* (pp. 158-167). Minneapolis, MN: ACM Press.

Kim, H. T., & Kim, E. Lee, & Ahn, C. W. (2010). A recommender system based on genetic algorithm for music data. In *Proceedings of the Computer Engineering and Technology (ICCET), 2010 2nd International Conference,* (vol. 6, pp. V6-414-V6-417). ICCET.

Kim, K. (2008). *A recommender system using GA K-means clustering in an online shopping market.* Seoul, South Korea: Dongguk University. doi:10.1016/j.eswa.2006.12.025

Konstan, J. A., Miller, B. N., & Riedl, J. (2004). PocketLens: Toward a personal recommender system. *ACM Transactions on Information Systems, 22*(3), 437–476.

Konstan, J. A., & Riedl, J. L. (1999). Recommender systems in e-commerce. In *Proceedings of the 1st ACM Conference on Electronic Commerce,* (pp. 158–166). New York, NY: ACM Press.

Kulkarni, U., & Shinde, S. K. (2011). *Hybrid personalized recommender system using centering-bunching based clustering algorithm.* Nanded, India: Bharati Vidyapeeth College of Engineering.

Li, J. Y. J., & Zhong, C. L. N. (2004). Bayesian networks structure learning and its application to personalized recommendation. In *Proceedings of the IEEE/WIC/ACM International Conference on Web Intelligence.* IEEE/WIC/ACM.

Li, P., & Yamada, S. (2004). A movie recommender system based on inductive learning. In *Proceedings of the IEEE Conference on Cybernetic Intelligence Systems,* (vol 1, pp. 318–323). IEEE Press.

Mitchell, M. (1998). *An introduction to genetic algorithm.* Cambridge, MA: MIT Press.

Mooney, R. J., & Roy, L. (2000). Content-based book recommending using learning for text categorization. In *Proceedings of the Fifth ACM Conference on Digital Libraries,* (pp. 195-204). ACM Press.

Papagelis, M., Plexousakis, D., & Kutsuras, T. (2005). Alleviating the sparsity problem of collaborative filtering using trust inferences. *Lecture Notes in Computer Science, 3477,* 224–239. doi:10.1007/11429760_16

Pazzani, M. J. (1999). A framework for collaborative, content-based and demographic filtering. *Artificial Intelligence Review, 13,* 394–408. doi:10.1023/A:1006544522159

Resnick, P., & Varian, H. R. (1997). Recommender system. *Communications of the ACM, 40*(3), 56–58. doi:10.1145/245108.245121

Takagi, H. (2001). Interactive evolutionary computation: Fusion of the capabilities of EC optimization and human evaluation. *Proceedings of the IEEE, 89,* 1275–1296. doi:10.1109/5.949485

Chapter 8
A Fuzzy Clustering Approach for Segmenting Retail Industry

M. Hemalatha
M.A.M. College of Engineering, India

ABSTRACT

The foremost theme of this chapter is to utilize the subtractive clustering concept for defining the market boundaries in the fuzzy-based segmentation. In this sense, the present work starts by analyzing the importance of segmenting the shoppers on the basis of store image. After reviewing the segmentation literature, the authors performed a segmentation analysis of retail shoppers in India. Researchers often use clustering analysis as a tool in market segmentation studies, the results of which often end with a crisp partitioning form, where one member cannot belong to two or more groups. This indicates that different segments overlap with one another. This chapter integrates the concept of application of subtractive clustering in fuzzy c means clustering for profiling the customers who perceive the retail store based on its image. Fuzzy clustering is also compared with hard clustering solutions. Then the authors predict the model using discriminate analysis. Further, the chapter concentrates on the answer tree model of segmentation to identify the best predictor. Main conclusions with implications for retailing management are shown.

INTRODUCTION

India is the ninth-largest retail market in the world. It is expected to grow further in the coming years. At present, organised retailing comprises only six percent of the market, but its share is expected to rise to 15 percent within two years. This growth is being driven by several factors. Retail demand in India is being fuelled by country's huge middle class, a large young working population that is less burdened than previous generations with educating children and providing healthcare for elderly parents, while retirement is still a long way off, Meanwhile, India's economy is increasing rapidly (Jindal, 2008). Shopping today is much more than just buying; it is an experience in itself. To best utilize the available time, Indian consumer is on the look-out for avenues that would give him the maximum value for his money and time spent (Parikh, 2006).

DOI: 10.4018/978-1-4666-2542-6.ch008

It has been well documented in the marketing literature that customer satisfaction is critical to any businesses' success. However, it is far less clear as on how marketers comprehend customer differences in customer satisfaction evaluations, and leverage such understanding in forming their marketing strategies. Recently researchers have begun to explore the notion of individual or segment differences in the formation of overall satisfaction judgments (Jianan & DeSarbo, 2005). In spite of the obvious importance of the retail innovation in India, little is known about the process of consumer acceptance responsible for the success or failure of a retail institution. To answer this question, a study of market segments, responsible for the success of a retail innovation was designed. This chapter concerned with identifying the characteristics of Indian market segments in selecting the retail outlet using fuzzy clustering technique.

Knowledge of the different types of shoppers can be very helpful to business in planning merchandising, promotion, pricing, and location activities (Lill, et al., 1981). Segmentation of shoppers has been explored by many academic researchers and business practitioners seeking to understand shopping behaviour and to develop marketing strategies for particular customer groups. Market segmentation holds the key to successful marketing strategy as it encourages understanding of the key variables that differentiate specific segments (Jarratt, 1996). The demographic variables (Allred, et al., 2006; Roos, et al., 2005; Yiyang, et al., 2007; Bruwer & Li, 2007), Psychographic variables (Allred, et al., 2006; Yiyang, et al., 2007), Shopping orientation (Sinha, 2003), benefit segmentation (Avi, et al., 2008), different roles (Fuller & Matzler, 2008), hierarchical self-organizing segmentation model (Hung & Tsai, 2008), purchasing behaviour (Simkin, 2008), and Product attribute (Sewall, 1978; Yiyang, et al., 2007) dimensions are generally used variables in the segmentation studies and in the design of marketing plans. Further, Yu and Zhou

(2010) explored potential regional differences by comparing young consumers from the better-developed coastal region and the less-developed inland region. Menzly and Ozbas (2010) presented evidence supporting the hypothesis that due to investor specialization and market segmentation.

However, segmentation criteria based on store image using fuzzy logic seems to be more realistic in order to explain the differences among consumers inside a market. So, it could be used as a segmentation variable of the market. Therefore, the objective of this study is to segment shoppers in India based on store image using fuzzy logic. A better understanding of shopper segments will encourage retailers to refine merchandise, store environments, and marketing programmes to consumers' precise desires. Market researchers have discussed on store image based market segmentation in the perspective of various partitioning and clustering methods, but such studies have toiled with unsupervised clustering approaches. But, no studies have identified the integration of fuzzy c-means with subtractive clustering for obtaining store image based market segmentation.

Store image is defined as the overall attitude towards the store based upon the perceptions of relevant store attributes. Store Image segmentation provides guidelines for a retail firm's marketing strategy and can increase profitability. The foremost theme of this research is to utilize the subtractive clustering concept for defining the market boundaries in the fuzzy based segmentation. Researchers often use clustering analysis as a tool in market segmentation studies, the results of which often ends with crisp partitioning form, in simple words, where one member cannot belong to two or more groups. This indicates that different segments overlap with one another. This study integrates the concept of application of subtractive clustering in fuzzy c means clustering for profiling the customers who perceive the retail store based on its image. Fuzzy clustering is also compared with hard clustering solutions. We have also predicted the model using discriminate analysis.

Further, it concentrates on answer tree model of segmentation to identify the best predictor.

As a first step in addressing the above said objective, the rest of the study is organized as follows. The next section reviews the existing literature in the field of segmenting the shoppers, trying to arrive a deeper understanding of the concept and structure. The following section describes the results of advanced data analysis with cluster analysis and development of a classification and regression tree. This section also describes various market segments of retail shoppers in India. After this, the future area of research is discussed. Finally, the last section of this chapter reports main conclusion with managerial implications to the retailers.

CONCEPTUAL BACKGROUND

In consumer marketing, a market segment is defined as a group of consumers with homogeneous needs. Market segmentation is based on the premise that most organisations cannot serve total populations, and therefore disaggregate these into more homogenous sub-groups to which marketing efforts can be targeted. The practice is generally common in consumer goods industries today (Pitt, et al., 1996). Segmenting consumer market is a creative act, which in itself is not always easy, so we suggest a clustering and a classification tree approach to the segmentation problem.

The past research in consumer shopping-decision styles, using these styles as the basis for market segmentation. Furthermore, Yu and Zhou (2010) explored potential regional differences by comparing young consumers from the better-developed coastal region and the less-developed inland region. The results indicate important differences not only among segments within each regional market, but also between the two regions. Menzly and Ozbas (2010) presented evidence supporting the hypothesis that due to investor specialization and market segmentation,

value-relevant information diffuses gradually in financial markets.

Different groups of consumers believe that different store attributes are important. Therefore, store attributes appears to be a promising market segmentation criterion. In this sense, Hemalatha et al. (2009) focused on store attributes as a possible criterion to segment the shoppers. Finally, three clusters of Indian shoppers, namely, economic shoppers, convenient shoppers and elegant shoppers are identified. Avi et al. (2008) used a benefit segmentation technique based on conjoint analysis in which the segments emerge simultaneously with the design based on certain design principles or "strategies."

Market segmentation has evoked the interests of both practitioners and academicians. Owing to their considerable potential for market segmentation studies, Sarstedt (2008) addressed the issue by evaluating how the interaction of the most important influencing factors for the measures' success sample and segment size affects the performance of four of the most widely used criteria for assessing the correct number of segments in mixture regression models. An application based on customer satisfaction data illustrates the relevance of the findings. The agencies conceal important characteristics of the offered services, such as hotel locations or flight schedules. Shapiro and Shi (2008) investigated the role of discount travel agencies such as Priceline and Hotwire in the market segmentation of the hotel and airline industries. This chapter explicitly model this opaque feature and show that it enables service providers to price discriminate between those customers who are sensitive to service characteristics and those who are not. Service providers can profit from such discrimination despite the fact that the opaque feature virtually erases product differentiation and thus intensifies competition.

In a segmented international capital market, Chan et al. (2008) studied the illiquidity of a country fund in the market in which its shares are traded affects only the share price of the fund

(*S*), while the illiquidity of its underlying assets in the market in which these are traded affects only the fund Net Asset Value (*NAV*). In an integrated market, illiquidity in one market can easily spill over to another and affect both the fund share price and its underlying asset value. It follows that the closed-end country fund premium, $P \equiv \ln(S) - \ln(NAV)$, is negatively (positively) affected by the fund (underlying asset) illiquidity in segmented capital markets, but has only an ambiguous association with either fund or underlying asset illiquidity in an integrated market. The results suggest that illiquidity plays a significant role in explaining closed-end country fund premia.

There is increasing evidence that product and service attributes fall into three factors (basic, performance, and excitement factors) which affect overall satisfaction differently. Fuller and Matzler (2008) reported an extensive empirical study which investigates the different roles of basic, performance and excitement factors in different market segments. The results clearly showed that significant differences can be found among lifestyle segments. King and Segal (2008) confirmed that Canadian and U.S. equity markets remain segmented and find no evidence that integration is increasing over time. They establish this result by comparing the valuation multiples assigned to the equity of Canadian firms listed exclusively in the home market with a matched sample of U.S. firms over the period 1989–2004. Canadian firms have lower valuations based on multiples of market-to-book, price-to-last 12-month earnings, Tobin's q, and enterprise value-to-EBITDA, despite exhibiting higher sales growth and profitability.

Customer relationship management aims at understanding and measuring the true value of customers. Hung and Tsai (2008) focused on approaches that provide a human manager with a visualized decision making tool for market segmentation. They proposed a novel market segmentation approach, namely the Hierarchical Self-Organizing Segmentation model (HSOS), for dealing with a real-world data set for market

segmentation of multimedia on demand in Taiwan. Simkin (2008) offered a solution for managers, focusing on customer purchasing behaviour, which evolves from the organisation's existing criteria used for grouping its customers. A straightforward process has been derived and applied, enabling organisations to practice market segmentation in an evolutionary manner, facilitating the transition to customer-led target market segments. This process also ensures commitment from the managers responsible for implementing the eventual segmentation scheme. This chapter outlines the six stages of this process and presents an illustrative example from the agrichemicals sector, supported by other cases.

To discover whether there are market segments for the fashion industry that cut across countries and responds differently to advertising messages. Ko et al. (2007) administered a survey to Korean, European, and US female consumers. Cluster analysis is used in an attempt to identify lifestyle segments that cut across cultures. Four cross-national market segments are identified. These segments were labeled as follows: "information seekers," "sensation seekers," "utilitarian consumers," and "conspicuous consumers." Findings also revealed that fashion lifestyle segment had a stronger effect on the reaction to a set of three ads for a major global fashion company than did consumer nationality. Dallen (2007) used cluster analysis, a form of a posteriori market segmentation, to understand the attitudes of tourists and the local community towards using the Looe Valley Branch Railway Line. The research revealed five segments of users distinguished by their attitudes towards using the train.

Appropriate modeling of Web use patterns may yield very relevant marketing and retailing information. Dias and Vermunt (2007) proposed a model-based clustering approach for market segmentation based on website users' search patterns. This chapter not only provide a detailed discussion of technical issues such as the problem of the selection of the number of segments, but also a very interesting empirical illustration of the potentials of the proposed approach. Verbeke et al. (2007) focused on consumer evaluation of fish quality and its association with fish consumption, risk and benefit beliefs and information processing variables. Cross-sectional data were collected from a sample of 429 consumers in March 2003 in Belgium. Two dimensions shape fish quality evaluation: personal relevance attached to fish quality and self-confidence in fish quality evaluation, which allow segmenting the market in four fish consumer segments. The segments are typified as Uninvolved, Uncertain, Self-confident and Connoisseurs, and have distinctive behavioural, attitudinal, and socio-demographic profiles.

The definition and scope of market segmentation is broader than the current marketing literature suggests. Quinn et al. (2007) first reviewed the marketing segmentation literature and its antecedents and identified an agenda for future research. In practice, based on evidence from this research, contemporary segmentation solutions include implicit assumptions, judgement and compressed experience, which are latent within the modelling processes. Koc and Altinay (2007) analyses seasonal variations in monthly per person tourist spending in Turkish inbound tourism from a market segmentation perspective. In this study, a seasonal unit root test and recently developed decomposition techniques are used. It is found that there is a stochastic and strong seasonality in per person tourist spending data. The findings interestingly show that the seasonal pattern in per person tourist spending is considerably different from the seasonal pattern in tourist arrivals.

Exploring consumer lifestyles and ethnocentrism is one way of investigating buyer behavior and market segmentation. John et al. (2007) studied consumer market segments existing among Peruvian consumers by using lifestyle patterns and ethnocentrism. Data for the study was collected through self-survey in two major cities located in Peru, South America. The results pointed out that there are nine style dimensions

among Peruvian consumers that influence their ethnocentric tendencies. Bruwer and Li (2007) compared and contrasted the composition and nature of the wine market segments with the earlier studies. The research confirms that there are five lifestyle related segments in the South Australian wine market, each differing in size and level of involvement with wine. This segmentation structure is relatively stable but continues to evolve as two new market segments were identified, namely mature time-rich wine drinker and young professional wine drinkers.

To compete in the marketplace, manufacturers have been seeking for expansion of their product lines by providing product families. Yiyang et al. (2007) proposed a fuzzy clustering-based market segmentation approach. With a focus on engineering characteristics, the fuzzy clustering based market segmentation helps plan the right products to target segments effectively and efficiently. Allred et al. (2006) classified Internet users into holiday shopper and non-shopper segments, and profiled the demographic, psychographic, and computer use characteristics of each segment. Finally, six important segments are identified in the data. Three of the segments characterize customers who resist online shopping, even though they engage in other online activities. Three of the segments describe active e-shoppers who are driven by a unique desire to socialize, minimize inconvenience, and maximize value.

Broderick et al. (2006) proposed a framework of alternative international marketing strategies, based on the evaluation of intra- and inter-cultural behavioural homogeneity for market segmentation. The framework developed in this study provides a generic structure to behavioural homogeneity, proposing consumer involvement as a construct with unique predictive ability for international marketing strategy decisions. A model-based segmentation process, using structural equation model, is implemented to illustrate the application of the framework. Roos et al. (2005) conducted a mail survey of Japanese post and beam builders to measure their level of ethnocentrism, market orientation, risk aversion, and price consciousness. The data were analyzed utilizing factor and cluster analysis. The results showed that Japanese post and beam builders can be divided into three distinct market segments: open to import, low price sensitivity, and conservative.

Studies on shoppers in India have largely been limited to their time and money spending pattern, demographic profile, and preferences for a particular format. Therefore, Sinha (2003) attempted to understand shoppers from their disposition towards shopping. He has been found useful as the differences between retailers are not significant in terms of value delivered. Based on the orientation of the Indian shoppers, 300 shoppers are clustered into two segments: Fun shoppers: Consisting of 39 percent of the sample, this segment enjoys shopping and is found to be involved. Work shoppers: This segment takes to shopping as an activity that needs to be finished with least effort. The two segments are found to be different in terms of their demographic and behavioural profile.

Organisations utilise and maximise marketing at various traditional events during the year. Gurau and Tinson (2003) attempted to investigate the response of customers to the Christmas commercial campaign. Based on customers' attitudes and behaviour, this study proposes an original segmentation of Christmas shoppers, and investigates the use of different advertising channels by different segments. Similarly fresh meat product retailing at traditional markets in Taiwan causes concerns over meat safety issues. Hsu and Chang (2002) utilized survey data to segment meat shoppers in Taiwan. Results indicate the shoppers who purchase meat products at supermarkets tend to continue shopping at that location. Potential shoppers of supermarkets, who may switch from traditional markets to supermarkets for meat products, are identified and the major concerns of this group are the meat safety issues. Factors that influence the possibilities of selecting supermarkets for meat products are examined.

Customer's commitment has become a main mediating goal for many companies. It appears to be a promising market segmentation criterion. In this sense, Iniesta and Sanchez (2002) focused on commitment as a possible criterion to segment the consumers' market. The study performs a segmentation analysis of bank customers and three clusters of clients are identified according to their level of commitment. Chen (2001) described a service quality study within a business to business environment and focuses on the use of expectations of service quality as a market segmentation tool. It is demonstrated that different members of buying centres have different expectations of the quality of service for a high-tech product and it is suggested that industrial marketers may wish to focus on these as an additional way of gaining customer insight for marketing strategy.

The importance of identification of market segments to the formulation of marketing strategy is widely accepted. There are two common approaches to defining market segments. One is to define some finite number of consumer categories frequently based on socioeconomic or demographic profiles and to relate purchase behavior to these categories. The other is to define purchasers of particular products or brands as segments and to attempt to relate this observed behavior to socioeconomic, demographic, personality, or lifestyle variables. Neither of these traditional approaches has been notably successful in establishing a relationship between defined segments and characteristics of consumers in the segments (Sewall, 1978). The best set of characteristics to define segments is the benefits sought by shoppers, often measured in terms of store attributes (Rinne & Swinyard, 1995). However, segmentation criteria based on store image using fuzzy logic seems to be more realistic in order to explain the differences among consumers inside a market. So, it could be used as a segmentation variable of the market. So this chapter describes a procedure for defining retail market segments based on consumer evaluations of store images using fuzzy logic technique.

RESEARCH ANALYSIS
AND RESULTS

Data analysis consisted of exploratory factor analysis, subtractive cluster analysis, fuzzy cluster analysis, k-means cluster analysis, multiple-discriminate analysis, and CHAID analysis. The result of appropriateness of the factor model indicates that the population correlation matrix is an identical matrix. The Bartlett's Test of Sphericity is based on approximate chi-square statistics transformation of the determinant of the correlation matrix. The approximate chi-square statistics is 12889.88 (larger value) with 1326 degree of freedom, which is significant at the 0.05 level proves the factor model is appropriate. Kaiser-Meyer-Olkin measure of sampling adequacy compares the magnitudes of the observed correlation coefficients to the magnitudes of the partial correlation coefficients. The Value of the KMO statistics is 0.941543, which is a larger value (>0.5) and indicates the sample size as adequate.

Previous related researches suggest that image dimensions produce factor. Factor analysis is used to reduce the image dimension scales into smaller, more manageable factors. This multivariate technique is also used to identify the underlying patterns or relationships for a large number of variables. Factor analysis was used to summarize the variables by examining correlations between the variables, and to create an entirely new set of variables to replace original variables. Factors were derived using principal components, which summarize the original information into factors for prediction. Only factors with eigenvalues greater than 1 were included. Total variance explained is 66.98 percent.

Factors were rotated using the varimax rotation method. Factor loadings at ± .30 are considered minimal, ± .40 more important, ± 0.50 or greater practically significant. In tune with this concept the variables with loadings greater than or equal to ± 0.50 were retained for this study. However, those with several high loadings on more than one factor have been deleted, and more so variables

with low loadings and those that were not loaded on any factor also were evaluated for possible deletion. Exclusion of variables was dependent upon their overall contribution to the research. In addition to the variable loading, the communality and the total amount of variance shared with other variables were evaluated duly before deleting the variables. Variables with loadings less than ± 0.50 and variables that did not load with communalities less than 0.50 were deleted. After the factors were formed, they were named according to those variables with higher factor loadings.

Subtractive Clustering and
Fuzzy C Means Clustering

The subtractive clustering method assumes that each data point is a potential cluster center and calculates a measure of the likelihood that each data point would define the cluster center, based on the density of surrounding data points. We performed Subtractive cluster in MatLab using the subclust function. We have also performed Fuzzy C- Means clustering in MatLab using the FCM function. To have an idea of "how fuzzy" the resulting clustering is, Dunn's partition coefficient is computed. Fuzziness helps the rule evaluation during the intermediate steps; the final desired output for each variable is generally a single number. However, the aggregate of a fuzzy set encompasses a range of output values, and so must be defuzzified in order to resolve a single output value from the set. Perhaps there are many defuzzification methods, we have used the most popular method of maximum likelihood method (see Tables 1 and 2).

Table 2 of minimum iteration section determines the number of clusters. The first column indicates the iteration number from the iteration report. The second column indicates the number of clusters reported. The percentage of variance column indicates the variance within the sum of squares with no clusters. Hence, by comparing second and third column the optimum number of clusters was determined as four because the point

Table 1. Fuzzy membership grade

Sample	Innovators	Loyalist	Female Dominant	Economic	Defuzzified Membership
1	0.0521	0.0001	0.0002	0.9476	4
2	0.0026	0.3796	0.6176	0.0001	3
3	0.0417	0.0001	0.0002	0.9580	4
4	0.0387	0.0002	0.0002	0.9610	4
5	0.0669	0.0002	0.0002	0.9327	4
6	0.0005	0.3541	0.6454	0.0000	3
7	0.0681	0.0001	0.0001	0.9318	4
8	0.0263	0.0001	0.0001	0.9734	4
9	0.0003	0.2308	0.7688	0.0000	3
10	0.0501	0.0002	0.0001	0.9495	4
11	0.3727	0.0005	0.0006	0.6262	4
12	0.7749	0.0003	0.0003	0.2245	1
13	0.9292	0.0054	0.0061	0.0593	1
14	0.9087	0.0183	0.0217	0.0513	1

at 57% fails to decrease dramatically. The cluster means exhibits the mean of each of the variables across each of the clusters. Based on the mean value and the demographic features, the clusters are labeled as Innovators, Female Dominant, Loyalist, and Economic. The last row shows the count or number of observations in the cluster.

The F- Ratio results of performing a one-way ANOVA on each variable, using the current defined clusters as the factor. The report helps us to investigate the importance of each variable in the clustering process. The one way ANOVA table indicates the most significant variables contribute to the most of the cluster solutions. The variables with large F value provide the greatest separation between clusters. According to the F- Ratio results, the variables like appealing, lighting, materials, temperature, architecture, physical facilities, wall and color, modern fixtures, privacy protected, attractive, overall design, trusting the store, easy layout, located closely, come in and shop, sensational, safe transactions are considered to be the greatest separation variables between the clusters. The variables like shopping gets me away, more

involvement, another world, exciting, less than other charge, helpful personnel and private labels are considered to be the least separation variables between the clusters (see Tables 3 and 4).

Using the FCM and Defuzzified segment results derived from all samples (358), the market size obtained from hard method are different from those of FCM and Defuzzified segments. The rule to identify and compare the fuzziness of the segments is that "The smaller the market size difference, the more stable the market, and vice-versa."

Based on the percentage of fuzziness, the Loyalist segment (18.509%) and Economic segments (27.92%) are considered to be more stable segment. Female Dominance segment (44.08%) and Innovators segment (36.19%) have greater fuzziness. Hence, these segments are considered to be unstable segments. The overall fuzziness of all the segments is estimated as 27.92 percent. Dunn's Partition normalized version of its coefficient (linear operation) lies between [0.62374 and 0.49832], so the fuzziness is between the range [0.62374 and 0.49832]. This indicates that the clusters have great amount of fuzziness.

Discriminant Analysis

Multi-group discriminant analysis is performed to examine the members belonging to different segments attach different relative importance to most important cluster separation variables. The dependent variables are the four different segments namely innovators, loyalist, female dominance and Economic. The independent variables are appropriate store light, products is attractive, visually appealing, convivial, fun to shop, service personnel helpfulness, overall design, expert merchandizing, frequent visit in future, music played in store and income of the respondent. The entire sample is divided into estimate sample and holdout sample. The estimated and holdout samples are selected randomly.

The distribution of the number of cases in the estimate and holdout sample is 80:20 in the ration of the percentage of the distributed cases for both the samples is similar in size. Leave-one-out cross-Validation method is performed to validate the model. The following are the results of estimating the four-group discriminant analysis. By examining the group statistics, the following variables, 1. The store lighting is appropriate, 2. Materials associated with this store's service (such as shopping bag, catalogue) are visually appealing, 3. My shopping at this store will be very frequent, separates the groups more widely than any other variables. Loyal and Female Dominance segments are very close in terms of, 1. This store plays music that I like, 2. It is really fun to shop at this store, 3. I think of this store as an expert in the merchandise it offers. The household income has a large standard deviation in relevant to the separations between the groups.

The pooled within-group correlation matrix indicates some correlation between, 1. The store lighting is appropriate and the way this store displays its products is attractive, 2. It is really fun to shop at this store and this store plays music that I like. It is found that there is no significant negative correlation between variables. Yet, these correlations are on the lower side which, indicates that although multi-collinearity may be of some concern, it is not likely to be a serious problem. As several functions are tested simultaneously, the Wilks' λ statistic and the univariate λ are used to assess the significance means of the independent variables for the groups. The significance attached to univariate F ratio indicates that when the predictors are considered individually the following variables, 1. The way this store displays its products is attractive, 2. The store lighting is appropriate, 3. Materials associated with this store's service (such as shopping bag, catalogue) are visually appealing are significant in differentiating between the groups.

Because there are four groups, a maximum of three functions can be extracted. Based on the eigenvalue associated with the first function is 6.185 which is accounted for 96.9 percent of the explained variance. Because the eigenvalue is large, the first function is likely to be superior. The second and third functions have a small eigenvalues of 0.165 and 0.054 respectively. Therefore, the second and the third functions do not much contribute significantly to group differences. The after function column above indicates that no function has been removed. The value of Wilks' λ for the 1 through 3 function is 0.104, which transforms to a chi-square of 629.928, with 33 degrees of freedom, which is significantly beyond the 0.05 level. The value of Wilks' λ for the 2 through 3 function is 0.814, which transforms to a chi-square of 57.335 with 20 degrees of freedom, which is significantly beyond the 0.05

Table 2. Iteration of k-means clustering

Minimum Iteration Secion		
Iteration No.	No. of Clusters	Percent of Variation
1	2	62.31
6	3	59.51
7	4	57

Table 3. A comparison of the subtractive clustering and fuzzy c means clustering solutions and defuzzified segment

Cluster and Clustering procedure	Innovators	Female Dominant	Loyalist	Economic	Total
Hard Segments (K-Means)	37	83	171	67	358
Soft Segment (FCM)	50.3926	119.591	139.349	48.666	357.998
Defuzzified segment	42	112	59	145	358

level. However, when the first and second functions are removed, the Wilks' λ associated with the third function does not contribute significantly to group differences.

Pooled within-groups correlations between discriminating variables and standardized canonical discriminant function variables are ordered by absolute size of correlation within function. A scattergram plot of all the groups based on function 1 and function 2. It can be seen that "Loyalist" segment has the highest value of function 1 and "Economic" segment has the lowest. The function 1 is associated with Lighting, Product attractiveness, Visual appearance of materials, Convivial and Fun. Those variables with high value on the above mentioned variables are most likely to associate with Loyalist segment. Conversely, those with the low value on these variables will mostly associate with Economic segment. Further the function 2, is associated with Courtesy and friendliness of sales personnel, Overall design and the mercnadize. It is found that the Innovators segment is expected to be higher value than any other segment. The group centroid is indicated with dark dots (see Tables 5 and 6).

Because there is a four-group discriminant analysis model, the three discriminant functions are calculated to discriminate among the four groups. The discriminate functions are based only on the variables which are included in the discriminant model.

The group means section helps us to profile each group by using the mean discriminant score for each function. The classification results based on the analysis sample indicate that 67.9 percent of the cases are correctly classified. The Leave-one-out cross validation method applied here correctly classifies 64.8 percent of the cases, whereas, when the classification analysis is conducted on the independent holdout sample, Innovators are accurately classified with 83.3% of the cases. The Loyalist with 79.3%, The Female Dominance segment with 54.5% being the least and the Economic based segment with 87.5%, which is the most accurately classified one. The incorrect classified Innovators are more likely to be classified as economic. The incorrect classified Loyalist is more likely to be classified as Female Dominating. The incorrect classified Female Dominating segment is more likely to be classified as Loyalist. The incorrect

Table 4. Stability of segments

Cluster	Innovators	Female Dominant	Loyalist	Economic	Total
Hard Segments (K-Means)	37	83	171	67	358
SoftSegment (FCM)	50.3926	119.591	139.349	48.666	357.998
Differences	13.3926	36.591	31.651	18.334	99.9686

Table 5. Unstandardized canonical discriminant function coefficients

Independent Variables	Function		
	1	2	3
The way this store displays its products is attractive.	0.285	0.122	0.023
The store lighting is appropriate	0.436	0.022	-0.156
The overall design of the store is interesting	0.265	-0.383	-0.024
Materials associated with this store's service are visually appealing	0.265	-0.515	0.173
This store plays music that I like	0.158	-0.124	0.29
It's really fun to shop at this store	0.157	0.182	0.188
This store always says, "come in and shop"	0.293	0.083	-0.289
I think of this store as an expert in the merchandise it offers.	0.186	0.285	0.063
The salespeople/ Customer service personnel in this store are quiet helpful	0.156	0.515	0.2
In future, my shopping at this store will be very frequent	0.181	0.096	-0.374
Household Income	-1.2E-07	7.93E-07	5.85E-06
(Constant)	-12.251	-1.314	-1.12

classified Economic is more likely to be classified as Innovators. A hit ratio of 73.23 percent is obtained, which indicates a satisfactory validity.

Chi-Squared Automatic Interaction Detection (CHAID) Analysis

At each step, CHAID chooses the independent (predictor) variable that has the strongest interaction with the dependent variable. Categories of each predictor are merged if they are not significantly different with respect to the dependent variable. Loyalist cluster was selected as target Category and Economic segment was excluded from the model. Table 6 indicates that the descriptive detail of estimate sample indicates that Economic segment does not much contribute to the Loyalty maintenance and development factors. So, Economic segment was excluded from the model. Cross validation was performed with 10 sample fold. To keep the tree fairly simple, the tree growth was limited by minimum number of cases in parent and child nodes as 75 and 25 respectively. The model estimates; the maximum number of 25 iterations, maximum change in expected cell frequencies to be 0.001, Significance level of

splitting nodes as 0.05 and the merging category at 0.05 level with the adjusting significance value using Bonferroni method.

The model summary provides very broad information about the specifications used to build the predictive model. The specifications section provides information on the settings used to generate the tree model, including the variables used in the analysis. The results section displays information on the total number of terminal nodes, depth of the tree (i.e., the number of levels below the root node), and independent variables included in the final model. As much as eleven independent variables are specified, but only three are included in the final model. The variables such as current working status, Number of Children, Gender has made significant contribution to the model. Rest of the variables are automatically dropped in the final model.

The tree diagram is a graphic representation of the tree model. This tree diagram (Figure 1) shows that, using CHAID method, The variable "Current working Status" is the best predictor of targeted segment of loyalists with the chi-square transformation of 7.570 and with the adjusted P-value of 0.012 in 1 degree of freedom. As such

Table 6. Canonical discriminant functions evaluated at group means (group centroids)

Fuzzy Cluster Solutions	Function		
	1	2	3
Innoators	-2.969	0.522	-0.337
Loyalist	1.773	-0.331	-0.134
Female Dominating	1.309	0.357	0.248
Economic	-5.41	-0.537	0.265

as two child nodes are estimated from the current working status. The Node 1 targets the maximum membership of female dominating segment account for 37.8%. Since there are no child nodes below it, this is considered as a terminal node.

On the other side of the same category, 57.4 percent of members fall in the loyalist segment. For this category, the next best predictor is "family is having number of Children less than one or more than one" with the chi-square transformation of 10.675 and with the adjusted P-value of 0.003 in 1 degree of freedom. Node 4 (i.e.) (Children less than one) targets the maximum membership of female dominance segment account for 57.5%. Since there are no child nodes below it, this is considered as a terminal node of the other side. On the other face (i.e. Children more than one) of the same category, Loyalist segment categorized with 98 members which account for 62.4 percent. To this category, the next best predictor is "Gender" with the chi-square transformation of 6.535 and with the adjusted P-value of 0.011 in 1 degree of freedom, which classifies into female and male with the node 5 and node 6 respectively. This leads to conclude that the node 6 contributes as much as 74.5 percentages of loyalists which are exclusively of "male." The content of the Tree diagram indicates the predicted category of dependent variables in the Loyalist Segment because it accounts for more than 50 percent. The column, Parent node indicates the parent node of each node.

The risk and classification analysis provide a quick evaluation of how well the model works.

The risk calculation based on Resubstitution method and Cross validation method indicates that the category (Loyalist Segment) estimates 0.462 (which is wrong for 46% of cases) and 0.525 (which is wrong for 52% of cases). Therefore, the approximate "risk" of misclassifying the members is 48%. The results of the classification analysis are consistent with the risk estimate. The model classifies approximately 54% of the members correctly. The classification reveals a potential problem in this model. For the Loyalists segment, the predicted loyalist rating is 53 percent, which means that 47 percent of the members with the loyalists segment are inaccurately classified with other segments. Therefore, the results from the foregoing give a clear indication of the closeness of the rate of classification of the terminal node as they have accomplished as much as 74.5% which has no much significant variation from the accepted level of classification rate which is 80%.

FUTURE RESEARCH DIRECTIONS

Shopping is perhaps one of the oldest activities that the human race has been performing with high level of regularity and involvement. Over the years, however, the shoppers' orientation towards this routine activity has been changing. The innovations brought by retailers and marketers in the practice of retailing have been providing new paradigms in the way shoppers have been disposed towards their act of shopping (Sinha, 2003). This has also led to a body of knowledge that aims to understand the classification of shoppers towards shopping and utilize it to develop typologies.

Target Population for this research was determined based on a parameter namely, male or female in the houschold who all visited the branded food and grocery retail chain. The sample frame has been effectively generated using random digit table and a simple random sample of respondents drawn up from each stratum excluding children and the respondents who do not know English. The sample size is determined by estimating the

Figure 1. Tree diagram

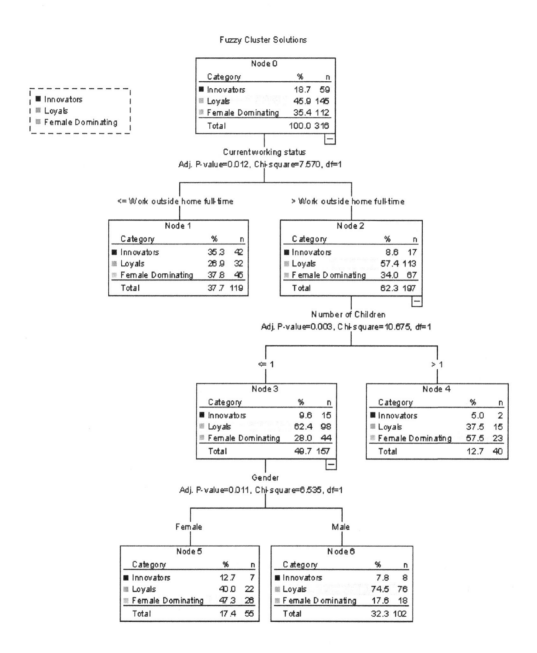

means for interval-scale variables. A pilot study was conducted to measure the store image attributes with 8 questions which was measured on a 7-point Likert-type scale. The ratings range from 1 to 7 (1 = strongly disagree, 7 = strongly agree). So the total sample size is determined as 358.

The instrument was designed and developed from the previous related researches using image attributes of outlets selling food and grocery. Items are decoded for the purpose of customizing the research for Indian retail conditions and later it was tested. To test the content of the questionnaire forty-five in-depth interviews were conducted with the shoppers of various retail stores and extensive discussions made with such retailer and merchandise managers. Respondents were evaluated as to how they understand, interact and respond to the structure, wordings, and ease of answering as well as the time taken to complete the questionnaire in all respect.

The eight-store image attributes were identified and later factored: they are visual appeal, retail preferences and future patronage intent, entertainment value, overall merchandise and service quality, intrinsic enjoyment, brand choice, escapism and economic value. All items are measured on a 7-point Likert-type scale. The ratings range from 1 to 7 (1 = strongly disagree and 7 = strongly agree). To establish the "face validity," merchandise managers of various retail store chains were asked to examine whether the scale items adequately cover the entire domain of store image dimensions with the research objectives. Whereas the construct validity was improved by using environmental dimensions studied in previous research, data were collected during the month of February, March, and April of 2010. Data were collected through mall intercept personal interviews. The respondents were intercepted while or after they shopped in the mall. The interviewer then administered the questionnaire. The usable questionnaires were received from the respondents with an average response rate of 67.57 percent.

This research is however not without any limitation, the first limitation is at the response rate, that is the entire food and grocery retail market in the country is under transition period. Every retail chain in the country is upgrading the retail formats. In this situation, the study on store image has achieved the response rate of only 67.57 percent. The next limitation is that, the indent of the research. According to the CII and McKinsey research on "Retailing in India," the food and grocery market size in the country has about 12 million outlets, where 96 percent of outlets are largely unorganized and only the remaining 4 percentage of the market is organized and the market does not have any clear base. Therefore, the samples of Food and grocery retail chains taken for the study cannot be claimed to have been from an organized sector as compared to developed countries. The scope of the research can further be widened by applying the approaches of the latest methods of segmentation like ANFIS and ANN, which can be used to predict and classify the market. The algorithms derived out of these methods may enable to perform clusters with natural thinking rule, to further lead to good pattern recognitions.

CONCLUSION

Segmenting consumer market is a creative act, which in itself is not always easy, so in our research, we suggest a fuzzy cluster based approach to the segmentation problem. A critical issue in successful market segmentation is the selection of segmentation variables. Segmentation variables can be broadly classified into general variables and product-specific variables. The general variables include the customer demographic, geographic, and psychographic characteristics. Many researchers have devoted themselves to using general variables to partition customers, because the general variables are intuitive and easy to operate. The purpose of grouping the customers by using general variables is to represent the diverse markets according to the customers' characteristics. Similarity in customers' characteristics performs as an indicator to provide retail offerings to the market where these customers belong. In practice, however, it is doubtful to assume that customers with similar demographic, geographic, and psychographic characteristics will exhibit similar purchasing behaviours.

Today's customers may gain abundant store and product information from various medium and channels. Even within a group with similar characteristics, the customers' preferences may vary a lot due to the uniqueness of personality. It is difficult to measure the customers' purchasing patterns using general variables alone. Furthermore, most general variables refer to personal or private information such as the income, occupation, and address, which make data collection inhibitive, thus jeopardizing the data credibility. Even though private information may be obtained, the information itself fluctuates and varies over time. All these issues make market segmentation using general variables questionable (Yiyang, et al., 2007). Customer preferences are reflected by their choices on different attribute value combinations. In this regard, market segmentation should take into account retail store image to cope with a high level of shopper's satisfaction.

The empirical result of the research shows that the subtractive cluster algorithm well separates each cluster in a better classified manner to determine the market boundaries. The clusters obtained from the subtractive clustering algorithm are four, which are rightly used for initializing iterative optimization-based clustering methods. Consequently, the study enhances the managers' job. In reality, marketing or merchandize managers in retail outlets find it difficult to frame the market boundaries and define the market. Integration of subtractive clustering in fuzzy clustering determines the exact boundaries of sub markets within the market. So managers' job is made easy to determine the number of segments.

Since effective validation could not be performed in "Jim Bezdek's FCM" algorithm to measure the range of fuzziness, we add a separate validity function called "Dunn's partition normalization coefficient" to determine the fuzziness of the cluster. The result of Dunn's Partition normalized coefficient indicates the existence of greater amount of fuzziness in the resulted segments. This proves that members in each segment often have multiple preferences and the stability of each segment is always a question mark. This leads to

go into the process of measuring the stability of the segments. To identify the crisp segments, it is essential to first defuzzify the fuzzy segments. Thereby, Crisp segments are formed based on the greater membership value in the fuzzy segment.

The stability of the segments has been measured by considering the mean value of various dimensions of the cluster. Results based on fuzzy clustering method and K-Means are similar. This denotes that the clusters are well separated and defined. However, the cluster size we obtained from the K-Means (Hard segmentation) is different from those in fuzzy clustering method (Soft Segmentation) which reflects the situation of the real world. By comparing the soft and hard segments, the managers can judge the market stability of each segment. Based on the research, it is found that the loyalist and the economic segments are considered to be stable. The interesting fact is that, the size of the economic segment is very low when it is compared with the size of loyalist segment. So based on the stability and the size of market, the managers can focus on loyalist segment and they can think of their market investment proposals like developing loyalty programs and taking advertising decision targeted towards loyalist, designing special prices for loyalists, reaching them on direct sales channel and so on.

To build a predictive model of group members based on the variables that provide the best discrimination between the groups, multi-group discriminant analysis has been performed. The F value variables, which separate the clusters within the K-Means cluster analysis are used as independent variables. It is found that the "loyalist segment" is differing from other segments based on the high value in lighting, product attractiveness, visual appearance of materials, convivial and fun. However, the "Economic segment" is differing from the other segments based on the low value of the attributes mentioned above. The "Innovators segment" is differing from other segments based on the high value of courtesy and friendliness of sales personnel, overall design, and merchandise. The "Female dominating" segment mostly overlaps the "Loyalist segment." The estimated discriminant model so helps managers predict easily the new unknown prospective customers.

The answer tree model rightly identifies the best predictor variable for loyalist segment. Instead of segmenting the market, market managers can easily grid the market to reach the target market. Thus, the rule and prediction of demographic variables on the Loyalist segment has been attained. The first best level of prediction is "working status" followed by "number of children" and "gender." If "Loyalist segment" is targeted, marketers can easily griddle the market based on variables like "people works outside home," "family having less than 1 child," and "gender" as well.

REFERENCES

Allred, C. R., Smith, S. M., & Swinyard, W. R. (2006). E-shopping lovers and fearful conservatives: A market segmentation analyses. *International Journal of Retail and Distribution Management*, *34*(4/5), 308–333. doi:10.1108/09590550610660251

Avi, G., Sridhar, S., & Christopher, L. T. (2008). Neo-Rawlsian fringes: A new approach to market segmentation and new product development. *Journal of Product Innovation Management*, *25*(5), 491–507. doi:10.1111/j.1540-5885.2008.00316.x

Broderick, A. J., Mueller, R. D., & Greenley, G. E. (2006). Applications of the behavioural homogeneity evaluation framework: The predictive ability of consumer involvement for international food market segmentation. *International Review of Retail, Distribution and Consumer Research*, *16*(5), 533–557. doi:10.1080/09593960600980154

Bruwer, J., & Li, E. (2007). Wine-related lifestyle (WRL) market segmentation: Demographic and behavioural factors. *Journal of Wine Research*, *18*(1), 19–34. doi:10.1080/09571260701526865

Chan, J. S. P., Jain, R., & Xia, Y. (2008). Market segmentation, liquidity spillover, and closed-end country fund discounts. *Journal of Financial Markets*, *11*(4), 377–399. doi:10.1016/j.finmar.2008.01.005

Chen, F. (2001). Market segmentation, advanced demand information, and supply chain Performance. *Manufacturing and Service Operations Management*, *3*(1), 53–67. doi:10.1287/msom.3.1.53.9993

Dallen, J. (2007). Sustainable transport, market segmentation and tourism: The Looe valley branch line railway, Cornwall, UK. *Journal of Sustainable Tourism*, *15*(2), 180–199. doi:10.2167/jost636.0

Dias, J. G., & Vermunt, J. K. (2007). Latent class modeling of website users' search patterns: Implications for online market segmentation. *Journal of Retailing and Consumer Services*, *14*(6), 359–368. doi:10.1016/j.jretconser.2007.02.007

Fuller, J., & Matzler, K. (2008). Customer delight and market segmentation: An application of the three-factor theory of customer satisfaction on life style groups. *Tourism Management*, *29*(1), 116–126. doi:10.1016/j.tourman.2007.03.021

Gurau, C., & Tinson, J. (2003). Early evangelist or reluctant Rudolph? Attitudes towards the Christmas commercial campaign. *Journal of Consumer Behaviour*, *3*(1), 48–62. doi:10.1002/cb.121

Hemalatha, M., Sivakumar, V. J., & Jayakumar, G. S. D. S. (2009). Segmentation of Indian shoppers based on store attributes. *International Journal of Business Innovation and Research*, *3*(6), 651–669. doi:10.1504/IJBIR.2009.027207

Hsu, J. L., & Chang, W. (2002). Market segmentation of fresh meat shoppers in Taiwan. *International Review of Retail, Distribution and Consumer Research, 12*(4), 423–436. doi:10.1080/09593960210151180

Hung, C., & Tsai, C. (2008). Market segmentation based on hierarchical self-organizing map for markets of multimedia on demand. *Expert Systems with Applications, 34*(1), 780–787. doi:10.1016/j.eswa.2006.10.012

Iniesta, M. A., & Sanchez, M. (2002). Retail-consumer commitment and market segmentation. *International Review of Retail, Distribution and Consumer Research, 12*(3), 261–279. doi:10.1080/09593960210139661

Jarratt, D. G. (1996). A shopper taxonomy for retail strategy development. *International Review of Retail, Distribution and Consumer Research, 6*(2), 196–215. doi:10.1080/09593969600000020

Jianan, W., & DeSarbo, W. S. (2005). Market segmentation for customer satisfaction studies via a new latent structure multidimensional scaling model. *Applied Stochastic Models in Business and Industry, 21*(4/5), 303–309.

Jindal, T. (2008). Ride the tiger. *Financial Management, 1*, 20–23.

John, E. S., Orsay, K., & Cesar, A. D. M. (2007). Profiling Peruvian consumers lifestyles, market segmentation, and ethnocentrism. *Latin American Business Review, 8*(4), 38–59.

Ko, E., Kim, E., Charles, R. T., Kim, K. H., & Kang, I. J. (2007). Cross - national market segmentation in the fashion industry. *International Marketing Review, 24*(5), 629–651. doi:10.1108/02651330710828022

Koc, E., & Altinay, G. (2007). An analysis of seasonality in monthly per person tourist spending in Turkish inbound tourism from a market segmentation perspective. *Tourism Management, 28*(1), 227–237. doi:10.1016/j.tourman.2006.01.003

Lill, D. J., Peterson, R. T., & Wall, L. C. (1981). How small business can use consumer shopping types as a planning tool. *American Journal of Small Business, 6*(1), 36–47.

Menzly, L., & Ozbas, O. (2010). Market segmentation and cross-predictability of returns. *The Journal of Finance, 65*, 1555–1580. doi:10.1111/j.1540-6261.2010.01578.x

Parikh, D. (2006). Measuring retail service quality: An empirical assessment of the instrument. *Vikalpa: The Journal for Decision Makers, 31*(2), 45–55.

Pitt, L., Morris, M. H., & Oosthuizen, P. (1996). Expectations of service quality as an industrial market segmentation variable. *Service Industries Journal, 16*(1), 1–9. doi:10.1080/02642069600000001

Quinn, L., Hines, T., & Bennison, D. (2007). Making sense of market segmentation: A fashion retailing case. *European Journal of Marketing, 41*(5/6), 439–465. doi:10.1108/03090560710737552

Rinne, H., & Swinyard, W. R. (1995). Segmenting the discount store market: The domination of the difficult discounter core. *International Review of Retail, Distribution and Consumer Research, 5*(2), 123–145. doi:10.1080/09593969500000010

Roos, J. A., Eastin, I. L., & Matsuguma, H. (2005). Market segmentation and analysis of Japan's residential post and beam construction market. *Forest Products Journal, 55*(4), 24–30.

Sarstedt, M. (2008). Market segmentation with mixture regression models: Understanding measures that guide model selection. *Journal of Targeting. Measurement and Analysis for Marketing, 16*(3), 228–246. doi:10.1057/jt.2008.9

Sewall, M. A. (1978). Market segmentation based on consumer ratings of proposed product designs. *JMR, Journal of Marketing Research, 15*(4), 557–564. doi:10.2307/3150625

Shapiro, D., & Shi, X. (2008). Market segmentation: The role of opaque travel agencies. *Journal of Economics & Management Strategy, 17*(4), 803–837. doi:10.1111/j.1530-9134.2008.00196.x

Simkin, L. (2008). Achieving market segmentation from B2B sectorisation. *Journal of Business and Industrial Marketing, 23*(7), 464–474. doi:10.1108/08858620810901220

Sinha, P. K. (2003). Shopping orientation in the evolving Indian market. *Vikalpa: The Journal for Decision Makers, 28*(2), 13–22.

Verbeke, W., Vermeir, I., & Brunso, K. (2007). Consumer evaluation of fish quality as basis for fish market segmentation. *Food Quality and Preference, 18*(4), 651–661. doi:10.1016/j.foodqual.2006.09.005

Yiyang, Z., Jiao, J. R., & Yongsheng, M. (2007). Market segmentation for product family positioning based on fuzzy clustering. *Journal of Engineering Design, 18*(3), 227–241. doi:10.1080/09544820600752781

Yu, J., & Zhou, J. X. (2010). Segmenting young Chinese consumers based on shopping-decision styles: A regional comparison. *Journal of International Consumer Marketing, 22*(1), 59–71. doi:10.1080/08961530902844964

Chapter 9
Rough Web Intelligent Techniques for Page Recommendation

H. Hannah Inbarani
Periyar University, India

K. Thangavel
Periyar University, India

ABSTRACT

Recommender systems represent a prominent class of personalized Web applications, which particularly focus on the user-dependent filtering and selection of relevant information. Recommender Systems have been a subject of extensive research in Artificial Intelligence over the last decade, but with today's increasing number of e-commerce environments on the Web, the demand for new approaches to intelligent product recommendation is higher than ever. There are more online users, more online channels, more vendors, more products, and, most importantly, increasingly complex products and services. These recent developments in the area of recommender systems generated new demands, in particular with respect to interactivity, adaptivity, and user preference elicitation. These challenges, however, are also in the focus of general Web page recommendation research. The goal of this chapter is to develop robust techniques to model noisy data sets containing an unknown number of overlapping categories and apply them for Web personalization and mining. In this chapter, rough set-based clustering approaches are used to discover Web user access patterns, and these techniques compute a number of clusters automatically from the Web log data using statistical techniques. The suitability of rough clustering approaches for Web page recommendation are measured using predictive accuracy metrics.

INTRODUCTION

The page recommendation process based on Web usage mining consists of three phases: data preparation and transformation, pattern discovery, and recommendation. Of these, only the latter

DOI: 10.4018/978-1-4666-2542-6.ch009

phase is performed in real-time. A variety of data mining techniques can be applied to this data in the pattern discovery phase, such as clustering, association rule mining, sequential pattern discovery, and probabilistic modelling. The results of the mining phase are transformed into aggregate user models, suitable for use in the recommendation phase (Bamshad Mobasher, et al., 2007). The recommendation engine considers the active user's profile in conjunction with the discovered patterns to provide personalized content. From an architectural and algorithmic point of view personalization systems fall into three basic categories: Rule-based systems, content-filtering systems, and collaborative filtering systems. Our primary focus in this chapter is on model-based approaches to collaborative filtering in which models are learned through a variety of data mining techniques.

Rough sets theory is applied to design smart Computational Web Intelligence (CWI) systems. Rough Web Intelligence (RWI) has two major techniques which are

1. Rough sets, and
2. Web Technology (WT).

The main goal is to design intelligent rough e-agents which can deal with roughness of data, information and knowledge for e-Business applications effectively.

Rough set theory introduced by Pawlak (1982) deals with uncertainty and vagueness. Rough set theory became popular among scientists around the world due to its fundamental importance in the field of artificial intelligence and cognitive sciences. Similar to fuzzy set theory it is not an alternative to classical set theory but it is embedded in it. Rough set theory can be viewed as a specific implementation of Frege's idea of vagueness, i.e., imprecision in the data is expressed by a boundary region of a set, and not by a partial membership, like in fuzzy set. The goal of this chapter is to develop robust techniques to model noisy data sets containing an unknown number of overlapping categories, and apply them for Web personalization and mining.

This chapter is organized as follows: the next section describes the background, followed by an explanation of the motivation behind this approach. Later, a description of the rough cluster-ing approaches for Web page recommendation is covered. After this, the experimental results are presented, and the last section concludes this chapter.

BACKGROUND

Web mining is the use of data mining techniques to automatically discover and extract information from World Wide Web documents and services. Web mining is a technique to discover and analyze the useful information from the Web data. Web data mining can be divided in three general categories: Web content mining, Web structure mining and finally Web usage mining (Zaiane, et al., 1999). Web mining can be defined roughly as data mining using data generated by the Web and includes the following sub areas: Web content mining, Web usage mining, and Web structure mining (Srivastava, et al., 2000). In Web Content Mining (WCM) useful information is extracted from the content of Web pages (Pal, et al., 2002) as e.g. free text inside a Web page, semi-structured data such as HTML code, pictures, and downloadable files. Web Structure Mining (WSM) aims at generating a structural summary about the Web site and Web pages. While Web content mining mainly focuses on the structure of inner document, Web structure mining tries to discover the link structure of the hyperlinks at the inter document level. Web Usage Mining (WUM) is applied to the data generated by visits to a Web site, especially those contained in Web log files. Other sources can be browser logs, user profiles, user sessions, bookmarks, folders, and scrolls (Pal, et al., 2002).

Personalization of Web sites is a very challenging field of both, current research as well as applications that have as goals e.g. individualized marketing for E-Commerce or dynamic recommendations to a Web visitor based on his/her profile and usage behavior (Dean, et al., 1999; Chen, et al., 2002). Analyzing Web data can also be used for system improvements providing the key to understanding Web traffic behavior. Advanced load balancing, data distribution or policies for Web caching as well as higher security standards are potential benefits of such improvements (Padmanabhan, et al. 1996; Schechter, et al., 1998). Similar analyses could be used for modification of Web sites. Understanding visitors' behavior in a Web site provides hints for adequate design and update decisions. Business intelligence covers the application of intelligent techniques in order to improve certain businesses, mainly in marketing.

Many Web mining techniques have been used in Web personalization systems to discover usage patterns from Web data such as clustering techniques, association rule mining, and click pattern analysis (Pawan Lingras, et al., 2003). Krishnapuram and Hathaway (Krishnapram, 2001; Hathaway, 1993) proposed to use fuzzy set theory to group Web users into several disjoint clusters. Some other researchers tried to explore clustering method by another soft computing technique, rough theory. The upper and lower approximations of rough sets are used to model the clusters (De, 2004; Lingras, 2002, 2004; Mitra, 2004). De et al. (2004) tries to use rough approximation to cluster Web transactions. Lingras (2002) applied the unsupervised rough set clustering based on genetic algorithms to group Web visitors. Later, Lingras (2004) proposed a modified rough K-Means method to cluster Web visitors. Mitra (2004) proposed a clustering algorithm based on rough K-Means and genetic algorithm.

In the data mining community, user profiling is often studied in the context of personalization (Adomavicius, et al., 2002; Mobasher, et al., 2002) and fraud detection (Burge, et al., 1997; Fawcett, et al., 1996; Hilas, et al., 2006; Hollmen, et al., 2000). In the information retrieval community, user profiles are used for personalized information retrieval or filtering (Fan, et al., 2005; Godoy, et al., 2006; Zigoris, et al., 2006). Constructing accurate and comprehensive user

profiles of individual users is one of the key issues in developing personalization applications. A user profile normally contains a list of variables (Cadez, et al., 2001; Cortes, et al., 1999) and/or conjunctive rules (e.g. association rules [Agrawal, et al., 1996; Aggarwal, et al., 2002] and classification rules [Breiman, et al., 1984]).

Adomavicius et al. (2004) studies user profiles as a set of rules. Their focus is on rule validation since there are large numbers of rules discovered for each user. Rules validated by experts serve as the user profiles. Instead of just individual user profiles for personalization, there has also been work on learning aggregate profiles, such as the work of Mobasher et al. (2002), which builds profiles that can apply across groups of users who may have similar interests. They use clustering to generate aggregate user profiles, which are evaluated in the context of providing recommendations as an integrated part of a personalization engine. Rather than learning profiles from click-stream data, Goecks et al. (2000) describes an approach that unobtrusively monitors user activity on pages (such as how much the user scrolls) to build profiles that capture user interest in specific pages or content. There is also other user profiling work based on Web usage data that is not associated with personalization. Mushtao et al. (2004) generates user profiles from various Web log files of a Web site. They assume that the owner of the Web site defines a list of topics and associates each Web page with one or more of these topics. A user profile is generated according to the time the user spent on the Web pages of different topics. Rafter et al. (2001) generates profiles from server logs of a career Web site. A user profile is generated from the number of clicks on job openings. Zhang et al. (2006) builds a rule-based Web user profiling platform that can be applied to different Web services to generate user profiles from their usage data, and the platform is not tied to any specific applications. None of the previous research on user profiling using Web usage data has considered user identification based on user-centric data.

Recommender systems are usually classified according to their approach to rating estimation and, in the next section, we will present such a classification that was proposed in the literature and will provide a survey of different types of recommender systems. The commonly accepted formulation of the recommendation problem was first stated in Hill et al. (1995), Resnick (1994), and Shardanand et al. (1995), and this problem has been studied extensively since then.

Moreover, recommender systems are usually classified into the following categories, based on how recommendations are made (Balabanovic, et al., 1997):

- **Content-based recommendations:** The user will be recommended items similar to the ones the user preferred in the past;
- **Collaborative recommendations:** The user will be recommended items that people with similar tastes and preferences liked in the past;
- **Hybrid approaches:** These methods combine collaborative and content-based methods.

In this chapter, model based collaborative filtering approach is used for page recommendation. Models are constructed using clustering approaches.

RESEARCH MOTIVATION

In applications such as Web mining, the categorization techniques need to satisfy the following requirements:

- The technique should be able to determine the appropriate number of components automatically, since a priori knowledge

about the number of components is rarely available.

- It needs to be robust. By robustness, it is meant that the categorization process (and hence the performance of a system) should not be affected drastically due to outliers (bad observations), provided there is enough good data to support the assumed model.
- The technique should be able to handle overlapping components.
- It needs to be scalable to extremely large high-dimensional data sets.

To address these challenges two rough clustering approaches, GRK and GRF, are proposed and compared with Rough K-Means approach proposed by Lingras.

METHODOLOGY

The Recommendation Process consists of two phases. The overall architecture of recommendation is shown in Figure 1.

- **Offline Phase:** The three steps of offline phase are
  - Preprocessing,
  - Construction of user model(Pattern Discovery)
  - User Profiling
- **Online Phase:** The two steps of online phase are
  - Match active session with user profiles
  - Recommend top N list of pages

CLUSTERING

The primary motivation behind the use of clustering (and more generally, model-based algorithms) in collaborative filtering (Guandong Xu, 2008) and Web usage mining is to improve the efficiency and

Figure 1. System architecture

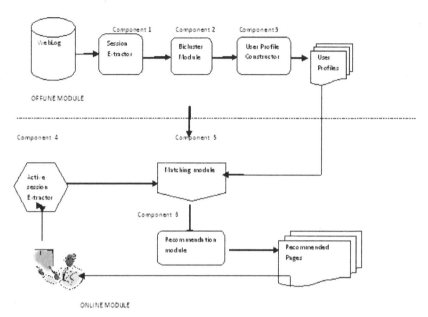

scalability of the real-time personalization tasks. In practical applications of clustering algorithms, several problems must be solved, including determination of the number of clusters and evaluation of the quality of the partitions. In order to increase the robustness of clustering and overlapping of user clusters, rough and rough fuzzy clustering techniques are applied for page recommendation.

ROUGH CLUSTERING

Rough sets theory is applied to design smart Computational Web Intelligence (CWI) systems. Rough Web Intelligence (RWI) has two major techniques which are

1.	Rough sets, and
2.	Web Technology (WT).

The main goal is to design intelligent rough e-agents which can deal with roughness of data, information and knowledge for e-Business applications effectively. Rough set theory introduced by Pawlak (1982) deals with uncertainty and vague-

ness. Rough set theory became popular among scientists around the world due to its fundamental importance in the field of artificial intelligence and cognitive sciences. Similar to fuzzy set theory it is not an alternative to classical set theory but it is embedded in it. Rough set theory can be viewed as a specific implementation of Frege's idea of vagueness, i.e., imprecision in this approach is expressed by a boundary region of a set, and not by a partial membership, like in fuzzy set. The goal of this chapter is to develop robust techniques to model noisy data sets containing an unknown number of overlapping categories, and apply them for Web personalization and mining. A rough cluster is defined in a similar manner to a rough set that is with a lower and upper approximation. The lower approximation of a rough cluster contains objects that only belong to that cluster. The upper approximation of a rough cluster contains objects in the cluster which are also members of other clusters (Qinbao Song, 2006; Sushmita Mitra, 2006).

An important distinction between rough clustering and traditional clustering approaches is that, with rough clustering, an object can belong to more than one cluster. This permits overlaps between clusters.

In this chapter, Gaussian Rough clustering (GR) and Gaussian Rough Fuzzy (GRF) clustering are proposed to cluster Web log transactions. The main goal of the proposed approaches is to handle the issues discussed in section 2. The resulting rough clusters are used for Web page recommendation. The metrics used for measuring the accuracy of the proposed approaches are Precision, Coverage, and F1.

GAUSSIAN ROUGH K-MEANS CLUSTERING (GRK)

In practice, each cluster can be mathematically represented by a parametric distribution, like a Gaussian (continuous) or a Poisson (discrete). The entire data set is therefore modeled by a mixture of these distributions. An individual distribution used to model a specific cluster is often referred to as a component distribution. Hence, Gaussian distribution is pertained in this approach to select the threshold value. The complete description of the algorithm is presented in Figure 2.

In this method, Web users are clustered based on Rough set theory and this algorithm is Intelligent in the sense that the optimum number of clusters is determined automatically this algorithm. Gaussian distribution function is employed to tune the threshold and relative importance of upper and lower approximations of the rough sets are used in modeling the clusters. First, Web user fuzzy subsets are created and similarity matrix is computed according to fuzzy set theory as defined in Mitra (2004) and Web server logs. In the first step, we create Web user fuzzy subsets and Web page fuzzy subsets according to fuzzy set theory and Web server logs. Let U be the set of users who access the Web site W during a period of time, and U is denoted as $U = \{u_i, u_2, ..., u_m\}$, where $1 \leq i \leq m$ m and m is the number of users.

Let P be the set of Web pages of the Web site W, the P is denoted as $P = \{P_1, P_2, ..., P_n\}$, where $1 \leq i \leq n$ n and n is the number of Web pages of the Web site W. The user fuzzy subset and Web page fuzzy subset are defined as follows:

The user fuzzy subset μ_{uj} of the jth user u_j that reflects the user's browsing behavior is defined as:

$$\mu_{uj}\left(p_i, f_{uuj}\left(p_i\right)\right) | p_i \in URL$$

and

$$1 \leq i \leq n$$

where $f_{uuj} : URL \rightarrow [0,1]$ is the membership function defined as

$$f_{uuj}(url_i)) = S(u_j, p_i) / \Sigma_{k=1}^{N} S(u_j, p_i) \qquad (1)$$

where $S(u_j, p_j)$ is the sequence of page accesses of u_j accesses of p_i. Similarly page fuzzy subset can be defined.

In the second step, fuzzy similarity matrix is derived using

$$Fsim\left(S_i, S_j\right) = \frac{\sum_{k=1}^{m} S_{ik} \wedge S_{ij}}{\sum_{k=1}^{m} S_{ik} \vee S_{ij}} \qquad (2)$$

In the third step, threshold value is computed using Gaussian distribution [97]. The density function of a univariate normal (or Gaussian) distribution is given by:

$$P\left(x, \mu, \sigma\right)^2 = \frac{1}{\sqrt{2\Pi\alpha}} \exp(-\frac{1}{2\alpha^2}\left(S - \mu\right)^2)$$

(3)

- μ = Mean of set of user sessions
- α = Standard deviation of set of user sessions

- S= Set of user session objects

In the fourth step, using the threshold determined by Gaussian distribution, centroids are computed. In the fifth step, using these centroids as initial seed points, users are clustered as in Rough K-Means (Sushmita Mitra, 2004).

GAUSSIAN ROUGH FUZZY CLUSTERING (GRF)

In this method, users are clustered based on Rough fuzzy clustering method and this algorithm is Intelligent in the sense that the optimum number of clusters is determined using Gaussian distribution automatically by this algorithm.

The hybrid notion of rough fuzzy sets comes from the combination of two models of uncertainty like vagueness by handling rough sets and fuzzy sets. First, Web user fuzzy subsets are created and similarity matrix is computed according to fuzzy set theory as defined in Eirinaki et al. (2003) and Web server logs. In the second step, number of clusters is determined using Gaussian distribution and then in the third step, users are clustered using rough fuzzy clustering method which is a slight modification of step 5 of the previous algorithm in the sense that instead of distance function, fuzzy membership value is used as in Song et al. (2006) and the value of fuzzy parameter m is taken as 2. The complete description of the algorithm is depicted in Figure 3.

USER PROFILING

User sessions (or clicks) can be extracted from Web log files and then submitted, offline, to clustering to discover typical user trends or profiles in the web click stream data. A profile can consist of a set of URLs that are relevant to the sessions assigned to a given cluster (Cheng, et al., 2000).

Once these profiles are discovered, they can be exploited as part of an automated personalization on the website, by treating them as summarized user models against which all future user sessions are compared. In rough clustering, cluster prototypes incorporate the concepts of upper and lower approximations. Since the patterns lying in the lower approximation definitely belong to a rough cluster, they are assigned a higher weight as specified by the parameter W_l. The patterns lying in boundary region are assigned a relatively lower weight as specified by the parameter W_u during computation. The user profiling approach is described in Figure 4.

RECOMMENDATION PROCESS

The goal of personalization based on anonymous web usage data is to compute a recommendation set for the current (active) user session, consisting of the objects (links, ads, text, products, etc.) that most closely match the current user profile. The recommendation engine is the online component of a usage-based personalization system.

In computing the matching score between aggregate profiles and the current active session, a variety of similarity measures can be used (Bamshad Mobasher, 2002). In traditional collaborative filtering domains (where feature weights are item ratings on a discrete scale), the Pearson r correlation coefficient is commonly used. This measure is based on the deviations of users' ratings on various items from their mean ratings on all rated items. However, this measure not appropriate in the context of anonymous personalization based on click-stream data.

Given the mapping of user transactions into a multi-dimensional space as vectors of page views, standard clustering algorithms, such as K-Means, generally partition this space into groups of transactions that are close to each other based on a measure of distance or instead other distance

Figure 2. Gaussian rough clustering

Algorithm	:	Gaussian Rough K-Means clustering (GRK)

Input : S - User Access Matrix
Output : **Users in Lower approximation** clusters and
Users in Boundary region clusters
Procedure :

Step 1: Compute Threshold α using Gaussian distribution function
  K = 1;
  For each user session $S_i \in S$
  If u_i not placed in any cluster k   (k= 1, 2, . . . , K)
  K++; i^{th} user session S_i is placed in cluster K;
    end
    For each user j <> i
      Compute the similarity of ith user with j^{th} user Sim(i, j)
      If (Sim (i, j) > threshold α place j in cluster k
    End
  End

Step 2: Compute means Z_k for the K clusters for I = 1, 2, . . . , K

Step 3: Assign each data object (pattern point) S_i to the lower approximation $\underline{C_k}$ or

Upper approximation $\overline{C_k}$ by computing the difference in its distance

$d(S_i - Z_p) - d(S_i - Z_q)$ from cluster centroid pairs Z_p and Z_q, 1<= j,q<=K

Step 4 : If distance is less than some   threshold ε ,then
    $S_i \in \overline{C_j}$ and $S_i \in \overline{C_i}$ cannot be a member of any lower approximation
  else
    $S_i \in \underline{C_i}$ such that distance is minimum over the K clusters

Step 5: Compute new mean for each cluster k using

$$Z_k = W_l \sum_{S_p \in \underline{C_i}} \frac{S_i}{|\underline{C_i}|} + W_u \sum_{S_p \in \overline{C_i}} \frac{S_i}{|\overline{C_i}|}$$

Based on distance and Iterate steps 3 to 4 until convergence, i.e., there are no more

or similarity measures which are applicable in the context of a vector space model can be used. In this thesis, the cosine coefficient, commonly used in information retrieval, is used to measure the cosine of the angle between two vectors. The cosine coefficient can be computed by normalizing the dot product of two vectors with respect to their vector.

EVALUATION MEASURES

Davies-Bouldin Index

The Davies-Bouldin (DB) index is based on similarity measure of clusters whose bases are the dispersion measure of a cluster and the cluster dissimilarity measure. The DB index measures

Figure 3. Gaussian rough fuzzy clustering

Algorithm   :Gaussian Rough Fuzzy clustering (GRF)

Input   :S - User Access Matrix
Output   : Lower approximation clusters and Boundary region clusters

Procedure:
Step 1:   For each user u_i
             Compute user fuzzy subset as defined in according to formula defined in
             Eqn.(4.2)
             Compute fuzzy similarity fsim
             K = 1;
               For each user u_i
                  K++;
               i^{th}user is placed in cluster k;
               For each user j <> i
               Compute fuzzy similarity of i^{th}user with j^{th}user fsim(i,j)
               If(fsim(i,j) > threshold α place j in cluster K
               End
               End
Step 2: Compute Fuzzy membership as defined in FCM

Step 3: Calculate means m_i for the K clusters.

Step 4: Assign each data object (pattern point) S_p to the lower approximation
           $\underline{C_i}$or upper approximation $\overline{C_i}$by computing the difference in its distance
           $d(S_p - \mu_i) - d(S_p-\mu_j)$from membership pairs μ_i and μ_j.

Step 5 : If distance is less than some threshold ε, then$S_p \in \overline{C_i}$ and $S_p \in \overline{C_i}$cannot
           Be a member of any lower approximation,
           else
               $Ses_p \in \underline{C_i}$, a member of lower approximation.

*Step 6:*Compute new mean for each cluster k using

the average of similarity between each cluster and its most similar one. As the clusters have to be compact and separated the lower DB index means better cluster configuration. It is a function of the ratio of the sum of within-cluster distance to between cluster separations. As clusters have to be compact and separated, the lower DB index means better cluster configuration. The DB index (Pal, et al., 1995; Davies, et al., 1979; Xuejian Xiong, 2004) is defined as:

$$DB = \frac{1}{K}\sum_{i=1}^{K}\left[\max_{\substack{j=1\ldots K, \\ i=1..K, i \neq j}}\left\{\frac{SU(Z_{i,}) + SU(Z_{j,})}{d_{(C_i, C_j)}}\right\}\right] \quad (1)$$

The formula to find the average distance between objects within the clusterfor crisp clusters is expressed as:

Figure 4. Building user profile based on rough and rough fuzzy clustering

Algorithm: Building user profile based on Rough and Rough Fuzzy Clustering
Input : A set of K user session clusters
Output : A set of user profiles
Procedure:
Step 1:   Apply Rough clustering algorithm for clustering sessions of web users
Step 2:   For each cluster K, furthermore, we calculate its mean vector as a) For users in Lower approximation, the weights of the pages visited by users are taken as W_l. b) For users in boundary region, the weight of the pages visited by users is taken as W_u.
Step 3:   For each page within the cluster, if the value is less than the threshold α, the corresponding page will be filtered out, otherwise be

$$SU(Z_i) = \frac{1}{K} \sum_{s_j TZ_i}^{c} d(s_j, C_i) \quad (2)$$

Similarly, the rough within-cluster distance is formulated based on W_l and W_u to find Rough DB index (Sushmita Mitra, 2006).

$$SU(Z_i) = \begin{cases} w_l \dfrac{\sum_{S_{k \in \underline{B U}_i} } u_{ik}^{m'} S_k}{\sum_{s_{k \in \underline{B U}_i}} u_{ik}^{m'}} + w_{up} \\[2ex] \dfrac{\sum_{s_{k/\left(\overline{B U}_i - \underline{B U}_i\right)}} u_{ik}^{m'} S_k}{\sum_{s_{k/\left(\overline{B U}_i - \underline{B U}_i\right)}} u_{ik}^{m'}} \\[2ex] if\ \underline{B U}_i \ne \varnothing \wedge B U_i - \underline{B U}_i \ne \varnothing, \\[1ex] \dfrac{\sum_{S_{k/\left(\overline{B U}_i - \underline{B U}_i\right)}} u_{ik}^{m'} S_k}{\sum_{s_{k/\left(\overline{B U}_i - \underline{B U}_i\right)}} u_{ik}^{m'}} \\[2ex] if\ \underline{B U}_i \ne \varnothing \wedge B U_i - \underline{B U}_i \ne \varnothing, \\[1ex] \dfrac{\sum_{S_{k \in \underline{B U}_i}} u_{ik}^{m'} S_k}{\sum_{s_{k \in \underline{B U}_i}} u_{ik}^{m'}}\ otherwise. \end{cases}$$

$$(3)$$

Cosine Similarity

The most extensively used similarity measures are based on correlation and cosine-similarity. Specifically, user-based clustering algorithms mainly use Pearson's correlation, whereas for page view clustering algorithms, the adjusted cosine measure is preferred. The adjusted cosine measure is a variation of the simple cosine formula that normalizes bias from subjective ratings of different users. Cosine similarity is used in this work for matching active session with user profiles.

Usage profiles are represented assets of page view-weight pairs. This allows both the active session and the profiles to be treated as n-dimensional vectors over the space of page views in the site. Thus, given a usage profile UP, we can represent UP as a vector:

$$UP_c = \left\{ wt_1^{\,C},\ wt_2^{\,C},\ \ldots,\ wt_n^{\,C} \right\}$$

where

$$Wt_i C = \begin{cases} Wt(p_i, C)\ if\ P_i \in C \\ 0\ ,otherwise \end{cases}$$

Table 1. User profiles generated using GR clustering

Cluster	Pages in Lower approximation	Pages in Upper approximation
1	/aboutus.html /microsoft.net-development.html /search-engine-optimization.html	/asp-development.html /database-driven-website.html

In computing the matching score between aggregate profiles and the current active session, a variety of similarity measures can be used. In our case, we use the cosine coefficient, commonly used in information retrieval, which measures the cosine of the angle between two vectors. The cosine coefficient can be computed by normalizing the dot product of two vectors with respect to their vector norm. The matching score is normalized for the size of the profiles and the active session.

This corresponds to the intuitive notion that we should see more of the user's active session before obtaining a better match with a larger cluster representing a user profile. The cosine coefficient between active session s_i and UP_k can be defined as:

$$Similarity\left(s_i, UP_k\right) = \frac{\sum_k w_k^c \cdot S_i}{\sqrt{\sum_i (S_i)^2 \cdot \sum_k (w_k^c)^2}}$$

(4)

Distance Measure

Euclidean distance between any two vectors X and Y of size n can be defined as:

$$d_E\left(x,y\right) = \sqrt{\sum_{i=1}^n \left(x_i - y_i\right)^2}$$

(5)

Table 2. Comparative performance of rough clustering algorithms

	No. of Users	Clustering Algorithm	No. of Clusters K (Input)	No. of Clusters Generated	DaviesBouldin Index
		RK		-	2.5354
	1000	GRK	10	23	1.8858
		GRF		23	1.8522
		RK		-	2.5354
	1500	GRK	7	25	1.7640
		GRF		25	1.6358
		RK		-	2.5354
	2000	GRK	8	28	1.8327
		GRF		28	1.6973
		RK		-	4.4425
	2500	GRK	9	29	1.8965
		GRF		29	1.8411
		RK		-	2.1229
	3000	GRK	9	32	1.8484
		GRF		32	1.6472

Table 3. Recommended list of pages

Active session	Recommended Pages	Recommendation score
/	/search-engine- optimization.html	1
/index.html	/microsoft.net- development.html	0.5000
/aboutus.html	/dbms.html	0.5000
/contact.html	/sitemap.html	0.7143
	/join.php	0.4286
/database-driven-	/drupal-development.html	0.7000
website.html	/graphics-design.html	1.0000
/asp-development.html	/web-development.html	1.0000
	/enterprise-web- pplications.html	0.5000
	/Webservices.html	1.0000
	/application-developments.html	1.0000
	/joomla-development.html	1.0000
	/content-management-system.html	0.5000
	/magento-development.html	0.5000

WEB PAGE RECOMMENDATION METRICS

Evaluation Methodology

The basic methodology used is as follows: For a given transaction t in the evaluation set, and an active session window size w, we randomly chose |t|−w+1 groups of items from the transaction as the surrogate active session windows, each having size n. For each of these active sessions, we produced a recommendation set based on aggregate profiles and compared the set to the remaining items in the transaction (i.e., t −w) in order to compute the precision, coverage, F1, and R scores. For each of these measures, the final score for the transaction t was the mean score over all of the |t|−w +1 surrogate active sessions associated with it. Finally, the mean over all transactions in the evaluation set was compute as the overall evaluation score for each measure.

Scalability

The performance and scalability dimension aims to measure the response time of a given recommendation algorithm and how easily it can scale to handle a large number of concurrent requests

Figure 5. Rough DB index values for the data sets

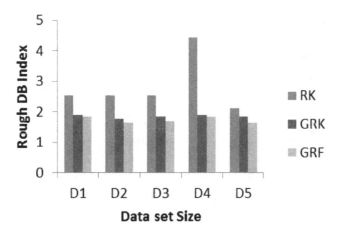

Figure 6. Users in lower approximation and boundary area for D1 (K=23)

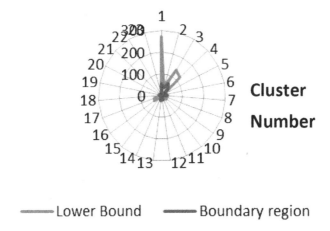

Figure 7. Users in the boundary area for D1

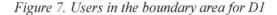

for recommendations. Typically, these systems need to be able to handle large volumes of recommendation requests without significantly adding to the response time of the web site that they have been deployed on. The proposed approaches in this thesis are scalable because the recommendation is performed online and user profile discovery is an offline process. The on-line parts concern the time it takes to create a recommendation list, based on the pages visited by the active user session. In offline processing, to measure the scalability of the proposed approaches in this thesis, various sizes of data sets have been taken and the accuracy has been measured.

Performance Accuracy Measures

The performances of clustering/biclustering approaches discussed in this thesis are measured using 3 different standard measures, namely, precision, coverage, and the F1-Measure.

Precision and Recall are standard metrics used in information retrieval. While precision measures the probability that a selected item is relevant, recall measures the probability that a relevant item is selected. Precision and recall are commonly used in evaluating the selection task. Coverage measures the percentage of the universe of items that the recommendation system is capable of

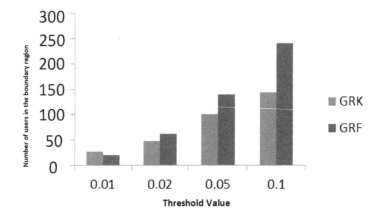

recommending. The F1-Measure that combines precision and coverage has also been used for this purpose task. In this thesis, precision, coverage, and F1-Measure are the metrics used for measuring the prediction process.

Each user session t is viewed as a set of page views and active window size $w \subseteq t$ (of size |w|) and the page views included in the recommendation set is R using the recommendation engine (Antonio Picariello, et al., 2008). A recommendation set based on aggregate profiles and compared the set to the remaining items in the transaction (i.e., t −w) in order to compute the precision, coverage, F1, and R scores. Then the precision of R with respect to t is defined as:

$$\Pr ecision\left(R, \; t\right)=\frac{\mid R \cap \; (t-w)\mid}{\mid R \mid}$$

(6)

and the coverage of R with respect to t is defined as:

$$Coverage\left(R,t\right)=\frac{\mid R \cap \; (t-w)\mid}{\mid t-w \mid}$$

(7)

These measures are adaptations of the standard measures, precision, and recall, often used in information retrieval. In this context, precision measures the degree to which the recommenda-

tion engine produces accurate recommendations (i.e., the proportion of relevant recommendations to the total number of recommendations). On the other hand, coverage measures the ability of the recommendation engine to produce all of the page views that are likely to be visited by the user (proportion of relevant recommendations to all page views that should be recommended).

Ideally, one would like high precision and high coverage. A single measure that captures both precision and coverage is F1-Measure

$$F1\left(R,t\right)=\frac{\begin{array}{c}(2\times precision(R,t)\times\\ \mathrm{cov}\, erage(R,t))\end{array}}{\begin{array}{c}(precision(R,t)+\\ \mathrm{cov}\, erage(R,t))\end{array}}$$

(8)

The F1-Measure attains its maximum value when both precision and coverage are maximized.

Predictive Accuracy

Web personalization is viewed as a data mining task. Hence the predictive accuracy of models learned for this purpose can be evaluated using a number of metrics that have been used in machine learning and data mining literature such as Mean Absolute Error (MAE) and Receiver Operating Characteristic (ROC) measure, depending on the formulation of the learning task. In this thesis, MAE is used to measure the predictive accuracy of Web page recommendation results.

Mean Absolute Error (MAE)

$$\mathrm{MAE} = \sum \frac{\left|X-X^{'}\right|}{N}$$

(9)

where X is the rating given by the user, X′ is the rating assigned by the system and N is the number of predictions.

Figure 8. Optimum number of clusters generated by GR and GRF

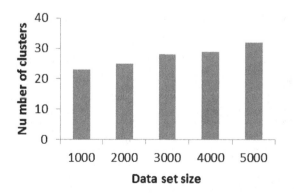

Figure 9. Performance of proposed approaches for D1

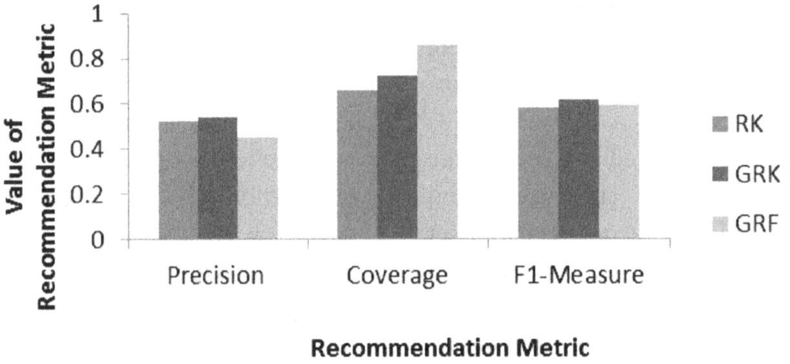

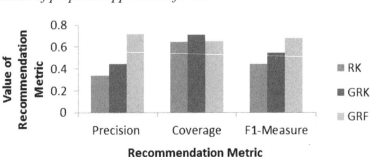

EXPERIMENTAL RESULTS

Data Source

The access logs from www.aimmtech.com were used for the analysis of proposed algorithms. After preprocessing and removing references by Web spiders, image files and style sheet files, a total of 3440 transactions were produced using the transaction identification process. The total number of URLs representing page views was 34 and we eliminated the page views appearing in less than 0.25% of the transactions. In order to evaluate the proposed algorithms, we applied it to the Web log collected from AIIMTECH.com by taking categories of pages visited by 1000, 1500, 2000, 2500, and 3000 users denoted by D1, D2, D3, D4, and D5. The Web pages after preprocessing is shown in Table 3.

USER PROFILES

Discovery of Aggregate Profiles Based on Rough User Clustering

In this method user profiles are generated as described in section 4 based on user transaction clustering. In generating the usage profiles, low-support page views (i.e. those with mean value below a certain threshold α) are filtered out. The value of α is taken as 0.3.

User profile is generated separately for page views in lower approximation clusters and page views in boundary region clusters. Each user profile is listed in ordered page views' sequence with weights, which means the greater weight of a page view contribution; the more likely it is to be visited. User profiles generated as a result of GR clustering is listed in Table 1.

Figure 10. Performance of proposed approaches for D2

Figure 11. Performance of proposed approaches for D3

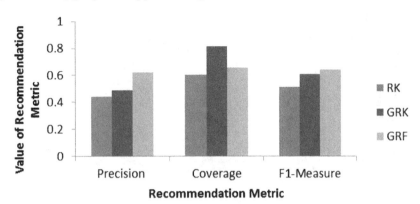

COMPARATIVE ANALYSIS

A comparative study of the performance of GR and GRF is made with Rough K-Means algorithm. The effectiveness of the algorithm is demonstrated in this section.

Cluster Validation

Cluster validation refers to procedures that evaluate the clustering results in a quantitative and objective function. The validation index is a single real value that can describe the quality of a complete cluster partition. Some kinds of validity indices are usually adopted to measure the adequacy of a structure recovered through cluster analysis. For the evaluation of RK, GR and GRF cluster-

ing techniques, Rough and Rough Fuzzy version of Davies-Bouldin's measure (DB) proposed in (Song et al. 2006) is used in this chapter. Table 2 lists sample results for rough clustering, by taking $W_l = 0.7$ and $W_u = 0.3$ and the results are reported for the DB index. The inherent roughness in this clustering mechanism handles the uncertainty (ambiguity) among the overlapping clusters in an appropriate manner.

It is observed that minimum value for DB index is obtained for GRF and GRK than for RK means algorithm which is illustrated in Figure 5.

Outliers

In the case of Rough clustering algorithms, the number of users in the boundary area decreases

Figure 12. Performance of proposed approaches for D4

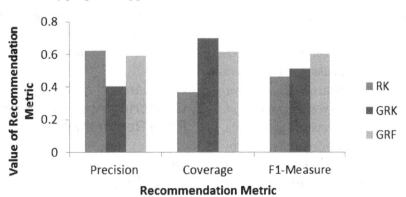

Figure 13. Performance of proposed approaches for D5

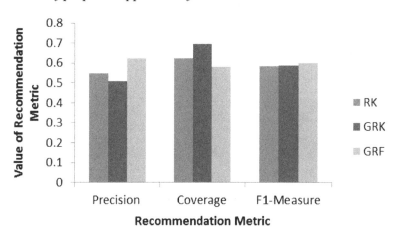

as the value of ε becomes < 0.1. The number of users in the Lower approximation and boundary region for D1 and number of clusters generated K=15 is shown in Figure 6. The number of users in the boundary region for various values of ε is shown in Figure 7. The larger the value of threshold ε, the more likely is the object lie within the rough boundary.

Optimum Number of Clusters

Figure 8 shows the optimum number of clusters determined by GR and GRF clustering algorithms based on Gaussian distribution. The number of clusters increases or remains constant depending upon the size of the data set.

PAGE RECOMMENDATION EXPERIMENT

The recommendation mechanism analyses previous activity of a user and calculates and assigns a rank value to each page profile used by the user.

The access logs from www.aimmtech.com were used for the analysis of proposed algorithms. After preprocessing and removing references by Web spiders, image files and style sheet files, a total of 6244 transactions were produced using

the transaction identification process. The total number of URLs representing page views was 34 and we eliminated the page views appearing in less than 0.25% of the transactions. Approximately 25% of these transactions were randomly selected as the testing set, and the remaining portion was used as the training set for page recommendation.

The Recommendation measures discussed in the previous chapters precision, coverage and F1-Measure were used for the evaluation of page recommendation results. Sample recommended list of pages along with recommendation score is listed in Table 3.

Parameter Setting

The values of number of clusters recommended *NC*, the number of pages in the recommendation set *R* and the sub session size were taken as 4, 4, 1 respectively. These optimum values are selected after several runs based on sensitivity analysis for the best performance in terms of F1-Measure.

Comparison of Rough Clustering Approaches for Page Recommendation

The evaluation results for the various rough clustering approaches RK, GRK, and GRF for various

Figure 14. Predictive accuracy of the proposed approaches for D1, D2, D3, D4, and D5

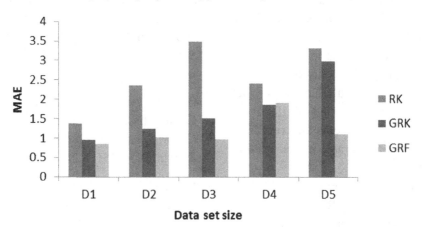

data set sizes are depicted in Figures 9 to 13 for an active session window size of 2. In terms of precision, GRK, and GRF prove good performance but RK shows only a poor performance. In terms of coverage, GRK shows a better performance than RK and GRF. However, the overall F1-Measure illustrates the best performance of GRK and GRF methods than RK method. There is no significant difference in the performance of GRK and GRF because of the slight change in algorithm.

Predictive Accuracy of the Proposed Approaches

The predictive accuracy of the proposed approaches can be measured by Mean Absolute Error (MAE) or Root Mean Square Error (RMSE). In this thesis, MAE is used as the metric for predictive accuracy. The predictive accuracy of RK is very low and so the value of MAE is very high than MAE of GRK and GRF. From Figure 14, it can be obeserved that MAE of GRF is lower than other two approaches, thus making GRF suitable for page recommendation.

CONCLUSION

The problem of predicting a user's behavior on a Web site has gained importance due to the rapid growth of the World Wide Web and the need to personalize and influence a user's browsing experience. In this chapter, two rough clustering approaches GRK and GRF for modeling user clusters are presented and the performance proposed approaches are compared with Lingras Rough K-Means algorithm. The relative importance of the upper and lower approximations of the rough clusters is optimized using DB index value.

The clusters are modeled as rough sets, expressed in terms of pages visited by users in lower approximations and boundary region. However, the optimal partitioning depends upon the suitable choice of threshold value, which is determined by Gaussian distribution. The choice of ε is a challenging one since it affects the number of outliers. The inherent roughness in this clustering mechanism handles the uncertainty among the overlapping clusters in an appropriate manner. So, rough clustering methods are used to retrieve effective user profiles from Web logs.

The empirical results also reveal the importance of using Intelligent Rough clustering methods for mining useful information from the Web log. Meanwhile, an evaluation metric DB Index is adopted to assess the quality of discovered clusters, and the experimental results have shown that the proposed approach is capable of effectively discovering user access patterns and revealing the underlying relationships among user visiting records as well.

Page recommendation experiments also exhibits the best performance of GRK and GRF user clustering approaches for page recommendation. RK shows a rather poor performance than GRK and GRF in terms of both precision and coverage since it does not estimate the number of clusters automatically. Hence the overall performance in terms F1-Measure for page recommendation is rather poor than GRK and GRF.

REFERENCES

Adomavicius, G., & Tuzhilin, A. (2001). Expert-driven validation of rule-based user models in personalization applications. *Data Mining and Knowledge Discovery, 5*(1/2), 33–58. doi:10.1023/A:1009839827683

Aggarwal, C. C., Sun, Z., & Yu, P. S. (2002). Fast algorithms for online generation of profile association rules. *IEEE Transactions on Knowledge and Data Engineering, 14*(5), 1017–1028. doi:10.1109/TKDE.2002.1033771

Agrawal, R., Mannila, H., Srikant, R., Toivonen, H., & Verkamo, A. I. (1996). Fast discovery of association rules. In *Advances in Knowledge Discovery and Data Mining* (pp. 307–328). AAAI Press.

Arayaa, S., Silvab, M., & Weberc, R. (2004). A methodology for web usage mining and its application to target group identification. *Fuzzy Sets and Systems, 148*, 139–152. doi:10.1016/j.fss.2004.03.011

Balabanovic, M., & Shoham, Y. (1997). Fab: Content-based, collaborative recommendation. *Communications of the ACM, 40*(3), 66–72. doi:10.1145/245108.245124

Breiman, L., Friedman, J. H., Olshen, R. A., & Stone, C. J. (1984). *Classification and regression trees*. London, UK: Wadsworth Publisher.

Burge, P., Shawe-Taylor, J., Cooke, C., Moreau, Y., Preneel, B., & Stoermann, C. (1997). Fraud detection and management in mobile telecommunications networks. In *Proceedings of the 2nd European Conference on Security and Detection*, (pp. 91–96). Security and Detection.

Cadez, I. V., Smyth, P., & Mannila, H. (2001). Probabilistic modeling of transaction data with applications to profiling, visualization, and prediction. In *Proceedings of the Seventh ACM SIGKDD International Conference on Knowledge Discovery and Data Mining (KDD)*, (pp. 37–46). ACM Press.

Chen, M., La Paugh, A. S., & Singh, J. P. (2002). Predicting category accesses for a user in a structured information space. In *Proceedings of the ACM SIGIR Conference on Research and Development in Information Retrieval*, (pp. 65–72). ACM Press.

Cortes, C., & Pregibon, D. (1999). Paper. In *Proceedings of the Fifth ACM SIGKDD International Conference on Knowledge Discovery and Data Mining (KDD)*, (pp. 327–331). ACM Press.

Davies, D. L., & Bouldin, D. W. (1979). A cluster separation measure. *IEEE Transactions on Pattern Analysis and Machine Intelligence, 1*(4), 224–227. doi:10.1109/TPAMI.1979.4766909

De, S., & Krishna, P. (2004). Clustering web transactions using rough approximation. *Fuzzy Sets and Systems, 148*, 131–138. doi:10.1016/j.fss.2004.03.010

Dean, J., & Henzinger, M. R. (1999). Finding related pages in the world wide web. In *Proceedings of the Eighth International Conference on World Wide Web,* (pp. 1467–1479). Toronto, Canada: Elsevier.

Fan, W., Gordon, M. D., & Pathak, P. (2005). Effective profiling of consumer information retrieval needs: A unified framework and empirical comparison. *Decision Support Systems, 40*(2), 213–233. doi:10.1016/j.dss.2004.02.003

Fawcett, T., & Provost, F. (1996). Combining data mining and machine learning for effective user profiling. In *Proceedings of the Second International Conference on Knowledge Discovery and Data Mining (KDD),* (pp. 8–13). ACM Press.

Godoy, D., & Amandi, A. (2006). User profiling in personal information agents: A survey. *The Knowledge Engineering Review, 20*(4), 329–361. doi:10.1017/S0269888906000397

Goecks, J., & Shavlik, J. (2000). Learning users' interests by unobtrusively observing their normal behavior. In *Proceedings of the 2000 ACM Intelligent User Interfaces Conference,* (pp. 129–132). ACM Press.

Hathaway, R., & Beadek, J. (1993). Switching regression models and fuzzy clustering. *IEEE Transactions on Fuzzy Systems, 1*(3), 195–204. doi:10.1109/91.236552

Hilas, C. S., & Sahalos, J. N. (2006). Testing the fraud detection ability of different user profiles by means of FF-NN classifiers. *Lecture Notes in Computer Science, 4132*, 872–883. doi:10.1007/11840930_91

Hill, W., Stead, L., Rosenstein, M., & Furnas, G. (1995). Recommending and evaluating choices in a virtual community of use. In *Proceedings of the Conference on Human Factors in Computing Systems,* (pp. 194-201). IEEE.

Hollmen, J. (2000). *User profiling and classification for fraud detection in mobile communications networks.* (PhD Dissertation). Helsinki University of Technology. Helsinki, Finland.

Krishnapram, R., & Joshi, A. (2001). Low complexity fuzzy relational clustering algorithms for web mining. *IEEE Transactions on Fuzzy Systems, 9*, 595–607. doi:10.1109/91.940971

Lingras, P. (2002). Rough set clustering for web mining. In *Proceedings of the 2002 IEEE International Conference on Fuzzy Systems (FUZZ-IEEE 2002),* (vol 2, pp. 1039-1044). IEEE Press.

Lingras, P., & West, C. (2004). Interval set clustering of web users with rough k-means. *Journal of Intelligent Information Systems, 23*(1), 5–16. doi:10.1023/B:JIIS.0000029668.88665.1a

Lingras, P., Yan, R., & West, C. (2003). Fuzzy c-means clustering of web users for educational sites. *Lecture Notes in Artificial Intelligence, 2671*, 557–562.

Liu, B. (2001). Fuzzy random dependent-chance programming. *IEEE Transactions on Fuzzy Systems, 9*(5), 721–726. doi:10.1109/91.963758

Liu, B. (2002). *Theory and practice of uncertain programming.* Berlin, Germany: Springer-Verlag.

Liu, B., & Liu, Y. (2002). Expected value of fuzzy variable and fuzzy expected value models. *IEEE Transactions on Fuzzy Systems, 10,* 445–450. doi:10.1109/TFUZZ.2002.800692

Mitra, S. (2004). An evolutionary rough partitive clustering. *Pattern Recognition Letters, 25,* 1439–1449. doi:10.1016/j.patrec.2004.05.007

Mitra, S. (2006). Rough fuzzy colloborative clustering. *IEEE Transactions on Systems, Man, and Cybernetics, 36*(4), 795–805. doi:10.1109/TSMCB.2005.863371

Mobasher, B., Brusilovsky, P., Kobsa, A., & Nejdl, W. (2007). Data mining for web personalization. *Lecture Notes in Computer Science, 4321,* 90–135. doi:10.1007/978-3-540-72079-9_3

Mobasher, B., Dai, H., Luo, T., & Nakagawa, M. (2002). Discovery and evaluation of aggregate usage profiles for web personalization. *Data Mining and Knowledge Discovery, 6,* 61–82. doi:10.1023/A:1013232803866

Mobasher, B., Dai, H., Luo, T., & Nakagawa, M. (2002). Discovery and evaluation of aggregate usage profiles for web personalization. *Data Mining and Knowledge Discovery, 6*(1), 61–82. doi:10.1023/A:1013232803866

Mushtao, N., Tolle, K., Werner, P., & Zicari, R. (2004). Building and evaluating non-obvious user profiles for visitors of web sites. In *Proceedings of IEEE International Conference on E-Commerce Technology,* (pp. 9-15). IEEE Press.

Pal, N. R., & Bezdek, J. C. (1995). On cluster validity for the fuzzy c-means model. *IEEE Transactions on Fuzzy Systems, 3,* 370–379. doi:10.1109/91.413225

Pal, S. K, Talwar, V., & Mitra, P. (2002). Web mining in soft computing framework: Relevance, state of the art and future directions. *IEEE Transactions on Neural Networks, 13*(I.5), 1163–1177.

Pawlak, Z. (1982). Rough sets. *International Journal of Computer and Information Sciences, 11*(1), 341–356. doi:10.1007/BF01001956

Pedmanabhan, V. N., & Mogul, J. C. (1996). Using predictive pre-fetching to improve worldwideweb latency. *Computer Communication Review, 26*(3), 22–36. doi:10.1145/235160.235164

Picariello, A., & Sansone, C. (2008). A web usage mining algorithm for web personalization. *Intelligent Decision Technologies, 2,* 219–230.

Rafter, R., & Smyth, B. (2001). Passive profiling from server logs in an online recruitment environment. In *Proceedings of the Workshop on Intelligent Techniques for Web Personalization,* (pp. 35–41). IEEE.

Resnick, P., Iacovou, N., Sushak, M., Bergstrom, P., & Riedl, J. (1994). An open architecture for collaborative filtering of netnews. In *Proceedings of the Computer Supported Collaborative Work Conference,* (pp. 175—186). IEEE.

Schechter, S., Krishnan, M., & Smith, M. D. (1998). Using path profiles to predict HTTP requests. In *Proceedings of the Seventh International Conference on World Wide Web,* (pp. 457–467). Elsevier.

Shardanand, U., & Maes, P. (1995). Social information filtering algorithms for automating word of mouth. In *Proceedings of the Conference on Human Factors in Computing Systems,* (pp. 210-217). IEEE.

Song, Q., & Shepperd, M. (2006). Mining web browsing patterns for e-commerce. *Computers in Industry, 57*(7), 622–630. doi:10.1016/j.compind.2005.11.006

Srivastava, J., Cooley, R., Deshpande, M., & Tan, P.-N. (2000). Web usage mining: Discovery and applications of usage patterns from web data. *SIGKDD Explorations, 1*(2), 12–23. doi:10.1145/846183.846188

Xiong, X., & Tan, K. L. (2004). Similarity-driven cluster merging method for unsupervised fuzzy clustering. In *Proceedings of the 20th Conference in Uncertainty in Artificial Intelligence*, (pp. 611-627). ACM.

Xu, G. (2008). *Web mining techniques for recommendation and personalization*. (Ph.D Thesis). Victoria University. Melbourne, Australia.

Zaiane, R. (1999). *Resource and knowledge discovery from the internet and multimedia repositories*. (Ph.D. Thesis). Simon Fraser University. Burnaby, Canada.

Zhang, J., & Shukla, M. (2006). Rule-based platform for web user profiling. In *Proceedings of the Sixth International Conference on Data Mining (ICDM)*, (pp. 1183–1187). ICDM.

Zigoris, P., & Zhang, Y. (2006). Bayesian adaptive user profiling with explicit & implicit feedback. In *Proceedings of the 15th ACM International Conference on Information and Knowledge Management*, (pp. 397–404). ACM Press.

Chapter 10
Hybrid Neural Architecture for Intelligent Recommender System Classification Unit Design

Emmanuel Buabin
Methodist University College Ghana, Ghana

ABSTRACT

The objective is intelligent recommender system classification unit design using hybrid neural techniques. In particular, a neuroscience-based hybrid neural by Buabin (2011a) is introduced, explained, and examined for its potential in real world text document classification on the modapte version of the Reuters news text corpus. The so described neuroscience model (termed Hy-RNC) is fully integrated with a novel boosting algorithm to augment text document classification purposes. Hy-RNC outperforms existing works and opens up an entirely new research field in the area of machine learning. The main contribution of this book chapter is the provision of a step-by-step approach to modeling the hybrid system using underlying concepts such as boosting algorithms, recurrent neural networks, and hybrid neural systems. Results attained in the experiments show impressive performance by the hybrid neural classifier even with a minimal number of neurons in constituting structures.

INTRODUCTION

From point of sale systems, through telecommunications data warehousing systems to space observation systems, computers have brought to the fore, a fair idea of the amount of data, humans generate each day. Bramer (2008) indicates that,

1. The current NASA earth observation satellites generates a terabyte size (i.e. 10^9 bytes) of data each day. The amount of data generated, is by far greater that the total amount of data ever transmitted by all previous observation satellites,

2. The Human Genome project stores thousands of bytes for each of several billion genetic bases, and

DOI: 10.4018/978-1-4666-2542-6.ch010

3.   As far back as 1990, the US Census collected over a million bytes of data.

The above-mentioned examples even suggest data explosion of structured and unstructured data across computer systems in all aspects of human endeavour. Researchers estimate that close to eighty percent (80%) of an institution's information lies in the form of unstructured data—emails, text files, graphs, etc. This means, for business entities to measure business performance over time, they need to take into consideration, unstructured data to arrive at a meaningful and appreciable management decision.

The introduction of the World Wide Web has also increased the volume of unstructured data stored by businesses and individuals. With every computer literate as potential author on the Web, new domains have been registered and corresponding website information added or updated to increase readership/viewership. News giants such as CNN, BBC etc have taken great advantage of the Internet to disseminate news to a wider reading/viewing public, by transmitting "breaking news" stories for example, within minutes for the public to access. Governments, public/private institutions and individuals, have also joined in the massive dissemination of huge amounts of unstructured data by publishing pages about business, jobs, goods, and services. Users have often times resorted to using text based publications mainly because

1.   They are easy to deploy,
2.   They have low runtime impact on servers—hence, loads faster,
3.   They use less hardware resources such as server disk space, and
4.   Much more information could be stored and published as compared to video, images etc.

For this reason, the Internet has become one of the large data repositories of unstructured data in the world. On one hand (i.e. human compre-

hension), Internet data has overwhelmed humans and become more of a "curse" than a "blessing." On the other hand, the same repository (i.e. the Internet) has become a "blessing" due to wealth of information it contains.

Many data mining systems have been built over the past few decades. To be specific, "Multi-" and "single-" classed text based classifiers have been built to ascertain their potential on real world news text corpora (Billsus & Pazzani, 1999b; Kroha & Baeza-Yates, 2005; Shaikh, et al., 2006; Garfield & Wermter, 2006, 2003a; Garfield & Wermte, 2003b; Wermter, et al., 2000b, 1999; Arevian, 2007; Arevian & Pachev, 2007) are examples of text classifiers. Text understanders (Hahn & Schnattinger, 1998), text categorizers (Taeho, 2009; Saha, 2010), text summarizers (Evans, et al., 2004; Mckeown, 2002; Takeda & Takasu, 2007; Radev, 2001; Chang-Shing, et al., 2005; McKeown, et al., 1995; Mingrong, et al., 2008; Wasson, 1998; Xindong, et al., 2010), Web classifiers (Jingwen, et al., 2009; Meijuan, et al., 2009; Meijuan & Jingwen, 2009b), Recommender systems (Chiang, et al., 2004; Wei, et al., 2009; Tintarev & Masthoff, 2006; Felden & Chamoni, 2007; Aciar, et al., 2006; Zhang, 2008; Zhang & Jiao, 2007) have also been built to support text based research—e.g. news domain. The rationale behind the usage of news text corpora is as a result of its inherent non-stationary features and ability to present similar challenges as the Internet. Therefore, successful implementation of a text-based classifier on news text corpora should be equally competitive on non-stationary platforms such as Really Simple Syndicated (RSS) feeds.

Classification and Recommender Systems

Classification and recommender systems have major commonalities across their design. Both

1.   Operate in search related domain,

2. Use search related mechanisms for finding optimal solutions to problems,
3. Use learning algorithms to extract knowledge from the training set into their structures.

In a typical text mining classification task, a set of training exemplars with corresponding targets are fed into the classification systems. The classifier acquires knowledge through the learning process and the learned information is used to predict novel text patterns. The process of finding optimal weights during training for onward classification of novel patterns in a test set, gives a clear indication of a search process. A text classifier meant to predict text based documents as "relevant," "equally relevant" or "irrelevant" must be trained into knowing what a relevant, equally relevant or an irrelevant document is. Knowledge acquired by the text classifier is used to determine whether a novel text document is worth considering for further processing or not.

Recommender systems, as high-level intelligent decision support systems, perform the task of reasoning and suggesting resources to users through learning. Recommender systems require expert training to enable flexibility in the suggestion process. A dynamic recommender system tasked to monitor stock performance across news text documents around the globe needs to

1. Identify which news text documents are relevant, equally relevant and not relevant, i.e. from a dataset,
2. Mine selected documents and compute document information score,
3. Select the top five stocks based on computed information score.

The first step of determining text document status is a pure classification task. Although classification ideas could be used in the second step, sophisticated approaches could be adopted to compute the information score of stocks. Using limited amount of textual information provided

in selected news text articles, the recommender system is expected to acquire in-depth knowledge though training so as to quantitatively determine which stocks performed better during the day. Since subsequent stages after stage 2, are heavily dependent on step 1, the argument therefore about classification being an integral part of recommender systems is justified and reasonable.

Bio-Inspired Intelligent Recommender Systems

The introduction of bio-inspired learning models such as, artificial neural networks, genetic algorithms, and reinforcement learning, has paid off in artificial intelligence research. These models have recorded improved performance in most experiments. The surge in performance has been as a result of their robustness, fault tolerance and level of adaptivity. In the case of artificial neural networks, improved performance stems from the fact that neural networks operate in a similar fashion as the brain, i.e. neurons are connected through synapses and learned information stored in synapse connections. In genetic algorithms, improved performance is due to imitation of natural and biological selection in humans, i.e. fit chromosomes within a given population are selected and genetically operated (e.g. mutation, crossover) upon to produce new and equally fit chromosomes. In reinforcement learning, improved performance is due to the imitation of human adaptation and communication within an environment, i.e. a learning agent performs the task of learning within an environment and the environment provides information to the agent through a reward function. The reward function determines how good a strategy is. Since human information processing is by far, the highest form of information processing, scientists believe that, getting machines to learn in the same manner as humans, could be of immense help in difficult and complex machine learning problems. Scientists are therefore finding ways to tap scientific theories underpinning human nature to buttress machine learning systems. Since the core aspect (i.e. learning and prediction) of recommender systems is akin to internal workings of classification systems, improvement in classification unit design would be an advantageous to recommender system design.

About Book Chapter

The book chapter aims at introducing and motivating neuroscience based hybrid neural architectures for intelligent recommender system design. In particular, a neuroscience based hybrid neural classifier modeled by Buabin (2011a) is introduced, explained in detail and examined on a benchmarked text corpus—modapte version of the Reuters news text corpus. The, so described neuroscience model is fully integrated with a novel boosting algorithm to augment real world news text document classification purposes. The model outperforms existing works and opens up an entirely new research field in the area of machine learning. In simple English language, a step-by-step explanation of the model is adopted. The work is also explained with less mathematical rigour in underpinning concepts. The concepts (boosting algorithms, recurrent neural networks and hybrid neural systems) are introduced and motivated along research lines for deeper understanding of the model. The level of comprehension of this book chapter is that of undergraduate computer science. Post-graduate students/tutors/lecturers and/or researchers who wish to study or research into the foundations, representations, concepts, theory and applications of boosted hybrid neural systems will also find this book chapter beneficial.

Arrangement of Book Chapter

The book chapter is arranged as follows. Section 1 describes the real world dataset used and how the text documents were pre-processed for the experiment. It also outlines ways of converting stochastic and discrete data formats into sequential

based formats for onward training in the hybrid model. Section 2 gives general introduction and research motivation into boosting. It mentions some of the boosting algorithms in existence and identifies sample research works in that area. Section 3 gives an insight into the back propagation algorithm whereas Section 4 ushers in artificial neural networks with in-depth discussion on simple recurrent neural networks. Hybrid neural systems are introduced in Section 5 and Section 6 combines artificial neural networks, boosting and hybrid neural techniques to produce a resultant neuroscience based hybrid neural classifier for the classification unit design of an intelligent recommender system. To demonstrate applicability of boosted hybrid neural networks, a list of industrial applications are enumerated in Section 7. Future directions are also hinted to motivate research in that area.

INTELLIGENT RECOMMENDER SYSTEMS: CLASSIFICATION UNIT DESIGN

Section 1: Dataset Preprocessing

The model (Buabin, 2011a) to be discussed in this book chapter sources its data from the modapte version of the Reuters news text corpus. The news text documents in this corpus appeared in the Reuters newswire in 1987 and were made available by Reuters and CGI for academic research purposes. Since its release, it has been used on many text-mining problems. Results obtained from the experiments could equally be compared with previous approaches for the task of text document classification. In addition, it is easier to analyze results as the content of the text is well known and structure is well understood. Many features sets can be extracted from the corpus (Lewis, 1992). There is also a degree of temporal structure present (Lewis & Ringuette, 1994) and a characteristic with possible time-ordered sequential information embedded in titles. It is as a result of these properties that, recurrent neural network experiments capitalize on to encode sequential information. Overall, the choice of dataset is influenced by the non-stationary characteristic it exhibits. On non-stationary platforms such as RSS feeds, limited amount of text document information is published, hence the sole responsibility of text classifiers to learn such and classify novel patterns appropriately within the shortest possible time. In all, one hundred and twenty-five (125) news text document titles of each category (i.e. currency, economy, etc.) were extracted and preprocessed. See Tables 1 and 2 for distribution and sample instances (see Table 3).

Abbreviations such as "nat'l," "int'l" were replaced with full words ("National," "International"). For a working lexicon, the three hundred and fifty thousand (350,000) simple English word-set from Infochimps.org was used. The lexicon base was automatically updated with new words encountered during the training session. For each word in the lexicon, the corresponding word frequencies in the training set were retrieved and normalized along and across document categories—as semantic vectors. The semantic vectors were then used to form numerical based training, validation and test sets. See Figure 1 for a chart on data preprocessing.

Other Data Forms: Conversion to Sequential Data Formats

In real life situations, data is also produced in stochastic and discrete forms. To ensure learning of such data (i.e. by the neuroscience based model), the data must be pre-processed into sequential data formats. See Figure 2.

Section 2: Boosting

Researchers believe that, by merging a number of weak classifiers (i.e. into an ensemble), the resultant classifier could perform better than the

Table 1. Text document distribution across categories

Category	# of news text documents		
	Train	Validate	Test
Money-fx	125	20	456
Ship	125	20	141
Interest	125	20	331
Economic	125	20	974
Currency	125	20	68
Corporate	125	20	6159
Commodity	125	20	1519
Energy	125	20	540

Table 2. Distribution across sets

Document Category	# of documents	Percentage (%)
Train Set	891	8.26
Validation Set	160	1.48
Test Set	9737	90.26

Table 3. Pre-processed sample instances

Category	An Instance
Money-fx	Baker Says United States Wants To Stabilize Exchange Rates
Ship	Ships Held Up At Calcutta
Interest	UAE Central Bank CD Yields Rise
Economic	United States February Trade To Be Reported On New Basis
Currency	Japan Business Leaders Say G 7 Accord Is Worrying
Corporate	United States West Incorporated USW Third Quarter Net
Commodity	Ghana Cocoa Purchases Slow
Energy	Triton Oil Says Paris Basin Reserves Up 39 Percent
Currency, Money-fx, Economics	Japan Panel Urges World Economic Adjustments
Money-fx, Interest	New Dutch Advances Total 65 Billion Guilders

Figure 1. Data processing

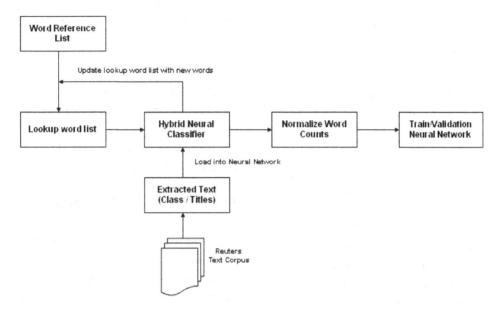

individual classifiers themselves. The notion of classifier ensembles (Abbott, 1999; Dietterich, 1998; Giacinto, 2000; Dietterich, 2000; Duin, 2002; Tumer & Ghosh, 1996; Garfield, et al., 2005; Lim & Goh, 2005; Boné, et al., 2003; Grubb & Bagnell, 2010; Schwenk & Bengio, 2000; McKee, 2001; Schapire, 1990; Cook & Robinson, 1996; Avnimelech & Intrator, 1999; Freund, 1990; Marsland, 2009) has proven true in data mining systems. The first family of boosting algorithms, introduced in Schapire (1990) for classification problems, exploited hierarchies of three classifiers, trained on progressively more difficult parts of the available data and their decisions combined by a

majority vote. Subsequent representatives of this family concern either classification or regression (Cook & Robinson, 1996; Avnimelech & Intrator, 1999). A second family of boosting algorithms was introduced in Freund (1990) and corresponds to the generic shown in Table 4.

Adaptive Boosting (AdaBoost)

Adaboost, a principal algorithm builds on the original 1990 boosting algorithm. In the original experiment, the training set was split into three. A classifier was trained on the first third and then tested on the second third. All of the data that was

Figure 2. Other data formats and conversion

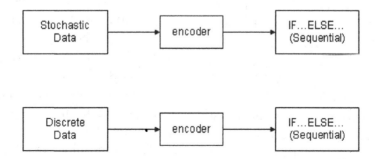

Table 4. Generic boosting algorithm

1. Setting the initial distribution on the training set
2. Iterating until the stopping criterion is reached
a. Develop a weak learner given the current distribution on the training se
b. Update the distribution on the training set
c. Evaluate the stopping criterion
3. Combine the weak learners

misclassified during that testing stage was used to form a new dataset, along with equally sized random selection of the data that was correctly classified. A second classifier was trained on this new dataset and then both of the classifiers were tested on the final third of dataset. The rationale was, should the two classifiers produce the same result, it would mean that, the random data points were ignored, otherwise the data point was added to yet another new dataset, which formed the training set for the third classifier. AdaBoost basically gives weights to each data point according to how difficult previous classifiers have found to get it correct. These weights are given to the classifier as part of the input when it is trained. For each iteration, a new classifier is trained on the training set. The corresponding weights are modified according to how the data point has been classified in the past. The error margin and alpha value are computed based on hypothesis generated by the indication function. Weights of correct examples are left alone and the whole set is normalized so that it sums up to 1. The training session terminates when a set of iterations is reached or when all data-points have been correctly classified. AdaBoost has been implemented in related works (Lim & Goh, 2005; Boné, et al., 2003; Grubb & Bagnell, 2010; Schwenk & Begio, 2000; McKee, 2001).

However, the major setbacks in these works are that, they do not integrate boosted weights into the classifier's weights. To be specific, a neural network classifier's weights does not benefit from the weight produced by the boosting algorithm. Meaning, there is not any scientific basis for integrating boosted weights into neural network weights. Marsland (2009) confirms this challenge between neural networks and boosting algorithms by making the following statement: "…boosting is not quite a stand-alone algorithm: the classifiers need to consider the weights when they perform their classifications. It is not always obvious how to do this for a particular classifier, but we have seen methods of doing it for a few classifiers…" (p. 157).

Section 3: Back-Propagation

The basic back-propagation algorithm was developed independently by Werbos (1974), Rumelhart et al. (1986), Werbos (1988), McClelland and Rumelhart (1981), and Rumelhart et al. (1995). Since its rediscovery, the back-propagation algorithm has been widely used as a learning algorithm in feed-forward MLPs. With a formal mathematical description in Rumelhart et al. (1986), Lippmann (1988), Haykin (1994), and Rumelhart et al. (1995), the back-propagation algorithm (e.g. also referred to as "truncated" gradient-descent algorithm), serves to minimize the mean square error between the actual and the desired output of a multi-layer perceptron. The error margin at the output layer is "back-propagated" to earlier ones, allowing incoming weights to be updated accordingly.

Section 4: Recurrent Neural Networks

Artificial neural networks in data mining systems has been motivated right from its inception by the recognition that, the human brain computes in an entirely different way from the conventional digital computer. According to Haykin (2008), the brain is a highly complex nonlinear, parallel computer (information processing system) that has the capability to organize its structural constituents, known as neurons, so as to perform certain computations (e.g. pattern recognition, perception and motor control). (Haykin, 2008) further defines a neural network

as a massively parallel distributed processor made up of simple processing units that has a natural propensity for storing experiential knowledge and making it available for use. It resembles the brain in two respects: 1) knowledge is acquired by the network from its environments through a learning process, 2) Interneuron connection strengths, known as synaptic weights are used to store the acquired knowledge (p. 5).

Artificial neural networks have a number of benefits. Below are some of the important general properties and advantages given by Haykin (1994) and Bengio (1996). They are

1. A neural network is non-linear, hence solves problems that are non-linear in nature. In other words, neural network models are able to learn real, discrete, and vector-valued functions from exemplars.
2. They are flexible in nature when compared to other non-parametric inference approaches.
3. They are able to generalize to small and large scale problems once they have been trained and tested properly.
4. They are adaptable and dynamic in operation; hence, they can be retrained to deal with changes of varying degrees in the operating environment. Their adaptability makes them robust to operate in noisy environments and on incomplete input data.
5. Depending on the task at hand and network architecture, they have proved (i.e. in scientific research) to be able to approximate many different arbitrary types of highly non-linear functions.
6. Although there is the eventual effect of the curse of high dimensionality, neural networks are able to make use of large input spaces with correlated features for improved model representation.

7. The robust nature of the neural network indirectly results in their parallel hardware and VLSI implementation.
8. Multi-class input/output mappings are inherently better learned by the hidden layers of NN models, with a distributed internal representation that is more compact; shared internal features and their representation, especially if there are related higher-order dependencies between the outputs, can improve generalization performance because fewer parameters are required.
9. Neural networks, especially the class of RNNs, are able to represent contextual information and sequential order.

Today, several neural network models have been built. Within the domain of supervised learning, Recurrent Neural Networks (RNN), coupled with their feedback loops and generalization capabilities have proven to be good candidates in encoding knowledge from sequential based formats such as text, speech etc. Their ability to encode knowledge from reasonably short sequences is as a result of recurrent connections found in the middle layer section of the network. In as much as their architectural layouts come in different forms, they incorporate a static Multilayer Perceptron (MLP) or parts thereof and exploit the nonlinear mapping capability of the MLP. RNNs are able to relate previous internal states and input to a desired response—especially acting as short-term incremental memories that take time and context into consideration. Scientific experiments have also established that, even the simplest form of recurrent neural networks (i.e. Elman Network or Simple Recurrent Network – SRN) has the capability to perform at par with high order recurrent networks on machine learning tasks. The works by Garfield and Wermter (2006, 2003a, 2003b), Wermter (1995, 1999), and Wermter et al. (2000a, 2000b, 1999a, 1999b) confirm this statement. The SRN is made up of at most four layers—input, hidden, output, and context. Whereas the input layer accepts numerical input data through its input units, the output units return limited activation values from the network. The hidden and context layers work interchangeably to affect the context learnt over the fixed or variable length of sequence. In this book chapter, neuronal activations at the hidden, context and output layers are limited with the logistic function. Bias nodes are also connected to the input and hidden layers to facilitate learning. In general, input to a hidden layer L_n is constrained by the underlying layer L_{n-1} as well as the incremental context layer C_n. The activation of a unit $L_{ni}(t)$ at time step t is calculated based on the weighted activation of the units in the previous layer $L_{(n-1)}(t)$ and the units in the current context of this layer $C_{ni}(t)$. The resultant is then limited by a logistic function. The computation provides a simple form of recurrence for training networks to perform sequential tasks over time.

$$C_{ni}(t) = (1 - \Psi_n) L_{ni}(t-1) + \Psi_n C_{ni}(t-1) \qquad (1)$$

$$L_{ni}(t) = f\left(\Sigma_k W_{ki} L_{(n-1)k}(t) + \Sigma_l W_{li} C_{(n)l}(t)\right) \qquad (2)$$

where Ψ_n is the hysteresis value.

The SRN prior to processing a sequence re-initializes its context layer activations to zero. For each input in a sequence, the hidden and context layer activations are computed and neural weights updated at the end of the sequence. The training action is performed repeated until the network encodes information from instances.

Section 5: Hybrid Neural Systems

Various scientific research works have found that knowledge-based neural networks train faster and better than standard neural networks (Berenji, 1991; Oliver & Schneider, 1988; Omlin & Giles, 1992; Shavlik & Towell, 1989). This is because

1. Initial information is used to choose a good starting point for the network,
2. Knowledge based networks generalize better to future examples than standard networks.

The improvement in generalization can be linked to two aspects of the insertion process. The domain theory produces a useful inductive bias by

1. Focusing attention on relevant input features, and
2. Indicating useful intermediate conclusions, which suggest a good network topology.

A lot of reasons have motivated researchers to move into the direction of hybrid connectionist systems. Below are some of the reasons.

Shavlik (1994) enumerates three reasons why connectionist symbolic ideas are necessary. They are

1. Trained neural networks have at least, comparable accuracies to induced decision trees on tasks that can be considered symbol oriented,
2. Neural network approaches have proven successful on a wide range of "real world" tasks, such as speech understanding (Lippmann, 1989), handwritten character recognition (Le Cun, et al., 1989), control of dynamic systems (Jordan & Rumelhart, 1992), gene finding (Uberbacher & Mural, 1991), language learning (Touretzky, 1991),
3. There are connectionist architectures beyond simple, feed-forward, single-hidden-layer neural networks.

In particular, recurrent networks with their feedback loops and "memory" are especially appealing for application to symbolic tasks that have a sequential nature.

Wermter and Weber (1997) also provides motivation for Hybrid connectionist symbolic architectures along the following reasons:

1. Hybrid connectionists are fault tolerant and support robustness (Rumelhart, et al., 1986; Sun, 1994),
2. They are known for their learning and generalization capabilities,

3. Learning induces regularities directly from examples,
4. Different knowledge sources can take advantage of the learning and capabilities of connectionist networks,
5. Other knowledge can be represented directly in symbolic representation,
6. They have the capability of shedding some light on human language processing.

It is in the respect of the sixth point makes hybrid connectionist-symbolic architectures different from other robust architectures such as statistical taggers, statistical ngrams.

According to Sun (1997)

1. Cognitive processes are not homogenous and whereas some parts of cognitive processes are best captured by symbolic models, others are best represented by connectionist models (Smolensky, 1988).
2. The development of intelligent systems for practical applications can benefit greatly from a proper combination of different techniques since no one single technique can do everything as this is the case in many application domains.
3. To develop a full range of capabilities in autonomous agents, an autonomous agent architecture needs to incorporate both symbolic and sub-symbolic processing for handling declarative and procedural knowledge respectively to effectively deal with a variety of environments in which an agent finds itself.

In all, these experiments strongly suggest that connectionist learning is a powerful approach and the use of neural networks with symbolic knowledge merits explosion. Recent research activities (Shavlik, 1994; Sun, 1997; Wermter, et al., 2000a, 1999b; Wermter, 1995; Vidhya & Aghila, 2010) suggest that they can be used effectively in real world classification purposes.

Limitations of Hybrid Neural Systems

Although the above-mentioned hybrid neural systems are relevant in their respective applications, they are limited from basic neuroscience perspective. Buabin (2011a) argues three basic neuroscience tendencies.

1. Localized neurons are similar in structure and perform related function (Haykin, 2008) provides a detailed representation of the human brain.
2. Minimal number of localized neurons are selected and put into an ensemble for information processing.
3. Results are enhanced to attain high throughput.

Aside the neuroscience contradictions, none of the boosting enabled systems (Lim & Goh, 2005; Boné, et al., 2003; Grubb & Bagnell, 2010; Schwenk & Begio, 2000; McKee, 2001) provide clear integration ability for updating learned neural network weights after boosting. Marsland (2009) confirms this by making the following statement: "…boosting is not quite a stand-alone algorithm: the classifiers need to consider the weights when they perform their classifications. It is not always obvious how to do this for a particular classifier, but we have seen methods of doing it for a few classifiers" (p. 157).

Section 6: About the Boosted Hybrid Recurrent Neural Classifier (Hy-RNC)

Motivated by the need to implement a hybrid neural based text classification system that:

1. Has similar localized constituents in an ensemble performing related function,
2. Uses minimal number of hidden layer neurons in constituting structures,

3. Is fully integrated with a boosting algorithm harnessed with back-propagation techniques,

4. Provides an obvious scientific basis for updating learned neural network weights, and

5. Is robust, adaptive, fault tolerant, etc.

The boosted Hybrid Recurrent Neural Classifier abbreviated Hy-RNC, was proposed and implemented in Buabin (2011a). In this book chapter, the general and special cases of Hy-RNC are explained and their capabilities in a real-world world text document classification task are also examined. Whereas the general Hy-RNC contains an ensemble of N Simple Recurrent Networks (SRNs), the special case Hy-RNC contains a single SRN. Both have a boosting unit fully integrated with the networks. The boosting unit, which contains an Adaboost-like algorithm herein termed NeuroBoost, operates by accepting network outputs from the hybrid neural classifier environment and extracting weak hypothesis from the outputs. The algorithm computes temporary weights based on extracted hypothesis and updates learned neural network weights through back-propagation approach. Having integrated the weights, the new neural weights are copied into the hybrid environment.

Hy-RNC: Architecture, Training, and Validation

Hy-RNC can be sub-divided into two (2) networks, namely general and special case. Each constituting SRN in the general case has i number of hidden neurons and k number of input/output units. They (individually) are fully connected and have bias connections at both Input and hidden layers. Similar to general case Hy-RNC, learned information in special case Hy-RNC is boosted and fed into the hybrid classifier environment through the NeuroBoost algorithm. The consti-

tuting SRN structure in special case Hy-RNC, is also similar to the network structure in general case Hy-RNC (i.e. k-i-k). In terms of operation, Hy-RNC initializes parameters such as hidden layers, hidden layer neurons, input-output units with default values. The input, output, context and hidden layer weights are randomly selected and used to initialize the hybrid network. For each news title in an epoch, Hy-RNC creates and initializes layer activations (context and hidden) with default values. The Layer activations are updated after every time step until the end of the sequence is reached. Having ended the sequence, Hy-RNC updates the hybrid network weights and re-initializes layer activations to default values. Hy-RNC is trained and validated repeatedly until an early stopping criterion is reached. The early stopping technique employed in this experiment so as to ensure a noise-free learning process.

NeuroBoost Algorithm

NeuroBoost uses back-propagation technique to integrate boosting weights into neural network weights. The algorithm which is AdaBoost-like, operates by

1. Accepting neural network weights and merged outputs,

2. Initializing temporary vectors such as weights, error, and alpha.

In one time step (i.e. T=1), NeuroBoost retrieves weak hypothesis from N classified examples and computes corresponding vectors error: (1*T), alpha: (1*T), boosting weights: ones (N*T), deltah and deltao. The algorithm's weights (i.e. boosting weights) are then integrated into the hybrid network weights through back-propagation approach. The new neural weights are subsequently transferred into the hybrid neural classifier environment for re-training and re-validation on exemplars. The algorithm's ability to integrate boosting weights into hybrid neural weights makes it unique and possible to measure deviation (i.e. of network outputs) on the Least Squares Error method. The integrating ability provides an obvious scientific basis for connecting boosting algorithms to neural based systems (see Tables 5 and 6).

Hy-RNC, NeuroBoost Integration

Hy-RNC and NeuroBoost can be performed in two ways. The first approach splits the boosting weight dimension (N*1) by 1) the number of output units (*k*) followed by 2) the number of hidden layer neurons (*i*), whilst the second approach splits by 1) the number of hidden layer neurons (*i*) and 2) subsequently number of output units (*k*).

First Approach: Split by Output Units and Then by Hidden Layer Neurons (i.e. "k" before "i")

Let (N*1) be the boosting weight dimension defined over N instances. For every generated hypothesis (h), there exists a set of network output units (*k*) that were employed in the computation of the boosting weights – i.e. N*1 = N*k | k*1. Secondly, output activations yield a set of hidden layer activations (i.e. "*i*") that were employed in the computation of the output activations – i.e.

$$N*1 = N*i \mid i*k \mid k*1. \tag{3}$$

Let matrices P = *N * 1*, Q = *N * i*, R = *i * k*, S = *k * 1*.
Using Matrix property A'A = AA' = I.

$$Q R S = P \tag{4}$$

To make R the subject, multiple through by Q'.

$$Q' (Q R S) = Q' P \tag{5}$$

$$I R S = Q' P \tag{6}$$

Multiplying through by S',

$$R S S' = Q' P S' \tag{7}$$

$$R I = Q' P S' \tag{8}$$

$$R = Q' P S' \tag{9}$$

In the case of this split, "N*1" is the boosted weight dimension, "N*i" is the hidden layer activations dimension for instances. "i*k" is the output weight dimension and "k*1" is the average of network outputs across instances.

$$R S S' = Q' P S' \tag{10}$$

$$R I = Q' P S' \tag{11}$$

$$R = Q' P S' \tag{12}$$

The output weight is therefore updated as follows

$$q = \eta * R' + (momentum * w^n) \tag{13}$$

$$w^{n+1} = w^n + q \tag{14}$$

where R' is the new parameter introduced in the learning formula. All other variables retain their standard definitions in the learning formula.

Second Approach: Split by Hidden Layer Neurons Then by Output Units ("i" before "k")

Similarly, the split could be done as follows N*1 = N * k | k * i | i * 1.
Let matrices P = N * 1, Q = N * *k*, R = *k * i*, S = *i * 1*.
Using Matrix property A'A = AA' = I.
Making R the subject, multiplying

$$Q'. Q R S = P \tag{15}$$

$$Q' (Q R S) = Q' P \tag{16}$$

Table 5. NeuroBoost algorithm

Initialization
• Accept neural weights and network outputs from hybrid environment
• Initialize temporary vectors: error, alpha, boosting weights
Repeat
• In one epoch
o Retrieve weak hypothesis from network outputs
o Compute Error, Alpha, Boosting weights
o Compute deltah, deltao
o Integrate boosting weights into
Final
• Copy neural weights into the hybrid environment

$$I\ R\ S = Q'\ P \tag{17}$$

Multiplying through by S',

$$R\ S\ S' = Q'\ P\ S' \tag{18}$$

$$R\ I = Q'\ P\ S' \tag{19}$$

$$R = Q'\ P\ S' \tag{20}$$

In the case of this split, "N*1" is the boosted weight dimension, "N*k" is the output dimension of all instances, "k*i" is the output weight dimension and "i*1" is the average of hidden layer activations across instances. The output weight is therefore updated as follows

$$q = \eta * R + (momentum * w^n) \tag{21}$$

$$w^{n+1} = w^n + q \tag{22}$$

where R is the new parameter introduced in the learning formula. All other variables retain their standard definitions in the learning formula

Evaluation with Confusion Matrix

Hy-RNC generates a corresponding k (i.e. eight) bit data for all instances in the test set. A predicted network output of a class is deemed to have been classified (i.e. 1), if the output activation is at least 0.50. Where a predicted network output is strictly less than 0.50, the resulting classification is set to 0. For example, a k bit output $[0,0,1,1,0,0,0,1]$ of an instance with corresponding target $[0,0,1,0,0,0,0,1]$, is represented in Hy-RNC as follows: $[0,0] = 5$, $[0,1] = 1$, $[1,0] = 0$, $[1,1] = 2$, where $[a,b]$ is interpreted as "a" classified as "b." Similarly, the confusion matrix is used to extract weak hypothesis from predicted network outputs. A predicted output (i.e. k bit data) of an instance is deemed to be classified if the number of correctly classified classes or bits is at least 50% or 0.5. Furthermore the confusion matrix is used to communicate the overall correct (i.e. $[0,0]$ and $[1,1]$) and incorrect (i.e. $[0,1]$ and $[1,0]$) classifications on the test set. Although the experiment uses a bit-wise approach to represent classifications, the approach could be modified

Table 6. Comparison of NeuroBoost and AdaBoost

Task	AdaBoost	NeuroBoost
Number of Time Steps	Arbitrary	1
Trains classifier and Returns WEAK Hypothesis?	YES	YES
Computes Error, Alpha and Weights?	YES	YES
Updates Neural Learned Weights with Computed Weights?	NO	YES
Uses Standard Back-Propagation?	N/A	YES
Uses Standard Neural Learning Formula?	N/A	YES
Obvious Connection to Recurrent Neural Networks?	N/A	YES
Obvious Applicability to other Supervised Learning Network Types	N/A	YES
Does connection allow for Least Square Error computation	N/A	YES

to generate classification results for each class across the dataset. In such a case, there will be a k*k confusion matrix.

Performance Measure

The F-Measure was used in evaluating classifier performance of Hy-RNC. The choice is informed by the fact that, the F-Measure metric is neither biased towards Recall or Precision. In data mining theory, Recall is defined as the number of True Positives over the sum of True Positives and False Negatives whereas Precision is defined as the number of True Positives over the sum of True Positives and False Positives. The F-Measure is therefore expressed as:

F = (2 * Recall * Precision)/(Recall + Precision)   (23)

Integration Requirement: NeuroBoost and Other Neural Network Family

NeuroBoost can be integrated into any supervised learning based neural network that uses back-propagation algorithm in updating its learned information—weights. The neural network family must be capable of feeding the NeuroBoost algorithm with learned network information (such as weights, outputs) and corresponding targets. Prior to passing the parameters, the ensemble section of the network must find a means of merging the networks outputs from constituting structures— i.e. if they are of different dimensions. In Buabin (2011a), constituting structures are assumed to have similar weight dimensions, hence merged by means of averaging.

Sample Experiment: Boosted Hy-RNC and Standard SRN

For each SRN classifier used in this experiment, a corresponding k-2-k, k-8-k and k-16-k network topologies were used. A k-2-k constituted Hy-RNC network was compared against a corresponding k-2-k standard SRN network. Similarly, a k-8-k and k-16-k constituted Hy-RNC networks were compared against k-8-k and k-16-k standard SRN networks respectively. Overall, three different kinds of classifiers were used – namely Hy-RNC (General Case), Hy-RNC (Special Case) and SRN. The general case consists of two (2) SRN classifiers. For every classifier type of a certain topology (k-i-k), three test runs were conducted. The experiments were conducted at fixed learning rate (0.01), momentum (0.9) and at an early stopping criterion (old error 1- new error >0.0000001) or (old error 2- old error 1 >0.0000001). The results are as follows—See Tables 7, 8, and 9.

Table 7 shows the three kinds of classifiers under investigation. Corresponding performance across three test runs is illustrated against classifier names. The constituting SRN network topology under consideration is K-2-K, where K is the number of input/output units. Hy-RNC (2GC) and Hy-RNC (SC) are boosted hybrid recurrent neural networks with two (2) and one (1) SRN classifiers respectively. The standard SRN is of type K-2-K.

Table 8 shows the three kinds of classifiers under investigation. Corresponding performance across three test runs is illustrated against classifier names. The constituting SRN network topology under consideration is K-8-K, where K is the number of input/output units. Hy-RNC (2GC) and Hy-RNC (SC) are boosted hybrid recurrent neural networks with two (2) and one (1) SRN

Table 7.

Classifier	Test Run (k-2-k)		
	1	*2*	*3*
Hy-RNC (2GC)	0.942235	0.950328	0.948067
Hy-RNC (SC)	0.946769	0.949775	0.950106
SRN (Standard)	0.927516	0.927898	0.928362

Table 8.

Classifier	Test Run (k-8-k)		
	1	2	3
Hy-RNC (2GC)	0.949101	0.949003	0.950401
Hy-RNC (SC)	0.950001	0.949996	0.950331
SRN (Standard)	0.930086	0.931326	0.930043

classifiers respectively. The standard SRN is of type K-8-K.

Table 9 shows the three kinds of classifiers under investigation. Corresponding performance across three test runs is illustrated against classifier names. The constituting srn network topology under consideration is K-16-K, where K is the number of input/output units. Hy-RNC (2GC) and Hy-RNC (SC) are boosted hybrid recurrent neural networks with two (2) and one (1) SRN classifiers, respectively. The standard SRN is of type K-16-K.

In all of the test runs, the hybrid networks performed better than the standard SRN. Although the classifiers were trained with different initial weights, the networks generated results that reflected information learnt over time. Meaning, classifier performances did not just occur by chance, but based on learned information. This provides a leveled platform for comparing the classifiers under investigation. From experimental result 1 (Table 7), Hy-RNC (2GC) performed better than the SRN by at least 1.471% and at-most 2.243%. The Hy-RNC (SC) performed at least 1.92% and at most 2.17% better than the standard SRN. From experimental result 2 (Table 8), Hy-RNC(2GC) performed at least 0.017677% and at most 0.020358%, Hy-RNC(SC) performed at least 0.018670% and at most 0.020288% than the standard SRN. From experimental result 3 (Table 9), Hy-RNC(2GC) performed at least 0.006% and at most 0.044%, Hy-RNC(SC) performed at least 0.028% and at most 0.091% than the standard SRN. From Tables 7, 8, and 9, it could be observed that, the hybrid network performance appreciated with increasing number of hidden layer

neurons. Although the standard SRN increased in performance, the hybrid networks still performed better than the SRN. Unlike Tables 8 and 9, Table 7 recorded high performance differences by the hybrid classifiers as compared to the SRN.

Industrial Applications

1. Autism is a neural development disorder characterized by impaired social interaction and communication, and by restricted and repetitive behavior. The signs begin prior to the child, attaining age of three. Autism affects information processing in the brain by altering how nerve cells and their synapses connect and organize. How this occurs, is not well understood by scientists. Since there has not been any cure for autism, health officials assign human assistants to engage the patient in interaction, communication and other activities with the sole aim of unlocking the patient's brain. The cost of hiring human assistants to cater for autistic patients has become very expensive, since the duty is tedious.

Question: How do Intelligent Recommender Systems Fit in This Setup?

In providing a solution for autistic patient care, an intelligent recommender system could be embedded in an assistive robot to recommend tasks to the patient. The choice of tasks could be based on patient performance on previous tasks. This would enable supervising doctors perform close examination on the autistic patient over time.

2. As part of war on terror, the US government is developing an adaptive missile defense technology to provide swift response against enemy missile intended for its home soil, foreign military bases, or allies around the globe. The intended system is expected to detect infrared and visible light from missiles launched from earth.

Table 9.

Classifier	Test Run (k-16-k)		
	1	*2*	*3*
Hy-RNC (2GC)	0.958947	0.958324	0.957333
Hy-RNC (SC)	0.959169	0.958788	0.957947
SRN (Standard)	0.958886	0.957879	0.957312

Question: How do Intelligent Recommender Systems Fit in This Setup?

Enemy missiles may come in different and complex forms. It behooves a humanoid missile defense system to learn missile related information or patterns effectively so as to yield the right response, i.e. no matter the form of the missile.

3. Thousands of flights are recorded all over the world each day. With some embarking on direct routes to destinations, others connect or make transits to enable passengers get to destinations. With the increasing business collaboration with flight companies and governments, flight information has increased tremendously.

Question: How Do Intelligent Recommender Systems Fit in This Setup?

Passengers, at some point might want to know which flights are of moderate price on a particular trip. An intelligent recommender system trained on requisite flight data could generate recommendations to the prospective passenger.

FURTHER DIRECTIONS

Owing to results attained by Hy-RNC, it is worth investigating novel approaches that have the possibility to improve classification results and widen performance margin over other networks. For this reason, robust and rigorous training regime on the revised boosted Hy-RNC classifier is worth exploring for its potential in classifying text

documents. One major approach worth exploring is (1) biologically motivated feature selection mechanisms for prolific pattern extraction prior to network training.

CONCLUSION

The book chapter demonstrates that

1. An ensemble of recurrent neural networks could used be in designing the classification unit of an intelligent recommender system,
2. Minimal number of hidden layer neurons could be used in constituting structures to attain high throughput or performance,
3. Network responses could be boosted to increase network performance,
4. Classification units of an intelligent recommender system could be boosted (i.e. a connection between boosting algorithms and neural based hybrid models is feasible and can be scientifically demonstrated),
5. The boosting-neural connection makes it possible for boosting weights to be integrated into neural based weights,
6. Back-propagation approach could help assist in integrating learned weights in intelligent recommender systems,
7. Newly integrated weights could be used on the validation set for onward measurement of deviation using least squares method.

The approach, adopted in this book chapter is different from most of the related approaches for natural language processing, in that, a boosted hybrid neural techniques have been used and yields better classification performance. Although the weight integration is explained for a recurrent neural network classifier (i.e. SRN), the engaged technique could be adequately used to update weights in other neural based supervised learning networks.

REFERENCE

Abbott, D. W. (1999). Combining models to improve classifier accuracy and robustness, In *Proceedings International Conference on Information Fusion*, (pp. 1-7). Sunnyvale, CA: Information Fusion.

Aciar, S., Zhang, D., Simoff, S., & Debenham, J. (2006). Informed recommender agent: Utilizing consumer product reviews through text mining. In *Proceedings of the WI-IATW*, (pp. 37 – 40). WI-IATW.

Al Masum, S. M., Islam, M. T., & Ishizuka, M. (2006). ASNA: An intelligent agent for retrieving and classifying news on the basis of emotion-affinity. In *Proceedings of the Web Technologies and Internet Commerce, International Conference*, (p. 133). IEEE.

Arevian, G. (2007). Recurrent neural networks for robust real-world text classification. In *Proceedings of the 2007 IEEE/WIC/ACM International Conference on Web Intelligence*. Silicon Valley, CA: IEEE/WIC/ACM.

Arevian, G., & Panchev, C. (2007a). Robust text classification using a hysteresis-driven extended SRN. In *Proceedings of the 2007 International Conference on Artificial Neural Networks*. Porto, Portugal: IEEE.

Arevian, G., & Panchev, C. (2007b). Optimizing the hystereses of a two context layer RNN for text classification. In *Proceedings of the International Joint Conference on Neural Networks*. Orlando, FL: IEEE.

Avnimelech, R., & Intrator, N. (1999). Boosting regression estimators. *Neural Computation, 11*, 491–513. doi:10.1162/089976699300016746

Bengio, Y. (1996). *Neural networks for speech and sequence recognition*. London, UK: International Thomson Computer Press.

Berenji, H. R. (1991). Refinement of approximate reasoning-based controllers by reinforcement learning. In *Proceedings of the Eighth International Machine Learning Workshop*, (pp. 475-479). Evanston, IL: IEEE.

Billsus, D., & Pazzani, M. (1999b). A hybrid user model for news story classification, user modeling. In *Proceedings of the Seventh International Conference (UM 1999)*, (pp. 98-108). Banff, Canada: UM.

Boné, R., Assaad, M., & Crucianu, M. (2003). Boosting recurrent neural networks for time series prediction. In Proceedings of the International Conference on Artificial Neural Nets and Genetic Algorithms, (pp. 18-22). Springer.

Bramer, M. (2008). *Principles of data mining*. London, UK: Springer-Verlag.

Buabin, E. (2011a). Boosted hybrid recurrent neural classifier for text document classification on the reuters news text corpus. In *Proceedings of the 3rd ICMLC 2011*. IEEE.

Chang-Shing, L., Zhi-Wei, J., & Lin-Kai, H. (2005). A fuzzy ontology and its application to news summarization. *IEEE Transactions on Systems, Man, and Cybernetics. Part B, 35*(5), 859–880.

Chiang, J.-H., & Yan-Cheng, C. (2004). An intelligent news recommender agent for filtering and categorizing large volumes of text corpus. *International Journal of Intelligent Systems, 19*, 201–216. doi:10.1002/int.10136

Cook, G. D., & Robinson, A. J. (1996). Boosting the performance of connectionist large vocabulary speech recognition. In *Proceedings of the International Conference on Spoken Language Processing*, (pp. 1305-1308). Philadelphia, PA: IEEE.

Dietterich, T. G. (1998). Approximate statistical tests for comparing supervised classification learning algorithms. *Neural Computation, 10*, 1895–1923. doi:10.1162/089976698300017197

Dietterich, T. G. (2000). Ensemble methods in machine learning. *Lecture Notes in Computer Science, 1857*, 1–15. doi:10.1007/3-540-45014-9_1

Duin, R. P. W. (2002). The combining classifier: to train or not to train. In *Proceedings of 16th International Conference on Pattern Recognition*, (vol. 2, pp. 765-770). Quebec, Canada: IEEE.

Evans, D. K., Klavans, J. L., & McKeown, K. R. (2004). Columbia newsblaster: Multilingual news summarization on the web. In *Proceedings of the Human Language Technology Conference and the North American Chapter of the Association for Computational Linguistics Annual Meeting*. ACL.

Felden, C., & Chamoni, P. (2007). Recommender systems based on an active data warehouse with text documents. In *Proceedings of the 40th HICSS 2007*, (p. 168a). HICSS.

Freund, Y. (1990). Boosting a weak learning algorithm by majority. In *Proceedings of the 3rd Annual Workshop on Computational Learning Theory*, (pp. 202-216). IEEE.

Garfield, S., & Wermter, S. (2003a). Comparing state vector machines, recurrent networks and finite state transducers for classifying spoken utterances. In *Proceedings of the International Conference on Artificial Neural Networks*, (pp. 646-653). Istanbul, Turkey: IEEE.

Garfield, S., & Wermter, S. (2003b). Recurrent neural learning for classifying spoken utterances. *Expert Update, 6*(3), 31–36.

Garfield, S., & Wermter, S. (2006). Call classification using recurrent neural networks, support vector machines and finite state automata. *Knowledge and Information Systems: An International Journal, 9*(2), 131–156. doi:10.1007/s10115-005-0198-5

Garfield, S., & Wermter, S. (2006). Call classification using recurrent neural networks, support vector machines and finite state automata. *Knowledge and Information Systems: An International Journal, 9*(2), 131–156. doi:10.1007/s10115-005-0198-5

Garfield, S., Wermter, S., & Devlin, S. (2005). Spoken language classification using hybrid classifier combination. *International Journal of Hybrid Intelligent Systems, 2*(1), 13–33.

Giacinto, G., Roli, F., & Fumera, G. (2000). Design of effective multiple classifier systems by clustering of classifiers. In *Proceedings of ICPR 2000 15th International Conference on Pattern Recognition*, (pp. 160-163). Barcelona, Spain: IEEE.

Grubb, A. J., & Bagnell, A. (2010). Boosted backpropagation learning for training deep modular networks. In *Proceedings of the 27th International Conference on Machine Learning*. Haifa, Israel: IEEE.

Hahn, U., & Schnattinger, K. (1998). A text understander that learns. In *Proceedings of the 17th COLING/ACL*, (pp. 476-482). Morgan Kaufmann.

Haykin, S. (1994). *Neural networks: A comprehensive foundation.* New York, NY: Macmillan College Publishing Company.

Haykin, S. (2008). *Neural networks and learning machines* (3rd ed.). Upper Saddle River, NJ: Pearson Prentice Hall.

Jingwen, T., & Meijuan, G. (2009). Research of web classification mining based on wavelet neural network. [JCAI.]. *Proceedings of JCAI, 2009*, 559–562.

Jingwen, T., Meijuan, G., & Yang, S. (2009). Study on web classification mining method based on fuzzy neural network. In *Proceedings of the ICAL*, (pp. 1781 – 1785). ICAL.

Jordan, M. I., & Rumelhart, D. (1990). *Forward models: Supervised learning with a distal teacher. Technical Report*. New York, NY: Center for Cognitive Science.

Kroha, P., & Baeza-Yates, R. (2005). A case study: News classification based on term frequency. In *Proceedings of the Sixteenth International Workshop on Database and Expert Systems Applications*, (pp. 428 – 432). IEEE.

Le Cun, Y., Boser, B., Denker, J., Henderson, D., Howard, R., Hubbard, W., & Jackel, L. (1989). Backpropagation applied to handwritten zip code recognition. *Neural Computation, 1*, 541–551. doi:10.1162/neco.1989.1.4.541

Lewis, D. D. (1992). Feature selection and feature extraction for text categorization. In *Proceedings of Speech and Natural Language Workshop*, (pp. 212-217). Morgan Kaufmann.

Lewis, D. D., & Ringuette, M. (1994). A comparison of two learning algorithms for text categorization. In *Proceedings of the Symposium on Document Analysis and Information Retrieval*, (pp. 81-93). Las Vegas, NV: ISRI.

Lim, C. P., & Goh, W. (2005). The application of an ensemble of boosted elman networks to time series prediction: A benchmark study. *International Journal of Computational Intelligence, 3*(2).

Lippmann, R. P. (1989). Review of neural networks for speech recognition. *Neural Computation, 1*, 1–38. doi:10.1162/neco.1989.1.1.1

Marsland, S. (2009). *Machine learning: An algorithmic perspective*. London, UK: Chapman & Hall.

McClelland, J. L., Rumelhart, D. E., & Hinton, G. E. (1986). The appeal of parallel distributed processing. In Rumelhart, D. E., & McClelland, L. (Eds.), *Parallel Distributed Processing (Vol. 1*, pp. 3–44). Cambridge, MA: MIT Press.

McClelland, L., & Rumelhart, D. E. (1981). An interactive activation model of context effects in letter perception. *Psychological Review, 88*, 375–407. doi:10.1037/0033-295X.88.5.375

McKee, D. W. (2001). *Boosting evolved artificial neural network to improve breast cancer classification accuracy*. Unpublished.

McKeown, K., & Radev, D. R. (1995). Generating summaries of multiple news articles. In *Proceedings of the 18th Annual International ACM SlGIR Conference on Research and Development in Information Retrieval*, (pp. 74-82). ACM Press.

McKeown, K. R., Barzilay, R., Evans, D., Hatzivassiloglou, V., Klavans, J. L., & Nenkova, A. … Sigelman, S. (2002). Tracking and summarizing news on a daily basis with Columbia's newsblaster. In *Proceedings of HLT 2002 Human Language Technology Conference*. San Diego, CA: HLT.

Meijuan, G., & Jingwen, T. (2009b). Web classification mining based on radial basic probabilistic neural network. In *Proceedings of the First International Workshop - DBTA*, (pp. 586 – 589). DBTA.

Meijuan, G., Jingwen, T., & Shiru, Z. (2009a). Research of web classification mining based on classify support vector machine. In *Proceedings of the Colloquim CCCM*, (pp. 21 – 24). CCCM.

Mingrong, L., Yicen, L., Liang, X., Xing, C., & Qing, Y. (2008). Single Chinese news article summarization based on ranking propagation. In *Proceedings of the International Symposium on Knowledge Acquisition and Modeling KAM 2008*, (pp. 779 – 783). KAM.

Oliver, W. L., & Schneider, W. (1988). Using rules and task division to augment connectionist learning. In *Proceedings of the Tenth Annual Conference of the Cognitive Science Society*, (pp. 55-61). Montreal, Canada: Erlbaum.

Omlin, C. W., & Giles, C. L. (1992). Training second-order recurrent neural networks using hints. In *Proceedings of the Ninth International Conference on Machine Learning*, (pp. 361-366). Aberdeen, Scotland: Morgan Kaufmann.

Radev, D. R., Blair-Goldensohn, S., Zhang, Z., & Raghavan, R. S. (2001). Newsinessence: A system for domain-independent, real-time news clustering and multi-document summarization. In *Proceedings of the Human Language Technology Conference*. IEEE.

Rumelhart, D., & McClelland, I. (1986). *Parallel distributed processing*. Cambridge, MA: MIT Press.

Rumelhart, D. E., Durbin, R., Golden, R., & Chauvin, Y. (1995). Backpropagation: The basic theory. In *Backpropagation: Theory, Architectures and Applications* (pp. 1–34). Hillsdale, NJ: Lawrence Erlbaum Associates.

Rumelhart, D. E., Hinton, G. E., & Williams, R. I. (1986). Learning internal representations by error propagation. In Rumelhart, D. E., & McClelland, I. L. (Eds.), *Parallel Distributed Processing (Vol. 1*, pp. 318–362). Cambridge, MA: MIT Press.

Saha, S., Sajjanhar, A., Shang, G., Dew, R., & Ying, Z. (2010). Delivering categorized news items using RSS feeds and web services. [CIT.]. *Proceedings of CIT, 2010*, 698–702.

Schapire, R. E. (1990). The strength of weak learnability. *Machine Learning, 5*, 197–227. doi:10.1007/BF00116037

Schwenk, H., & Bengio, Y. (2000). Boosting neural networks. *Neural Computation, 12*, 1869–1887. doi:10.1162/089976600300015178

Shaikh, M. A. M., & Mitsuru, I. (2006). ASNA: An intelligent agent for retrieving and classifying news on the basis of emotion-affinity. In *Proceedings of the International Conference on Intelligent Agents, Web Technologies and Internet Commerce (IAWTIC 2006)*, (pp. 133-138). Sydney, Australia: IAWTIC.

Shavlik, J. W. (1994). Extended abstract: Combining symbolic and neural learning. *Machine Learning, 14*, 321–331. doi:10.1007/BF00993982

Shavlik, J. W., & Towell, G. G. (1989). An approach to combining explanation-based and neural learning algorithms. *Connection Science, 1*, 233–255. doi:10.1080/09540098908915640

Smolensky, P. (1988). On the proper treatment of connnectionism. *The Behavioral and Brain Sciences, 11*(1), 1. doi:10.1017/S0140525X00052432

Sun, R. (1994). *Integrating rules and connectionism for robust common sense reasoning*. New York, NY: Wiley and Sons.

Sun, R. (1997). Introduction to connectionist symbolic integration. In Sun, R., & Alexandre, F. (Eds.), *Connectionist-Symbolic Integration*. Mahwah, NJ: Lawrence Erlbaum Associates.

Taeho, J. (2009). Categorization of news articles using neural text categorizer. In *Proceedings to FUZZY* (pp. 19–22). FUZZY.

Takeda, T., & Takasu, A. (2007). Update news: A news clustering and summarization system using efficient text processing. In *Proceedings of International Conference Digital Libraries*. IEEE.

Tintarev, N., & Masthoff, J. (2006). Similarity for news recommender systems. In *Proceedings of the AH 2006 Workshop on Recommender Systems and Intelligent User Interfaces*. AH.

Touretzky, D. S. (Ed.). (1991). Special issue on connectionist approaches to language learning. *Machine Learning, 7.*

Tumer, K., & Ghosh, J. (1996). Analysis of decision boundaries in linearly combined neural classifiers. *Pattern Recognition, 29*(2), 341–348. doi:10.1016/0031-3203(95)00085-2

Uberbacher, E. C., & Mural, R. J. (1991). Locating protein coding regions in human DNA sequences by a multiple sensor - Neural network approach. *Proceedings of the National Academy of Sciences of the United States of America, 88*, 11261–11265. doi:10.1073/pnas.88.24.11261

Vidhya, K. A., & Aghila, G. (2010). Hybrid text mining model for document classification. In *Proceedings of the ICCAE*, (pp. 210 – 214). ICCAE.

Wasson, M. (1998). Using leading text for news summaries: Evaluation results and implications for commercial summarization applications. In *Proceedings of the Joint 17th International Conference on Computational Linguistics and 36th Annual Meeting of the Association for Computational Linguistics*. IEEE.

Wei, C., Li-Jun, Z., Chun, C., & Jia-Jun, B. (2009). A hybrid phonic web news recommender system for pervasive access. In *Proceedings of the International Conference on Communications and Mobile Computing*, (vol 3, pp. 122-126). WRI.

Werbos, P. I. (1974). *Beyond regression: New tools for regression and analysis in the behavioral sciences*. (PhD Thesis). Boston, MA: Harvard University.

Werbos, P. I. (1988). Backpropagation and neuro-control: A review and prospectus. In *Proceedings of the Joint Conference on Neural Networks*, (vol 1, pp. 209-216). IEEE Press.

Wermter, S. (1995). *Hybrid connectionist natural language processing*. London, UK: Chapman and Hall Thomson International.

Wermter, S. (1999). Preference moore machines for neural fuzzy integration. In *Proceedings of the International Joint Conference on Artificial Intelligence*, (pp. 840-845). Stockholm, Sweden: IEEE.

Wermter, S., Arevian, G., & Panchev, C. (1999). Recurrent neural network learning for text routing. In *Proceedings of the International Conference on Artificial Neural Networks*, (pp. 898-903). Edinburgh, UK: IEEE.

Wermter, S., Arevian, G., & Panchev, C. (2000a). Towards hybrid neural learning internet agents. In Wermter, S., & Sun, R. (Eds.), *Hybrid Neural Systems* (pp. 160–176). Berlin, Germany: Springer. doi:10.1007/10719871_11

Wermter, S., Arevian, G., & Panchev, C. (2000b). Network analysis in a neural learning internet agents. In *Proceedings of the International Conference on Computer Intelligence and Neuroscience*, (pp. 880-884). Atlantic City, NJ: IEEE.

Wermter, S., Panchev, C., & Arevian, G. (1999b). Hybrid neural plausibility networks for news agents. In *Proceedings of the National Conference on Artificial Intelligence AAAI*, (pp. 93-98). Orlando, FL: AAAI.

Wermter, S., & Weber, V. (1997). SCREEN: Learning a flat syntactic and semantic spoken language analysis using artificial neural networks. *Journal of Artificial Intelligence Research, 6*(1), 35–85.

Xindong, W., Gong-Qing, W., Fei, X., Zhu, Z., & Xue-Gang, H. (2010). News filtering and summarization on the web. *IEEE Intelligent Systems, 25*(5), 68–76. doi:10.1109/MIS.2010.11

Zhang, D., Simoff, S., Aciar, S., & Debenham, J. (2008). A multi agent recommender system that utilises consumer reviews in its recommendations. *International Journal of Intelligent Information and Database Systems*, *2*(1), 69–81. doi:10.1504/IJIIDS.2008.017245

Zhang, Y., & Jiao, J. R. (2007). An associative classification-based recommendation system for personalization in B2C e-commerce applications. *Expert Systems with Applications*, *33*(2). doi:10.1016/j.eswa.2006.05.005

Chapter 11
Newly Developed Nature-Inspired Algorithms and their Applications to Recommendation Systems

Utku Köse
Usak University, Turkey

ABSTRACT

Because of their mathematical backgrounds and coherent structures, Artificial Intelligent-based methods and techniques are often used to find solutions for different types of problems encountered. In the related context, nature-inspired algorithms are also important for providing more accurate solutions. Because of their nature-based, flexible process structures, the related algorithms can be applied to different types of problems. At this point, recommendation systems are one of the related problem areas where nature-inspired algorithms can be used to get better results. In the literature there are many research studies that are based on using nature-inspired algorithms within recommendation systems. This chapter aims to discuss usage of some newly developed nature-inspired algorithms in typical recommendation systems. In this aim, features and functions of some new nature-inspired algorithms will be explained first. Later, using the related algorithms in recommendation systems will be discussed. Following that, there will be a discussion on future of nature-inspired algorithms and also their roles in the recommendation approach or system-based applications.

INTRODUCTION

Today, in the field of Computer Science, there is a remarkable research effort especially on solving real world based challenging, difficult problems. At this point, different types of intelligent approaches, methods, and techniques are designed and developed to find necessary solutions for the related problems. In this context, nature-inspired algorithms have also an important role on finding optimal solutions by using more advanced approaches, which were developed according to some dynamics, functions, or events that are occurred within the nature.

DOI: 10.4018/978-1-4666-2542-6.ch011

Because of obtained successful results, there has been an increasing interest on nature-inspired algorithms and currently, there is also a big effort on designing and developing newer ones that aim to find better solutions for encountered problems. Some popular algorithms like Particle Swarm Optimization (PSO), Ant Colony Optimization (ACO), and Artificial Bee Colony (ABC) are already applied to different types of problems to get better results. Additionally, some researchers also try to improve features and functions of these algorithms to obtain more optimal results. But on the other hand, some researchers also design more effective and efficient algorithms that provide more optimal and accurate calculation approaches rather than the mentioned ones. As a result of the related studies, some newer algorithms like River Formation Dynamics (RFD) Algorithm, Intelligent Water Drops (IWDs) Algorithm, Gravitational Search Algorithm (GSA), Firefly Algorithm and Charged System Search (CSS) Algorithm have taken place in the related literature.

As mentioned before, nature-inspired algorithms are used for solving real-world based difficult, challenging problems. However, as different from real-world based problems, the related algorithms can also be used within different user-based systems or environments. For instance, recommendation systems are one of these environments that nature-inspired algorithms can be used to provide better experiences for users.

In this chapter, some newly developed nature-inspired algorithms and their using in recommendation systems will be discussed. In this sense, objectives of the chapter can be listed as below:

- Introducing features and functions of some newly developed nature-inspired algorithms.
- Showing how nature-inspired algorithms can be used within recommendation systems.
- Discussing about the future of nature-inspired algorithms and their roles on appli-

cations associated with recommendation approaches or systems.

SOME NEWLY DEVELOPED NATURE-INSPIRED ALGORITHMS

As it was mentioned before, there is an increasing interest and effort on developing newer and more effective nature-inspired algorithms in recent years. The related researchers, who try to develop new algorithms, aim to provide more accurate and efficient approaches in order improve process performances in finding optimal solutions. In this sense, three of these newly developed nature-inspired algorithms will be explained in this section. Before discussing about applications on recommendation systems, it is better to introduce basics and working mechanisms of the related algorithms.

Intelligent Water Drops (IWDs) Algorithm

In general terms, Intelligent Water Drops (IWDs) Algorithm is a nature-inspired algorithm, which is based on the observation of the behavior of water drops. It is an algorithm, which was developed on the dynamic of a natural river system, reactions, and actions that happen among water drops in a natural river (Shah-Hosseini, 2007, 2008, 2009).

In the nature, it can be seen that natural rivers have many different turns and twists along their paths and at this point, it can be thought that why these turns and twists are created and is there any logic or some kind of intelligence behind them? Furthermore, it can also be thought that is it possible to design and develop intelligent algorithms according to the related mechanisms within natural rivers? All of these thought have been starting point for Shah-Hosseini to design and develop IWDs algorithm. IWDs Algorithm tries to model the related mechanisms in a natural river and implement them in an algorithm structure. Within the algorithm, intelligent water drops work together to reach an optimal solution for the given problem. In this context, some important coefficients and parameters are used to design and develop intelligent water drop scheme and the related problem-solving environment.

Basics of the Algorithm

In a typical IWD algorithm, some Intelligent Water Drops (IWDs) are created first and the related IWDs are based on two main properties: velocity and soil during the problem solving process. Velocity and soil properties are changed during the lifetime of a typical IWD. Within the algorithm steps, an IWD flows from a source to a destination. At this point, an IWD starts its flow with a zero soil and an initial velocity value.

While travelling from one point to another one, the related IWD removes some soil and consequently, it can gain some speed. At this point, the amount of the removed soil is added to the related IWD and this soil is non-linearly proportional to the inverse of the time needed for the IWD to flow from its current point to the next point. The related time interval is calculated by using some simple laws of physics (linear motion). Thus, the time taken is proportional to the velocity of the IWD and inversely proportional to the distance between the related two points (Shah-Hosseini, 2009). As it can be understood, both IWDs and the problem-solving environment (for instance each path between two different points) have memories to track soil information.

During the problem solving process, an IWD has discrete flowing steps. While travelling between two different points, the IWD velocity value is increased by the amount nonlinearly proportional to the inverse of the soil between the two points (As a result, a path with less soil let an IWD to become faster than a path having more soil). At this point, the IWD prefers the paths having low soils to the paths having high soils (In other words, paths with lower soils have more chance

to be selected by an IWD). This path selection behavior is implemented by imposing a uniform random distribution on the soils of the available paths. Then, the probability of the next path to select is inversely proportional to the soils of the available paths (Shah-Hosseini, 2009).

General Algorithm Structure

Within IWDs algorithm, a typical problem is shown as the form of a graph (*N*: node set and *E*: edge set). After starting to problem solving steps, each created IWD begins constructing its solution by navigating on the nodes of the graph along the edges. This navigation continues until the related IWD completes its own solution. At this point, each IWD tries to find an optimal solution for the current iteration. When all IWDs in the solution space have completed their solutions, the current iteration of the algorithm is ended. At the end of every iteration, the best solution of the related iteration: T^{LB} (local best) is used to update the global best solution T^{GB}. This global best solution is stored until the end of the whole problem solving process. On the other hand, the amount of soil on the related edges of the T^{LB} is reduced according to quality of the solution. Following that, the next iteration is started with new IWDs (However, last remaining soils on the paths are kept) and the mentioned steps are repeated. The IWDs algorithm is stopped when a stopping criteria is ensured. The stopping criterion can be a "maximum number of iterations value" or "a specific, expected solution value."

The mentioned algorithm steps can be explained in more detail as below (Shah-Hosseini, 2009):

Step 1: Initialization of static parameters.
- The graph (*N*, *E*) of the chosen problem is given to the algorithm. The quality of the global best solution T^{GB} is initially set to the worst value: $q(T^{GB}) = -\infty$.

- The stopping criterion (for instance; the maximum number of iterations) is determined by the user.
- The number of water drops N_{IWD} is set to a positive integer value, which is usually set to the number of nodes N_c of the graph.
- For velocity updating, the parameters are $a_v = 1$, $b_v = .01$ and $c_v = 1$.
- For soil updating, the parameters are $a_s = 1$, $b_s = .01$ and $c_s = 1$.
- The local soil updating parameter ρ_n, which is a small positive number less than one, is set as 0.9. On the other hand, the global soil updating parameter ρ_{IWD}, which is chosen from [0, 1], is set as $\rho_{IWD} = 0.9$.
- The initial soil on each path (edge) is determined with the constant: *InitSoil* such that the soil of the path between every two nodes i and j is set by $soil(i, j) = InitSoil$.
- The initial velocity of each IWD is determined with the constant: *InitVel*.

Step 2: Initialization of dynamic parameters.

- Every IWD has a visited node list $vc(IWD)$, which is initially empty: $vc(IWD) = \{ \}$.
- Each IWD's velocity is set to *InitVel*.
- All IWDs are set to have zero amount of soil.

Step 3: Spread the IWDs randomly on the nodes of the graph as their first visited nodes.

Step 4: Update the visited node list of each IWD, so they can include the nodes just visited.

Step 5: Repeat the calculations below for those IWDs with partial solutions:

- For the IWD residing in node i, choose the next node j, which does not violate any constraints of the problem and is not in the visited node list the related IWD, using the following probability equation:

$$p_i^{IWD}(j) = \frac{f(soil(i, j))}{\sum_{k \notin vc(IWD)} f(soil(i, k))} \quad (1)$$

such that

$$f(soil(i, j)) = \frac{1}{\varepsilon_s + g(soil(i, j))} \quad and$$

$$g(soil(i, j)) = \begin{cases} soil(i, j) & if \\ \min_{l \notin vc(IWD)} (soil(i, l)) \geq 0 \\ soil(i, j) - \\ \min_{l \notin vc(IWD)} (soil(i, l)) & else \end{cases}$$

Following that, add the newly visited node j to the list $vc(IWD)$.

- For each IWD flowing from node i to node j, update its velocity $vel^{IWD}(t)$ with the following equation:

$$vel^{IWD}(t + 1) = vel^{IWD}(t) + \frac{a_v}{b_v + c_v . soil^2(i, j)} \quad (2)$$

($vel^{IWD}(t + 1)$ is the updated velocity of the IWD)

- For the IWD flowing on the path from node i to j, compute the soil value $\Delta soil(i, j)$ that the IWD loads from the path by using the following equation:

$$\Delta soil(i, j) = \frac{a_s}{b_s + c_s . time^2(i, j; vel^{IWD}(t + 1))} \quad (3)$$

such that

$$time(i, j; vel^{IWD}(t + 1)) = \frac{HUD(j)}{vel^{IWD}(t + 1)}$$

(The heuristic undesirability: *HUD(j)* is defined appropriately for the chosen problem).

- Update the soil $soil(i, j)$ of the path from node i to j traversed by the related IWD and also update the soil that the IWD carries $soil^{IWD}$ by using the following equations:

$$soil(i, j) = (1 - \rho_n) . soil(i, j) - \rho_n . \Delta soil(i, j) \quad (4)$$

$$soil^{IWD} = soil^{IWD} + \Delta soil(i, j) \quad (5)$$

Step 6: Find the local (iteration) best solution T^{LB} from all the solutions T^{IWD} found by the IWDs by using the following equation:

$$T^{LB} = \arg\max_{\forall T^{IWD}} q(T^{IWD}) \qquad (6)$$

($q()$ is used to get quality of the obtained solution)

Step 7: Update the soils on the paths that form the current local best solution T^{LB} with the following equation:

$$soil(i,j) = (1 + \rho_{IWD}) \cdot soil(i,j) -$$

$$\rho_{IWD} \cdot \frac{1}{(N_{LB} - 1)} \cdot soil_{LB}^{IWD} \qquad \forall (i,j) \in T^{LB}$$

$$(7)$$

(N_{LB} is used for the number of nodes in the solution: T^{LB}).

Step 8: Update the global best solution T^{GB} by the (current iteration) local best solution T^{LB} with the following equation:

$$T^{GB} = \begin{cases} T^{GB} & if \quad q(T^{GB}) \geq q(T^{LB}) \\ T^{LB} & otherwise \end{cases} \qquad (8)$$

Step 9: Control the stopping criterion. If it has not been reached yet, go to the Step 2.

Step 10: The IWDs algorithm is ended here with the global best solution: T^{GB}.

The whole IWDs algorithm is worked according to the explained algorithm steps. At this point, there may only need for some modifications on some of the provided equations in order to fit the algorithm structure for more specific problem types.

Gravitational Search Algorithm (GSA)

Gravitational Search Algorithm (GSA) is another nature-inspired algorithm, which was first introduced in a Master Thesis in 2007 (Rashedi, 2007) and published internationally in 2009 (Rashedi, et al., 2009). GSA is an algorithm, which was developed based on Newtonian laws of gravity and motion. Within the algorithm, the related laws are applied to find the optimum solution by using a set of agents, which are also called as "masses" (Rashedi, et al., 2011; Ghalambaz, et al., 2011). As it was explained by Rashedi *et al.* (2009), the related masses obey the following rules during the problem solving process:

- **Law of gravity:** "A particle attracts every other particle and the gravitational force between two particles is directly proportional to the product of their masses and also inversely proportional to the distance between them."
- **Law of motion:** "The current velocity value of any mass is equal to the sum of the fraction of its previous velocity and the variation in the velocity. Variation in the velocity or acceleration of any mass is equal to the force acted on the system divided by mass of inertia."

In order to understand GSA, it is better to explain basics of the algorithm and the general problem solving steps (the algorithm structure), respectively.

Basics of the Algorithm

The GSA comes with some conjectures and specific mathematical basics. First, it is clear that every masses must obey rules provided with "Law of gravity" and also "Law of motion" explained before. Additionally; in GSA, every mass (agent) has four specifications: "position, active gravitational mass, passive gravitational mass and inertial mass." At this point, each mass provides a solution for the problem, by using its position. On the other hand, the problem solving steps are continued by using gravitational and inertial masses, which are determined with a chosen fitness function. Finally, it is also expected that masses in the solution space can be attracted by the "heaviest mass." As it can be understood, the heaviest mass is the one providing an optimal solution for the problem (Rashedi, et al., 2009; Ghalambaz, et al., 2011).

General Algorithm Structure

Generally, the whole GSA is based on the following mathematical representations and the related equations (Rashedi, et al., 2009; Ghalambaz, et al., 2011):

- In GSA, the following definition is used to determine position of each (ith) mass:

$$X_i = (x_i^1, ..., x_i^d, ..., x_i^n), i = 1, 2, ..., s \quad (9)$$

(Here, x_i^d is position of the ith mass in the dth dimension. Additionally, n is the dimension of solution search space).

- Mass of each agent is calculated after computing the current population's fitness. It can be done with the following equations:

$$q_i(t) = \frac{fit_i(t) - the\ worst(t)}{the\ best(t) - the\ worst(t)} \quad (10)$$

$$M_i(t) = \frac{q_i(t)}{\sum_{j=1}^{s} q_j(t)} \quad (11)$$

(In the related equations, $M_i(t)$ represents the mass whereas $fit_i(t)$ is the fitness value of the agent i at t).

The related *the worst(t)* and *the best(t)* functions are also defined as follows:

$$the\ best(t) = \min_{j \in \{1,...,s\}} fit_j(t) \quad (12)$$

$$the\ worst(t) = \max_{j \in \{1,...,s\}} fit_j(t) \quad (13)$$

- In order to calculate acceleration of an agent, total forces from a set of heavier masses that apply on an agent should be considered based on the law of gravity (Equation [14]). This calculation is followed by the calculation of agent acceleration by using the law of motion (Equation [15]). Next, velocity and also position of an agent are updated by using Equation (16) and Equation (17) respectively:

$$F_i^d(t) = \sum_{j \in kbest\ j \neq i} rand_j G(t) \frac{M_j(t) . M_i(t)}{R_{ij}(t) + \varepsilon} \quad (14)$$
$$\cdot \left(x_j^d(t) - x_i^d(t) \right)$$

$$a_i^d(t) = \frac{F_i^d(t)}{M_i(t)} = \sum_{j \in kbest\ j \neq i} rand_j G(t) \frac{M_j(t)}{R_{ij}(t) + \varepsilon} \quad (15)$$
$$\cdot \left(x_j^d(t) - x_i^d(t) \right)$$

$$v_i^d(t+1) = rand_i \times v_i^d(t) + a_i^d(t) \quad (16)$$

$$x_i^d(t+1) = x_i^d(t) + v_i^d(t+1) \quad (17)$$

In the equations, $rand_i$ and $rand_j$ are two uniformly distributed random numbers in the interval [0, 1], ε is a small value, $Rij(t)$ is the Euclidean distance between two agents i and j, calculated with $\left\| X_i(t), X_j(t) \right\|_2$, *kbest* is the set of first K agents with the best fitness value and biggest mass, which is a function of time, initialized to K0 at the beginning and decreasing with time. Here K0 is set to s (total number of agents) and is decreased linearly to 1. In GSA, the gravitational constant, G, will take an initial value, G0, and it will be reduced with time:

G(t) = G(G₀, t) (18)

With respect to the mentioned equations, the problem solving steps of the GSA can be expressed as follows (Rashedi, et al., 2009; Ghalambaz, et al., 2011):

Step 1: Search space identification.

Step 2: Randomized initialization.

Step 3: Fitness evaluation of agents.

Step 4: Update *G(t), the best(t), the worst(t)* and $M_i(t)$ for $i = 1, 2,...,N$.

Step 5: Calculate the total force in different directions.

Step 6: Calculate acceleration and velocity.

Step 7: Update agents' positions.

Step 8: Control the stopping criterion. If it has not been reached yet, go to the Step 3.

Charged System Search (CSS) Algorithm

The Charged System Search (CSS) Algorithm was first introduced in 2010 (Kaveh & Talatahari, 2010a) and as similar to the GSA, it is a nature-inspired algorithm, which is based on physical laws. The algorithm is designed and developed according to electrostatic and Newtonian mechanics laws. Because of this, working mechanism of CSS includes mathematical equations inspired from the related laws.

As general, the algorithm is formed on a multi-agent based structure in which each agent is also called as "Charged Particle (CP)." In this context, every CP is evaluated as a charged sphere with a specified radius, having a uniform volume charge density, which can insert an electric force to the other related CPs (Kaveh & Talatahari, 2010c).

Basics of the Algorithm

As it was explained, the first basic feature of the CSS is that it includes some kind of CPs interacting with each other to reach optimal solutions during the problem solving steps. The further mathematical basics about CSS can be expressed as follows (Halliday, et al., 2008; Kaveh & Talatahari, 2010a, 2010c):

- The Coulomb and Gauss laws provide the magnitude of the electric field at a point inside and outside a charged insulating solid sphere, respectively, as expressed with the following equation:

$$E_{ij} = \begin{cases} \dfrac{k_e q_i}{a^3} r_{ij} & \text{if } r_{ij} < a \\ \dfrac{k_e q_i}{r_{ij}^2} & \text{if } r_{ij} \geq a \end{cases} \quad (19)$$

(In the equation, k_e is a constant, which is also called as the "Coulomb constant." On the other hand, r_{ij} is the separation of the center of sphere and the selected point, q_i

is the magnitude of the charge and a is the radius of the charged sphere).

- As a result of using the "principle of super-position," the resulting electric force due to N charged spheres is equal to the following equation:

$$F_j = k_e q_j \sum_{i=1}^{N} \frac{\left(\dfrac{q_i}{a^3} r_{ij} \cdot i_1 + \dfrac{q_i}{r_{ij}^2} \cdot i_2 \right)}{\cdot \dfrac{r_i - r_j}{\|r_i - r_j\|}} \quad (20)$$

$$\begin{cases} i_1 = 1, \ i_2 = 0 \Leftrightarrow r_{ij} < a \\ i_1 = 0, \ i_2 = 1 \Leftrightarrow r_{ij} \geq a \end{cases}$$

- Furthermore, according to the Newtonian mechanics, the following equations can also be expressed:

$$\Delta r = r_{new} - r_{old} \quad (21)$$

$$v = \frac{r_{new} - r_{old}}{\Delta t} \quad (22)$$

$$a = \frac{v_{new} - v_{old}}{\Delta t} \quad (23)$$

(In Equation [21] – [23], r_{old} and r_{new} are the initial and final position of a particle, respectively. Additionally, v is the velocity of the particle whereas a corresponds to the acceleration of the particle).

- By using the expressed equations above and applying "Newton's second law," the displacement of any object as a function of time can be obtained with the following equation:

$$r_{new} = \frac{1}{2} \cdot \frac{F}{m} \cdot \Delta t^2 + v_{old} \cdot \Delta t + r_{old} \quad (24)$$

General Algorithm Structure

After expressing the related mathematical equations, it is easier to form general algorithm structure of the CSS. In the literature, problem-solving steps within CSS are defined under three different sections, which are called as "levels." In this sense, the related steps can be expressed as follows (Kaveh & Talatahari, 2010a, 2010b, 2010c):

- **Level 1:** Initialization
  - ◦ **Step 1:** Initialize parameters of the CSS. Initialize an array of CPs with random positions. The initial velocities of the related CPs are taken as zero value. Each CP has a charge of magnitude (q) defined considering the quality of its solution as:

$$q_i = \frac{fit(i) - fit\ the\ worst}{fit\ the\ best - fit\ the\ worst} \qquad (25)$$

$$i = 1, 2, ..., N$$

(In the equation, fit the best and fit the worst are the best and the worst fitness of all particles and *fit(i)* is the fitness of agent *i*).

The separation distance: r_{ij} between two CPs is defined with the following equation:

$$r_{ij} = \frac{\|X_i - X_j\|}{\|(X_i - X_j)/2 - X_{best}\| + \varepsilon} \qquad (26)$$

(Here, X_i and X_j are the positions of the ith and jth CPs, respectively. Also, X_{best} is the position of the best current CP and ε is a small positive number, which is used to avoid singularities).

  - ◦ **Step 2:** Evaluate the values of the fitness function for the related CPs and compare with each other ones to sort them in an increasing order.
  - ◦ **Step 3:** Store the number of the first CPs equal to the Charged Memory Size (CMS) and their related values of the fitness functions in the Charged Memory (CM).

- **Level 2:** Searching
  - ◦ **Step 1:** Determine the probability of moving each CP toward the others considering the following probability equation:

$$p_{ij} = \begin{cases} 1 & \dfrac{fit(i) - fit\ the\ best}{fit(j) - fit(i)} > \\ rand \vee fit(j) > fit(i) \\ 0\_ else \end{cases} \qquad (27)$$

Afterwards, calculate the attracting force vector for each CP by using the following equation:

$$F_j = q_j \sum_{i, i \neq j} \left(\frac{q_i}{a^3} r_{ij} \cdot i_1 + \frac{q_i}{r_{ij}^2} \cdot i_2 \right)$$
$$\cdot p_{ij} \cdot (X_i - X_j) \qquad (28)$$

$$\begin{cases} j = 1, 2, ..., N \\ i_1 = 1,\ i_2 = 0 \Leftrightarrow r_{ij} < a \\ i_1 = 0,\ i_2 = 1 \Leftrightarrow r_{ij} \geq a \end{cases}$$

(Here, F_j is the resultant force, which affects the jth CP).

  - ◦ **Step 2:** Move each CP to the new position and find its velocity by using the following equations:

$$X_{j,new} = rand_{j1} \cdot k_a \cdot \frac{F_j}{m_j} \cdot \Delta t^2 + \qquad (29)$$
$$rand_{j2} \cdot k_v \cdot v_{j,old} \cdot \Delta t + X_{j,old}$$

$$v_{j,new} = \frac{X_{j,new} - X_{j,old}}{\Delta t} \qquad (30)$$

In these equations, $rand_{j1}$ and $rand_{j2}$ are two random numbers, which are uniformly distributed in the range (0, 1). Additionally, m_j is the mass of the CPs, Δt is the time step (it is set to 1), k_a is the acceleration coefficient, k_v is the velocity coefficient to control the influence of the previous velocity (both of k_a and k_v are taken as 0.5).

  - ◦ **Step 3:** If each CP exits from the allowable search space, correct its position by using the HS-based handling approach as described for the HPSACO algorithm (Kaveh & Talatahari, 2009a, 2009b).
  - ◦ **Step 4:** Evaluate and compare the values of the fitness function for the new CPs and sort them in an increasing order.
  - ◦ **Step 5:** If some new CP vectors are better than the worst ones in the CM, in terms of their objective function values, include the better vectors in

the CM and exclude the worst ones from the CM.

- **Level 3:** Stopping criterion control
  Control the stopping criterion. If it has not been reached yet, repeat the "Level 2: Searching" steps (until the stopping criterion is reached).

CSS and also other explained algorithms employ wide range mathematical basics and flexible algorithmic structures. Because of this, they can be used to design and develop some kind of recommendation systems. This subject is devoted to the next title.

APPLICATIONS ON RECOMMENDATION SYSTEMS

Within this chapter, some typical recommendation systems, which are based on the explained nature-inspired algorithms, have been developed. Because of their similarities, both GSA and CSS algorithm has been used for a similar recommendation system structure whereas the IWDs algorithm has been employed for developing another one.

Using IWDs Algorithm to Develop a Recommendation System

IWDs algorithm has been used for providing a "Web page recommender system." In this system, new users' navigation behaviors on the Web page system is predicted according to the active users' previous actions, current point, and also previous navigation trends, by using structure of a previously formed hierarchical page navigation tree. At this point, some kind of Web logs that keep previous users' navigation styles are used to develop a page navigation tree first. The related tree is then updated adaptively with the support of the IWDs algorithm. In order to understand working mechanism of this recommendation system, the related processes must be explained in detail.

As it was mentioned, previously stored navigation Web logs are used for designing a hierarchical navigation tree first. The related Web log data must be cleaned and suitable data fields must be filtered by using some kind of "data mining" approaches. After getting the "clean navigation data," it can be used to form a hierarchical navigation tree structure by using "clustering" methods. As it can be understood, the recommendation system, which has been developed within this chapter, is some kind of hybrid system that employs both data mining approaches and a nature-inspired algorithm to obtain desired results. However, at this point, data mining approaches and methods used for data preparing and clustering are subjects of different research studies rather than this study.

Generally, the remaining working processes of the system can be explained as below (see Figure 1):

- After getting the navigation tree structure once, the whole tree can be updated by using results that will be obtained after each user's navigation. In this sense, the whole recommendation problem can be evaluated as similar to a "Travelling Salesman Problem (TSP)." At this point, the IWDs algorithm starts its work by giving feedback to the active user after evaluating the user's current page visiting situation.
- Each user is evaluated by the IWDs algorithm (and by the recommendation system in this context) as an Intelligent Water Drop (IWD).
- As it can be remembered from the general algorithm structure, this IWD must flow through suitable nodes by evaluating some factors like "soil" and "velocity." Because of this, each connection between the related Web pages contains soil values and these values are changed according to IWDs algorithm calculations to change recommendation trend of the system after each user's navigation session.

Figure 1. Working mechanism of the IWDs based recommendation system

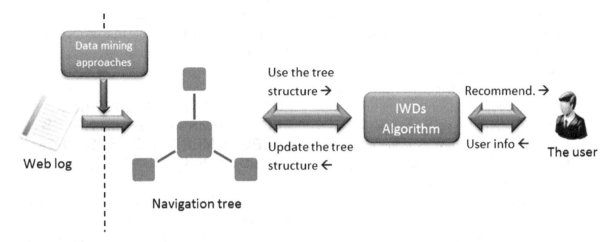

- In this way, the hierarchical structure of the navigation tree is also updated at the end of active user's session and consequently, an adaptive recommendation system structure is ensured to give more accurate recommendations for each new visit.

Using GSA and CSS Algorithm to Develop Recommendation Systems

As it was mentioned before, both GSA and CSS algorithm has been used to develop similar recommendation systems. GSA and CSS algorithm include similar approaches to develop intelligent systems that evaluate data and return feedbacks. Because of this, two "social profile recommendation systems," which have similar interface and working mechanisms, have been designed and developed by using the related algorithms. As it can be understood, evaluating processes of these systems are changed as a result of different algorithmic structures of GSA and CSS algorithm.

Briefly, the working processes of the related systems can be explained as below:

- In the systems, each social profile gains some scores according to the mentioned properties that must be taken into evalu-

ation. At this point, the person's properties like age, gender, height, weight... etc. can have some user defined weights. Additionally, according to the structure of any social profile, some specific properties like hobbies, interests, etc. can be evaluated with some numbers and by giving different user defined weights, they can be enable to be taken into consideration to calculate a general profile score. Mathematically, for a total of *i* social profile, this approach can be expressed as follows:

$$P^i_{score} = w_1 . age\, v_i + w_2 . gender\, v_i + ...$$
$$+ \sum_{j=1}^{n_1} wh_j . hobby\, v_j + ... \tag{31}$$

(It is important that active user's social profile score is also calculated in order to use it during further evaluation processes).

- After calculating scores of each social profile, the related values are used while creating agents ("masses" in GSA and "CPs" in CSS algorithm) in the algorithms. As it can be understood, position of any agent in GSA or CSS algorithm is associated with a social profile score. Thus, except from other initial values or specific coefficients, the connection between GSA or CSS algorithm and social profile structure is ensured in this way (definitely, as different from the expressed approach in this chapter, more accurate ones can also be discovered experimentally).

- The remaining evaluation processes are continued within different problem solving steps of the related algorithms. In this context, social profile(s) that will be recommended are determined by using a fitness function in which active user's social profile score and each other scores are taken into consideration to get a recommendation value (result). At this point, execution of both GSA and CSS algorithm is ended after evaluating each social profile and the active user's profile. As a result, some social profiles having better recommendation values than others are given as feedback to the user (number of social profiles that will be recommended is initially defined with a constant). The fitness function, which is used within both GSA and CSS algorithm is expressed as follows:

$$fitness(i) = \frac{\sqrt{(P_{score}^{active\ user} - agent_{position}^{i})^2} - \min P_{score}}{\left|\min P_{score}\right| + \left|\max P_{score}\right|} \quad (32)$$

(In the equation, $agent_{position}^{i}$ is the position value of ith mass of GSA or ith CP of CSS) (see Figure 2).

As it can be seen from the explained systems, the related nature-inspired algorithms can be easily employed to design and develop a typical recommendation system. Furthermore, as different from the mentioned approaches, using features and functions of such recommendation systems can also be improved by combining different Web based functions, applications, scripts or any other technologies. It is also possible to provide more accurate and flexible systems by modifying database structures or using additional functions. Consequently, these studies are also some kind of references for possible future studies. On the other hand, in respect with the future studies, it is also important to discuss about future of such algorithms and their possible role on recommendation systems based applications.

FUTURE OF NATURE-INSPIRED ALGORITHMS AND THEIR ROLES IN RECOMMENDATION SYSTEMS-BASED APPLICATIONS

In today's modern world, there is a need for more intelligent approaches or systems that try to provide more effective solutions for people to solve their real-world based problems or enable them to have more meaningful and practical life standards. Thus, Artificial Intelligence techniques are widely used in many different fields to achieve the mentioned objectives. In this sense, more efficient and effective techniques are also employed more in order to obtain optimal solutions in specific problems. Within the context of this chapter, nature-inspired are also some kind of the related techniques, which have been implemented in different research studies, as it can be seen from the literature. However, at this point, future of these techniques (mostly of nature-inspired algorithms) should be discussed to think more objective about future of the world and evaluate environmental factors that form this future.

According to the performed research studies and newly developed approaches or systems, it seems that there will be more need for Artificial Intelligence techniques in the future of the world. Furthermore, it can be expressed that the future of the modern world will be based on mostly intelligent systems enabling higher life standards. In this world, more advanced intelligent techniques will take active roles to ensure desired situations. At this point, nature-inspired algorithms will also have important roles on solving encountered problems and supporting people to adapt them to the future of the world.

Figure 2. Working mechanism social profile recommendation systems

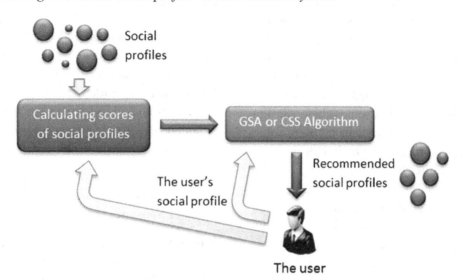

It seems that there will be more nature-inspired techniques that are based on more different laws or rules from the nature. In the future of the world, today's popular nature-inspired algorithms will be replaced by more advanced and efficient ones and these algorithms will have more complex mathematical basics to provide intelligent approaches or systems. Probably, they will provide more functions to design and develop intelligent systems, which are suitable to the structure of the future world. At this point, it can also be expressed that they will simulate human-thinking or human intelligence better according to today's algorithms. However, in spite of everything, the trend of inspiring from the nature and developing nature-inspired algorithms will be continued in the future.

In the daily life of the future world, recommendation approaches and so systems will also have more important roles and functions. In this sense, people will need more assistance to determine their needs and general trends to adapt themselves to the flow of the life. At this point, there will be more advanced recommendation systems, which will help people during travelling, shopping, or just having a lunch at a restaurant. As different from today's world, this kind of systems will be more accurate, objective, flexible, and fast on giving recommendations. Furthermore, it will be easier to keep recommendation systems in a mobile device. On the other hand, people will also be enabled to reach this type of systems whenever and wherever they go. In the terms of nature-inspired algorithms, it will also be possible to design recommendation systems based on the related algorithms. Definitely, it is possible to develop more advanced Artificial Intelligence techniques that can be specially used within recommendation systems in the future. But on the other hand, it seems that as a result of larger usage scope of newer nature-inspired algorithms in the future, it will always possible to implement them such intelligent approaches or systems.

CONCLUSION

Nowadays, nature-inspired algorithms are widely used to get optimal solutions for encountered problems and design intelligent systems for specific usage areas. Because of their mathematical basics and nature-based rules, it is always possible to simulate human-thinking behavior or human intelligence better to ensure more advanced and accurate Artificial Intelligence based applications. As it was discussed within this chapter, recommendation systems are one of these applications. In the literature, there are many different research studies, which aim to design and develop recommendation systems based on nature-inspired algorithms. Additionally, it is also possible to design and develop this type of systems by using some newly developed nature-inspired algorithms, as it was shown in the chapter.

As it was mentioned before, currently there is a big effort on designing newer and more accurate nature-inspired algorithms to obtain better results on solving specific problems or getting more effective intelligent approaches or systems. Because of this, it is always for researchers to develop more effective nature-inspired algorithms that provide desired results within the related concept. Furthermore, it is also possible to obtain better results on recommendation system applications, by using different types of nature-inspired algorithms or hybrid systems that combine more than one Artificial Intelligence approaches, methods, or techniques.

In the future, it seems that recommendation systems will be more popular because of increasing need for assistance during the flow of the life. Thus, there will be more need for Artificial Intelligence based techniques, as it was explained before. Consequently, it will also be possible for nature-inspired algorithms to take active roles on designing more advanced recommendation approaches or systems. In this context, it can also be said that as a result of using different laws and functions of the nature, more accurate and advanced nature-inspired algorithms will also take place in the modern life and provide more advanced intelligent approaches to simulate human-thinking behavior or human intelligence and cause more desired results in the related works or studies.

REFERENCES

Ghalambaz, M., Noghrehabadi, A. R., Behrang, M. A., Assareh, E., Ghanbarzadeh, A., & Hedayat, N. (2011). A hybrid neural network and gravitational search algorithm (HNNGSA) method to solve well known Wessinger's equation. *World Academy of Science. Engineering and Technology*, *6*(73), 803–807.

Halliday, D., Resnick, R., & Walker, J. (2008). *Fundamentals of physics*. Hoboken, NJ: John Wiley & Sons Inc.

Kaveh, A., & Talatahari, S. (2009a). Particle swarm optimizer, ant colony strategy and harmony search scheme hybridized for optimization of truss structures. *Computers & Structures*, *87*(5/6), 267–283. doi:10.1016/j.compstruc.2009.01.003

Kaveh, A., & Talatahari, S. (2009b). A particle swarm ant colony optimization algorithm for truss structures with discrete variables. *Journal of Constructional Steel Research*, *65*(8/9), 1558–1568. doi:10.1016/j.jcsr.2009.04.021

Kaveh, A., & Talatahari, S. (2010a). A novel heuristic optimization method: Charged system search. *Acta Mechanica*, *213*(3/4), 267–289. doi:10.1007/s00707-009-0270-4

Kaveh, A., & Talatahari, S. (2010b). A charged system search with a fly to boundary method for discrete optimum design of truss structures. *Asian Journal of Civil Engineering*, *11*(3), 277–293.

Kaveh, A., & Talatahari, S. (2010c). Charged system search for optimum grillage system design using the LRFD-AISC code. *Journal of Constructional Steel Research*, *66*(6), 767–771. doi:10.1016/j.jcsr.2010.01.007

Rashedi, E. (2007). *Gravitational search algorithm*. (M.Sc. Thesis). Shahid Bahonar University of Kerman. Kerman, Iran.

Rashedi, E., Nezamabadi-Pour, H., & Saryazdi, S. (2009). GSA: A gravitational search algorithm. *Information Sciences, 179*(13), 2232–2248. doi:10.1016/j.ins.2009.03.004

Rashedi, E., Nezamabadi-Pour, H., & Saryazdi, S. (2011). Filter modelin using gravitational search algorithm. *Engineering Applications of Artificial Intelligence, 24*(1), 117–122. doi:10.1016/j.engappai.2010.05.007

Shah-Hosseini, H. (2007). Problem solving by intelligent water drops. In *Proceedings of the 2007 IEEE Congress on Evolutionary Computation,* (pp. 3226-3231). Singapore, Singapore: IEEE.

Shah-Hosseini, H. (2008). Intelligent water drops algorithm: A new optimization method for solving the multiple knapsack problem. *International Journal of Intelligent Computing and Cybernetics, 1*(2), 193–212. doi:10.1108/17563780810874717

Shah-Hosseini, H. (2009). The intelligent water drops algorithm: A nature-inspired swarm-based optimization algorithm. *International Journal of Bio-Inspired Computation, 1*(1/2), 71–79. doi:10.1504/IJBIC.2009.022775

ADDITIONAL READING

Alpaydin, E. (2009). *Introduction to machine learning.* Cambridge, MA: The MIT Press.

Ansari, A., Essegaier, S., & Kohli, R. (2000). Internet recommendation systems. *JMR, Journal of Marketing Research, 37*(3), 363–375. doi:10.1509/jmkr.37.3.363.18779

Blum, C., & Merkle, D. (2010). *Swarm intelligence: Introduction and applications.* Berlin, Germany: Springer-Verlag.

Bonabeau, E., Theraulaz, G., & Dorigo, M. (1999). *Swarm intelligence: From natural to artificial systems.* Oxford, UK: Oxford University Press.

Brighton, H., & Selina, H. (2007). *Introducing artificial intelligence.* Cambridge, UK: Icon Books Ltd.

Brownlee, J. (2011). *Clever algorithms: Nature-inspired programming recipes.* Raleigh, NC: Lulu.

Butalia, A. (2010). *Recommendation system for matchmaking: Strategies for match making using similarity matrix and correlation factor.* Berlin, Germany: VDM Verlag Dr. Müller.

Cawsey, A. (1997). *The essence of artificial intelligence.* Upper Saddle River, NJ: Prentice Hall.

Chiong, R. (2009). *Nature-inspired algorithms for optimization.* Berlin, Germany: Springer-Verlag. doi:10.1007/978-3-642-00267-0

Chiong, R. (2009). *Nature-inspired informatics for intelligent applications and knowledge discovery: Implications in business, science and engineering.* Hershey, PA: IGI Global. doi:10.4018/978-1-60566-705-8

Cruz, C., Gonzalez, J., Krasnogor, N., Pelta, D. A., & Terrazas, G. (2010). *Nature inspired cooperative strategies for optimization.* Berlin, Germany: Springer-Verlag.

Dorigo, M., Birattari, M., & Stutzle, T. (2006). Ant colony optimization. *IEEE Computational Intelligence Magazine, 1*(4), 28–39.

Drineas, P., Kerenidis, I., & Raghavan, P. (2002). Competitive recommendation systems. In J. Reif (Ed.), *The 2002 ACM Symposium on Theory of Computing,* (pp. 82-90). New York, NY: ACM Press.

Eberhart, R. C., Shi, Y., & Kennedy, J. (2001). *Swarm intelligence.* San Francisco, CA: Morgan Kaufmann Publishers.

Ekbia, H. R. (2008). *Artificial dreams: The quest for non-biological intelligence.* Cambridge, UK: Cambridge University Press. doi:10.1017/CBO9780511802126

Engelbrecht, A. P. (2006). *Fundamentals of computational swarm intelligence*. Hoboken, NJ: John Wiley & Sons Inc.

Fesenmaier, D. R., Wöber, K. W., & Werthner, H. (2006). *Destination recommendation systems: Behavioral foundations and applications*. CABI. doi:10.1079/9780851990231.0000

Floreano, D., & Mattiussi, C. (2008). *Bio-inspired artificial intelligence: Theories, methods and technologies*. Cambridge, MA: The MIT Press.

Garnier, S., Gautrais, J., & Thereulaz, G. (2007). The biological principles of swarm intelligence. *Swarm Intelligence*, *1*(1), 3–31. doi:10.1007/s11721-007-0004-y

Gonzalez, T. F. (2007). *Handbook of approximation algorithms and metaheuristics*. Boca Raton, FL: Chapman & Hall/CRC. doi:10.1201/9781420010749

He, H. (2011). *Self-adaptive systems for machine intelligence*. Hoboken, NJ: John Wiley & Sons Inc. doi:10.1002/9781118025604

Jannach, D., Zanker, M., Flfernig, A., & Friedrich, G. (2010). *Recommender systems: An introduction*. New York, NY: Springer.

Jones, M. T. (2005). *AI application programming. Newton Center*. MA: Charles River Media.

Jones, M. T. (2008). *Artificial intelligence: A systems approach*. Hingham, MA: Infinity Science Press.

Karaboga, D., & Akay, B. (2009). A comparative study of artificial bee colony algorithm. *Applied Mathematics and Computation*, *214*(1), 108–132. doi:10.1016/j.amc.2009.03.090

Konar, A. (2005). *Computational intelligence: Principles, techniques and applications*. Berlin, Germany: Springer-Verlag.

Liu, J., & Tsui, K. C. (2006). Toward nature-inspired computing. *Communications of the ACM*, *49*(10), 59–64. doi:10.1145/1164394.1164395

Luger, G. F. (2008). *Artificial intelligence: Structures and strategies for complex problem solving*. Boston, MA: Addison Wesley.

Marmanis, H., & Babenko, D. (2009). *Algorithms of the intelligent web*. Greenwich, CT: Manning Publications.

Marrow, P. (2000). Nature-inspired computing technology and applications. *BT Technology Journal*, *18*(4), 13–23. doi:10.1023/A:1026746406754

McDonald, D. W., & Ackerman, M. S. (2000). Expertise recommender: A flexible recommendation system and architecture. In W. Kellogg & S. Whittaker (Eds.), *The 2000 ACM Conference on Computer Supported Cooperative Work*, (pp. 231-240). New York, NY: ACM Press.

Mourlas, C., & Germanakos, P. (2008). *Intelligent user interfaces: Adaptation and personalization systems and technologies*. Hershey, PA: IGI Global. doi:10.4018/978-1-60566-032-5

Negnevitsky, M. (2004). *Artificial intelligence: A guide to intelligent systems*. Boston, MA: Addison Wesley.

Nilsson, N. J. (2009). *The quest for artificial intelligence*. Cambridge, UK: Cambridge University Press.

Perner, P. (2002). *Advances in data mining: Applications in e-commerce, medicine, and knowledge management*. Berlin, Germany: Springer-Verlag.

Poli, R., Kennedy, J., & Blackwell, T. (2007). Particle swarm optimization – An overview. *Swarm Intelligence*, *1*(1), 33–57. doi:10.1007/s11721-007-0002-0

Poole, D. L. (2010). *Artificial intelligence: Foundations of computational agents.* Cambridge, UK: Cambridge University Press. doi:10.1017/CBO9780511794797

Resnick, P., & Varian, H. R. (1997). Recommender systems. *Communications of the ACM, 40*(3), 56–58. doi:10.1145/245108.245121

Ricci, F., Rokach, L., Shapira, B., & Kantor, P. B. (2010). *Recommender systems handbook.* Cambridge, UK: Cambridge University Press.

Roberts, P. (2009). *Mind making: The shared laws of natural and artificial intelligence.* New York, NY: CreateSpace.

Russell, S. (2009). *Artificial intelligence: A modern approach.* Upper Saddle River, NJ: Prentice Hall.

Stützle, T., Grün, A., Linke, S., & Rüttger, M. (2000). A comparison of nature inspired heuristics on the travelling salesman problem. In M. Schoenauer, K. Deb, G. Rudolph, X. Yao, E. Lutton, J. J. Merelo, & H. Schwefel (Eds.), *The 6th International Conference on Parallel Problem Solving from Nature,* (pp. 661-670). London, UK: Springer-Verlag.

Stützle, T., Grün, A., Linke, S., & Rüttger, M. (2000). Toward nature-inspired computing. *Communications of the ACM, 49*(10), 59–64.

Winston, P. H. (1992). *Artificial intelligence.* Boston, MA: Addison Wesley.

Yang, X.-S. (2008). *Nature-inspired metaheuristic algorithms.* Frome, UK: Luniver Press.

Zomaya, A. Y. (2010). *Handbook of nature-inspired and innovative computing: Integrating classical models with emerging technologies.* New York, NY: Springer.

KEY TERMS AND DEFINITIONS

Artificial Intelligence: (1) A term that is used to describe the feature, function or characteristic of computer systems or machines that try to simulate human-thinking behavior or human intelligence. (2) A field of Computer Science, which is based on research studies or developments on providing intelligent systems simulating the human-thinking behavior or human intelligence.

Intelligent System: A term that is used to define a system, which was designed and developed based on Artificial Intelligence approach(es), method(s) or technique(s).

Nature-Inspired Algorithm: A type of algorithm, which employs some mathematical equations and computing approaches obtained from some nature laws or derived from actions or reactions that happen in a natural system.

Nature-Inspired: A term that is used to define something, which includes some features or functions inspired from the nature or a specific natural system.

Recommendation System: A type of intelligent system, which recommends some information items that are likely to be interest of the related user.

Chapter 12
Modelling Clearance Sales Outshopping Behaviour Using Neural Network Model

M. Hemalatha
M.A.M. College of Engineering, India

ABSTRACT

The neural network is a very useful tool for approximation of a function, time series prediction, classification, and pattern recognition. If there is found to be a non-linear relationship between input data and output data, it is difficult to analyse the system. A neural network is very effective to solve this problem. This chapter studies the applied neural network model in relation to clearance sales outshopping behaviour. Since neural network theory can be applied effectively to this case, the authors have used neural network theory to recognise the retail area satisfaction and loyalty. To measure the impact among the retail area attributes, retail area satisfaction, and retail area loyalty, the authors have used the neural network model. In this chapter, they have treated twenty seven factors as the input signals into the input layer. Therefore, they find the weights between nodes in the relationship between the value of all twenty seven factors and the retail area satisfaction and loyalty. The development of the model by retail area attributes, and their interpretation, was facilitated by a collection of data across three trading areas. This neural network modeling approach to understand clearance sales outshopping behaviour provides retail managers with information to support retail strategy development.

INTRODUCTION

Clearing sale is a dominant part of modern retailing worldwide. As a marketing tool, it has always had an important and legitimate role in creating consumer excitement and in clearing surplus or obsolete stock (Merrilees & Fam, 1999). Retail

items that are "cleared" at the end of its season are referred to as seasonal merchandise. When merchandise is cleared, it is often sold below cost, at a price that will be called the residual value (Smith, et al., 1998). Retail promotions or special sales events are designed to increase store traffic and sales and, ultimately, store profits (Walters, 1988). Retail stores start the season without knowing which designs they have, if any, will be fashion-

DOI: 10.4018/978-1-4666-2542-6.ch012

able. Stores initially charge a fashion premium in hopes of capturing their fashion market, but as the end of the season approaches with designs still on the shelves, they adjust their expectations downward. At some point in the season, it becomes more profitable to have sales to capture the discount market. Retailers have higher prices early in the season, followed by deeper markdowns in the clearance period (Courty & Li, 1999). Further, inventory sensitivity makes it more desirable to have leftover merchandise at the end of the clearance period (Smith & Achabal, 1998).

Shopping today is much more than just buying—it is an experience in itself. To best utilize the available time, the Indian consumer is on the lookout for avenues that would give him the maximum value for his money and time spent (Parikh, 2006). Clearance sale stimulates the response from consumers in a cyclical seasonality, viz. summer and post-Christmas winter – spring clearances offered by the self-service retail stores. Theoretically, it is suggested that consumers will react favourably to a clearance sale. Clearance sales act as stimulus to consumers who are likely to elicit a positive response. Further, it is predicted that the magnitude of this positive response will be proportional to the value of an option to select the discount sales alternative. Individual consumer behaviour to a discount sales option is a function of preference for the option, whether it is a considered option or any choice constraint is personally directed. The consumer response is also affected by search associated with making a decision on a clearance sale. Consumer response to clearance sales is positively related to the importance of price advantage while is inversely related to the change in decision difficulty or intimidation of search costs (Rajagopal, 2007). Outshopping is quite common during clearance sales and this study covers the modelling of clearance sales outshoppers.

Customer outshopping is defined as customer buying goods away from home that could be purchased locally (Anderson & Kaminsky, 1985). Outshopping was found to be less frequent among lower-income families, and families with younger children or a large number of children. The desire for access to larger and more varied selections of men's and women's clothing was the principal factor motivating out-of-town shopping. Dissatisfaction with local selections was most common among the higher-income families, while concern over local prices was most common among the lower-income families (Herrmann & Beik, 1968). Outshopping behaviour is of concern to regional retailers as they recognize competitive forces coming not only from within their own regional trading community, but also from larger, distant regional or urban trading communities (Jarratt, 1998). Outshopping is generally accepted as a benefit for urban retailers and it results in a net financial profit to the urban retailers.

As a result, outshopping behaviour has recently emerged as a significant focus of retailing research. Lennon et al. (2009) investigate rural consumers' online shopping for food and fiber products as a function of satisfaction with local retailing and outshopping. Lee et al. (2009) investigated the relationship between consumer outshopping-related characteristics and preference for Internet shopping. Ricks and Pettypool (2008) investigated the perception of the small retailers regarding the impact of the superstores in the area and student opinions of shopping in the area. Hui and Wan (2008) compared the travel frequencies of 203 Singapore residents who travelled to Malaysia for shopping purposes. Findlay and Sparks (2008) analysed three comparable consumer surveys of shopping behaviour in the Scottish Borders. Lennon et al. (2007) predicted and found that clothing outshopping behaviour could be significantly predicted by the degree of satisfaction with local retailing and number of children remaining in the home. Paddison and Calderwood (2007) reviewed the dynamic forms of rural retailing, by location, that have innovated through a mixture of actions leading to growth, adaptation, diversification and differentiation.

Based on the existing literature, Guo et al. (2006) confirmed previous findings that product quality, service quality, fashion consciousness, and shopping enjoyment are four motives positively related to outshopping frequency. McEachern and Warnaby (2006) compared and contrasted the food shopping behaviour of customers in rural and urban areas in Scotland. Bygvra and Westlund (2004) described the level and character of cross-border shopping by the residents of the oresund region before and after the opening of the fixed link. Perceived economic benefits appear a solid motivator for outshopping (Piron, 2001). Jarratt (2000) developed models explaining outshopping behaviour by shopper motivation segment. City household respondents appear to be more satisfied with retailing overall and suburban households are more satisfied with their standard of living (Smith, 1999). Jarratt (1998) developed an explanatory model of regional outshopping behavior. Taylor (1997) examined a problem that many hospitals in rural parts of the U.S. are dealing with. Moreover, all shopping variables were significantly affected by some dimensions of religiousness (Siguaw & Simpson, 1997).

In their article, Sullivan and Savitt (1997) presented results from a study on outshopping grocery patterns relates to rural shoppers. Gooding (1994) pursued an enhanced understanding of health care outshopping. Jarratt and Polonsky (1993) explored the determinants of rural to rural outshopping in Australia. McDaniel et al. (1992) measured the extent of outshopping for hospital care in a rural environment. Yavas and Abdul-Gader (1991) reported intermarket patronage in an international context. Many believe that outshoppers are attracted mostly towards out-of-town retailers who carry products of better quality, lower prices, or that cannot be purchased at home (Anderson & Kaminsky, 1985). The consumer outshopping behaviour is not only product specific, but also influenced by the product form and the price level of the product (Ho-Fuk & Oliver, 1985).

In the intraurban area, Nevin and Houston (1980) examined the importance retail image in attracting consumers to competitive intraurban shopping areas. Papadopoulos (1980) in his article

goes beyond this to discuss outshopping behavior as it relates to the size and degree of geographic isolation. Outshoppers may tend to use more sources of information in evaluating their purchase alternatives (Darden, et al., 1978). Heavy outshoppers are more dissatisfied with the local shopping facilities than the other groups (Samli & Uhr, 1974). Reynolds and Darden (1972) analysed the psychographic profile of women who frequently outshop. Thompson (1971) reported the findings of a ten-part study of consumer outshopping. Based on a survey of the residents of a small Pennsylvania city, Herrmann and Beik (1968) investigated the factors affecting shopping outside a local retail area.

Past research in the area of outshopping behaviour has dealt mainly with shopping satisfaction (Lennon, et al., 2009; Smith, 1999), frequency (Guo, et al., 2006; Hui & Wan, 2008; Piron, 2001), motives (Guo, et al., 2006; Jarratt, 2000), shopping characteristics of the outshoppers (Bygvra & Westlund, 2004; McEachern & Warnaby, 2006), demographic variables (Piron, 2001), psychographic variable (Reynolds & Darden, 1972), choice behavior (Gooding, 1994), rural to rural outshopping (Jarratt & Polonsky, 1993), intermarket patronage (Yavas & Abdul-Gader, 1991), store image components (Nevin & Houston, 1980), product form and the price level of the product (Ho-Fuk & Oliver, 1985), and size and degree of geographic isolation (Papadopoulos, 1980). However, no studies have explored the modelling of clearance sales outshopping behaviour. This could also imply that modelling of outshopping behaviour with respect to clearance sales on the basis of retail area attributes have been left out in the previous outshopping behaviour literature. This research attempts to fill this gap in the literature. Therefore, this study has incorporated all retail area attributes into the research and developed a model of clearance sales outshopping behaviour using neural network technique.

The architecture of the neural network is the multi-layer neural network. There are five hidden layers between the input layer and the output layer.

We have used neural network model to measure the impact among the retail area attributes, retail area satisfaction, and retail area loyalty. This chapter describes the impact of twenty-seven input layers on five hidden layers. Then the impact of hidden layers on retail area loyalty and retail area satisfaction of the clearance sales outshoppers is obtained. The model fitness indices revealed that the proposed full neural network model to measure the clearance sales outshopping behaviour is significant. The development of model by retail area attributes, and their interpretation, was facilitated by collection of data across three trading areas. This neural network modeling approach to understand clearance sales outshopping behaviour provides retail managers with information to support retail strategy development.

THE CONCEPT OF OUTSHOPPING BEHAVIOUR

Outshopping is defined as the purchase of goods by consumers outside their local shopping area (Jarratt, 2000). Shopping area preferences are reflected in the phenomena known as outshopping which occurs when consumers shop outside their local trade area. Retail apparel stores offer product lines that generally attract a high degree of consumer outshopping. Approximately twenty-five percent of the upscale target audience preferred to shop at locations outside their local trade area for clothing purchases. Outshoppers thus represent a significant market segment for retailers to better understand. Within the general population, outshoppers are younger, better educated with higher incomes. Outshoppers perceived the specialty store as having better clothing styles but it was less convenient and required more driving time than corresponding evaluations by non-outshoppers. The association among store image attributes and store visits indicates that outshoppers are influenced by merchandise features such as clothing selection and styles. Store location elements seem

to have no significant influence on store visits by outshoppers (Stephen, 1991).

Consumers' quality perceptions play a vital role in explaining outshopping behavior (Gooding, 1994). Highly visible products with high unit costs exhibiting fashion characteristics were purchased out-of-town more frequently, the presence of children in the household also influences when consumers do their holiday shopping (Smith, 1999). The consumer outshopping behaviour is not only product specific, but also influenced by the product form and the price level of the product (Ho-Fuk & Oliver, 1985). A random telephone survey of 338 participating residents of five small towns centering around Ruston, Louisiana, indicated that each dimension of religiousness had a significant effect on one or more Sunday shopping and outshopping variables. Moreover, all shopping variables were significantly affected by some dimensions of religiousness (Siguaw & Simpson, 1997).

An out-shopper is defined as a consumer who has made at least one out-of-town purchase in the previous six months. The characteristics of outshoppers examined are consumer demographic characteristics, attitudes toward their own local shopping conditions, the same type of products are purchased out of town regardless of the shopping conditions in the hometown retailers and consumers for out-shopping (Thompson, 1971). Socio economic, attitudinal and informational source variable were found to differ significantly for the four points on the outshopping spectrum: heavy outshoppers, outshoppers, inshoppers and loyal inshoppers. The attitudinal index clearly displays the outshopping spectrum. Heavy outshoppers are more dissatisfied with the local shopping facilities than the other three groups. In addition, the degree of dissatisfaction decreases when moving towards the loyal inshopper end of the spectrum (Samli & Uhr, 1974).

Outshoppers generally had higher incomes than inshoppers. Outshoppers were dispersed throughout most of the occupational areas. Over one-third of the outshoppers were willing to make a one to two hour trip to a larger city for shopping and entertainment. Twenty-three percent were willing to drive for over two hours. The profile of these individuals suggests that their financial status and schedules may permit extended shopping trips or that aspects of the local retailing mix may not appeal to them. It would appear that the primary focus of an outshopping trip is clothing, that the outshopper may complete clothing purchases with shoes and other accessories, and use the opportunity to eat and drink away from home. Many believe that outshoppers are attracted mostly towards out-of-town retailers who carry products of better quality, lower prices, or that cannot be purchased at home (Anderson & Kaminsky, 1985).

There are different kinds of outshoppers, that is, some consumers shop for certain types of products outside of their local trading area while others outbuy quite different kinds of products. The outshopping behavior is in large measure determined by unique socioeconomic, lifestyle, and economic factors as well as by the quality of local retail facilities. If the genesis of much outshopping behavior is socio-psychological in nature, then interurban shoppers may have media exposure patterns, which are unlike those of buyers in the local trade area. Outshopping thus, may mean being cosmopolitan and having an extra local world view. Outshoppers in general have more exposure to magazines and television programs than do consumers who shop in local retail stores. They consult all sources of information to a greater extent than do local shoppers to help in evaluating specific shopping choices. Another reason outshoppers may tend to use more sources of information in evaluating their purchase alternatives is their innovative nature (Darden, et al., 1978).

Outshopping has actually been occurring for quite some time. Rural retailers need to implement innovative marketing approaches in order to retain these customers (Taylor, 1997). Urban consumers are more likely to be satisfied with their retail provision locally (McEachern & Warnaby, 2006). Jarratt and Polonsky (1993) explored determinants of rural to rural outshopping in the Central Western region of NSW, Australia. The results of the study indicated significant psychographic and demographic variables associated with outshoppers to another rural trading area. These outshoppers tend to be more socially active, innovative, have one to two children living at home and are younger than those people who tend to shop in their local trading area. Polonsky and Jarratt (1992) focused on rural to rural outshopping examined the net retail trade flow of two towns within a specific area, and combines this with data previously gathered on the level of outshopping from one town to the other, and, as well, examined the net retail trade flow of the specific area encompassing both towns.

International outshopping frequency is influenced by demographic variables such as age, marital status, highest educational level attained occupation, and ethnicity. Perceived economic benefits appear a solid motivator for outshopping. Outshopping may be strongly motivated by qualitative characteristics pertaining to the joy and fun of the shopping experience. Overwhelmingly, Singaporeans outshop internationally for economic reasons, in spite of superior retail conditions at home (Piron, 2001). Yavas and Abdul-Gader (1991) reported intermarket patronage in an international context. The results of the study concluded that the dissatisfaction with the local trading area leads to outshopping behaviour. Product purchase behaviours also differ among the light, moderate, and heavy outshoppers. The international outshopping purchases are generally dominated by taxed products being purchased with the lowest prices (Bygvra & Westlund, 2004).

Outshopping results in an outflow of retail revenues and profits from local merchants to non-local trade centers. Merchants located in small towns and sparsely settled communities may face a more severe problem as a result of a net financial outflow caused by the outshoppers. To understand the behavior of the consumer in purchasing practices, the events that precede and follow the purchase act must be examined. Intermarket patronage is important in at least two respects. One, it provides information which helps to delineate the size of trade areas. Two, it provides information helpful in adjusting marketing activities designed to increase the inflow of shopping trade from other areas (Reynolds & Darden, 1972). Outshopping behaviour has been explored by many academic researchers and business practitioners seeking to understand shopping behaviour and to develop marketing strategies for particular customer groups. No research project has systematically and exclusively explored the modelling with regard to clearance sales outshopping behaviour. Hence, this research contributes to better understanding of clearance sales outshopping behaviour using neural network model.

NEURAL NETWORK MODELLING TO OUTSHOPPING BEHAVIOUR

Research Model

We have selected Aadi clearance sales event celebrated in Tamilnadu, India to study the clearance sales outshopping behaviour. The Aadi clearance sales is mainly celebrated by clothing and apparel, electronics and gold items selling retailers. Since clothing and apparel is a product purchased by all segments, we wish to develop clearance sales outshopping behaviour model based on clothing and apparel shopping activity. A preliminary qualitative study has been performed based on focus group interview with customers who are frequently visiting the outside their local trading area during the clearance sales. Each focus group consisted of 10 shoppers were focused on their clearance sales outshopping experience. Each focus group interview lasted for 60 minutes.

Finally, retail area attributes, retail area satisfaction and retail area loyalty of outshoppers of clearance sales were determined and listed in

the questionnaire. All items related to the clearance sales outshopping behaviour were measured using a 5-point Likert scale. We have tested the questionnaire using a pilot study with 52 clearance sales outshoppers and modified the questionnaire based on the consumer suggestions. Mall intercept method is widely used in studies related to the shopping behavior of the respondents. So we have used mall intercept method for data collection during the clearance sales event.

Likewise, we have used systematic sampling technique for data collection in three major cities of Tamilnadu, India. These cities are Chennai, Coimbatore, and Tiruchirappalli. We have collected data during the clearance sales event that is Aadi clearance sales which is celebrated in these cities of Tamilnadu, India. The reason for including three different shopping areas was to increase the external validity of the results. A total of 216 outshoppers were surveyed during clearance sales event. First, we have checked the missing values prior to data analysis. We have used somewhat larger sample size of 216 respondents. Normality was tested based on the skewness and kurtosis of the observed variables. Finally, we tested for the existence of outliers. Our analyses revealed that there was no observation that might be considered as outliers.

First reliability and validity of the constructs were evaluated. In particular, we are looking for consistency among the scales used to evaluate the retail area attributes, retail area loyalty and retail area satisfaction of the outshopping behaviour. In this study, Cronbach's alpha is used to assess the reliability of measurement scales with multi-point items relating to the components of outshopping behaviour. The coefficient alpha based on the standardised items is above 0.806 which indicates satisfactory internal consistency among the items of all dimensions.

The validity is measured using confirmatory factor analysis. The construct validity of the items is systematically evaluated by a team of academic and retail industry practitioners. The Goodness of Fit Index (GFI) is found to be 0.930 which confirms a good fit of 93 per cent for the model. The Adjusted Goodness of Fit Index (AGFI) is 0.91 which takes the degrees of freedom into consideration. This indicates that the 27 indicators is a good fit in measuring the retail area attributes and their dimensions. Both goodness of fit and adjusted goodness of fit are close to the recommended level of one. The RMR of 0.042 and RMSEA of 0.05 suggest that the error involved in calculating the parameter was close to the recommended level of zero. In addition the result of chi square test is good. All the above said model fitness indices and the test of model fitness revealed that 27 indicators mentioned in the study are good fit in measuring the outshopping behaviour. We have used a neural network model for the analysis. Outshopping is quite common during clearance sales and this study covers the outshopping behaviour of the clearance sales shoppers. We propose following hypotheses to study the outshopping behaviour of clearance sales shoppers.

H1: There is no impact of input layers on hidden layers of the clearance sales outshoppers.

H2: There is no impact of hidden layers on retail area satisfaction of the clearance sales outshoppers.

H3: There is no impact of hidden layers on retail area loyalty of the clearance sales outshoppers.

Neural Network Model

The neural network is a program or system, which is modelled mathematically for information processing based on a connection approach to computation, particularly the process of learning. Learning is to change the weight by an amount proportional to the difference between the desired output and the actual output. The original inspiration for the technique was from examination of bioelectrical networks in the brain formed by neurons and their synapses. The neural network is a very useful tool for approximation of a function, time series prediction, classification, and pattern recognition. If there is found to be a non-linear relationship between input data and output data, it is difficult to analyse the system. A neural network is very effective to solve this problem. The aim of neural network model is to train the network to achieve the balance between the ability to respond correctly to the input patterns that are used for training and the ability to give reasonable responses to input that is similar, but not identical, to that used in training (Huang, et al., 2004).

A central phase in Artificial Neural Network (ANN) analysis is 'learning.' During this phase, the network learns by adjusting the relationships between its nodes. 'Learning' occurs through thousands of iterations, in which the network's ability to predict the output correctly on the basis of the input data constantly improves through continuous adjustments of the relationships until convergence occurs. In this chapter, we use this three-layer architecture. In satisfaction and loyalty modelling, outputs can be seen as effects, measured as satisfaction or loyalty (dependent variables), and inputs are the drivers (explanatory variables). The hidden layer handles non-linearities in the dataset. Such Artificial Neural Network architecture, specially developed for analysing customer data and it is a new analysis and management decision tool (Gronholdt & Martensen, 2005).

One of the most common neural network architectures is so-called three-layer perceptrons architecture, as illustrated in Figure 1. The first layer is called the input layer and is the only layer exposed to external signals. The input layer transmits signals to the nodes in the next layer, which is called a hidden layer. The hidden layer extracts relevant features or patterns from the received signals. Those features or patterns that are considered important are then directed to the output layer, the final layer of the network (Gronholdt & Martensen, 2005).

Since neural network theory can be applied effectively to this case, we have used neural network theory to recognise the retail area satisfaction and loyalty. Moreover, the Guass Newton algorithm is selected to learn the pattern of the

Figure 1. A neural network model for clearance sales outshopping behaviour

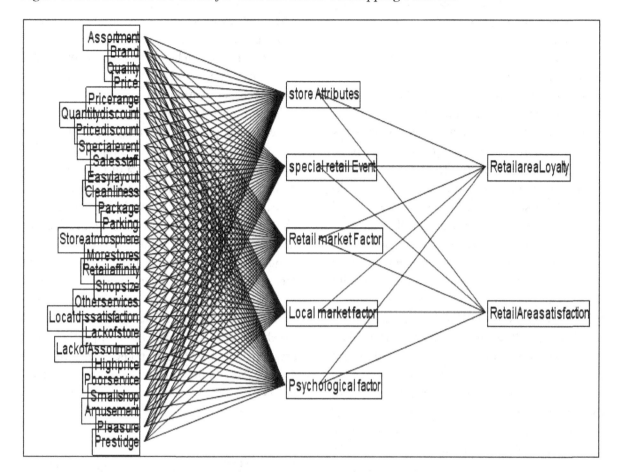

surveyed information. The architecture of this neural network is the multi-layer neural network. There are five hidden layers between the input layer and the output layer as described in Figure 1. Through the learning process, the weights between nodes in the neural network are modified in such a way to improve the desired representation between input and output data.

To measure the impact among the retail area attributes, retail area satisfaction and retail area loyalty, we have used neural network model. To analyse the data collected, we have used SAS JMP version 8.0 software. Figure 1 illustrates the neural network model of the clearance sales outshopping behaviour. The R square of the full neural network model found to be 0.968 which confirms a good fit of 96 per cent for the model.

The R square confirms that this model is a good fit in measuring retail area attributes, retail area satisfaction, retail area loyalty and their dimensions. R square is close to the recommended level of one. Similarly, the R square of the retail area loyalty is found to be 0.97 and the retail area satisfaction is found to be 0.95. The Root Mean Square Error (RMSE) of retail area loyalty is 0.12 and retail area satisfaction is 0.16 suggest that the error involved in calculating the parameter was close to the recommended level of zero. The Root Mean Square Error (RMSE) scaled of retail area loyalty is 0.15 and retail area satisfaction is 0.20 suggest that the error involved in calculating the parameter was close to the recommended level of zero. All the above said model fitness indices revealed that the proposed full neural network model to measure the clearance sales outshopping behaviour is significant (see Table 1).

In this study, we have treated twenty-seven factors as the input signals into the input layer. Therefore, we will find the weights between nodes in the relationship between the value of all twenty-seven factors and the retail area satisfaction and loyalty. The twenty seven input layers includes assortment, brand, quality, price, price range, quantity discount, price discount, special event, sales staff, easy layout, cleanliness, package, parking, store atmosphere, more stores, retail affinity, shop size, other services, local dissatisfaction, lack of store, lack of assortment, high price, poor service, small shop, amusement, pleasure and prestige. All input signals are multiplied with the weight between the input node and a node in the following layer. Then, these are summed for a node in the following layer, and transformed by an activation function. This is continued until it reaches the nodes in the final layer. Then, each activated value in the final layer is compared with that in the output layer, and each weight is modified to synchronise the value of nodes in the input layer and the output layer. This process is continued until the change of the weights among nodes is ignorable. The calculated weights are used to represent the relationship between the input layer and the output layer (Lee, et al., 2006).

First, we have studied the impact of twenty-seven input layers on five hidden layers. The five hidden layers are store attributes special event, retail market factor, local market factor, and psychological factor. Finally, we have identified that input layers such as prestige, quality, cleanliness, price range, parking, more stores, poor service, and small shop have more impact on hidden layer store attributes. At the mean time, we have also found out that input layers such as price discount, special event, package, other services, lack of store, and lack of assortment have more impact on hidden layer special event. The input layers such as more stores, retail affinity, local dissatisfaction, poor service, and prestige have

more impact on hidden layer retail market factor. The input layers such as store atmosphere, sales staff, special event, more stores, retail affinity, and local dissatisfaction have more impact on hidden layer local market factor. Finally the input layers such as store atmosphere, more stores, retail affinity, high price, small shop and amusement have more impact on hidden layer psychological factor. Hence, hypothesis H1 is rejected, and it is proved that there is an impact of input layers on hidden layers of the clearance sales outshoppers.

Similarly, among the five hidden layers psychological factor, store attributes and special event have more impact on retail area loyalty. Hence, hypothesis H3 is rejected and it is proved that there is an impact of hidden layers on retail area loyalty of the clearance sales outshoppers. At the same time, hidden layers such as special event and psychological factor have more impact on retail area satisfaction. Hence, hypothesis H2 is rejected and it is proved that there is an impact of hidden layers on retail area satisfaction of the clearance sales outshoppers (see Table 2).

FUTURE RESEARCH DIRECTIONS

Clearance sale stimulates the response from consumers in a cyclical seasonality, viz. summer and post-Christmas winter – spring clearances offered by the self-service retail stores. Theoretically, it is suggested that consumers will react favourably to a clearance sale. Clearance sales act as stimulus to consumers who are likely to elicit a positive response. Further, it is predicted that the magnitude of this positive response will be proportional to the value of an option to select the discount sales alternative (Rajagopal, 2007). Outshopping is quite common during clearance sales and this study modelled the outshopping behaviour of the clearance sales shoppers using neural network technique of business intelligence. Retailers implement many strategies such as extensive collection of merchandise, low price, and excellent retail

Table 1. The impact of retail area attributes on hidden layers

Retail Area Attributes	Store Attributes	Special Event	Retail Market Factor	Local Market Factor	Psychological Factor
Intercept	-0.409663363	-0.568029496	0.6745012839	-1.614054861	2.6499751707
Assortment	-0.942805333	-1.884074191	-0.108201864	0.2663054853	0.7455628479
Brand	0.0381362355	1.0625491214	-0.063241021	-1.052669231	-0.998203548
Quality	1.9782072717	0.5111808728	0.2575780224	-1.131515719	-0.128122771
Price	1.0560203938	0.3733335573	0.1265746184	-2.80338108	-0.206293137
Price range	1.1204066542	0.9988636278	0.353156749	-0.527153382	-0.533220478
Quantity discount	-0.52493221	-0.285484909	-0.101713896	0.1066266101	-0.359002146
Price discount	-0.395721226	1.5003581331	0.2923529106	0.5926497156	0.3763790499
Special event	-0.273186325	1.3374985458	-0.202977451	1.4579707292	-0.790267513
Sales staff	0.2205753427	1.0298003542	-0.132046728	2.7586477181	-0.418197912
Easy layout	0.448643801	-0.237451856	-0.226760074	-7.028529712	-3.029604514
Cleanliness	1.6991027451	-2.012498712	-0.125856549	-0.389386512	-0.738723918
Package	0.3168886755	1.9088132906	0.0112104257	2.1773471432	-1.327014735
Parking	1.1389373583	1.1691963834	0.3539733305	-0.749711835	0.241712444
Store atmosphere	-5.640950497	-0.7274272	-1.07394213	3.5421139352	1.2836323077
More stores	1.961212371	-1.332957389	0.7568310568	1.9460871041	1.3031605863
Retail affinity	-0.14729692	-2.021102301	0.4568580451	2.5074624102	4.3975750616
Shop size	-0.275001511	3.1565925692	-0.265727891	-2.214103114	-2.82334764
Other services	-1.229958489	1.1651380506	-0.567178643	-0.832816486	-1.834357407
Local dissatisfaction	0.0145387626	0.5310801367	0.4111356298	1.723057057	0.6967275463
Lack of store	-0.578843896	1.8065287691	-0.433072856	-0.751408013	-2.952112856
Lack of Assortment	-2.955850315	1.8365910704	-0.955352513	0.2469558232	-2.645159563
High price	-0.064581876	-3.645619005	-0.364285574	-0.552315669	1.4181226875
Poor service	1.2389623091	-0.415195188	0.3969700766	-1.605665106	0.689485126
Small shop	1.1121791062	-1.360744117	0.2106934749	0.4310535398	2.1976330925
Amusement	0.2216466153	0.4879684968	0.0586876365	0.9202743192	1.184433901
Pleasure	0.1240213601	-0.750568617	-0.170416795	-0.906559211	-1.409405666
Prestige	2.6208250244	0.5994314427	0.6542663424	-3.581077895	0.3018643591

services to attract the shoppers during clearance sales. Therefore, the retailers should know the shopper's preference towards clearance sales retail area attributes, based on which they can modify their offerings and services. Therefore, it is essential to develop model, which assists the retailers in understanding and measuring the effect of the clearance sales outshopping behaviour.

Retail apparel stores offer product lines that generally attract a high degree of consumer out-

shopping. Overall, the outshoppers are evaluated on the basis of various retail area attributes such as merchandise, price, discount sales, retail services, market factor and local market factor. Outshoppers thus represent a significant market segment for retailers to better understand. The underlying factors of consumer outshopping patterns have drawn attention, both from scholars and practitioners. Outshopping is a significant retailing phenomenon, not only because of its managerial

Table 2. The impact of hidden layers on retail area loyalty and retail area satisfaction

Hidden Layers	Retail area Loyalty	Retail Area satisfaction
Intercept	-1.177652253	0.0769000034
Store Attributes	5.211430153	0.1142342408
Special Event	4.9022222661	4.109740417
Retail Market Factor	-11.40399264	-5.593596928
Local Market Factor	-0.932484349	-3.451478881
Psychological Factor	5.5662173234	4.0297176303

implications to retailers but also because of its influence on urban planning. The outshopping behaviour must be monitored to identify the favourable reasons about the outshopping situation. This provides a basis for the formulation of strategic plans to maximize the favourable aspect of the store attributes to satisfy and retain the shoppers.

However, this study has few limitations that can be considered opportunities for both theoretical and empirical work. The present study was an exploratory one, with Aadi clearance sales from India. The samples of this study are taken from the southern India and the applicability of the result is limited. Retail area satisfaction and loyalty determinants may vary among different customer segments. Treating the whole market as a homogenous segment would lead to market failure. Subsequent replication research is, therefore, needed to enhance the robustness of the relationships between the performances of retail area attributes and retail area satisfaction and loyalty. That is, the further verification of model with other clearance sales like great Singapore sale festival is required to enhance the generalization of the study. Further study on the effect of different types of non-retail area attributes such as complaints and waiting time on clearance sales retail area satisfaction and loyalty is required. Similarly, the study is conducted in the context of the clothing and apparel product. Future studies

should incorporate additional products or multiple product categories such as electronics and gold items to examine differences in consumer shopping segments between products.

CONCLUSION AND MANAGERIAL IMPLICATIONS

This chapter examines clearance sales outshopping behaviour decisions and attempts to expand the traditional analysis of outshoppers. Findlay and Sparks (2008) developed a neural network classification model to identify factors which are concerned by different types of consumers. A questionnaire survey was conducted to collect data among consumers of hospitals in southern Taiwan. Then, a neural network classification model was used to recognize consumers' demographic data into different types consuming orientation. Based on the results of the research, the evidence is enough to suggest that the neural network model is useful in identifying existing patterns of the data. Authors believe that the model is useful and suitable as an analyzing tool for marketing planners on the market strategy planning. Meanwhile, the powerful classification power will be helped to understand what goes on between input and output layers. In this study, we have studied the clearance sales outshopping behaviour in apparel and clothing industry, and developed the neural network model for the clearance sales outshopping behaviour.

Outshopping, that is, consumers' purchasing from outside their normal trading area has a long and colorful history, but has not been measured in the context of clearance sales events. Retail apparel stores offer product lines that generally attract a high degree of consumer outshopping. Outshoppers thus represent a significant market segment for retailers to better understand. Early research into outshopping behaviour concentrated on understanding the contribution of demographic and socio-economic variables to outshopping behaviour. Subsequent researchers combined these variables with psychographic profiles and attitudes to trading areas in an attempt to explain the outshopping phenomenon further. Others sought an understanding of the type of goods purchased, while some adopted an economics perspective and concentrated on measuring the total impact of outshopping on retail trading communities. Shopping orientation and general lifestyle factors have been examined in the role of influencing both shopping and outshopping behaviour. Few researchers have examined the concept of 'loyalty to the local trading area' as a variable influencing the level of outshopping activity. Models specific to retailing and outshopping behaviour are less evident in the literature (Jarratt, 2000).

Outshopping is a complex phenomenon, influenced by a flurry of personal, situational, and marketer-dependent factors. With a better understanding of outshoppers, marketers can develop specific marketing offerings to stimulate local and international patronage, thereby fostering a competitive retailing environment. However, as most of studies were conducted in North America, it is conceivable that the factors influencing consumer outshopping may vary between countries and regions. Outshopping is a complex phenomenon involving many variables (Piron, 2001). This research seeks to strengthen our understanding of some of these variables, and specifically offer fresh insight on the clearance sales outshopping behaviours. The findings from this study should be informative to strategic decision-makers in retail areas.

Many believe that outshoppers are attracted mostly towards out-of-town retailers who carry products of better quality, lower prices, or that cannot be purchased at home. This may not be true for all outshoppers. While the product and its attributes are important to potential buyers, the outshopping phenomenon seems to go beyond that. Not too surprisingly, the data indicated that outshoppers prefer to shop in larger metropolitan areas, even if they have to drive a considerable distance. A third of the outshoppers stated that

they just want to "get away" to do their shopping, even when identical products can be purchased at the same price closer to home. The strong attraction of out-of-town retailers may be due to a desire to possess things that are perceived as "different" from what everyone else has, even though many of those identical products can be purchased locally. Perhaps there is more of a special feeling in purchasing goods away from home, making the shopping trip more of an occasion. There are indications that many small retailers are providing these psychological dimensions for outshopping customers who come to them from outside trading areas. Interestingly, outshoppers do not enjoy shopping as much as inshoppers do, implying a preference for a concentration of stores and larger merchandise assortments. A large retail mix enables the outshopper to combine purchases in one major shopping event rather than numerous short trips closer to home (Anderson & Kaminsky, 1985).

This chapter describes the impact of twenty-seven input layers on five hidden layers. The twenty seven input layers includes assortment, brand, quality, price, price range, quantity discount, price discount, special event, sales staff, easy layout, cleanliness, package, parking, store atmosphere, more stores, retail affinity, shop size, other services, local dissatisfaction, lack of store, lack of assortment, high price, poor service, small shop, amusement, pleasure and prestige. The five hidden layers are store attributes, special event, retail market factor, local market factor and psychological factor. Then the impact of hidden layers on retail area loyalty and retail area satisfaction of the clearance sales outshoppers is obtained using neural network analytical technique. A neural network modeling approach to understanding clearance sales outshopping behaviour provides retail managers with information to support retail strategy development. The development of model by retail area attributes, and their interpretation, was facilitated by collection of data across three trading areas. When anticipated linkages were supported in the clearance sales outshopping behaviour model through model indices, it can be concluded that among the five hidden layers psychological factor, store attributes and special event have more impact on retail area loyalty. At the same time, hidden layers such as special event and psychological factor have more impact on retail area satisfaction.

From a managerial perspective, outshoppers are significant to retailers who face competition. The neural network model emerging through this research was developed with the objective of providing retail management with a framework to assist managers to understand specific issues relating to the trading area and develop strategies to maximise outshopping activity. This model has linked, retail area attributes for the first time with retail area satisfaction and retail area loyalty of the clearance sales outshopping behavior. This study also facilitates the understanding of hidden layers such as store attributes, special event, retail market factor, local market factor and psychological factor behind the clearance sales outshopping behavior. This approach allows retail management to determine the factors, which have impact on retail area loyalty and retail area satisfaction of the clearance sales outshopping activity. Based on the result of our neural network model, Managers will need to address psychological factor, store attributes and special event to increase the retail area loyalty and special event and psychological factor to increase the retail area satisfaction. As a result, retailing strategies would be improved, while keeping outshoppers' various needs satisfied. In sum, we intend to offer retailers better insight into formulating retailing mix strategies to compete more effectively in the outshoppers segment. The outshopping behaviour model must be developed and monitored to identify the favourable reasons about the outshopping situation. This provides a basis for the formulation of strategic plans to maximize the favourable aspect of the retail mix to satisfy and retain the shoppers. Hence, this research contributes to better understanding of clearance sales outshopping behaviour.

REFERENCES

Anderson, C. H., & Kaminsky, M. (1985). The outshopper problem: A group approach for small business retailers. *American Journal of Small Business*, *9*(4), 34–45.

Bygvra, S., & Westlund, H. (2004). Shopping behaviour in the Oresund region before and after the establishment of the fixed link between Denmark and Sweden. *GeoJournal*, *61*, 41–52. doi:10.1007/s10708-004-0876-y

Courty, P., & Li, H. (1999). Timing of seasonal sales. *The Journal of Business*, *72*(4), 545–572. doi:10.1086/209627

Darden, W. R., Lennon, J. J., & Darden, D. K. (1978). Communicating with interurban shoppers. *Journal of Retailing*, *54*(1), 51–64.

Findlay, A., & Sparks, L. (2008). Weaving new retail and consumer landscapes in the Scottish borders. *Journal of Rural Studies*, *24*(1), 86–97. doi:10.1016/j.jrurstud.2007.05.007

Gooding, S. K. S. (1994). Hospital outshopping and perceptions of quality: Implications for public policy. *Journal of Public Policy & Marketing*, *13*(2), 271–280.

Gronholdt, L., & Martensen, A. (2005). Analysing customer satisfaction data: A comparison of regression and artificial neural networks. *International Journal of Market Research*, *47*(2), 121–130.

Guo, C., Vasquez-Parraga, A. Z., & Wang, Y. (2006). An exploratory study of motives for Mexican nationals to shop in the US: More than meets the eye. *Journal of Retailing and Consumer Services*, *13*(5), 351–362. doi:10.1016/j.jretconser.2005.11.002

Herrmann, R. O., & Beik, L. L. (1968). Shoppers' movements outside their local retail area. *Journal of Marketing*, *32*(4), 45–51. doi:10.2307/1249337

Ho-Fuk, L., & Oliver, H. M. Y. (1985). Consumer outshopping behaviour and its implications for channel strategy: A study of the camera patronage pattern in Hong Kong. *European Journal of Marketing, 19*(6), 12–23. doi:10.1108/EUM0000000004731

Huang, Z., Chen, H., Hsu, C. J., Chen, W. H., & Wu, S. (2004). Credit rating analysis with support vector machines and neural networks: A market comparative study. *Decision Support Systems, 37*(4), 543–558. doi:10.1016/S0167-9236(03)00086-1

Hui, T. K., & Wan, D. (2008). The cross-border shoppers' behaviour: The case of Singapore. *International Journal of Data Analysis Techniques and Strategies, 1*(1), 104–115. doi:10.1504/IJDATS.2008.020025

Jarratt, D. G. (1998). Modelling outshopping behaviour: A non-metropolitan perspective. *International Review of Retail, Distribution and Consumer Research, 8*(3), 319–350. doi:10.1080/095939698342805

Jarratt, D. G. (2000). Outshopping behaviour: An explanation of behaviour by shopper segment using structural equation modeling. *International Review of Retail, Distribution and Consumer Research, 10*(3), 287–304. doi:10.1080/095939600405983

Jarratt, D. G., & Polonsky, M. J. (1993). Causal linkages between psychographic and demographic determinants of outshopping behavior. *International Review of Retail, Distribution and Consumer Research, 3*(3), 303–319. doi:10.1080/09593969300000020

Lee, D., Paswan, A. K., Ganesh, G., & Xavier, M. J. (2009). Outshopping through the Internet: A multicountry investigation. *Journal of Global Marketing,* 53–66.

Lee, Y. H., Jung, J. W., Eum, S. C., Park, S. M., & Nam, H. K. (2006). Production quantity allocation for order fulfilment in the supply chain: A neural network based approach. *Production Planning and Control, 17*(4), 378–389. doi:10.1080/09537280600621909

Lennon, S. J., Baugh, D., Chatterton, J., & Larkin, J. (2007). Clothing outshopping in a rural western community. *Journal of Consumer Studies & Home Economics, 11*(4), 369–374. doi:10.1111/j.1470-6431.1987.tb00147.x

Lennon, S. J., Ha, Y., Johnson, K. K. P., & Jasper, C. R. (2009). Rural consumers' online shopping for food and fiber products as a form of outshopping. *Clothing & Textiles Research Journal, 27*(1), 3–30. doi:10.1177/0887302X07313625

McDaniel, C., Gates, R., & Lamb, C. W. (1992). Who leaves the service area? Profiling the hospital outshopper. *Journal of Health Care Marketing, 12*(3), 2–9.

McEachern, M. G., & Warnaby, G. (2006). Food shopping behaviour in Scotland: The influence of relative rurality. *International Journal of Consumer Studies, 30*(2), 189–201. doi:10.1111/j.1470-6431.2005.00475.x

Merrilees, B., & Fam, K. S. (1999). Effective methods of managing retail sales. *International Review of Retail, Distribution and Consumer Research, 9*(1), 81–92. doi:10.1080/095939699342697

Nevin, J. R., & Houston, M. J. (1980). Image as a component of attraction to intraurban shopping areas. *Journal of Retailing, 56*(1), 77–93.

Paddison, A., & Calderwood, E. (2007). Rural retailing: A sector in decline? *International Journal of Retail and Distribution Management, 35*(2), 136–155. doi:10.1108/09590550710728093

Papadopoulos, N. G. (1980). Consumer outshopping research: Review and extension. *Journal of Retailing, 56*(4), 41–58.

Parikh, D. (2006). Measuring retail service quality: An empirical assessment of the instrument. *Vikalpa: The Journal for Decision Makers, 31*(2), 45–55.

Piron, F. (2001). International retail leakages: Singaporeans outshopping in Malaysia. *Singapore Management Review, 23*(1), 35–58.

Polonsky, M. J., & Jarratt, D. G. (1992). Rural outshopping in Australia: The Bathurst-Orange region. *European Journal of Marketing, 26*(10), 5–16. doi:10.1108/EUM0000000000647

Rajagopal. (2007). Stimulating retail sales and upholding customer value. *Journal of Retail and Leisure Property, 6*(2), 117-135.

Reynolds, F. D., & Darden, W. R. (1972). Intermarket patronage: A psychographic study of consumer outshoppers. *Journal of Marketing, 36*(4), 50–54. doi:10.2307/1250427

Ricks, J., & Pettypool, D. (2008). Pilot study of the perceptions of small downtown retailers regarding the impact of mega stores: An optimum balance desired. *Proceedings of the Academy of Marketing Studies, 13*(1), 59–64.

Samli, A. C., & Uhr, E. B. (1974). The outshopping spectrum: Key for analyzing intermarket leakages. *Journal of Retailing, 50*(2), 70–105.

Siguaw, J. A., & Simpson, P. M. (1997). Effects of religiousness on Sunday shopping and outshopping behaviours: A study of shopper attitudes and behaviours in the American South. *International Review of Retail, Distribution and Consumer Research, 7*(1), 23–40. doi:10.1080/095939697343111

Smith, M. F. (1999). Urban versus suburban consumers: a contrast in holiday shopping purchase intentions and outshopping behavior. *Journal of Consumer Marketing, 16*(1), 58–73. doi:10.1108/07363769910250778

Smith, S. A., & Achabal, D. D. (1998). Clearance pricing and inventory policies for retail chains. *Management Science, 44*(3), 285–300. doi:10.1287/mnsc.44.3.285

Smith, S. A., Agrawal, N., & McIntyre, S. H. (1998). A discrete optimization model for seasonal merchandise planning. *Journal of Retailing, 74*(2), 193–221. doi:10.1016/S0022-4359(99)80093-1

Stephen. (1991). *Developing a retail strategy for an upscale target audience: The influence of outshopping and store.* Retrieved from http://www.sbaer.uca.edu/research/ssbia/1991/PDF/02.pdf

Sullivan, P., & Savitt, R. (1997). Store patronage and lifestyle factors: Implications for rural grocery retailers. *International Journal of Retail and Distribution Management, 25*(10/11), 351–364.

Taylor, S. L. (1997). Outshopping: The battle between rural and urban medical services. *Marketing Health Services, 17*(3), 42–44.

Thompson, J. R. (1971). Characteristics and behavior of out-shopping consumers. *Journal of Retailing, 47*(1), 70–80.

Walters, R. G. (1988). Retail promotions and retail store performances: A test of some key hypotheses. *Journal of Retailing, 64*(2), 153–180.

Yavas, U., & Abdul-Gader, A. (1991). Transborder outshopping: An Arabian Gulf study. *International Review of Retail, Distribution and Consumer Research, 1*(4), 455–468. doi:10.1080/09593969100000003

Chapter 13
Hybrid Neural Genetic Architecture:
New Directions for Intelligent Recommender System Design

Emmanuel Buabin
Methodist University College Ghana, Ghana

ABSTRACT

The objective is a neural-based feature selection in intelligent recommender systems. In particular, a hybrid neural genetic architecture is modeled based on human nature, interactions, and behaviour. The main contribution of this chapter is the development of a novel genetic algorithm based on human nature, interactions, and behaviour. The novel genetic algorithm termed "Buabin Algorithm" is fully integrated with a hybrid neural classifier to form a Hybrid Neural Genetic Architecture. The research presents GA in a more attractive manner and opens up the various departments of a GA for active research. Although no scientific experiment is conducted to compare network performance with standard approaches, engaged techniques reveal drastic reductions in genetic operator operations. For illustration purposes, the UCI Molecular Biology (Splice Junction) dataset is used. Overall, "Buabin Algorithm" seeks to integrate human related interactions into genetic algorithms as imitate human genetics in recommender systems design and understand underlying datasets explicitly.

INTRODUCTION

Data explosion across business platforms has necessitated the call for efficient storage mechanisms. Research scientists estimate that close to 80% of a business's data lies in amorphous data format. This means, management decisions are likely to be optimized should unstructured data formats be considered in decision-making processes. Since its inception, the Internet has grown to become one of the largest data repositories in the world. With every computer literate as potential author on the Web, new domains have been registered and corresponding Website information added or updated to increase readership/viewership. News producing giants such as

DOI: 10.4018/978-1-4666-2542-6.ch013

CNN, BBC etc have taken great advantage of the Internet to disseminate news to a wider reading/viewing public. By transmitting news stories on the Internet, "breaking news" for example, can be accessed across the globe by the within a matter of minutes. Governments, institutions (public or private) and individuals, have also joined in the production of unstructured data by publishing pages about business, jobs, goods, and services. Text is easily to deployed, have low runtime impact on servers, and load faster. They use less hardware resources (e.g. server disk space) and much more information likely to be published—as compared to video, images, etc. The growing nature of the Internet has prompted researchers to mine the data therein to ascertain hidden trends and heuristics.

Classification based learning agents have been built to extract, mine and perform exploratory tasks on large text data in non-stationary platforms. Among approaches used, neural based methods have proved to be better candidates than their counterparts. Buabin (2011a, 2012) are typical examples of such systems. Buabin (2012) argues that, classification and recommender systems have major commonalities across their design. They both

1. Operate in search related domains,
2. Use search related mechanisms for finding optimal solutions to problems,
3. Use learning algorithms to extract knowledge from the training set into their structures and most importantly train on the exemplars.

With the aim of improving classifier performance, researchers have extracted features prior to performing classification tasks. Although implemented in many data mining systems, feature selection has taken many forms, some of which are statistical approaches (Perkins, et al., 2003; Hermes & Buhmann, 2000; Dash & Liu, 1997; Forman, 2003; Krishnapuram, et al., 2004; Piramuthu, 2004; Yang, 1999; Liu & Yu, 2005; Song, et al., 2007; Weston, et al., 2003) and neural based

approaches (Gabrilovich & Markovitch, 2004; Rakotomamonjy, 2003; Froehlich, 2002; Liu & Zheng, 2005; Taira & Haruno, 1999; Hardin, et al., 2004; Zhang, et. al., 2006; Huang & Wang, 2006; Chen, 2007; Warmuth, et al., 2003; Suna, 2004).

Biological or bio-inspired approaches have been adopted and implemented in problem domains where the solution space is extremely large, unknown, and complex. With its core principles deeply rooted in genetics, Genetic Algorithms have proven to perform better than other techniques in complex search related problems. A GA essentially comprises of a set of individual solutions or chromosomes (called the population) and some biologically inspired operators that create a new and potentially better population from an old one. It seeks to find optimal solutions for complex search problems with little knowledge of the solution space. In differentiating GAs from other techniques, GAs work by encoding the parameter set and simultaneously searching with multiple points. Whereas other approaches use deterministic rules, GAs use stochastic operators in finding optimal solutions. Feature selection is a typical search related problem and GAs tend to be good candidates. Although much work has been done in the domain of feature selection (i.e. with GAs) and are relevant, they are limited in terms of human nature, interactions and behaviour. In this book chapter, existing works in the area of feature selection and genetic based methods are investigated. In simple English language, a step by step approach to critiquing existing GA based techniques is adopted. Among others, new directions aimed at

1. Relating human nature, interactions and behaviour to search based problems,
2. Enhancing genetic operations,
3. Introducing further genetic operator restrictions, and
4. Making GA research appealing for active research.

Underpinning concepts of general feature selection algorithms, statistical, neural and evolution-based algorithms will be also introduced. Although no explicit scientific experiment is conducted in this book chapter, newly introduced directions reveal

1.   Deeper similarity to human nature, interactions, and behaviour,
2.   Reduced number of genetic operator operations,
3.   Increased understanding of internal interactions in the underlying dataset.

The level of comprehension of this text is at undergraduate level education. Post-graduate students and researchers who wish to study and/or to research into the foundations, representations, concepts, theory and applications of genetic based intelligent recommender system design would also find the text beneficial. In terms of arrangement, the book chapter starts by introducing specialized systems called Recommender Systems. The underlying dataset, evolutionary algorithms, and feature selection are introduced and discussed respectively. Based on limitations in GA related works, new directions are discussed with the sole aim of opening up research work within GAs. A novel GA is modeled as a result, and justification for possible integration with a hybrid neural classifier to form a hybrid neural genetic architecture. In all Underpinning scientific theory is introduced to get readers appreciate, understand, be motivated and mostly importantly have firm foundations for high-level discussions in neuro-genetic feature selection recommender systems. The underlying dataset used in the book chapter is the UCI Molecular Biology Splice Junction Dataset.

RECOMMENDER SYSTEMS

Recommender systems (Huang, et al., 2004; Mobasher, et al., 2000; Miller, et al., 2004; Buczak, et al., 2002; Massa & Avesani, 2007; Adomavicius & Tuzhilin, 2005; Avery & Zeckerhauser, 1997; Zhang & Iyengar, 2002; Schmidt-Thieme, 2005; Setten, et al., 2003; Jahrer, et al., 2010; Fong, et al., 2009; Sobecki, 2006; Cristache, 2009; OLSSON, 2003; Ansari, et al., 2000; Iyengar & Zhang, 2001; Ziegler, et al., 2004; Herlocker & Konstan, 2001; Setten, 2003; Burke, 2002; Cho, et al., 2002; Kim & Kim, 2003; Lawrence, et al., 2001; Lin, et al., 2002; Middleton, et al., 2004; Sarwar, et al., 2000; Kogel, 2002; Ricci, et al., 2001), as high level intelligent decision support systems, perform the task of suggesting resources to users through some form of learning. The technique emerged as an autonomous research fraternity in the 1990s. In the field of eCommerce (Goy, et al., 2007; Tran & Cohen, 2000; Sarwar, et al., 2000), they play an important role. Due to its advantages, many media firms now deploy recommender systems to buttress services they provide to subscribers. Conferences, workshops and other events have been dedicated towards the advancement of research in this area. To be specific, ACM Recommender Systems instituted in the late 2000s is now a leading annual event in recommender research and applications. A lot of research work has gone on in this area with a sizeable number of works attempting to classify recommender systems - content, collaborative filtering, demographic, knowledge based, community based, and hybrid recommender system. Content-based recommender systems learn to recommend items that are similar to the ones that a different user liked in the past. For example, if a user has 5-star rated a math book published by XYZ publishers, the system can learn to recommend other math books from this publisher. Collaborative filtering (Sarwar, et al., 2001; Herlocker, et al., 2004; Jin, et al., 2003; Ricci, et al., 2012; Sarwar, et al., 2001; Koren, 2009; Paterek, 2007; Billsus, 1998; Billsus & Pazzani, 1998; Lin, 2000; Massa & Avesani, 2004; Li, et al., 2010) recommends items that other users with similar interests liked in the past to an active user. The similarity in interest is computed based on the similarity in the rating history of the users. Collaborative filtering is considered to be the most popular and widely implemented technique in RS. Demographic kinds of recommender systems recommend items based on demographic profiles of users. With this form of system, different recommendations are generated for different demographic sections. Many eCommerce Websites adopt simple and effective personalization solutions based on demographics. For example, German speakers are dispatched to particular Web sites based on the German language. In other domains, suggestions may be customized according to the age of the user. Knowledge-based recommender systems recommend items based on specific domain knowledge. They do so based on how certain item features meet user-needs and preferences and, ultimately, how the item is useful for the user. Knowledge-based recommender systems tend to work better than others at the beginning of their deployment but if they are not equipped with learning components they may be surpassed by other shallow methods that can exploit the logs of the human/computer interaction (as in CF). Community-based recommender systems recommend items based on the preferences of the user's friends. In real life, it is sometimes likely for friends to like a particular set of items. With the introduction of social networking platforms like facebook, tweeter etc, there has been growing interest in community based recommender system research to ascertain items of interest between users. Hybrid recommender systems are a combination of the above-mentioned techniques. The combination is as a result of compensating the weakness of a type with the strengths of another type. In other cases, the rationale for combination had stemmed from the fact that the hybrid form would combine the strengths is yield a more formidable recommender system.

Classification Unit: An Integral Unit of Recommender Systems

Classification and recommender systems have major commonalities across their design. Both

1. Operate in search related problems,
2. Use search related mechanisms for finding optimal solutions to problems,
3. Use learning algorithms to extract knowledge from the training domain into their structures.

In a typical text mining classification task, a set of training exemplars with corresponding targets are fed into the classification systems. The classifier acquires knowledge and the learned information is used to predict novel text patterns. The process of finding optimal weights during training for onward classification of novel patterns gives a clear indication of a search process. A text classifier meant to predict text based documents as relevant, equally relevant, or irrelevant must be trained into knowing what a relevant, equally relevant or an irrelevant document is. Knowledge acquired by the text classifier is used to determine whether a text document is worth considering for further processing or not. Recommender systems, as high level intelligent decision support systems, perform the task of suggesting resources to users through learning. Recommender systems require expert training to enable flexibility in the suggestion process. A dynamic recommender system meant to monitor stock performance across news text documents around the globe needs to

1. Identify which news text documents are relevant, equally relevant, and not relevant—i.e. from a dataset,
2. Mine selected documents and compute document information score,
3. Select the top five stocks based on computed information score.

The first step of determining text document status is a pure classification task. Although classification ideas could be used in the second step, sophisticated approaches could be adopted to compute the information score of stocks. Using limited amount of textual information provided in selected news text articles, the recommender system is expected to acquire in-depth knowledge though training so as to quantitatively determine which stocks performed better during the day. Since subsequent stages (i.e. stage 2 onwards), are heavily dependent on step 1, the argument about classification being an integral part of recommender systems is justified and meaningful.

MOLECULAR BIOLOGY (SPLICE JUNCTION) DATASET

Splice junctions are points on a DNA sequence at which 'superfluous' DNA is removed during the process of protein creation in higher organisms. The problem posed in the splice junction dataset is to recognize the boundaries between exons and introns, given a sequence of DNA. The problem consists of two subtasks. They are

1. Recognizing exon/intron boundaries (referred to as EI sites),
2. Recognizing intron/exon boundaries (IE sites).

In biological terms, IE borders are referred to as "acceptors" whereas EI borders are referred to as "donors." The dataset has since been used on many data mining problems—e.g. Knowledge Based Artificial Neural Networks (KBANN) (Towell, et al., 1991; Zheng & de Sa, 2003; Chen, et al., 2004).

Dataset Description and Distribution

The dataset has three thousand one hundred and ninety (3190) gene sequences with sixty-one (61)

attributes. The first and second attributes define the gene sequence class (EI, IE, N) and names, respectively. The third to the sixty-first attribute represent the gene sequence. In this book chapter, all three thousand one hundred and ninety instances are used (see Tables 1 and 2).

In this book chapter, gene constituents (A, C, G, T, D, R, N, and S) are termed gene components. The first four constituents (i.e. A, C, G, T) are termed primary gene components, whereas the remainder of the list is termed secondary gene components. The main difference between primary and secondary genes is that, primary gene components are strictly definite and unambiguous. Secondary gene component (1) D – is either A or G or T (2) R – A or G (3) N – is either A or G or C or T (4) S – is either C or G

Data Encoding

The binary digit coding system is adopted and used to represent each of the gene components. The binary digits of gene components are randomly selected to form the primary basis for gene sequences in the dataset. Corresponding classes of gene sequences are also preprocessed into binary digits to form a complete bit coded dataset (see Table 3).

The classes are pre-processed as Table 4.

The raw dataset is then converted to the binary dataset shown in Table 5.

Attributes three to sixty-one are merged into one-bit system of length 480 (see Table 6).

EVOLUTIONARY ALGORITHMS

Scientists have over time, tried to explain evolution with different theories. Over the last four decades, different kinds of evolutionary algorithms have evolved:

1. Genetic algorithm was developed by J. H. Holland in the US,

2. Evolutionary strategies by I. Rechenberg in Germany, and

3. Evolutionary programming by H.-P. Schwefel.

Each approach solves problems in a different fashion but inspired by the same principles of natural evolution.

Genetic Algorithms (GAs) in the field of Evolutionary Algorithms (EAs) is the most widespread method. The main feature of GAs is the use of a recombination (or crossover) operator as the primary search tool. The rationale is that, different parts of the optimal solution can be independently discovered, and be later combined to create better solutions. Genetic operators such mutation are also used to introduce new information into the population.

Evolution Strategies (ESs) were built mainly to solve engineering problems and characterized by handling massive floating-point arrays. A very attractive characteristic of this technique is the utilization of self-adaptive mechanisms for controlling the application of mutation.

Evolutionary Programming (EP) focuses on the adaptation of individuals rather than the evolution of their genetic information. As opposed to manipulation of genes, this form implies a much more abstract view of the evolutionary process. Complex data structures such as finite state automata, graphs are used to model their behaviors.

Evolutionary Algorithms (EAs) are generally stochastic based search methods that imitate human natural biological evolution. EAs work on a population of potential solutions applying the principle of fitness to produce optimal approximations to a solution. In each generation, a new set of approximations is created by selecting individuals according to fitness levels and genetically operating population constituents using operators such as crossover and mutation. The process leads to the evolution of populations of individuals that are better suited to their environment than the individuals that, they were created from an initial

Table 1. A dataset distribution

Class	Total
EI	767
IE	768
NG	1655
Total	**3190**

Table 2. Raw splice dataset

Class	Gene name	Attribute 3	Attribute 4...	Attribute 61
EI	Name 1	A	C...	T
EI	Name 2	G	T...	G
	...	....	......	....
IE	Name (W-1)	G	G...	T
N	Name W	C	C...	A

Table 3. Gene sequence component: bit pair data

Gene Component	Corresponding Binary Digit
A	001011
C	111001
G	000010
T	110000
D	000001
R	111100
N	011001
S	100010

Table 4. Gene sequence component class: bit pair data

Gene Sequence Class	Corresponding Binary Digit
EI	101010
IE	101001
NG	001010

Table 5. Processed splice dataset

Class	Attribute 3	Attribute 4...	Attribute 61
101010	001011	111001...	110000
101010	000010	110000...	000010
	....	.....	......
101001	000010	000010...	110000
001010	111001	111001...	001011

population. Evolutionary algorithms basically model the three most important human natural processes—selection, crossover and mutation. At the beginning, a set of individuals are randomly selected into a population. Individuals in the initial population/generation are evaluated using an objective function to extract a set of individuals for breeding. The breeding process and fitness check continues until the optimal results are met. Having met the optimization criteria, all fit individuals are extracted as results.

Genetic Algorithms

Genetic algorithms (Bandyopadhyay, et al., 1995; Palaniappan, et al., 2002; Rovithakis, et al., 2004; Chouaib, et al., 2008; Lin, et al., 2006; Hussein, et al., 2001; Reeves & Rowe, 2003; Bandyopadhyay & Pal, 2007) were invented by John Holland in the 1960s. The technique was developed by Holland and his group in the 1960s and the 1970s. As opposed to evolution strategies and evolutionary programming, Holland's main aim was to implement algorithms to formally study the

phenomenon of adaptation as it occurs in nature and to develop ways in which the mechanisms of natural adaptation might be imbibed into computer systems. In his book Adaptation in Natural and Artificial Systems, Holland presents the GA as an abstraction of human biological evolution and gave theoretical foundations for adaptation under the concept. Holland's GA method moves one population of chromosomes to a new population by using a kind of "natural selection" together with genetic inspired operators of crossover and mutation. The selection process chooses chromosomes that will be allowed for breeding in a population. As the name suggests, crossover exchanges parts of two chromosomes by roughly imitating biological recombination of chromosomes. The process of mutation randomly changes allele values of some locations in the chromosome. Holland's introduction of a population based algorithm with crossover and mutation was a major innovation. Rechenberg's evolution strategies had earlier on focused on an initial population of two individuals—one parent and one offspring, where the offspring is a mutated version of the parent.

Table 6. Processed splice dataset

Instance	Class	Attribute 3...61	Bit Length
1	101010	001011111001...110000	480
2	101010	000010110000...000010	480
....		....	....
3189	101001	000010000010...110000	480
3190	001010	111001111001...001011	480

GAs are particularly suited for such complex applications where knowledge about the solution space is unnecessarily huge and uncertain. With its core principles deeply rooted in genetics, GAs have proven to perform better than other techniques in complex search related problems. A GA essentially comprises of a set of individual solutions or chromosomes (called the population) and some biologically inspired operators that create a new and potentially better population from an old one. It seeks to find optimal solutions for complex search problems with little knowledge of the solution space. In differentiating GAs from other techniques, GAs works by encoding the parameter set and simultaneously searching with multiple points. Whereas other approaches use deterministic rules, GAs use stochastic operators in finding optimal solutions. Due to the evidential performance of GAs, the technique has been widely used in hybrid (Kim, et al., 2007; El-Mihoub, et al., 2006; Silva & Soma, 2008; Loh, et al., 2004; Fatourechi, et al., 2005; Lobo & Goldberg, 1997; Kanoh & Hara, 2008; Loukil, et al., 2009) and neural based (Sheikhan & Movaghar, 2009; Tian & Noore, 2005; Armano, et al., 2005; Kim & Shin, 2007; Leung, et al., 2003; Hochman, et al., 1996; Yao, 1993; McDonnell & Waagen, 1994; Maniezzo, 1994; Angeline, et al., 1994; Ishigami, et al., 1995; Alsultanny & Aqel, 2003; Dasgupta & Mcgregor, 1992; Cho, 1999; Delgado, et al., 2006; Lin & Huang, 2006; Whitley, 1995; Yamany, et al., 1997; Sziranyi & Csapodi, 1998; Yao, 1999; Lessmann, et al., 2006) systems.

FEATURE SELECTION

Feature selection, also termed as variable selection, feature reduction, attribute selection or variable subset selection, is the technique of selecting a subset of relevant features from a data repository for training learning models. Feature selection helps to improve learning model performance by

1. Enhancing generalization capability,
2. Reducing or alleviating noise from a train set,
3. Increasing the speed of the learning process, and
4. Enhancing model interpretability.

A lot of feature selection models have been implemented over the past decades—statistical (e.g. Perkins, et al., 2003; Krishnapuram, et al., 2004), neural (e.g. Gabrilovich & Markovitch, 2004; Miller, et al., 2003; Sun, et al., 2004; Froehlich, 2002; Huang & Wang, 2005; Liu & Zheng, 2005; Taira & Haruna, 1999; Byvatov & Schneider, 2004; Hardin, et al., 2004; Hermes & Buhmann, 2000), others (Dash & Liu, 1997; Liu & Yu, 2005; Song, et al., 2007; Piramuthu, 2004; Forman, 2003). Feature selection, ideally is a search problem. One area of study which has become popular due to its biological underpinnings and tenacity, in difficult and complex search related problems is GA (Salcedo-Sanz, et al., 2004; Rajavarman & Rajagopalan, 2007). Although GAs have been used in feature selection tasks, not much advancement has been done. In this book chapter, a novel GA based on human nature, interactions and behavior is introduced.

HUMAN NATURE, INTERACTION, AND BEHAVIOUR: SOME FACTS

The world is made up of different kinds of people with different lifestyles. Each member of the population has a sex—male, female, or hermaphrodite. Each member has a birth reference point from which the member's age could be determined. Each member of the population is skilled in at least in one thing. The skill or skill set is acquired over time and may be

1. On the increase,
2. On the decrease,

3. In equilibrium, or
4. Behave otherwise, for a given period of time.

Each member at a certain stage in life relies on partner preference information to select a partner for procreation purposes. Each new born inherits traits from the parents in addition to its unique traits. Although the traits are present at birth, they become more visible as the newborn grows into a toddler, teenager, or a young adult. During growth stages, the individual (i.e. the child) acquires skills in different areas of human endeavour but gradually moves towards domains of utmost interest. At puberty and beyond, the sexual reproductive organs of the child might have become matured and fertile enough to engage in mating for reproduction purposes. The member at a point in time may adapt to certain habits, behaviors, and lifestyles due to peer pressure, environment, and personal instincts. Similarly, certain decisions, behaviors, and lifestyles are likely to affect fertility leading to a restriction in procreation. Occurrence such death be it (human or non-human induced), hormonal changes (e.g. menopause) are also likely to affect reproduction in a generation.

LIMITATIONS OF EXISTING GA WORKS

The underlying principle in most GA algorithms include

1. Generating N random chromosomes of length L from a chosen alphabet, and
2. Repeating the actions of selecting, recombining, mutating and replacing the current population with new population.

Current day research works within the field of GAs have NOT strongly tied human nature, interactions, and behaviour to GA design. This has resulted in GA research advancement still in its infancy. Although completed works are relevant in their respective applications, implemented works are limited in significant ways.

In this section, a step-wise comparison of current GA approach and "human nature, interactions and behaviour" is made. The rationale is to demonstrate that human nature, interactions and behaviors have great influence in restricting reproduction and should be considered in GA based system design (see Tables 7-9).

Table 7. Current GA limitations

With Respect to GA Initial population	
Current GA Approaches	**Human Nature, Interaction and Behaviour (Real Life)**
Do not distinguish between members in a given population	A member of a population is male, female, hermaphrodite. This is necessary for procreation
Do not explicitly interpret the age of population members – as it is in the case of humans	Each member of a real life population has an age. Age plays a factor in procreation – e.g. a feminine member might want to have children with an older male.
Do not explicitly show an initially acquired (random) fitness values for members in a population	Each member of a real life population is fit is at least one thing. For example, a feminine member might want to have children with an established business tycoon. In this case, the business tycoon is extremely fit in the business he does.
Do not show any preference list for mating partner selection for a member	Each member of a real life population has preferences. For example, a male member celebrity may want to have children with a fellow celebrity who is female.
Do not contain bio-data of population members	Each member in a real life population has bio-data. This bio-data in some cases affects reproduction. For example, a male member might want to have children with a female from the same country, educational background, same interest etc.

Table 8. Current GA limitations

With Respect "GA Learning Section"	
Current GA method Approaches	**Human Nature, Interaction and Behaviour (Real life)**
Do not implement selective mating based on sexual orientation, preferences and/or others	In real life, a member selects partner based on some factors in order to reproduce - sexual orientation, preferences and/or others. A homosexual never goes to another homosexual to reproduce.
Do not put restrictive mating orders on newly born members.	In real life, a new born goes through stages to reach puberty. The new born does not start having children immediately after birth. It will have to wait till the reproductive organ is matured before it can reproduce. Maturity of the sexual organ is age based.
Do not show explicit transfer of traits (inherited or unique)	In real life, a new born inherits traits from the parent in addition to its unique ones. In other words, a child may have its own traits in addition to those transferred from the parents.
Do not show a fertility pedigree of members.	In real life, the fertility status of a member can be tracked over a period of time. For example, the fertility status of a child at age 1 is by far lower than the fertility at puberty. Even at adulthood, a member's fertility status could be affected by personal habits – such as smoking, drinking etc
Do not model decisions, lifestyle and/or behavior acquisition pedigree	In real life, certain life styles, decision and behaviors affect choice of partners for reproduction. Example, family planning, becoming a catholic priest etc.
Do not model death, biological related issues that is likely to affect reproduction	In real life, members are born and they also die. Similarly, hormonal changes such as menopause (in women) set in to stop reproduction.

MOTIVATION FOR NEW DIRECTIONS

Eshelman (1991) developed the CHC algorithm which uses a number of mechanisms to get maximum power from crossover. The two most unique mechanisms are "incest prevention" and "soft restarts." The novel contributions, work in conjunction with the cross generational rank selection. The first (i.e. incest prevention) is a self-adjusting mechanism aimed at preventing members of a given population from being mated. The second (i.e. soft-restarts) replaces mutation and the only operator used in each generation to generate offspring, is crossover. At converging point, the best individual found is used as a template to generate a new population of partially randomized individuals and the algorithm is restarted. This is continued until a suitable number of individuals are found. Problems that are considered easy in nature are solved without a restart and harder problems are solved with multiple restarts.

Undoubtedly, Eshelman's work brings a lot of insight and benefits to GA research.

1. Incest prevention indirectly means some crossover operations will have to be ignored,
2. By ignoring a number of crossover operations, computational overhead is reduced,
3. Population size could be increased to make room for more equally good solutions to be added.

Table 9. Current GA limitations

With Respect to "GA Stopping criteria"	
Current GA methods	**Fact - Human Nature & Interaction based (Real life)**
Only check whether the number of strings (i.e. solutions) or the number of epochs has been attained	In real life, reproduction is likely to stop based on a number of factors – e.g. death of all members, all homosexual population, all lesbian population etc

Motivated by the need to further relate human nature, interactions, and behaviors to GA design, the "Buabin Algorithm" is proposed in this book chapter.

NEW DIRECTIONS FOR GENETIC ALGORITHM DESIGN

In this book chapter, a number of human related characteristics are identified and integrated in a novel GA. The characteristics are those that affect reproduction are those that were selected (see Tables 10 and 11).

Offspring Determination

The offspring determination technique adopted below

1. Helps the designer to determine which life styles are likely to yield offspring upon mating. For example, in Tables 12 and 13, twelve sexual orientation combinations are considered. Out of One hundred and forty-four possible crossover combinations,

ONLY eighteen combinations proved viable for offspring production. Depending on the choice of the population, characteristics such as preference set and bio-data could introduce certain restrictions in mating,

2. Helps the designer to determine which life styles ought to be given priority during selection for a given population,

3. Provides scientific basis based on natural interaction in humans.

Let N be the result of a pair NOT yielding an off-spring; Y be the result of a pair yielding an off-spring; X(Y): be the result of a pair yielding an off-spring should they meet. In real life situation, the pair does not or cannot meet.

GA Initialization Section: Population Member Representation

In modeling population members, every member must be explicitly assigned:

1. **A sexual orientation:** Male, female, hermaphrodite, or acquired status such as homosexual or lesbian;

Table 10. Characteristics

#	Characteristics	Possibilities	Description
1	Sexual Orientation	{SO1=0, SO2=1}	Single Valued Choice {Male, Female, Hermaphrodite}. One value can be selected (i.e. "1") at a time. All others turn to "0"
2	Age	f(Year Of Birth)	31 – i.e.(function of year of birth)
3	Fitness Set Values	{FV1, FV2, …, FVN}	Multiple Valued Choice {0.02, 0.01,…., 0.34}
4	Preference Set Values	{PR1, PR2, …, PRN}	Multiple Valued Choice {Education, Religion, Work} ; where Education set could be {Bachelor, Master, PhD, Other}; Religion could be {Christian, Hindu, Moslem, Other}; Work as {Official, Unofficial, Private, Public, Other},..
5	Bio-data	{BD1, BD2, …,BDN}	Multiple Valued choice. More than one value can be selected at a time.
6	Fertility	{LS1=0, LS2=1}	Single Valued Choice {Fertile, Un-Fertile}. One value can be selected (i.e. "1") at a time. All others turn to "0"
7	Death	DTH Value	0.002 – on a scale of [0 - 1.0]. Must be threshold based
8	Adopted Sexual Orientation Life-Style set	{LS1=0, LS2=1}	Single Valued Choice {Lesbian, Homosexual}. One value can be selected (i.e. "1") at a time. All others turn to "0"

Table 11. Sexual orientation coding

Sexual Orientation	Name of Sexual
M	A fertilized Male
F	A fertilized Female
MH	A masculine feeling fertilized Hermaphrodite
FH	A feminine feeling fertilized Hermaphrodite
H	A fertilized Homosexual
L	A fertilized Lesbian
uM	An unfertilized Male
uF	An unfertilized Female
uMH	An unfertilized male feeling Hermaphrodite
uFH	An unfertilized female feeling Hermaphrodite
uH	An unfertilized Homosexual
uL	An unfertilized Lesbian

2. **An age:** Specific value;
3. **An initial fitness value set:** This set contains random fitness values within the scale of [0-1] for the N number of objective functions under consideration;
4. **A preference set:** A preference set value may be a set on its own. For example, a preference set value "education" might have sub-values (Bachelors, Masters, Doctorate, Other);
5. **Biodata:** This could be any set of values that are likely to match up with another member's preference;
6. **A fertility value:** This value (range: 0-1), determines the fertility rate of member at every point in time;
7. **A death value:** This value between 0-1, determines the likelihood of death of a member at every point in time.

This is modeled so as to monitor a member's likelihood of dying at a given time.

GA Learning Section: Population Member Representation

In real life, newly born members in a given population are assigned the following at birth:

1. A sex: male, female, or hermaphrodite;
2. An age;
3. A fitness value set;
4. A preference set;
5. Bio-data;
6. Fertility value;
7. Death value.

Computational genetics with the help of probabilities make it possible to determine the sexual orientation of the newborn child. The age of a member is computed based on the year in which he/she was born. With regards to fitness, initial fitness values of 0.005 for all objective functions under consideration are worth awarding. In real life, some preferences may be inherited. A member in adulthood may prefer things that are similar to that of his/her parents. The Hamming distance could be used to determine the distance between the parents of newborn and naively pass resultant set values onto newly born members.

Fertility, in humans increase, decrease, or stay in equilibrium, over time. Although a child in real life, cannot readily produce other new borns, its fertility status is NOT entirely zero. At least a fertility value of 0.005 is worth awarding to members at birth.

RESULT OF NEW DIRECTIONS: THE BUABIN ALGORITHM

Although more human characteristics can be identified in real life, to strengthen human characteristics based GA design, the characteristics identified in previous sections are used to model a novel algorithm called "Buabin Algorithm." Prior to discussing the algorithm in detail, a couple of

Table 12. Crossover operations: among fertilized and unfertilized members

	M	F	MH	FH	H	L	uM	uF	uMH	uFH	uH	uL
M	N	Y	N	Y	N	X(Y)	N	N	N	N	N	N
F	Y	N	Y	N	X(Y)	N	N	N	N	N	N	N
MH	N	Y	N	Y	N	X(Y)	N	N	N	N	N	N
FH	Y	N	Y	N	X(Y)	N	N	N	N	N	N	N
H	N	X(Y)	N	X(Y)	N	X(Y)	N	N	N	N	N	N
L	X(Y)	N	X(Y)	N	X(Y)	N	N	N	N	N	N	N
uM	N	N	N	N	N	N	N	N	N	N	N	N
uF	N	N	N	N	N	N	N	N	N	N	N	N
uMH	N	N	N	N	N	N	N	N	N	N	N	N
uFH	N	N	N	N	N	N	N	N	N	N	N	N
uH	N	N	N	N	N	N	N	N	N	N	N	N
uL	N	N	N	N	N	N	N	N	N	N	N	N

functions are discussed. The scope of this book chapter does not cover the implementation of the functions but present a fair idea of the task each function handles.

Function 1: Reproduction Viability Test (String1, String2): This function accepts two string parameters and tests whether mating is feasible between them. It returns a Boolean result. A true result means, the two strings can be mated to produce two (2) new strings, whereas false result means the two strings cannot be mated. This unit may perform series of tests that are mating related.

Function 2: Substring Test (String1, String2): This function accepts a list of string parameters and tests whether there is at least one substring in the dataset. The function terminates as soon as a substring is detected. This is to prevent adding strings which will definitely yield zero-valued fitness value. If ALL of the strings return a true value, it means ALL strings have at least 1 substring in the dataset. If one of them returns a true value, it means that string has at least one substring in the dataset. If none of the strings returns a true value, it means the strings have NO substrings are available in the dataset

Function 3: Assign Characteristics (): This function assigns human related characteristic values to newly born children. The function is called during the GA initialization and

Table 13. Crossover operations: among fertilized members

	M	F	MH	FH	H	L
M	N	Y	N	Y	N	X(Y)
F	Y	N	Y	N	X(Y)	N
MH	N	Y	N	Y	N	X(Y)
FH	Y	N	Y	N	X(Y)	N
H	N	X(Y)	N	X(Y)	N	X(Y)
L	X(Y)	N	X(Y)	N	X(Y)	N

Learning processes. In the GA initialization process, the characteristics are assigned randomly. Depending on the characteristic to be assigned, Hamming distance or probabilities is used. Issues related to acquisition of characteristics could be placed under this unit.

Function 4: Update Characteristics (): This function updates characteristic values of members. Values such as fertility, death, etc. are impacted upon steadily with time. Anything that changes in the lifetime of the member's life in the GA is worth considering under this function.

Initialization Stage

1. Generate a list of random strings
2. For each string
   a. Assign Characteristics ().

Learning Stage

Please refer to Box 1.

Stopping Criteria

The stopping criteria of "Buabin Algorithm" could be triggered by any of the following:

1. When the population is made up of ALL Males: fertilized or unfertilized;
2. When the population is made up of ALL Females: fertilized or unfertilized;
3. When the members of the population are ALL Male Hermaphrodites: fertilized or unfertilized;
4. When the members of the population are ALL Female Hermaphrodites: fertilized or unfertilized;
5. When the members of the population are ALL Homosexuals: fertilized or unfertilized;
6. When the members of the population are ALL Lesbians: fertilized or unfertilized;
7. When the members of the population are ALL dead;
8. The requisite number of strings or chromosomes have been reached.

Box 1.

```
Create an initially new population
    Repeat
        1. Select two strings - as String 1, String 2
        2. IF Perform Reproduction Viability Test (String 1, String 2) <> OK
                a. Move to step (1) above
        3. ELSE
                a. Recombine to produce 2 new strings
                b. IF Perform Substring Test (String 1, String 2) <> OK
                        i. Move to step (1) above
                c. ELSE
                i. Assign Characteristics()for String 1 and String 2
                ii. Mutate parsed String or String(s) – i.e. String 1 or String 2 or both.
                iii. IF Perform Substring Test (newly mutated strings) <> OK
                        1. Move to step (1) above
                iv. ELSE
                        1. Mutate Characteristics of String or String(s).
                        2. IF new_characteristic <> OK
                                a. Move to (3)(c)(iv)(1)
                        3. ELSE
                                a. Update Characteristics()
                                b. Add to current population or use elitism
                                c. Keep track of best strings
        4. Repeat Step 1 until ALL string combinations are done.
        5. Replace the current population with new population
        6. Repeat Step 1 until the number of generations is reached.
```

HUMAN BASED FEATURE SELECTION AND CLASSIFICATION

Humans unconsciously use feature selection and classification to solve many real world problems. For example, to extract stock related information for analysis, the human being (user) identifies a large text data repository such as the Internet. Prior to extracting files from the repository, the user acquires fair knowledge of stocks, learns key terms etc. For each stock related document in the large text corpora, the user's brain uses the "fair knowledge" it has learnt, to compute the information score of the stock document. Based on an implicit threshold value the user might have assigned, the user's brain, tags the document as selected or not-selected. The process of feature selection is fully integrated to classification. In computing the information scores of the documents in the repository,

1. The human brain searches for localized neurons in the classification region of the brain. The neurons used is based on the level of difficulty of the task at hand;
2. The human brain then puts selected localized neurons into an ensemble.

The ensemble of localized neurons, scan through the stock documents whilst applying the "fair knowledge." During the scanning processing, constituting localized neuronal structures keep adjusting and enhancing information learnt over time until an acceptable information score is determined—i.e. at early stopping stage.

JUSTIFICATION FOR HYBRID NEURAL INTEGRATION

It has been established in earlier sections of this book chapter that, genetic algorithms perform best in complex search related problems. Selecting features from a large text corpus for subsequent training in a classifier is a difficult task. Whereas some schools of thought use GAs purely on problems, others have combined the technique with artificial neural networks to form hybrid forms or generated corresponding neural networks topologies from GA results.

Many researchers have made suggestions as to how GAs should be used with neural networks. (Marsland, 2009) suggests that, "A more sensible use for GAs with neural networks is to use the GA to choose the topology of the network" (p. 285). Marsland (2009, p. 285) also admits that ONLY the mutation genetic operator will be of interest: "We can use a GA for this problem, although the crossover operator doesn't make a great deal of sense, so we just consider mutation. However, we allow for four different types of mutation: delete a neuron, delete a weight connection, add a neuron, add a connection. The delete operators bias the learning towards simple networks."

Although suggestions by Marsland (2009) are relevant, the suggestions would introduce major setbacks. To be specific, recurrent neural networks have been used extensively in real world text and speech classification applications, some of which have been identified in Buabin (2011a, 20011b). Recurrent Neural Networks (RNNs) use feedback loops connections, context and hidden layers. RNNs are have input, output, hidden and context weights which are periodically updated through backpropagation technique. The questions are

1. How will a GA perform the task of encoding sequential context from sequential data formats?
2. How will a GA systematically show the computation of hidden and context layer activations for each sequence or pattern?
3. How will a GA update learned weights after each sequence?
4. How will a GA compensate the loss of gradient information?
5. Will the conversion of a GA result to a neural network, imitate human information processing?

In this book chapter, a more rewarding approach to using GAs with neural networks is modeled. The approach resultant model is a hybrid neural genetic architecture that imitates human based feature selection and classification as described in the previous section. The model maintains all benefits accompanied by neural networks and GAs. The GA section basically, performs the task of extracting features from the text corpus (in this case the pre-processed UCI Molecular Biology Splice junction Dataset) and the Hy-RNC section of the architecture trains on extracted features.

HYBRID RECURRENT NEURAL CLASSIFIER (HY-RNC)

Buabin (2011a, 2012) contends that, for classifiers to imitate human information processing they must possess certain basic principles in neuroscience.

1. Localized neurons are similar in structure and perform related function—Haykin (2008) provides a detailed representation of the human brain.
2. Minimal number of localized neurons are selected and put into an ensemble for information processing.
3. Results are enhanced to attain high throughput.

Aside the neuroscience contradictions, none of the boosting enabled systems (Lim & Goh, 2005; Boné, et al., 2003; Grubb & Bagnell, 2010; Schwenk & Begio, 2000; McKee, 2001) provide clear integration ability for updating learned neural network weights after boosting. Marsland (2009) confirms this by making the following statement: "...boosting is not quite a stand-alone algorithm: the classifiers need to consider the weights when they perform their classifications. It is not always obvious how to do this for a particular classifier, but we have seen methods of doing it for a few

classifiers" (p. 157). Motivated by the need to implement a hybrid neural based text classification system that:

1. Has similar localized constituents in an ensemble performing related function,
2. Uses minimal number of hidden layer neurons in constituting structures,
3. Is fully integrated with a boosting algorithm harnessed with backpropagation techniques,
4. Provides an obvious scientific basis for updating learned neural network weights, and
5. Is robust, adaptive, fault tolerant, etc., the boosted Hybrid Recurrent Neural Classifier abbreviated Hy-RNC was proposed and implemented in Buabin (2011a, 2012).

The general and special cases of Hy-RNC are explained. Whereas the general Hy-RNC contains an ensemble of N simple recurrent networks (SRNs), the special case Hy-RNC contains a single SRN. Both have a boosting unit fully integrated with the networks. The boosting unit, which contains an Adaboost-like algorithm (termed NeuroBoost), operates by

1. Accepting network outputs from the hybrid neural classifier environment, and
2. Extracting weak hypothesis from the outputs.

The algorithm computes temporary weights based on extracted hypothesis and updates learned neural network weights through backpropagation approach. Having integrated the weights, the new neural weights are copied into the hybrid environment.

Hy-RNC: Architecture, Training, and Validation

Hy-RNC can be sub-divided into two (2) networks: namely general and special case. Each constituting SRN in the general case has *i* number of hidden neurons and *k* number of input/output units. They (individually) are fully connected and have bias connections at both Input and hidden layers. Similar to general case Hy-RNC, learned information in special case Hy-RNC is boosted and fed into the hybrid classifier environment through the NeuroBoost algorithm. The constituting SRN structure in special case Hy-RNC, is also similar to the network structure in general case Hy-RNC (i.e. *k-i-k*). In terms of operation, Hy-RNC initializes parameters such as hidden layers, hidden layer neurons, input-output units with default values. The input, output, context, and hidden layer weights are randomly selected and used to initialize the hybrid network. For each news title in an epoch, Hy-RNC creates and initializes layer activations (context and hidden) with default values. The Layer activations are updated after every time step until the end of the sequence is reached. Having ended the sequence, Hy-RNC updates the hybrid network weights and re-initializes layer activations to default values. Hy-RNC is trained and validated repeatedly until an early stopping criterion is reached. The early stopping technique employed in this experiment so as to ensure a noise-free learning process.

NeuroBoost Algorithm

NeuroBoost uses back-propagation technique to integrate boosting weights into neural network weights. The algorithm, which is AdaBoost-like, operates by

1. Accepting neural network weights and merged outputs,
2. Initializing temporary vectors such as weights, error, and alpha.

In one time step (i.e. T=1), NeuroBoost retrieves weak hypothesis from N classified examples and computes corresponding vectors error: (1*T), alpha: (1*T), boosting weights: ones (N*T), deltah and deltao. The algorithm's weights (i.e. boosting weights) are then integrated into the hybrid network weights through back-propagation approach. The new neural weights are subsequently transferred into the hybrid neural classifier environment for re-training and re-validation on exemplars. The algorithm's ability to integrate boosting weights into hybrid neural weights makes it unique and possible to measure deviation (i.e. of network outputs) on the Least Squares Error method. The integrating ability provides an obvious scientific basis for connecting boosting algorithms to neural based systems (see Table 14).

Evaluation with Confusion Matrix

Hy-RNC generates a corresponding *k* (i.e. eight) bit data for all instances in the test set. A predicted network output of a class is deemed to have been

Table 14. NeuroBoost algorithm

Initialization:
• Accept neural weights and network outputs from hybrid environment • Initialize temporary vectors: error, alpha, boosting weights

Repeat
• In one epoch
    o Retrieve weak hypothesis from network outputs
    o Compute Error, Alpha, Boosting weights
    o Compute deltah, deltao
    o Integrate boosting weights into

Final • Copy neural weights into the hybrid environment

classified (i.e. 1), if the output activation is at least 0.50. Where a predicted network output is strictly less than 0.50, the resulting classification is set to 0. For example, a *k* bit output [0,0,1,1,0,0,0,1] of an instance with corresponding target [0,0,1,0,0,0,0,1], is represented in Hy-RNC as follows: [0,0] = 5, [0,1] = 1, [1,0] = 0, [1,1] = 2, where [*a*, *b*] is interpreted as "*a*" classified as "*b*." Similarly, the confusion matrix is used to extract weak hypothesis from predicted network outputs. A predicted output (i.e. *k* bit data) of an instance is deemed to be classified if the number of correctly classified classes or bits is at least 50% or 0.5. Furthermore the confusion matrix is used to communicate the overall correct (i.e. [0, 0] and [1, 1]) and incorrect (i.e. [0, 1] and [1, 0]) classifications on the test set. Although the experiment uses a bit-wise approach to represent classifications, the approach could be modified to generate classification results for each class across the dataset. In such a case, there will be a *k**k confusion matrix

Performance Measure

The F-Measure was used in evaluating classifier performance of Hy-RNC. The choice is informed by the fact that, the F-Measure metric is neither biased towards Recall or Precision. In data mining theory, Recall is defined as the number of True Positives over the sum of True Positives and False Negatives whereas Precision is defined as the number of True Positives over the sum of True Positives and False Positives. The F-Measure is therefore expressed as:

$$F = (2 * Recall * Precision)/(Recall + Precision) \tag{24}$$

HYBRID NEURAL GENETIC ARCHITECTURE

The resulting integration between the human nature and interactions based GA and Hy-RNC is shown below. The GA section extracts features from a collection of labeled documents. The features are used to train and validate Hy-RNC repeatedly until an early stopping criterion is reached. Having trained and validated Hy-RNC, the network is tested on novel examples to ascertain classifier performance. Since real world problems are non-stationary in nature, the data pool from which features are extracted is monitored for change in status. A change in the data pool state results in the re-extraction (i.e. of features), re-training, re-validation, and re-testing of examples (see Figures 1 and 2).

LIMITATIONS

Like any other system, the hybrid neural genetic architecture described in this book chapter has limitations. Although human nature and interaction characteristics have been discussed, there are many other issues that affect human genetics. Some of these issues have strong underpinnings in human biology and ought to be investigated to stimulate GA research.

Figure 1. Hybrid neural genetic model

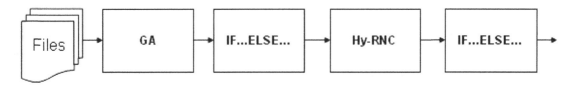

Figure 2. Hybrid neural genetic architecture operation

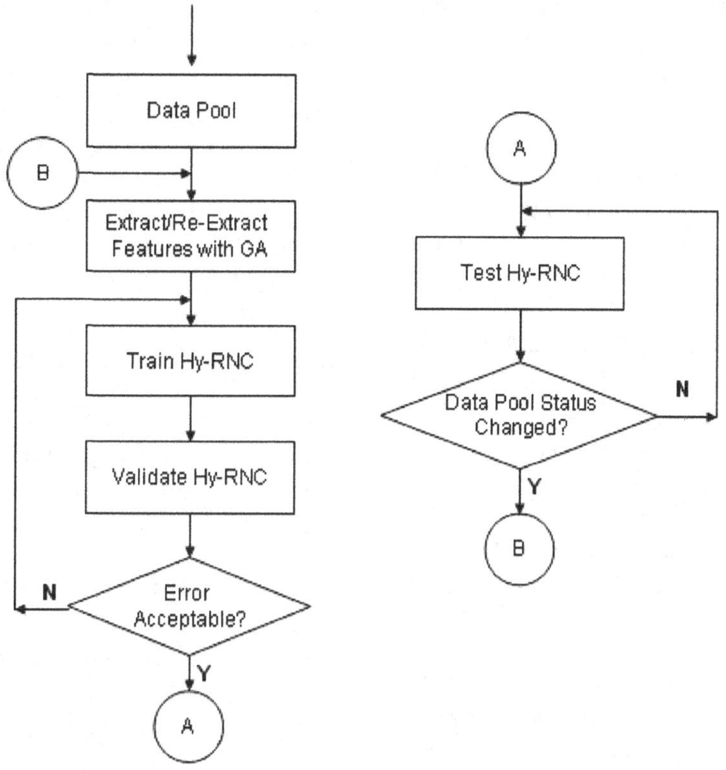

CONCLUSION

This book chapter demonstrates:

1. The modeling of a human-like GA,
2. A rewarding approach for using GAs with neural networks,
3. Integration ability between the novel GA and the Hybrid Recurrent Neural Classifier—Hy-RNC with losing quality information on both sides,
4. The repetitive task of extracting feature from a non-stationary domain,
5. Applicability of human centered characteristic in GA research.

The approach, adopted in this book chapter is different from most of the related approaches for feature selection and data classification, in that, a hybrid neural genetic architecture has been used which stands to imitate basic human related characteristics and yield positive results when implemented. Although the approach is explained for a fewer number of characteristics, the engaged technique could be used to introduce more human characteristics into GA design.

REFERENCES

Adomavicius, G., & Tuzhilin, A. (2005). Toward the next generation of recommender systems: A survey of the state-of-the-art and possible extensions. *IEEE Transactions on Knowledge and Data Engineering, 17*(6). doi:10.1109/TKDE.2005.99

Alsultanny, Y. A., & Aqel, M. M. (2003). Pattern recognition using multilayer neural-genetic algorithm. *Neurocomputing, 51*, 237–247. doi:10.1016/S0925-2312(02)00619-7

Angeline, P. J., Saunders, G. M., & Pollack, J. B. (1994). An evolutionary algorithm that constructs recurrent neural networks. *IEEE Transactions on Neural Networks*, *5*(1), 54–65. doi:10.1109/72.265960

Ansari, A., Essegaier, S., & Kohli, R. (2000). Internet recommendation systems. *JMR, Journal of Marketing Research*, *37*, 363–375. doi:10.1509/jmkr.37.3.363.18779

Armano, G., Marchesi, M., & Murru, A. (2005). A hybrid genetic-neural architecture for stock indexes forecasting. *Information Sciences*, *170*, 3–33. doi:10.1016/j.ins.2003.03.023

Avery, C., & Zeckerhauser, R. (1997). Recommender systems for evaluating computer messages. *Communications of the ACM*, *40*(3). doi:10.1145/245108.245127

Bandyopadhyay, S., Murthy, C. A., & Pal, S. K. (1995). Pattern classification with genetic algorithms. *Pattern Recognition Letters*, *16*, 801–808. doi:10.1016/0167-8655(95)00052-I

Bandyopadhyay, S., & Pal, S. K. (2007). *Classification and learning using genetic algorithms: Applications in bioinformatics and web intelligence*. Berlin, Germany: Springer.

Billsus, D., & Pazzani, M. J. (1998). Learning collaborative information filters. In *Proceedings of the 15th International Conference on Machine Learning*, (pp. 46–54). IEEE.

Boné, R., Assaad, M., & Crucianu, M. (2003). Boosting recurrent neural networks for time series prediction. In *Proceedings of the International Conference on Artificial Neural Nets and Genetic Algorithms. France*, (pp. 18-22). Roane, France: Springer.

Buabin, E. (2011a). Boosted hybrid recurrent neural classifier for text document classification on the reuters news text corpus. In *Proceedings of the 3ʳᵈ ICMLC 2011*. IEEE Press.

Buabin, E. (2012). Hybrid neural architecture for intelligent recommender system classification unit design . In Dehuri, S., Patra, M. R., Misra, B. B., & Jagadev, A. K. (Eds.), *Intelligent Techniques in Recommendation Systems: Contextual Advancements and New Methods*. Hershey, PA: IGI Global.

Buczak, A. L., Zimmerman, J., & Kurapati, K. (2002). Personalization: Improving ease-of-use, trust and accuracy of a TV show recommender. [Malaga, Spain: IEEE.]. *Proceedings of Personalization in Future TV*, *2002*, 3–12.

Burke, R. (2002). Hybrid recommender systems: survey and experiments. *User Modeling and User-Adapted Interaction*, *12*, 331–370. doi:10.1023/A:1021240730564

Byvatov, E., & Schneider, G. (2004). SVM-based feature selection for characterization of focused compound collections. *Journal of Chemical Information and Computer Sciences*, *44*, 993–999. doi:10.1021/ci0342876

Chen, T.-M., Lu, C.-C., & Li, W.-H. (2004). *Prediction of splice sites with dependency graphs and their expanded Bayesian networks*. Oxford, UK: Oxford University Press. doi:10.1093/bioinformatics/bti025

Chen, Y.-W. (2007). *Combining SVMs with various feature selection strategies. (Master of Science)*. Taipei, Taiwan: National Taiwan University.

Cho, S.-B. (1999). Pattern recognition with neural networks combined by genetic algorithm. *Fuzzy Sets and Systems*, *103*, 339–347. doi:10.1016/S0165-0114(98)00232-2

Cho, Y. H., Kim, J. K., & Kim, S. H. (2002). A personalized recommender system based on web usage mining and decision tree induction. *Expert Systems with Applications*, *23*, 329–342. doi:10.1016/S0957-4174(02)00052-0

Chouaib, H., Terrades, O. R., Tabbone, S., Cloppet, F., & Vincent, N. (2008). Feature selection combining genetic algorithm and Adaboost classifiers. In *Proceedings of the 19ᵗʰ International Conference on Pattern Recognition*. IEEE Press.

Cristache, A. (2009). *Hybrid recommender system using association rules*. (Master Thesis). Auckland University of Technology. Auckland, New Zealand.

Dasgupta, D., & Mcgregor, D. R. (1992). Designing application specific neural networks using the structured genetic algorithm . In *Proceedings Cogann 1992*. IEEE Computer Society Press. doi:10.1109/COGANN.1992.273946

Dash, M., & Liu, H. (1997). Feature selection for classification. *Intelligent Data Analysis, 1*, 131–156. doi:10.1016/S1088-467X(97)00008-5

Delgado, M., Pegalajar, M. C., & Cu'ellar, M. P. (2006). Evolutionary training for dynamical recurrent neural networks: An application in financial time series prediction. *Mathware & Soft Computing, 13*, 89–110.

El-Mihoub, T. A., Hopgood, A. A., Nolle, L., & Battersby, A. (2006). Hybrid genetic algorithms: A review. *Engineering Letters, 13*(2).

Eshelman, L. J. (1991). The CHC adaptive search algorithm: how to have safe search when engaging in nontraditional genetic recombination. *Foundations of Genetic Algorithms, 1*, 265–283.

Fatourechi, M., Bashashati, A., Ward, R. K., & Birch, G. E. (2005). A hybrid genetic algorithm approach for improving the performance of the LF-ASD brain computer interface. In *Proceedings of ICASSP 2005*. ICASSP.

Fong, S., Si, Y.-W., & Biuk-Aghai, R. P. (2009). Applying a hybrid model of neural network and decision tree classifier for predicting university admission. In *Proceedings of ICICS*. IEEE Press.

Forman, G. (2003). An extensive empirical study of feature selection metrics for text classification. *Journal of Machine Learning Research, 3*, 1289–1305.

Froehlich, H. (2002). *Feature selection for support vector machines by means of genetic algorithms*. (Thesis). Philipps-University. Marburg, Germany.

Gabrilovich, E., & Markovitch, S. (2004). Text categorization with many redundant features: Using aggressive feature selection to make SVMs competitive with C4.5. In *Proceedings of the 21st International Conference on Machine Learning*. Banff, Canada: IEEE.

Goy, A., Ardissono, L., & Petrone, G. (2007). Personalization in e-commerce applications. *Lecture Notes in Computer Science, 4321*, 485–520. doi:10.1007/978-3-540-72079-9_16

Grubb, A. J., & Bagnell, A. (2010). Boosted backpropagation learning for training deep modular networks. In *Proceedings of the 27th International Conference on Machine Learning*. Haifa, Israel: IEEE.

Hardin, D., Tsamardinos, I., & Aliferis, C. F. (2004). A theoretical categorization of linear SVM based feature selection. In *Proceedings of the 21st International Conference on Machine Learning*. Banff. Canada: IEEE.

Haykin, S. (2008). *Neural networks and learning machines* (3rd ed.). Upper Saddle River, NJ: Pearson Prentice Hall.

Herlocker, J. (2000). *Understanding and improving automated collaborative filtering systems*. Minneapolis, MN: University of Minnesota.

Herlocker, J., & Konstan, J. A. (2001). Content-independent task-focused recommendation. *IEEE Internet Computing, 5*(6), 40–47. doi:10.1109/4236.968830

Herlocker, J. L., Konstan, J. A., Terveen, L. G., & Riedl, J. T. (2004). Evaluating collaborative filtering recommender systems. *ACM Transactions on Information Systems, 22*(1), 5–53. doi:10.1145/963770.963772

Hermes, L., & Buhmann, J. M. (2000). Feature selection for support vector machines. In *Proceedings of the ICPR 2000*, (vol. 2, pp. 716-719). ICPR.

Hochman, R., Khoshgoftaar, T. M., Allen, E. B., & Hudepohl, J. P. (1996). Using the genetic algorithm to build optimal neural networks for fault-prone module detection. In *Proceedings of the 7th International Symposium on Software Reliability Engineering*, (pp. 152-162). IEEE.

Huang, C.-L., & Wang, C.-J. (2005). A GA-based feature selection and parameters optimization for support vector machines. *Expert Systems with Applications, 31*, 231–240. doi:10.1016/j.eswa.2005.09.024

Huang, Z., Chen, H., & Zeng, D. (2004). Applying associative retrieval techniques to alleviate the sparsity problem in collaborative filtering. *ACM Transactions on Information Systems, 22*(1), 116–142. doi:10.1145/963770.963775

Hussein, F., Kharma, N., & Ward, R. (2001). Genetic algorithms for feature selection and weighting: A review and study. In *Proceedings of the International Conference on Document Analysis and Recognition*, (pp. 1240-1244). IEEE Press.

Ishigami, H., Fukuda, T., Shibata, T., & Arai, F. (1995). Structure optimization of fuzzy neural networks by genetic algorithm. *Fuzzy Sets and Systems, 71*, 257–264. doi:10.1016/0165-0114(94)00283-D

Iyengar, V. S., & Zhang, T. (2001). Empirical study of recommender systems using linear classifiers. In *Proceedings of the 5th Pacific-Asia Conference on Knowledge Discovery and Data Mining*, (pp. 16–27). London, UK: Springer-Verlag.

Jahrer, M., Töscher, A., & Legenstein, R. (2010). *Combining predictions for accurate recommender systems*. Paper presented at KDD 2010. Washington, DC.

Jin, R., Si, L., Zhai, C., & Callan, J. (2003). Collaborative filtering with decoupled models for preferences and ratings. In *Proceedings of the Twelfth International Conference on Information and Knowledge Management, CIKM 2003*, (pp. 309-316). ACM Press.

Kanoh, H., & Hara, K. (2008). *Hybrid genetic algorithm for dynamic multi-objective route planning with predicted traffic in a real-world road network*. Paper presented at GECCO 2008. Atlanta, GA.

Kim, C., & Kim, J. (2003). A recommendation algorithm using multi-level association rules. In *Proceedings of the IEEE/WIC International Conference on Web Intelligence*. IEEE/WIC.

Kim, D. H., Abraham, A., & Cho, J. H. (2007). A hybrid genetic algorithm and bacterial foraging approach for global optimization. *Information Sciences, 177*, 3918–3937. doi:10.1016/j.ins.2007.04.002

Kim, H., & Shin, K. (2007). A hybrid approach based on neural networks and genetic algorithms for detecting temporal patterns in stock markets. *Applied Soft Computing, 7*, 569–575. doi:10.1016/j.asoc.2006.03.004

Koren, Y. (2009). Factor in the neighbors: Scalable and accurate collaborative filtering. In *Proceedings of the 15th ACM SIGKDD International Conference on Knowledge Discovery and Data Mining*. IEEE.

Krishnapuram, B., Hartemink, A. J., Carin, L., & Figueiredo, M. A. T. (2004). Bayesian approach to joint feature selection and classifier design. *IEEE Transactions on Pattern Analysis and Machine Intelligence, 26*(9). doi:10.1109/TPAMI.2004.55

Lawrence, R. D., Almasi, G. S., Kotlyar, V., Viveros, M. S., & Duri, S. S. (2001). Personalization of supermarket product recommendations. *Data Mining and Knowledge Discovery, 5,* 11–32. doi:10.1023/A:1009835726774

Lessmann, S., Stahlbock, R., & Crone, S. F. (2006). Genetic algorithms for support vector machine model selection. In *Proceedings of the 2006 International Joint Conference on Neural Networks,* (pp. 16-21). Vancouver, Canada: IEEE.

Leung, F. H. F., Lam, H. K., Ling, S. H., & Tam, P. K. S. (2003). Tuning of the structure and parameters of a neural network using an improved genetic algorithm. *IEEE Transactions on Neural Networks, 14,* 79–88. doi:10.1109/TNN.2002.804317

Lin, F. J., & Huang, P. K. (2006). Recurrent fuzzy neural network using genetic algorithm for linear induction motor servo drive. In *Proceedings of ICIEA 2006.* ICIEA.

Lin, W. (2000). *Association rule mining for collaborative recommender systems.* Retrieved on 29 September 2008 from http://www.wpi.edu

Lin, W., Alvarez, S. A., & Ruiz, C. (2002). Efficient adaptive-support association rule mining for recommender systems. *Data Mining and Knowledge Discovery, 6,* 83–105. doi:10.1023/A:1013284820704

Liu, H., & Yu, L. (2005). Toward integrating feature selection algorithms for classification and clustering. *IEEE Transactions on Knowledge and Data Engineering, 17*(4).

Liu, Y., & Zheng, Y. F. (2005). FS_SFS: A novel feature selection method for support vector machines. In *Proceedings of the Pattern Recognition Society.* Elsevier.

Lobo, F. G., & Goldberg, D. E. (1997). *Decision making in a hybrid genetic algorithm.* Washington, DC: IEEE Press. doi:10.1109/ICEC.1997.592281

Loh, S., Lorenzi, F., Saldaña, R., & Licthnow, D. (2004). A tourism recommender system based on collaboration and text analysis. *Information Technology & Tourism, 6,* 157–165. doi:10.3727/1098305031436980

Loukil, L., Mehdi, M., Melab, N., Talbi, E.-G., & Bouvry, P. (2009). A parallel hybrid genetic algorithm-simulated annealing for solving Q3AP on computational grid. In *Proceedings of the International Symposium on Parallel and Distributed Processing.* IEEE Press.

Maniezzo, V. (1994). Genetic evolution of the topology and weight distribution of neural networks. *IEEE Transactions on Neural Networks, 5*(1), 39–53. doi:10.1109/72.265959

Marsland, S. (2009). *Machine learning: An algorithmic perspective.* Boca Raton, FL: Chapman & Hall/CRC.

Massa, P., & Avesani, P. (2007). *Paper.* Paper presented at Trust-Aware Recommender Systems. Minneapolis, MN.

McDonnell, R., & Waagen, D. (1994). Evolving recurrent perceptrons for time-series modeling. *IEEE Transactions on Neural Networks, 5*(1), 24–38. doi:10.1109/72.265958

McKee, D. W. (2001). *Boosting evolved artificial neural network to improve breast cancer classification accuracy.* Unpublished.

Middleton, S. E., Shadbolt, N. R., & de Roure, D. C. (2004). Ontological user profiling in recommender systems. *ACM Transactions on Information Systems, 22*(1), 54–88. doi:10.1145/963770.963773

Miller, B. N., Konstan, J. A., & Riedl, J. (2004). PocketLens: Toward a personal recommender system. *ACM Transactions on Information Systems, 22*(3), 437–476. doi:10.1145/1010614.1010618

Miller, M. T., Jerebko, A. K., Malley, J. D., & Summers, R. M. (2003). Feature selection for computer-aided polyp detection using genetic algorithms, medical imaging 2003: Physiology and function: Methods, systems, and applications. *Proceedings of the Society for Photo-Instrumentation Engineers*, 5031.

Mobasher, B., Cooley, R., & Srivastava, J. (2000). Automatic personalization based on web usage mining. *Communications of the ACM, 43*(8), 142–151. doi:10.1145/345124.345169

O'Donovan, J., & Smyth, B. (2005). Trust in recommender systems. In *Proceedings of the 2005 Conference on Intelligent User Interfaces*, (pp. 167-174). IEEE.

Olsson, T. (2003). *Bootstrapping and decentralizing recommender systems. (IT Licentiate Theses)*. Uppsala, Sweden: Uppsala University.

Palaniappan, R., Raveendran, P., & Omatu, S. (2002). Vep optimal channel selection using genetic algorithm for neural network classification of alcoholics. *IEEE Transactions on Neural Networks, 13*(2). doi:10.1109/72.991435

Paterek, A. (2007). Improving regularized singular value decomposition for collaborative filtering. In *Proceedings of KDD Cup and Workshop*. IEEE.

Perkins, S., Lacker, K., & Theiler, J. (2003). Grafting: Fast, incremental feature selection by gradient descent in function space. *Journal of Machine Learning Research, 3*, 1333–1356.

Piramuthu, S. (2004). Evaluating feature selection methods for learning in data mining applications. *European Journal of Operational Research, Computing, Artificial Intelligence, and Information Technology, 156*, 483–494.

Rajavarman, V. N., & Rajagopalan, S. P. (2007). Feature selection in data-mining for genetics using genetic algorithm. *Journal of Computer Science, 3*(9), 723–725. doi:10.3844/jcssp.2007.723.725

Rakotomamonjy, A. (2003). Variable selection using SVM-based criteria. *Journal of Machine Learning Research, 3*, 1357–1370.

Reeves, C. R., & Rowe, J. E. (2003). *Genetic algorithms: Principles and perspectives a guide to GA theory*. Dordrecht, The Netherlands: Kluwer Academic Publishers.

Ricci, F., et al. (Eds.). (2011). *Recommender systems handbook*. Berlin, Germany: Springer Science + Business Media.

Rovithakis, G. A., Maniadakis, M., & Zervakis, M. (2004). A hybrid neural network/genetic algorithm approach to optimizing feature extraction for signal classification. *IEEE Transactions on Systems, Man, and Cybernetics. Part B, Cybernetics, 34*(1), 695–702. doi:10.1109/TSMCB.2003.811293

Salcedo-Sanz, S., Camps-Valls, G., Pérez-Cruz, F., Sepúlveda-Sanchis, J., & Bousoño-Calzón, C. (2004). Enhancing genetic feature selection through restricted search and Walsh analysis. *IEEE Transactions on Systems, Man and Cybernetics. Part C, Applications and Reviews, 34*(4). doi:10.1109/TSMCC.2004.833301

Sarwar, B., Karypis, G., Konstan, J., & Riedl, J. (2000). *Application of dimensionality reduction in recommender systems: A case study*. Paper presented at the ACM WebKDD Workshop. New York, NY.

Sarwar, B., Karypis, G., Konstan, J., & Riedl, J. (2000). Analysis of recommendation algorithms for e-commerce. In *Proceedings of the 2nd ACM Conference on Electronic Commerce*, (pp. 158-167). ACM Press.

Sarwar, B., Karypis, G., Konstan, J. A., & Riedl, J. T. (2001). Item-based collaborative filtering recommendation algorithms. In *Proceedings of the 10th International World Wide Web Conference*, (pp. 285–295). IEEE.

Schmidt-Thieme, L. (2005). Compound classification models for recommender systems. In *Proceedings of the Fifth IEEE International Conference on Data Mining (ICDM 2005)*. IEEE Press.

Schwenk, H., & Bengio, Y. (2000). Boosting neural networks. *Neural Computation, 12*, 1869–1887. doi:10.1162/089976600300015178

Setten, M. V. (2003). Prediction strategies in a TV recommender system: Framework and experiments. In *Proceedings of IADIS WWW/Internet 2003*. Algarve, Portugal: IADIS.

Setten, M. V., Veenstra, M., Nijholt, A., & Dijk, B. V. (2004). Case-based reasoning as a prediction strategy for hybrid recommender systems. *Lecture Notes in Computer Science, 3034*, 13–22. doi:10.1007/978-3-540-24681-7_4

Sheikhan, M., & Movaghar, B. (2009). Exchange rate prediction using an evolutionary connectionist model. *World Applied Sciences Journal, 7*, 8–16.

Silva, J. L. C., & Soma, N. Y. (2008). A constructive hybrid genetic algorithm for the flowshop scheduling problem. *International Journal of Computer Science and Network Security, 8*(9), 219–223.

Sobecki, J. (2006). Implementations of web-based recommender systems using hybrid methods. *International Journal of Computer Science & Applications, 3*(3), 52–64.

Song, L., Smola, A., Gretton, A., Borgwardt, K., & Bedo, J. (2007). Supervised feature selection via dependence estimation. In *Proceedings of the 24th International Conference on Machine Learning*. Corvallis, OR: IEEE.

Sun, Z., Bebis, G., & Miller, R. (2004). Object detection using feature subset selection. *Pattern Recognition, 37*, 2165–2176. doi:10.1016/j.patcog.2004.03.013

Suna, Z., Bebisa, G., & Millerb, R. (2004). Object detection using feature subset selection. In *Proceedings of the Pattern Recognition Society*. Elsevier.

Sziranyi, T., & Csapodi, M. (1998). Texture classification and segmentation by cellular neural networks using genetic learning. *Computer Vision and Image Understanding, 71*(3), 255–270. doi:10.1006/cviu.1997.0646

Taira, H., & Haruno, M. (1999). Feature selection in SVM categorization. In *Proceedings of AAAI 1999*. AAAI.

Tian, L., & Noore, A. (2005). On-line prediction of software reliability using an evolutionary connectionist model. *Journal of Systems and Software, 77*, 173–180. doi:10.1016/j.jss.2004.08.023

Towell, G. G., Craven, M. W., & Shavlik, J. W. (1991). Constructive induction in knowledge-based neural networks. In L. Birnbaum & G. Collins (Eds.), *Machine Learning: Proceedings of the Eighth International Workshop*. San Mateo, CA: Morgan Kaufmann.

Tran, T., & Cohen, R. (2000). Hybrid recommender systems for electronic commerce. In *Proceedings of the Seventeenth National Conference on Artificial Intelligence (AAAI-2000) Workshop on Knowledge-Based Electronic Markets*, (pp. 78–84). AAAI Press.

Warmuth, M. K., Liao, J., Raetsch, G., Mathieson, M., Putta, S., & Lemmen, C. (2003). Active learning with support vector machines in the drug discovery process. *Journal of Chemical Information and Computer Sciences, 43*(2), 667–673. doi:10.1021/ci025620t

Weston, J., & Perez-Cruz, F., Bousquet1, O., Chapelle, O., Elisseeff, A., & Schoelkopf, B. (2003). Feature selection and transduction for prediction of molecular bioactivity for drug design. *Bioinformatics (Oxford, England), 19*(6), 764–771. doi:10.1093/bioinformatics/btg054

Whitley, D. (1995). Genetic algorithms and neural networks . In Periaux, J., & Winter, G. (Eds.), *Genetic Algorithms in Engineering and Computer Science*. New York, NY: John Wiley & Sons Ltd.

Yamany, S. M., Khiani, K. J., & Farag, A. A. (1997). Application of neural networks and genetic algorithms in the classification of endothelial cells. *Pattern Recognition Letters*, *18*, 1205–1210. doi:10.1016/S0167-8655(97)00140-2

Yang, Y. (1999). An evaluation of statistical approaches to text categorization. *Information Retrieval*, *1*, 69–90. doi:10.1023/A:1009982220290

Yao, X. (1993). A review of evolutionary artificial neural networks. *International Journal of Intelligent Systems*, *4*, 203–222.

Yao, X. (1999). Evolving artificial neural networks. *Proceedings of the IEEE*, *87*(9), 1423–1447. doi:10.1109/5.784219

Zhang, T., & Iyengar, V. S. (2002). Recommender systems using linear classifiers. *Journal of Machine Learning Research*, *2*, 313–334.

Zhang, X., Lu, X., Shi, Q., Xu, X.-Q., Leung, H.-C. E., & Harris, L. N. (2006). Recursive SVM feature selection and sample classification for mass-spectrometry and microarray data. *BMC Bioinformatics*, *7*(197).

Zheng, C. L., & de Sa, V. R. (2003). On selecting features from splice junctions: An analysis using information theoretic and machine learning approaches. *Genome Informatics*, *14*, 73.

Ziegler, C., Schmidt-Thieme, L., & Lausen, G. (2004). Exploiting semantic product descriptions for recommender systems. In *Proceedings of the 2nd ACM SIGIR Semantic Web and IR WS (SWIR 2004)*. Sheffield, UK: ACM Press.

Chapter 14
Web Usage Mining Approaches for Web Page Recommendation:
A Survey

H. Hannah Inbarani
Periyar University, India

K. Thangavel
Periyar University, India

ABSTRACT

The technology behind personalization or Web page recommendation has undergone tremendous changes, and several Web-based personalization systems have been proposed in recent years. The main goal of Web personalization is to dynamically recommend Web pages based on online behavior of users. Although personalization can be accomplished in numerous ways, most Web personalization techniques fall into four major categories: decision rule-based filtering, content-based filtering, and collaborative filtering and Web usage mining. Decision rule-based filtering reviews users to obtain user demographics or static profiles, and then lets Web sites manually specify rules based on them. It delivers the appropriate content to a particular user based on the rules. However, it is not particularly useful because it depends on users knowing in advance the content that interests them. Content-based filtering relies on items being similar to what a user has liked previously. Collaborative filtering, also called social or group filtering, is the most successful personalization technology to date. Most successful recommender systems on the Web typically use explicit user ratings of products or preferences to sort user profile information into peer groups. It then tells users what products they might want to buy by combining their personal preferences with those of like-minded individuals. However, collaborative filtering has limited use for a new product that no one has seen or rated, and content-based filtering to obtain user profiles might miss novel or surprising information. Additionally, traditional Web personalization techniques, including collaborative or content-based filtering, have other problems, such as reliance on subject user ratings and static profiles or the inability to capture richer semantic relationships among Web objects. To overcome these shortcomings, the new Web personalization tool, nonintrusive personalization, attempts to increasingly incorporate Web usage mining techniques. Web usage mining can help improve the scalability, accuracy, and flexibility of recommender systems. Thus, Web usage mining can reduce the need for obtaining subjective user ratings or registration-based personal preferences. This chapter provides a survey of Web usage mining approaches.

DOI: 10.4018/978-1-4666-2542-6.ch014

INTRODUCTION

Web mining is the use of data mining techniques to automatically discover and extract information from World Wide Web documents and services. Web mining is a technique to discover and analyze the useful information from the Web data. Web mining can be defined roughly as data mining using data generated by the Web and includes the following sub areas: Web content mining, Web usage mining, and Web structure mining (Srivastava, et al., 2000). In Web Content Mining (WCM) useful information is extracted from the content of Web pages (Pal, et al., 2002), as e.g. free text inside a Web page, semi-structured data such as HTML code, pictures, and download-able files. Web Structure Mining (WSM) aims at generating a structural summary about the Web site and Web pages. While Web content mining mainly focuses on the structure of inner document, Web structure mining tries to discover the link structure of the hyperlinks at the inter document level. Web Usage Mining (WUM) is applied to the data generated by visits to a Web site, especially those contained in Web log files. Other sources can be browser logs, user profiles, user sessions, bookmarks, folders and scrolls (Pal, et al., 2002; Arayaa, et al., 2004). Personalization of Web sites is a very challenging field of both, current research as well as applications that have as goals e.g. individualized marketing for E-Commerce or dynamic recommendations to a Web visitor based on his/her profile and usage behavior. Analyzing Web data can also be used for system improve-ments providing the key to understanding Web traffic behavior. Advanced load balancing, data distribution or policies for Web caching as well as higher security standards are potential benefits of such improvements. Similar analyses could be used for modification of Web sites. Understanding visitors' behavior in a Web site provides hints for adequate design and update decisions. Business intelligence covers the application of intelligent techniques in order to improve certain businesses, mainly in marketing.

The rest of this chapter is organized as follows: section 2 discusses the applications of Web usage mining techniques, section 3 presents a detailed review of various association rule mining tech-niques, section 4 provides a review of sequential pattern mining techniques for Web personaliza-tion, section 5 provides a detailed review of various clustering techniques for Web page recommenda-tion, section 6 presents a review of graph theoretic modeling techniques for Web personalization, section 7 presents a review of Latent variable model for Web personalization, and section 8 provides a review of bi-clustering techniques for Web personalization in the literature.

APPLICATIONS OF WEB USAGE MINING

Personalization

Web Personalization simply means to understand the needs and interests of the visitors of the site and respond accordingly. Such a Web site recognizes each visitor and customizes itself by various ways such as determining the information that should be shown to the visitor or automatically changing the site structure in a way that will be useful and attractive for the current user. Personalization is attractive research topic, because it is critically im-portant for the success of e-commerce companies.

Making dynamic recommendations to a Web user, based on her/his profile in addition to usage behavior is very attractive to many applications, e.g. cross sales and up-sales in e-commerce. Web usage mining is an excellent approach for achieving this goal, as illustrated in Cooley et al. (1999). The WebWatcher (Joachims, et al., 1997), SiteHelper (Ngu, et al., 1997), Letizia (1995) and Yan et al. (1996) have all concentrated on providing Web site personalization based on us-age information. The system proposed in Yan et al. (1996) consists of an offline module that will perform cluster analysis and an online module, which is responsible for dynamic link generation of Web pages.

System Improvement

Research on system improvement aims to use Web usage mining for improving the Web traffic and increasing the speed at which the visitors are responded. One way to do this is to provide the Web server with the capability of predicting the pages that may be retrieved by the visitors next and generate the dynamic content of these pages before user retrieves them. For predicting the pages, the system proposed by Schecter et al. makes use of the concept of path profile, which is constructed from the data contained in the Web logs (Schecter, et al., 1998). In Pedmanabhan et al. (1996) and Cunha et al. (1997), prefetching is proposed in order to improve Web latency. This technique is useful if pre-fetched object or page is the target of the next request of the user. As long as a matching path whose maxima. Another prediction technique is named as point based prediction in which the next page is predicted only by considering the last page retrieved not the whole path. Experiments with the system show that agreement prediction technique gives the most accurate results.

Site Modification

Another way of benefiting from the usage data discovered from the logs is to use it to improve the design of the Web site. In personalization, Web sites are dynamically customizing themselves differently for each visitor. On the other hand, site modification systems offer static changes in the structure and content of the Web sites to meet the needs of all visitors (Perkowitz, et al., 1998). IndexFinder is one example for that kind of tools. It aims to discover index pages whose addition is very likely to improve the site design. These pages, which are created offline, consist of links to the conceptually related, but currently unlinked pages,

which coexist in most of the user sessions. The addition of automatically created index pages to the site is performed with the authorization of the WebMaster. Index page creation in IndexFinder is performed in three phases: processing logs, cluster mining, and conceptual clustering. In the first stage of the algorithm, a log is processed to be divided into visits. What comes next is the calculation of the co-occurrence frequencies between each pair of pages to determine to what extent these pages are related.

WEB USAGE MINING

In Web usage mining, all users' Web access activities of a Website are recorded by the WWW server of the Website and stored into the Web server logs. Each user access record contains the client IP address, request time, requested URL, user ID, HTTP status code, etc. In the offline processing, after obtaining the Web server logs, the clustering/biclustering component is applied to mine the user access sequences from the Web server logs and the user profiles are generated. In online processing, current active session of the user is matched with user profiles and the most similar profiles are used for page recommendation.

In general, Web usage mining consists of three stages, namely data preprocessing, pattern discovery and pattern analysis. Web data collected in the first stage of data mining are usually diverse and voluminous. These data must be assembled into a consistent, integrated, and comprehensive view, in order to be used for pattern discovery (Cooley, 2000). As in most applications of data mining, data preprocessing involves removing and filtering redundant and irrelevant data, predicting and filling in missing values, removing noise, transforming and encoding data, as well as resolving any inconsistencies. The task of data transformation and encoding is particularly important for the success of data mining. In Web usage mining, this stage includes the identification of users and user sessions, which are to be used as the basic building blocks for pattern discovery.

Data Preprocessing

The purpose of analyzing Web logs is to understand the user's browsing behavior. Based on the result of perceived user's behavior, user's page searching time may be reduced by recommending pages customers may be interested in. The most important information revealed by analyzing customer's clickstream is the user's current interest.

Common Web Log Format

A Web server log file contains requests made to the Web server, recorded in chronological order. The most popular log file formats are the Common Log Format (CLF) and the extended CLF.

A common log format file is created by the Web server to keep track of the requests that occur on a Web site. The format of a common log file (http://www.w3.org/Daemon/User/Config/Logging.html#common-logfile-format, 1995) is shown in Table 1.

A sample Web log file in the common log file format is shown in Table 2.

Clustering analysis is widely used to establish object pro-files on the basis of objects' variables. Objects can be customers, Web documents, Web users, or facilities (Inbarani, et al., 2009). In this

Table 1. Common log file format

remotehost	Remote hostname
Rfc931	The remote log name of the user.
Authuser	The username as which the user has authenticated himself
date	Date and time of the request.
request	The request line exactly as it came from the client
status	The HTTP status code returned to the client
Bytes	The content-length of the document transferred

chapter, clustering algorithms are applied on Web clickstreams to analyze user access trends. On one hand, the profiles can be used for predicting the navigation behavior of current users, thus aiding in Web personalization. On the other hand, Webmasters can improve the design and organization of Websites based on the acquired profiles

Data Cleaning

The purpose of data cleaning is to eliminate irrelevant items, and these kinds of techniques are of importance for any type of Web log analysis not only data mining.

Data Filtering

Most Web log records are irrelevant and require cleaning because they do not refer to pages clicked by visitors (Pabarskaite, et al., 2007). A user's request to view a particular page often results in several log entries for a single Web page access since graphics and scripts are downloaded. Removing these irrelevant items can reduce the data that will be analyzed and increase the analysis's speed. It also can decrease the irrelevant items' negative influence to the mining process.

Feature Selection

Log files usually contain nonessential information from the analytical point of view. Thus, the first data pre-processing step is the selection of features. Moreover, reducing the number of features at this stage decreases the memory usage and improves performance (Selamat, et al., 2004). It is also beneficial from the computational point of view, since log files contain thousands of megabytes of data. The final output of the pre-processing must be divided into sessions. The key attributes to build sessions are page ID, computer's IP address (or host) and page request time. These are the main features to work with in Web usage mining. Other features are less relevant unless participating in some specific tasks.

Table 2. Sample web log file

```
124.49.105.224 -- [29/Nov/2000:18:02:26 +0200] "GET /index.html HTTP/1.0" 200 1159

124.49.105.224 -- [29/Nov/2000:18:02:27 +0200] "GET /PtitLirmm.gif HTTP/1.0" 200 1137

124.49.105.224 -- [29/Nov/2000:18:02:28 +0200] "GET /acceuil_fr.html HTTP/1.0" 200 1150

124.49.105.225 -- [29/Oct/2000:18:03:07 +0200] "GET /index.html HTTP/1.0" 200 1051

124.49.105.225 -- [16/Oct/2000:20:34:32 +0100] "GET /formation.html HTTP/1.0" 200

124.49.105.225 -- [31/Oct/2000:01:17:40 +0200] "GET /formation.html HTTP/1.0" 304

124.49.105.225 -- [31/Oct/2000:01:17:42 +0200] "GET /theses2000.html HTTP/1.0" 304

124.49.105.56 -- [22/Nov/2000:11:06:11 +0200] "GET /lirmm/bili/ HTTP/1.0" 200 4280

124.49.105.56 -- [22/Nov/2000:11:06:12 +0200] "GET /lirmm/rev_fr.html HTTP/1.0" 200

124.49.105.56 -- [07/Dec/2000:11:44:15 +0200] "GET /ress/ressources.html HTTP/1.0" 200
```

In Inbarani et al. (2007), Quick Reduct and Variable Precision Rough Set (VPRS) Algorithms are proposed for feature selection from the Web log file. These feature selection algorithms are used for selecting significant attributes (features) for describing a session, which is suitable for pattern discovery phase.

User's Identification

User's identification is meant to identify those who access the Web site and which pages are accessed. If users have logged in their information, it is easy to identify them. In fact, there is lot of users who do not register their information. What's more is there are several users who access Web sites through agent, several users use the same computer, firewall's existence, one user use different browsers, and so forth. All of these problems make this task greatly complicated and it is very difficult, to identify every unique user accurately.

Session Identification

For logs that span long periods of time, it is very likely that users will visit the Web site more than once. The goal of session identification is to di-

vide the page accesses of each user at a time into individual sessions. A session is a series of Web pages user browse in a single access. The simplest method of achieving session is through a timeout, where if the time between page requests exceeds a certain time limit, it is assumed that the user is starting a new session. Many commercial products use 30 minutes as a default timeout.

Data Formatting

Data formatting (Cooley, et al., 1999) consists of mapping the number of valid URLs on a Website to distinct indices. A user's clickstream consists of accesses originating from the same IP address within a predefined time period. Each URL in the site is assigned a unique number. Thus the pages visited by the users are encoded as binary attribute vectors.

Path Completion

Another critical step in data preprocessing is path completion. There are some reasons, which result in path's incompletion, for instance, local cache, agent cache, "post" technique and browser's "back" button can result in some important accesses not recorded in the access log file, and the number of URLs recorded in log may be less than the real one. This problem is referred to path completion, which will influence next steps' efficiency and accuracy if it is not solved properly.

Pattern Discovery

In the pattern discovery stage, machine learning, and statistical methods are used to extract patterns of usage from the preprocessed Web data (Baumgarten, et al., 2000). A variety of machine learning methods have been used for pattern discovery in Web usage mining. These methods represent the four approaches that most often appear in the data mining literature: clustering, classification, association discovery, and sequential pattern discovery. Similar to most of the work in data mining, classification methods were the first to be applied to Web usage mining tasks (Pierrakos, et al., 2003). However, the difficulty of labeling large quantities of data for supervised learning has led to the adoption of unsupervised methods, especially clustering.

Pattern Analysis

Pattern Analysis is the final stage of the whole Web usage mining. The goal of this process is to eliminate the irrelative rules or patterns and to extract the interesting rules or patterns from the output of the pattern discovery process. The output of Web mining algorithms is often not in the suitable form for direct human consumption, and thus need to be transformed to a format that can be assimilated easily. There are two most common approaches for the patter analysis. One is to use the knowledge query mechanism such as SQL, while another is to construct multi-dimensional data cube before perform Online Analytical Processing (OLAP) operations. All these methods assume that the output of the previous phase has been structured.

REVIEW OF WEB USAGE MINING TECHNIQUES FOR WEB PERSONALIZATION

Web usage mining uses data mining algorithms to automatically discover and extract patterns from Web usage data and predict user behavior while users interact with the Web. Although Web usage mining has exposed limitations—sparsity in usage data or regular changes in site content, for example—personalization based on Web usage mining has several advantages over traditional techniques. For example, it can dynamically develop user profiles from user patterns while reducing the need to explicitly obtain subjective user ratings or registration-based personal preferences, which are prone to biases. Therefore, the personalization system's performance does not degrade over time. These systems incorporate data mining techniques to discover interesting patterns in Web usage data. The data source for Web usage mining is generally the server access log, but sometimes a client-side agent collects data. The increasing focus on Web usage data is due to several factors. The input is not a subjective description of the users, and thus it is not prone to biases and is not intrusive. Such systems obtain user profiles dynamically from usage patterns, and thus their performance does not degrade over time as the profiles age.

The usage mining tasks can involve the discovery of association rules, sequential patterns, page view clusters, user clusters, probabilistic models, biclustering or any other pattern discovery method (Anand, et al., 2007). The discovered patterns are used by the online component to provide personalized content to users based on their current navigational activity. The personalized content can take the form of recommended links or products, targeted advertisements, or text and graphics tailored to the user's preferences. The Web server keeps track of the active server session as the user's browser makes HTTP requests. The recommendation engine considers the active server session in conjunction with the discovered patterns to provide personalized content.

REVIEW OF ASSOCIATION RULE MINING TECHNIQUES

One problem for association rule recommendation systems is that a system cannot give any recommendations when the dataset is sparse (Agarwal, et al., 1999). The result of association rule mining can be used in order to produce a model for recommendation or personalization systems. The first solution is to rank all discovered rules calculated by the degree of intersection between the left-hand-side of rule and a user's active session and then to generate the top K recommendations. The second solution is to utilize collaborative filtering: the system finds "close neighbors" who have similar interest to a target user and makes recommendations based on the close neighbor's history. Table 3 provides a review of association rule mining techniques for Web personalization.

In Mobasher et al. (2000), four types of association rules among products or product categories were derived.

In Choa et al. (2002), an automatic discovery method that discovers frequent access patterns was presented for unique clients. It extracts the sets of all predictive access sequences from semi-structured Web access logs.

In Ha et al. (2002), the authors have suggested a personalized recommendation methodology based on association rule mining and decision tree induction for E-Commerce applications.

In Thor et al. (2005), four types of association rules among products or product categories is derived.

Relational Fuzzy Subtractive Clustering was proposed in Suryavanshi et al. (2005) which is a highly scalable technique for extracting usage profiles. It does not require any user specified parameters, works well on large datasets, and also reduces the concern over the prohibitively long time taken for compiling the data into a model and a fuzzy hybrid Collaborative Filtering (CF) Technique was for page recommendation.

Algorithms on mining sequential association rules, based on different sequence and temporal

Table 3. Summary of association rule mining techniques for web personalization

S. No	Author	Year	User/ Page	Method	Recommendation Method
1.	Bamshad Mobasher et al.,	2000	-	Association rule mining	Classification
2.	Bamshad Mobasher	2001	-	Association rule mining	K-nearest-neighbor strategy
3.	Yoon Ho Choa et al.,	2002	-	Association rule mining and decision tree induction	Agent and data warehousing technology
4.	Sung Ho Ha	2002	-	Association rule mining	-
5.	Andreas Thor et al.,	2005		Association rule mining	Data warehouse-based recommendation
6.	SutheeraPuntheeramurak et al.,	2005	-	Sequential association rules	Association rule matching

constraint combination were discussed in G´ery et al. (2003). The authors also proved that the sequence constrains, the temporal constrains and the interaction between these two constrains can affect the precision of prediction.

REVIEW OF SEQUENTIAL PATTERN MINING TECHNIQUES

Sequential pattern mining algorithm is used to identify frequent sequential Web access patterns. The access patterns are then stored in a compact tree structure, called Pattern-tree, which is then used for matching and generating Web links for recommendations. Unlike association rule mining techniques, sequential pattern mining algorithms (Xiaoqiu, et al., 2004) also considers the sequential characteristic of access patterns, which is very suitable for predicting the next Web pages. An empirical evaluation of association and sequential pattern based recommendation showed that site characteristics such as site topology and degree of connectivity can have a significant impact on the usefulness of sequential patterns over non-sequential association) patterns.

A technique related to the use of sequential rules is that of modeling Web interactions as Markov Chain models. In Markov model, the transition matrix associated with the Markov process keeps the information regarding the user's site access patterns (Lee, et al., 2010). According to the model, a user occupying a given state can make a transition with certain probability to another state with his or her next request. Searching for an optimal policy in such an accessible stochastic environment is a sequential decision problem known as the Markov decision problem. Table 4 provides a review of sequential pattern mining techniques for Web personalization.

Mathias et al. (2003) describes three Web mining approaches Association Rules (AR), frequent sequences and frequent generalized sequences are applied for the generation of asso-ciation rules. For page recommendation, discovered rules are matched using Highest Confidence (HC) and Last Sequence methods.

An intelligent Web recommender system known as SWARS (Sequential Web Access-based Recommender System) that uses sequential access pattern mining is discussed in Xiaoqiu et al. (2004). The access patterns are then stored in a compact tree structure, called Pattern-tree, which is then used for matching and generating Web links for recommendations.

Periodic Web personalization (Xiaoqiu, et al., 2004) aims to recommend the most relevant resources to a user during a specific time period by analyzing the periodic access patterns of the user from Web usage logs The proposed approach first constructs a user behavior model, called Personal Web Usage Lattice, from Web usage logs using the fuzzy Formal Concept Analysis technique. Based on the Personal Web Usage Lattice, resources that the user is most probably interested in during a given period can be deduced efficiently.

In Yang (2005), the authors proposed a new approach based on sequential pattern mining to discover user access patterns form usage data and the patterns are highly compressed into a tree structure. Nearest access subsequence from current user session is matched with sub paths of the tree during personalization recommendation stage.

In Jenamani et al. (2002) the authors had introduced the use of a multi-instance genetic programming algorithm for modeling user preferences in Web index recommendation systems. The algorithm learns user interest by means of rules, which add comprehensibility and clarity to the discovered model.

In Lee et al. (2010), Web personalization approach is based on Markov process model which generates links based on the aggregate profile of visitors based on navigational data created during past visits to the site and visitors navigation pattern during a session.

In Xu et al. (2006), an efficient prediction model called Two-Level Prediction Model (TLPM) was

Table 4. Summary of sequential pattern mining techniques for web personalization

S. No	Author	Year	User/ Page	Method	Recommendation Method
1.	Mathias G´ery, et al.,	2003	-	association rules, sequential rules and generalised sequential rules.	Rule matching based on high confidence and Last sequence
2.	Baoyao Zhou	2004	-	sequential access pattern mining	Rule matching based on pattern tree
3.	TAN Xiaoqiu et al.,	2004	-	sequential pattern mining	Frequently accessed sequence tree matching
4.	Baoyao Zhou et al.,	2006	-	sequential pattern mining	Rule generation
5.	WANG Xiao-Gang	2009	-	Sequential Pattern mining	Pattern tree based recommendation
Survey – Markov Process Model					
6.	MamataJenamani et al.,	2002	-	Markov process model	Recommendation engine using matching score
7.	Chu-Hui Lee et al.,	2010	-	Markov model Bayesian theorem	Relevance matrix model

proposed, using a novel aspect of natural hierarchical property from Web log data. In the TLPM, in level one, Markov model was used to predict the next possible category at time t.In level two, Bayesian theorem is used to predict the next possible page which belongs to the predicted category.

REVIEW OF LATENT VARIABLE MODELS

The user intended tasks are characterized by the latent factors through probabilistic inference, to represent the user navigational interests (Ishikawa, et al., 2003). Moreover, the active user's intuitive task-oriented preference is quantized by the probabilities, by which pages visited in current user session are associated with various tasks as well.

REVIEW OF GRAPH THEORETIC APPROACHES

Using these pair-wise similarity values between users, a graph is constructed whose vertices are user sessions (Aggarwal, et al., 1999). An edge connecting two vertices in the graph has a weight equal to the similarity between these two user sessions. Using an efficient graph-based clustering algorithm, the user sessions are clustered, and each cluster is then represented by a click-stream tree whose nodes are pages of user sessions of that cluster.

REVIEW OF CLUSTERING TECHNIQUES FOR WEB PERSONALIZATION

Traditional collaborative filtering techniques are often based on real-time matching of the current user's profile against similar records (nearest neighbors) obtained by the system over time from other users (Menon, et al., 2003). However, as noted in recent studies, it becomes hard to scale collaborative filtering techniques to a large number of items (for example, pages or products), while maintaining reasonable prediction performance and accuracy. Part of this is due to the increasing sparsity in the data as the number of items increase. One potential solution to this problem is to first cluster user records with similar characteristics, and focus the search for nearest neighbors only in the matching clusters.

User Clustering

In the context of Web personalization, this task involves clustering user sessions identified in the preprocessing stage. A variety of clustering techniques can be used for clustering similar sessions based on occurrence patterns of URL references. User sessions can be mapped into a multidimensional space as vectors of URL references (so, the dimensions—or features—are the URLs appearing in the session file). Standard clustering algorithms generally partition this space into groups of items that are close to each other based on a measure of distance or similarity. Dimensionality reduction techniques may be employed to focus only on relevant or significant features. Ideally, each cluster represents a group of users with similar navigational patterns. However, session clusters by themselves are not an effective means of capturing an aggregated view of common user profiles. Each session cluster may potentially contain thousands of user sessions involving hundreds of URI references. In Web usage mining framework, the ultimate goal in clustering user sessions is to obtain actionable usage profiles, which can be represented as weighted collections of URIs.

The representation of user sessions as vectors of URL references can provide a number of advantages and a great deal of flexibility. For instance, the distance or similarity among sessions can be computed using standard vector operations. Furthermore, depending on the goals of Web usage mining, a variety of weights can be chosen for each URL in a session vector. Weights can be based on the amount of time users spend on pages referenced by each URL, or they can be based on prior domain knowledge specified by the site owner (for example, in an online catalog, the site owner may wish to weigh product pages referenced by URIs more heavily than other informational pages within the site) behavior of users who are more specifically interested in conferences and journals related to consumer psychology. Note that the behavior of a single user may match both profiles during the same or different sessions.

Page View Clustering

Another approach for obtaining aggregate usage profiles is to directly compute (overlapping) clusters of page view references based on how often they occur together across user sessions (rather than clustering sessions, themselves). We call the usage profiles obtained in this way page view clusters. In general, this technique will result in a different type of aggregate profiles as compared to the session clustering technique. The usage profiles derived from session clusters group together pages that co-occur commonly across similar sessions. On the other hand, clusters tend to group together frequently co-occurring items across sessions, even if these sessions are themselves not deemed to be similar. This technique allows one to obtain clusters that potentially capture overlapping interests of different types of users. The question of which type of clusters are most appropriate for personalization tasks is an open research issue. However, the answer to this question, in part, depends on the structure and content of the specific site, as well as the goals of personalization actions.

The difficulty in clustering URIs directly comes from the high dimensionality of the feature space. The user sessions, measured in tens to hundreds of thousands in a typical application, must be used instead of the URIs as features. Traditional clustering techniques, such as distance-based methods, generally cannot handle this type of clustering. Furthermore, dimensionality reduction in this context may not be appropriate, as removing a significant number of sessions as features may result in losing too much information. In the next section we discuss an approach based on Association Rule Hyper graph Partitioning, which has been found to be particularly suitable for this task. Table 5 provides a review of user/page clustering techniques for Web personalization.

Personalized Web Advertisement Recommendation method proposed is divided into three parts customer clustering, fuzzy inference, and Web advertisement matching. Customer clustering uses the Self-Organizing Map (SOM) to mine Web server log files, split customers into different segments on the basis.

In Ishikawa et al. (2003), dynamic clustering approach is introduced by the authors to cluster user sessions. They had also proposed a novel similarity measure for Feature Matrices (FM) Model to discover and interpret user access patterns.

In Wanga et al. (2004), user access patterns are clustered and pages are recommended using frequent access patterns.

In Nasraoui et al. (2004), an efficient prediction model called Two-Level Prediction Model (TLPM) was proposed, using a novel aspect of natural hierarchical property from Web log data. In the TLPM, in level one, Markov model was used to predict the next possible category at time t. In level two, Bayesian theorem was used to predict the next possible page, which belongs to the predicted category.

In Castellano et al. (2006), User access patterns were clustered and then auto associative memory Hopfield Networks was used for page recommendation.

In Wang et al. (2008), Web recommendation based on maximum entropy was presented. It converts each user session into a sequence of tasks since on comparison with page-level patterns, task-level patterns can capture Web users' underlying interests and their Web users' underlying interests and their temporal changes, providing better understanding of users' diverse behaviors. It picks the pages with highest probabilities as recommendations.

In Wang et al. (2009), the sequential pattern mining component then mines the server logs to extract sequential Web-access pattern. A pattern-tree, which was based on the true data structure, compactly stores sequential Web-access patterns. The recommendation rules generation component searches for the best-matching access path in the pattern-tree according to a mobile user's current Web-access sequence.

An efficient sequential pattern mining approach (Baraglia, et al., 2007) to identify frequent sequential Web access patterns was presented. The access patterns were then stored in a compact tree structure, called Pattern-tree, which is then used for matching and generating Web links for recommendations.

In Mobasher et al. (2002), an efficient prediction model called Two-Level Prediction Model (TLPM) was proposed, using a novel aspect of natural hierarchical property from Web log data. In the TLPM, in level one, Markov model was used to predict the next possible category at time t. In level two, Bayesian theorem was used to predict the next possible page, which belongs to the predicted category.

Two techniques were presented in Gunduz et al. (2003) based on clustering of user transactions and clustering of page views, in order to discover overlapping aggregate profiles that can be effectively used by recommender systems for real-time Web

Table 5. Summary of user/page clustering techniques for web personalization

No	Author	Year	User/ Page	Method	Recommendation Method
1.	Hiroshi Ishikawa	2002	User clustering	L-R system for classification of users and Clustering(Ward's method)	Probability based methods
2.	Kartik Menon	2003	User clustering	Neuro Clustering (self organizing map)	-
3.	Sung Min Bae et al.,	2003	User clustering	Neuro clustering (self organizing map)	Fuzzy inference engine
4.	Cyrus Shahabi et al.,	2003	User clustering	Dynamic clustering	Classification
5.	Hiroshi Ishikawa	2003	User clustering	clustering	Frequent access patterns
6.	Feng-Hsu Wanga, et al,	2004	User clustering	Clustering and Association rule mining	Window sliding Maximal matching
7.	OlfaNasraouiMrud ulaPavuluri	2004	User clustering	Clustering	Auto associative Memory Hopfield Networks
8.	G. Castellano et al.	2006	User clustering	Fuzzy clustering	Neuro fuzzy network
9.	Youwei Wang et al.,	2008	User clustering	Clustering	navigation graph-based recommendation system
10.	Taowei Wang et al,	2009	User clustering	K-Means clustering	Similarity based recommendation
11.	RanieriBaraglia et al.,	2007	-	Least Recently Used(LRU) based algorithm	
Survey – User / Page Clustering					
12.	Bamshad Mobasher et al,	2002	User and Pageview clustering	Clustering Association Rule Hypergraph Partitioning (ARHP) technique	-
13.	SuleGunduz et al.,	2003	User /session clustering	Clustering by Graph partitioning	Click stream tree For top –N clusters
14.	FabrizioSilvestri	2004	User /session clustering	Clustering by Graph partitioning	Suggestion Building algorithm
15.	Bhushan Shankar Suryavanshi	2005	-	Relational Fuzzy Subtractive Clustering	Hybrid CF technique
16.	Xin Jin et al.	2005	-	Maximum Entropy	Probability based recommendation
17.	Baoyao Zhou et al,	2006	-	Personal Web usage Lattice sing Fuzzy formal concept analysis	Personalized Resources Generation
18.	Ming Jia et al,	2007	User and Pageview clustering	Clustering	K-Nearest Neighbor (KNN) approach
19.	Antonio Picariello et al,	2008	-	classification	Reclassification
20.	XiongHaijun et al.,	2008	-	Rough set rules based on Information entropy	rough set important attribute mining
21.	A. Zafra et al.,	2009	-	multi-instance genetic programming	Rule generation

personalization. Multivariate K-Means clustering approach was used for clustering user transactions and Association Rule Hyper graph Partitioning (ARHP) technique was used for clustering page views. This chapter also explained the methods for the discovery of aggregate user profiles based on transaction clustering and page view clustering.

In Silvestri et al. (2004), a classification algorithm for Web personalization was presented based on Web usage mining techniques. The algorithm takes into account both static information, by means of classical clustering techniques, and dynamic user behavior, thus proposing a novel and effective re-classification algorithm.

Different from previously proposed WUM systems, SUGGEST 2.0 (Suryavanshi, 2005), finds groups of strongly correlated pages by partitioning the graph according to its connected component. Suggest consists of only one component (online) that is able to update incrementally and automatically the knowledge obtained from historical data and generate personalized content online. After the clustering step, actual suggestions list was constructed by finding the cluster, which has the largest intersection with the Page Window correspondent to the current session.

In Jin et al. (2005), the recommendation module builds a knowledge base of navigation patterns by first clustering users based on the time-framed navigation sessions over the historical navigation database using HBM (Hierarchical Bisecting Medoids Algorithm) then establishes the access patterns for each user group using the association-mining technique. To produce personalized recommendations for a user, window sliding method and maximal matching method were presented.

A new recommendation method (Zhou, et al., 2006) was proposed to be applied to Web log mining by integrating user clustering and association rule mining techniques to improve the effectiveness of electronic commerce recommendation. Similarity degree between users was used for page recommendation.

In Jia et al. (2007), a new framework based on Web logs mining for building a personalized recommender system was proposed.

Periodic Web personalization (Picariello, et al., 2008) aims to recommend the most relevant resources to a user during a specific time period by analyzing the periodic access patterns of the user from Web usage logs The proposed approach first constructs a user behavior model, called Personal Web Usage Lattice, from Web usage logs using the fuzzy Formal Concept Analysis technique. Based on the Personal Web Usage Lattice, resources that the user was most probably interested in during a given period can be deduced efficiently.

In order to solve the accuracy and speed problems of page recommendation in Haijun et al. (2008), the authors had used information entropy of data in positive domain to find out the rough set rules. A new rough set important attribute mining algorithm based on information entropy was used, for Web page recommendation.

In Zafra et al. (2009), a navigation graph-based recommendation system was proposed, in which the navigation patterns of previous Website visitors are utilized to provide recommendations for newcomers.

In Inbarani et al. (2011), K-Means clustering approach was used for clustering user transactions a similarity based approach was used for page recommendation

REVIEW OF BICLUSTERING APPROACH

A clustering process needs to meet a number of challenges to be efficient. These challenges involve the definition of appropriate similarity or distance measures that will adequately capture the

Table 6. Summary of biclustering technique for web personalization

S. No	Author	Year	User/ Page	Method	Recommendation Method
1.	Hannah Inbarani et al.	2011	-	Biclustering	Similarity based recommendation

relations between data objects and guide properly the clustering process. The application of specific similarity (distance) measures depends on the underlying data nature and the data structures used for their representation. Hence, biclustering approaches were introduced for simultaneous clustering of users and pages. Most of the data mining approaches for Web personalization proposed in the previous works were based on either clustering or association rule mining. However, biclustering approach efficiently retrieves co occurrence navigation patterns of users. It proficiently combines the advantages clustering and association rule mining approaches. Hence, this thesis proposes approaches to solve the problems with clustering approaches and introduces new biclustering approaches for Web personalization. Table 6 provides a review of biclustering technique for Web personalization.

In Ouamani et al. (2007), Web personalization based on novel biclustering approach was proposed.

In Suryavanshi et al. (2005), a recommendation system prototype which suggests Web sites was presented. It collects browsing events from routers without neither user nor Web site effort. It used user clustering and page view clustering approaches for extracting patterns and KNN approach was used for page recommendation.

Recommendation Engine

The recommendation engine is the online component of a Web personalization system. The task of the recommendation engine is to compute a recommendation set for the current (active) user session, consisting of the objects (links, ads, text, products, and so forth) that most closely match the current user profile. The essential aspect of computing a recommendation set for a user is matching the current user's activity against aggregate usage profiles. The recommendation engine must be an online process, providing results quickly enough to avoid any perceived delay by the users.

CONCLUSION

In this chapter, a comprehensive discussion on the survey of various Web usage mining techniques for Web personalization process is provided. A key part of the personalization process is the generation of user models. This survey clearly describes the various Web usage mining techniques such as association rule mining, sequential pattern mining, clustering, and biclustering approaches used for creating user models. Another important and difficult challenge is the approach adopted for Web page recommendation. This survey also explains the approach adopted for Web page recommendation such as classification, rule generation, and probability based methods.

REFERENCES

Aggarwal, C. C., Wolf, J. L., Wu, K., & Yu, P. (1999). Horting hatches an egg: A new graph-theoretic approach to collaborative filtering. In *Proceedings of the ACM KDD Conference*, (pp. 201–212). ACM Press.

Anand, S. S., & Mobasher, B. (2007). Intelligent techniques for web personalization. *ACM Transactions on Internet Technology*, 7(4), 1–36. doi:10.1145/1278366.1278367

Arayaa, S., Silvab, M., & Weberc, R. (2004). A methodology for web usage mining and its application to target group identification. *Fuzzy Sets and Systems*, 148, 139–152. doi:10.1016/j.fss.2004.03.011

Bae, S. M., Ha, S. H., & Park, S. C. (2003). Fuzzy web ad selector based on web usage mining. *IEEE Proceedings on Intelligent Systems, 18*(6), 62-69.

Baraglia, R., & Silvestri, F. (2007). Dynamic personalization of web sites without user intervention. *Communications of the ACM, 50*(2), 63–67. doi:10.1145/1216016.1216022

Baumgarten, M., Bchner, A. G., Anand, S. S., Mulvenna, M. D., & Hughes, J. G. (2000). Navigation pattern discovery from internet data. In *Advances in Web Usage Analysis and User Profiling*. Berlin, Germany: Springer-Verlag. doi:10.1007/3-540-44934-5_5

Castellano, G., Fanelli, A. M., & Torsello, M. A. (2008). A web personalization system based on a neuro-fuzzy strategy. In *Proceedings of the Industrial Engineering and Management Systems Conference*, (pp. 1784-1785). IEEE.

Choa, Y. H., Kimb, J. K., & Kim, S. H. (2002). A personalized recommender system based on web usage mining and decision tree induction. *Expert Systems with Applications*, *23*, 329–342. doi:10.1016/S0957-4174(02)00052-0

Consortium, W. W. W. (1995). *The common log file format*. Retrieved from http://www.w3.org/Daemon/User/Config/Logging.html#common-logfile-format1995

Cooley, R. (2000). *Web usage mining: Discovery and application of interesting patterns from web data*. (Ph.D. Thesis). University of Minnesota. Minneapolis, MN.

Cooley, R., Mobasher, B., & Srivastava, J. (1999). Data preparation for mining world wide web browsing patterns. *Journal of Knowledge and Information Systems*, *1*(1), 5–32.

Cunha, C. R., & Jaccoud, C. F. B. (1997). Determining www user's next access and its application to prefetching. In *Proceedings of Computers and Communication* (pp. 1–3). IEEE Press.

G'ery, M., & Haddad, H. (2003). Evaluation of web usage mining approaches for user's next request prediction. [New Orleans, LA: WIDM.]. *Proceedings of WIDM, 2003*, 74–81.

Gunduz, S., & Ozsu, M. T. (2003). A web page prediction model based on click-stream tree representation of user behavior. In *Proceedings of ACM SIGKDD International Conference on Knowledge Discovery and Data Mining, KDD 2003*, (pp. 188-194). ACM Press.

Ha, S. H., Selamat, A., & Sigeru, O. (2004). Web page feature selection and classification neural networks. *Information Sciences*, *158*, 69–88. doi:10.1016/j.ins.2003.03.003

Haijun, X., Qi, Z., & Baoyi, W. (2008). Rough set page recommendation algorithm based on information entropy, In *Proceedings of the International Conference on Computer Science and Software Engineering*, (pp. 735 – 738). IEEE.

Inbarani, H., & Thangavel, K. (2009). Mining and analysis of clickstream patterns. In *Proceedings of the Foundations of Computational, Intelligence - Data Mining, Studies in Computational Intelligence*, (pp. 3-27). Springer.

Inbarani, H., & Thangavel, K. (2011). A robust biclustering approach for effective web personalization. In *Proceedings of the Visual Analytics and Interactive Technologies: Data, Text and Web Mining Applications*, (pp. 186-201). IEEE.

Inbarani, H., Thangavel, K., & Pethalakshmi, A. (2007). Rough set based feature selection for web usage mining. In *Proceedings of the Computational Intelligence and Multimedia Applications*, (pp. 33-38). IEEE.

Ishikawa, H., Ohta, M., Watanabe, T., Yokoyama, S., & Katayama, K. (2003). Toward active web usage mining for page recommendation and restructuring. [I-Know.]. *Proceedings of I-Know*, *2003*, 492–499.

Jenamani, M., Mohapatra, P. K. J., & Ghose, S. (2002). Online customized index synthesis in commercial web sites. In *Proceedings of IEEE Intelligent Systems*, (pp. 20-26). IEEE Press.

Jia, M., Yey, S., Liz, X., & Dickerson, J. (2007). Web site recommendation using HTTP traffic. In *Proceedings of the Seventh IEEE International Conference on Data Mining,* (pp. 535—540). IEEE Press.

Jin, X., Mobasher, B., & Zhou, Y. (2005). A web recommendation system based on maximum entropy. In *Proceedings of the International Conference on Information Technology: Coding and Computing (ITCC 2005),* (pp. 213 – 218). ITCC.

Joachims, T., Freitag, D., & Mitchell, T. (1997). WebWatcher: A tour guide for the world wide web. In *Proceedings of IJCAI,* (pp. 770-777). IJCAI.

Lee, C.-H., Lo, Y.-L., & Fu, Y.-H. (2010). A novel prediction model based on hierarchical characteristic of web site. In *Proceedings of Expert Systems with Applications* (pp. 3422–3430). IEEE. doi:10.1016/j.eswa.2010.08.128

Letizia, H. L. (1995). An agent that assists web browsing. In *Proceedings of International Conference on Artificial Intelligence.* IEEE.

Menon, K., & Dagli, C. H. (2003). Web personalization using neuro-fuzzy clustering algorithms. In *Proceedings of the Fuzzy Information Processing Society,* (pp. 525-529). Fuzzy Information Processing Society.

Mobasher, B., Cooley, R., & Srivastava, J. (2000). Automatic personalization based on web usage mining. *Communications of the ACM, 43*(8), 142–151. doi:10.1145/345124.345169

Mobasher, B., Dai, H., Luo, T., & Nakagawa, M. (2001). Effective personalization based on association rule discovery from web usage data. In *Proceedings of Web Information and Data Management* (pp. 9–15). IEEE.

Mobasher, B., Dai, H., Luo, T., & Nakagawa, M. (2002). Discovery and evaluation of aggregate usage profiles for web personalization. *Data Mining and Knowledge Discovery, 6,* 61–82. doi:10.1023/A:1013232803866

Nasraoui, O., & Pavuluri, M. (2004). Accurate web recommendations based on profile-specific URL-predictor neural networks. [New York, NY: IEEE.]. *Proceedings of the WWW, 2004,* 17–22.

Ngu, D. S. W., & Xindong. (1997). SiteHelper: A localized agent that helps incremental exploration of the world wide web. *Computer Networks and ISDN Systems, 29*(8-13), 1249-1255.

Ouamani, F., Jrad, Z., Aufaure, M. A., Zghal, H. B., & Ghezala, H. B. (2007). PWUM: A web usage mining multi-agent architecture for web personalization. In *Proceedings of the IADIS International Conference WWW/Internet,* (pp. 272-276). IADIS.

Pabarskaite, Z., & Raudys, A. (2007). A process of knowledge discovery from weblog data: Systematization and critical review. *Journal of Intelligent Information Systems, 28,* 79–104. doi:10.1007/s10844-006-0004-1

Pal, S. K., Talwar, V., & Mitra, P. (2002). Web mining in soft computing framework: Relevance, state of the art and future directions. *IEEE Transactions on Neural Networks, 13*(I.5), 1163–1177.

Pedmanabhan, V. N., & Mogul, J. C. (1996). Using predictive pre-fetching to improve world wide web latency. *Computer Communication Review, 26*(3), 22–36. doi:10.1145/235160.235164

Perkowitz, M., & Etzioni, O. (1998). Adaptive sites: Automatically synthesizing web pages. In *Proceedings of Artificial Intelligence* (pp. 727–732). IEEE.

Picariello, A., & Sansone, C. (2008). A web usage mining algorithm for web personalization. *Intelligent Decision Technologies, 2,* 219–230.

Pierrakos, D., Paliouras, G. O., Papatheodorou, C., & Spyropoulos, C. D. (2003). Web usage mining as a tool for personalization: A survey. *User Modeling and User-Adapted Interaction, 3,* 311–372. doi:10.1023/A:1026238916441

Puntheeranurak, S., & Tsuji, H. (2005). Mining web logs for a personalized recommender system. In *Proceedings of International Conference on Information Technology: Research and Education,* (pp. 445 – 448). IEEE Press.

Schecter, M. K. S., & Smith, M. (1998). Using path profiles to predict HTTP request. In *Proceedings of 7th International WWW Conference,* (pp. 457-467). IEEE.

Shahabi, C., & Banaei-Kashani, F. (2003). Efficient and anonymous web-usage mining for web personalization. *INFORMS Journal on Computing.* Retrieved from http://www.csee. umbc.edu/~kolari1/Mining/papers/Shahabi-WebKDD2001-BookChapter.pdf

Silvestri, F., Baraglia, R., Palmerini, P., & O, M. S. (2004). On-line generation of suggestions for web users. In *Proceedings of Information Technology: Coding and Computing,* (pp. 1-3). IEEE.

Srivastava, J., Cooley, R., Deshpande, M., & Tan, P.-N. (2000). Web usage mining: Discovery and applications of usage patterns from web data. *SIGKDD Explorations, 1*(2), 12–23. doi:10.1145/846183.846188

Suryavanshi, B. S., Shiri, N., & Mudur, S. P. (2005). A fuzzy hybrid collaborative filtering technique for web personalization. In *Proceedings of Intelligent Techniques for Web Personalization.* IEEE.

Tan, X., Yao, M., & Xu, M. (2004). An effective technique for personalization recommendation based on access sequential patterns. In *Proceedings of Asia – Pacific Conference on Services Computing,* (pp. 42 – 46). IEEE.

Thor, A., Golovin, N., & Rahm, E. (2005). Adaptive website recommendations with AWESOME. *The VLDB Journal, 14*(4), 357–372. doi:10.1007/s00778-005-0160-x

Wang, T., & Ren, Y. (2009). Research on personalized recommendation based on web usage mining using collaborative filtering technique. *WSEAS Transactions on Information Science and Applications, 1*(6), 62–72.

Wang, Y., Dai, W., & Yuan, Y. (2008). Website browsing aid: A navigation graph-based recommendation system. *Decision Support Systems, 45,* 387–400. doi:10.1016/j.dss.2007.05.006

Wang, Y., Li, Z., & Zhang, Y. (2005). Mining sequential association-rule for improving web document prediction. In *Proceedings of the Sixth International Conference on Computational Intelligence and Multimedia Applications (ICCIMA 2005),* (pp. 146 – 151). ICCIMA.

Wanga, F.-H., & Shaob, H.-M. (2004). Effective personalized recommendation based on time-framed navigation clustering and association mining. *Expert Systems with Applications, 27,* 365–377. doi:10.1016/j.eswa.2004.05.005

Xu, G., Zhang, Y., & Zhou, X. (2006). Discovering task-oriented usage pattern for web recommendation. In *Proceedings of the Seventeenth Australasian Database Conference,* (pp. 167-174). IEEE.

Yan, T. W., Jacobsen, M., Garcia-Molina, H., & Dayal, U. (1996). From user access patterns to dynamic hypertext linking. *Journal of Computer Networks and ISDN Systems, 28,* 7–11.

Zafra, A., Romero, C., Ventura, S., & Viedma, E. H. (2009). Multi-instance genetic programming for web index recommendation. *Expert Systems with Applications, 36,* 11470–11479. doi:10.1016/j.eswa.2009.03.059

Zhou, B., Hui, S. C., & Chang, K. (2006). Enhancing mobile web access using intelligent recommendations. *IEEE Intelligent Systems*, *21*(1), 28–34. doi:10.1109/MIS.2006.5

Zhou, B., Hui, S. C., & Fong, A. C. M. (2006). An effective approach for periodic web personalization. In *Proceedings of IEEE/WIC/ACM International Conference on Web Intelligence*, (pp. 284-292). IEEE/WIC/ACM.

Compilation of References

Abbar, S., Bouzeghoub, M., & Lopez, S. (2009). Context-aware recommender systems: A service-oriented approach. In *Proceedings of the 35ᵗʰ Conference on Very Large Data-Bases.* IEEE.

Abbasi, A., Chen, H., & Salem, A. (2008). Sentiment analysis in multiple languages: Feature selection for opinion classification in web forums. *ACM Transactions on Information Systems.* Retrieved from http://ai.arizona.edu/intranet/papers/AhmedAbbasi_SentimentTOIS.pdf

Abbott, D. W. (1999). Combining models to improve classifier accuracy and robustness, In *Proceedings International Conference on Information Fusion*, (pp. 1-7). Sunnyvale, CA: Information Fusion.

Aberg, J. (2002). *Live help systems: An approach to intelligent help for web information system*s. (Ph.D. Thesis). Linköpings Universitet. Linköping, Sweden.

Aciar, S., Zhang, D., Simoff, S., & Debenham, J. (2006). Informed recommender agent: Utilizing consumer product reviews through text mining. In *Proceedings of the WI-IATW*, (pp. 37 – 40). WI-IATW.

Addis, A., Armano, G., & Vargiu, E. (2010). Assessing progressive filtering to perform hierarchical text categorization in presence of input imbalance. In *Proceedings of International Conference on Knowledge Discovery and Information Retrieval*, (pp. 14-23). IEEE.

Addis, A., Armano, G., Giuliani, A., & Vargiu, E. (2010). A recommender system based on a generic contextual advertising approach. In *Proceedings of ISCC 2010: IEEE Symposium on Computers and Communications*, (pp. 859–861). IEEE Press.

Addis, A., Armano, G., Giuliani, A., & Vargiu, E. (2010). A novel recommender system inspired by contextual advertising approach. In *Proceedings of IADIS International Conference Intelligent Systems and Agents 2010*, (pp. 67-74). IADIS.

Addis, A., Armano, G., & Vargiu, E. (2009). A novel semantic approach to document collections. *IADIS International Journal on Computer Science and Information Systems, 4*(2), 73–85.

Adetunmbi, A. O., Falaki, S. O., Adewale, O. S., & Alese, B. K. (2008). Network intrusion detection based on rough set and k-nearest neighbor. *International Journal of Computing and ICT Research, 2*(1), 60–66.

Adomavicius, G., & Tuzhilin, A. (1999). User profiling in personalization applications through rule discovery and validation. In *Proceedings of the 5ᵗʰ ACM SIGKDD International Conference on KDD*, (pp. 377-381). San Diego, CA: ACM Press.

Adomavicius, G., & Tuzhilin, A. (2008). Context-aware recommender systems. In *Proceedings of the 2008 ACM Conference on Recommender Systems*, (pp. 335–336). New York, NY: ACM.

Adomavicius, G., Sankaranarayanan, R., Sen, S., & Tuzhilin, A. (2005). Incorporating contextual information in recommender systems using a multidimensional approach. *ACM Transactions on Information Systems, 23*(1), 103–145. doi:10.1145/1055709.1055714

Adomavicius, G., & Tuzhilin, A. (2001). Expert-driven validation of rule-based user models in personalization applications. *Data Mining and Knowledge Discovery, 5*(1/2), 33–58. doi:10.1023/A:1009839827683

Adomavicius, G., & Tuzhilin, A. (2005). Toward the next generation of recommender systems: A survey of the state-of-the-art and possible extensions. *IEEE Transactions on Knowledge and Data Engineering*, *17*(6). doi:10.1109/TKDE.2005.99

Aerts, A., Bierhoff, P., & De Bra, P. (1999). Web-CS: Infrastructure for web-based competitions. In *Proceedings of the WebNet 1999 Conference*, (pp. 69-74). WebNet.

Agelli, M., Armano, G., Cherchi, G., Clemente, M. L., & Ghironi, D. (2008). Experimenting combinations of content-based and collaborative filtering with a photo recommender system. *Communications of SIWN, 5*, 33–38.

Aggarwal, C. C., Wolf, J. L., Wu, K., & Yu, P. (1999). Horting hatches an egg: A new graph-theoretic approach to collaborative filtering. In *Proceedings of the ACM KDD Conference*, (pp. 201–212). ACM Press.

Aggarwal, C. C., Sun, Z., & Yu, P. S. (2002). Fast algorithms for online generation of profile association rules. *IEEE Transactions on Knowledge and Data Engineering*, *14*(5), 1017–1028. doi:10.1109/TKDE.2002.1033771

Agrawal, R., Mannila, H., Srikant, R., Toivonen, H., & Verkamo, A. I. (1996). Fast discovery of association rules. In *Advances in Knowledge Discovery and Data Mining* (pp. 307–328). AAAI Press.

Ahn, H., & Kim, K. (2004). Using a clustering genetic algorithm to support customer segmentation for personalized recommender systems. *Artificial Intelligence Simulations*, *3397*, 409–415.

Ahn, H., & Kim, K. (2008). A recommender system using GA K-means clustering in an online Shopping market. *Expert Systems with Applications*, *34*(2), 1200–1209. doi:10.1016/j.eswa.2006.12.025

Al Masum, S. M., Islam, M. T., & Ishizuka, M. (2006). ASNA: An intelligent agent for retrieving and classifying news on the basis of emotion-affinity. In *Proceedings of the Web Technologies and Internet Commerce, International Conference*, (p. 133). IEEE.

Alcala, J., Bobadilla, J., Hernando, A., & Ortega, F. (2011). *Improving collaborative filtering recommender system results and performance using genetic algorithms*. Madrid, Spain: Universidad Politecnica de Madrid.

Alcala, J., Bobadilla, J., Hernando, A., & Ortega, F. (2011). Improving collaborative filtering recommender system results and performance using genetic algorithms. *Knowledge-Based Systems, 24*, 1310–1316. doi:10.1016/j.knosys.2011.06.005

Alcala, J., Bobadilla, J., Hernando, A., & Ortega, F. (2012). A collaborative filtering similarity measure based on singularities. *Information Processing & Management, 48*(2).

Aleksander, I., & Morton, H. (1995). *An introduction to neural computing*. New York, NY: International Thompson Computer Press.

Allred, C. R., Smith, S. M., & Swinyard, W. R. (2006). E-shopping lovers and fearful conservatives: A market segmentation analyses. *International Journal of Retail and Distribution Management*, *34*(4/5), 308–333. doi:10.1108/09590550610660251

Al-Shamri, & Bharadwaj, K. K. (2008). Fuzzy-genetic approach to recommender systems based on a novel hybrid user model. *Expert Systems with Applications*, *35*(3), 1386–1399. doi:10.1016/j.eswa.2007.08.016

Al-Shamri. Bharadwaj, K. K., & Yahya, H. M. (2008). *Fuzzy-genetic approach to recommender systems based on a novel hybrid user model*. New Delhi, India: Jawaharlal Nehru University.

Al-Smadi, M., Guetl, C., & Helic, D. (2009). Towards a standardized e-assessment system: Motivations, challenges and first findings. In *Proceedings of the 4th International Conference on Mobile and Computer Aided Learning, ICML*. Amman, Jordan: ICML.

Alspector, J., Kolez, A., & Karunanithi, N. (1998). Comparing feature based and clique-based user models for movie selection. In *Proceedings of the 3rd ACM Conference on Digital Libraries*, (pp. 11-18). Pittsburgh, PA: ACM Press.

Alsultanny, Y. A., & Aqel, M. M. (2003). Pattern recognition using multilayer neural-genetic algorithm. *Neurocomputing*, *51*, 237–247. doi:10.1016/S0925-2312(02)00619-7

Amandi, A., & Schiaffino, S. N. (2000). User profiling with case-based reasoning and Bayesian networks. In *Proceedings of the IBERAMIA-SBIA 2000 Open Discussion Track*, (pp. 12–21). IBERAMIA-SBIA.

Amiel, T., & Reeves, T. C. (2008). Design-based research and educational technology: Rethinking technology and the research agenda. *Journal of Educational Technology & Society, 11*(4), 29–40.

Anagnostopoulos, A., Broder, A. Z., Gabrilovich, E., Josifovski, V., & Riedel, L. (2007). Just-in-time contextual advertising. In *Proceedings of the 16th ACM Conference on Information and Knowledge Management,* (pp. 331–340). New York, NY: ACM Press.

Anand, D., & Bharadwaj, K. K. (2011). *Utilizing various sparsity measures for enhancing accuracy of collaborative recommender systems based on local and global similarities.* New Delhi, India: Jawaharlal Nehru University. doi:10.1016/j.eswa.2010.09.141

Anand, S. S., & Mobasher, B. (2007). Contextual recommendation. In *Discovering and Deploying User and Content Profiles* (pp. 142–160). Berlin, Germany: Springer. doi:10.1007/978-3-540-74951-6_8

Anand, S. S., & Mobasher, B. (2007). Intelligent techniques for web personalization. *ACM Transactions on Internet Technology, 7*(4), 1–36. doi:10.1145/1278366.1278367

Anderson, C. (2006). *The long tail: Why the future of business is selling less of more.* Berlin, Germany: Hyperion Verlag.

Anderson, C. H., & Kaminsky, M. (1985). The outshopper problem: A group approach for small business retailers. *American Journal of Small Business, 9*(4), 34–45.

Anderson, J. P. (1985). *Computer security threat monitoring and surveillance. Technical Report.* Fort Washington, PA: J.P. Anderson Company.

Andre, E., & Rist, T. (2002). Form adaptive hypertext to personalized web companions. *Communications of the ACM, 45*(5), 43–46. doi:10.1145/506218.506243

Angeline, P. J., Saunders, G. M., & Pollack, J. B. (1994). An evolutionary algorithm that constructs recurrent neural networks. *IEEE Transactions on Neural Networks, 5*(1), 54–65. doi:10.1109/72.265960

Ansari, A., Essegaier, S., & Kohli, R. (2000). Internet recommendation systems. *JMR, Journal of Marketing Research, 37*, 363–375. doi:10.1509/jmkr.37.3.363.18779

Antonopoulus, N., & Salter, J. (2006). Cinema screen recommender agent: Combining collaborative and content-based filtering. *IEEE Intelligent Systems, 21*(1), 35–41. doi:10.1109/MIS.2006.4

Apte, C., Grossman, E., Pednault, E., Rosen, B., Tipu, F., & White, B. (1999). *Insurance risk modeling using data mining technology.* Report RC-21314. Yorktown Heights, NY: IBM Research Division.

Arayaa, S., Silvab, M., & Weberc, R. (2004). A methodology for web usage mining and its application to target group identification. *Fuzzy Sets and Systems, 148*, 139–152. doi:10.1016/j.fss.2004.03.011

Arevian, G. (2007). Recurrent neural networks for robust real-world text classification. In *Proceedings of the 2007 IEEE/WIC/ACM International Conference on Web Intelligence.* Silicon Valley, CA: IEEE/WIC/ACM.

Arevian, G., & Panchev, C. (2007). Robust text classification using a hysteresis-driven extended SRN. In *Proceedings of the 2007 International Conference on Artificial Neural Networks.* Porto, Portugal: IEEE.

Arevian, G., & Panchev, C. (2007). Optimizing the hystereses of a two context layer RNN for text classification. In *Proceedings of the International Joint Conference on Neural Networks.* Orlando, FL: IEEE.

Armano, G., & Vargiu, E. (2010). A unifying view of contextual advertising and recommender systems. In *Proceedings of International Conference on Knowledge Discovery and Information Retrieval,* (pp. 22–28). IEEE.

Armano, G., Giuliani, A., & Vargiu, E. (2011). Experimenting text summarization techniques for contextual advertising. In *Proceedings of the Italian Workshop on Information Retrieval, CEUR Workshop,* (Vol. 704). CEUR.

Armano, G., Giuliani, A., & Vargiu, E. (2011). Semantic enrichment of contextual advertising by using concepts. In *Proceedings of International Conference on Knowledge Discovery and Information Retrieval.* IEEE.

Armano, G., Giuliani, A., & Vargiu, E. (2011). Studying the impact of text summarization on contextual advertising. In *Proceedings of 8th International Workshop on Text-Based Information Retrieval.* IEEE.

Armano, G., de Gemmis, M., Semeraro, G., & Vargiu, E. (Eds.). (2010). *Intelligent information access*. Berlin, Germany: Springer-Verlag. doi:10.1007/978-3-642-14000-6

Armano, G., Marchesi, M., & Murru, A. (2005). A hybrid genetic-neural architecture for stock indexes forecasting. *Information Sciences*, *170*, 3–33. doi:10.1016/j.ins.2003.03.023

Aroyo, L., Cristea, A., & Dicheva, D. (2002). A layered approach towards domain authoring support. [ICAI.]. *Proceedings of the ICAI*, *2002*, 615–621.

Asnicar, F. A., & Tasso, C. (1999) ifWeb: A prototype of user model-based intelligent agent for document filtering and navigation in the world wide web. In *Proceedings of the Workshop Adaptive Systems and User Modeling on the World Wide Web, Sixth International Conference on User Modeling*. IEEE.

Avery, C., Resnick, P., & Zeckhauser, R. (1999). The market for evaluations. *The American Economic Review*, *89*(3), 564–584. doi:10.1257/aer.89.3.564

Avery, C., & Zeckerhauser, R. (1997). Recommender systems for evaluating computer messages. *Communications of the ACM*, *40*(3). doi:10.1145/245108.245127

Avi, G., Sridhar, S., & Christopher, L. T. (2008). Neo-Rawlsian fringes: A new approach to market segmentation and new product development. *Journal of Product Innovation Management*, *25*(5), 491–507. doi:10.1111/j.1540-5885.2008.00316.x

Avnimelech, R., & Intrator, N. (1999). Boosting regression estimators. *Neural Computation*, *11*, 491–513. doi:10.1162/089976699300016746

Bae, S. M., Ha, S. H., & Park, S. C. (2003). Fuzzy web ad selector based on web usage mining. *IEEE Proceedings on Intelligent Systems*, *18*(6), 62-69.

Balabanovic, M., & Shoham, Y. (1997). Fab: Content-based, collaborative recommendation. *Communications of the ACM*, *40*(3), 66–72. doi:10.1145/245108.245124

Bandyopadhyay, S., Murthy, C. A., & Pal, S. K. (1995). Pattern classification with genetic algorithms. *Pattern Recognition Letters*, *16*, 801–808. doi:10.1016/0167-8655(95)00052-I

Bandyopadhyay, S., & Pal, S. K. (2007). *Classification and learning using genetic algorithms: Applications in bioinformatics and web intelligence*. Berlin, Germany: Springer.

Baraglia, R., & Silvestri, F. (2007). Dynamic personalization of web sites without user intervention. *Communications of the ACM*, *50*(2), 63–67. doi:10.1145/1216016.1216022

Barker, K. (1999). *Quality guidelines for technology assisted distance education*. New York, NY: FuturEd Consulting Education Futurists.

Basu, C., Hirsh, H., & Cohen, W. W. (1998). Recommendation as classification: Using social and content-based information in recommendation. In *Proceedings of the 15th National Conference on Artificial Intelligence*, (pp. 714–720). IEEE.

Baumgarten, M., Bchner, A. G., Anand, S. S., Mulvenna, M. D., & Hughes, J. G. (2000). Navigation pattern discovery from internet data. In *Advances in Web Usage Analysis and User Profiling*. Berlin, Germany: Springer-Verlag. doi:10.1007/3-540-44934-5_5

Belkin, N. J., & Croft, W. B. (1992). Information filtering and information retrieval: Two sides of the same coin? *Communications of the ACM*, *35*(12), 29–38. doi:10.1145/138859.138861

Benamara, F., Cesarano, C., Picariello, A., Reforgiato, D., & Subrahmanian, V. (2007). Sentiment analysis: Adjectives and adverbs are better than adjectives alone. In *Proceedings of the International Conference on Weblogs and Social Media (ICWSM)*, (pp. 203–206). ICWSM.

Bengio, Y. (1996). *Neural networks for speech and sequence recognition*. London, UK: International Thomson Computer Press.

Bennett, J., & Lanning, S. (2007). *The Netflix prize*. San Jose, CA: ACM Press.

Berenji, H. R. (1991). Refinement of approximate reasoning-based controllers by reinforcement learning. In *Proceedings of the Eighth International Machine Learning Workshop*, (pp. 475-479). Evanston, IL: IEEE.

Bernal, J., Bobadilla, J., & Serradilla, F. (2010). A new collaborative filtering metric that improves the behaviour of recommender systems. *Knowledge-Based Systems, 23*(6), 520–528. doi:10.1016/j.knosys.2010.03.009

Berry, J. A. M., & Linoff, G. (1997). *Data mining techniques for marketing sales and customer support*. New York, NY: John Wiley & Sons Inc.

Berry, M. J., & Linoff, G. (1997). *Data mining techniques*. New York, NY: John Wiley.

Biggam, J. (2010). Using automated assessment feedback to enhance the quality of student learning in universities: A case study. In *Technology Enhanced Learning: Quality of Teaching and Educational Reform* (pp. 188–194). Athens, Greece: Springer. doi:10.1007/978-3-642-13166-0_27

Bilgic, M. (2004). *Explanation for recommender systems: Satisfaction vs. promotion.* (PhD Thesis). University of Texas at Austin. Austin, TX.

Billsu, D. S., & Pazzani, M. (1997). Learning and revising user profiles: The identification of interesting. *Machine Learning, 27*, 313–331. doi:10.1023/A:1007369909943

Billsus, D., & Pazzani, M. (1999). A hybrid user model for news story classification, user modeling. In *Proceedings of the Seventh International Conference (UM 1999)*, (pp. 98-108). Banff, Canada: UM.

Billsus, D., & Pazzani, M. J. (1998). Learning collaborative information filters. In *Proceedings of the 15th International Conference on Machine Learning*, (pp. 46–54). IEEE.

Birenbaum, M., Kimron, H., Shilton, H., & Shahaf-Bar, R. (2009). Cycles of inquiry: Formative assessment in service of learning in classrooms and in school-based professional communities. *Studies in Educational Evaluation, 35*, 130–149. doi:10.1016/j.stueduc.2010.01.001

Black, P., & Wiliam, D. (2009). Developing the theory of formative assessment. *Assessment. Evaluation and Accountability, 21*(1), 5–31. doi:10.1007/s11092-008-9068-5

Bobadilla, J., & Serradilla, F. (2009). The incidence of sparsity on collaborative filtering metrics. In *Proceedings of the Australian Database Conference ADC 92*. ADC.

Bobadilla, J., Hernando, A., & Serradilla, F. (2009). Collaborative filtering adapted to recommender systems of e-learning. *Knowledge-Based Systems, 22*, 261–265. doi:10.1016/j.knosys.2009.01.008

Bodea, C., & Dascalu, M. (2009). A parametrized web-based testing model for project management. In *Proceedings of the Advances in Web-Based Learning, ICWL,* (pp. 68–72). Aachen, Germany: Springer.

Bodea, C., & Dascalu, M. (2010). Competency-based e-assessment in project management and firm performance: A case study. In *Proceedings of the 4th Conference on European Computing Conference,* (pg. 76-81). Bucharest, Romania: WSEAS.

Boné, R., Assaad, M., & Crucianu, M. (2003). Boosting recurrent neural networks for time series prediction. In *Proceedings of the International Conference on Artificial Neural Nets and Genetic Algorithms. France,* (pp. 18-22). Roane, France: Springer.

Boratto, L., & Carta, S. (2010). State-of-the-art in group recommendation and new approaches for automatic identification of groups. In Soro, A., Vargiu, E., Armano, G., & Paddeu, G. (Eds.), *Information Retrieval and Mining in Distributed Environments* (pp. 1–20). Berlin, Germany: Springer-Verlag. doi:10.1007/978-3-642-16089-9_1

Bramer, M. (2008). *Principles of data mining*. London, UK: Springer-Verlag.

Breese, J., Heckerman, D., & Kadie, C. (1998). Empirical analysis of predictive algorithms for collaborative filtering. In *Proceedings of the 14ᵗʰ Conference on Uncertainty in Artificial Intelligence,* (pp. 43–52). San Francisco, CA: Morgan Kaufmann.

Breiman, L., Friedman, J. H., Olshen, R. A., & Stone, C. J. (1984). *Classification and regression trees*. London, UK: Wadsworth Publisher.

Broder, A., Fontoura, M., Josifovski, V., & Riedel, L. (2007). A semantic approach to contextual advertising. In *Proceedings of the 30ᵗʰ Annual International ACM SIGIR Conference on Research and Development in Information Retrieval,* (pp. 559–566). New York, NY: ACM Press.

Broderick, A. J., Mueller, R. D., & Greenley, G. E. (2006). Applications of the behavioural homogeneity evaluation framework: The predictive ability of consumer involvement for international food market segmentation. *International Review of Retail, Distribution and Consumer Research, 16*(5), 533–557. doi:10.1080/09593960600980154

Bruke, R. (2002). Hybrid recommender systems: Survey and experiments. *Journal of User Modelling and User Adapted Interaction, 12*(4), 331–370. doi:10.1023/A:1021240730564

Brusilovsky, P. (2001). Adaptive educational hypermedia. In *Proceedings of the 10ᵗʰ International Peg Conference (Peg 2001)*, (pp. 8-12). Peg.

Brusilovsky, P., & Cooper, D. (1999). ADAPTS: Adaptive hypermedia for a web-based performance support system. In *Proceedings of 2ⁿᵈ Workshop on Adaptive Systems and User Modeling on WWW at 8ᵗʰ International Word Wide Web Conference and 7ᵗʰ International Conference on User Modeling.* Retrieved October 15, 2002 from http://wwwis.win.tue.nl/asum99/brusilovsky/brusilovsky.html

Brusilovsky, P., & Schwartz, E. (1997). User as student: Towards an adaptive interface for advanced web-based applications. In *Proceedings of the 6ᵗʰ International Conference on User Modeling,* (pp. 177-188). IEEE.

Bruwer, J., & Li, E. (2007). Wine-related lifestyle (WRL) market segmentation: Demographic and behavioural factors. *Journal of Wine Research, 18*(1), 19–34. doi:10.1080/09571260701526865

Buabin, E. (2011). Boosted hybrid recurrent neural classifier for text document classification on the reuters news text corpus. In *Proceedings of the 3ʳᵈ ICMLC 2011.* IEEE Press.

Buabin, E. (2011). Boosted hybrid recurrent neural classifier for text document classification on the reuters news text corpus. In *Proceedings of the 3ʳᵈ ICMLC 2011.* IEEE.

Buabin, E. (2012). Hybrid neural architecture for intelligent recommender system classification unit design. In Dehuri, S., Patra, M. R., Misra, B. B., & Jagadev, A. K. (Eds.), *Intelligent Techniques in Recommendation Systems: Contextual Advancements and New Methods.* Hershey, PA: IGI Global.

Buczak, A. L., Zimmerman, J., & Kurapati, K. (2002). Personalization: Improving ease-of-use, trust and accuracy of a TV show recommender. [Malaga, Spain: IEEE.]. *Proceedings of Personalization in Future TV, 2002, 3*–12.

Burge, P., Shawe-Taylor, J., Cooke, C., Moreau, Y., Preneel, B., & Stoermann, C. (1997). Fraud detection and management in mobile telecommunications networks. In *Proceedings of the 2nd European Conference on Security and Detection,* (pp. 91–96). Security and Detection.

Burke, R. (2002). *Hybrid recommender systems: Survey and experiments.* Fullerton, CA: California State University.

Burke, R. (2002). Hybrid recommender systems: survey and experiments. *User Modeling and User-Adapted Interaction, 12,* 331–370. doi:10.1023/A:1021240730564

Burke, R. (2007). Hybrid web recommender systems. *Lecture Notes in Computer Science, 4321,* 377–408. doi:10.1007/978-3-540-72079-9_12

Butler, D., & Sellbom, M. (2002). Barrier to adopting technology for teaching and learning. *EDUCAUSE Quarterly, 2.* Retrieved March 16, 2003 from http://www.educause.edu/ir/library/pdf/EQM0223.pdf

Butz, C. (2002). Exploiting contextual independencies in web search and user profiling. In *Proceedings of World Congress on Computational Intelligence,* (pp. 1051–1056). IEEE.

Buzzetto-More, N., & Alade, A. J. (2006). Best practices in e-assessment. *Journal of Information Technology Education, 5,* 251–269.

Bygvra, S., & Westlund, H. (2004). Shopping behaviour in the Oresund region before and after the establishment of the fixed link between Denmark and Sweden. *GeoJournal, 61,* 41–52. doi:10.1007/s10708-004-0876-y

Byvatov, E., & Schneider, G. (2004). SVM-based feature selection for characterization of focused compound collections. *Journal of Chemical Information and Computer Sciences, 44,* 993–999. doi:10.1021/ci0342876

Cadez, I. V., Smyth, P., & Mannila, H. (2001). Probabilistic modeling of transaction data with applications to profiling, visualization, and prediction. In *Proceedings of the Seventh ACM SIGKDD International Conference on Knowledge Discovery and Data Mining (KDD),* (pp. 37–46). ACM Press.

Callan, J., Smeaton, A., Beaulieu, M., Borlund, P., Brusilovsky, P., & Chalmers, M. … Toms, E. (2003). *Personalisation and recommender systems in digital libraries*. Joint NSF-EU DELOS Working Group Report. Retrieved April 24, 2004 from http://www.dli2.nsf.gov/internationalprojects/working_group_reports/perso-nalisation.htm

CALM. (2012). *Website*. Retrieved from http://clamproject.org/

Candillier, L., Meyer, F., & Fessant, F. (2008). *Designing specific weighted similarity measures to improve collaborative filtering systems*. Paper presented at the Industrial Conference on Data Mining. Leipzig, Germany.

Capobianco, A. (2002). *Stratégies d'aide en ligne contextuelles: Acquisition d'expertises, modélisation et évaluation expérimentale*. (Thèse de Doctorat). Université Henri Poincaré. Nancy, France.

Cardie, C., Rogers, S., Schroedl, S., & Wagstaff, K. (2001). Constrained k-means clustering with background knowledge. In *Proceedings of the 18th International Conference on Machine Learning*, (pp. 577-584). IEEE.

Carrasco, J., Fain, D., Lang, K., & Zhukov, L. (2003). Clustering of bipartite advertiser-keyword graph. In *Proceedings of the Workshop on Clustering Large Datasets, IEEE Conference on Data Mining*. IEEE Computer Society Press.

Castellano, G., Fanelli, A. M., & Torsello, M. A. (2008). A web personalization system based on a neuro-fuzzy strategy. In *Proceedings of the Industrial Engineering and Management Systems Conference*, (pp. 1784-1785). IEEE.

Celma, O. (2008). *Music recommendation and discovery in the long tail*. Barcelona, Spain: Universitat Pompeu Fabra.

Chakrabarti, S., Dom, B. E., Kumar, S. R., Raghaban, P., Rajgopalan, S., & Tomkins, A. (2000). Mining the web's link structure. *IEEE Computer*, *32*(8), 60–67. doi:10.1109/2.781636

Chang, H. Y. A., & Zhang, F. (2006). Collaborative filtering algorithm employing genetic clustering to ameliorate the scalability issue. In *Proceedings of the IEEE International Conference on e-Business Engineering*, (pp. 331–338). IEEE Press.

Chang-Shing, L., Zhi-Wei, J., & Lin-Kai, H. (2005). A fuzzy ontology and its application to news summarization. *IEEE Transactions on Systems, Man, and Cybernetics. Part B*, *35*(5), 859–880.

Chan, J. S. P., Jain, R., & Xia, Y. (2008). Market segmentation, liquidity spillover, and closed-end country fund discounts. *Journal of Financial Markets*, *11*(4), 377–399. doi:10.1016/j.finmar.2008.01.005

Chen, M., La Paugh, A. S., & Singh, J. P. (2002). Predicting category accesses for a user in a structured information space. In *Proceedings of the ACM SIGIR Conference on Research and Development in Information Retrieval*, (pp. 65-72). ACM Press.

Chen, F. (2001). Market segmentation, advanced demand information, and supply chain Performance. *Manufacturing and Service Operations Management*, *3*(1), 53–67. doi:10.1287/msom.3.1.53.9993

Chen, T.-M., Lu, C.-C., & Li, W.-H. (2004). *Prediction of splice sites with dependency graphs and their expanded Bayesian networks*. Oxford, UK: Oxford University Press. doi:10.1093/bioinformatics/bti025

Chen, Y.-W. (2007). *Combining SVMs with various feature selection strategies. (Master of Science)*. Taipei, Taiwan: National Taiwan University.

Chiang, J.-H., & Yan-Cheng, C. (2004). An intelligent news recommender agent for filtering and categorizing large volumes of text corpus. *International Journal of Intelligent Systems*, *19*, 201–216. doi:10.1002/int.10136

Chidanand, A., Edna, G., Edwin, P. D., Pednault, B. K. R., Fateh, A. T., & Brian, W. (1999). Probabilistic estimation-based data mining for discovering insurance risks. *IEEE Intelligent Systems*, *14*(6), 49–58. doi:10.1109/5254.809568

Choa, Y. H., Kimb, J. K., & Kim, S. H. (2002). A personalized recommender system based on web usage mining and decision tree induction. *Expert Systems with Applications*, *23*, 329–342. doi:10.1016/S0957-4174(02)00052-0

Cho, S.-B. (1999). Pattern recognition with neural networks combined by genetic algorithm. *Fuzzy Sets and Systems*, *103*, 339–347. doi:10.1016/S0165-0114(98)00232-2

Chouaib, H., Terrades, O. R., Tabbone, S., Cloppet, F., & Vincent, N. (2008). Feature selection combining genetic algorithm and Adaboost classifiers. In *Proceedings of the 19ᵗʰ International Conference on Pattern Recognition.* IEEE Press.

Cho, Y. H., Kim, J. K., & Kim, S. H. (2002). A personalized recommender system based on web usage mining and decision tree induction. *Expert Systems with Applications, 23,* 329–342. doi:10.1016/S0957-4174(02)00052-0

Ciaramaita, M., Murdock, V., & Plachouras, V. (2008). Online learning from click data for sponsored search. In *Proceeding of the 17ᵗʰ International Conference on World Wide Web.* ACM Press.

Ciaramaita, M., Murdock, V., & Plachouras, V. (2008). Semantic associations for contextual advertising. *Journal of Electronic Commerce Research, 9*(1), 1–15.

Commission of the European Communities. (2005). *Proposal for a recommendation of the European parliament and of the council on key competences for lifelong learning.* Brussels, Belgium: European Commission.

Consortium, W. W. W. (1995). *The common log file format.* Retrieved from http://www.w3.org/Daemon/User/Config/Logging.html#common-logfile-format1995

Cook, G. D., & Robinson, A. J. (1996). Boosting the performance of connectionist large vocabulary speech recognition. In *Proceedings of the International Conference on Spoken Language Processing,* (pp. 1305-1308). Philadelphia, PA: IEEE.

Cooley, R. (2000). *Web usage mining: Discovery and application of interesting patterns from web data.* (Ph.D. Thesis). University of Minnesota. Minneapolis, MN.

Cooley, R., Mobasher, B., & Srivastava, J. (1999). Data preparation for mining world wide web browsing patterns. *Journal of Knowledge and Information Systems, 1*(1), 5–32.

Cortes, C., & Pregibon, D. (1999). Paper. In *Proceedings of the Fifth ACM SIGKDD International Conference on Knowledge Discovery and Data Mining (KDD),* (pp. 327–331). ACM Press.

Cortés, U., Moreno, A., Armengol, E., Béjar, J., Belanche, L., & Gavaldá, R. … Sánchez, M. (1994). *Aprendizaje automático.* Catalina, Spain.

Costagliola, G., Ferrucci, F., & Francese, R. (2002). Web engineering: Model and methodologies for the design of hypermedia applications. In Chang, S. K. (Ed.), *Handbook of Software Engineering & Knowledge Engineering (Vol. 2,* pp. 181–199). Singapore, Singapore: World Scientific. doi:10.1142/9789812389701_0009

Courty, P., & Li, H. (1999). Timing of seasonal sales. *The Journal of Business, 72*(4), 545–572. doi:10.1086/209627

Craven, P. (2009). *History and challenges of e-assessment: The Cambridge approach perspective – e-Assessment research and development 1989 to 2009.* Cambridge, UK: Cambridge University Press.

Cremonesi, P., Koren, Y., & Turrin, R. (2010). Performance of recommender algorithms on top-N recommender tasks. In *Proceedings of the Fourth ACM Conference on Recommender System (RecSys'10).* Barcelona, Spain: ACM Press.

Cristache, A. (2009). *Hybrid recommender system using association rules.* (Master Thesis). Auckland University of Technology. Auckland, New Zealand.

Cristea, A., & Mooij, A. (2003). LAOS: Layered WWW AHS authoring model and their corresponding algebraic operators. In *Proceedings of the 12ᵗʰ International World Wide Web Conference (WWW 2003).* Retrieved March 23, 2004 from http://wwwis.win.tue.nl/~acristea/HTML/Minerva/papers/WWW03-cristea-mooij.doc

Cristea, A., & Garzotto, F. (2004). Designing patterns for adaptive of adaptable educational hypermedia: A taxonomy. [AACE.]. *Proceedings of ED-MEDIA, 2004,* 808–813.

Crow, J. F., & Kimura, M. (1979). Efficiency of truncation selection. *Proceedings of the National Academy of Sciences of the United States of America, 76*(1), 396–399. doi:10.1073/pnas.76.1.396

Cunha, C. R., & Jaccoud, C. F. B. (1997). Determining www user's next access and its application to prefetching. In *Proceedings of Computers and Communication* (pp. 1–3). IEEE Press.

Dallen, J. (2007). Sustainable transport, market segmentation and tourism: The Looe valley branch line railway, Cornwall, UK. *Journal of Sustainable Tourism, 15*(2), 180–199. doi:10.2167/jost636.0

Darden, W. R., Lennon, J. J., & Darden, D. K. (1978). Communicating with interurban shoppers. *Journal of Retailing, 54*(1), 51–64.

Dasgupta, D., & Mcgregor, D. R. (1992). Designing application specific neural networks using the structured genetic algorithm. In *Proceedings Cogann 1992.* IEEE Computer Society Press. doi:10.1109/COGANN.1992.273946

Dash, M., & Liu, H. (1997). Feature selection for classification. *Intelligent Data Analysis, 1,* 131–156. doi:10.1016/S1088-467X(97)00008-5

David, M. (2003). An example inference task: Clustering. In *Information Theory, Inference and Learning Algorithm* (pp. 284–292). Cambridge, UK: Cambridge University Press.

Davidson, J., Liebald, B., & Liu, J. (2010). The You-Tube video recommendation system. In *Proceedings of the Fourth ACM Conference on Recommender System (RecSys'10).* Barcelona, Spain: ACM Press.

Davies, D. L., & Bouldin, D. W. (1979). A cluster separation measure. *IEEE Transactions on Pattern Analysis and Machine Intelligence, 1*(4), 224–227. doi:10.1109/TPAMI.1979.4766909

De Bra, P., Aerts, A., Berden, B., De Lange, B., Rousseau, B., & Santic, T. ... Stash, N. (2003). AHA! The adaptive hypermedia architecture. In *Proceedings of the ACM Hypertext Conference,* (pp. 81-84). ACM Press.

de Campos, L. M., Fernandez-Luna, J. M., & Huete, J. F. (2005). Generalizing e-bay.net: An approach to recommendation based on probabilistic computing. In *Proceedings of the 1st Workshop on Web Personalization, Recommender Systems and Intelligent User Interface,* (pp. 24–33). IEEE.

de Campos, L. M., Fernandez-Luna, J. M., & Huete, J. F. (2005). A decision-based approach for recommending in hierarchical domains. *Lecture Notes in Computer Science, 3571,* 123–135. doi:10.1007/11518655_12

de Campos, L. M., Fernandez-Luna, J. M., & Huete, J. F. (2008). *A collaborative recommender system based on probabilistic inference from fuzzy observations. Granada, Spain: Departamento de Ciencias de la Computacin e Inteligencia Artificial E.T.S.I.*

de Campos, L. M., Fernandez-Luna, J. M., & Huete, J. F., & RuedaMorales, M. A. (2010). Combining content-based and collaborative recommendations: A hybrid approach based on Bayesian networks. *International Journal of Approximate Reasoning, 51,* 785–799. doi:10.1016/j.ijar.2010.04.001

Dean, J., & Henzinger, M. R. (1999). Finding related pages in the world wide web. In *Proceedings of the Eighth International Conference on World Wide Web,* (pp. 1467–1479). Toronto, Canada: Elsevier.

Deepayan, C., Deepak, A., & Vanja, J. (2008). Contextual advertising by combining relevance with click feedback. In *Proceeding of the 17th International Conference on World Wide Web,* (pp. 417–426). ACM Press.

DeLacey, B., & Leonard, D. (2002). Case study on technology and distance in education at the Harvard Business School. *Journal of Educational Technology & Society, 5*(2), 13–28.

Delcea, C., & Dascalu, M. (2009). Knowledge strategies tools for managing enterprise crisis. In Proceedings of *the 4th International Conference on Knowledge Management: Projects, Systems and Technologies,* (pp. 115-117). Bucharest, Romania: Carol I National Defense University.

Delgado, M., Pegalajar, M. C., & Cu'ellar, M. P. (2006). Evolutionary training for dynamical recurrent neural networks: An application in financial time series prediction. *Mathware & Soft Computing, 13,* 89–110.

Delisle, S., & Moulin, B. (2002). User interfaces and help systems: From helplessness to intelligent assistance. *Artificial Intelligence Review, 18*(2), 117–157. doi:10.1023/A:1015179704819

Denis, H. (2007). Managing collaborative learning processes, e-learning applications. In *Proceedings of the 29th International Conference on Information Technical Interfaces,* (pp. 345–350). IEEE.

Denning, D. E. (1987). An intrusion detection model. *IEEE Transactions on Software Engineering, 13*(2), 222–232. doi:10.1109/TSE.1987.232894

Denning, D. E., & Neumann, P. G. (1985). *Audit trail analysis and usage collection and processing. Technical Report Project 5910.* Menlo Park, CA: SRI International.

Derrig, R. A., & Ostaszewski, K. M. (1995). Fuzzy techniques of pattern recognition in risk and claim classification. *The Journal of Risk and Insurance, 62*(3), 447–482. doi:10.2307/253819

De, S., & Krishna, P. (2004). Clustering web transactions using rough approximation. *Fuzzy Sets and Systems, 148,* 131–138. doi:10.1016/j.fss.2004.03.010

Deshpande, M., & Karypis, G. (2004). Item-based top-N recommendation algorithms. *ACM Transactions on Information Systems, 22*(1), 143–177. doi:10.1145/963770.963776

Dias, J. G., & Vermunt, J. K. (2007). Latent class modeling of website users' search patterns: Implications for online market segmentation. *Journal of Retailing and Consumer Services, 14*(6), 359–368. doi:10.1016/j.jretconser.2007.02.007

Dietterich, T. G. (1998). Approximate statistical tests for comparing supervised classification learning algorithms. *Neural Computation, 10,* 1895–1923. doi:10.1162/089976698300017197

Dietterich, T. G. (2000). Ensemble methods in machine learning. *Lecture Notes in Computer Science, 1857,* 1–15. doi:10.1007/3-540-45014-9_1

Ding, X., & Liu, B. (2007). The utility of linguistic rules in opinion mining. In *Proceedings of the 30ᵗʰ Annual International ACM SIGIR Conference on Research and Development in Information Retrieval,* (pp. 811–812). ACM Press.

Draper, S. (1999). Supporting use, learning, and education: Commentary on Guzdial's supporting learners as users. *Journal of Computer Documentation, 23*(2), 19–24.

Duin, R. P. W. (2002). The combining classifier: to train or not to train. In *Proceedings of 16th International Conference on Pattern Recognition,* (vol. 2, pp. 765-770). Quebec, Canada: IEEE.

Ehlers, U.-D., Goertz, L., Hildebrandt, B., & Pawlowski, J. (2005). *Quality in e-learning - Use and dissemination of quality approaches in European e-learning - A study by the European quality observatory.* Luxembourg, Luxembourg: Office for Official Publications of the European Communities.

Ehlert, P. (2003). *Intelligent user interfaces: Introduction and survey.* Research Report DKS03-01/ICE01. Delft, The Netherlands: Delft University of Technology. Retrieved November 7, 2002 from ftp://ftp.kbs.twi.tudelft.nl/pub/ice/Ehlert.P.A.M-report_IUI.pdf

Eirinaki, M., & Vazirgianis, M. (2003). Web mining for web personalization. *ACM Transactions on Internet Technology, 3*(1), 1–27. doi:10.1145/643477.643478

El-Mihoub, T. A., Hopgood, A. A., Nolle, L., & Battersby, A. (2006). Hybrid genetic algorithms: A review. *Engineering Letters, 13*(2).

Encarnação, M. (1997). Multi-level user support through adaptive hypermedia: A highly application-independent help component. In *Proceedings of the International Conference on Intelligent User Interfaces (IUI 1997),* (pp. 187-194). IUI.

Erkol, E. (1998). *A multi-agent extension of Negoplan and its application to a business strategy game.* (Master Degree Thesis). University of Ottawa. Ottawa, Canada.

Eshelman, L. J. (1991). The CHC adaptive search algorithm: how to have safe search when engaging in nontraditional genetic recombination. *Foundations of Genetic Algorithms, 1,* 265–283.

Evans, D. K., Klavans, J. L., & McKeown, K. R. (2004). Columbia newsblaster: Multilingual news summarization on the web. In *Proceedings of the Human Language Technology Conference and the North American Chapter of the Association for Computational Linguistics Annual Meeting.* ACL.

Fan, W., Gordon, M. D., & Pathak, P. (2005). Effective profiling of consumer information retrieval needs: A unified framework and empirical comparison. *Decision Support Systems, 40*(2), 213–233. doi:10.1016/j.dss.2004.02.003

Fatourechi, M., Bashashati, A., Ward, R. K., & Birch, G. E. (2005). A hybrid genetic algorithm approach for improving the performance of the LF-ASD brain computer interface. In *Proceedings of ICASSP 2005.* ICASSP.

Fawcett, T., & Provost, F. (1996). Combining data mining and machine learning for effective user profiling. In *Proceedings of the Second International Conference on Knowledge Discovery and Data Mining (KDD),* (pp. 8–13). ACM Press.

Felden, C., & Chamoni, P. (2007). Recommender systems based on an active data warehouse with text documents. In *Proceedings of the 40th HICSS 2007*, (p. 168a). HICSS.

Findlay, A., & Sparks, L. (2008). Weaving new retail and consumer landscapes in the Scottish borders. *Journal of Rural Studies, 24*(1), 86–97. doi:10.1016/j.jrurstud.2007.05.007

Fischer, S., & Steinmetz, R. (2000). Automatic creation of exercises in adaptive hypermedia learning systems. In *Proceedings of the Eleventh ACM Conference on Hypertext and Hypermedia*, (pp. 49 – 55). ACM Press.

Fischer, G. (2001). User modeling in human computer interaction. *User Modeling and User-Adapted Interaction, 11*(1-2), 65–86. doi:10.1023/A:1011145532042

Fleming, M., & Cohen, R. (1999). User modeling in the design of interactive interface agents. In *Proceedings of the 7th International Conference (UM 1999)*, (pp. 67-76). IEEE.

Fong, S., Si, Y.-W., & Biuk-Aghai, R. P. (2009). Applying a hybrid model of neural network and decision tree classifier for predicting university admission. In *Proceedings of ICICS*. IEEE Press.

Forman, G. (2003). An extensive empirical study of feature selection metrics for text classification. *Journal of Machine Learning Research, 3*, 1289–1305.

Freund, Y. (1990). Boosting a weak learning algorithm by majority. In *Proceedings of the 3rd Annual Workshop on Computational Learning Theory*, (pp. 202-216). IEEE.

Frey, N., & Fisher, D. (2009). Using common formative assessments as a source of professional development in an urban American elementary school. *Teaching and Teacher Education, 25*, 674–680. doi:10.1016/j.tate.2008.11.006

Froehlich, H. (2002). *Feature selection for support vector machines by means of genetic algorithms*. (Thesis). Philipps-University. Marburg, Germany.

Fuller, J., & Matzler, K. (2008). Customer delight and market segmentation: An application of the three-factor theory of customer satisfaction on life style groups. *Tourism Management, 29*(1), 116–126. doi:10.1016/j.tourman.2007.03.021

G'ery, M., & Haddad, H. (2003). Evaluation of web usage mining approaches for user's next request prediction. [New Orleans, LA: WIDM.]. *Proceedings of WIDM, 2003*, 74–81.

Gabrilovich, E., & Markovitch, S. (2004). Text categorization with many redundant features: Using aggressive feature selection to make SVMs competitive with C4.5. In *Proceedings of the 21st International Conference on Machine Learning*. Banff, Canada: IEEE.

Gao, L. Q., & Li, C. (2008). Hybrid personalized recommended model based on genetic algorithm. In *Proceedings of the International Conference on Wireless Communications Networks and Mobile Computing*, (pp. 9215–9218). IEEE.

García, F. (2000). CACTUS: Automated tutorial course generation for software applications. In *Proceedings of the 5th International Conference on Intelligent User Interfaces*, (pp. 113–120). IEEE.

Garfield, S., & Wermter, S. (2003). Comparing state vector machines, recurrent networks and finite state transducers for classifying spoken utterances. In *Proceedings of the International Conference on Artificial Neural Networks*, (pp. 646-653). Istanbul, Turkey: IEEE.

Garfield, S., & Wermter, S. (2003). Recurrent neural learning for classifying spoken utterances. *Expert Update, 6*(3), 31–36.

Garfield, S., & Wermter, S. (2006). Call classification using recurrent neural networks, support vector machines and finite state automata. *Knowledge and Information Systems: An International Journal, 9*(2), 131–156. doi:10.1007/s10115-005-0198-5

Garfield, S., Wermter, S., & Devlin, S. (2005). Spoken language classification using hybrid classifier combination. *International Journal of Hybrid Intelligent Systems, 2*(1), 13–33.

Ghalambaz, M., Noghrehabadi, A. R., Behrang, M. A., Assareh, E., Ghanbarzadeh, A., & Hedayat, N. (2011). A hybrid neural network and gravitational search algorithm (HNNGSA) method to solve well known Wessinger's equation. *World Academy of Science. Engineering and Technology, 6*(73), 803–807.

Giacinto, G., Roli, F., & Fumera, G. (2000). Design of effective multiple classifier systems by clustering of classifiers. In *Proceedings of ICPR 2000 15th International Conference on Pattern Recognition,* (pp. 160-163). Barcelona, Spain: IEEE.

Giaglis, G. M., & Lekakos. (2006). Improving the prediction accuracy of recommendation algorithms: Approaches anchored on human factors. *Interacting with Computers, 18*(3), 410–431. doi:10.1016/j.intcom.2005.11.004

Gilbert, L., Gale, V., Warburton, B., & Willis, G. (2008). *Report on summative e-assessment quality (REAQ).* Southampton, UK: Joint Information Systems Committee.

Godoy, D., & Amandi, A. (2006). User profiling in personal information agents: A survey. *The Knowledge Engineering Review, 20*(4), 329–361. doi:10.1017/S0269888906000397

Goecks, J., & Shavlik, J. (2000). Learning users' interests by unobtrusively observing their normal behavior. In *Proceedings of the 2000 ACM Intelligent User Interfaces Conference,* (pp. 129–132). ACM Press.

Göksedef, M., & Gündüz-Ögüdücü, S. (2010). Combination of web page recommender systems. *Expert Systems with Applications, 37,* 2911–2922. doi:10.1016/j.eswa.2009.09.046

Goldberg, D., & Thierens, D. (1994). Elitist recombination: An integrated selection recombination GA. In *Proceedings of the First IEEE Conference on Evolutionary Computation,* (pp. 508–512). IEEE Press.

Goldberg, D. E., & Holland, J. H. (1988). Genetic algorithms and machine learning. *Machine Learning, 3*(2-3), 95–99. doi:10.1023/A:1022602019183

Gooding, S. K. S. (1994). Hospital outshopping and perceptions of quality: Implications for public policy. *Journal of Public Policy & Marketing, 13*(2), 271–280.

Goy, A., Ardissono, L., & Petrone, G. (2007). Personalization in e-commerce applications. *Lecture Notes in Computer Science, 4321,* 485–520. doi:10.1007/978-3-540-72079-9_16

Grasha, A. (1996). *Teaching with style.* New York, NY: Alliance Publishers.

Gronholdt, L., & Martensen, A. (2005). Analysing customer satisfaction data: A comparison of regression and artificial neural networks. *International Journal of Market Research, 47*(2), 121–130.

Grubb, A. J., & Bagnell, A. (2010). Boosted backpropagation learning for training deep modular networks. In *Proceedings of the 27th International Conference on Machine Learning.* Haifa, Israel: IEEE.

Gunduz, S., & Ozsu, M. T. (2003). A web page prediction model based on click-stream tree representation of user behavior. In *Proceedings of ACM SIGKDD International Conference on Knowledge Discovery and Data Mining, KDD 2003,* (pp. 188-194). ACM Press.

Guo, C., Vasquez-Parraga, A. Z., & Wang, Y. (2006). An exploratory study of motives for Mexican nationals to shop in the US: More than meets the eye. *Journal of Retailing and Consumer Services, 13*(5), 351–362. doi:10.1016/j.jretconser.2005.11.002

Gurau, C., & Tinson, J. (2003). Early evangelist or reluctant Rudolph? Attitudes towards the Christmas commercial campaign. *Journal of Consumer Behaviour, 3*(1), 48–62. doi:10.1002/cb.121

Guzdial, M. (1999). Supporting learners as users. *Journal of Computer Documentation, 23*(2), 3–13.

Hackerman, D. (1995). *A tutorial on learning with bayesian networks microsoft research. MSR-TR-95-06.* Seattle, WA: Microsoft.

Hae-Sang, & Jun, C. (2009). A simple and fast algorithm for K-medoids clustering. *Expert Systems with Applications, 36*(2), 3336–3341. doi:10.1016/j.eswa.2008.01.039

Hahn, U., & Schnattinger, K. (1998). A text understander that learns. In *Proceedings of the 17th COLING/ACL,* (pp. 476-482). Morgan Kaufmann.

Haijun, X., Qi, Z., & Baoyi, W. (2008). Rough set page recommendation algorithm based on information entropy, In *Proceedings of the International Conference on Computer Science and Software Engineering,* (pp. 735 – 738). IEEE.

Halliday, D., Resnick, R., & Walker, J. (2008). *Fundamentals of physics.* Hoboken, NJ: John Wiley & Sons Inc.

Han, E. H., & Karypis, G. (2000). Centroid-based document classification: Analysis and experimental results. In *Proceedings of the 4th European Conference on Principles of Data Mining and Knowledge Discovery, PKDD 2000*, (pp. 424–431). London, UK: Springer-Verlag.

Hanani, U., Shapira, B., & Shoval, P. (2001). Information filtering: Overview of issues, research and systems. *User Modeling and User-Adapted Interaction, 11*, 203–259. doi:10.1023/A:1011196000674

Han, J., & Kamber, M. (2000). *Data mining: Concepts and techniques*. San Francisco, CA: Morgan Kaufmann.

Hardas, M. (2006). *A novel approach for test problem assessment using course ontology*. Kent, OH: Kent State University.

Hardin, D., Tsamardinos, I., & Aliferis, C. F. (2004). A theoretical categorization of linear SVM based feature selection. In *Proceedings of the 21st International Conference on Machine Learning*. Banff. Canada: IEEE.

Hartley, R. (2003). An interactive computer-based simulation environment for supporting and developing complex decision-making skills. *International Journal of Continuing Engineering Education and Lifelong Learning, 13*(3-4), 212–231. doi:10.1504/IJCEELL.2003.003279

Ha, S. H., Selamat, A., & Sigeru, O. (2004). Web page feature selection and classification neural networks. *Information Sciences, 158*, 69–88. doi:10.1016/j.ins.2003.03.003

Hathaway, R., & Beadek, J. (1993). Switching regression models and fuzzy clustering. *IEEE Transactions on Fuzzy Systems, 1*(3), 195–204. doi:10.1109/91.236552

Haykin, S. (1994). *Neural networks: A comprehensive foundation*. New York, NY: Macmillan College Publishing Company.

Haykin, S. (2008). *Neural networks and learning machines* (3rd ed.). Upper Saddle River, NJ: Pearson Prentice Hall.

Hemalatha, M., Sivakumar, V. J., & Jayakumar, G. S. D. S. (2009). Segmentation of Indian shoppers based on store attributes. *International Journal of Business Innovation and Research, 3*(6), 651–669. doi:10.1504/IJBIR.2009.027207

Henze, N., & Nejdl, W. (1999). Student modeling in an active learning environment using Bayesian networks. In *Proceedings of 7th Conference User Modelling*. Retrieved March 23, 2003 from http://www.cs.usask.ca/UM99/Proc/posters/Henze.htm

Herlocker, J., Konstan, J., & Riedl, J. (2000). Explaining collaborative filtering recommendations. In *Proceedings of the ACM Conference on Computer Supported Cooperative Work*. ACM Press.

Herlocker, J. (2000). *Understanding and improving automated collaborative filtering systems*. Minneapolis, MN: University of Minnesota.

Herlocker, J. L., Konstan, J. A., Terveen, L. G., & Riedl, J. T. (2004). Evaluating collaborative filtering recommender systems. *ACM Transactions on Information Systems, 22*(1), 5–53. doi:10.1145/963770.963772

Herlocker, J., & Konstan, J. A. (2001). Content-independent task-focused recommendation. *IEEE Internet Computing, 5*(6), 40–47. doi:10.1109/4236.968830

Hermes, L., & Buhmann, J. M. (2000). Feature selection for support vector machines. In *Proceedings of the ICPR 2000*, (vol. 2, pp. 716-719). ICPR.

Herrera, F., Lozano, M., & Verdegay, J. L. (1998). Tackling real-coded genetic algorithms: Operators and tools for behavioural analysis. *Artificial Intelligence Review, 12*, 265–319. doi:10.1023/A:1006504901164

Herrera-Viedma, E., & Porcel, C. (2009). A multidisciplinary recommender system to advice research resources in university digital libraries. *Expert Systems with Applications, 36*, 12520–12528. doi:10.1016/j.eswa.2009.04.038

Herrera-Viedma, E., & Porcel, C. (2010). Dealing with incomplete information in a fuzzy linguistic recommender system to disseminate information in university digital libraries. *Knowledge-Based Systems, 23*(1), 32–39. doi:10.1016/j.knosys.2009.07.007

Herrmann, R. O., & Beik, L. L. (1968). Shoppers' movements outside their local retail area. *Journal of Marketing, 32*(4), 45–51. doi:10.2307/1249337

Hilas, C. S., & Sahalos, J. N. (2006). Testing the fraud detection ability of different user profiles by means of FF-NN classifiers. *Lecture Notes in Computer Science*, *4132*, 872–883. doi:10.1007/11840930_91

Hill, & Terveen, L. (2001). Beyond recommender systems: Helping people help each other. In *HCI in the New Millennium*, (pp. 487–509). Reading, MA: Addison-Wesley.

Hill, W., Stead, L., Rosenstein, M., & Furnas, G. (1995). Recommending and evaluating choices in a virtual community of use. In *Proceedings of the SIGCHI Conference on Human Factors in Computing Systems*, (pp. 194–201). ACM Press.

Ho, Y., Fong, S., & Yan, J. (2007). A hybrid ga-based collaborative filtering model for online recommenders. In *Proceedings of the International Conference on e-Business*, (pp. 200–203). IEEE.

Hochman, R., Khoshgoftaar, T. M., Allen, E. B., & Hudepohl, J. P. (1996). Using the genetic algorithm to build optimal neural networks for fault-prone module detection. In *Proceedings of the 7th International Symposium on Software Reliability Engineering*, (pp. 152-162). IEEE.

Ho-Fuk, L., & Oliver, H. M. Y. (1985). Consumer outshopping behaviour and its implications for channel strategy: A study of the camera patronage pattern in Hong Kong. *European Journal of Marketing*, *19*(6), 12–23. doi:10.1108/EUM0000000004731

Ho, K., & Lin, H. M. T. (2012). Design and implementation of an intelligent recommendation system for tourist attraction: The integration of EBM model, Bayesian network and Google maps. *Expert Systems with Applications*, *39*, 3257–3264. doi:10.1016/j.eswa.2011.09.013

Hollmen, J. (2000). *User profiling and classification for fraud detection in mobile communications networks*. (PhD Dissertation). Helsinki University of Technology. Helsinki, Finland.

Housmann, V., & Kaskela, E. (1996). State of the art in selective dissemination of information. In *Proceedings of IEEE Transactions on Engineering and Writing Speech*, (pp. 100-112). Stanford, CA: AAAI Press.

Hsu, I.-C. (2009). SXRS: An xlink-based recommender system using semantic web technologies. *Expert Systems with Applications*, *36*, 3795–3804. doi:10.1016/j.eswa.2008.02.062

Hsu, J. L., & Chang, W. (2002). Market segmentation of fresh meat shoppers in Taiwan. *International Review of Retail, Distribution and Consumer Research*, *12*(4), 423–436. doi:10.1080/09593960210151180

Hsu, M.-H. (2009). A personalized English learning recommender system for ESL students. *Expert Systems with Applications*, *34*, 683–688. doi:10.1016/j.eswa.2006.10.004

Hu, M., & Liu, B. (2004). Mining and summarizing customer reviews. In *Proceedings of the Tenth ACM SIGKDD International Conference on Knowledge Discovery and Data Mining*, (pp. 168–177). ACM Press.

Huang, C.-L., & Wang, C.-J. (2005). A GA-based feature selection and parameters optimization for support vector machines. *Expert Systems with Applications*, *31*, 231–240. doi:10.1016/j.eswa.2005.09.024

Huang, Z., Chen, H., Hsu, C. J., Chen, W. H., & Wu, S. (2004). Credit rating analysis with support vector machines and neural networks: A market comparative study. *Decision Support Systems*, *37*(4), 543–558. doi:10.1016/S0167-9236(03)00086-1

Huang, Z., Chen, H., & Zeng, D. (2004). Applying associative retrieval techniques to alleviate the sparsity problem in collaborative filtering. *ACM Transactions on Information Systems*, *22*(1), 116–142. doi:10.1145/963770.963775

Hui, T. K., & Wan, D. (2008). The cross-border shoppers' behaviour: The case of Singapore. *International Journal of Data Analysis Techniques and Strategies*, *1*(1), 104–115. doi:10.1504/IJDATS.2008.020025

Hung, C., & Tsai, C. (2008). Market segmentation based on hierarchical self-organizing map for markets of multimedia on demand. *Expert Systems with Applications*, *34*(1), 780–787. doi:10.1016/j.eswa.2006.10.012

Hussein, F., Kharma, N., & Ward, R. (2001). Genetic algorithms for feature selection and weighting: A review and study. In *Proceedings of the International Conference on Document Analysis and Recognition*, (pp. 1240-1244). IEEE Press.

Hyun-Tae, K., Jang-Hyun, L., & Wook, C. (2011). A recommender system based on interactive evolutionary computation with data grouping. *Procedia Computer Science, 3*, 611–616. doi:10.1016/j.procs.2010.12.102

Inbarani, H., & Thangavel, K. (2009). Mining and analysis of clickstream patterns. In *Proceedings of the Foundations of Computational, Intelligence - Data Mining, Studies in Computational Intelligence,* (pp. 3-27). Springer.

Inbarani, H., & Thangavel, K. (2011). A robust biclustering approach for effective web personalization. In *Proceedings of the Visual Analytics and Interactive Technologies: Data, Text and Web Mining Applications,* (pp. 186-201). IEEE.

Inbarani, H., Thangavel, K., & Pethalakshmi, A. (2007). Rough set based feature selection for web usage mining. In *Proceedings of the Computational Intelligence and Multimedia Applications,* (pp. 33-38). IEEE.

Ingoo, H., Kyong, J. O., & Tae, H. R. (2003). The collaborative filtering recommendation based on SOM cluster-indexing CBR. *Expert Systems with Applications, 25*, 413–423. doi:10.1016/S0957-4174(03)00067-8

Iniesta, M. A., & Sanchez, M. (2002). Retail-consumer commitment and market segmentation. *International Review of Retail, Distribution and Consumer Research, 12*(3), 261–279. doi:10.1080/09593960210139661

International Project Management Association. (2006). *IPMA competence baseline*. Nijkerk, The Netherlands: IPMA.

Ishigami, H., Fukuda, T., Shibata, T., & Arai, F. (1995). Structure optimization of fuzzy neural networks by genetic algorithm. *Fuzzy Sets and Systems, 71*, 257–264. doi:10.1016/0165-0114(94)00283-D

Ishikawa, H., Ohta, M., Watanabe, T., Yokoyama, S., & Katayama, K. (2003). Toward active web usage mining for page recommendation and restructuring. [I-Know.]. *Proceedings of I-Know, 2003*, 492–499.

Iyengar, V. S., & Zhang, T. (2001). Empirical study of recommender systems using linear classifiers. In *Proceedings of the 5th Pacific-Asia Conference on Knowledge Discovery and Data Mining,* (pp. 16–27). London, UK: Springer-Verlag.

Jahrer, M., Töscher, A., & Legenstein, R. (2010). *Combining predictions for accurate recommender systems*. Paper presented at KDD 2010. Washington, DC.

Jameson, A., & Smyth, B. (2007). Recommendation to groups. *Lecture Notes in Computer Science, 4321*, 596–627. doi:10.1007/978-3-540-72079-9_20

Jarratt, D. G. (1996). A shopper taxonomy for retail strategy development. *International Review of Retail, Distribution and Consumer Research, 6*(2), 196–215. doi:10.1080/09593969600000020

Jarratt, D. G. (1998). Modelling outshopping behaviour: A non-metropolitan perspective. *International Review of Retail, Distribution and Consumer Research, 8*(3), 319–350. doi:10.1080/095939698342805

Jarratt, D. G. (2000). Outshopping behaviour: An explanation of behaviour by shopper segment using structural equation modeling. *International Review of Retail, Distribution and Consumer Research, 10*(3), 287–304. doi:10.1080/095939600405983

Jarratt, D. G., & Polonsky, M. J. (1993). Causal linkages between psychographic and demographic determinants of outshopping behavior. *International Review of Retail, Distribution and Consumer Research, 3*(3), 303–319. doi:10.1080/09593969300000020

Jenamani, M., Mohapatra, P. K. J., & Ghose, S. (2002). Online customized index synthesis in commercial web sites. In *Proceedings of IEEE Intelligent Systems,* (pp. 20-26). IEEE Press.

Jennings, A., & Higuchi, H. (1992). A personal news service based on a user model neural network. *IEICE Transactions on Information and Systems. E (Norwalk, Conn.), 75-D*(2), 198–210.

Jennings, A., & Higuchi, H. (1993). A user model neural network for a personal news service. *User Modeling and User-Adapted Interaction, 3*(1), 1–25. doi:10.1007/BF01099423

Jia, M., Yey, S., Liz, X., & Dickerson, J. (2007). Web site recommendation using HTTP traffic. In *Proceedings of the Seventh IEEE International Conference on Data Mining,* (pp. 535—540). IEEE Press.

Jianan, W., & DeSarbo, W. S. (2005). Market segmentation for customer satisfaction studies via a new latent structure multidimensional scaling model. *Applied Stochastic Models in Business and Industry, 21*(4/5), 303–309.

Jiang, L., Eberlein, A., Far, B., & Mousavi, M. (2008). *A methodology for the selection of requirements engineering techniques*. Berlin, Germany: Springer. doi:10.1007/s10270-007-0055-y

Jin, R., Si, L., Zhai, C., & Callan, J. (2003). Collaborative filtering with decoupled models for preferences and ratings. In *Proceedings of the Twelfth International Conference on Information and Knowledge Management, CIKM 2003*, (pp. 309-316). ACM Press.

Jin, X., Mobasher, B., & Zhou, Y. (2005). A web recommendation system based on maximum entropy. In *Proceedings of the International Conference on Information Technology: Coding and Computing (ITCC 2005)*, (pp. 213 – 218). ITCC.

Jindal, T. (2008). Ride the tiger. *Financial Management, 1*, 20–23.

Jinghua, H., Kangning, W., & Shaohong, F. (2007). A survey of e-commerce recommender systems. In *Proceedings of the International Conference on Service Systems and Service Management*, (pp. 1–5). IEEE.

Jingwen, T., Meijuan, G., & Yang, S. (2009). Study on web classification mining method based on fuzzy neural network. In *Proceedings of the ICAL*, (pp. 1781 – 1785). ICAL.

Jingwen, T., & Meijuan, G. (2009). Research of web classification mining based on wavelet neural network. [JCAI.]. *Proceedings of JCAI, 2009*, 559–562.

JISC. (2010). *Methods of assessment*. Retrieved February 25, 2011, from http://www.jiscinfonet.ac.uk/InfoKits/effective-use-of-VLEs/e-assessment/assess-methods

Joachims, T. (2002). Optimizing search engines using clickthrough data. In *Proceedings of the ACM Conference on Knowledge Discovery and Data Mining (KDD)*. ACM Press.

Joachims, T., Freitag, D., & Mitchell, T. (1997). Web-Watcher: A tour guide for the world wide web. In *Proceedings of IJCAI*, (pp. 770-777). IJCAI.

Joachims, T. (1999). Making large-scale support vector machine learning practical. In *Advances in Kernel Methods: Support Vector Learning* (pp. 169–184). New York, NY: ACM Press.

Johansson, A. (2001). *Authoring tools for developing intelligent tutoring systems*. Uppsala, Norway: Uppsala University. Retrieved October 11, 2002 from http://www.csd.uu.se/~alj/ATDITS.html

John, E. S., Orsay, K., & Cesar, A. D. M. (2007). Profiling Peruvian consumers lifestyles, market segmentation, and ethnocentrism. *Latin American Business Review, 8*(4), 38–59.

Jordan, M. I., & Rumelhart, D. (1990). *Forward models: Supervised learning with a distal teacher. Technical Report*. New York, NY: Center for Cognitive Science.

Kanayama, H., & Nasukawa, T. (2006). Fully automatic lexicon expansion for domain-oriented sentiment analysis. In *Proceedings of the 2006 Conference on Empirical Methods in Natural Language Processing*, (pp. 355–363). IEEE.

Kanoh, H., & Hara, K. (2008). *Hybrid genetic algorithm for dynamic multi-objective route planning with predicted traffic in a real-world road network*. Paper presented at GECCO 2008. Atlanta, GA.

Kantardžić, M. (2003). *Data mining: Concepts, models, methods and algorithms*. New York, NY: John Wiley & Sons. doi:10.1115/1.2123107

Kantor, P. B., Boros, E., Melamed, B., Menkov, V., Shapira, B., & Neu, D. J. (2000). Capturing human intelligence in the net. *Communications of the ACM, 43*(8), 112–115. doi:10.1145/345124.345162

Kardan, A., Abbaspour, S., & Hendijanifard, F. (2009). A hybrid recommender system for e-learning environments based on concept maps and collaborative tagging. In *Proceedings of the 4th International Conference on Virtual Learning*, (pp. 200-207). ICVL.

Karsenti, T. (2004). Prof branches: Un sondage révèle que 71% des formateurs emploient les TIC. *Forum, 38*(31), 1–2.

Karypis, G. (2001). Evaluation of item-based top-N recommendation algorithms. In *Proceedings of the 10th International Conference on Information and Knowledge Management*, (pp. 247–254). IEEE.

Karypis, G., Konstan, J., Riedl, J., & Sarwar, B. (2000). Analysis of recommendation algorithms for ecommerce. In *Proceedings of the 2nd ACM Conference on Electronic Commerce,* (pp. 158-167). Minneapolis, MN: ACM Press.

Kaveh, A., & Talatahari, S. (2009). Particle swarm optimizer, ant colony strategy and harmony search scheme hybridized for optimization of truss structures. *Computers & Structures, 87*(5/6), 267–283. doi:10.1016/j.compstruc.2009.01.003

Kaveh, A., & Talatahari, S. (2009). A particle swarm ant colony optimization algorithm for truss structures with discrete variables. *Journal of Constructional Steel Research, 65*(8/9), 1558–1568. doi:10.1016/j.jcsr.2009.04.021

Kaveh, A., & Talatahari, S. (2010). A novel heuristic optimization method: Charged system search. *Acta Mechanica, 213*(3/4), 267–289. doi:10.1007/s00707-009-0270-4

Kaveh, A., & Talatahari, S. (2010). A charged system search with a fly to boundary method for discrete optimum design of truss structures. *Asian Journal of Civil Engineering, 11*(3), 277–293.

Kaveh, A., & Talatahari, S. (2010). Charged system search for optimum grillage system design using the LRFD-AISC code. *Journal of Constructional Steel Research, 66*(6), 767–771. doi:10.1016/j.jcsr.2010.01.007

Keller, F. (2002). *Naive Bayes classifiers.* Saarlandes, Germany: Universit"at des Saarlandes. Retrieved January 16, 2004 from http://homepages.inf.ed.ac.uk/keller/teaching/connectionism/lecture10_4up.pdf

Kim, C., & Kim, J. (2003). A recommendation algorithm using multi-level association rules. In *Proceedings of the IEEE/WIC International Conference on Web Intelligence.* IEEE/WIC.

Kim, H. T., & Kim, E. Lee, & Ahn, C. W. (2010). A recommender system based on genetic algorithm for music data. In *Proceedings of the Computer Engineering and Technology (ICCET), 2010 2nd International Conference,* (vol. 6, pp. V6-414-V6-417). ICCET.

Kim, S. M., & Hovy, E. (2006). Automatic identification of pro and con reasons in online reviews. In *Proceedings of the COLING/ACL on Main Conference Poster Sessions,* (pp. 483–490). COLING/ACL.

Kim, D. H., Abraham, A., & Cho, J. H. (2007). A hybrid genetic algorithm and bacterial foraging approach for global optimization. *Information Sciences, 177,* 3918–3937. doi:10.1016/j.ins.2007.04.002

Kim, H., & Shin, K. (2007). A hybrid approach based on neural networks and genetic algorithms for detecting temporal patterns in stock markets. *Applied Soft Computing, 7,* 569–575. doi:10.1016/j.asoc.2006.03.004

Kimiavi, S. (1998). *ITS author: A framework for building hypermedia-based intelligent tutoring systems for the world wide web.* (Ph.D. Dissertation). George Washington University. Washington, DC.

Kim, K. (2008). *A recommender system using GA K-means clustering in an online shopping market.* Seoul, South Korea: Dongguk University. doi:10.1016/j.eswa.2006.12.025

Kinshuk, H. (2003). State-of-the-art in adaptive learning: Keynote address pedagogies & communication. In *Proceedings of the International Conference on Open & Online Learning (ICOOL 2003).* Retrieved March 18, 2004 from http://icool.uom.ac.mu/2003/papers/file/keynote/kinshuk.zip

Kinshuk, H., & Patel, A. (2001). Extended ITS framework with human teacher model. In C. H. Lee, S. Lajoie, R. Mizoguchi, Y. Yoo, & B. du Boulay (Eds.), *Enhancement of Quality Learning Through Information & Communication Technology (ICT), Proceedings of ICCE/SchoolNet 2001 Conference,* (pp. 1259-1262). ICCE/SchoolNet.

Kinshuk, H., Patel, A., & Russell, D. (1999). HyperITS: A web-based architecture for evolving a configurable learning environment. *Staff and Educational Development International Journal, 3*(3), 265–280.

Klepac, G. (2005). *Time series rule discovering with unique model of transformation.* (Unpublished Doctoral Dissertation). University of Zagreb FOI. Varaždin, Croatia.

Klepac, G., & Mršić, L. (2006). *Poslovna inteligencija kroz poslovne slučajeve.* Zagreb, Croatia: Liderpress.

Kobayakawa, T. S., Kumano, T., Tanaka, H., Okazaki, N., Kim, J.-D., & Tsujii, J. (2009). Opinion classification with tree kernel SVM using linguistic modality analysis. In *Proceeding of the 18th ACM Conference on Information and Knowledge Management,* (pp. 1791–1794). ACM Press.

Kobsa, A. (1993). *User modeling: Recent work, prospects, and hazards*. Retrieved from http://www.isr.uci.edu/~kobsa/papers/1993-aui-kobsa.pdf

Kobsa, A., Koenemann, J., & Pohl, W. (2001). Personalized hypermedia presentation techniques for improving online customer relationships. *The Knowledge Engineering Review, 16*(2), 111–155. doi:10.1017/S0269888901000108

Koc, E., & Altinay, G. (2007). An analysis of seasonality in monthly per person tourist spending in Turkish inbound tourism from a market segmentation perspective. *Tourism Management, 28*(1), 227–237. doi:10.1016/j.tourman.2006.01.003

Koch, N. (1999). *A comparative study of methods for hypermedia development*. Technical Report 9905. Munich, Germany: Ludwig Maximilians–Universitt. Retrieved November 20, 2002 from http://www.dsic.upv.es/~west2001/iwwost01/files/contributions/NoraKoch/hypdev.pdf

Ko, E., Kim, E., Charles, R. T., Kim, K. H., & Kang, I. J. (2007). Cross - national market segmentation in the fashion industry. *International Marketing Review, 24*(5), 629–651. doi:10.1108/02651330710828022

Kohonen, T. (2001). *Self-organizing maps*. Berlin, Germany: Springer. doi:10.1007/978-3-642-56927-2

Kolcz, A., Prabakarmurthi, V., & Kalita, J. (2001). Summarization as feature selection for text categorization. In *Proceedings of the 10th International Conference on Information and Knowledge Management*, (pp. 365–370). ACM Press.

Kolyshkina, I. (2002). *Modeling insurance risk: A comparison of data mining and logistic regression approaches*. London, UK: PricewaterhouseCoopers.

Konstan, J. A., & Riedl, J. L. (1999). Recommender systems in e-commerce. In *Proceedings of the 1st ACM Conference on Electronic Commerce*, (pp. 158–166). New York, NY: ACM Press.

Konstan, J. A., Miller, B. N., & Riedl, J. (2004). PocketLens: Toward a personal recommender system. *ACM Transactions on Information Systems, 22*(3), 437–476.

Koolen, M., & Kamps, J. (2011). Are semantically related links more effective for retrieval? In *Proceedings of the 33rd European Conference on Advances in Information Retrieval*, (pp. 92-103). Berlin, Germany: Springer-Verlag.

Koren, Y. (2009). Factor in the neighbors: Scalable and accurate collaborative filtering. In *Proceedings of the 15th ACM SIGKDD International Conference on Knowledge Discovery and Data Mining*. IEEE.

Koren, Y. (2010). Factors in the neighbors: Scalable and accurate collaborative filtering. *ACM Transactions on Knowledge Discovery from Data, 4*(1), 1–24. doi:10.1145/1644873.1644874

Koychev, I. (2002). Tracking changing user interests through prior-learning of context. *Lecture Notes in Computer Science, 2347*, 223–232. doi:10.1007/3-540-47952-X_24

Krishnapram, R., & Joshi, A. (2001). Low complexity fuzzy relational clustering algorithms for web mining. *IEEE Transactions on Fuzzy Systems, 9*, 595–607. doi:10.1109/91.940971

Krishnapuram, B., Hartemink, A. J., Carin, L., & Figueiredo, M. A. T. (2004). Bayesian approach to joint feature selection and classifier design. *IEEE Transactions on Pattern Analysis and Machine Intelligence, 26*(9). doi:10.1109/TPAMI.2004.55

Kroha, P., & Baeza-Yates, R. (2005). A case study: News classification based on term frequency. In *Proceedings of the Sixteenth International Workshop on Database and Expert Systems Applications*, (pp. 428 – 432). IEEE.

Kulkarni, U., & Shinde, S. K. (2011). *Hybrid personalized recommender system using centering-bunching based clustering algorithm*. Nanded, India: Bharati Vidyapeeth College of Engineering.

Kuschel, J. A. (2006). *Conceptual framework for remote vehicle diagnostics services - Customer experienced needs as core business*. Paper presented at the 5th International Conference on Mobile Business. Copenhagen, Denmark.

Lacerda, A., Cristo, M., Goncalves, M. A., Fan, W., Ziviani, N., & Ribeiro-Neto, B. (2006). Learning to advertise. In *Proceedings of the 29th Annual International ACM SIGIR Conference on Research and Development in Information Retrieval*, (pp. 549–556). ACM Press.

Lam, S. K., & Riedl, J. S. (2004). Recommender systems for fun and profit. In *Proceedings of the International World Wide Web Conference*, (pp. 393-402). New York, NY: ACM Press.

Lawrence, R. D., Almasi, G. S., Kotlyar, V., Viveros, M. S., & Duri, S. S. (2001). Personalization of supermarket product recommendations. *Data Mining and Knowledge Discovery, 5,* 11–32. doi:10.1023/A:1009835726774

LeCun, Y., Boser, B., Denker, J., Henderson, D., Howard, R., Hubbard, W., & Jackel, L. (1989). Backpropagation applied to handwritten zip code recognition. *Neural Computation, 1,* 541–551. doi:10.1162/neco.1989.1.4.541

Lee, D., Paswan, A. K., Ganesh, G., & Xavier, M. J. (2009). Outshopping through the Internet: A multicountry investigation. *Journal of Global Marketing,* [REMOVED HYPERLINK FIELD]*22*(1), 53–66.

Lee, C.-H., Lo, Y.-L., & Fu, Y.-H. (2010). A novel prediction model based on hierarchical characteristic of web site. In *Proceedings of Expert Systems with Applications* (pp. 3422–3430). IEEE. doi:10.1016/j.eswa.2010.08.128

Lee, W., & Stolfo, S. J. (2000). A framework for constructing features and models for intrusion detection systems. *ACM Transactions on Information and System Security, 3*(4), 227–261. doi:10.1145/382912.382914

Lee, Y. H., Jung, J. W., Eum, S. C., Park, S. M., & Nam, H. K. (2006). Production quantity allocation for order fulfilment in the supply chain: A neural network based approach. *Production Planning and Control, 17*(4), 378–389. doi:10.1080/09537280600621909

Lennon, S. J., Baugh, D., Chatterton, J., & Larkin, J. (2007). Clothing outshopping in a rural western community. *Journal of Consumer Studies & Home Economics, 11*(4), 369–374. doi:10.1111/j.1470-6431.1987.tb00147.x

Lennon, S. J., Ha, Y., Johnson, K. K. P., & Jasper, C. R. (2009). Rural consumers' online shopping for food and fiber products as a form of outshopping. *Clothing & Textiles Research Journal, 27*(1), 3–30. doi:10.1177/0887302X07313625

Lessmann, S., Stahlbock, R., & Crone, S. F. (2006). Genetic algorithms for support vector machine model selection. In *Proceedings of the 2006 International Joint Conference on Neural Networks,* (pp. 16-21). Vancouver, Canada: IEEE.

Letizia, H. L. (1995). An agent that assists web browsing. In *Proceedings of International Conference on Artificial Intelligence.* IEEE.

Leung, M. (2001). *Towards a generic approach to providing proactive task support.* (Ph.D. Dissertation). University of Waterloo. Waterloo, Canada.

Leung, F. H. F., Lam, H. K., Ling, S. H., & Tam, P. K. S. (2003). Tuning of the structure and parameters of a neural network using an improved genetic algorithm. *IEEE Transactions on Neural Networks, 14,* 79–88. doi:10.1109/TNN.2002.804317

Lewis, D. D. (1992). Feature selection and feature extraction for text categorization. In *Proceedings of Speech and Natural Language Workshop,* (pp. 212-217). Morgan Kaufmann.

Lewis, D. D., & Ringuette, M. (1994). A comparison of two learning algorithms for text categorization. In *Proceedings of the Symposium on Document Analysis and Information Retrieval,* (pp. 81-93). Las Vegas, NV: ISRI.

Li, J. Y. J., & Zhong, C. L. N. (2004). Bayesian networks structure learning and its application to personalized recommendation. In *Proceedings of the IEEE/WIC/ACM International Conference on Web Intelligence.* IEEE/WIC/ACM.

Li, P., & Yamada, S. (2004). A movie recommender system based on inductive learning. In *Proceedings of the IEEE Conference on Cybernetic Intelligence Systems,* (vol 1, pp. 318–323). IEEE Press.

Lill, D. J., Peterson, R. T., & Wall, L. C. (1981). How small business can use consumer shopping types as a planning tool. *American Journal of Small Business, 6*(1), 36–47.

Lim, C. P., & Goh, W. (2005). The application of an ensemble of boosted elman networks to time series prediction: A benchmark study. *International Journal of Computational Intelligence, 3*(2).

Lin, F. J., & Huang, P. K. (2006). Recurrent fuzzy neural network using genetic algorithm for linear induction motor servo drive. In *Proceedings of ICIEA 2006.* ICIEA.

Lin, W. (2000). *Association rule mining for collaborative recommender systems.* Retrieved on 29 September 2008 from http://www.wpi.edu

Linacre, J. (2000). *Computer - Adaptive testing: A methodology whose time has come.* Chicago, IL: MESA Psychometric Laboratory.

Linden, G., Smith, B., & York, J. (2003). Amazon.com recommendations: Item-to-item collaborative filtering. *IEEE Internet Computing, 7*(1), 76–80. doi:10.1109/MIC.2003.1167344

Lingras, P. (2002). Rough set clustering for web mining. In *Proceedings of the 2002 IEEE International Conference on Fuzzy Systems (FUZZ-IEEE 2002),* (vol 2, pp. 1039-1044). IEEE Press.

Lingras, P., & West, C. (2004). Interval set clustering of web users with rough k-means. *Journal of Intelligent Information Systems, 23*(1), 5–16. doi:10.1023/B:JIIS.0000029668.88665.1a

Lingras, P., Yan, R., & West, C. (2003). Fuzzy c-means clustering of web users for educational sites. *Lecture Notes in Artificial Intelligence, 2671,* 557–562.

Lin, W., Alvarez, S. A., & Ruiz, C. (2002). Efficient adaptive-support association rule mining for recommender systems. *Data Mining and Knowledge Discovery, 6,* 83–105. doi:10.1023/A:1013284820704

Lippmann, R. P. (1989). Review of neural networks for speech recognition. *Neural Computation, 1,* 1–38. doi:10.1162/neco.1989.1.1.1

Liu, Y., & Zheng, Y. F. (2005). FS_SFS: A novel feature selection method for support vector machines. In *Proceedings of the Pattern Recognition Society.* Elsevier.

Liu, B. (2001). Fuzzy random dependent-chance programming. *IEEE Transactions on Fuzzy Systems, 9*(5), 721–726. doi:10.1109/91.963758

Liu, B. (2002). *Theory and practice of uncertain programming.* Berlin, Germany: Springer-Verlag.

Liu, B., & Liu, Y. (2002). Expected value of fuzzy variable and fuzzy expected value models. *IEEE Transactions on Fuzzy Systems, 10,* 445–450. doi:10.1109/TFUZZ.2002.800692

Liu, H., & Singh, P. (2004). ConceptNet: A practical commonsense reasoning tool-kit. *BT Technology Journal, 22,* 211–226. doi:10.1023/B:BTTJ.0000047600.45421.6d

Liu, H., & Yu, L. (2005). Toward integrating feature selection algorithms for classification and clustering. *IEEE Transactions on Knowledge and Data Engineering, 17*(4).

Lobo, F. G., & Goldberg, D. E. (1997). *Decision making in a hybrid genetic algorithm.* Washington, DC: IEEE Press. doi:10.1109/ICEC.1997.592281

Loh, S., Lorenzi, F., Saldaña, R., & Licthnow, D. (2004). A tourism recommender system based on collaboration and text analysis. *Information Technology & Tourism, 6,* 157–165. doi:10.3727/1098305031436980

Lops, P., de Gemmis, M., & Semeraro, G. (2010). Content-based recommender systems: State of the art and trends. In Ricci, F., Rokach, L., Shapira, B., & Kantor, P. B. (Eds.), *Recommender Systems Handbook* (pp. 73–105). New York, NY: Springer. doi:10.1007/978-0-387-85820-3_3

Lorés, J., Abascal, J., Cañas, J., Gea, M., Gil, A., & Martínez, A. ... Vélez, M. (2002). *Introducción a la interacción persona-ordenador.* Retrieved August 6, 2003 from http://griho.udl.es/ipo/descarga.html

Loukil, L., Mehdi, M., Melab, N., Talbi, E.-G., & Bouvry, P. (2009). A parallel hybrid genetic algorithm-simulated annealing for solving Q3AP on computational grid. In *Proceedings of the International Symposium on Parallel and Distributed Processing.* IEEE Press.

Lynch, P., & Horton, S. (2001). *Web style guide: Basic design principles for creating website.* Retrieved June 22, 2004 from http://www.webstyleguide.com/type/lines.html

Lysagh, R. M., & Altschuld, J. W. (2000). Beyond initial certification: The assessment and maintenance of competency in professions. *Evaluation and Program Planning, 23,* 95–104. doi:10.1016/S0149-7189(99)00043-9

Magnini, B., & Cavagli, G. (2000). Integrating subject field codes into WordNet. In *Proceedings of LREC-2000, 2nd International Conference on Language Resources and Evaluation,* (pp. 1413-1418). LREC.

Mahoney, M., & Chan, P. (2003). An analysis of the 1999 DARPA/Lincoln lab: Evaluation data for network anomaly detection. In *Proceedings of Recent Advances in Intrusion Detection* (pp. 220–238). Berlin, Germany: Springer. doi:10.1007/978-3-540-45248-5_13

Malone, T., Grant, K., Turbak, F., Brobst, S., & Cohen, M. (1987). Intelligent information sharing systems. *Communications of the ACM, 30*(5), 390–402. doi:10.1145/22899.22903

Maniezzo, V. (1994). Genetic evolution of the topology and weight distribution of neural networks. *IEEE Transactions on Neural Networks, 5*(1), 39–53. doi:10.1109/72.265959

Marsland, S. (2009). *Machine learning: An algorithmic perspective*. Boca Raton, FL: Chapman & Hall/CRC.

Marsland, S. (2009). *Machine learning: An algorithmic perspective*. London, UK: Chapman & Hall.

Martell, K., & Calderon, T. (2005). Assessment of student learning in business schools: What it is, where we are, and where we need to go next. *Assessment of Student Learning in Business Schools: Best Practices Each Step of the Way, 1*(1), 1–22.

Massa, P., & Avesani, P. (2007). *Paper*. Paper presented at Trust-Aware Recommender Systems. Minneapolis, MN.

Mathiassen, L. (2002). Collaborative practice research. *Information Technology & People, 15*(4), 321–345. doi:10.1108/09593840210453115

Mayer, R., & Moreno, R. (2003). Nine ways to reduce cognitive load in multimedia learning. *Educational Psychologist, 38*, 43–52. doi:10.1207/S15326985EP3801_6

McCalla, G., Searwar, F., Thomson, J., Collins, J., Sun, Y., & Zhou, B. (1996). Analogical user modeling: A case study in individualized information filtering. In *Proceedings of the 5th International Conference on User Modeling*, (pp. 13-20). IEEE.

McClelland, J. L., Rumelhart, D. E., & Hinton, G. E. (1986). The appeal of parallel distributed processing. In Rumelhart, D. E., & McClelland, L. (Eds.), *Parallel Distributed Processing* (*Vol. 1*, pp. 3–44). Cambridge, MA: MIT Press.

McClelland, L., & Rumelhart, D. E. (1981). An interactive activation model of context effects in letter perception. *Psychological Review, 88*, 375–407. doi:10.1037/0033-295X.88.5.375

McDaniel, C., Gates, R., & Lamb, C. W. (1992). Who leaves the service area? Profiling the hospital outshopper. *Journal of Health Care Marketing, 12*(3), 2–9.

McDonnell, R., & Waagen, D. (1994). Evolving recurrent perceptrons for time-series modeling. *IEEE Transactions on Neural Networks, 5*(1), 24–38. doi:10.1109/72.265958

McEachern, M. G., & Warnaby, G. (2006). Food shopping behaviour in Scotland: The influence of relative rurality. *International Journal of Consumer Studies, 30*(2), 189–201. doi:10.1111/j.1470-6431.2005.00475.x

McHugh, J. (2000). Testing intrusion detection system: A critique of the 1998 and 1999 DARPA intrusion detection system evaluations as performed by Lincoln laboratory. *ACM Transactions on Information and System Security, 3*(4), 262–294. doi:10.1145/382912.382923

McKee, D. W. (2001). *Boosting evolved artificial neural network to improve breast cancer classification accuracy*. Unpublished.

McKeown, K. R., Barzilay, R., Evans, D., Hatzivassiloglou, V., Klavans, J. L., & Nenkova, A. … Sigelman, S. (2002). Tracking and summarizing news on a daily basis with Columbia's newsblaster. In *Proceedings of HLT 2002 Human Language Technology Conference*. San Diego, CA: HLT.

McKeown, K., & Radev, D. R. (1995). Generating summaries of multiple news articles. In *Proceedings of the 18th Annual International ACM SIGIR Conference on Research and Development in Information Retrieval*, (pp. 74-82). ACM Press.

McNee, S., Riedl, J., & Konstan, J. (2006). Being accurate is not enough: How accuracy metrics have hurt recommender systems. In *Proceedings of the 2006 ACM Conference on Human Factors in Computing Systems*. ACM Press.

Meijuan, G., & Jingwen, T. (2009). Web classification mining based on radial basic probabilistic neural network. In *Proceedings of the First International Workshop - DBTA*, (pp. 586 – 589). DBTA.

Meijuan, G., Jingwen, T., & Shiru, Z. (2009). Research of web classification mining based on classify support vector machine. In *Proceedings of the Colloquim CCCM*, (pp. 21 – 24). CCCM.

Melville, P., Mooney, R. J., & Nagarajan, R. (2002). Content–boosted collaborative filtering for improved recommendations. In *Proceedings of the 18th National Conference on Artificial Intelligence*, (pp. 187-192). Edmonton, Canada: AAAI Press.

Menon, K., & Dagli, C. H. (2003). Web personalization using neuro-fuzzy clustering algorithms. In *Proceedings of the Fuzzy Information Processing Society*, (pp. 525-529). Fuzzy Information Processing Society.

Menzly, L., & Ozbas, O. (2010). Market segmentation and cross-predictability of returns. *The Journal of Finance, 65*, 1555–1580. doi:10.1111/j.1540-6261.2010.01578.x

Merrilees, B., & Fam, K. S. (1999). Effective methods of managing retail sales. *International Review of Retail, Distribution and Consumer Research, 9*(1), 81–92. doi:10.1080/095939699342697

Middleton, S. E., Shadbolt, N. R., & de Roure, D. C. (2004). Ontological user profiling in recommender systems. *ACM Transactions on Information Systems, 22*(1), 54–88. doi:10.1145/963770.963773

Miller, B. N., Konstan, J. A., & Riedl, J. (2004). PocketLens: Toward a personal recommender system. *ACM Transactions on Information Systems, 22*(3), 437–476. doi:10.1145/1010614.1010618

Miller, G. A. (1995). WordNet: A lexical database for English. *Communications of the ACM, 38*(11), 39–41. doi:10.1145/219717.219748

Miller, M. T., Jerebko, A. K., Malley, J. D., & Summers, R. M. (2003). Feature selection for computer-aided polyp detection using genetic algorithms, medical imaging 2003: Physiology and function: Methods, systems, and applications. *Proceedings of the Society for Photo-Instrumentation Engineers*, ▪▪▪, 5031.

Mingrong, L., Yicen, L., Liang, X., Xing, C., & Qing, Y. (2008). Single Chinese news article summarization based on ranking propagation. In *Proceedings of the International Symposium on Knowledge Acquisition and Modeling KAM 2008*, (pp. 779 – 783). KAM.

Mitchell, M. (1998). *An introduction to genetic algorithm*. Cambridge, MA: MIT Press.

Mitra, S. (2004). An evolutionary rough partitive clustering. *Pattern Recognition Letters, 25*, 1439–1449. doi:10.1016/j.patrec.2004.05.007

Mitra, S. (2006). Rough fuzzy colloborative clustering. *IEEE Transactions on Systems, Man, and Cybernetics, 36*(4), 795–805. doi:10.1109/TSMCB.2005.863371

Miyahara, K., & Pazzani, M. (2002). Improvement of collaborative filtering with the simple Bayesian classifier. *IPSJ Journal, 43*(11). Retrieved May 6, 2004 from http://www.ics.uci.edu/~pazzani/Publications/IPSJ.pdf

Mobasher, B., Brusilovsky, P., Kobsa, A., & Nejdl, W. (2007). Data mining for web personalization. *Lecture Notes in Computer Science, 4321*, 90–135. doi:10.1007/978-3-540-72079-9_3

Mobasher, B., Cooley, R., & Srivastava, J. (2000). Automatic personalization based on web usage mining. *Communications of the ACM, 43*(8), 142–151. doi:10.1145/345124.345169

Mobasher, B., Dai, H., Luo, T., & Nakagawa, M. (2001). Effective personalization based on association rule discovery from web usage data. In *Proceedings of Web Information and Data Management* (pp. 9–15). IEEE.

Mobasher, B., Dai, H., Luo, T., & Nakagawa, M. (2002). Discovery and evaluation of aggregate usage profiles for web personalization. *Data Mining and Knowledge Discovery, 6*(1), 61–82. doi:10.1023/A:1013232803866

Mobasher, B., Dai, H., Luo, T., & Nakagawa, M. (2002). Discovery and evaluation of aggregate usage profiles for web personalization. *Data Mining and Knowledge Discovery, 6*, 61–82. doi:10.1023/A:1013232803866

Mooney, R. J., & Roy, L. (2000). Content-based book recommending using learning for text categorization. In *Proceedings of the Fifth ACM Conference on Digital Libraries*, (pp. 195-204). ACM Press.

Mooney, R., & Roy, L. (2000). Content based book recommending using learning for text categorization. In *Proceedings of the 5ᵗʰ ACM Conference on Digital Libraries*, (pp. 195-204). San Antonio, TX: ACM Press.

Mooney, R., & Roy, L. (2010). Content-based book recommending using learning for text categorization. In *Proceedings of the ACM International Conference on Digital Libraries*, (pp. 195-204). San Antonio, TX: ACM.

Murdock, V., Ciaramita, M., & Plachouras, V. (2007). A noisy-channel approach to contextual advertising. In *Proceedings of the Workshop on Data Mining and Audience Intelligence for Advertising (ADKDD)*. IEEE.

Murray, T. (1999). Authoring intelligent tutoring systems: An analysis of the state of the art. *International Journal of Artificial Intelligence in Education, 10*, 98–129.

Mushtao, N., Tolle, K., Werner, P., & Zicari, R. (2004). Building and evaluating non-obvious user profiles for visitors of web sites. In Proceedings *of IEEE International Conference on E-Commerce Technology,* (pp. 9-15). IEEE Press.

Nasraoui, O., & Pavuluri, M. (2004). Accurate web recommendations based on profile-specific URL-predictor neural networks. [New York, NY: IEEE.]. *Proceedings of the WWW, 2004,* 17–22.

Nevin, J. R., & Houston, M. J. (1980). Image as a component of attraction to intraurban shopping areas. *Journal of Retailing, 56*(1), 77–93.

Newell, S. C. (1997). User models and filtering agents for improved internet information retrieval. *User Modeling and User-Adapted Interaction, 7*(4), 223–237. doi:10.1023/A:1008292003163

Ngu, D. S. W., & Xindong. (1997). SiteHelper: A localized agent that helps incremental exploration of the world wide web. *Computer Networks and ISDN Systems, 29*(8-13), 1249-1255.

Nicol, D. (2007). E-assessment by design: Using multiple-choice tests to good effect. *Journal of Further and Higher Education, 31*(1), 53–64. doi:10.1080/03098770601167922

Nuseibeh, B., & Easterbrook, S. (2002). Requirements engineering: A roadmap. In *Proceedings of the Conference on the Future of the Software Engineering,* (pp. 35-46). Limerick, Ireland: IEEE.

O'Donovan, J., & Smyth, B. (2005). Trust in recommender systems. In *Proceedings of the 2005 Conference on Intelligent User Interfaces,* (pp. 167-174). IEEE.

O'Mahoney, M., Silvestre, G., & Hurley, N. (2004). Collaborative recommendations: A robustness analysis. *ACM Transactions on Internet Technology, 4*(4), 344–377.

O'Reilly, T. (2005). *O'reilly network: What is web 2.0.* Retrieved from http://www.oreillynet.com/lpt/a/6228

Oard, W. D. (1998). Implicit feedback for recommender systems. In *Proceedings of the American Association for Artificial Intelligent Workshop of Collaborative Systems (AAAI 1998),* (pp. 80-83). AAAI.

Oliver, W. L., & Schneider, W. (1988). Using rules and task division to augment connectionist learning. In *Proceedings of the Tenth Annual Conference of the Cognitive Science Society,* (pp. 55-61). Montreal, Canada: Erlbaum.

Olsson, T. (2003). *Bootstrapping and decentralizing recommender systems. (IT Licentiate Theses).* Uppsala, Sweden: Uppsala University.

Omlin, C. W., & Giles, C. L. (1992). Training second-order recurrent neural networks using hints. In *Proceedings of the Ninth International Conference on Machine Learning,* (pp. 361-366). Aberdeen, Scotland: Morgan Kaufmann.

Ouamani, F., Jrad, Z., Aufaure, M. A., Zghal, H. B., & Ghezala, H. B. (2007). PWUM: A web usage mining multi-agent architecture for web personalization. In *Proceedings of the IADIS International Conference WWW/ Internet,* (pp. 272-276). IADIS.

Oza, N. C. (2004). AdaBoost2: Boosting with noisy data. In F. Roli, J. Kittler, & T. Windeatt (Eds.), *Proceedings of the 5th International Workshop on Multiple Classifier Systems,* (pp. 31-40). Berlin, Germany: Springer-Verlag.

Pabarskaite, Z., & Raudys, A. (2007). A process of knowledge discovery from weblog data: Systematization and critical review. *Journal of Intelligent Information Systems, 28,* 79–104. doi:10.1007/s10844-006-0004-1

Paddison, A., & Calderwood, E. (2007). Rural retailing: A sector in decline? *International Journal of Retail and Distribution Management, 35*(2), 136–155. doi:10.1108/09590550710728093

Pal, S. K., Talwar, V., & Mitra, P. (2002). Web mining in soft computing framework: Relevance, state of the art and future directions. *IEEE Transactions on Neural Networks, 13*(I.5), 1163–1177.

Palaniappan, R., Raveendran, P., & Omatu, S. (2002). Vep optimal channel selection using genetic algorithm for neural network classification of alcoholics. *IEEE Transactions on Neural Networks, 13*(2). doi:10.1109/72.991435

Pal, N. R., & Bezdek, J. C. (1995). On cluster validity for the fuzzy c-means model. *IEEE Transactions on Fuzzy Systems, 3,* 370–379. doi:10.1109/91.413225

Panda, M., & Patra, M. R. (2009). Ensemble voting system for detecting anomaly based network intrusions. *International Journal of Recent Trends in Engineering*, *2*(5), 8–13.

Pang, B., Lee, L., & Vaithyanathan, S. (2002). Thumbs up? Sentiment classification using machine learning techniques. In *Proceedings of the ACL-02 Conference on Empirical Methods in Natural Language Processing*, (pp. 79–86). ACL.

Papadimitriou, C. H., Raghavan, P., Tamaki, H., & Vempala, S. (1998). Latent semantic indexing: A probabilistic analysis. In *Proceedings of the 17ᵗʰ ACM Symposium on Principles of Database Systems*, (pp. 159-168). ACM Press.

Papadopoulos, N. G. (1980). Consumer outshopping research: Review and extension. *Journal of Retailing*, *56*(4), 41–58.

Papagelis, M., Plexousakis, D., & Kutsuras, T. (2005). Alleviating the sparsity problem of collaborative filtering using trust inferences. *Lecture Notes in Computer Science*, *3477*, 224–239. doi:10.1007/11429760_16

Parikh, D. (2006). Measuring retail service quality: An empirical assessment of the instrument. *Vikalpa: The Journal for Decision Makers*, *31*(2), 45–55.

Patel, A., Russell, D., Oppermann, K., & Rashev, R. (1998). An initial framework of contexts for designing usable intelligent tutoring systems. *Information Services & Use*, *18*(1-2), 65–76.

Paterek, A. (2007). Improving regularized singular value decomposition for collaborative filtering. In *Proceedings of KDD Cup and Workshop*. IEEE.

Pawlak, Z. (1982). Rough sets. *International Journal of Computer and Information Sciences*, *11*(1), 341–356. doi:10.1007/BF01001956

Payr, S. (2003). The virtual university's faculty: An overview of educational agents. *Applied Artificial Intelligence*, *17*, 1–19. doi:10.1080/713827053

Pazzani, M. J. (1999). A framework for collaborative, content-based and demographic filtering. *Artificial Intelligence Review*, *13*, 394–408. doi:10.1023/A:1006544522159

Pedmanabhan, V. N., & Mogul, J. C. (1996). Using predictive pre-fetching to improve worldwideweb latency. *Computer Communication Review*, *26*(3), 22–36. doi:10.1145/235160.235164

Perkins, S., Lacker, K., & Theiler, J. (2003). Grafting: Fast, incremental feature selection by gradient descent in function space. *Journal of Machine Learning Research*, *3*, 1333–1356.

Perkowitz, M., & Etzioni, O. (1998). Adaptive sites: Automatically synthesizing web pages. In *Proceedings of Artificial Intelligence* (pp. 727–732). IEEE.

Perugini, S., Goncalves, M. A., & Fox, E. A. (2004). Recommender system research: A connection centric survey. *Journal of Intelligent Information Systems*, *23*(2), 107–143. doi:10.1023/B:JIIS.0000039532.05533.99

Picariello, A., & Sansone, C. (2008). A web usage mining algorithm for web personalization. *Intelligent Decision Technologies*, *2*, 219–230.

Pierrakos, D., Paliouras, G. O., Papatheodorou, C., & Spyropoulos, C. D. (2003). Web usage mining as a tool for personalization: A survey. *User Modeling and User-Adapted Interaction*, *3*, 311–372. doi:10.1023/A:1026238916441

Pierre, S. (1998). Inferring new design rules by machine learning: A case study of topological optimization. *IEEE Transactions on Man, Systems, and Cybernetics*, *28A*(5), 575–585. doi:10.1109/3468.709602

Pierre, S., & Elgibaoui, A. (1997). A tabu search approach for designing computer network topologies with unreliable components. *IEEE Transactions on Reliability*, *46*(3), 350–359. doi:10.1109/24.664006

Pierre, S., & Gharbi, I. (2001). A generic object-oriented model for representing computer network topologies. *Advances in Engineering Software*, *32*(2), 95–110. doi:10.1016/S0965-9978(00)00081-8

Pierre, S., & Legault, G. (1998). A genetic algorithm for designing distributed computer network topologies. *IEEE Transactions on Man, Systems, and Cybernetics*, *28*(2), 249–258. doi:10.1109/3477.662766

Piramuthu, S. (2004). Evaluating feature selection methods for learning in data mining applications. *European Journal of Operational Research, Computing, Artificial Intelligence, and Information Technology*, *156*, 483–494.

Piron, F. (2001). International retail leakages: Singaporeans outshopping in Malaysia. *Singapore Management Review, 23*(1), 35–58.

Pitt, L., Morris, M. H., & Oosthuizen, P. (1996). Expectations of service quality as an industrial market segmentation variable. *Service Industries Journal, 16*(1), 1–9. doi:10.1080/02642069600000001

Poirier, D., Fessant, F., & Tellier, I. (2010). Reducing the cold-start problem in content recommendation through opinion classification. In *Proceedings of Web Intelligence* (pp. 204–207). Toronto, Canada: IEEE. doi:10.1109/WI-IAT.2010.87

Polonsky, M. J., & Jarratt, D. G. (1992). Rural outshopping in Australia: The Bathurst-Orange region. *European Journal of Marketing, 26*(10), 5–16. doi:10.1108/EUM0000000000647

Porter, M. (1980). An algorithm for suffix stripping. *Program, 14*(3), 130–137. doi:10.1108/eb046814

Power, R. (2002). CSI/FBI computer crime and security survey. *Computer Security Journal, 18*(2), 7–30.

Pratt, K. (2001). *Locating patterns in discrete time series*. (M.Sc. Thesis). University of South Florida. Tampa, FL.

Puntheeranurak, S., & Tsuji, H. (2005). Mining web logs for a personalized recommender system. In *Proceedings of International Conference on Information Technology: Research and Education,* (pp. 445 – 448). IEEE Press.

Pyle, D. (1999). *Data preparation for data mining*. San Francisco, CA: MKP.

Quinn, L., Hines, T., & Bennison, D. (2007). Making sense of market segmentation: A fashion retailing case. *European Journal of Marketing, 41*(5/6), 439–465. doi:10.1108/03090560710737552

Radev, D. R., Blair-Goldensohn, S., Zhang, Z., & Raghavan, R. S. (2001). Newsinessence: A system for domain-independent, real-time news clustering and multi-document summarization. In *Proceedings of the Human Language Technology Conference.* IEEE.

Rafter, R., & Smyth, B. (2001). Passive profiling from server logs in an online recruitment environment. In *Proceedings of the Workshop on Intelligent Techniques for Web Personalization,* (pp. 35–41). IEEE.

Rajagopal. (2007). Stimulating retail sales and upholding customer value. *Journal of Retail and Leisure Property, 6*(2), 117-135.

Rajavarman, V. N., & Rajagopalan, S. P. (2007). Feature selection in data-mining for genetics using genetic algorithm. *Journal of Computer Science, 3*(9), 723–725. doi:10.3844/jcssp.2007.723.725

Rakotomamonjy, A. (2003). Variable selection using SVM-based criteria. *Journal of Machine Learning Research, 3*, 1357–1370.

Ramaswamy, L., Polavarapu, R., Gunasekera, K., Garg, D., Visweswariah, K., & Kalyanaraman, S. (2009). Caesar: A context-aware, social recommender system for low-end mobile devices. *IEEE International Conference on Mobile Data Management,* (pp. 338–347). IEEE Press.

Rao, K. N., & Talwar, V. G. (2008). Application domain and functional classification of recommender systems - A survey. *Journal of Library Information Technology, 28*(3), 17–35.

Rashedi, E. (2007). *Gravitational search algorithm*. (M.Sc. Thesis). Shahid Bahonar University of Kerman. Kerman, Iran.

Rashedi, E., Nezamabadi-Pour, H., & Saryazdi, S. (2009). GSA: A gravitational search algorithm. *Information Sciences, 179*(13), 2232–2248. doi:10.1016/j.ins.2009.03.004

Rashedi, E., Nezamabadi-Pour, H., & Saryazdi, S. (2011). Filter modelin using gravitational search algorithm. *Engineering Applications of Artificial Intelligence, 24*(1), 117–122. doi:10.1016/j.engappai.2010.05.007

Ratsch, G., Onoda, T., & Muller, K. R. (2001). Soft margins for AdaBoost. *Machine Learning, 42*, 287–320. doi:10.1023/A:1007618119488

Raymond, L., Croteau, A.-M., & Bergeron, F. (2009). The integrative role of IT in product and process innovation: Growth and productivity outcomes for manufacturing. In *Proceedings of the Enterprise Information Systems, 11th International Conference,* (pp. 27-39). Berlin, Germany: Springer-Verlag.

Reeves, C. R., & Rowe, J. E. (2003). *Genetic algorithms: Principles and perspectives a guide to GA theory*. Dordrecht, The Netherlands: Kluwer Academic Publishers.

Resnick, P., Iacovou, N., Suchak, M., Bergstrom, P., & Riedl, J. (1994). Grouplens: An open architecture for collaborative filtering of netnews. In *Proceedings of the Conference on Computer Supported Cooperative Work,* (pp. 175–186). ACM Press.

Resnick, P., Iacovou, N., Sushak, M., Bergstrom, P., & Riedl, J. (1994). An open architecture for collaborative filtering of netnews. In *Proceedings of the Computer Supported Collaborative Work Conference,* (pp. 175—186). IEEE.

Resnick, P., & Varian, H. R. (1997). Recommender system. *Communications of the ACM, 40*(3), 56–58. doi:10.1145/245108.245121

Reynolds, F. D., & Darden, W. R. (1972). Intermarket patronage: A psychographic study of consumer outshoppers. *Journal of Marketing, 36*(4), 50–54. doi:10.2307/1250427

Ribeiro-Neto, B., Cristo, M., Golgher, P. B., & Silva de Moura, E. (2005). Impedance coupling in content-targeted advertising. In *Proceedings of the 28th Annual International ACM SIGIR Conference on Research and Development in Information Retrieval,* (pp. 496–503). New York, NY: ACM Press.

Ricci, F., et al. (Eds.). (2011). *Recommender systems handbook.* Berlin, Germany: Springer Science + Business Media.

Ricci, F., Rokach, L., Shapira, B., & Kantor, P. B. (Eds.). (2010). *Recommender systems handbook.* New York, NY: Springer.

Rich, E. (1998). User modeling via stereotypes. In Maybury, M. T., & Wahlster, W. (Eds.), *Readings in Intelligent User Interfaces* (pp. 329–342). San Francisco, CA: Morgan Kaufmann Publishers Inc.

Ricks, J., & Pettypool, D. (2008). Pilot study of the perceptions of small downtown retailers regarding the impact of mega stores: An optimum balance desired. *Proceedings of the Academy of Marketing Studies, 13*(1), 59–64.

Rinne, H., & Swinyard, W. R. (1995). Segmenting the discount store market: The domination of the difficult discounter core. *International Review of Retail, Distribution and Consumer Research, 5*(2), 123–145. doi:10.1080/09593969500000010

Rocchio, J. (1971). Relevance feedback in information retrieval. In *The SMART Retrieval System: Experiments in Automatic Document Processing* (pp. 313–323). Upper Saddle River, NJ: Prentice Hall.

Rodríguez, A. (2011). Teacher model for an educational adaptive hypermedia that supports the teaching of decision-making. In *Proceedings of INTED 2011 Conference,* (pp. 91-100). INTED.

Rodríguez, A., Aïmeur, E., & Vázquez-Abad, F. (2003). Training teachers in teaching decision-making skills. In *Proceedings of the 2nd International Conference on Multimedia and Information & Communication Technologies in Education,* (pp. 1964-1968). IEEE.

Rodríguez, A., Aïmeur, E., & Vázquez-Abad, F. (2004). Adaptive help techniques to reduce the teachers' cognitive overload. In *Proceedings of the International Conference on Computers in Education (ICCE 2004),* (pp. 1741-1750). ICCE.

Rodríguez, A., Aïmeur, E., & Vázquez-Abad, F. (2004). E-learning for complex decision-making with the support of a web-based adaptive ITS. In *Proceedings of the International Conference on Knowledge Engineering and Decision Support (ICKEDS 2004),* (pp. 47-54). ICKEDS.

Rodríguez, A. (2007). Evaluación de un tipo de ayuda en línea destinada a profesores que deseen crear sitios educativos en Internet. *Intersedes, 7*(11), 99–117.

Rodríguez, A. (2008). Generation, testing and recommendation of teaching materials using classification learning. *International Journal of Advanced Media and Communication, 2*(3), 308–324. doi:10.1504/IJAMC.2008.020182

Roos, J. A., Eastin, I. L., & Matsuguma, H. (2005). Market segmentation and analysis of Japan's residential post and beam construction market. *Forest Products Journal, 55*(4), 24–30.

Rothrock, L., Koubek, R., Fuchs, F., Haas, M., & Salvendy, G. (2002). Review and reappraisal of adaptive interfaces: Toward biologically-inspired paradigms. *Theoretical Issues in Ergonomics Science, 3*(1), 47–84. doi:10.1080/14639220110110342

Rovithakis, G. A., Maniadakis, M., & Zervakis, M. (2004). A hybrid neural network/genetic algorithm approach to optimizing feature extraction for signal classification. *IEEE Transactions on Systems, Man, and Cybernetics. Part B, Cybernetics, 34*(1), 695–702. doi:10.1109/TSMCB.2003.811293

Rumelhart, D. E., Durbin, R., Golden, R., & Chauvin, Y. (1995). Backpropagation: The basic theory. In *Backpropagation: Theory, Architectures and Applications* (pp. 1–34). Hillsdale, NJ: Lawrence Erlbaum Associates.

Rumelhart, D. E., Hinton, G. E., & Williams, R. I. (1986). Learning internal representations by error propagation. In Rumelhart, D. E., & McClelland, I. L. (Eds.), *Parallel Distributed Processing* (*Vol. 1*, pp. 318–362). Cambridge, MA: MIT Press.

Rumelhart, D., & McClelland, I. (1986). *Parallel distributed processing*. Cambridge, MA: MIT Press.

Saha, S., Sajjanhar, A., Shang, G., Dew, R., & Ying, Z. (2010). Delivering categorized news items using RSS feeds and web services. [CIT.]. *Proceedings of CIT, 2010*, 698–702.

Salcedo-Sanz, S., Camps-Valls, G., Pérez-Cruz, F., Sepúlveda-Sanchis, J., & Bousoño-Calzón, C. (2004). Enhancing genetic feature selection through restricted search and Walsh analysis. *IEEE Transactions on Systems, Man and Cybernetics. Part C, Applications and Reviews, 34*(4). doi:10.1109/TSMCC.2004.833301

Salton, G., & McGill, M. (1984). *Introduction to modern information retrieval*. Columbus, OH: McGraw-Hill Book Company.

Samli, A. C., & Uhr, E. B. (1974). The outshopping spectrum: Key for analyzing intermarket leakages. *Journal of Retailing, 50*(2), 70–105.

Samson, D. (1986). Designing an automobile insurance classification system. *European Journal of Operational Research, 27*, 235–241. doi:10.1016/0377-2217(86)90065-2

Samson, D., & Thomas, H. (1987). Linear models as aids in insurance decision making: The estimation of automobile insurance claims. *Journal of Business Research, 15*, 247–256. doi:10.1016/0148-2963(87)90027-0

Sarstedt, M. (2008). Market segmentation with mixture regression models: Understanding measures that guide model selection. *Journal of Targeting. Measurement and Analysis for Marketing, 16*(3), 228–246. doi:10.1057/jt.2008.9

Sarwar, B., Karypis, G., Konstan, J. A., & Riedl, J. T. (2001). Item-based collaborative filtering recommendation algorithms. In *Proceedings of the 10th International World Wide Web Conference*, (pp. 285–295). IEEE.

Sarwar, B., Karypis, G., Konstan, J., & Riedl, J. (2000). Analysis of recommendation algorithms for e-commerce. In *Proceedings of the 2nd ACM Conference on Electronic Commerce*, (pp. 158-167). ACM Press.

Sarwar, B., Karypis, G., Konstan, J., & Riedl, J. (2000). *Application of dimensionality reduction in recommender systems: A case study*. Paper presented at the ACM Web-KDD Workshop. New York, NY.

Sarwar, B., Karypis, G., Konstan, K. A., & Riedl, J. (2001). Item based collaborative filtering recommendation algorithms. In *Proceedings of the 10th International Conference on World Wide Web*, (pp. 115-153). IEEE.

Schacter, J. (1999). *The impact of education technology on student achievement: What the most current research has to say*. Santa Monica, CA: Milken Exchange on Education Technology.

Schafer, J. B., Konston, J. A., Borchers, A., Sarwar, B., Herlocker, J., & Riedl, J. (1999). Combining collaborative filtering with personal agents for better recommendations. In *Proceedings of 16th National Conference on Artificial Intelligence*, (pp. 439-446). AAAI Press.

Schapire, R. E. (1990). The strength of weak learnability. *Machine Learning, 5*, 197–227. doi:10.1007/BF00116037

Schechter, S., Krishnan, M., & Smith, M. D. (1998). Using path profiles to predict HTTP requests. In *Proceedings of the Seventh International Conference on World Wide Web*, (pp. 457–467). Elsevier.

Schecter, M. K. S., & Smith, M. (1998). Using path profiles to predict HTTP request. In *Proceedings of 7th International WWW Conference*, (pp. 457-467). IEEE.

Schein, A., Popescul, A., Ungar, L., & Pennock, D. (2002). Methods and metrics for cold-start recommendations. In *Proceedings of the 25th Annual International ACM SIGIR Conference on Research and Development in Information Retrieval,* (pp. 253-260). ACM Press.

Schmidt-Thieme, L. (2005). Compound classification models for recommender systems. In *Proceedings of the Fifth IEEE International Conference on Data Mining (ICDM 2005).* IEEE Press.

Schwenk, H., & Bengio, Y. (2000). Boosting neural networks. *Neural Computation, 12,* 1869–1887. doi:10.1162/089976600300015178

Schwenk, H., & Bengio, Y. (2000). Boosting neural networks. *Neural Computation, 12,* 1869–1887. doi:10.1162/089976600300015178

Selbach, M., Sieckenius, C., & Barbosa, S. (2003). A method of semiotic engineering for the online help systems construction. In *Proceedings of the Latin American Conference on Human-Computer Interaction,* (pp. 167-177). IEEE.

Self, T. (1998). Implementing a web-based help system. In *Proceedings of the Help for the Web Symposium.* Retrieved May 6, 2004 from http//:www.help4web.org/publication/self1.htm

Setten, M. V. (2003). Prediction strategies in a TV recommender system: Framework and experiments. In *Proceedings of IADIS WWW/Internet 2003.* Algarve, Portugal: IADIS.

Setten, M. V., Veenstra, M., Nijholt, A., & Dijk, B. V. (2004). Case-based reasoning as a prediction strategy for hybrid recommender systems. *Lecture Notes in Computer Science, 3034,* 13–22. doi:10.1007/978-3-540-24681-7_4

Sewall, M. A. (1978). Market segmentation based on consumer ratings of proposed product designs. *JMR, Journal of Marketing Research, 15*(4), 557–564. doi:10.2307/3150625

Shahabi, C., & Banaei-Kashani, F. (2003). Efficient and anonymous web-usage mining for web personalization. *INFORMS Journal on Computing.* Retrieved from http://www.csee.umbc.edu/~kolari1/Mining/papers/Shahabi-WebKDD2001-BookChapter.pdf

Shah-Hosseini, H. (2007). Problem solving by intelligent water drops. In *Proceedings of the 2007 IEEE Congress on Evolutionary Computation,* (pp. 3226-3231). Singapore, Singapore: IEEE.

Shah-Hosseini, H. (2008). Intelligent water drops algorithm: A new optimization method for solving the multiple knapsack problem. *International Journal of Intelligent Computing and Cybernetics, 1*(2), 193–212. doi:10.1108/17563780810874717

Shah-Hosseini, H. (2009). The intelligent water drops algorithm: A nature-inspired swarm-based optimization algorithm. *International Journal of Bio-Inspired Computation, 1*(1/2), 71–79. doi:10.1504/IJBIC.2009.022775

Shaikh, M. A. M., & Mitsuru, I. (2006). ASNA: An intelligent agent for retrieving and classifying news on the basis of emotion-affinity. In *Proceedings of the International Conference on Intelligent Agents, Web Technologies and Internet Commerce (IAWTIC 2006),* (pp. 133-138). Sydney, Australia: IAWTIC.

Shapira, B., Hanani, U., Raveh, A., & Shoval, P. (1997). Information filtering: A new two-phase model using stereotypic profiling. *Journal of Intelligent Information Systems, 8,* 155–165. doi:10.1023/A:1008676625559

Shapiro, D., & Shi, X. (2008). Market segmentation: The role of opaque travel agencies. *Journal of Economics & Management Strategy, 17*(4), 803–837. doi:10.1111/j.1530-9134.2008.00196.x

Shapiro, V., & Varian, H. R. (1999). *Information rules: A strategic guide to the network economy.* Boston, MA: Harvard Publisher School Press.

Shardanand, U., & Maes, P. (1995). Social information filtering: Algorithms for automating "word of mouth". In *Proceedings of the SIGCHI Conference on Human Factors in Computing Systems,* (pp. 210–217). ACM Press.

Shavlik, J. W. (1994). Extended abstract: Combining symbolic and neural learning. *Machine Learning, 14,* 321–331. doi:10.1007/BF00993982

Shavlik, J. W., & Towell, G. G. (1989). An approach to combining explanation-based and neural learning algorithms. *Connection Science, 1,* 233–255. doi:10.1080/09540098908915640

Sheikhan, M., & Movaghar, B. (2009). Exchange rate prediction using an evolutionary connectionist model. *World Applied Sciences Journal*, *7*, 8–16.

Shiri-Ahmadabadi, M. (1999). *Étude et modélisation des connaissances et raisonnement de l'apprenant dans un STI.* (PhD Dissertation). Université de Montréal. Montreal, Canada.

Siguaw, J. A., & Simpson, P. M. (1997). Effects of religiousness on Sunday shopping and outshopping behaviours: A study of shopper attitudes and behaviours in the American South. *International Review of Retail, Distribution and Consumer Research*, *7*(1), 23–40. doi:10.1080/095939697343111

Silva, J. L. C., & Soma, N. Y. (2008). A constructive hybrid genetic algorithm for the flowshop scheduling problem. *International Journal of Computer Science and Network Security*, *8*(9), 219–223.

Silvestri, F., Baraglia, R., Palmerini, P., & O, M. S. (2004). On-line generation of suggestions for web users. In *Proceedings of Information Technology: Coding and Computing*, (pp. 1-3). IEEE.

Simkin, L. (2008). Achieving market segmentation from B2B sectorisation. *Journal of Business and Industrial Marketing*, *23*(7), 464–474. doi:10.1108/08858620810901220

Sinha, P. K. (2003). Shopping orientation in the evolving Indian market. *Vikalpa: The Journal for Decision Makers*, *28*(2), 13–22.

Sitthiworachart, J., Joy, M., & Sutinen, E. (2008). Success factors for e-assessment in computer science education. In *Proceedings of World Conference on E-Learning in Corporate, Government, Healthcare, and Higher Education*, (pp. 2287-2293). Chesapeake, VA: AACE.

Smith, K. A., Willis, R. J., & Brooks, M. (2000). An analysis of customer retention and insurance claim patterns using data mining: A case study. *The Journal of the Operational Research Society*, *51*(5), 532–541.

Smith, M. F. (1999). Urban versus suburban consumers: a contrast in holiday shopping purchase intentions and outshopping behavior. *Journal of Consumer Marketing*, *16*(1), 58–73. doi:10.1108/07363769910250778

Smith, S. A., & Achabal, D. D. (1998). Clearance pricing and inventory policies for retail chains. *Management Science*, *44*(3), 285–300. doi:10.1287/mnsc.44.3.285

Smith, S. A., Agrawal, N., & McIntyre, S. H. (1998). A discrete optimization model for seasonal merchandise planning. *Journal of Retailing*, *74*(2), 193–221. doi:10.1016/S0022-4359(99)80093-1

Smolensky, P. (1988). On the proper treatment of connnectionism. *The Behavioral and Brain Sciences*, *11*(1), 1. doi:10.1017/S0140525X00052432

Sobecki, J. (2006). Implementations of web-based recommender systems using hybrid methods. *International Journal of Computer Science & Applications*, *3*(3), 52–64.

Song, L., Smola, A., Gretton, A., Borgwardt, K., & Bedo, J. (2007). Supervised feature selection via dependence estimation. In *Proceedings of the 24th International Conference on Machine Learning*. Corvallis, OR: IEEE.

Song, Q., & Shepperd, M. (2006). Mining web browsing patterns for e-commerce. *Computers in Industry*, *57*(7), 622–630. doi:10.1016/j.compind.2005.11.006

Spool, J. (1999). *Web site usability: A designer's guide*. San Francisco, CA: Morgan Kauffman Publishers Inc.

Srivastava, J., Cooley, R., Deshpande, M., & Tan, P.-N. (2000). Web usage mining: Discovery and applications of usage patterns from web data. *SIGKDD Explorations*, *1*(2), 12–23. doi:10.1145/846183.846188

Stefani, A., & Strapparava, C. (1999). Exploiting NLP techniques to build user model for web sites: The use of WordNet in SiteIF project. In *Proceedings of the Second Workshop on Adaptive Systems and User Modeling on the World Wide Web, 8th International World Wide Web Conference*. ACM Press.

Stefanidis, K., & Pitoura, E. (2008). Fast contextual preference scoring of database tuples. In *Proceedings of EDBT*, (pp. 344-355). Nantes, France: EDBT.

Stephanidis, C. (2001). Adaptive techniques for universal access. *User Modeling and User-Adapted Interaction*, *11*, 159–179. doi:10.1023/A:1011144232235

Stephen. (1991). *Developing a retail strategy for an up-scale target audience: The influence of outshopping and store.* Retrieved from http://www.sbaer.uca.edu/research/ssbia/1991/PDF/02.pdf

Stevens, F. C. (1993). *Knowledge-based assistance for accessing large, poorly structured information spaces.* (PhD Thesis). University of California. Boulder, CO.

Stone, M. (1977). Asymptotics for and against cross-validation. *Biometrika, 64*, 29–35. doi:10.1093/biomet/64.1.29

Suikki, R., Tromstedt, R., & Haapasal, H. (2006). Project management competence development framework in turbulent business environment. *Technovation, 26*, 723–738. doi:10.1016/j.technovation.2004.11.003

Sullivan, P., & Savitt, R. (1997). Store patronage and lifestyle factors: Implications for rural grocery retailers. *International Journal of Retail and Distribution Management, 25*(10/11), 351–364.

Suna, Z., Bebisa, G., & Millerb, R. (2004). Object detection using feature subset selection. In *Proceedings of the Pattern Recognition Society.* Elsevier.

Sun, R. (1994). *Integrating rules and connectionism for robust common sense reasoning.* New York, NY: Wiley and Sons.

Sun, R. (1997). Introduction to connectionist symbolic integration. In Sun, R., & Alexandre, F. (Eds.), *Connectionist-Symbolic Integration.* Mahwah, NJ: Lawrence Erlbaum Associates.

Sun, Z., Bebis, G., & Miller, R. (2004). Object detection using feature subset selection. *Pattern Recognition, 37*, 2165–2176. doi:10.1016/j.patcog.2004.03.013

Suryavanshi, B. S., Shiri, N., & Mudur, S. P. (2005). A fuzzy hybrid collaborative filtering technique for web personalization. In *Proceedings of Intelligent Techniques for Web Personalization.* IEEE.

Su, X., & Khoshgoftaar, T. M. (2009). A survey of collaborative filtering techniques. In *Proceedings of Advances in Artificial Intelligence.* IEEE.

Sweller, J. (1988). Cognitive load during problem solving: Effects on learning. *Cognitive Science, 12*, 257–285. doi:10.1207/s15516709cog1202_4

Sziranyi, T., & Csapodi, M. (1998). Texture classification and segmentation by cellular neural networks using genetic learning. *Computer Vision and Image Understanding, 71*(3), 255–270. doi:10.1006/cviu.1997.0646

Taeho, J. (2009). Categorization of news articles using neural text categorizer. In *Proceedings to FUZZY* (pp. 19–22). FUZZY.

Taira, H., & Haruno, M. (1999). Feature selection in SVM categorization. In *Proceedings of AAAI 1999.* AAAI.

Takagi, H. (2001). Interactive evolutionary computation: Fusion of the capabilities of EC optimization and human evaluation. *Proceedings of the IEEE, 89*, 1275–1296. doi:10.1109/5.949485

Takeda, T., & Takasu, A. (2007). Update news: A news clustering and summarization system using efficient text processing. In *Proceedings of International Conference Digital Libraries.* IEEE.

Tan, X., Yao, M., & Xu, M. (2004). An effective technique for personalization recommendation based on access sequential patterns. In *Proceedings of Asia – Pacific Conference on Services Computing,* (pp. 42 – 46). IEEE.

Taraskina, A., & Cheremushkin, E. (2006). The modified fuzzy c-means method for clustering of microarray data. In *Proceedings of the Fifth International Conference on Bioinformatics of Genome Regulation and Structure,* (pp. 180-183). Novosibirsk, Russia: IEEE.

Tavallaee, M., Bagheri, E., Lu, W., & Ghorbani Ali, A. (2009). A detailed analysis of the KDDCup 1999 dataset. In *Proceedings of 2009 IEEE International Symposium on Computational Intelligence in Security and Defense Applications,* (pp. 1-6). IEEE Press.

Taylor, S. L. (1997). Outshopping: The battle between rural and urban medical services. *Marketing Health Services, 17*(3), 42–44.

Terveen, L., Hill, W., Amento, B., McDonald, D., & Creter, J. (1997). Phoaks: A system for sharing recommendations. *Communications of the ACM, 40*(3), 59–62. doi:10.1145/245108.245122

Thomas, C., & Fisher, G. (1996). Using agents to improve the usability an usefulness of the WWW. In *Proceedings of the 5th International Conference on User Modeling,* (pp. 5-12). IEEE.

Thomas, L., Edelman, D., & Crook, J. (2002). *Credit scoring and its application.* New York, NY: SIAM. doi:10.1137/1.9780898718317

Thompson, J. R. (1971). Characteristics and behavior of out-shopping consumers. *Journal of Retailing, 47*(1), 70–80.

Thor, A., Golovin, N., & Rahm, E. (2005). Adaptive website recommendations with AWESOME. *The VLDB Journal, 14*(4), 357–372. doi:10.1007/s00778-005-0160-x

Tian, L., & Noore, A. (2005). On-line prediction of software reliability using an evolutionary connectionist model. *Journal of Systems and Software, 77*, 173–180. doi:10.1016/j.jss.2004.08.023

Tintarev, N., & Masthoff, J. (2006). Similarity for news recommender systems. In *Proceedings of the AH 2006 Workshop on Recommender Systems and Intelligent User Interfaces.* AH.

Touretzky, D. S. (Ed.). (1991). Special issue on connectionist approaches to language learning. *Machine Learning, 7.*

Towell, G. G., Craven, M. W., & Shavlik, J. W. (1991). Constructive induction in knowledge-based neural networks. In L. Birnbaum & G. Collins (Eds.), *Machine Learning: Proceedings of the Eighth International Workshop.* San Mateo, CA: Morgan Kaufmann.

Towle, B. (2001). *Authoring tools for building how-to simulations.* (Ph.D. Dissertation). Northwestern University. Evanston, IL.

Tran, T., & Cohen, R. (2000). Hybrid recommender systems for electronic commerce. In *Proceedings of the Seventeenth National Conference on Artificial Intelligence (AAAI-2000) Workshop on Knowledge-Based Electronic Markets,* (pp. 78–84). AAAI Press.

Tryfos, P. (1980). On classification in automobile insurance. *The Journal of Risk and Insurance, 47*(2), 331–337. doi:10.2307/252336

Tumer, K., & Ghosh, J. (1996). Analysis of decision boundaries in linearly combined neural classifiers. *Pattern Recognition, 29*(2), 341–348. doi:10.1016/0031-3203(95)00085-2

Turney, P. D. (2002). Thumbs up or thumbs down? Semantic orientation applied to unsupervised classification of reviews. In *Proceedings of the 40th Annual Meeting of the Association for Computational Linguistics,* (pp. 417–424). ACL.

Tuttle, H. G. (2007). *Formative assessment cycle in your classroom: Your technology use.* Retrieved March 13, 2011, from http://eduwithtechn.wordpress.com/2007/10/31/formative-assessment-cycle-in-your-classroom-your-technology-use/

Uberbacher, E. C., & Mural, R. J. (1991). Locating protein coding regions in human DNA sequences by a multiple sensor - Neural network approach. *Proceedings of the National Academy of Sciences of the United States of America, 88*, 11261–11265. doi:10.1073/pnas.88.24.11261

Valient, L. G. (1984). A theory of learnable. *Communications of the ACM, 27*(11), 1134–1142. doi:10.1145/1968.1972

Van Joolingen, W. (1999). Cognitive tools for discovering learning. *International Journal of Artificial Intelligence in Education, 10*, 385–397.

Vaughan, E. J., & Vaughan, T. M. (1996). *Fundamentals of risk and insurance* (7th ed.). New York, NY: Wiley.

Vázquez-Abad, F., Rodríguez, A., & Aïmeur, E. (2003). Training the teacher: A new approach for authoring ITSs for teaching decision-making. In *Proceedings of the International Conference on Open & Online Learning (ICOOL 2003).* Retrieved May 18, 2004 from http://icool.uom.ac.mu/2003/papers/file/Rodriguez.pdf

Vázquez-Abad, F., Rodríguez, A., Ng, A., Zukerman, M., & Warfield, R. (2001). Bridging theory and practice in network design using web-based simulation. In *Proceedings of the 12th Annual Conference of the Australasian Association for Engineering Education (AaeE 2001),* (pp. 40-45). AaeE.

Verbeke, W., Vermeir, I., & Brunso, K. (2007). Consumer evaluation of fish quality as basis for fish market segmentation. *Food Quality and Preference, 18*(4), 651–661. doi:10.1016/j.foodqual.2006.09.005

Vidhya, K. A., & Aghila, G. (2010). Hybrid text mining model for document classification. In *Proceedings of the ICCAE,* (pp. 210 – 214). ICCAE.

Virvou, M., & Moundridou, M. (2002). Adding an instructor modelling component to the architecture of ITS authoring tools. *International Journal of Artificial Intelligence in Education, 12*, 185–211.

Vose, D. (2000). *Quantitative risk analysis*. New York, NY: John Wiley & Sons.

Walters, R. G. (1988). Retail promotions and retail store performances: A test of some key hypotheses. *Journal of Retailing, 64*(2), 153–180.

Wang, J. (2001). *Toward the usability of hypermedia adaptive intelligent interfaces*. (PhD. Dissertation). The George Washington University. Washington, DC.

Wang, Y., Li, Z., & Zhang, Y. (2005). Mining sequential association-rule for improving web document prediction. In *Proceedings of the Sixth International Conference on Computational Intelligence and Multimedia Applications (ICCIMA 2005)*, (pp. 146 – 151). ICCIMA.

Wanga, F.-H., & Shaob, H.-M. (2004). Effective personalized recommendation based on time-framed navigation clustering and association mining. *Expert Systems with Applications, 27*, 365–377. doi:10.1016/j.eswa.2004.05.005

Wang, T.-H. (2008). Web-based quiz-game-like formative assessment: Development and evaluation. *Computers & Education, 51*, 1247–1263. doi:10.1016/j.compedu.2007.11.011

Wang, T., & Ren, Y. (2009). Research on personalized recommendation based on web usage mining using collaborative filtering technique. *WSEAS Transactions on Information Science and Applications, 1*(6), 62–72.

Wang, Y., Dai, W., & Yuan, Y. (2008). Website browsing aid: A navigation graph-based recommendation system. *Decision Support Systems, 45*, 387–400. doi:10.1016/j.dss.2007.05.006

Warmuth, M. K., Liao, J., Raetsch, G., Mathieson, M., Putta, S., & Lemmen, C. (2003). Active learning with support vector machines in the drug discovery process. *Journal of Chemical Information and Computer Sciences, 43*(2), 667–673. doi:10.1021/ci025620t

Wasson, M. (1998). Using leading text for news summaries: Evaluation results and implications for commercial summarization applications. In *Proceedings of the Joint 17th International Conference on Computational Linguistics and 36th Annual Meeting of the Association for Computational Linguistics*. IEEE.

Webb, G., Pazzani, M., & Billsus, D. (2001). Machine learning for user modeling. *User Modeling and User-Adapted Interaction, 11*, 19–20. doi:10.1023/A:1011117102175

Weber, J. (2000). Editing online help. *WeberWoman's Wrevenge*. Retrieved from http://www.wrevenge.com

Wei, C., Li-Jun, Z., Chun, C., & Jia-Jun, B. (2009). A hybrid phonic web news recommender system for pervasive access. In *Proceedings of the International Conference on Communications and Mobile Computing*, (vol 3, pp. 122-126). WRI.

Weiss-Lambrou, R., & Raymond, D. (2002). *Rapport du sondage sur: L'utilisation de WebCT à l'Université de Montréal et l'appréciation du soutien offert par le programme SUITE*. Montreal, Canada: Université de Montréal. Retrieved October 12, 2003 from http://www.cefes.umontreal.ca/Documents/CEFES_SondageA01_Resultats.pdf

Wei, Y. Z., Jennings, N. R., Moreau, L., & Hall, W. (2000). User evaluation of a market-based recommender system. *Autonomous Agents and Multi-Agent Systems, 17*, 251–269. doi:10.1007/s10458-008-9029-x

Werbos, P. I. (1974). *Beyond regression: New tools for regression and analysis in the behavioral sciences*. (PhD Thesis). Boston, MA: Harvard University.

Werbos, P. I. (1988). Backpropagation and neurocontrol: A review and prospectus. In *Proceedings of the Joint Conference on Neural Networks*, (vol 1, pp. 209-216). IEEE Press.

Wermter, S. (1999). Preference moore machines for neural fuzzy integration. In *Proceedings of the International Joint Conference on Artificial Intelligence*, (pp. 840-845). Stockholm, Sweden: IEEE.

Wermter, S., Arevian, G., & Panchev, C. (1999). Recurrent neural network learning for text routing. In *Proceedings of the International Conference on Artificial Neural Networks,* (pp. 898-903). Edinburgh, UK: IEEE.

Wermter, S., Arevian, G., & Panchev, C. (2000). Network analysis in a neural learning internet agents. In *Proceedings of the International Conference on Computer Intelligence and Neuroscience,* (pp. 880-884). Atlantic City, NJ: IEEE.

Wermter, S., Panchev, C., & Arevian, G. (1999). Hybrid neural plausibility networks for news agents. In *Proceedings of the National Conference on Artificial Intelligence AAAI,* (pp. 93-98). Orlando, FL: AAAI.

Wermter, S. (1995). *Hybrid connectionist natural language processing.* London, UK: Chapman and Hall Thomson International.

Wermter, S., Arevian, G., & Panchev, C. (2000). Towards hybrid neural learning internet agents. In Wermter, S., & Sun, R. (Eds.), *Hybrid Neural Systems* (pp. 160–176). Berlin, Germany: Springer. doi:10.1007/10719871_11

Wermter, S., & Weber, V. (1997). SCREEN: Learning a flat syntactic and semantic spoken language analysis using artificial neural networks. *Journal of Artificial Intelligence Research, 6*(1), 35–85.

Weston, J., & Perez-Cruz, F., Bousquet1, O., Chapelle, O., Elisseeff, A., & Schoelkopf, B. (2003). Feature selection and transduction for prediction of molecular bioactivity for drug design. *Bioinformatics (Oxford, England), 19*(6), 764–771. doi:10.1093/bioinformatics/btg054

Whitley, D. (1995). Genetic algorithms and neural networks. In Periaux, J., & Winter, G. (Eds.), *Genetic Algorithms in Engineering and Computer Science.* New York, NY: John Wiley & Sons Ltd.

Wieling, M., & Hofman, W. (2010). The impact of online video lecture recordings and automated feedback on student performance. *Computers and Education.* Retrieved from http://www.martijnwieling.nl/files/onlinevideo.pdf

Williams, J. G., Weiqian, L., & Mehmet, O. (2001). Temporal data mining using hidden Markov local polynomial models. *Lecture Notes in Artificial Intelligence, 2035.*

Williams, J. G., Weiqiang, L., & Mehmet, A. O. (2002). An overview of temporal data mining. In *Proceedings of the 1st Australian Data Mining Workshop (ADM 2002),* (pp. 83-90). Canberra, Australia: University of Technology.

Witten, I. H., & Eibe, F. (2005). *Data mining -Practical machine learning tools and techniques* (2nd ed.). London, UK: Elsevier.

Wolinski, F., Vichot, F., & Stricker, M. (2000). Using learning-based filters detect rule-based filtering obsolescence. In *Proceedings of the RIAO 2000 Conference,* (vol 2, pp. 1208-1220). RIAO.

Wu, H., Houben, G., & De Bra, P. (1998). AHAM: A reference model to support adaptive hypermedia authoring. In *Proceedings of the Zesde Interdisciplinaire Conferentie Informatiewetenschap,* (pp. 77-88). Academic Press.

Xindong, W., Gong-Qing, W., Fei, X., Zhu, Z., & Xue-Gang, H. (2010). News filtering and summarization on the web. *IEEE Intelligent Systems, 25*(5), 68–76. doi:10.1109/MIS.2010.11

Xiong, X., & Tan, K. L. (2004). Similarity-driven cluster merging method for unsupervised fuzzy clustering. In *Proceedings of the 20th Conference in Uncertainty in Artificial Intelligence,* (pp. 611-627). ACM.

Xsniaping, G. (1998). *Pattern matching in financial time series data.* Retrieved from http://www.datalab.uci.edu/people/xge/chart

Xu, G. (2008). *Web mining techniques for recommendation and personalization.* (Ph.D Thesis). Victoria University. Melbourne, Australia.

Xu, G., Zhang, Y., & Zhou, X. (2006). Discovering task-oriented usage pattern for web recommendation. In *Proceedings of the Seventeenth Australasian Database Conference,* (pp. 167-174). IEEE.

Yamany, S. M., Khiani, K. J., & Farag, A. A. (1997). Application of neural networks and genetic algorithms in the classification of endothelial cells. *Pattern Recognition Letters, 18,* 1205–1210. doi:10.1016/S0167-8655(97)00140-2

Yang, S.-Y. (2010). Developing an ontology-supported information integration and recommendation system for scholars. *Expert Systems with Applications, 37,* 7065–7079. doi:10.1016/j.eswa.2010.03.011

Yang, Y. (1999). An evaluation of statistical approaches to text categorization. *Information Retrieval, 1,* 69–90. doi:10.1023/A:1009982220290

Yan, T. W., & Garcia-Molina, H. (1999). The SIFT information dissemination system. *ACM Transactions on Database Systems, 24*(4), 529–565. doi:10.1145/331983.331992

Yan, T. W., Jacobsen, M., Garcia-Molina, H., & Dayal, U. (1996). From user access patterns to dynamic hypertext linking. *Journal of Computer Networks and ISDN Systems, 28,* 7–11.

Yao, X. (1993). A review of evolutionary artificial neural networks. *International Journal of Intelligent Systems, 4,* 203–222.

Yao, X. (1999). Evolving artificial neural networks. *Proceedings of the IEEE, 87*(9), 1423–1447. doi:10.1109/5.784219

Yavas, U., & Abdul-Gader, A. (1991). Trans-border outshopping: An Arabian Gulf study. *International Review of Retail, Distribution and Consumer Research, 1*(4), 455–468. doi:10.1080/09593969100000003

Yih, W. T., Goodman, J., & Carvalho, V. R. (2006). Finding advertising keywords on web pages. In *Proceedings of the 15th International Conference on World Wide Web,* (pp. 213–222). ACM Press.

Yiyang, Z., Jiao, J. R., & Yongsheng, M. (2007). Market segmentation for product family positioning based on fuzzy clustering. *Journal of Engineering Design, 18*(3), 227–241. doi:10.1080/09544820600752781

Yu, H., & Hatzivassiloglou, V. (2003). Towards answering opinion questions: Separating facts from opinions and identifying the polarity of opinion sentences. In *Proceedings of the 2003 Conference on Empirical Methods in Natural Language Processing,* (pp. 129–136). ACM.

Yu, T. (2002). *Empirical study to cognitive load and the PI theory with well-designed products for procedure skills and parallel instruction*s. Retrieved July 25, 2004 from http://projects.edte.utwente.nl/pi/Papers/indexYu.html

Yu, T., Min, R., & Spenkelink, G. (2003). E-learning environments on the world wide web, based on the concept of parallelism. In *Proceedings of the EARLI Conference.* Retrieved March 23, 2004 from http://wwwis.win.tue.nl/~acristea/HTML/Minerva/papers/report4jOfCompAssLearning-YuMinSpenkelink.doc

Yu, J., & Zhou, J. X. (2010). Segmenting young Chinese consumers based on shopping-decision styles: A regional comparison. *Journal of International Consumer Marketing, 22*(1), 59–71. doi:10.1080/08961530902844964

Zafra, A., Romero, C., Ventura, S., & Viedma, E. H. (2009). Multi-instance genetic programming for web index recommendation. *Expert Systems with Applications, 36,* 11470–11479. doi:10.1016/j.eswa.2009.03.059

Zaiane, R. (1999). *Resource and knowledge discovery from the internet and multimedia repositories.* (Ph.D. Thesis). Simon Fraser University. Burnaby, Canada.

Zhang, J., & Shukla, M. (2006). Rule-based platform for web user profiling. In *Proceedings of the Sixth International Conference on Data Mining (ICDM),* (pp. 1183–1187). ICDM.

Zhang, D., Simoff, S., Aciar, S., & Debenham, J. (2008). A multi agent recommender system that utilises consumer reviews in its recommendations. *International Journal of Intelligent Information and Database Systems, 2*(1), 69–81. doi:10.1504/IJIIDS.2008.017245

Zhang, T., & Iyengar, V. S. (2002). Recommender systems using linear classifiers. *Journal of Machine Learning Research, 2,* 313–334.

Zhang, X., Lu, X., Shi, Q., Xu, X.-Q., Leung, H.-C. E., & Harris, L. N. (2006). Recursive SVM feature selection and sample classification for mass-spectrometry and microarray data. *BMC Bioinformatics, 7*(197).

Zhang, Y., & Jiao, J. R. (2007). An associative classification-based recommendation system for personalization in B2C e-commerce applications. *Expert Systems with Applications, 33*(2). doi:10.1016/j.eswa.2006.05.005

Zheng, C. L., & de Sa, V. R. (2003). On selecting features from splice junctions: An analysis using information theoretic and machine learning approaches. *Genome Informatics, 14*, 73.

Zhen, L., Huang, G., & Jiang, Z. (2010). An inner-enterprise knowledge recommender system. *Expert Systems with Applications, 37*, 1703–1712. doi:10.1016/j.eswa.2009.06.057

Zhou, B., Hui, S. C., & Fong, A. C. M. (2006). An effective approach for periodic web personalization. In *Proceedings of IEEE/WIC/ACM International Conference on Web Intelligence*, (pp. 284-292). IEEE/WIC/ACM.

Zhou, B., Hui, S. C., & Chang, K. (2006). Enhancing mobile web access using intelligent recommendations. *IEEE Intelligent Systems, 21*(1), 28–34. doi:10.1109/MIS.2006.5

Ziegler, C., Schmidt-Thieme, L., & Lausen, G. (2004). Exploiting semantic product descriptions for recommender systems. In *Proceedings of the 2nd ACM SIGIR Semantic Web and IR WS (SWIR 2004)*. Sheffield, UK: ACM Press.

Ziegler, C.-N., McNee, S., Konstan, J., & Lausen, G. (2005). Improving recommendation lists through topic diversification. In *Proceedings of the 14th International World Wide Web Conference*, (pp. 22–32). IEEE.

Zigoris, P., & Zhang, Y. (2006). Bayesian adaptive user profiling with explicit & implicit feedback. In *Proceedings of the 15th ACM International Conference on Information and Knowledge Management*, (pp. 397–404). ACM Press.

About the Contributors

Satchidananda Dehuri is a Director of the Center for Distance and Continuing Education, Fakir Mohan University, Vyasa Vihar, Balasore, Odisha. He received his M.Sc. degree in Mathematics from Sambalpur University, Odisha, in 1998, and the M.Tech. and Ph.D. degrees in Computer Science from Utkal University, Vani Vihar, Odisha, in 2001 and 2006, respectively. He completed his Post Doctoral Research in Soft Computing Laboratory, Yonsei University, Seoul, Korea, under the BOYSCAST Fellowship Program of DST, Govt. of India. In 2010, he received the Young Scientist Award in Engineering and Technology for the year 2008 from Odisha Vigyan Academy, Department of Science and Technology, Govt. of Odisha. He was at the Center for Theoretical Studies, Indian Institute of Technology Kharagpur as a Visiting Scholar in 2002. During May-June 2006, he was a Visiting Scientist at the Center for Soft Computing Research, Indian Statistical Institute, Kolkata. His research interests include Evolutionary Computation and Data Mining. He has already published about 100 research papers in reputed journals and refereed conferences, has published three text books for undergraduate and post graduate students, and edited five books, and is acting as an editorial member of various journals. He has already guided 2 Ph. D. scholars in the area of Computer Science.

Alok Kumar Jagadev obtained his Ph.D. degree from Siksha O Anusandhan University, Odisha, in the year 2011. He has served as faculty member in various institutes in the state of Odisha. Presently, he is working as an Associate Professor in the Department of Computer Science and Engineering of Siksha O Anusandhan University, Odisha. His area of research is wireless ad-hoc networks and applications of soft computing techniques in data mining. He has contributed around 30 papers in journals and conferences of national and international repute. He has also contributed four textbooks in the area of computer science.

B. B. Misra is currently working as Dean (Research) at Silicon Institute of Technology, Bhubaneswar, India. He received Bachelor degree in Textiles from Kanpur University, India, in 1984, Master of Technology in Computer Science from Utkal University, Bhubaneswar, India, in 2002, and Ph.D. in Engineering from Biju Pattanaik University of Technology, Rourkela, India, in 2011. His areas of interest include data mining, sensor network, bioinformatics, evolutionary computation, bio-inspired computation, and computational intelligence. He has published one book, three book chapters, and fifty-six papers in different journals and conferences of national and international repute. He has been a keynote speaker and session chair of different national and international conferences.

Manas Ranjan Patra born on 4th June 1963, holds a Ph.D. degree in Computer Science from the Central University of Hyderabad. He has been teaching in the Post Graduate Department of Computer Science, Berhampur University, since 1987. As a United Nations Visiting Fellow, he carried out research at the International Institute for Software Technology, United Nations University, Macau, in the year 2000. He worked as an Assistant Professor at the Institute for Development and Research in Banking Technology (Reserve Bank of India), Hyderabad, during 2005-2006. Currently, he heads the Department of Computer Science, Berhampur University. He is a life member of CSI, ISTE, and OITS, and a Fellow of ACEEE. He has published more than 100 research articles in various international and national journals and conferences. His active area of research include data mining, intrusion detection and prevention, e-governance, etc.

* * *

Giuliano Armano is currently Associate Professor of Computer Engineering at the Dept. of Electrical and Electronic Engineering (DIEE), University of Cagliari, where he leads the Intelligent Agents and Soft-Computing Group (IASC Group). At the Faculty of Engineering, Prof. Armano teaches courses on Fundamentals of Databases and Bioinformatics, on Fundamentals of Computer Science, and on Object-Oriented Programming Languages. His educational background ranges over expert systems and machine learning. His research activity is focused on machine learning (in particular classifier ensembles), on bioinformatics (in particular protein secondary structure prediction), and on information retrieval/filtering (in particular, hierarchical text categorization, user profiling, and recommender systems). Author or co-author of several international journals, Prof. Armano has organized various international events (conferences, symposia, and workshops), mainly on software agents and bioinformatics, and has also been guest editor in special issues of the following international journals: *MultiAgent and Grid Systems*, *International Transactions on Systems Science and Applications*, *IEEE Transactions on Nanobiosciences*.

Sagarika Bakshi has obtained her B.Tech. in Computer Science and Engineering from B.P.U.T., Odisha, India. Presently she is pursuing her M.Tech. in the same from Siksha O Anusandhan University, Odisha. Her interest lies in the areas of data mining and machine learning. She is also most likely to continue her exploration in the recommendation systems.

Constanta-Nicoleta Bodea is Professor at the Academy of Economic Study Bucharest (ASE), Faculty of Cybernetics, Statistics, and Economic Informatics, Economic Informatics Department. Currently, she teaches Artificial Intelligence, Data Mining, and Project Management. She coordinates numerous research projects at national level and achieved a high expertise in managing projects with multiple consortia. She is author of 11 books and more than 50 papers on project management, information systems, and artificial intelligence, being honored by IPMA with the Outstanding Research Contributions in 2007.

Emmanuel Buabin is a Lecturer in the Department of Information Technology at the Methodist University College Ghana, Ghana. As part of his professional activities, Emmanuel has been an Executive Member of the IEEE Ghana Section since 2010. He has worked in the capacity as Software Engineer on both local and international projects. His current research interests include machine learning with artificial neural networks, natural language processing, reinforcement learning, and cognitive neuroscience. Emmanuel holds a BSc Honours degree in Computer Science and Statistics and an MEng degree in Electrical Engineering and Information Technology (Technical Computer Science option) from the University of Ghana and Deggendorf University of Applied Sciences, respectively.

Maria-Iuliana Dascălu has a Master Degree in Project Management from the Academy of Economic Studies, Bucharest, Romania (2008), and a Bachelor Degree in Computer Science from the Alexandru-Ioan Cuza University, Iasi, Romania (2006). She obtained a PhD in Economic Informatics at the Academy of Economic Studies (July 2011), after combining her work experience as a programmer with numerous research activities. Her research relates to computer-assisted testing with applications in e-learning environments for project management, competences development systems, and their benefits to adult education. Maria Dascălu is a Certified Project Management Associate (2008). She also conducted a research stage at the University of Gothenburg, Sweden, from October 2009 to May 2010.

Françoise Fessant is a Research Engineer in Data Mining and Machine Learning. She works in the international telecommunication company Orange in the team "profiling and data mining." Her research areas include data mining, statistical learning, and artificial neural networks. Her main interests are for exploratory data analysis with non-supervised techniques like Kohonen self organizing map and for feature selection methods. Her most recent research applications concern the network quality of service and content recommendation. She has published more than 40 scientific articles and book chapters in these areas. Dr. Fessant received her PhD in Signal Processing and Telecommunications in 1995 from Rennes University France.

Alessandro Giuliani is a Ph.D. student in Electronics and Computer Engineering. Currenlty, he is attending the third (and last) year Ph.D course at the University of Cagliari, Italy, under the supervision of Prof. G. Armano. His main research interests are in the field of information retrieval. In particular, he is investigating several algorithms, techniques, and applications on contextual advertising.

M. Hemalatha completed her Doctorate in the field of Data Mining from National Institute of Technology, Trichy, India. She has completed M.B.A., Marketing and Systems from Bharathidasan University, India. She worked as a Business Consultant in Pearl Feasibility Studies and Consultancy, Dubai, U.A.E. for a period of 5 years in the area of business plan formulation and marketing research, and she also worked as a Business Analyst in a Micro Finance Company, India. She has presented papers in 25 international conferences and has published 30 articles in the international and national journals. Her area of interest includes retailing, shopping behaviour, and data analytics.

H. Hannah Inbarani is currently working an Assistant Professor, Department of Computer Science, Periyar Uinversity, Salem, India. She received M.Sc degree in Computer Science from Bharathidasan University, Trichy, India, in 1991, M.Phil degree from MS University, Tirunelveli, India, in 2001, and M.Tech Degree from AAI Deemed University, Allahabad, India, in 2005. Her research interest lies in rough sets, fuzzy systems, Internet technologies, swarm intelligence, and Web mining. She has published several research papers in the areas like Web usage mining, rough sets, and ant clustering in reputed international journals.

Goran Klepac, Ph.D., works as a Head of Strategic and Reporting Department in Sector of Credit Risk in Raiffeisen Bank Austria, in Croatia. In several universities in Croatia, he lectures subjects in Domain of Data Mining, Predictive Analytics, Decision Support System, Banking Risk, Risk Evaluation Models, Expert System, Database Marketing, and Business Intelligence. As a team leader, he successfully finished many data mining projects in different domains like retail, finance, insurance, hospitality, telecommunications, and production. He is an author/coauthor of several books published in Croatian and English in the domain of data mining.

Utku Köse was born on March 26, 1985 in Afyon, Turkey. He was educated at Gazi Anatolian Profession High School (Department of Computer-Software) and entered Gazi University in 2004. He graduated as a Faculty Valedictorian in 2008 with a B. S. degree in Computer Education, and afterwards, he received a M.S. degree in Computer from Afyon Kocatepe University (2010). Currently, he continues Ph. D. at Selcuk University in the field of Computer Engineering. Between 2009 - 2011, he has worked as a Research Assistant in Afyon Kocatepe University. Following, he has also worked as a Lecturer in Afyon Kocatepe University between 2011 - 2012. Currently, he is a Lecturer in Usak University, Turkey. His research interests focus on artificial intelligence techniques, the chaos theory, distance education and electronic learning applications, computer education, blended learning, virtual learning environments, online / virtual laboratories, new learning / teaching models, mobile / wireless technologies, animation and 3D systems, and cryptography.

Frank Meyer graduated in 1995 from the University of Montpellier in Computer Science and Artificial Intelligence, and then he joined the France Telecom Group (Orange). Since 2000, he worked as Research Engineer, specializing in profiling, recommender systems, and automatic classification in a data mining research team at Orange Labs, focusing on customer classification and customer segmentation projects, and on decision trees and clustering. Since 2007, he worked simultaneously on a PhD thesis "Recommender Systems in Industrial Contexts" presented in January 2012 at the University of Grenoble II, and at Orange on Automatic Recommender System's Developments. He designed two automatic recommender engines: Reperio-C and -E, one Web-service-based, the other one embedded on Java-based devices (Google Android OSTM). These engines are currently used for prototype frameworks or for real services in several Orange projects: Lecteur.com (books), VideoParty (videos on demand), LiveRadio (radios).

Mrutyunjaya Panda born on 7th June 1974, holds a Ph.D degree in Computer Science from Berhampur University. He obtained his Master in Communication System Engineering from Sambalpur University, MBA in HRM from IGNOU, New Delhi, Bachelor in Electronics and Tele-Communication Engineering from Utkal University in 2002, 2009, 1997, respectively. He has 13 years of teaching and research experience. He is presently working as Professor and Head, Department of ECE, Gandhi Institute for Technological Advancement (GITA), Bhubaneswar, Odisha, India. He is a member of IEEE (USA), KES (Australia), IAENG (Hong Kong), ACEEE (I), IETE (I), CSI (I), ISTE (I). He has published about 45 papers in International and national journals and conferences. He has also published 5 book chapters. He is a program committee member of various international conferences. He is acting as a member of various international journals. His active area of research include data mining, intrusion detection and prevention. social networking, mobile communication, wireless sensor networks, etc.

Damien Poirier is a Research Engineer in Computational Linguistic and Information Retrieval. In 2007, after getting his Master's degree in Computer Science with honors at the University of Bordeaux (France), he was employed by the international company Orange during three years as Research Engineer. His works in collaboration with the University of Orléans (France) and the University of Paris 6 (France) resulted in the obtaining of a Ph.D. in Computer Science with highest honors in 2011. The subject of his thesis focused on the analysis and the extraction of information from Internet reviews in order to feed a beginner recommender system. After that, he was employed at the University of Orléans as Assistant Professor in Computer Science and Mathematics. His research themes are about opinion mining, natural language processing, information retrieval, text mining, machine learning, and recommender systems.

Arnoldo Rodríguez is an Associate Professor in the Sede del Atlántico (Atlantic Branch) at Universidad de Costa Rica (University of Costa Rica). He received a M.Sc. degree in Computer Science from Instituto Tecnonológico de Costa Rica (Costa Rica Institute of Technology), Costa Rica, in 1997. He received the Ph.D. in Computer Science from the Université de Montréal, Canada, in 2006. His research interests include recommender systems, artificial intelligence, adaptive educational hypermedia, multimedia, human computer interaction, robotics, tourism, and digital literacy. He has taught courses related to multimedia, information technology planning, and social issues in computer sciences since 1993.

Sweta Sarkar has obtained her B.Tech. in Computer Science and Engineering from W.B.U.T., West Bengal, India. Presently, she is pursuing M.Tech. in the same from Siksha O Anusandhan University, Odisha. Her area of research work lies in data mining and soft computing applications. She is continuing her thesis work in the recommender system.

Isabelle Tellier was born in 1968 in Nantes, France. She has been from September 2011 Professor of Computational Linguistics in Paris 3 – Sorbonne Nouvelle, member of the LaTTiCe laboratory (http://www.lattice.cnrs.fr/). She obtained a PhD in Computer Science in 1996 at the ENS de Cachan and an habilitation in Lille in 2005. She was, when this chapter was written, Professor of Computer Science in Orléans, member of the LIFO laboratory (http://www.univ-orleans.fr/lifo/). Her research concern is machine learning for natural language processing, both from a symbolic and a statistic point of view. She has worked on grammatical inference, classification, information retrieval, conditional random fields, and other subjects. She supervised 4 PhDs and contributed to many publications.

K. Thangavel received M. Sc., and M. Phil in Mathematics from the Bharathidasan University, Tiruchirappalli, India, in 1986 and 1988, respectively. He received Ph. D degree from Gandhigram Rural University, Gandhigram, India in 1999. His research area is optimization algorithms. He received M. C. A degree from Madurai Kamaraj University, Madurai, India, in 2001. Currently, he is a Professor and Head, Department of Computer Science, Periyar University, Salem, India. He authored and co-authored for more than 80 research papers published in international journals. He has edited three books. Five Ph.D degrees have been awarded under his research supervision. His research interests include digital medical image processing, data mining, mobile computing, and pattern recognition. He has been bestowed with Tamilnadu State Scientist Award for the year 2010.

Eloisa Vargiu obtained her Ph.D. in Electronic and Computer Engineering at the University of Cagliari, Italy, in 2003. During her PhD, she studied the pro-active and adaptive behavior of agents, and she developed hierarchical agent architecture. In the same period, she collaborated with the CRS4 (an interdisciplinary research center located in Sardinia). During her post-doc activity, she worked on projects on bioinformatics and information retrieval. After a collaboration of about 11 years with the Intelligent Agents and Soft-Computing (IASC) at the Dept. of Electrical and Electronic Engineering (DIEE), of Cagliari, since December 2011, she is currently a Researcher at Digital (bDigital) in the group Health R&D&I. She is co-author of more than 50 peer-reviewed publications in international journals and conferences, as well as co-editor of 3 books.

Index

A

AdaBoost 56, 61, 197-198, 204, 265
adaptation 1, 3, 5, 13, 15-17, 20-21, 29, 34, 42, 64, 194, 228, 231, 250-251
Adaptive Educational Hypermedia (AEH) 1
Adjusted Goodness of Fit Index (AGFI) 236
ARIALE 2-3, 5-15, 17, 19-21
Artificial Intelligence (AI) 1
Artificial Neural Network (ANN) 236
attacks
 DoS 54, 58
 probing 54, 58
 Root to Local (R2L) 54
 User to Root (U2R) 54
authorial mathematical model 84
authoring tool 1-9, 13-16, 20, 22, 29
automatic generation 1-3, 9, 20-21, 29

B

back-propagation 198, 202, 205, 207, 261
Bayesian networks 3, 24, 27, 65, 84, 87-89, 103-104, 129, 141, 148-150, 264
benchmarks 63-64
biclustering 182, 271, 273, 276, 283-285
binary digits 249
Buabin Algorithm 245, 255-256, 258

C

Case Base Reasoning 1, 3, 29
CertExam 33, 36-39, 42-43
Charged Memory Size (CMS) 221
Charged Particle (CP) 220
Charged System Search (CSS) Algorithm 215, 220
Chi-Squared Automatic Interaction Detection (CHAID) 162
classification
 Bayesian 1-2, 10-11, 29
 cost sensitive 57, 60
 opinion 63, 77-79, 81-83

Classification-based Features (CF) 112
Clearance Sales 230-233, 235-242
clustering
 center-bunching based 138, 150
 fuzzy c means 152-153, 158, 161
 Gaussian rough fuzzy 176
 Gaussian rough k-means 175
 k-mean 146
 subtractive 152-153, 158, 161, 166, 277
Common Log Format (CLF) 274
Computational Web Intelligence (CWI) 171, 174
Computer Science 3, 24, 32, 46, 51, 61, 123, 125, 148-150, 189-190, 195, 209, 214, 229, 265, 268-270, 285
conditional probability 11, 29, 84, 88-89, 104, 141
 table 84, 104
confusion matrix 57, 204-205, 261-262
connection 22, 33, 54, 61, 199, 207, 211, 222-223, 236, 259
 contains 6, 30, 34, 41, 58, 74, 76-77, 93, 172, 174, 193, 202, 222, 256, 260, 273-274
 if-then 30, 41
 switch 18, 30, 43, 132, 157
contextual advertising 105-106, 110-111, 116, 118, 122-124, 126-127
cosine distance 115, 136-137
cosine-similarity 179
Cross-validation 19, 26-27, 70, 160

D

data mining 51, 59-60, 62, 82, 84-86, 90-91, 102-104, 107, 124-126, 146-147, 170-172, 183, 188-191, 193, 197-198, 205, 208, 222, 228, 246, 249, 262, 266-269, 272-274, 276, 284-286
 temporal 103
 time series 84-85
Davies-Bouldin (DB) index 177
decision-making 1-2, 5-6, 9, 15, 21, 24-26, 63, 102, 245
Decision Trees (DT) 55